THE LEVELLERS

AND THE ENGLISH REVOLUTION

THE LEVELLERS
AND THE ENGLISH
REVOLUTION

By H. N. Brailsford

Edited and prepared for publication

By Christopher Hill

STANFORD UNIVERSITY PRESS

CALIFORNIA: 1961

Stanford University Press
Stanford, California.
© *1961 by Evamaria Brailsford*
All rights reserved
Library of Congress Catalog Card Number 61-11501

Printed in Great Britain

Editorial Note

When H. N. Brailsford died on 23 March, 1958, he left the manuscript of a large book on the Levellers. Of the book as he planned it, four chapters were still unwritten. One on the Diggers has been replaced by an article which Brailsford wrote in 1945 (Chapter XXXIV below). Another missing chapter would have dealt with the careers of the Leveller leaders after the suppression of their party. I have added a few additional facts to the author's Appendix B at the end of Chapter XXXI; this does a little to fill the gap. More serious is the absence of either an Introduction or a Conclusion. One can see why the author of *The War of Steel and Gold* and of *Property or Peace*, the devoted worker for women's suffrage, for the emancipation of the Balkan, Irish and Indian peoples, the steadfast advocate of internationalism and socialism—one can see why Brailsford devoted to the Levellers the last years of his dedicated life. He thought of this book not as a mere history, but as a profoundly political study, which would convey a message from him to the younger generation. For this reason it is sad not to have his mature reflections on the Levellers' place in English history. He himself thought that one of the main achievements of his book was to prove that, at decisive moments in the seventeenth-century English Revolution, the intellectual and political initiative lay with the Levellers, and that Cromwell and the Independent Grandees followed their lead. Without this Leveller initiative the course of English history might have been very different. But it is impossible now to reconstruct the Conclusion which Brailsford never wrote. His book must speak for itself. The political and moral overtones are there for those who can hear them; but Brailsford was a scrupulous and conscientious historian, and nothing in his telling of the story is imposed with historical hindsight.

In preparing the book for the press, editorial additions and corrections have been kept to a minimum. Chapter I had to be recast, because much of it was repeated in Chapter XIX. In the manuscript there was also considerable overlap between the second and third chapters, whole sentences being repeated *verbatim*. The present Chapter II has been formed by fusing these two and omitting repetitions: virtually everything that Brailsford wrote has been retained. The reader is asked to bear in mind this use of scissors and paste if he finds that the first two chapters read less smoothly than Brailsford's writing normally does.

Otherwise the text is as Brailsford left it. Some references were missing: these have been inserted wherever possible, except in the case of well-known works like the *Verney Memoirs* or the writings of Baxter and Clarendon. A very few references proved impossible to trace, but I believe these can be taken on trust. I have not checked every date and every quotation, but enough to be confident that they are always substantially accurate. Brailsford had modernised seventeenth-century spelling, punctuation and capitalisation throughout, even in titles of books and pamphlets. I have not interfered with this. His spelling of proper names like Monk, Peters, Rainsborough, has been retained. The only significant alterations concern Brailsford's use of religious labels, which was not always consistent. Sometimes he spoke of 'nonconformists' or 'dissenters' before 1660: I have substituted 'sectaries', in accordance with Brailsford's usage on other occasions. Similarly I have occasionally altered 'Congregationalist' to 'Independent', 'Anglican' to 'Episcopalian' or 'Prelatist' (during the years when the state church was not episcopalian), in the interests of consistency. Brailsford would no doubt have made similar changes himself in revising for publication. An appendix was promised on the authorship of *Tyranipocrit*, which Brailsford attributed to Walwyn. Laski apparently found his arguments convincing, but the appendix has not been found (see p. 71 below).

Two debts of gratitude must be acknowledged. The first is to Mr Kingsley Martin, with whom Brailsford worked for many years on the *New Statesman*, and who helped to get this book published. The second is to Mrs Brailsford, who shared in the creation of her husband's book from its inception; I am deeply indebted to her help and guidance throughout.

C. H.

Abbreviations

The following abbreviations have been used in the notes, which are grouped at the end of each chapter:

Abbott—Ed. W. C. Abbott, *The Writings and Speeches of Oliver Cromwell* (Harvard U.P., 4 vols., 1937-47).

C.S.P.—*Calendar of State Papers.*

C.P.—*The Clarke Papers*, ed. C. H. Firth (Camden Soc., 4 vols., 1891-1901).

Declaration—*A Declaration of the Engagements, Remonstrances . . . and Resolutions from H. E. Sir Thomas Fairfax and the General Council of the Army* (27 September, 1647).

H. and D.—Ed. W. Haller and G. Davies, *The Leveller Tracts, 1647-53* (Columbia U.P., 1944).

Rushworth—John Rushworth, *Historical Collections* (7 volumes, 2nd ed., 1721).

Wolfe—Ed. D. M. Wolfe, *Leveller Manifestoes of the Puritan Revolution* (Nelson, 1944).

Woodhouse—Ed. A. S. P. Woodhouse, *Puritanism and Liberty* (Dent, 1938).

Author's Preface

To our generation fell the good fortune of re-discovering the Levellers. To the classical liberal historians they meant rather less than nothing. J. R. Green's *Short History* is still the most readable and sympathetic biography of the English people: it dismissed John Lilburne in half a line and assigned to the Levellers six lines in its crowded volume of 820 pages. In style and vitality few books of its kind equal G. M. Trevelyan's *England under the Stuarts*; it dismissed the Levellers in a patronising footnote. This neglect is puzzling. At the crisis of the Revolution it was from the Levellers and not from its commanders that the victorious New Model Army derived its political ideas and its democratic drive. Even on a superficial glance the Leveller leaders are as personalities unusual and, indeed, unique. King Charles had Lilburne flogged as a youngster from Ludgate Hill to Palace Yard; Cromwell banished him in middle age to a dungeon in Jersey. Was there any other man in English history so well-beloved that London juries twice saved his life by acquitting him against the clearest evidence of treason and felony? Finally, this spirited soldier who led the dragoons to victory at Marston Moor was among the first of their converts whom the Quakers buried at Bunhill Fields.

Dick Overton, protagonist of toleration, ranks as the most popular satirist and pamphleteer of the left, until Defoe surpassed him. In the arch-conspirator Wildman even Macaulay was interested. But the man of them all who means most for our day is William Walwyn. An enquirer, familiar with Lucian and steeped in Montaigne, who dared to subject the Puritans to Socratic questioning, he is none the less one of the few men of his age whose undogmatic Christianity is still gracious and fragrant after three centuries. He could write a satire against intolerance so witty in its fantasy that Voltaire might have penned it. His prose style is as well mannered as his social thinking is humane. He was more generous than Gladstone in his proposal to recognise Ireland as 'a free state', and went rather farther than Keir Hardie in advocating the representation of labouring men in Parliament. But what we have rediscovered is not merely the fact that the Levellers anticipated our fathers in most of the social and political reforms of the next three hundred years; the theme of this book is rather that they were, until Cromwell crushed them, the dynamic pioneers, who had the initiative during the most formative years of the Interregnum. They would have won for our peasants in the mid-seventeenth century what the Great Revolution gained for those of France at the close of the eighteenth. I have tried (if the reader can forgive some repetition) to make good this estimate in my first chapter.

This book is addressed to the general reader. For that reason I have placed references and other matters of interest only to specialists in the notes at the end of chapters. While specialists will find that much of my material is familiar and uncontroversial, they may discover among it a few finds that my spade brought up while digging in the buried treasures of the Thomason Tracts in the British Museum. I say farewell with regret to the many scholars, the dead as well as the living, in whose company I have passed the years spent upon this book. I feel towards the classical historians, Gardiner and Firth, a gratitude that borders on veneration, in spite of the fact that they would disagree with most of my conclusions—as also would Godwin, the first, and Abbott, the last, of them. The happiest hours of my studies were spent with the men and women who helped me to organise my picture of the social background of Cromwell and the Levellers—my old friend R. H. Tawney, G. P. Gooch, E. Lipson, the economic historian, Margaret James, whose pioneer researches influenced me deeply, George Unwin, and in a neighbouring field, Ernst Troeltsch and Belfort Bax. But the chief of my debts is to the scholars, most of them Americans, whose pioneering work in recent years on the Levellers and Diggers lightened my own labours immeasurably. On the other side of the Atlantic I would thank more especially T. C. Pease with William Haller, Godfrey Davies and Don Wolfe who have republished the salient Leveller documents, G. H. Sabine to whom we owe a model edition of Winstanley, D. W. Petegorsky, and lastly A. S. P. Woodhouse who re-edited the debates between Levellers and 'Grandees' with Cromwell in the chair. On this side of the Atlantic I would single out Eduard Bernstein, the forerunner of us all, whom I had the good fortune to count my friend, W. Schenk and M. A. Gibb, of whose biography of Lilburne I have made constant use.

Contents

CHAPTER I

Seen in Perspective

What was the Civil War about? How are we to explain this
unique event in English history? Unique it was. The Wars of
the Roses were only a prolonged vendetta between rival
aristocratic houses. The calm of the Tudor century was broken
only by a few local risings. After the 'crowning mercy' of
Worcester in 1651 which finally confirmed Cromwell's victory,
the few encounters in which our ancestors did gird on their
swords may be regarded as belated rear-guard actions of the
great Civil War itself—Monmouth's Rebellion, the bloodless
Whig Revolution of 1688, and the two Jacobite risings of 1715
and 1745. The political earthquakes of the Industrial Revolution led to no organised warfare in our busy island, save for
the pitiful Chartist rising at Newport in 1838, crushed between
midnight and dawn. Only once did our fathers insist on fighting
out their quarrel to the bitter end, though it cost the English
belligerents by the official parliamentary reckoning 100,000
killed in a population of some five millions—not to mention
the maimed, the invalids and the thousands of prisoners sold
into temporary slavery. The Scots were bled white. As for
Ireland, it lost, by Sir William Petty's reckoning, over 40% of
its population. Englishmen, whatever they may have done in
the way of organised slaughter beyond their own shores, have
never been quick to cut one another's throats. What, then, was
the quarrel that in this century alone routed the peacemakers
and frustrated every attempt at compromise?

The official propaganda, profuse though it was in the early
years of the war, helps us not at all. The polemics of King and

Parliament, as Clarendon reports them, are the only pages in his *History of the Rebellion* which one reads with something less than breathless attention. While each side vowed its unshakable loyalty to King and constitution, there must have been thousands who felt, like Sir Edmund Verney, that there was nothing to choose between them. It has never been the habit of English gentlemen to thrust their swords into each other's bowels because lawyers were at odds over questions of constitutional theory. Then shall we dignify with the name of causes the many economic grievances that inspired so much eloquence of voice and pen before the war broke out—ship money, forced loans, monopolies, and the antiquated feudal exactions levied on the owners of great forests and those who held their estates under knight's service? Assuredly in this century it is never amiss to look for economic motives. It was a venal and mercenary age. In the propertied classes most marriages were arranged for money or land. Friends, if one reads the diaries and letters of the time, commonly expected some form of payment for services rendered. A great gentleman like Ashburnham, whom the King called 'Jack' and treated as an intimate, would charge a meritorious royalist soldier £500 for recommending him for a peerage. Lesser gentlemen like Sir Arthur Haslerig's private secretary would charge ten 'shillings a time for an interview with the great man. Nearly everything was for sale, even the degree of Doctor of Divinity at Cambridge. The evidence that Lenthall, Speaker of the Long Parliament, took bribes is painfully clear. Leading politicians like Bradshaw and brilliant soldiers like Lambert seemed to expect a *pourboire* in land or money from time to time to keep them loyal to the 'good old cause'. In this atmosphere economic grievances undoubtedly frayed men's loyalty to the crown. It was no less a person than Milton who asked 'What . . . stirs the Englishmen sooner to rebellion than violent and heavy hands upon their goods and purses?' Yet economic grievances did not cause the war. The King had met all these complaints between the meeting of the Long Parliament in 1640 and the outbreak of war in 1642. Some who were to be his loyal supporters in the fighting had previously suffered from his exactions as severely as those on the other side.

Would it be more accurate to say that this was a rebellion against the arbitrary rule of one man's will? That phrase with endless verbal variations recurs throughout the debates and pamphlets of the period. It stands out, underlined in blood, from the indictment that summed up the indignation of the victorious Army against the man Charles Stuart: 'Out of a wicked design to erect and uphold in himself an unlimited and tyrannical power to rule according to his will, and to overthrow the rights and liberties of the people, . . . he . . . hath traitorously and maliciously levied war against the present Parliament and the people therein represented.' Certainly the Puritan half of the propertied class looked on the King's eleven years of personal rule, prosperous though they were, with deep resentment. But to think of this King as a personal dictator is a grave mistake. From his belief that he was God's anointed he derived an heroic steadfastness; he even dared to say to his people (in 1628): 'I must avow that I owe the account of my actions to God alone.' We think of him as Van Dyck painted him, a melancholy but majestic figure. He loved good art and this master responded by idealising him. Physically he was not impressive and he stammered when he spoke. By temperament an aloof introvert, he had no magnetism, no gift to inspire and lead. But it cannot fairly be said of him that he strayed very far from English political tradition. Even the detested Star Chamber was conducted pretty much as it had been under the Tudors. This 'arbitrary' king was rather more careful to keep within the known laws of the land than the Puritan régimes that followed him. Modern historians discarded long ago the Whig accusations of despotism and misgovernment.

The Star Chamber, to be sure, had a piebald record. It was a political tribunal, which inflicted on some of its opponents, more especially the Puritans, savage and vindictive punishments and crippling fines. But it was the boast of Wentworth's Council in the North that it would hear 'the petition of the poorest man against the richest or against the greatest lord'. The Privy Council, whose organs both Star Chamber and Council in the North were, was capable of acting with prompt humanity. More especially during the period of personal government, it maintained an elaborate system of inspection and control to 'quicken' the zeal of the Justices of the Peace in caring for the needy under the Elizabethan poor law. It would even impose in times of scarcity or during a visitation of the plague a special rate, levied weekly, to provide food for the hungry and nurses for the sick. One typical example of its policy is worth retelling. At Colchester in 1637 a cloth manufacturer who used to pay his workers in goods was ordered by the mayor and justices to pay their wages in money, including the arrears. He refused and boasted that he would carry the case from court to court rather than make restitution. The Privy Council made an example of him by sending him to prison until he paid his workers twice the amount due, together with the costs of the prosecution.[1]

Archbishop Laud was the last English statesman who tried hard to stop depopulation by the enclosure of common land. His was not an attractive personality, but we should not forget his services to scholarship and his love for oriental art and literature. One need not be a high churchman to respect his determination to bring back order, decency and beauty into the worship of God. In that paradoxical century, men who would slaughter multitudes of their fellows in the name of religion would without shame allow the rain to drip through the roof of St Paul's cathedral. Laud had to deal with bishops who would lease the church's land to their kinsmen for a song, and with a vicar who used his church to shelter his cattle. He made enemies as much by his virtues as by his intolerance. It has been suggested that he and Wentworth (to use Strafford's family name) were the first Tory democrats. Certainly they headed the party of social reform in the Privy Council, but they looked on democracy of any kind with distaste. They were the King's servants, who did all their governing and reforming from above. Of the movement of public opinion they were disastrously ignorant; they cared nothing for it and did nothing to win it. Laud would tune the pulpits to preach passive obedience, but it would never have occurred to him or to Wentworth to enlist the support of their poorer fellow-countrymen, whose interests these two had served in the secrecy of the King's cabinet. But once more we have run into difficulties in the effort to discover what the Civil War was about. After the

Long Parliament had met, the King made little attempt to
preserve the Star Chamber and the other 'prerogative' organs
of government; and he sacrificed Strafford's life to appease the
ruling class, which regarded him as a deserter from its ranks.
And so it happened, when it came to the test of arms, that this
uninspired and lonely King could count at the drawn battle of
Edgehill on the swords of a good half of the governing class of
England.

What we have to explain is not merely a great rebellion, but
the division of this governing class. Up till the eve of the Civil
War men born within it had regarded loyalty to the King as
one of the native qualities of a gentleman, a part of his heritage
that one took for granted like his sword, his coat of arms and
his ancestral lands. Clarendon (still at this time plain Edward
Hyde) records his astonishment when some little while before
the outbreak of the war he discovered an exception to this rule.
In a talk with Henry Marten, the noted wit who afterwards
acted with the Levellers and commanded a regiment of horse
for the Parliament, he had to hear from his fellow member's
lips this remark about the King: 'I do not think one man wise
enough to govern us all.' It was strange, he comments, that such
an idea should enter the head of 'a gentleman possessed of a
very great fortune and having great credit in his country'
(county). A few months later, when he reached the story of
Edgehill, Clarendon made the interesting statement that 'most
of the persons of quality' in the cavalier army served in the
King's troop of Guards:

> Upon a very modest computation the estate and revenue of
> that single troop might justly be valued at least equal to all
> theirs who then voted in both Houses under the name of
> Lords and Commons of Parliament, and so made and
> maintained that war.

When he came to describe Cromwell's rise to power as Lord
Protector eleven years later, Clarendon ventured on another
calculation equally revealing:

> In this manner and with so little pains this extraordinary
> man, . . . without the assistance and against the desire of
> all noble persons or men of quality, or of three men who in

the beginning of the troubles were possessed of £300 land by the year, mounted himself into the throne of three kingdoms, without the name of King but with a greater power and authority than had ever been exercised or claimed by any King.[2]

Evidently for Clarendon the struggle in which he was engaged was a class war. In two stages the aristocratic oligarchy of great landowners, which was at its start the ruling class, was replaced in its last phase by a group with no pretensions to birth and only a modest qualification in the acres it owned. James Harrington, the most original political thinker of that century, whose prose at its best could match Clarendon's (though there are deserts of obscure prolixity between his happier pages) took much the same view of it. Himself born in the upper class, though he was a convinced republican, he tells us in *Oceana* that in the Civil War 'the people' under Cromwell (to whom he dedicated his book) 'have overthrown the nobility'. A pioneer in the economic interpretation of history, he argues that this came about because the 'balance' of class power, as measured by the ownership of land, had been 'falling' for some time past 'to the people'. He aims at ending the extreme inequality of landed property and would begin by fixing an upper limit of 2-3,000 acres, worth £2,000 per annum; but these estates would diminish rapidly, since he would abolish the 'flinty custom' of primogeniture, which he likened to the drowning of five pups in a litter of six. He reckoned that only about 300 great landowners exceeded this allowance.[3] His 300 families were the opulent Cavaliers of Clarendon's reckoning, who formed the King's bodyguard.

This reading of the split in the governing, land-owning class can at best be only roughly true; there were wealthy commoners like John Hampden and aristocrats like Lord Brooke and Lord Saye and Sele on the wrong side of the barricades. Can we bring this division according to class into relation with the territorial division favoured by liberals? Liberal historians are as shy in facing the fact of class as were the novelists of the last century in facing the fact of sex. Since our schooldays we have been familiar with the maps that show the dividing line between the loyal West of England and the rebellious East.

The exceptions were few, but significant; for all the sea-ports fell to Parliament save in the Celtic fringe of Cornwall and Wales, and so did the industrial salient of Somerset with its wool trade, and two or three busy towns like Gloucester and Manchester. In the northern and western borderlands, a good century behind the times, men still felt a feudal loyalty towards their nobility and the King. Puritanism had not yet begun to penetrate Wales, while the rural parishes of Lancashire, the Lakes and the Border were still largely Catholic. The King of course had Oxford, while Hobbes looked on Cambridge as the bottomless well of republican poison; for him, indeed, the only question was whether Aristotle or Calvin was chiefly responsible for the Civil War. Parliament had the industrial areas of the West Riding and East Anglia, and the great mercantile centres of London, Bristol, Norwich, Hull and Newcastle. If the millionaire noblemen, Worcester, Winchester, Derby and Newcastle (the first two of them Catholics) fought for the crown, Parliament had on its side the more enterprising type of landowner, some with titles and some without, who invested the surplus they drew from their rents in draining the Fens, colonising Massachusetts or Providence Island, sharing in joint-stock trading ventures, financing the slave trade, and lending money at interest on good landed security. This half of England had a good deal of capital locked up in the holds and hulls of its ships, and its mind was quickened by intercourse with Europe, above all with the Netherlands.

On the whole, then, the territorial division had a basis in economics; the mercantilist East went to war with the feudal West. But then as now, men will fight only when their collective emotions have been roused by fear or hate, by envy or a galling sense of inferiority. In this case, if we are asking what went on in the daylight of men's conscious emotions, the answer is, of course, that their differences over religion raised the temperature to battle point. Once more Clarendon gives us a clue. He was dining one day with the leaders of the opposition, the group round Pym and Hampden, who kept a common table at Westminster, when Nathaniel Fiennes (the son of Lord Saye and Sele) joined them and predicted that if the King defended the bishops, it would occasion 'as sharp a war as had ever been in England'. Many he said, were already 'resolved to lose their lives before they would ever submit'.[4] Why the control of the pulpit, whether by bishops or presbyteries, was vital for the maintenance of the social pyramid, we shall see in the next chapter. What rather concerns us here is the psychological power of religion to create a mood of fear and hate. The fear of God has always worked in this way, in Edinburgh and London as in Thebes and Argos. Laud and Prynne both believed that a jealous God would avenge upon the whole nation any tolerance by its rulers of blasphemy, heresy or schism, much as the Greeks who listened to the classical tragedies thought it natural and inevitable that the subjects of Oedipus and Clytaemnestra should pay for the incests and murders of their rulers.

The climate of war was created well before the Long Parliament met. The Scots were the first to make it, when they mobilised to resist the imposition of episcopacy and the Prayer Book, and crossed the border under arms. Strafford unwittingly awakened the fears of Protestant England when he proposed to bring over an Irish army to crush—was it the Scots, or, as the Puritans suspected, the English? The massacre of Protestants in Ireland, grossly exaggerated as it was, raised the temperature by many degrees of holy anger. When Archbishop Laud, Bishop Juxon and their lay colleagues of the Star Chamber forced the horrified crowd of Londoners to witness the public mutilation—by cutting off their ears—of the Presbyterian militants, William Prynne, Dr Bastwick and Henry Burton the popular divine, they satisfied their own sacred sadism, but they awakened it also in their opponents. Those ears cried out for blood, and before long it flowed in torrents. Englishmen in that century were used to the sight of cruelty. Any day, in passing Tyburn, one might chance to witness a mass hanging, and comment as a contemporary journalist did, 'the 23 were all very proper gentlemen'. In walking across Smithfield one might happen to see, as Evelyn the diarist did, the burning alive of a woman who had murdered her husband.[5] But to shed the blood of God's saints was another matter altogether.

A deeply interesting document, *Persecutio Undecima*, written from the standpoint of a royalist churchman, concedes the folly of these savage punishments. So indignant, he reports, were Londoners, that a divine could not walk the streets in his clerical habit without being reproached as 'Baal's priest'.[6] For Puritans of all shades, and assuredly for their army, the final and sufficient justification for the ten years of war was that they were fighting for liberty of conscience. One still senses in retrospect the climate of fear, when Cromwell in the security of 1658 looked back upon the past. 'Nay,' he exclaimed, 'who could have forethought, when we were plunged into the midst of our troubles, that ever the people of God should have had liberty to worship God without fear of enemies?'[7]

Up to 1646 two classes and two churches faced each other, the Episcopalian nobility and gentry on the one side, the Presbyterian gentry and merchants on the other. They had to fight, because both churches were intolerant and exclusive; or as some of us would put it, they were intolerant, because for other reasons they had to fight. On either interpretation, religion was in England the paramount fact of social and political life. The Reformation culminated in the Civil War and in Oliver's brief reign. After the Restoration, religion rapidly dwindled as a political force, and survived rather as a subjective fact in the personal life of individuals. Under Oliver, as under Charles I, England was a theocracy. The Lord Protector was as sure as the hereditary and anointed King of his divine right to rule. The God of Battles had made His will clear, by granting to the Saints victory after victory in an unbroken series of triumphs. These 'dispensations' and 'providences' gave Cromwell the same assurance of God's favour that Mahomet drew from revelation. Others might prate about the sovereignty of the people: he trusted to the sovereignty of God.

Round about 1646, towards the end of the first Civil War, the Levellers emerged as an independent group. There had been peasant revolts in the past. The first claim of the Levellers to originality lay in this, that they organised as a modern party, run on democratic lines, a third force, drawn from the lower middle class, the skilled craftsmen and the small farmers. Their followers ranged from some well-to-do merchants to the weavers of Spitalfields and the lead-miners of Derbyshire.

Sometimes Lilburne spoke of them as 'the middle sort of people', sometimes as 'the hobnails, clouted shoes, the private soldiers, the leather and woollen aprons and the laborious and industrious people in England'.[8] The Levellers were the first political party which dared to make complete religious toleration a chief plank in their platform. By 1647 they had behind them most of the rank and file of the New Model Army and many of its junior officers.

Characteristic of Leveller propaganda was the inspiring historical myth they wove about the Norman Conquest (see Chapter VII below). They drew a highly idealised picture of Anglo-Saxon democracy under Alfred the Great and Edward the Confessor, and maintained that it was William the Bastard who brought in serfdom. This was the Leveller way of calling for an end to feudalism, and a most effective way it was, for it linked the class-consciousness of the 'laborious and industrious people' with the emotional force of English nationalism. The nobles and gentlemen who opposed their Revolution derived their privileges from a foreign invasion.

The Levellers went on to demand the end of the 'negative voices' or vetoes of the King and the House of Lords on legislation. Hitherto the leaders of the parliamentary Revolution had been content with the traditional muddle of the unwritten English constitution, which recognised the sovereignty of King, Lords and Commons. 'Can there be three supremes?' the Levellers asked, and went on to proclaim the sovereignty of the people. They understood very well that the Long Parliament, which looked like sitting for ever, was merely the organ of the landowning classes. Lilburne tore in pieces its claim to be representative, exposed the scandal of the 'decayed', or as the next century called them, the 'rotten' boroughs, and called boldly for manhood suffrage. The Levellers' first draft of a written constitution, the Agreement of the People, defined in black and white what the annual Parliaments of the future might do and what they were forbidden to do. Their notion of democratic self-government began, however, in the parish and the hundred. They would have ended the reign of the ruling landed oligarchy by insisting on the election of every officer and magistrate, from the sheriffs down to the clergy and the

regimental officers of the militia. We shall see, as we go on,
how they proposed to humanise the savage criminal law, to end
imprisonment for debt and abolish tithes. What they proposed
in 1646, the Army under their teaching realised in 1649:
England became a Commonwealth without King or House of
Lords. But the lawyers thwarted the social reforms which the
Levellers called for; and Cromwell's opposition defeated their
demands for manhood suffrage. Worst of all (to use their own
language), their suppression confirmed the Norman Conquest
in the village. The Levellers' policy had been to make independent citizens of the peasantry by winning for them the freehold
of the acres they tilled. Within a few generations of their defeat
the English peasantry had ceased to exist.

Have we stumbled, then, on a chief issue of the Civil War?
What was at stake was the ownership of the soil of England,
including its 'waste' and common lands. Clarendon makes this
clear. At the start the two Houses declared that the costs of the
war, advanced by loans from the 'well-affected', should be
repaid 'out of the estates of . . . delinquents and of the malignant
and disaffected party in this kingdom'. The result was that 'all
persons of honour and quality plainly discerned that they had
no safety but in the preservation of the regal power', since
Parliament could declare whom it would 'delinquents'. As we
all know, the 'well-affected' did acquire as the fruits of victory a
large part of the surface of England, and to the indignation of
the Cavaliers even contrived to retain a considerable proportion of it after the Restoration. We are apt to forget that the
King's party were driven by the same greed of land. Whenever
they felt themselves in secure possession of a district, they
also confiscated their opponents' estates. Clarendon tells us
that the King conferred on Sir Richard Grenville, a turncoat
whom the historian detested hardly less than the more notorious
Goring, all the estates of the Earl of Bedford and Sir Francis
Drake in Devon, with other valuable properties in Cornwall.[9]
It is significant that the brief treaty of neutrality which the
royalist gentry of Cornwall concluded with the parliamentarian
gentry of Devon for a year's duration, contained this clause:

> I do solemnly vow . . . that I am without any intention (by
> fomenting this unnatural war) to gain or hope to advantage

myself with the real or personal estate of any person whatsoever.

One knows what a war is about only when it is over. The only
clearly definable fruits of the Parliament's victory were that the
crown, when it was restored, lost some of its ancient feudal
rights, and its supporters some part of their ancestral estates.

But there was, under Leveller leadership, a third claimant,
the peasantry, who did not gain a single acre. We know much
more about the activities of the Levellers in London and the
Army than about their doings in the villages. Their name,
however, recalled many a local rebellion of the countrymen,
when they rose to 'level' the fences which encroaching landlords had erected to turn their common fields into sheepwalks.
When the Long Parliament had taught the Levellers the futility
of petitioning, their strategy was to win the Army, in the last
resort by mutiny. Twice they tried and twice they failed. If
Lilburne had taught it to think, Fairfax and Cromwell had
taught it to obey. Had the rebels won the day in 1647 or 1649,
they would have forced a dissolution and a general election
under manhood suffrage, with toleration and the emancipation
of the peasants from their 'base tenures' as the biggest items in
their programme. This was not, up to Cromwell's final victory
at Worcester in 1651, a hopelessly unrealisable dream. Thereafter the officers of the victorious Army were chiefly busied in
acquiring landed estates for themselves in all three kingdoms.
Cromwell, who had been in his younger days the champion of
the commoners of the Fens against the encroachments of the
great nobles, had now made Pym's watchword, 'liberty and
property', his own. The Lord Protector's speeches to his
Parliaments show that he rejected Leveller democracy on
specifically social grounds (see p. 417 below). When Lilburne
returned from exile in 1653, aflame with plans to play the
Gracchus and carry a revolutionary Agrarian Law, Cromwell
held him a prisoner for the rest of his brief life. The bourgeois
revolution in England failed to do what its counterpart did in
France; it did not give the land to those who tilled it.

But with all their pioneering foresight, were the Levellers,
with the little group on their Left, the Diggers, ever anything
more than 'a few visionaries' (Gardiner's phrase)?[10] That is

the traditional Whig view of them; we shall see reason to discard it as we go along. Certainly the Levellers were a minority; so were the Cromwellians. But of the several parties in the crucial year 1649, it is conceivable that the Levellers for a time were the largest and that they had the best organisation. To secure 100,000 signatures, as in that year they did, in and around London to a highly seditious petition, at a time when the population of London and its 'liberties' was perhaps 450,000 was a remarkable achievement. Even after their suppression, neither the Protector nor the Royalists treated them as a negligible power. Oliver, to be sure, poured contempt upon them as 'a company of mean fellows, alas, not a lord nor a gentleman, nor a man of fortune, nor this nor that amongst them', but he also described them as 'pretty numerous' and added the advice: 'Do not despise them.'[11]

To understand this period, the most exciting chapter in our national history, we have to realise that the mass, the great majority of the English population, were political illiterates who had endured the Civil War as neutrals, understanding nothing of the issues. There was evidently hot excitement in London during the struggle at Westminster which preceded the outbreak of hostilities: but several of the more distant counties were so undecided, or so evenly divided, that they tried to contract out of the war by declaring their neutrality. The volunteers, who fought gladly, were on either side a minority: from 1643 onwards both King and Parliament had to fill their ranks with pressed men, snatched from civilian life, often with harsh violence. At a later stage, in regions of the south and west, the farmers and peasants organised themselves as 'Clubmen', whose purpose was to keep both sides at bay. Hobbes insisted on the indifference of the masses. 'There were very few of the common people that cared much for either of the causes, but would have taken any side for pay or plunder.'[12] Sir Arthur Haslerig, the republican leader, said the same thing about the majority in less offensive language: 'They care not what government they live under, so as they may plough and go to market.' The lines that divided classes and parties were fluid, and a surprisingly long list can be compiled of important politicians and soldiers who changed

sides during the struggle. It opens with the three most brilliant
of the King's servants, Strafford, Montrose and Clarendon.
Throughout the war, it was the practice of both sides to offer
the rank and file of their prisoners the chance of enlisting in
their own ranks, and many took advantage of it. In these
conditions, a third party, which knew how to talk to the
common man about the realities of daily life, his debts, his
tithe, and the exactions of the lord of the manor, should have
had a future before it. But it had first to win a vote for the
'hobnails and woollen aprons'. It could persuade the private
soldiers to don the sea-green ribbons that were its colours, but
without trained officers of their own way of thinking they were
helpless.

The verdict of the classical historians on the Levellers has
been accepted too readily. Lilburne's list of the reforms which
he hoped to carry in a few months was in reality, they tell us,
a programme for three centuries. Behind this judgment lurks
the liberal idea of progress. History, in this view, marches at
its own predestined pace; you cannot hurry it. The rotten
boroughs had to go on rotting till 1832; they could not have
been swept away a day earlier. And so one may go on, with the
abolition of the death penalty for petty theft, Catholic emancipation, the bestowal of the vote on the agricultural labourers,
the clipping of the veto of the House of Lords, and the recognition of the Irish Free State. Each came in its due season.
Today we know better. Just as anthropologists have discarded
the evolutionary theories of Lewis Morgan, Tylor and Frazer,
so historians have abandoned the belief in the steady, imper-
turbable advance of civilisation. Degeneration may be our
lot as well as progress, and we may have to reckon with long
periods of stagnation. Eight and twenty inglorious years of
reaction followed the end of the Commonwealth. The reign of
the Saints, as Macaulay put it, was followed by the rule of the
strumpets. But when the misgovernment became at last
intolerable, the sons of the men who fought at Marston Moor
and Naseby lacked the manhood to rebel against a much
worse King than Charles I, and had to be liberated by a
Dutch army. The only men of that generation who had the
courage to rebel were the peasants of the West Country, who

wore the Leveller sea-green ribbons when they rallied to the luckless adventure of the Duke of Monmouth. It was not the strumpets who brought about this degeneration. It began under the Rump and the Protectorate. The men whom Captain Cromwell enlisted in his troop of horse because they 'made some conscience of what they did'[13] were no longer the same men when he promoted them to his House of Lords and saw to it that they had rent rolls long enough to sustain their dignity as the new ruling caste. The idealism of the Puritan Revolution went to pieces in a society as ruthlessly acquisitive as any this island has ever witnessed.

We can understand what happened more easily than the historians of the nineteenth century. We have learned from contemporary experience to recognise a police state when its records lie before us, and we do not doubt that in the seventeenth century, as in our own, it sapped the moral courage and perverted the public spirit alike of those who submitted to it and of those who actively supported it. The tragedy was not so much that Cromwell managed to suppress the Levellers; it was rather that they had no successors, until the radicals of the London Corresponding Society came together during the French Revolution. The brief moment when English institutions under the flame of revolution were malleable passed with the consolidation of Oliver's dictatorship. Thereafter, unable to fight either with sword or pen, the kind of Englishmen who had begun under the sea-green flag to work for a true Commonwealth sought salvation, as did Lilburne himself, in some form of subjective religion—in his century in the Society of Friends, in the next in Methodism.

The nineteenth century, at the apex of its imperial glory, revelled in the tale of Cromwell's victories, his influence on the continent, his acquisition of Jamaica and Dunkirk, his megalomaniac dream of sharing world-wide empire with the other great sea-power, the Dutch. For our generation this story has lost its glamour; our values have changed. The stature of the man still impresses us, as it impressed our fathers. We still rank him as a great leader, for he learned, in a war in which everything had to be improvised, to combine inspiration with organisation. But his was not a creative or constructive mind.

Throughout a decade he held England in the hollow of his hand, yet he left it no better or happier than he found it. Not a single social reform stands to his credit—not even the simplest and most obvious of all, the abolition of the death penalty for petty crimes, which in words he favoured.

There are wicked and abominable laws which it will be in your power to alter. To hang a man for sixpence, threepence, I know not what . . . this is a thing God will reckon for.[14]

As he neared the end of his Protectorate, he looked back on its record and found two things good. 'We have made great settlements; that we have.' First he put the plantation of Ireland, and then the erection (through the Triers) of an established Puritan church. 'There hath not been such a service to England since the Christian religion was professed.'[15] There, summed up in his own words, the tragedy of his reign stares us in the face. His Puritan church crumbled when the Stuarts returned; his Irish settlement survived, to curse vanquished and victors alike. The record of the Levellers is one of failure and defeat. But if history still takes account of moral values, it may rate higher than Cromwell's victories at Drogheda and Wexford the daring of men who risked their lives to prevent the re-conquest of Ireland. The day when a group of Englishmen first publicly asked the question: By what right are we preparing to appropriate the lands and suppress the religion of the Irish?—that day, in the late summer of 1649, deserves to be remembered in our annals.

NOTES TO CHAPTER I

1. E. Lipson, *Economic History of England*, III, pp. 277-8.

2. Edward, Earl of Clarendon, *Life* (1759), I, p. 82; *History of the Rebellion and Civil Wars in England* (1888), II, p. 348; V, pp. 287-8.

3. J. Harrington, *Oceana* (Morley's Universal Library), pp. 49, 104-14. See Appendix to this Chapter.

4. Clarendon, *Life*, I, pp. 80-1.

5. *A Modest Narrative* (7-14 April, 1649); John Evelyn, *Diary*, 5 May, 1652.

6. [Anon.], *Persecutio Undecima* (1648).

7. Abbot, IV, p. 706.

8. J. Lilburne, *The Upright Man's Vindication* (1653), p. 15; cf. p. 239 below.

9. T. Hobbes, *Behemoth* (ed. F. Tönnies), p. 115; Clarendon, *History,* IV. p. 66.

10. S. R. Gardiner, *History of the Great Civil War*, III, p. 388.

11. Abbott, IV, p. 265.

12. Hobbes, *Behemoth*, p. 2.

13. Abbott, IV, p. 271.

14. *Ibid.*, p. 274; cf. p. 650, below.

15. *Ibid.*, p. 495.

APPENDIX

What, the reader may ask, was the value of such a sum as £2000 in the sterling of today? Only a very rash economist would risk an answer. The ways of life of the seventeenth and twentieth centuries differ so widely that it would be very difficult, if not impossible, to construct a weighted cost of living index that would apply to both. Yet some rough and ready ratio one must carry in one's mind. If one takes as a basis the ratio worked out in the last century by Thorold Rogers, which Firth accepted in his day, and adjusts it in accordance with the fall in the purchasing power of sterling, it is now (1953) necessary to multiply the seventeenth-century figure by twelve, or let us say, to avoid exaggeration, by ten. Even so, the result requires some interpretation. Thus £100 was regarded as a fair professional income; Harrington fixed it as the standard stipend of the clergy in *Oceana*. But it was worth far more than £1,000 today, since before 'the troubles' there was no direct taxation. The princely incomes drawn by the nobility from land paid neither income tax nor surtax and only a moderate poor rate. By way of contrast, the usual income of a village schoolmaster—£10 or £12 per annum—must have meant penury, even if, as is likely, he had a cottage rent free. Sometimes the tenfold ratio seems to work out correctly. Thus one learns from the *Memoirs of the Verney Family* that Miss Betty's boarding school cost £25 p.a. Today a fashionable boarding school for girls charges £225, with riding and music extra. Betty's letters are a poor testimonial to her teachers, but riding and music may have had pride of place in their curriculum, for in the case of Master Jack Verney, whose boarding school charged 12s. a week, the chief stress was on his playing of the viol and guitar. The scamp of the family, Tom, had to pay 10s. 6d. a week for his diet in the debtor's prison at the Fleet, 'which is as low as any one that is born a gentleman can possibly live at'. If one was born an orphan in the working class, one managed on less. In *London's*

Charity Enlarged (1650), the famous educational reformer, Samuel Hartlib, reckons that in an orphanage run on his principles a child could be fed on 10*d.* a week. The diet consisted of bread, beer, pottage, herring and turnips: there is no mention of milk, meat, cheese, green vegetables or fruit. Normally beef might cost 2*d.* and mutton 3*d.* per lb., but in years of scarcity these prices might be doubled. But no rule or ratio will apply all round. While labour was scandalously cheap, transport over the execrable roads was relatively dear. Travel by stage coach cost 1*s.* for 5 miles. Lastly I will add a group of figures which suggest that the tenfold ratio may be rather too high. Justices of the Peace were allowed 4*s.* a day for their expenses while attending Quarter Sessions. Lilburne in a letter to Cornelius Holland in one of his pamphlets says that King Charles allowed £3 or even £4 a week to his prisoners in the Tower (usually the prison for the nobility and gentry), whereas he had been offered a beggarly £1, 'which I scorned'. This agrees with the sum which the Long Parliament paid its members for their expenses at Westminster—£4 a week. This is in round figures a fifth, not a tenth of the amount paid today. But it was lavish in voting money on every conceivable pretext to its members, on a scale that no modern House of Commons would dare to propose.

CHAPTER II

Pulpits and Taverns

At mid-summer 1646, the first Civil War came to an end. Parliament was victorious and nothing whatever was settled. The indifferent mass seems to have blamed first the King and then Parliament for the steady deterioration of the country's economic case. Though Charles had sought refuge with the Scots, the political world expected his early restoration—on terms. It had still to discover how far his faith in God and his disastrous talent for intrigue would sustain him, even after total defeat. Above the wreckage of traditional England Parliament's New Model Army stood out, the most astonishing creation of the age. There had been nothing like the New Model in the history of our island, nor has it had a successor. English, none the less, it was in its sobriety, its scruples, its relative humanity. Victory, in Clarendon's phrase, was entailed to it, yet it never lost its inherited instinct of self-restraint. To its good conduct even its vanquished foes bore witness. The high level of intelligence of its officers, drawn though many of them were from the self-educated 'middle sort of people', yeomen, tradesmen and craftsmen, impresses us still, when we read in the *Clarke Papers* the records of their political debates.

The effect of victory on the minority of Parliament's convinced supporters, and on the New Model, was on the whole one of exhilaration. But indeed, throughout the twenty years of crisis, England was living under high pressure, so that alike in the fields of action and thought her people reached a stature, moral and intellectual, which dwarfed their normal selves.

'Liberty,' as Milton put it, 'which is the nurse of all great wits
. . . hath enfranchised, enlarged and lifted up our apprehensions
degrees above themselves.' Talent and even genius flowered
profusely among a population that probably did not exceed
five millions. Cromwell and Blake had several lieutenants not
very far below them in military and naval talent. When
Secretary Milton's eyes could see his pen no longer, there was
an Andrew Marvell to pick it up. Montrose and Lovelace were
only two among many cavaliers who sang as well as they fought.
From Hobbes and Harrington to Walwyn and Roger Williams,
was there ever in the vaster population of later days a bolder
group of speculative pioneers? Milton wrote at the time what
we feel as we look back on these crowded years:

> Behold now this vast city: a city of refuge, the mansion house
> of liberty, encompassed and surrounded with His protec-
> tion; the shop of war hath not there more anvils and hammers
> waking, to fashion out the plates and instruments of armed
> Justice in defence of beleaguered Truth, than there be pens
> and heads there, sitting by their studious lamps, musing,
> searching, revolving new notions and ideas wherewith to
> present, as with their homage and fealty, the approaching
> reformation.

Milton himself, hoping at one stroke 'to wipe away ten thousand tears out of the life of man', fought in the first *Tractate
on Divorce* the most tyrannous repressions of his age and race
with a courage no other Englishman dared to imitate through
the best part of the next two hundred years. If he defied the
inhibitions of his day on the perilous subject of sex, Winstanley
challenged it as boldly over property and organised religion.
Military talent, speculative audacity, poetic genius, saintly
insight in Fox and Bunyan, style in Clarendon, an elevation of
character in men like Brooke, Hampden, Vane, Falkland and
Hutchinson which ennobled the nation that bred them, heroic
obstinacy in Charles Stuart—what did this generation lack
save pedestrian common sense? What was it that made them
bigger than their fathers and nobler than their sons? Was it
the tension of a struggle in which men had tossed away the
scabbard? Or was it the sense, which no generation has felt
with the same assurance and sincerity, that God was among

them and very near to each of them? To some, like Fox,
Bunyan and Winstanley, He spoke in audible or visible signs.
Cromwell read His will in the providences and dispensations
that assured his unbroken career of victory. Milton had the
Holy Spirit for muse. This 'nation of prophets, of sages and of
worthies', this nation of Englishmen, to whom God, 'as his
manner is', had revealed himself first, was resolved that she
would not 'forget her precedence of teaching nations how to
live'. This generation believed that God Himself had chosen it
to complete a reformation of religion that would endure for
all time. It did not flinch when royal blood dripped from its
axe. More than ever in this hour of challenges, while Europe
averted its face in horror, it believed that it was destined to lead
civilised mankind.

In the summer of 1646 Parliament was by a substantial
majority Presbyterian. Clarendon, who can have been personally familiar only with the upper-class Presbyterians (for he
was a notable snob), wrote that they were addicted to luxury
and voluptuousness, and despised 'the thrift, sordidness and
affected ill-breeding of the Independents'.[1] He believed that
the severer standards of the Independents in matters of conduct
favoured the Cromwellian cause. It should be noted that both
'Presbyterian' and 'Independent' were used in a double sense,
religious and political. The word 'Presbyterian' in its current
English usage might mean merely a politician of the landowning or mercantile classes, who opposed the extremer claims of
the crown, and wished to be rid of episcopacy and to transfer
the control of the church and religious belief to Parliament.
Evelyn the diarist drew an amusing distinction between
'politic' and 'conscientious' Presbyterians. The word 'Independent' had also a wider political meaning and was often
used to include all, from the Levellers, republicans and
sectaries on the left to the Cromwellians on the right, who
opposed the Presbyterian conservatives.

The political problem in 1646 was, would the conservative
majority in Parliament be able, with the backing of the Scots
and the City, to impose its intolerant creed on the Army, to
which it owed everything? Before we consider the memorable
controversy over toleration, which engaged men's minds

throughout this year, we must face the new distribution of power which the victories of Fairfax and Cromwell brought about. The strength of the Presbyterians lay in their economic power, but from 1642 onwards the decision lay with the sword. In the early phases of the Civil War, Presbyterian leadership had been ineffective for the simple reason that neither the parliamentary oligarchy nor its leaders in the field really aimed at a decision. Their purpose was to check the King and bring the feudal and episcopalian party to terms, but they dreaded a revolution even more than they disliked arbitrary monarchy. By the end of the year 1644 their general, the Earl of Essex had already vowed to 'devote his life to repressing the audacity of the people'.[2]

This centre party, as all its actions no less than the frank words of its leaders show, was as much aware of the threat from below as of the incubus above it. The Presbyterians were the older wing of the Puritan host. They had a big following among the peers, drawn largely from those new-rich families which had sacked the church, appropriated the abbey lands and enclosed the commons during the previous century. But their main strength lay in the House of Commons and among the governing families of London and the chief commercial cities. They formed a plutocratic oligarchy, closely knit by marriage ties which frequently implied some degree of partnership in business, and also by their sincere attachment to the Protestant cause which had given them their lands. As a convenient measure of the economic power of this new upper-middle class of intermarried merchant and landowning families, the contemporary reckoning that the House of Commons of 1628 represented three times the wealth of the House of Lords is sufficiently familiar.

The lower House was in fact the wealth of England, and in so far as it was representative, what it represented was property —in the counties the free-holders only, and in the boroughs normally the close corporations. Though in its quarrel with the King it always claimed to speak for the nation, it did not in fact take its representative capacity very seriously. So little was it effectively responsible, even to the limited electorate which had nominally chosen it, that constituencies had no

right to know how their members had voted. To publish
the details of a division was a punishable breach of privilege.
Attendance in the overcrowded and uncomfortable chamber
was slack, and even in highly critical divisions it often
happened that only half the members voted. Membership
was then what it was destined so long to remain, a valuable
and often hereditary privilege in the gift of great and wealthy
families. An attempt to stir the electorate to exercise a real
choice between policies on a national scale was made for the
first time only in 1640, when Pym and Hampden rode round as
many constituencies as they could personally visit, to promote
the election of members who could be trusted to stand by the
Parliament's cause.

This daring innovation could not at one stroke alter the
outlook and atmosphere of the Commons. Secured against
dissolution save by its own consent, the Long Parliament came
to regard itself as a privileged governing caste, which enjoyed
collectively almost unlimited rights over against the nation.
This tendency was by no means confined to the Presbyterians:
the Independents inherited it when power came into their
hands. The perpetual senate which Milton advocated, in which
members would be removable only by resignation or death, was
not the mere eccentricity of a speculative mind: it reflected
pretty closely what the Long Parliament, without theorising,
meant to be.

The ultimate distinction between the Presbyterian and
Independent parties in England may have been, to put it
crudely, that between the arrived and the arriving. Only a
handful of peers adhered to the political Independents, while
the wealthy City of London was decidedly and often bitterly
opposed to them. Their typical leaders both in the field and in
the House were country gentlemen like Cromwell and Ireton,
well-to-do rather than wealthy members of relatively 'recent'
families. Behind the Independents in Parliament stood the
Independent and sectarian congregations, which varied in
doctrine as in social composition. These were the fighting men
of the Puritan Revolution. What was unique about the Independent political leaders was that they were sure enough of
themselves—or, as they would have said, of God's support—

to be relatively tolerant of the extremer and socially inferior sects on their left.

What these had in common, according to Lord Brooke and William Walwyn, who both as tolerant outsiders defended even the heretical groups on and beyond their fringe, was a habit of free discussion, which included the practice of questioning the preacher after his discourse. They shaded off into many sects or tendencies, Brownists, Anabaptists of several hues who now preferred to call themselves Baptists, the dwindling Family of Love, Seekers, Ranters and presently Quakers, and, standing latterly apart, the Fifth Monarchy men.

To the Presbyterians, free and tolerant discussion seemed absolutely sinful. Calvinism, it is true, was never for long wholly congenial to any large number of Englishmen. The Presbyterian majority in Parliament might dread episcopacy, and turn away with a curiously violent horror from the verbal beauty of the Prayer-book; but they retained something of the nationalist and Erastian tradition which the Tudors had imposed on the Church of England. They were on their guard against the extremer pretensions of Calvinist clericalism, and meant to retain over the church the supremacy of a Parliament which represented property. But like the divines, they were bent on uniformity and stoutly rejected toleration.

It is vital to grasp the significance of the disputes over church government and the right to persecute, which were the core of English history throughout this century. In their conscious minds the divines and pamphleteers who argued these questions out were doubtless sincerely trying to arrive at an understanding of God's will in this matter, by torturing texts from the Scriptures and basing themselves loyally on the model set by Old Testament magistrates and the Kings of Judah. Their ideal was to build England on the pattern of culture reached by a minor and rather backward Levantine people in the early Iron Age. It is not uncharitable to suspect that under the surface other considerations influenced them. England was in fact in the van of contemporary economic development, only a little behind the Dutch. It was a land in which real power was divided between the great capitalistic farming-landowners and the merchants of the world-wide trading corporations. Calvinists could not plead, as Catholics did, that they persecuted to save souls: souls were either damned from all eternity or they were inescapably elect. The utmost they could and did say was that a society which tolerated improper beliefs or rituals might draw down on its head the wrath of God. In its antique Hebraic dialect, this century was fighting out in its own way our modern issue of propaganda.

If we were planning a *coup d'état* anywhere in the modern world our list of objectives would include the airfield, the power-house and the railway terminus, but first of all we should make sure of the broadcasting station. With that in our control the mass of the population would accept as fact what we wished it to believe; our slogans and our promises would reach its ears and we could use our monopoly of the air to draw our own picture of our opponents. In the seventeenth century, wars were fought to secure control of the pulpit. That was a major objective in the English Civil War, as it was in the Thirty Years War which devastated the continent at the same time.

The pulpit was in this age incomparably the most effective means of winning and fettering men's minds. The press, indeed, was beginning to come into its own. Silenced under Laud, it sprang to life when the Long Parliament met. The weekly 'news-books', which had never been allowed to print domestic news, were now, after a period of total suppression, both numerous and relatively free. At the height of their influence the Levellers had their own weekly newspaper. Pamphlets poured both from the licensed and the 'underground' presses. The tavern, where men met to discuss the affairs of the day over a tankard of ale or a glass of sack, was becoming an important political institution, in effect a party club. Pym, it was said, had a tavern devoted to his interests in every ward of the City. The Leveller party was organised from certain taverns where it held its meetings. But these could rarely take more than about 200 persons. As yet neither press nor tavern could compete with the church. The public meeting on a secular platform was with rare exceptions an invention that still lay in the future. Pamphlets were, indeed, competing actively with the pulpit, but they could not reach the poor and the unlettered: some of the ablest of them, written in a heavy periodic English and packed with classical allusions and quotations, could appeal only to the learned few. Paper, moreover, must have been scarce and dear, for at a penny (the equivalent, more or less, of a shilling today) the miniature newspapers were not cheap.

In rural England—and England was still a green land of villages—the church was the one social centre the scattered population possessed, and to it in the happier days before the Puritan victory yeoman and labourer, pedlar and squire, resorted gladly for church ales and sports as well as sermons. Attendance was, moreover, compulsory and could be enforced by fines. Then as now, but more then than now, the spoken word with the drama of human contact and the mass emotion of an assenting congregation was more powerful than the printed page: only from the pulpit could the speaker, in a robe that marked him off from the common run of men, claim some measure of divine inspiration.

Hobbes tells us in *Behemoth* that when the Presbyterian divines made their long improvised prayers their hearers believed that their words were 'dictated by the spirit of God within them'.[3] Walwyn said the same thing about their sermons also. Something we have never experienced, something very strange and terrible must have happened in these English churches, when a sincere and gifted preacher, who himself believed he was inspired, spoke to a congregation which accepted him as God's messenger. He might, and often did, range over all the disputed social and political issues of the day—enclosures, usury, the right of resistance to tyrants, the divine institution of property or the equally divine precedent for holding all things in common. Even if he evaded directly contentious issues, he must promote one outlook or the other, acquiescence or rebellion, passive obedience or the questioning habit. Inevitably then, the control of the pulpit and the choice of the preachers had become throughout the centuries of faith a central political issue and a class issue.

The first victim of Parliament's triumph in the Civil War was the episcopal organisation of the Church of England. It vanished for fourteen years when Oxford surrendered. The King had always believed that 'people are governed by pulpits more than the sword in times of peace'. In this year 1646, he wrote that 'if the pulpits teach not obedience, the King will have but small comfort of the militia'. Yet it is doubtful whether the Church of England could ever have been a good instrument for his purpose. There were in this generation not a few talented men, there were even men of genius among its clergy, poets, philosophers and scholars. But the Puritans probably told the truth when they maintained that many of the rural clergy were too ignorant to compose a sermon. Most of them were content to mumble a printed sermon from the Book of Homilies. Few of them were popular preachers capable of swaying the multitude.

Laud came too late to reverse the flowing tide of Puritanism. The laity would not swallow his 'popish' doctrine of the sacrifice of God upon the altar. He did not encourage preaching and if ever his priests tried to win the good will of the masses, they failed completely. It was on ritual and coercion that he relied. In the towns, at least, the younger generation had come to despise ritual and resented the coercion of the ecclesiastical courts and the Star Chamber as something alien and un-English. Laud paid for his errors of judgment with his head; during the first four years of war and the deceptive sequel of nominal peace, the royalist clergy were swept away and forbidden either to preach or teach, to the number of over 2,000 out of a total of 9,000. Tried Puritans filled the places of the dismissed 'malignants', and the rest conformed, more or less sincerely.

By traditions based on the models of Geneva and Scotland, Presbyterianism also was a national church, which sought to stabilise the existing social order. But it understood far better than Laud's high church how to win and dominate the masses. During the critical years before 'the troubles' began, the wealthier Puritan merchants and gentry, who had not separated themselves from the Church of England, raised large sums of money to endow 'lecturers'—ordained clergy of their own way of thinking. Tradition has handed down to us a mistaken estimate of these Puritan preachers. It is true that their sermons were often inordinately long. Many of the specimens to be found among the Thomason Tracts seem to a modern reader pedantic and dull, with their mosaic of quotations in Hebrew,

Greek and Latin. But many of these were written to impress Parliament or the Lord Mayor on a prescribed fast day. On less solemn occasions the Puritans, when they preached *ex tempore*, let themselves go in a much more popular style. Hobbes, to quote from *Behemoth* again, tells us that they prided themselves on their powers of gesture and elocution. Thanks to 'their long-practised histrionic faculty' they could fill the church of a market town on working days in the morning. In this way their influence reached even the country folk. Thanks to their zeal and their understanding of popular psychology, Hobbes estimates that at the outbreak of the Civil War the 'greatest part' of the urban population of England as a whole, as well as the citizens of London, were devoted to Presbyterianism.[4] Pym relied largely on these ministers to organise his forces at the general election in the autumn of 1640. Under the Protectorate, the Presbyterian ministers were still a formidable electioneering force.

Sermons can do much when the devout accept them as inspired. But the Presbyterian church was before all else a system of discipline. The first duty of its ministers was to watch over the morals of their flock. With the assent of lay elders, they could refuse the sacraments to a sinner or a heretic, impose a public penance on him, excommunicate him and even hand him over to the civil magistrate. They could summon whom they would before them for examination. The setting up of a presbytery with such rights as these meant an immense shift of power from bishops and the old-world feudal gentry to the ministers and the elected elders, who were usually the well-to-do inhabitants of the parish—'men whom God has blessed', to quote a cant expression still in daily use among dissenters in the last century. Wealth was coming to be regarded as a sign of God's favour; it afforded a presumption, though not an infallible proof, that those so blessed were among the Elect.

What morality was it that the Presbyterians enforced by these formidable sanctions? Hobbes tells us in the same passage that their preachers assailed only 'carnal lusts and vain swearing'. 'Nothing else was sin', not even 'malice or greed'. They 'did never inveigh against the lucrative vices of men of trade or handicraft.' Hobbes was a shrewd but hostile witness. There is, however, objective confirmation for his account of Puritan discipline. Rendered confident by victory, Parliament passed, on 20 October 1645, an ordinance concerning suspension from the Lord's Supper. Anyone could be suspended, or eventually excommunicated, either (1) for failure to understand or refusal to accept a rather elaborate creed, which defined the Calvinist view of the Trinity, the sacraments and similar mysteries, or (2) for scandalous conduct. There follows a typical Puritan moral code. By far the longest part of it are the rules for keeping the Sabbath. Many sins are enumerated, which range from the making of an image of any person of the Trinity to marrying a Papist. There is no mention of the sin of exploiting one's servants. Misconduct in business is expressly exluded from review:

> The Presbytery or eldership shall not have cognisance of anything wherein any matter of payment, contract or demand is concerned.

This unlovely mercantilist morality, so lax in its indifference to 'lucrative vices', so austere in its enforcement of archaic Hebrew tabus, based the authority of the victorious Puritans firmly on the fear of Jehovah. For a time, thanks to the rendering into English of the Old Testament, and its acceptance as the word of God, English civilisation was partially eclipsed by this antique shadow. The outlook for humanity had been happier in the previous century, when More and Erasmus wrote. Presbyterians in France and Scotland gave proof enough of an heroic and militant courage, but the English sect in this generation had the defensive mind of a wealthy community which has arrived. The Presbyterians were the totalitarians of the time, who would have retained in their own exclusive hands all the machinery that formed opinion through a controlled pulpit and a licensed press. They would admit to the pulpit only men trained within a tightly organised church, and tamed by the discipline of closely regulated universities. From time to time an item of news reveals to the astonished reader the perversity of the moral values of this generation. Thus we learn that on a Sunday in 1648, the boys of Westminster School were playing after the sermon in the cloisters. They there 'abused a maid of sixteen' and about twenty of them 'fell on the top of her and hurt her'. When this story of adolescent brutality was reported to the House of Lords, it ordered the schoolmaster 'to take care of the scholars for the future and not suffer them so to abuse the Lord's day.'[5]

With the Independents and Anabaptists we shall grow familiar as we go along. In outlook, temperament and social composition these sects differed widely from the Presbyterians. The word 'Independent' (used in the religious sense) covers those like Oliver Cromwell who were prepared to accept a national church, but with greater congregational independence than the Genevan organization of presbytery, classis and synod allowed. It is also used to cover 'Congregationalists' (to give them their modern name). Known at first as Brownists, these sectaries had originally separated themselves from the church of their parish, to form what was called a 'gathered church'— it might be under a minister who had been forced out of his first pulpit, or one who after 1640 had returned from exile in the Netherlands or New England. The Independents and the radical sects—Anabaptists and many others—were the advance guard of the Puritan Revolution, who claimed more freedom of movement than they could enjoy in a church subject in the last resort to regulations laid down by Parliament. Each Independent congregation was an autonomous unit, which elected its pastor. Independent ministers were ordained, and were paid, by their congregations, whereas the Presbyterians relied on the tithes which had maintained their episcopal predecessors.

The level of learning and ability among the Independent divines was high, and it was their habit to preach boldly on political themes. Many of their congregations in London, Norwich, Newcastle and the larger towns were (as Clarendon tells us) wealthy. But there still survive in rural England, here and there, a few of their barn-like little meeting-houses, bearing a date from the years of the Interregnum, which suggest modest congregations of straitened means, a few yeomen farmers and craftsmen gathered round a lay preacher. In theology most Independents were at first orthodox Calvinists. Their adherents were by profession the elect, who felt within them the assurance that they were among the few 'called' to salvation. Inevitably,

it may be, in this God-intoxicated generation, the 'Saints'
came to think of themselves as a godly *élite* summoned by
Providence to rule, and complete the work of reformation, in
Oliver's phrase, 'in the world as well as at home'. This cos-
mopolitan phase of the Puritan Revolution came, however,
only in its riper years.

A very few of the political Independents, like Henry Marten,
Algernon Sydney and James Harrington, were deists; a few
like the younger Sir Harry Vane and eventually Milton were
'Seekers', and many were Anabaptists. How numerous and
influential the latter were is not generally realised. Thus, in
the Army three generals were said to be Anabaptists, Fleetwood, Harrison and latterly Ludlow, and at least seven
colonels, Alured, Hutchinson, Robert Lilburne, Okey, Robert
Overton, Rich and Saunders. In the army of occupation in
Ireland in 1655 ten colonels were Anabaptists.[6]

Behind the Anabaptists (i.e. 'again—baptisers', *Wiedertäufer*,
the name for the Baptists still usual in this generation) lay a
long and tragic history of persecution and struggle, which
neither they nor their opponents ever forgot. First heard of in
Zürich round about 1522, they spread rapidly down the Rhine
to the Netherlands and over much of south Germany and the
Tyrol. Whereas most of the Puritans were attracted especially
by the Old Testament they fixed their minds on the New,
bent on reviving the primitive church and on living as the
Gospels taught. They were originally pacifists, who would
neither fight, nor pay military taxes, nor go to law, nor serve as
magistrates. They condemned capital punishment altogether.
They would never take an oath, for (like Tolstoy) they would
not surrender their consciences to another's keeping. They had
no paid or professional ministry and partook of the Lord's
Supper only as a fraternal act of commemoration. They
rejected infant baptism, since they held that the act of joining
the community of believers involved an individual choice, of
which only an adult was capable.

These fraternal communities were closely knit and in some
sense had 'all things in common'. This might mean only that
they kept a common purse to relieve the needs of their poorer
members, but in Moravia up to 1620, and afterwards in

Hungary, Anabaptists lived, without money or wages, in thriving communal settlements (resembling the *Kibbutzim* of modern Israel) which were famous for their skill and honesty in several crafts and which evolved a system of education in many ways progressive. Anabaptists trusted to the 'inner light' of God's direct inspiration. They ardently believed in human equality and would neither bend the knee nor remove their hats for any human being—honours reserved for God: in other words, they respected the dignity of human personality. They taught and practised the equality of women and men. They set a high value on silence. They argued for toleration as a universal principle.

Their stricter leaders stood aloof, as pacifists, from the German Peasant War in 1525, but Thomas Münzer, the most famous of the few intellectuals who led the peasants, was very near to the Anabaptists, if not exactly one of them. In the barbarous repression which followed the peasants' defeat, the Anabaptists were all but exterminated, for Catholics, Lutherans and Calvinists behaved with an equal intolerance. But in Münster, under magnetic leaders of whom Jan of Leyden was the most famous, they threw over their pacifism, made an end of private property, adopted communism and drew their swords to hasten the millennium promised in the Apocalypse. Fighting for their lives with signal gallantry through a siege of sixteen months (1534-5), they gave way in some matters to fanaticism and adopted polygamy as their way of life. Was it this Biblical extravagance or their communism that made them a byword of horror to posterity? The Bishop who besieged them and tortured their leaders to death behaved with a savagery which no one censured. After the heroic tragedy of Münster, the Anabaptists in the Netherlands, known henceforward as Mennonites, abandoned communism and reverted to the original pacifism of the movement.

Spreading in its early days to England, this heresy was cruelly persecuted. In 1535 as many as 25 Anabaptists were burned alive in one day. Queen Elizabeth was no more merciful. The Family of Love, a harmless little sect which originated in Flanders, also spread across the Channel and survived with dwindling numbers down to the Whig Revolution. Commonly reckoned as a branch of the Anabaptist movement, it was both pacifist and communist. After severe persecution, it sought safety by avoiding publicity. The main body of English Baptists were at first akin to the Dutch Mennonites, and some few were in communion with them during their exile in Amsterdam. They multiplied rapidly during the Civil War and shed both their original pacifism and their traditional doctrine that no Christian could be a magistrate. Many of them fought for the Parliament and some (as we have seen) rose to high rank in the New Model and the navy.

By 1644 they had seven churches in the City alone, were strong in Southwark and were spreading in East Anglia and the home counties. They still retained their traditional objection to a paid, professional ministry and to the taking of oaths. The dialectic of faith created within this movement, in England as on the continent, the same contrasted extremes of conduct and belief. Some Baptists, like those of Münster, convinced that the Second Coming—the Fifth Monarchy as they called it— was at hand, were militants, who wished to use their swords only to ensure the reign of King Jesus and the Saints—that is to say of themselves. Under the flamboyant General Harrison they had for a time influence with Cromwell. It was the Quakers, in the next decade, who revived the quietist and pacifist traditions of the Anabaptists. Though it discarded baptism with all the sacraments, 'the Society of Friends', as Troeltsch has put it, 'represents the final expression in its purest form of the Anabaptist movement'.[7]

This digression may be pardoned, because the Levellers can hardly be understood without reference to the Anabaptist tradition that lay behind them. The party was translating into a political programme the ethics of a religious movement. The profound belief of the Anabaptists in human equality, including the equality of the sexes, their faith in toleration, their horror at the thought of capital punishment, their rejection of any form of priesthood—all this and much more the Levellers inherited. John Lilburne and Richard Overton were Anabaptists. Clarendon, who knew John Wildman personally, says that his father was an Anabaptist. In later life, if we may trust Bishop Burnet, he was if anything a deist. Walwyn would join no sect, but he defended the Anabaptists and even the despised Family of Love with warm sympathy.

With the Anabaptists and their kindred sects, the Seekers and ere long the Quakers, we have left behind us the authoritative, dogmatic pulpit. The Baptists had their lay preachers, but it was their habit after the sermon to invite questions and permit discussion. In the ferment of revolution, ephemeral sects and congregations multiplied beyond counting, often under 'mechanic preachers', self-taught laymen, who worked with their hands and dared to interpret the Scriptures without the ability which the Presbyterians demanded from their divines to translate at sight from Hebrew into Latin. Among them there were radicals in politics as well as religion, who were suspected by the timid rich of advocating 'anarchy and community'. This world of the sects was dynamic: it was in motion, straining towards new visions of man's relation to God and new forms of human society. By contrast Presbyterianism was static. It sought no new or developing reformation. It stood by the reformation of Geneva. Once for all, Calvin had laid down God's plan of damnation, and with it the theocratic system of discipline that befitted this creed.

It is significant of the temper of these sects that the Independents and Baptists survived the persecutions of the two succeeding reigns and the invidious discriminations that vexed them down to the last century, while the much more numerous Presbyterians vanished from English soil. (The Presbyterian churches existing in England today are immigrant branches from the Scottish churches.) As a political force they went under in 1649, and though they enjoyed a brief revival after Cromwell's death, it was only to experience after the Restoration the disillusionment they merited. But, as we shall see, their economic interests found a mighty protector in Cromwell himself.

So in 1646 the Presbyterians had arrived; the Independents were arriving. But they were still struggling, with the Baptists and other sectaries as their allies, for the right to exist.

NOTES TO CHAPTER II

1. Clarendon, *Life*, I, p. 41.

2. The Venetian envoy quotes Essex to this effect (16 December, 1644): 'Is this the liberty which we claim to vindicate by shedding our blood? . . . Our posterity will say that to deliver them from the yoke of the King we have subjected them to that of the common people. If we do this the finger of scorn will be pointed at us and so I am determined to devote my life to repressing the audacity of the people' (*C.S.P., Venetian, 1643-7*, p. 162).

3. Hobbes, *Behemoth*, p. 25.

4. *Ibid.*, pp. 22-5.

5. *Perfect Occurrences of every day's Journal*, 4-11 February, 1648.

6. A letter to Thurloe from Dublin, dated 17 October, 1655, reported that 12 governors of towns, 10 colonels, 3 or 4 lieut.-colonels, 10 majors, 19 or 20 captains and 23 officers in the civil list, are Anabaptists, 'and many more' (*Thurloe State Papers*, IV, pp. 90-1).

7. E. Troeltsch, *The Social Teaching of the Christian Churches* (English translation), II, p. 781.

CHAPTER III

The Case for Intolerance

Among the notable happenings of the eventful year 1646 was the publication of a book as scandalous as it was pious, by a Presbyterian minister, Thomas Edwards. *Gangraena* appeared in three instalments, in February, May and December. It was addressed with a fulsome dedication to the Lords and Commons, and its purpose was to warn them of the wrath to come, if they failed to suppress the countless heresies proclaimed by unordained preachers and unlicensed books. Edwards informed the Presbyterian rulers of England that their ordinances forbidding laymen to preach had had no effect. The sects were steadily growing, and 'all sorts of illiterate, mechanic preachers, yea of women and boy preachers', were thriving at their very doors. In a single parish of the City no less than eleven sectarian congregations were meeting. At all this 'our dear brethren of Scotland stand amazed'. From exhortation he turned to threats. 'God who is said to scatter kings can scatter you.' With much quoting of the Church Fathers, including both Luther and Calvin, he predicted that the judgment of God, perhaps in the shape of a pestilence, would fall upon a land which tolerated such doings.

Edwards made good this general indictment in minute detail. Many godly ministers had sent him precise evidence about the heretics, backed in some cases by sworn statements. In his first instalment he enumerated no less than 176 heresies and errors preached in England during the previous four years; in his third the total rose to 300. Some of them were charming eccentricities, the belief for example that all beasts and birds will be resurrected and live for ever. Then as now there were humanitarians who not only opposed war, but even held that it is unlawful to kill a chicken. Others held that it was unlawful to keep days of thanksgiving for victories, that is to say for one man's killing another. Some believed that the souls of the departed Saints are present with their friends on earth. There were actually sectaries who held that it was lawful to use organs and other musical instruments in worship, and to sing hymns. Worse still, 'a great sectary', whom Edwards did not name, would tolerate stage plays and even witches.

But it was against graver heresies than these that Edwards pointed his heavier guns. Some sectaries held that John's baptism by water ended with the coming of Christ, who instituted no baptism at all. A lieutenant in the Army argued in his sermons that the Sabbath was for the Jews and not for Christians. An apothecary who preached at Yarmouth, one John Boggis, went further and denied that Christians are subject to the Old Testament. He was imprisoned for blasphemy and Edwards sympathised with the Recorder, who wished he had the power to hang him. The worst of all heresies, however, was to rob the Puritans of their hell. So Edwards attacked the scholar, poet and mystic John Saltmarsh, for long a chaplain in the Army, who believed that all shall be saved at last, even Judas and Cain. It was scandalous that his *Smoke in the Temple* should have been licensed for publication. Another 'Universalist', Henry Denne (whom we shall meet again at Burford), an Anabaptist and Arminian, was justly imprisoned at Cambridge but released 'by influence'. He taught that Christ died for Judas as well as Peter, and for the Turks and Pagans also; all sins were forgiven when Christ shed his blood. The same heresy was preached by the Anabaptist preacher Thomas Lamb (by trade a soap-boiler and afterwards a Leveller) whose church in Coleman Street was specially dear to youths and wenches. He travelled as far as York and Bristol preaching and he too, though sent to prison by the Lord Mayor of London, was released after a time by influence.

Edwards was shocked by the habit of some of these preachers to invite questions after their sermons. He attacked another famous Anabaptist preacher, William Kiffin, who practised faith healing by the laying on of hands and anointing with oil. Sometimes he succeeded, but 'the man is base'. Again we are told that several women died, soon after they had been 'dipped' by the Anabaptist Oates of Colchester, for which he was justly imprisoned. In the eyes of posterity his graver sin was that he begat Titus. In one way or another, God's judgments fell visibly on the sectaries; thus John Lilburne, shortly after publishing his reply to William Prynne in a pamphlet, all but lost the sight of one of his eyes by accidentally running into a pike in the street. Again, a married couple of Colchester (whom Edwards named) resolved that if they had any more children, they should not be baptised. Thereafter, the woman bore two children, both dead, of which one was a monster.

Edwards's chief delight was, however, to accuse the sectaries (often by name) of drunkenness and a rich variety of sexual sins, including incest. He revelled in a suggestive description of the doings of a preacher who insisted on baptising his converts naked as St John did, the women as well as the men. Edwards's vulgarity reached its climax when he described the private lives of the women preachers. One of them, a lacemaker whom he named, deserted her 'unsanctified husband . . . that did not speak the language of Canaan' and ran off with another woman's husband. Another, Mrs Katherine Chidley (whom he describes as 'a brazen-faced, audacious old woman') set up with her son ('a pragmatical fellow'), a Brownist church at Bury in Suffolk, and together they wrote some pamphlets. We shall meet her as the leader of the Leveller women; evidently she was a pioneer of women's emancipation.

Gangraena culminated in an attack on the advocates of toleration. Foremost among them is Hugh Peters, the Independent minister, who had been an exile in Laud's day, first in the Netherlands and then in New England. He was a chaplain to the New Model, and evidently a popular preacher, whom the royalist journalists accused of playing the buffoon in the pulpit. He had angered Edwards by attacking the greediness of the Presbyterian divines, some of whom drew incomes of £200 or £300 from tithes (in contemporary values say £2,000 to £3,000, virtually tax-free). Dr Annesley, Susannah

Wesley's father, drew an income of £700 from his Presbyterian church in the City. Edwards admitted that one of them had £400 *per annum*, but retorted by estimating that from various sources Peters himself earned no less. In general he maintained that Independent ministers were as grasping as the Presbyterians. One of them expected 4*s.* or 5*s.* a year even from the maid servants in his congregation, while its wealthier members paid him £15 or £20.

With these side-lights on the professional jealousies of the ordained divines, it is easy to understand the respect of the Levellers for the Anabaptist preachers, who earned their own living. One of them, Hanserd Knollys, could draw, according to Edwards, a congregation of a thousand, and he had the audacity to pray from the pulpit for the release of John Lilburne from Newgate. Edwards summarises a typical sermon by Hugh Peters.[1] He declared that the word 'uniformity' was not to be found in all the Scriptures (nor the demand for uniformity either, on which the Presbyterians insisted): the Scriptural ideal was 'unity'. He went on to declare that in Holland, Anabaptists, Brownists, Independents and Papists could all live quietly together; why should they not do so here? In the Army there were twenty several opinions and they too could live quietly together.

The Army was never long out of Edwards's thoughts and he massed conclusive evidence about its shocking state of mind. A certain lieutenant would not actually deny, yet he doubted the resurrection of Jesus Christ. A godly minister affirmed that there were whole troops among the horse which denied the resurrection of the dead and the existence of hell. A colonel at Oxford said he was against fighting the Irish, because they did but fight for their religion and liberty of conscience and for their lands and estates; nor was he alone, another great sectary in the Army said the same thing. Two godly witnesses testified that a captain in Colonel Hammond's regiment said (on 12 August, 1646) that the House of Commons was the Parliament of England and not only a part of it—an opinion which the rest of the Army shared. 'He spake of the City of London with much detestation, saying he was persuaded [it] hated that Army.' A chief cause of this 'detestation', which led to the Army's occupation of London a year later, is mentioned in Edwards's own pages, for he cites the City's petition, which prayed that all heretics, Anabaptists, Brownists, Independents and the like 'be removed from all places of public trust, both martial and civil'.[2]

This prosperous man was plagued by many fears. 'Within five days,' he wrote, 'as many books came out for a toleration.' He compiled a long and alarming list of such books, which should all be burned by the public hangman. 'O what a burnt offering, a sweet-smelling sacrifice would this be to God.' Among the advocates of toleration whom he names, together with the veteran Saltmarsh, is Roger Williams, whose claim to our grateful remembrance is not merely that he wrote *The Bloody Tenent of Persecution*, but also that he founded the colony of Rhode Island on a footing of toleration, and set an example of justice and friendship in his dealings with the Indians as remarkable as William Penn's. It is worth noting that there is no mention in *Gangraena* of *Areopagitica*, which for all its noble eloquence fell still-born from the press, unregarded either by friends or foes.

Edwards is most voluble in his attacks on Overton, Walwyn and Lilburne, whom he treats as a group, though the nick-name Leveller was not yet in use. He summarised some of their early democratic pamphlets not unfairly, argued (as Cromwell afterwards did) that they would make for anarchy and put some shrewd questions to John Lilburne, which were duly answered (as we shall note in a later chapter) as his political programme evolved. So much was fair argument—there are about ten pages of argument in a book of over 500 pages—but Edwards served it up with some of his characteristic person-alities. We need pay no attention to his silly slander that Lilburne merely wrote for money, or that after Walwyn and Lilburne had failed to secure nomination as M.P.s for South-wark, the former wrote his pamphlets in order to commend himself to the Independents and so secure nomination for the pair of them for a pocket borough in Cornwall. The history of the Interregnum might have run somewhat differently if these two unusual men had sat in the Commons.

About Walwyn Edwards wrote in genuine alarm: he was 'a

Seeker and a dangerous man and a strong head': moreover he was 'Jesuitical'. He denied the Scriptures to be the word of God—the only one of Edwards's accusations which Walwyn condescended to answer. According to Edwards, Walwyn had said it was a sin to pray for the King; he even argued that the kingdom could not be safe under the government of a king. He described the Presbyterian divines Marshall, Calamy and Sedgwick as 'mountebanks' who would soon leave their trade if they had no tithes; cobblers, weavers or soap-boilers were as much entitled to preach as they. About the Irish he said that they 'did no more but what we would have done ourselves, if it had been our case'. 'What,' he asked, 'had the English to do in their kingdom?' Again he said that 'they were a better natured people than we', and asked, 'Why should not they enjoy the liberty of their consciences?'

As for Lilburne, 'a darling of the sectaries . . . and a great stickler in the meeting at the Windmill Tavern', his 'insolency and contempt of authority' were unparalleled. Though he 'pretends great piety, holiness and suffering for the truth of God', Edwards's 'godly ministers' reported him to be 'a man of loose life, profaning the Lord's day in sports, . . . a player at cards . . . who will sit long with company at wine and tippling'. Coming down to details Edwards can prove that Lilburne played cards several times at Oxford. In this instance the godly witnesses are referring to one of the most tragical moments in John's eventful life, when he lay in a royalist prison under sentence of death. Let us hope that in fact he had this distraction. Finally Richard Overton is dismissed as a 'desperate sectary, one of Lilburne's breed and followers', notorious for the 'profanity' of his pen. But Edwards has the satisfaction of reporting that for printing scandalous things against the House of Lords, his press was seized and he was thrown into Newgate 'as he most justly deserved'. His pamphlets aim at the overthrow of the constitution based as it is on King, Lords and Commons, and would in their place 'set up the body of the common people as the sovereign Lord and King'. In short 'the desperate wickedness' of Overton lay in this, that he attacked both 'the Lords and the ministers'.[3]

The reader, it may be, has had more than enough of this

book, famous and influential though it was. Its purpose was to start a reign of terror at the expense of the 'sectaries', and to some extent it succeeded, for many of their preachers spent some time in prison. Edwards is forgotten today: the only English Presbyterian divine of his generation whom posterity remembers is Richard Baxter.[4] He too was a conservative who feared the radicals of the Army and there were definite limits to his tolerance. But he was not a stranger to Christian charity and he had the moral courage to write on behalf of the peasants evicted by enclosing landlords in the Midlands. A much smaller and meaner man, Edwards was probably more typical of the orthodox Calvinist clergy of his day. He thinks of himself as a member of a privileged caste, a Brahmin threatened by the anti-clericalism of the Levellers and sectaries, and he rallies to the support of the other privileged caste which they menaced, the Lords with the King at their head. His church is for him first of all a buttress for authority, and he sees the doctrine of toleration as the most dangerous solvent of the social structure, the class society in which he occupied a respected and enviable position.

But second rate though his mind was, Edwards was shrewd enough to understand that authority is something more intimate and pervasive than a House of Lords or an established church. Here is a passage more significant than the whole of the rest of his book. It is a cry from the heart:

> Oh! let the ministers, therefore, oppose toleration, . . .
> possess the magistrates of the evil of it, yea and the people
> too, showing them how if a toleration were granted, they
> should never have peace in their families more, or ever after
> have command of wives, children, servants.[5]

What was at stake, then, was the authority every head of a middle- or upper-class household enjoyed over wife, children and employees. Unless Baptists, Brownists and Levellers were suppressed, the immemorial hierarchy of every respectable home in the patrilinear society of that day would be destroyed.

To grasp the full meaning of this argument against toleration, we must somehow contrive to measure the crushing weight of authority in the seventeenth century. We must start, where everything in social life has its beginning, with the relations of parents and children. Aubrey put it on record that till his own generation 'the child perfectly loathed the sight of his parents'.[6] Sons, even when they were thirty or forty years of age, had to stand in their presence; daughters must either stand or kneel on a cushion. Towards the end of the reign of King James the Venetian ambassador described

> the admirable custom of the country, well worthy of imitation, for every child on first meeting his parents each day to kneel and ask their blessing. This happens in the public streets and in the most frequented and conspicuous places of the City, no matter what their age.[7]

Prince Charles, he added, did not like to be long in the country, for fear of missing his father's blessing. This subordination of sons to fathers startles us in the memoirs of this generation. Sir Simonds d'Ewes, the perfect type of the sincere upper-class Puritan, was under the absolute authority of his father until long after he had finished his studies at Cambridge and been called to the bar. His father began and dropped several treaties for his marriage without ever consulting him, and finally chose a bride for him whom he had never met, though he had an indistinct recollection of seeing her once as a child of seven. He did not question his father's right to treat him in this way, though he did criticise his faulty technique in these negotiations, his 'inconstancy'. At Oxford it was the custom to use the rod on students until they graduated as Bachelors of Arts.

In this context there is much to be learned from the vivid autobiography of Thomas Ellwood, an early Quaker convert, who served Milton as secretary and friend. He describes the tests to which his moral courage was subjected, when he first obeyed the rules of the Society of Friends which forbade him to lift his hat in honour of any man, to use such titles as master, sir and my lord, or to say 'you' instead of plain 'thou' and 'thee'. At first he could not bring himself to keep his hat on in his father's presence, or to address him as 'thou'. When at last his conscience forced him to obey, his father, though he was a 'professor of godliness' and a Justice of the Peace under the

Protectorate, struck him with both fists and beat him over the head with his cane, wounding him severely. Then, though Thomas was a young man of twenty, his father took his hat and money and kept him indoors the whole winter.[8] The suggestion that a prime function of religion, whether the King's high church or the Parliament's Presbyterianism, was to maintain authority, including parental authority, is rendered the more probable by a negative instance. Clarendon, in the famous passage in his *Life* in which he laments the corruption that sapped the younger generation of Cavaliers during the Interregnum, starts with the decay of 'pietas', submission. 'Children asked not blessing of their parents. . . . Parents had no measure of authority over their children.' The church, which helped to keep the King's contemporaries tractable, was crushed, but the lads whose fathers rode behind Prince Rupert would not kneel to the Roundhead God. They grew up godless and undisciplined.

If the sons of the middle and upper classes were kept in subjection with an arrogance that might turn to brutality, it is not difficult to guess what 'servants' (a word which in this century included all employees) had to endure from authority. There are in this case no memoirs to inform us; 'servants', even if they were literate, were too busy, or too poor, or too modest to publish any record of their obscure lives. But we get glimpses, none the less, even at times in official documents, of the manners of the day. The Merchant Adventurers drew up the most elaborate rules to govern the behaviour of their members, who enjoyed a monopoly for the import of English cloth, lead and tin in various continental ports in succession (Antwerp, Hamburg and now Rotterdam), together with extra-territorial rights, freedom from taxation, and other valuable privileges. These rules punished sexual irregularities, drunkenness and gaming and then went on to forbid any 'person of this fellowship [to] call any other of the fellowship—not being his servant—knave, false knave or any other vile or opprobrious name . . . [or] . . . to strike, beat or wound any other person of the fellowship'. The eloquent words 'not being his servant' inform us that it was in no way contrary to the strict code of manners of this proud oligarchy to beat one's employees and scold them in insolent language, even in the presence of foreigners.[9]

At home in England when a 'gentleman' (meaning a person entitled to a heraldic coat of arms) faced a 'servant' of whatever degree, there was no need to draw up rules to enforce a dual code of manners. Gentlemen carried swords; servants had only their naked hands. On this fundamental difference the class society of seventeenth-century England was based. Here and there in the *Verney Memoirs* the beating of servants is mentioned as a usual occurrence. In one instance a cavalier refugee in France who had forced his French servant to 'unbutton' and endure a whipping on his naked person was surprised that such treatment met with disapproval from the French. A Verney of the next generation whipped his valet repeatedly. Things were, it may be, appreciably worse before the Civil War. It was then that Laud forbade the practice of drinking the Redeemer's blood in two qualities, a vintage wine for the gentry, *vin ordinaire* for servants. In those days it was not unusual for the squire to sit throughout the service in his high fenced pew with his hat on his head.

We should learn a good deal of the truth about class in this century, if we could grasp the whole etiquette of hats. The first principle was that the master of the house, and no one else, had the right to wear his hat in his own home. That is why members of Parliament sat 'covered', and are still supposed to do so. The second principle was that social inferiors 'uncovered' before their superiors—a practice still recalled by the elderly rural labourer's habit of 'touching his cap'.

Against this recognition of class distinctions the Quaker refusal to uncover to any man was a conscious protest. Liberal historians are apt to treat this habit of theirs as a meaningless breach of good manners, a tasteless eccentricity. On the contrary, it meant the boldest thing in social life. It was a revolutionary act. Taken over, like most of the Quaker beliefs and practices, from the Anabaptist tradition, it was an affirmation of human equality, a revolt against class. Though the English Anabaptists were much less strict in observing the rule than were the early Quakers, there is ample evidence that the bolder of them did observe it. Edwards mentions a sectary at

Bedford who insisted on remaining covered before the County Committee. The Diggers, when they met Sir Thomas Fairfax in 1649, refused to uncover before the Lord General, 'because he was their fellow-creature'. Again in 1657, when Venner, the militant Anabaptist preacher and Fifth Monarchist, was interrogated with his fellow-conspirators by Cromwell as Lord Protector, they would not 'put off hats to him and thou'd him at every word they spake to him'.[10] These simple men proclaimed with a gesture the equalitarian doctrine which the Leveller leaders defended in their pamphlets.

There is yet another witness whom we may call to complete our survey of the sociology of hats, a man of a very different origin and outlook. Colonel Harry Marten lives in history as the wit of the Long Parliament, an audacious pioneer of republicanism, a regicide and also a determined opponent of Cromwell's usurpation. He was, with the veteran Selden, the earliest and boldest advocate in the House of the toleration of Catholics and five years before Cromwell's effort he asked the Commons (albeit in vain) to re-admit the Jews to England. The inheritor of a big estate in the Vale of the White Horse, he was, to quote Aubrey's character-sketch,

> as far from a Puritan as light from darkness. . . . He was a great and faithful lover of his country and never got a farthing by the Parliament. He was of an incomparable wit for repartees, not at all covetous, humble, not at all arrogant as most of them were, a great cultor of justice and did always in the House take the part of the oppressed.

Marten was an intimate friend of the Leveller leaders and collaborated with them closely during the three critical years before the King's execution. One of the early Leveller pamphlets, of which he was part author, remarks that in the early days of the Long Parliament hardly would its members 'permit men to stand bareheaded' before them in their committee rooms; as the years went on they grew more arrogant. In 1648, giving the charge to the Quarter Sessions at Reading, Marten 'would not suffer the jury or the people to stand bare before the bench, telling them they ought not, because they were the supreme majesty and authority of England'.[11] Marten thought and spoke in secular terms, but he meant the same thing as the Anabaptists and the Quakers. All of them stood for social equality.

With what wit and courage the Levellers fought we shall see in later chapters. But we must first note how near the Presbyterians came to success. On 2 September, 1646, the fruit of two instalments of *Gangraena* and of two petitions from the City against toleration was duly harvested. One of the most monstrous bills in English history was welcomed by the Commons and got its second reading without a division. At Westminster the Independents, realising that on such questions they were in a hopeless minority, had almost ceased to fight. The Blasphemy Ordinance (finally passed 2 May, 1648), began by classing as felonies, punishable with death, the publishing or maintaining any heresy concerning the complicated mysteries of the Trinity and the Incarnation. The threat of being hanged, drawn and quartered was launched not only at Unitarians and Arians, but at many less radical heretics as well. It would be enough, moreover, that two of Mr Edwards's godly ministers should give evidence of words spoken in private conversation. Secondly for blaspheming the name of God, or any of the Trinity, or impugning the word of God, the offender was to be branded with a B on his left cheek; for a second offence the punishment was death.

Thirdly came a long list of lesser but still damnable heresies —those chiefly with which Mr Edwards has made us familiar. The doors of some foetid prison would close for life on any man who dared to hope that the sacrifice of the Son of God might avail to save all mankind; or 'that a man by nature hath free will to turn to God'; 'that a man is bound to believe no more than by his reason he can comprehend'; 'that the baptising of infants is unlawful'; 'that the church government by Presbytery is anti-Christian or unlawful'; 'that the use of arms for public defence is unlawful' and many similar deviations from Calvinist orthodoxy. Any accused person must renounce his error publicly in church. If he failed to do so, he was to be imprisoned until he found two sureties who would undertake that he would not publish or maintain the said error any more. On a strict reading this barely credible bill was directed against the majority of the English nation—all Episcopalians, Arminians, Independents and Baptists, to mention only the Protestants. Unless they made a public recantation of their beliefs, they were threatened with imprisonment for ever. The English nation was at the moment helpless; the New Model Army, however, took note of the fact that in this bill Parliament had condemned most of its officers and men to jail for life.

In this way, then, the Presbyterians sought to secure for middle- and upper-class householders 'command of wives, children, servants.'

NOTES TO CHAPTER III

1. T. Edwards, *The Second Part of Gangraena*, p. 183. One cannot infer from this sermon that Hugh Peters was himself prepared to tolerate Papists. How near he was at this time to the Levellers is clear from his *God's Doings and Man's Duty* (1646), briefly summarised in S. R. Gardiner's *History of the Great Civil War*, III, p. 85. See also p. 644 below.

2. The City presented two petitions against toleration in this year, on 15 January and 19 December. The latter was directed specially against the Army (Gardiner, *op. cit.*, III, p. 183).

3. Edwards's attacks on the Leveller leaders are in *Gangraena*, Part I, p. 53, Part II, p. 30 and Part III, pp. 148, 159-60.

4. [Baxter denied that he was a Presbyterian (*Reliquiae Baxterianae*, pp. 55-6); but his theological and political positions at this time were virtually indistinguishable from those of the Presbyterians.—Ed.]

5. *Gangraena*, Part III, p. 156.

6. J. Aubrey, *Brief Lives* (ed. A. Powell), p. 11.

7. *C. S. P. Venetian, 1621-3*, p. 451.

8. Ed. S. Graveson, *The History of the Life of Thomas Ellwood* (1906), p. 56.

9. E. Lipson, *Economic History of England*, II, pp. 218-19.

10. *Gangraena*, Part I, p. 106; ed. G. H. Sabine, *The Works of Gerrard Winstanley*, p. 15; Abbott, IV, p. 465.

11. *A Remonstrance of many thousand citizens*, in Wolfe, p. 126; *Mercurius Pragmaticus*, 22 August, 1648. See also p. 342 below.

CHAPTER IV

Richard Overton

The Leveller pioneers were not intimidated by *Gangraena*.
The big battalions at Westminster and the coercive machine of
the state were against them. But Overton and Walwyn possessed
a weapon, both offensive and defensive, rarely found in the
armoury of the Puritans; they had a lively sense of humour. If
they kept their serenity, there was yet another explanation;
each of them inhabited a private world of his own, far above the
pestilential atmosphere congenial to Mr Edwards. Walwyn
was a humanist who could retire to his cherished library.
Overton had his memories of the formative years he spent in
the Netherlands. At this time the United Provinces led western
civilisation, as much by the glory of their art and the daring of
their experiments in the natural sciences, as by the liberality of
their statesmanship. When Overton recalled the tolerant
republic of Grotius and Rembrandt, in which Huygens and
Spinoza were getting ready to enlighten ages to come, Thomas
Edwards must have looked like a puny barbarian long since
outmoded.

Of Richard Overton's early life we know little more than
the fact that he was a member of the congregation of English
refugees established in Amsterdam, until the meeting of the
Long Parliament emboldened many of them to return. Originally Brownists, they became Anabaptists and were in communion with a branch of the Dutch Mennonites who were
Arminians and pacifists. A document in Latin has survived in
the records of the latter in which Overton, after summarising
the creed of this church, adopts it as his own belief, repents his

sins and applies for membership.[1] A few years later, in one of his satirical pamphlets, he wrote a humorous page in Latin, which if not elegant is at least grammatically correct.[2] Evidently he had had a good grammar school education, but whether in England or Holland we do not know. He seems also to have spent some time in Germany and knew High German, for in *The Arraignment of Mr Persecution* he quotes a German proverb correctly, though his spelling is eccentric. He was a printer by trade, perhaps an inherited calling, for Henry Overton, a printer who kept within the law (which Richard did not) seems to have been a relative.[3]

In his mental development Overton travelled, as the years went on, far beyond the thinking of these simple, idealistic refugees, but something of the climate of opinion in which he grew up remained with him in his maturity. This realm of thought is worth exploring, for here lie the roots of the Leveller movement. The beliefs of John Smith's congregation were set out some time before 1614, in a creed of 102 articles. The two clauses on toleration declared:

§71. That all repenting and believing Christians are brethren in the communion of the outward, visible church . . . be they Roman Catholics, Lutherans, Zwinglians, Calvinists, Brownists, Anabaptists or any other pious Christians, who in truth and by godly zeal strive for repentance and faith, although they are implicated in great ignorance and weakness. Nevertheless we greet them all together with a holy kiss, deploring that we should be so divided . . .
§86. That the magistrate by virtue of his office is not to meddle with religion or matters of conscience, nor to compel men to this or that form of religion or doctrine, but to leave the Christian religion to the free conscience of every one, and to meddle only with political matters . . . because Christ alone is the king and lawgiver of the church and the conscience.

This creed then went on to reject the whole idea of punishment. A Christian must 'love his enemies, and not kill them. . . . He must visit them in prison but not throw them there. . . . He must suffer persecution with Christ . . . which it is impossible to do and to keep the sword of vengeance.' It follows that

Christ's disciples must compose all their own differences among themselves, and may not go to law nor take an oath. The experience of these Anabaptist communities which dispensed with lawyers and settled their disputes among themselves was evidently the background of the proposals which the Levellers were soon to make to substitute neighbourly arbitration, in all but the gravest cases, for professional courts of law. This was not a reformer's daydream, or an antiquarian's fancy. It was a rule of life they had seen at work from boyhood.

Finally the creed declared that to meet the necessities of 'poor brethren' and of the church itself 'all things ought to be common'. The usual practice was that each of these communities, the English and the Dutch alike, maintained a bakery where food was prepared for their needy members. These kitchens were also hostels, in which the needy, the sick and the aged were housed. At Amsterdam it seems that many perhaps most of the English Anabaptists lived together in their 'cake-house'.

The first of Richard Overton's writings that have come down to us are two topical satires in verse dated January and March 1642. His heroic couplets are fluent if rough, as the manner of his generation was. They are far superior to the general run of contemporary satirical verse and were well calculated to flatter the mood and tickle the taste of Puritan London. It would be churlish to complain that the salt of these amusing trifles retains little of its savour today. *Articles of High Treason exhibited against Cheapside Cross* celebrates the destruction of this relic of medieval 'idolatry' with its sculptured Pope and its Virgin. The modern reader cannot repress a shudder as he pictures this act of vandalism. *New Lambeth Fair* describes an auction of relics and indulgences offered by the Pope himself to raise a ransom for Archbishop Laud—a grim subject for joking.

Overton's most daring publication was a little book entitled *Man's Mortality*, which horrified his contemporaries hardly less than Milton's pamphlets on divorce. It endeavours to prove from scriptural texts, in the customary style of the day, that man's soul perishes with his body at death and has no existence until the Last Day, when soul and body will both be restored in the miracle of the resurrection. In short, as the title page runs, 'man as a rational creature is a compound wholly mortal, contrary to that common distinction of soul and body'.[4] Some not very impressive arguments drawn from natural history are used to confirm this negative view of the immortality of the soul. William Godwin, who had a violent prejudice against the Levellers, said that Overton and Walwyn were 'unbelievers', and maintained that Overton's use of Biblical texts and his very brief profession of faith in the resurrection of the body on the last page of the book were merely a device to escape capital punishment for atheism.[5] Eduard Bernstein, whose pioneering work in re-discovering the Levellers and Diggers was of the first importance, adopted Godwin's guess. Their view is plausible and yet they failed to penetrate Overton's secret, for they overlooked a fact which suggests a different interpretation. This opinion that the soul perishes at death and comes to life again only with the body in the miracle of the resurrection had been for more than a century the tenet of the Anabaptists, proclaimed in Switzerland and professed by all their persecuted branches in Germany and the Netherlands. *Gangraena* contains a lively description of a debate on this subject in one of their chapels in the City at which Overton was present. All that he did was to repeat their heresy with the addition of confirmation drawn from biology.

Overton, in short, was a pioneer in that type of apologetical literature common in the next two centuries, which aimed at proving that science and revelation are, in spite of appearances, really in agreement. So much, indeed, he tells us himself. In his indignant narrative of the conduct of the soldiers who arrested him in May 1649, he tells us that they robbed him of the manuscript of a book which he had begun to write, entitled *God's Word confirmed by his Works*.[6] Its theme was that the main truths of revelation can be demonstrated from the facts of nature. In this he 'endeavoured the probation of a God, a creation, a state of innocency, a fall, a resurrection, a restorer, a Day of Judgment, etc., barely from the consideration of things visible and created'. This seems conclusive. Milton and Sir Thomas Browne also held the 'soul-sleeping' heresy, and they assuredly were no crypto-atheists. Sir Thomas at the start of

Religio Medici even refers to it as 'the African heresy', and so traces it back to antiquity. About Walwyn Godwin was even more grossly mistaken. Overton's affirmation of his faith in the resurrection, brief though it is, rings sincere. He was no 'unbeliever', yet he had strong rationalist tendencies.

In his moods of high spirits, what Overton wrote with the greatest zest were his anti-clerical satires against the Presbyterian divines. These he modelled on the performances of the Elizabethan Martin Marprelate. He calls himself young Martin Marpriest and aims his darts from his shop in Toleration Street at Sir John Presbyter and Sir Simon Synod. The humour is broad, and he repeats his favourite inventions rather too often. A cherished theme of his, as ancient as the popular anti-clericalism of the medieval *Land of Cockayne* and as modern as the *Pickwick Papers*, is the gluttony of the divines, their 'godly care for their own guts' and their love of 'delicate, toothsome tithes'. Jokes about their consumption of tithe pigs and geese alternate with shrewd comments on topical themes. He reminds us that the men who are Presbyterian 'persecutors today' got their benefices from Laud, wore surplices, 'crouched and cringed to their altars yesterday' and delivered up those less servile than themselves to the High Commission's tyranny. The record of these Vicars of Bray under Tudors and Stuarts goes far to explain the contemptuous anti-clericalism of the Levellers. While creeds and rituals swung to and fro, backwards and forwards, from Rome to Canterbury and from Canterbury to Geneva under Henry and his three children, the two Charleses and Cromwell, the majority of the beneficed clergy always contrived to adapt themselves to the abruptest of changes. The proportions varied from generation to generation, but two in three of God's salaried servants would always profess whatever creed their rulers paid them to preach.

Sometimes, however, Overton strikes a graver note and contrasts the opulence of the Presbyterian clergy with the misery of the maimed soldiers, who are given a ticket permitting them to beg. Here is his picture, put into the mouth of a divine, of the triumph of the Presbyterian cause:

> Oh! then our church would shine most gloriously in their satin doublets and cloaks, lined throughout with plush, their

wives and children flourish like young princes, their spits filled with pigs, geese and capons, their cauldrons with beef, their prisons with heretics; widows, orphans and lame soldiers standing with their pitchers begging pottage at others' doors, and the Independents, Brownists and Anabaptists driven into augur-holes as it was in the primitive times.[7]

Overton wrote five of these Marpriest satires during 1645 and a sixth early in 1646. *The Ordinance for Tithes dismounted* (29 December, 1645) is typical of them all. He starts with an attack on tithes, which he treats as a Jewish institution that has no rightful place in a Christian society: 'therefore, reverend brethren, you must not think to do Christ's work and exact Moses his wages'. He goes on to show how the Presbyters, 'the brisk and spermatick sons of the bishops, took over from their fathers when they grew decrepid', and then he attacks the whole Presbyterian organisation newly prescribed by an ordinance of the Long Parliament, with its provinces, classes and parishes.

Here's like to be Inquisition after Inquisition, worse than the Spanish, after the blood of the people. . . . The bishops' courts stripped us of our clothes, but the presbyters' courts will strip us of coats, skins, lives and all.

There is enough of Overton's usual fun in this piece to lure the indifferent citizen into reading it, but when he comes to his main argument against regimentation and intolerance, one is aware that the man is in deadly earnest.

The most popular and influential of these Marpriest pamphlets was the first of them, *The Arraignment of Mr Persecution*.[8] The first of three editions was published by Overton's own illicit press on 8 April, 1645. Mr God's-Vengeance prosecutes Mr Persecution, who is defended by Sir Simon Synod and Sir John Presbyter, before the judge Lord Parliament and a Jury of Life and Death, among whom sit Good Samaritan (Walwyn) and Truth-and-Peace (Roger Williams). Such allegories, with their castes of abstractions, seem tedious to the modern reader, but Overton captures our attention at the start and through fifty closely packed pages our interest rarely flags. He makes adroit use throughout of the procedure of English justice—

so well, indeed, did he do it that Bunyan evidently used this trial as his model for similar scenes in *Pilgrim's Progress* and the *Holy War*.[9] He jests in his usual style about the greed of the Presbyterian divines; he is irreverent at the expense of Mr Edwards, Mr Calamy and, indeed, of the whole Westminster Assembly. He jokes grimly about the 'mickle army' of the Scots and their Calvinist instruments of torture. Yet he so manages his comic interludes that they in no way lessen the force of his argument for toleration.

Part of the case against Persecution is historical; Overton's picture of the ruin (which he may have seen) that followed the war of religion in Germany is specially moving; more briefly his witnesses point also to Ireland. He must have startled his Puritan readers, when he proved that in cruelty and intolerance there was nothing to choose between Protestants and Catholics. He argues, of course, for toleration for Brownists, Independents and Anabaptists. But he is no less emphatic in putting the case for the Jews. The real proof of his moral courage is that (like Roger Williams and Walwyn) he pleads for peace and understanding between Catholics and Protestants. If they would but cease to force one another's consciences,

> in a short time the enmity of heart between the Papist and Protestant would be quite worn out. Why should we hate and destroy one another? Are we not all the creatures of one God, redeemed by one Lord Jesus Christ? This should provoke us to love and peace, one towards another. If God have revealed more light of the Gospel to one than another shall the more knowing trample the ignorant under his feet?

In these questions Overton is echoing the case for toleration based on Christian charity which he had learned as a youth among the Anabaptists of Amsterdam. But as he goes on, one can perceive how his mind has matured. Here in a few lines is the gist of his own case for toleration:

> He [Mr Persecution] is an utter enemy to all spiritual knowledge, a hinderer of its increase and growth. For no man knoweth but in part, and what we know we receive it by degrees, now a little and then a little. He that knows the most was once as ignorant as he that knows the least. Nay,

is it not frequent among us, that the thing that we judged heresy we now believe is orthodox?

This is the secular case for toleration, or part of it. It is the fruit of self-criticism, there is even a note of healthy scepticism in it. Toleration begins when it occurs to us that we may possibly be mistaken. The man who wrote these limpidly simple lines had learned something from history.

If Overton had written nothing more than this popular indictment of Persecution, he would deserve an honourable place in the intellectual history of England. But he became in the course of this year, 1646, the devoted friend and lieutenant of John Lilburne, and his pen was henceforward at the service of the Leveller movement.

John's was the more original and creative mind of the two, but it worked by sudden flashes, without method or sequence. Overton's was a more disciplined intelligence, and he was much the better writer. It happened more than once that he gave an incomparably more convincing statement of an idea which Lilburne was the first to engender in his chaotic pages. Overton's political writings are the work of a sturdy and competent journalist with a modern outlook, which convey their meaning to the reader of today instantly and directly, almost as if they were contemporary documents. His view of the state is completely secular. He was one of the few men of his day who had ceased to live in Judaea. It is tempting, for example, to contrast him with John Goodwin, one of the most liberal and scholarly of the Independent divines. Both defend the right and duty of resistance to tyrants. Goodwin reminds us vividly —as if it had happened yesterday—that the Prophet Elisha resisted Ahab, when that tyrant tried to behead him, and that David resisted King Saul.[10] The only thing that worries him is that the early Christians did not resist their Roman persecutors. Probably they were too weak to do so. To be sure, Tertullian says that they were non-resisters on principle: but he was an unreliable witness whom we may dismiss, for in later life he became a Montanist and an open heretic. Overton also felt that he ought to quote a precedent or two for resistance. No ancient Jews for him. He cites the heroic resistance of the Dutch to their Spanish tyrants, and the spirited behaviour of the

Scots when they rose in arms against Archbishop Laud.[11] It is hardly surprising that his contemporaries mistook this man for an atheist.

As we go along we shall meet this pioneer in several character-istic postures—stubbornly resisting arrest, defying Cromwell in person and at odds with the more solemn Puritans in his own Leveller party. He did not take himself too seriously. He could even write of himself in an open letter as 'little Dick Overton'. That letter, penned in captivity in the Tower, annoyed his comrades, 'the sea-green gallants', when it was read out to them at one of their meetings in the Whalebone Tavern, because of the tastelessness of one of its jokes. Unabashed, in a second letter, he offered to put a little water in his wine, if they would put some wine in their water.[12] A wit always pays a heavy penalty for amusing Anglo-Saxons; he is classed among the not quite respectable. That may have been Overton's case. He must have lived a precarious life as a heretic scribbler and an unlicensed printer, with a wife to keep and three children. Did he do it chiefly with his pen, or with that illicit press which was eventually seized? We do not know, but we get the impression of poverty endured with gaiety and spirit, as we meet him in his overcrowded lodging in the spring of 1649, when he was arrested with the other leaders of the party. Was his character as steadfast as his intellect was clear? When Puritanism degen-erated in its totalitarian phase under the Protectorate, some of the Levellers got entangled in cobwebs of royalist conspiracy. Sexby made shocking errors of judgment, but he kept his honour. Although the evidence is uncertain, some have thought Overton's record in those days as dirty as Wildman's. Let us remember, none the less, that in the early years of the Revolu-tion, he lived recklessly and fought bravely. [See also p. 624 below.]

NOTES TO CHAPTER IV

1. Overton's creed is reprinted in an Appendix by the Dutch Baptist Prof. Müller to Dr B. Evans's *The Early English Baptists* (1862), I, p. 254. To this Appendix (pp. 211 sq.) I am indebted for the facts I have given about the English refugees in Amsterdam. The creed quoted is in modern English, because Dr Müller had to translate it from the Dutch archives of the Waterland Church.

2. *A Sacred Decretal* (June 1645).

3. It is unlikely that Colonel Robert Overton was a relative, though both men were Anabaptists. both wrote well and both were imprisoned in the Tower. But the Colonel was the head of a well-to-do landed family in the neighbourhood of Hull. Milton wrote of him as a friend who shared his literary interests.

4. On the soul-sleeping heresy see D. Saurat, *Milton, Man and Thinker*, Part IV, section iii.

5. W. Godwin, *History of the Commonwealth of England* (1824-8), III, p. 53. Godwin's big four-volume history is, in spite of mistakes, prejudices and some pedantic moralising, a work worthy of his abilities and industry. He was the first student of this period who used the Thomason Tracts, which had as yet no catalogue. He found and read some of Lilburne's pamphlets, but cannot have discovered any of Walwyn's. On the other hand, he made good use of the Journals of Commons and Lords, still at this date little studied by historians. His hostility to the Levellers, though they held many of his own opinions, is to be explained by his dislike of all organised agitation.

6. *The Picture of the Council of State* (4 April, 1649), H. and D., pp. 214-32.

7. *Martin's Echo* (27 June, 1645), p. 7.

8. W. Haller, *Tracts on Liberty in the Puritan Revolution*, III, p. 203.

9. The suggestion comes from T. C. Pease, *The Leveller Movement*, p. 100, n. 21.

10. J. Goodwin, *Anti-Cavalierism*, in Haller, *Tracts on Liberty*, II.

11. *An Appeal from the Commons*, in Woodhouse, p. 323.

12. *Overton's Defiance of the Act of Pardon* (2 July, 1649); *The Baiting of the Great Bull of Bashan* (16 July, 1649).

CHAPTER V

William Walwyn

A surprising figure in this Puritan age, Walwyn seems to have strayed into it from the humanist Renaissance. His intellectual contemporaries were rather Erasmus and Montaigne than Edwards and Prynne. More completely than any of his Leveller comrades he threw away the dogmas of the churches, yet he was at once the most charitable and the most revolutionary of Christians. In one sense or another of the word, all the Levellers aimed at equality; his goal was equality for all men in their incomes, as well as in legal status and education.[1] By its wit, its verbal felicity and the range of its thought the best of his writing deserves the rank of literature.

William Walwyn was born at Newland in Worcestershire in 1600, the second son of a well-to-do landowner. His maternal grandfather was a bishop. Though his elder brother was entered at his Oxford college as a gentleman (*armiger*), it is significant that unlike Lilburne, who often used this word to describe himself, Walwyn was content to call himself a merchant. Like Lilburne, also a younger son, he was sent to London and apprenticed to the cloth trade. As a member of the Merchant Adventurers' Company, whose privileges the Levellers incessantly attacked, he belonged to the prosperous middle class. He and his family, he tells us, lived simply and dressed 'in plain apparel'; it was his habit to go on foot from his home in Moorfields when he had business in Westminster. He and his family were 'tender one of another'; he was devoted to his 'dear and ancient mother whom he had the greatest cause to love' and also to his wife and children 'whom he valued tenfold above his life'.

His son-in-law, the physician Dr Humphrey Brooke, after 'eight years abode' under his roof, wrote with admiration of the 'innocency and real goodness that is so visible in his life and conversation', noted his 'inward sweetness and calmness of spirit' and pronounced him the man 'the most averse from contention' and 'the most cheerful and pleasant' he had ever known. So modest was he that he 'blushed', if he heard an 'obscene word'. Never, Brooke adds, did 'a hasty word' pass between him and his wife. She (to return to Walwyn's own account) was never in good health for a week together, which may have some connection with the fact that she bore him 'almost twenty children', of whom several daughters survived. He took pleasure in his garden, but his chief delight was in his library, stocked with translations of the classics, ancient and modern. To the horror of his Puritan critics, his favourite authors were pagans and Catholics, whom he would read on the Sabbath day—Plutarch, Thucydides, Lucian, Seneca, Charron and above all Montaigne.[2]

Walwyn led a stay-at-home life, never travelled abroad and never left London save to visit his native county and—a significant exception—the New Model Army. He was content to remain a member of his parish church and never joined a sect, though he was a decided Antinomian. When the troubles began, he 'spent himself' (to use Dr Brooke's phrase) for the Parliament. As he tells us himself, he was active in his ward and parish, notably in drafting for the Common Council and Parliament a 'remonstrance' which set forth 'certain infallible maxims of free government'; this was 'stifled'. Later, when things went ill for the Parliament, he joined what we should call today the 'ginger groups' at Salters' Hall and the Windmill Tavern, and petitioned for a *levée en masse* of all the well-affected in the kingdom. He must have served in his local train-band, for as he tells us he practised his arms in his garden, but if ever he was called up, he cannot have been a combatant on active service. 'Although possibly nature'—so he runs in *The Fountain of Slander Discovered*—'would prevail with me to kill rather than be killed, yet to my judgment and conscience to kill a man is so horrid a thing that upon deliberation I cannot resolve I should do it'. He believed that it is lawful to kill 'to free a nation from bondage and tyranny', yet only after 'all means used for prevention', and then 'with   dismal a sadness exempt from that usual vapouring and gallantry (accustomed in mere mercenary soldiers) as should testify to the world that their hearts took no pleasure therein'. The man who wrote these words was rather more adult than most of his contemporaries.

Dr Brooke's sketch of Walwyn was written for a purpose— to answer the calumnies of the clergy. Accordingly it stressed his innocence and gentleness. That was not the whole truth about this far from simple character. John Lilburne estimated his 'choicest comrade and fellow-sufferer' as a man 'as able in parts as any is in England'. Even more remarkable than his ability was his self-reliance, his readiness to stand alone and defy the majority. The only portrait we have of him is an engraving dated 1680, which shows us his broad shoulders and his handsome head under a perruque at eighty years of age. If we may trust the artist, who could draw a strong and confident line, he carried the weight of his years easily. His singularly attractive features are clean-shaven, regular and well proportioned. We are at a loss to say which aspect of the man strikes us most forcibly—his strength, his intelligence, his serenity or his kindliness.[3]

Walwyn was never what Lilburne was, a popular leader and orator. He seems to have disliked publicity, for most of his pamphlets were unsigned, save those written in self-defence. Behind the scenes, however, and on committees he wielded great influence as an *éminence grise*. This power of his, precisely because it was anonymous and disinterested, infected his opponents with a morbid blend of hatred and fear. Edwards's attack resembles flattery when one compares it with the picture Dr John Bastwick drew of him. What impressed this Presbyterian martyr was that Walwyn seemed to dominate the sectarian 'toads', who shared his activities 'in the very suburbs of hell'. Among them he was 'one of the properest gentlemen . . . and the most remarkable and taken notice of by reason of his habit and his busy diligence'; yet he was notoriously 'bankrupt of all goodness' and a 'knave from his mother's womb'. The man who wrote this was no vulgar fanatic, but a physican who had studied in Padua as well as Cambridge, and a scholar capable of writing classical Latin.[4]

The more conservative Puritans were convinced that Walwyn was a Jesuit (born, as some said, in Spain) and by some freak of natural history an atheist as well. With a formidable attack published in 1649 by the pastors of seven Independent and Anabaptist chapels, under the title *Walwyn's Wiles*, we shall be concerned in a later chapter. The malignity which Walwyn inspired is the more remarkable in that he never wrote a harsh word about any man, until he answered the slanders in this pamphlet. What set the seven godly scavengers muck-raking was his anti-clericalism and his supposed communism. To see him as his contemporaries saw him, we must remind ourselves that the arts of rousing public opinion and organising men into parties were new discoveries in that generation. Pym had practised them but his methods were obvious and rather clumsy; Hugh Peters understood them more or less, but Walwyn's subtlety terrified his opponents, for this master-craftsman pulled wires silently in the dark. Finally, he questioned all the accepted truths about everything from heaven to hell. Not content with attacking the clergy, he would have liked to sweep away all the organised churches as they then existed.[5] Worst of all, he would have made an end of class itself —an insufferable challenge both to the Presbyterians in power and the Independents who jostled their sluggish rear. But we have dwelt on Walwyn's reputation long enough; let us turn to the man's own writings.

It is typical of Walwyn that the earliest of his writings that has come down to us is a plea for toleration. *The Humble Petition of the Brownists* dates from the troubled years before the outbreak of the Civil War. It is much more than a defence of one persecuted sect; it states the case for toleration without exception. One by one it mentions the peculiarities of the various sects; 'if the Brownists will separate themselves' . . . 'if the Puritans will not use the service book' . . . and so on through a list that includes Socinians, Arminian high churchmen and even Adamites and the despised Family of Love, who

'give each other the sweet kiss of peace'; . . . 'great pity it were
to hinder their mutual charity'. His occasional jokes (which
never hurt) about the more eccentric heretics are characteristic
of the author. The bravest thing in this pamphlet is its unequivocal statement of the case for the Catholics:

> If the Papists will have altars, priests, sacrifice and cere-
> monies and the Pope for their supreme head in spiritual
> affairs . . . the matter imports not, so they obey the king as
> temporal head and humbly submit to the state and civil
> laws and live quietly together.[6]

This was written while Pym was lashing the City mob into
fury against the Catholics, much as Shaftesbury did in the next
generation. Toleration, Walwyn argues, will not breed confusion, 'considering the good natures and sweet dispositions
of our English nation'. Given freedom of discussion, he is convinced that what is erroneous will in time wither and perish.
A year later, when he wrote *Some Considerations* (10 November,
1642), the war had already begun and he argues that the
dissensions between Protestants (meaning low churchmen)
and Puritans are the main obstacle to an early victory for the
Parliament. He lays the chief blame for these quarrels on the
clergy, who are the hirelings of the politicians, bought by tithes
and preferment and trained up in the universities for such disputes. He attacks the clergy also for preaching peace before
liberty had been won. 'There is peace in a dungeon.'

Another year passed and the Walwyn we now meet has
grown into a mature artist who can find the most moving
words to express his deepest feelings of compassion and indignation. In *The Power of Love* he assumes the character of a
preacher of the hunted Anabaptist sect, the Family of Love.
In his preface he supposes the reader, when he sees the title,
will sneer: 'Here's one of the Family of Love.' To which comes
the unexpected retort: 'Well, what family are you of?' There
follows a sermon on inequality which deserves to be quoted:

> Consider our Saviour saith: 'He that hath this world's goods
> and seeth his brother lack, how dwelleth the love of God in
> him?' Judge then by this rule, who are of God's family.
> Look about and you will find in these woeful days thousands

of miserable, distressed, starved, imprisoned Christians. See how pale and wan they look; how coldly, raggedly and unwholesomely they are clothed. Live one week with them in their poor houses, lodge as they lodge, eat as they eat and no oftener, and be at the same pass to get the wretched food for a sickly wife and hunger-starved children. If you dare do this for fear of death or diseases, then walk abroad and observe the general plenty of all necessaries, observe the gallant bravery of multitudes of men and women abounding in all things that can be imagined. Observe likewise the innumerable numbers of those that have more than sufficeth. . . . Observe the whole body of religious people . . . and see whether they have not this world's goods. Their silks, their beavers, their rings and other devices will testify they have; aye and the wants and distresses of the poor will testify that the love of God they have not.

This is William Walwyn speaking in his own person, though he wears the cloak of a sectary. Again and again, in all his more personal writings this note recurs, to find its final expression in his longest and most memorable work, *Tyranipocrit*. The Familist's sermon is followed by a reminder that the first Christians had all things in common.[7] One cannot infer that this was Walwyn's own ideal and still less that he thought of it as an aim realisable in his own day. That, as we shall see, he denied, six years later, in a a formal manifesto of the Leveller party. But from this and much clearer evidence to come, we may conclude that he was by temperament inclined to 'community', whereas Lilburne was an aggressive individualist.

It is obvious throughout Walwyn's writings, but especially in *The Power of Love*, that he sympathised with the belief known in our day as 'universalism', though he would not have proclaimed even this as a dogma—the belief that all men will be saved. This was to sap the entire Calvinist structure of terrorism. An assertion of the goodness of God was the sin which in these days Christians found unpardonable. His imaginary preacher is made to say:

The work of your redemption was perfected when Christ died. . . . Neither infidelity nor impenitency nor unthankfulness nor sin nor anything whatsoever can make void his purchase; no, though with the Jews you should deny the Lord that bought you.

It is clear that at this time Walwyn did hold this extreme antinomian position, with its corollary that no such thing as hell exists, save indeed the psychological hell a man must endure in remorse for his sins. But Dr Brooke has told the painful story of the test to which, somewhat later, he and his father-in-law subjected themselves; they found indisputable proof in three passages of Scripture that a blazing, physical hell does exist. 'Though it seems contrary to reason that a man should be punished everlastingly for a little sinning in this world . . . yet have we both submitted our reasons to God's word, the places forementioned being express for the same.'[8]

We meet the same Walwyn, as mature in his style as in his reasoning, once more in *The Compassionate Samaritan*, another of his pleas for toleration, this time on behalf of all the separatists—the Brownists, Anabaptists and other sectaries. He applauds them for their faith in free discussion, which they invite in their meetings. He points to the proud record of the Dutch as a proof that diversity in religious belief neither hinders prosperity nor prevents effective unity in action, as the Spaniards can testify. He sweeps away the case for the authority of the Westminster Assembly of Divines (or for that matter of any church council) by reminding it that the liturgy it rejected had been approved both by an equally venerable assembly (Convocation) and by Parliament as well. As for the iniquity of schism, he tells the Presbyterians bluntly that their breach with the Church of England was as schismatical as the Tudor revolt against Rome. There cannot, he argues, be two governments in one commonwealth. 'The end of government being to promote virtue, restrain vice and to maintain to each particular his own, one sort of government which we call the civil, either is sufficient or by the wisdom of Parliament may be made sufficient for these ends.' He is arguing, in short, for a secular republic.[9]

Walwyn is never vituperative, as most of his contemporaries were, but when he discusses the clergy he can hit hard and speak plainly. He traces to professional egoism the claim of the

Presbyterian clergy to punish and persecute those who differ from them. To beget awe in their flocks they must base their monopoly of preaching on divine right, or in other words on the apostolical succession, though for centuries it passed through the hands of the Popes. Without this the people would not take on trust what the ministers give them. The clergy's living depends on their keeping up the belief that their specialised knowledge and especially their familiarity with the original tongues is necessary for the interpretation of the Scriptures. Christ had been satisfied with fishermen and tentmakers to preach his Gospel. But they, to maintain their power and prestige, must pose as a 'peculiar tribe of nearer relation to God than other men'. And so (unlike the Anabaptists who teach and preach for nothing) they levy their tithes and 'hover about dying men for their fee and hope of legacy'. History proves that the clergy have been 'the chief causers of most of the wars of Christendom'. What these divines lack is 'love and lowliness of mind', the main evidences of the Gospel. But since there is no liberty of reply in their churches and they control the press, they can confute all opinions unless men will run the hazard of imprisonment ('as I do now'). He ends with a plea for freedom of the press.

How many men, since writing was invented, have given out the best that was in them when they had to reply to a vulgar and scandalous opponent? Walwyn was one of the very few. The five pamphlets in which he answers Mr Edwards's serial *Gangraena*, brief and slight though they are, are enough to stamp him as one of the most attractive and original minds of his generation. In the first of them, *A Whisper in the ear of Mr Thomas Edwards*, Walwyn takes the attack more or less seriously yet with perfect good temper, and condescends to answer it by giving a few facts about his own public activities. But it is with Edwards's slanders against his fellow-Christians of the various sects that Walwyn is really concerned. Edwards, he tells us, is 'quite deaf on the right Christian ear, deaf to all that is good'. He then diagnoses his malady in some detail; it is because he fears the loss of his craft and its gains, together with his authority over his flock, that he assails the sectaries with such cruelty. 'I am as much grieved', Walwyn comments, 'that any man should be so unhappy as to be cruel or unjust, as that any man should suffer by cruelty or injustice.' Finally he whispers the remedy in Mr Edwards's ear:

> [Love is the] balsam that often and well rubbed in may cure your gangrene, and though at first your distemper may cause you to loathe it, yet take a little and a little of it, use inwardly and outwardly, constantly, and you will find your disposition to alter . . . until you come to be a strong and healthful Christian.

There is much in this wise yet humorous pamphlet one might be tempted to quote, but one passage in which he sums up his good advice to Mr Edwards is enough to show its quality. Protesting against the use of force to ensure religious conformity, he declares that God himself only persuades the heart. 'Compulsion and enforcement may make a confused mass of dissembling hypocrites, not a congregation of believers.'[10]

A prediction of Master Edwards his conversion and recantation is a masterly essay in sustained irony. In a long imaginary speech Edwards describes the pride, the greed and the disdain he now repents—his foibles of a sad countenance and a black garb, his preference for ignorant and superstitious people, since these admired his parts and learning as gifts of the Holy Ghost and believed his erring sermons to be the very word of God. Walwyn keeps up the fun with unflagging zest through nineteen pages of merciless exposure. In wit and invention doubtless Voltaire surpassed him, but one cannot read this punishment of Edwards for his cruelty and injustice without recalling the penalty that Maupertuis incurred in the *Diatribe of Dr Akakia* for the same sins. But is wit the right name for Walwyn's talent? Certainly in this piece he is in deadly earnest. It is intolerance rather than Master Edwards that he scourges, and in yet another style he preaches a deeply moving sermon on his own heart's theme that love is the one thing needful.[11]

In spite of 'all the labour bestowed upon him', Edwards in due course produced yet another instalment of *Gangraena*. In *An Antidote against Mr Edwards his old and new poison* (10 June, 1646) Walwyn had to admit that he had 'cast his pearl

amiss'; Edwards (as he put it) acted on Machiavelli's observation: 'Cast dirt enough upon them, some of it will stick.' But
Walwyn made yet another attempt 'to wash the blackamore
white'. *A Parable* (29 October, 1646), in an allegorical manner
that recalls Overton's *Arraignment of Mr Persecution*, is at once
the most amusing and the most deadly of his polemical tracts.
The physicians hold a consultation on Master Edwards's case.
Dr Love tells him his distemper is grave and Dr Patience
agrees. Policy cannot deny that he is sick, but asks for time, so
that he may first 'build God's own house, sweeping out the
heretics and schismatics, stopping the mouths of illiterate,
mechanical preachers and beautifying this holy building with
the glorious ornament of uniformity, the mother of peace'.
Conscience replied that no sin is more odious in God's sight
than to enforce men to worship contrary to their belief; he then
called on Drs Justice and Love to join him in turning Policy
out and closing the door upon him. After pulling the curtains to
allow Edwards to fall asleep, the physicians withdraw and Dr
Patience diagnoses his disease as a fistula in the brain, which
vents itself once a month. For the matter that is discharged,
though odious and stinking, he has a market among Superstition and his like, much as beggars live by their sores.

Edwards now begins to talk in his sleep and is heard wel-
coming the doctors, whom he mistakes for godly informers. 'I
see you labour faithfully in the sweeping of God's house; come,
what rubbish have you discovered? Is there none of the sectaries
addicted to drunkenness, or whoredom or thievery? Haven't
you something against Hugh Peters and John Goodwin?
A woman was dipped and died ten days after; what was the
party's name that dipped her? Never fear the loss of your trade.'
His slumbers deepen into ecstacy, and the matter pours out.
The doctors operate and remove the fistula. Never was as big a
one seen, except in 'the late head of the great Canterbury'
(Laud). Conscience remains to watch over Edwards.

In the consulting room the doctors discuss Conscience. He
was never at a university nor yet at court. He is always warning
the people not to be content 'with the cheapest parts of religion',
as going to church and fasting; they should 'deliver the captive,
set the oppressed free and visit the fatherless and widows'.

Superstition then warns the doctors that they may have killed Master Edwards.

Presently, however, Edwards is heard praying. Conscience holds him up, and he preaches from the text: 'The whole commandment is fulfilled in this one word, Love.' After discoursing on John, the disciple whom Jesus loved, he makes his confession. 'No man hath been more earnest than I for compelling all to uniformity, and for punishment of all contrary practisers. But I now see my error and will do all to make amends for the evil I have done. The books I have written I will burn with my own hand, for I judge no opinion so evil as molestation in religion.'

Though it was published a year later (1647), it is relevant to say something here of another pamphlet which helps us to understand something more of Walwyn's development. He wrote *A still and soft voice from the Scriptures, witnessing them to be the word of God* in the hope (vain, as it turned out) of silencing the dangerous rumour that he was an atheist who rejected the Bible. The fact is, as he tells us, that it was his habit to go about asking Socratic questions to discover how we know that there is a God and that the scriptures are His word. When he disputed the validity of the weak arguments commonly advanced to establish these truths, the usual answer was: 'Do you deny them; it seems you do? Otherwise why do you ask such questions?' He was fortunate in escaping the gallows, the penalty prescribed by law for such curiosity; Puritans would not have let him off with a cup of hemlock.[12]

Walwyn was not a sophist who put such questions to score a point in debate. The fact is that, at some time before the Long Parliament met, he passed through a painful crisis in his religious life, 'much disconsolation', to use his own words, 'great uncertainty and at last extreme affliction of mind, the Law and Gospel fighting for victory in me'.[13] The seven Puritans who wrote *Walwyn's Wiles* quoted him as saying to an intimate friend that sometimes he believed the Bible was the word of God and sometimes he believed it was not. 'All those passages therein that declare the nature of God, viz. his grace and goodness to men, I believe are the Word of God', but 'the

Scripture is plainly and directly contradictory to itself'. In the end he solved his problem by ignoring the obscure and uncongenial chapters, which may have been addressed to another age than ours, and concentrating on passages which called forth a spontaneous echo from his own heart. He ceased to puzzle over difficult doctrines. Faith for him meant love; 'that,' he might have said if he could have anticipated Keats, 'is all we know on earth and all we need to know'; 'so much faith so much love; so much love so much pure and undefiled religion'.[14] He dismissed all the arguments for the inspiration of the Scriptures. For him as for Elijah, God was not in the wind nor the earthquake nor the fire. 'I believe them through an irresistible persuasive power that from within them (like unto the soft still voice wherein God was) hath pierced my judgment and affection.'

From this standpoint of intuition, where at last he felt secure and at peace, Walwyn could look round with perfect tolerance on his fellows. 'I have no quarrel to any man, either for unbelief or misbelief, because I judge no man believeth anything but what he cannot choose but believe.' He reserved his opposition for those who believed nothing at all from inner conviction or experience, those who were content to accept the traditional, customary religion in which they were bred. The 'superstitious' people as he called them, are 'deadly enemies to examination and trial of things'. They 'think of God as a severe and spiteful judge, with difficulty appeased, and so they go trembling with fear'. Politicians know that their sort of religion offers 'the easiest means to lead a multitude'. The superstitious man will drive 'his poor neighbour out of all he hath, yea out of the nation', in order to drive him into his own opinion.

As for his body or estate, that's no part of his care; he is not so hasty to run into his poor neighbour's house, to see what is wanting there. He may be upon a bed, or no bed, covering or no covering, be starved through cold and hunger, overburdened with labour, be sick, lame or diseased, and all this troubles not the superstitious man's . . . conscience. He may through want and necessity go into what prison he will, and lie and rot and starve there, and these kind of religious people are not half so much moved at it, as if he go to another church or congregation than what they approve. If he do so, up starts their zeal; and after him, watch, spy, accuse and inform, and all for the good of his soul and for the glory of God.

If this is customary and superstitious religion, he reminds us that pure religion and undefiled is to feed the hungry, clothe the naked, visit the sick, relieve the prisoner, deliver the captive and set the oppressed free, 'especially the oppressed for conscience sake'. This he tells us will 'empty the fullest bags and pluck down the highest plumes'. Here in a sentence was Walwyn's message to his age. Henceforward it rings out from everything he writes like a *motif* in a symphony. His 'practical Christianity', as he called it, became more revolutionary as time went on. Two years later, after he had spoken of the hungry, the naked, the sick, the aged, the weak and impotent, he went on to stress as the essentials of a Christian's duty, 'the delivering of prisoners, supporting of poor families' and the 'freeing a commonwealth from all tyrants, oppressors and, deceivers'.[15] Until Lamennais wrote his *Paroles d'un Croyant*, this gospel was seldom heard for two centuries to come.

NOTES TO CHAPTER V

1. I am assuming here what I have tried to demonstrate in Appendix A, that Walwyn wrote *Tyranipocrit*. [This Appendix has not been found. Brailsford assumes Walwyn's authorship of this anonymous tract throughout—e.g. pp. 64, 254, 287, 463, 534. *Tyranipocrit* (1649) is reprinted in G. Orwell and R. Reynolds, *British Pamphleteers*—Ed.]

2. The quotations from Walwyn are from *The Fountain of Slander Discovered* (30 May, 1649); from *A Whisper in the Ear of Mr. Thomas Edwards, Minister*, reprinted in Haller's *Tracts on Liberty*, III, pp. 319-35; and from *Walwyn's Just Defence*, reprinted in H. and D., pp. 350-98. Those from Dr Brooke are from *The Charity of Churchmen* (H. and D., esp. pp. 337 and 339).

3. Reproduced in W. Schenk, *The Concern for Social Justice in the Puritan Revolution*. Brooke speaks of Walwyn's 'ruddy complexion'. At this time he wore a beard. Bastwick describes his 'great white and brown basket-hilted beard' and his unusually 'white and clear teeth, each far apart from the other'.

4. *A Just Defence of John Bastwick* (30 August, 1645), p.17.

5. There will be no peace, he wrote in *The Vanity of the Present Churches*, 'until the mock churches are overturned and laid flat' (H. and D., p. 271).

6. Dated by Thomason November 1641. Though Prof. Haller doubts the

ascription of this pamphlet to Walwyn (*Tracts on Liberty*, I, p. 126), Pease's arguments seem to me convincing (*The Leveller Movement*, p. 256).

7. Haller, *Tracts on Liberty*, II, pp. 273-306 (19 September, 1643). For *Tyranipocrit*, see note 1 above.

8. *The Charity of Churchmen*, H. and D., p. 334.

9. Haller, *Tracts on Liberty*, III, pp. 61-104 (June or July 1644).

10. *Ibid.*, III, pp. 321-35 (13 March, 1646).

11. *Ibid.*, III, pp. 339-48 (11 August, 1646).

12. Reprinted in D. M. Wolfe, *Milton in the Puritan Revolution*, pp. 363-74.

13. *A Whisper in the Ear*, Haller, *Tracts on Liberty*, III, p. 323.

14. H. and D., pp. 297-8, 266.

15. *Ibid.*, p. 272.

CHAPTER VI

John Lilburne

Three men could hardly have been less alike than Overton, Walwyn and Lilburne, yet they made a perfect team. Among them Lilburne was the man of action, a figure as gallant and vital as ever strode through English history. With his ready tongue and supple wrist, he was equally formidable in fence and debate. As a stripling under the old régime, he defied all the grandees in church and state, and when they fell he defied their successors, again and yet again, while the revolution devoured its children. Clarendon noted his appetite for martyrdom, but always in the depth of suffering he knew how to strike back. Religion was in early life his sole concern, and still when he became absorbed in politics he believed that he acted under the direct inspiration of God. Walwyn and Overton had left the terrors and glories of predestination far behind them, but Lilburne, until he turned Quaker, was a convinced Calvinist. There was nothing of the sour and negative side of Puritanism in his nature: Mr Edwards's godly spies may have told the truth when they said that he enjoyed a glass of wine and on occasion even played a game of cards.

Each in his own manner, Lilburne's two colleagues were literary artists. He wrote rapidly, much as he might have talked in a rambling monologue among his followers in the Windmill Tavern. He had no trace of a sense of humour, nor was wit among his weapons. He published in his short lifetime several score of pamphlets, which flew from him, to borrow a phrase from G. M. Young, like sparks from an anvil. His style, when he writes about ideas, is often clumsy, for his wordy sentences are apt to be both ill-organised and of interminable length; yet when he turns on the next page to a concrete subject he will manage to be admirably simple and direct, so that something of his militant and dynamic personality always emerges. The reader must listen to this eager, vehement voice, sure of itself and full of its theme. Certainly the masses read gladly everything he wrote, and some of these pamphlets, printed with worn and dirty types on miserable paper, had for those days an immense circulation. This man was an extrovert who spoke out all that was in him, his hatreds and his vanity, his idealism and his courage. We know the worst there is to know about him; he blurted it all out. His friend Walwyn described his simplicity and his emotional susceptibility:

> being to my knowledge . . . a very lamb in conversation . . . whom goodness and love and piety, justice and compassion shall as soon melt and that into tears (I hope he will pardon my blabbing) as any man in the world; but he hates all kind of baseness with a perfect hatred.[1]

In or out of gaol, this man was irrepressible. He harangued the citizens with his head in the pillory: from his prisons he addressed them in vehement pamphlets, printed somehow without the censor's licence. In these he was rapidly educating himself no less than his readers, and hurrying, as experience opened his eyes, from one advanced position to another. From the pillory, the battlefield and the Tower of London, much may be learned about the nature of democratic institutions, but the revelation will tend to come in flashes of anger and the final product may lack system. The defect of Lilburne's qualities was that his eager, self-reliant, combative mind lacked a sense of proportion and perspective. Worse than this was his tendency to exaggerate a personal grievance, a weakness that was in the end his ruin. He was wholly lacking in common sense—that radar-like gift which enables the average man to find his way, as bats do, in a dark and hostile world, without bumping into lethal obstacles. These are not the qualities that make a good political strategist. He could rally a big and eager army behind him, but he could not plan a campaign. His genius was for single combat.

Lilburne was a man of strong passions, given as a youth to hero-worship, and in later life to warm friendships and furious enmities. His language is intemperate, after the fashion of the time, but not more so than Milton's. In those days Englishmen were not inclined to under-statement. Lilburne's vocabulary of abuse, as he said by way of apology, came straight out of the Bible. Any fair estimate of his character must take account of the gross wrongs he suffered. Sir Charles Firth, in his just and not unkindly verdict, speaks of his 'passionate egotism', but instantly adds that he was 'ready to assail any abuse at any cost to himself'.[2] He sometimes wearies us by dwelling incessantly on the wrongs and injuries he endured. But in defending his own he was the champion of every man's rights, for as he put it in a phrase that might serve as the motto of his life's work, 'what is done to anyone may be done to everyone'.[3] He who keeps silence in the face of wrong, because he shuns 'the censure of turbulency, incurs the guilt of treachery to the present and future generations'.

The bigness of the man was that his whole life, from first to last, was an unyielding battle for his ideal of liberty. If it was for freedom of conscience that he first enlisted, he went on to conceive of liberty in the widest and simplest terms. Here is his definition of it, based as he claims not only on the word of God, but on the fundamental laws of the land, which provide

> that no man be questioned or molested or put to answer for anything but wherein he materially violates the person, goods or good name of another.[4]

Rash though it is in its militant individualism, this definition stands out from the records of the seventeenth century as one of the earliest and one of the boldest statements of the liberal creed. Strictly interpreted, it would deny the right of society to exact from the individual citizen his contribution to the welfare and even to the safety of the whole organism. Needless to say, that was not what Lilburne meant; he was not an anarchist. How the Levellers conceived the relationship of the individual to the state we shall see as this narrative proceeds; they ignored neither the duties of the citizen nor the rights of the community. 'Freeborn John', as his Cockney admirers nicknamed him, lived up to his difficult creed. He fought as furiously to right the wrongs of others as ever he did for the redress of his own injuries.

John Lilburne was human, engagingly human in his tendency to dramatise every phase of this struggle as the duel of *Lilburnius contra Mundum.* He was a romantic who strove to realise Aristotle's ideal of the magnanimous, the great-souled man—'a man', as he put it, 'of a gallant, ennobled and heroic mind'.[5] As he once told Cromwell, he would never strike him down when he was low, but only when he was in his full glory. His zest in quarrelling amused his contemporaries, witness the epigram on his death which versified a joke of Henry Marten's:

> *Is John departed and is Lilburne gone?*
> *Farewell to Lilburne and farewell to John.*
> *But lay John here; lay Lilburne there about,*
> *For if they ever meet, they will fall out.*

Some men in their day-dreams get their satisfaction by imagining amorous triumphs. Others climb the Himalayas in fancy, or swim the Hellespont. In John's day-dreams he posed as the hero in gallant deeds of violence, which he would record with a cock-crow audible upon the printed page. Because he had a life-long feud with the Merchant Adventurers, he dreamed in broad daylight a romantic plan by which he would defeat their monopoly. He would cause a ship to be loaded in a continental port with the goods they alone were privileged to import. As she sailed up the Thames, he would board her 'with half a dozen lusty resolved blades' and then

> with my own hand give the chief monopoliser a brace of pistol bullets in his guts, or a prick with my rapier or dagger, in case he came to take away my goods.

After this exploit he would confidently take his chance before a jury in a court of common law. In sober fact he never did resort to direct action in this style, nor did he ever fight a duel or strike down a tyrant, though these also were among the heroic deeds that figured in his day-dreams.

Quarrelsome though John was, it is fair to note that he never fell out with his closer comrades, Walwyn and Overton;

if he did once quarrel with Marten, he made it up very hand-
somely. He knew how to keep the love of his elder brother,
Colonel Robert. His wife was devoted to him, though he must
have been the most ruinous head of a family that any luckless
mother could have had. His physical personality must have
been pleasing. The best portrait of him, an engraving by
Wenceslas Hollar, shows a young man with a high brow, a
rather long nose, regular features, dark eyes and a slight, dark
moustache. The whole effect is agreeable, even handsome and
rather pensive. The sloping shoulders suggest a slight frame and
remind us that he died of consumption. He may have had some
pride in his appearance, for he would show himself in public
in his dragoon's scarlet coat long after he had left the Army. He
must have possessed the personal magnetism that dominates
the many and enslaves the few. To women he was evidently
attractive. During his many imprisonments, thousands of them
signed petitions on his behalf again and again. On one occasion
hundreds of them marched from the City to Westminster to
demand his release. Contemporary records suggest that he was
easily the most popular man in the England of his day. Even
Godwin, in spite of his violent disapproval, conceded that he
was 'to an unexampled degree popular'.[6] Cromwell, who took
some pains to win him, came in the end to fear him. When
Cromwell feared a man, he struck him down, were he monarch
or Leveller.

Such a man was marked for leadership.

John Lilburne, the second of the three sons of Richard and
Margaret Lilburne, was born in the royal palace at Green-
wich, round about 1616. Both parents had seen service at
court. Theirs, as he described it, was 'an ancient and worshipful
family', which owned land in County Durham. His uncle
George was wealthy; was interested in coal mines near Sunder-
land and had sat in Parliament, as under the Protectorate his
cousin Thomas also did. Both father and uncle were in the
parliamentary camp during the troubles, and later served on
the Committee of their county. John lost his mother in infancy.
One need not be a psychologist to understand the consequences
of such a loss. Deprived of the mother's tenderness, the child

suffers from frustration, and turns with hostility and aggression upon a world that perpetually disappoints him. As the boy developed, the decisive influence on his character would be his father's.

What manner of man was Richard Lilburne? The little that we know of him is suggestive. He nearly ruined himself by interminable litigation with a neighbour over the ownership of land. In the end the case came before the Privy Council, and he was the last Englishman who claimed the obsolete privilege of ordeal by battle in a civil lawsuit. Champions were actually brought into court, but the suit was decided peacefully. Though this did not happen till 1636, long after John had left home, we can divine from this affair the sort of man his father was—a reckless, obstinate fighting man, who rejoiced in aggression, an exhibitionist, an original who would go his own way and swim for choice against the tide. This pattern of behaviour the motherless boy imitated in after life with improvements of his own. Yet a third circumstance would aggravate John's tendency to aggression. The Lilburnes in their county belonged to a small minority. The majority of their neighbours were churchmen and Royalists and many of them were Catholics. Even at school in such an environment the boy would learn that only by fearless militancy could he hold his own. In this way John grew up the very genius of rebellion.

John went to school first at Bishop Auckland and then at Newcastle, where he learned some Greek as well as Latin. He can have been barely fifteen when he was apprenticed to a merchant in the cloth trade in the City of London. Though he tells us that he worked honestly and hard, he had some leisure, which he spent in reading. First on his scanty bookshelf, after the Bible, came Foxe's Book of Martyrs, which may have influenced his emotional habits profoundly by confirming his tendency to masochism. Then came Luther, Calvin, Béza, Cartwright and other lesser divines, together with some histories of England, foremost among them Speed's. Like so many of the earnest young men of his generation, he found in religion with a strong Calvinistic tinge the stimulus and discipline that fired his emotions and satisfied his intellect.

The autobiography of the leading Baptist preacher of this

age, William Kiffin, a close friend of John's, gives a vivid idea of how these lads spent their scanty leisure on Sundays. He and his fellow apprentices would attend a morning lecture on religion at 6 a.m. But they met for prayer an hour earlier, and in addition spent much time together in reading and discussing the Scriptures.[7] The process that led up to conversion was often stormy and prolonged, and the enquirer might pass from one teacher to another and sample several sects before he found rest for his soul. The search for salvation was under Laud a perilous quest, for every prayer-meeting broke the law. Religion in these dangerous years called to all that was mettlesome and romantic in youth. The heroes of these apprentices were the martyrs whom the Star Chamber mutilated and imprisoned.

John felt deeply honoured when he was allowed to visit in his prison Dr Bastwick, whom we have met already (p. 8). 'For his service,' he wrote, 'I could have laid down my life.' Next he got to know the most famous Puritan champion of them all, William Prynne, also a prisoner. Prynne was a man of boundless courage and vast antiquarian learning, which ranged widely over the common law, the English constitution, theology and church history, but he was a fanatic so intemperate and intolerant that any reader who does succeed in getting through two or three of his books, as tedious as they are furious, will end by asking the question: was this man sane? 'I accounted it my duty,' Lilburne wrote, 'to do William Prynne and Dr Bastwick all the free offices of love and service that lay in my power during all the time that I conceived they stood either for God, goodness or justice.'[8] Prynne's statement some years later, which John greatly resented, that he had been his servant or clerk, must have been due to a slip of memory. From this learned barrister, he may have picked up his first notions of law, while acting in the Tower as his volunteer amanuensis.

Bastwick has left us an amusing record of his intimacy with this generous young man, whom he describes as 'honest and religious' with 'very considerable abilities'. Bastwick was his tutor in theology and greatly improved 'his language and dialect', for even after six years in the City John was still

a mere country courtier and very rough hewn; so that he could neither make a leg with grace nor put off his hat seemly, till I had polished him and taught him all his postures of courtship, and now he is become a very gallant fellow. I made him fit for all gentlemen's and noblemen's society, and who but John among the controllesses of dripping pans, the Independent sisters?[9]

John was near the end of his apprenticeship, but had no prospect of work in front of him, presumably (to hazard a guess) because his father was too poor to pay the £100 entrance fee of the Merchant Adventurers' monopoly. To help him earn some money, Bastwick gave his young friend the manuscript of the first of his attacks on the bishops and the institution of episcopacy which he had written in English, the most violent and popular of them all, his *Litany*. This was to be printed in Holland and smuggled back. John spent several months there, and speaks of his stay as his 'banishment'. He never learned Dutch but may none the less have profited from his sojourn, for the republic sheltered a big English colony.

On his return he was betrayed to the bishops' catchpoles by two of his confederates, one of whom, Edmund Chillenden, was afterwards an Agitator, officer and preacher in the parliament-ary army. John resisted arrest, until he was disarmed. First before the King's Attorney, then before the Star Chamber itself and finally before the Lord Keeper and the Lord Privy Seal, John refused to incriminate himself by answering questions, would not pay the customary clerk's fee, and objected that he had not been served with a *subpoena*, nor had any charge been preferred against him. Finally he refused to take the usual *ex officio* oath, on which the procedure of the prerogative courts was based. Nothing quite like this had ever happened before in England, for here was a youngster of 22 who defied all the greatest in the land. John was sentenced to a fine of £500, a public flogging and the pillory, and to imprisonment until he should submit to the court's procedure. A second sentence passed next day aggravated his imprisonment by putting him in irons and denying him any food save what he could get from the prison's poor-box. Among those who passed one or other of these sentences were Laud, Bishop Juxon, the elder Sir Harry Vane, the then Earl of Manchester, three other earls, three members of the inner Privy Council and the Lord Chief Justice.

In *A Work of the Beast* John Lilburne told the story of his ordeal, not with pathos but in a psalm of triumph. He refers to himself at the start as 'one of His chosen ones'; it was this assurance that he held God's commission which sustained not his courage only, but his physical strength. Stripped to the waist and tied to the tail of a cart, he was flogged from the Fleet prison, through Fleet Street and the Strand, past Whitehall to the Palace Yard at Westminster. The instrument was a whip with three knotted cords and from this he received two hundred strokes. In words that were by accident an echo of Sir Thomas More's, he wrote: 'I went to my suffering with as willing and joyful a heart as if I had been going to solemnise the day of my marriage with one of the choicest creatures this world could afford.' At the first stripe he called out 'Blessed be thy name, O Lord my God, that hast counted me worthy to suffer for Thy glorious name's sake'. At the second he shouted 'Hallelujah'. Standing in great pain under a hot sun with his head in the pillory, he made a defiant speech to a big crowd, warmly commended Dr Bastwick's pamphlet and then with one of the most magnificent gestures in history, flung three copies of it to his hearers. When he persisted in arguing that the bishops derived their apostolical succession from Anti-Christ, a 'fat lawyer' had him cruelly gagged.[10]

There was drama and excitement to carry John Lilburne through the sufferings of this day, 18 April, 1638, and he sensed the sympathy and admiration of the crowded streets. In prison, with heavy irons on both wrists and ankles, he had to endure first fever and then semi-starvation for four months without a friend in sight, though his fellow prisoners, neglected criminals though most of them were, sometimes contrived to feed him and to check the worst brutalities of the warders. From his dungeon the indomitable young man sent through the Chief Warden a challenge to the Archbishop of Canterbury to meet him in public debate on the whole question of episcopacy, in the presence of all the nobles and peers of the kingdom. He staked his own life on a victory over Laud. This was John's characteristic variation on his father's theme of ordeal by battle. In the depths of his suffering in prison he could still write:

I am as merry, yea more cheerful than ever I was in any

D

condition in my life and can sleep as soundly in my boots and irons as Peter did between the two soldiers when he was in prison.

Life was made rather easier for him after the first four months; he was transferred to a less dismal part of the prison, and could receive food and visitors. But throughout the three years of his captivity, as on his day of torment, he was deserted by his family. His father was angry because he feared that his son's defiance would turn the Privy Council against him in the lawsuit in which he was still engaged. So passed for John Lilburne what should have been the three best years of his youth. Soon his wounded back was whole again, but the weals this experience inflicted on his mind were never cured. The rulers of Caroline England flogged him; the rulers of parliamentary England were their sons. His shoulders must have smarted when he heard the names of Vane and Manchester.

Was it worth it? Flogging, pillory and irons were a high price to pay for the satisfaction of arguing that bishops wore their mitres *jure diabolico*. There was more at issue than this juvenile thesis, very much more. In the first place young Lilburne testified, with health and even life at stake, for the liberty of unlicensed printing, and repeated his testimony over and over again in all the prisons of London, as the years went on. Milton did it a few years later in a slender volume of immortal prose, but he went a long way towards unwriting his masterpiece when he spent his genius in supporting a dictator who destroyed the press. But Lilburne's chief purpose when he defied the Star Chamber was to establish a basic civil right— the right of an accused person to refuse to incriminate himself. It was characteristic of the so-called 'prerogative courts' that their procedure was based on the examination of the arrested person, who was required to take an oath even before he was charged. The purpose of these courts was to secure a conviction by extracting a confession, rather than by building up a case against him on the evidence of others. Wherever confession is regarded as the ideal form of proof which every officer of justice is bent on achieving, not all of them will resist the temptation to use illegitimate forms of pressure, ranging from bullying and trickery to physical torture. The dictatorships of yesterday and today have always used such methods, and in mitigated forms they occur too often in the criminal jurisprudence of some of our continental neighbours. The basis of our British system (mingled as it is with defects peculiar to itself) which must be reckoned among the bulwarks of our liberty is the recognised right to refuse to submit to interrogation, or to go into the witness box.

In the seventeenth century it was touch and go which system would prevail in England. Selden, perhaps the wisest and sanest, as he was certainly the most learned lawyer of his age, held the opinion that the English use of torture was worse in his day than that prevailing in continental countries. 'Here in England they take a man and rack him, I do not know why nor when—not in time of judicature, but when somebody bids.' He mentions the contemporary use of the well-known totalitarian trick of telling a man (falsely) that someone else has already confessed and implicated him. There are some grounds for thinking that torture was still applied on occasion to political prisoners under the Protectorate.[11]

There is good reason to believe that it is Lilburne whom we have to thank for the gradual acceptance of what our fathers have long regarded as an established English tradition. He was the first to publicise by word and deed the claims of this civil right. Overton and Walwyn followed his example in action, and both of them wrote arresting pages on the subject. Presently the organised Leveller party inscribed this right to refuse to answer incriminating questions in its programmes and petitions. Soon afterwards it was mentioned in petitions from soldiers and sectaries. Finally, on the eve of the Whig Revolution, the Seven Bishops sanctified the legacy which the arch-rebel of the previous generation left behind him, by refusing to answer questions when they were charged with treason. And so, thanks to the daring of this stripling, English law does not aim from first to last at the extraction of confessions. To Americans this right appeared so fundamental that they embodied it by the Fifth Amendment in the constitution of the United States.

During these years in prison John's mind was active, and his opinions were taking a new shape. He had already his inner assurance of his 'calling and election', in other words his

conversion, some two years before his imprisonment. Soon
after his ordeal he wrote:

> I honour and glorify my God, who hath passed by so many
> thousands as He hath done, and left them in their sins, and
> yet hath chosen me freely before the foundation of the world
> was laid.[12]

Dr Bastwick may have cured him of his northern burr, but he
did not make a Presbyterian of him. No one could ever deprive
him for long together of pen and ink and among the pamphlets
which he wrote in the Fleet is one, *Come out of her my People*,
which gives a surprising impression of his loyalty and quietism
in political matters. He was as yet a rebel only in his rejection
of episcopacy and in his insistence on the way of total separation from the 'Antichristian' Church of England, 'commonly
but falsely called Brownism'. The pamphlet is the work of an
immature, self-educated, but very confident youngster, who has
as yet nothing constructive to say and only wants to attack the
bishops. He repeats in all its austerity Calvin's doctrine of
passive obedience to the secular power, precisely as it was laid
down in the *Institutes*. The bolder spirits of the second generation of Calvinists, du Plessis-Mornay (in *Vindiciae contra
Tyrannos*) among the Huguenots and Buchanan among the
Scots, had begun to preach resistance to tyrants. As yet their
influence had not reached him.

He declares that he would always refuse to obey the bishops'
officers and 'would not go to prison with them', unless they
carried him by force (in fact he drew his sword to resist arrest),

> yet if it were the meanest officer in the kingdom that took
> me, that were made an officer by virtue of the King's
> authority and power, I would submit unto him . . . for I
> know the King's authority is from God. . . . But if they
> command me anything that is dishonourable to God or his
> truth, I dare not in the least obey them actively. . . . Yet I
> will submit my body to them and suffer cheerfully . . . any-
> thing they shall inflict on me. For I do hold it unlawful for
> any of God's people in their greatest oppression by the
> magistrate to rebel or to take up any temporal arms against
> them, whether the oppression be in spiritual or temporal

things, but only to pray and make use of God's two-edged sword.[13]

After a year in prison his attitude became more militant. Though he was so weak that he could not stand or walk without help, he managed to write a stirring appeal to his fellow-apprentices, which a maid-servant helped him to smuggle out so that it could be distributed among them during their Whitsun holidays in 1639. He believed that in the Fleet his life was actually in danger. His plea was for a public trial and removal to another prison. He did not ask the apprentices to take to rioting, but his words moved them so deeply that they did so, and for a moment Laud's person was in some danger. John's petition ended with a renewal of his vow 'to fight it out' for the good of future generations, 'for I have a soldier's heart in my innocent breast'. We know that Lord Brooke was at this time taking an interest in the spirited prisoner in the Fleet. Was his the influence that made John ready, before he was much older, to use 'temporal arms' against the King? However that may be, it was in Brooke's regiment that his 'soldier's heart' fought it out with carnal weapons.

The meeting of the Long Parliament on 3 November, 1640, brought freedom to all Laud's victims. On that day Lilburne presented a petition and was at once granted his liberty to press it. On this petition, on 9 November, Oliver Cromwell chose to make his first speech in this Parliament. No one is likely to forget the impressions of this speech recorded by the royalist Member, Sir Philip Warwick. He noted Cromwell's 'sharp and untunable voice', his unfashionable clothes and the fervour of his eloquence. 'He aggravated the imprisonment of this man . . . unto such height that one would have believed the very government itself had been in great danger by it. . . . He was very much hearkened unto.' The Commons accordingly passed on 4 May, 1641, a resolution which condemned Lilburne's judgment and imprisonment as 'illegal, . . . bloody, wicked, cruel, barbarous and tyrannical', and recognised his right to financial reparation; the Lords, however, delayed their consent till 1 December, 1645. To Cromwell above all men in England John looked up, from this day in 1641 for six years to come, with gratitude, hero-worship and ere long with affection.

Lilburne's uncle George, meanwhile, found the capital to set him to work as a master brewer, and he married Elizabeth Dewell. She must have been a woman of exceptional courage. Even before their marriage she must have shared John's opinions, for we know that she visited him in the Fleet prison. It seems that the apprentices who had rioted to set him free in 1639 still looked to him for leadership, and on the eve of the Civil War they stood behind him in defending Parliament against the King's bravo, Thomas Lunsford, and his 'roaring boys'. Lunsford drew on John in Westminster Hall, and they fought it out with some bloodshed.

On the outbreak of the war, Lilburne received a commission in the regiment of foot raised by Robert Greville, Lord Brooke. This idealistic young scholar, immortal because Milton praised him in *Areopagitica*, fell early in the war in an attack on Lichfield. He had been a student of Plato, but with Pym and Hampden he acted as one of the little inner group which organised the parliamentary party for the decisive struggle. On its eve he wrote one of the most memorable of the early pleas for toleration, *A Discourse opening the Nature of that Episcopacy, which is exercised in England* (1641).[14] 'Truth or the broken gleams of truth,' as he put it, 'appear diversely in the minds of all men.' He would have order, indeed, but 'not by fire and faggot'. He called for 'a fair hearing' for the persecuted Brownists, covered even 'preaching cobblers' with his sympathy, expounded the position of the extremer sects, though without adopting it, more persuasively than they could have done it themselves, and ended with the conclusion that 'so far as Christ is in us, we shall . . . honour . . . the least particle of his image in others'. How much, one asks, did John gain in his mental development from association with this noble mind?

It so happens that a vivid record of Brooke's regiment, drawn from the City apprentices, has come down to us in the letters of Sergeant Nehemiah Wharton. In these early days it was as ill-disciplined as it was pious. It sacked the houses of papists, wrecked what offended its Puritan conscience in the churches along its route, mutinied against an unpopular officer and poached fat bucks from the parks of 'malignant' gentry. But it relished as keenly the sermons of its Puritan chaplains. Its purple-coats with Lilburne in charge of a company fought well at Edgehill. At Brentford, where in the temporary absence of Lord Brooke Captain Lilburne was the senior officer in command of his regiment, he rallied it when it nearly took to flight and led it with distinction in an engagement where, with Denzil Holles's red coats, it bore the full weight of a furious attack. These two regiments stood their ground and saved Essex's army from disaster; but they were cut in pieces (12 November 1642) and John was taken prisoner and carried to the King's headquarters at Oxford.

There, after a vain attempt to seduce him from his loyalty to the Parliament, he was tried for treason (6 December). After insisting that the indictment which described him as 'yeoman, should be amended to 'gentleman', he defended himself with his usual intrepidity. He owed his life to his wife. She 'rushed violently into the House', addressed the Commons from the bar, and won from Parliament a threat of retaliation if the King should execute his prisoners. She then made her way, though she was with child, 'through all the strong courts of guard' to Oxford, and arranged an exchange of prisoners. The City welcomed Lilburne back as a hero and he was offered a civilian post under Parliament, but he still thought it his duty to 'fight it out'.

Essex, always kindly and generous, gave him a purse of £300, but pressed him to take the Covenant. This he would not do, since he read it in its plain meaning as a promise to extirpate schism and heresy by force. Walwyn's subtler mind was able to take it, because he argued that the qualification which Vane inserted—'according to the word of God'—meant that heretics must be won over in the only Christian way, 'by love, light and argument'. Lilburne had another good reason for refusing. Strict Anabaptists, like Quakers and Tolstoyans, took the Commandment 'swear not at all' literally and seriously, and this, as one of his pamphlets tells us, was John's belief. In this difficulty, Cromwell again came to his help and in October 1643 offered him a commission as major in a regiment of foot under the Eastern Association. Unluckily Cromwell thought ill of its commander, Colonel Edward King, a Presbyterian, and instructed Lilburne to watch him and report—surely a thing no subordinate should be asked to do. There is no doubt that King was a shockingly incompetent soldier; whether he also embezzled public money we do not know, but this both Lilburne and some members of the County Committee of Lincoln firmly believed. Cromwell was satisfied when he got Manchester to cashier him for incompetence, but John, like the headstrong young man he still was, wanted (as the local sectaries also did) to have him tried for treason, Manchester's was not a harmonious army.

One of the secrets of Cromwell's success as a soldier was his liking for spirited young men, even if and perhaps especially if they had minds of their own. He had a quick eye for such types and when he found them he promoted them rapidly, whether like Lilburne they were 'gentlemen', or came like Joyce and Sexby from tradesmen in the ranks. If they belonged to the 'People of God' that sufficed to obliterate class distinctions—at all events in this period of his life. He must have taken a liking to John from his first acquaintance and they were soon so intimate that they were often 'bedfellows' at the front—for it was a habit of Cromwell's to talk things over in bed with men whom he trusted. He seems to have talked over everything and everybody with John, who had no inhibitions.

After settling the awkward business of Colonel King, Cromwell got Manchester to promote Lilburne to the command of his own regiment of dragoons (mounted infantry) with the rank of Lieutenant-Colonel. John fought well at the storming of Sir Francis Wortley's castle near Wakefield, where he was wounded in the arm. A month later he distinguished himself on Marston Moor. Shortly after this victory, which might have been decisive under any commander less supine and half-hearted than Manchester, John underwent at Tickhill Castle, near Doncaster, the experience that in effect ended his career as a soldier. Acting independently at the head of his dragoons, he took the town by a series of rapid and skilful movements and drove the garrison into the castle. Since he had good reason to believe that it was demoralised, he asked leave from Manchester to take this fortress. Manchester, timid as he always was, would not sanction any move that entailed the slightest risk, but the talk ended with an ambiguous, jocular phrase, which, on Ireton's advice, Lilburne interpreted as a tacit permission to act on his own judgment. He did so and took the castle without losing a man. For this Manchester, who would not listen to his explanation, overwhelmed him with vulgar abuse before a large audience, and even threatened to hang him. Lilburne was tempted to resign at once, but Cromwell persuaded him to remain in the Army and presently made great use of him as a valuable witness in his political campaign against Manchester. When the New Model was formed, Lilburne felt obliged to refuse an offer of a high command, for once more the Covenant stood in his way. This oath, which troubled many an honest soldier, required loyalty to Genevan orthodoxy as well as to King Charles—if any man could reconcile these incompatibles. And so, on the last day of April 1645 he handed over his dragoons to Colonel Okey.

On his return to civil life John still 'fought on', but with other weapons. He soon had his following at the Windmill Tavern and again he was busy with his pen. Cromwell made one more attempt, through his younger brother Henry, to draw him back into the Army. Accordingly he visited Fairfax's headquarters in Somerset and witnessed the destruction of Goring's army at Langport on 10 July, 1645. Though Cromwell failed to re-enlist him, he gave him on that date a warm letter of commendation to the Speaker for his 'good service', in which he backed John's claim for his arrears of pay amounting to £880, which dated from two years back—to say nothing of the compensation promised him for his cruel imprisonment. 'Truly,' wrote Cromwell, 'it is a grief to see men ruin themselves through their affection and faithfulness to the public, and so few lay it to heart.' After a moving plea for the neglected widows and orphans of his men, he asked once more that John's petition should be read. 'Hereby you shall lay a special obligation upon your servant, Oliver Cromwell.'[15] The Lieutenant-General chose him to carry 'a true and punctual relation' of the latest victory to Westminster, which John did, riding as fast through dangerous country as his horse could carry him. He may have hoped for the gratuity which Parliament in those days commonly paid to the bearers of good tidings. There was none for him. Instead, he found himself trapped in a complicated web of sectarian jealousies, and on 19 July, 1645, he was arrested in Westminster Hall by a vote of that House of Commons for which he had so often risked his life. The men to whose enmity he owed this misfortune were Bastwick and Prynne, his heroes of yesterday.

Lilburne was still in the Army when he wrote the brief but unusual pamphlet that started all this trouble. Addressed to William Prynne, *A Copy of a Letter* is a challenge to him to debate their fundamental differences over toleration.[16] John's instinct for drama never failed him. It was not his way to write a treatise on this or any other subject. He threw down his gauntlet, and the man at whom he hurled it had been his fellow-sufferer when Laud was the arch-persecutor. Now it was Prynne who insisted on uniformity in religion, with all the powers of the civil magistrate to enforce it.

Lilburne, when he wrote these characteristic pages, was the inhabitant of a climate of thought and feeling from which Walwyn and Overton, if ever they breathed it, had long ago escaped. Their arguments for toleration—the fallibility of all authority and the necessity of free discussion—were as secular as any that Voltaire used in the next century. Lilburne's argument is, on the contrary, an echo of the primitive Anabaptist separation of the Saints from the world. 'No parliament, council, synod, emperor, king nor magistrate'—so he declares—'hath any authority or jurisdiction' over Christ's spiritual kingdom or the subjects thereof.

> For, Sir, let me tell you, it is the incommunicable prerogative of Jesus Christ alone to be king of his Saints and law-giver to his church and people, and to reign in the souls and consciences of his chosen ones.

From which it follows that 'to persecute for conscience', whether Laud does it or Prynne, is 'from Antichrist'. Happily the exemption of the Saints from all secular control in spiritual matters was so interpreted as to emancipate the whole of mankind, including the vast majority who have not been 'chosen'.

Lilburne is at his best in this pamphlet when he protests against the 'stopping of the press', by the Blackcoats, so that only one side in this controversy could be heard. Though he sent his challenge to Prynne—'Go you, and tell the tall cedar the little shrub will have a bout with him'—he guessed that his tall adversary, instead of meeting him in debate, would 'run and complain to Parliament and press them upon their Covenant to take vengeance' upon him, which is precisely what Prynne did. The experience of having both one's ears twice sawn off in public did not make for magnanimity.

John was in fact twice haled before the Commons' Committee of Examinations for the offence of writing this and other pamphlets, but the charges were soon dropped. By the merest accident he presently gave two of Prynne's allies the chance of involving him in a much uglier complication. In Westminster Hall, the hub of the political world in those days, he happened to join a group which included Ireton, Walwyn, and several members of the Committee from Salters' Hall, who were engaged in stating a case against Speaker Lenthall, to the effect that he and his brother Sir John had transmitted £60,000 to the King at his headquarters in Oxford. Lenthall was a notorious opportunist, addicted to corruption, and the charge, as Gardiner puts it, is not 'intrinsically improbable', but Lilburne had nothing to do with it, save that he happened to find himself in a group that was discussing it.

In another group not far away was John's old tutor in manners and theology, Dr Bastwick, and his new enemy, Colonel King. They saw their chance of injuring an opponent of the Presbyterian cause, and with the help of Denzil Holles, the Presbyterian leader whose regiment had once fought gallantly beside Lilburne's at Edgehill and Brentford, they promptly took it, by sending a note to the Speaker informing him that John was spreading this scandal about him in the Hall. They might have accused General Ireton with as much or as little reason, but Cromwell's son-in-law would have been a dangerous enemy to provoke. The Serjeant-at-arms arrested Lilburne, and a few days later he was interrogated by the Commons' Committee of Examinations. He challenged its right to try him, accused it of reviving all the old practices of the Star Chamber, protested against the secrecy of its proceedings, argued that he was entitled under Magna Carta to a trial by due process of law, and refused to incriminate himself by answering the Committee's questions. After he had explained his reasons for this defiance in yet another pamphlet (*A Letter to a Friend*), Parliament committed him to Newgate. When he had spent three months in prison the charge against him, which could not have been proved, was withdrawn and he was freed (14 October, 1645).

Hardly had Lilburne escaped from the resentment of the Speaker of the lower House of the Long Parliament, when he found himself involved in a legal duel with the Speaker of the Lords—Manchester, the general who had threatened to hang him, son of the Earl who had him flogged. How this came about is a long and complicated story, of which the details may be left to Lilburne's biographer. Suffice it to say that John had been pleading in vain before the Committee of Accounts to which the Commons referred his petition for arrears of pay and compensation for the Star Chamber's outrages. Its Chairman was his personal enemy Prynne, who behaved with a vindictiveness which the modern reader finds barely credible. He first dismissed John's claim for his arrears and later ruled (although the Lords had at last voted Lilburne £2,000 compensation) that even this was not due to him. In the wretched business of Colonel King two cross actions were pending—against King for treason and against Lilburne for slander—but were never pressed to a conclusion.

In the meanwhile John, who always appealed directly to the public when he was wronged, infuriated the Presbyterian majority still further by publishing two more unlicensed pamphlets, *The Just Man's Justification* and *The Freeman's Freedom Vindicated*. In these, though he had much to say that was reasonable, he had the folly to provoke Manchester, first by accusing him of protecting Colonel King because he was 'glued' to the Presbyterian interest, and then by a threat to publish all Cromwell's evidence against the Earl, 'whose head hath stood too long upon his shoulders'. For this he was called before the Lords, with Manchester himself in the chair. Naturally he protested that the plaintiff should not be his judge; of course he refused to answer incriminating questions; then, taking his stand on Magna Carta, he claimed that he should be judged by his peers. He argued, in other words, that the Lords had no jurisdiction over a commoner, a contention for which he could quote the high authority of Coke's *Institutes*. He, therefore, appealed for protection to the Commons. For this the Lords sent him to Newgate. (The modern reader has, first of all, to realise that no one, until Lilburne did it, had ever questioned the right of either house to act as a criminal court. In our day it is, of course, only the law lords, i.e. the judges raised to the peerage, who sit as a court of appeal.)

Called before the Lords again, on 11 July, 1646, John refused to kneel at their bar, remained covered and stopped his ears, so that he should not hear the charge read out against him. Then in a passionate speech he counter-attacked his judges.

> All you intended when you set us a-fighting was merely to unhorse and dismount our old riders and tyrants, that so you might get up, and ride us in their stead. And therefore, my Lords . . . if you shall be so unworthy as to persevere . . . in the destruction of the fundamental laws and liberties of England . . . I will venture my life and heart's blood against you, with as much zeal and courage as ever I did against any of the King's party.

To this declaration of war the Lords replied by sentencing John Lilburne to a fine of £2,000, with seven years' imprisonment in the Tower, and by declaring him for ever incapable of holding any office, civil or military, while his pamphlets were to be burned by the common hangman.

Such a sentence rings like the end of a gallant career. It was, instead, the beginning of a revolutionary movement which within three years swept away the House of Lords itself. Lilburne's contemporaries could understand his gesture when he refused to obey Black Rod's order to kneel at the bar of the Lords. There is an engraving of this period which shows us the pitiful little figure of some citizen whom the Commons had determined to humiliate. Bareheaded, he approaches the bar. The seated rows of legislators, imposing personages in their tall beavers, seem to dwarf him into nullity, while the Speaker makes ready to rebuke him for some opinion uncongenial to the ruling class. Men whose names scholars still honour today submitted to this indignity. An interesting case is that of the scholar and theologian William Chillingworth, who had spoken in private conversation of 'the other side' in Parliament, meaning the group round Hyde and Falkland. He had to kneel while the Speaker rebuked him for implying that there were sides, parts and divisions in the House.

'Freeborn John', was the first to refuse, as he had been the first to defy the Star Chamber. He did so because he was a young man of unusual mettle, but also because he had the Anabaptist tradition behind him. Here is the comment of one of his comrades, probably Walwyn:

> He had learned better religion and manners than to kneel to any human or mortal power, how great so ever, whom he had never offended, and far less to them whom he had defended with the adventure both of his life and estate.[17]

That a man should kneel only to his God had a clear significance in the dialect of the seventeenth century. In our day when we talk of the dignity and worth of the individual we mean the same thing. Lilburne's gesture was much more than a defiance of the House of Lords. It shook, symbolically, from the shoulders of his generation an intolerable load of authority— the leaden weight of the class structure, which rested on its twin foundations, parental discipline and clerical control.

There was a pioneering vanguard that backed John Lilburne at once. The first of countless petitions for his release was signed by two to three thousand Londoners. Women organised by his spirited wife, Elizabeth, presented their petition and waited for days in the lobbies till it was referred to a committee of the Commons. Walwyn and Overton wrote telling pamphlets in his defence.[18] The latter did even more to back him. When he too was challenged by the Lords for his pamphlet, he repeated Lilburne's tactics of defiance, until with his wife and brother he was brutally dragged through the streets to Newgate. Passive disobedience 'awakened the drowsy spirits of [their] fellow commoners' (as Walwyn put it) and soon in their tens of thousands they fell into step behind the radical van. What was of more importance to history, thanks to the stimulus of this struggle, the leaders between them refashioned the foundations of political democracy.

NOTES TO CHAPTER VI

1. *Walwyn's Just Defence*, H. and D., p. 370.

2. *Dictionary of National Biography*.

3. H. and D., p. 455.

4. *Ibid.*, p. 457.

5. *Legal Fundamental Liberties* (8 June, 1649), p. 28.

6. Godwin, *History of the Commonwealth*, III, p. 101.

7. Ed. W. Orme, *Remarkable Passages in the Life of William Kiffin* (1823), pp. 11-12.

8. *Innocency and Truth Justified* (6 January, 1646), p. 7.

9. *A Just Defence of John Bastwick*, pp. 15 sqq.

10. Haller, *Tracts on Liberty*, II, pp. 1-34.

11. John Selden, *Table Talk*, under 'Trial'. [Brailsford gave no reference for his remark about torture under the Protectorate.—Ed.]

12. *An Answer to Nine Arguments*, p. 35. (Written in 1638, though published in 1645.)

13. *Come out of her, my People* (1639), p. 14.

14. Printed in Haller, *Tracts on Liberty*, II, pp. 35-163.

15. Abbott, I, p. 363.

16. Haller, *Tracts on Liberty*, III, pp. 179-88 (7 January, 1645).

17. *The Just Man in Bonds* (29 June, 1646).

18. *A Pearl in a Dunghill* (23 June, 1646) and *A Remonstrance of Many Thousand Citizens* (7 July, 1646). The latter is in Wolfe, pp. 109-30.

CHAPTER VII

The Leveller Challenge

While Lilburne lay in Newgate prison awaiting the sentence of the House of Lords, three of his comrades were drafting a manifesto that gave a new drive and direction to the Revolution. Hitherto the pamphleteers of the left had written as individuals; in this *Remonstrance* they claimed to be addressing 'their own House of Commons' on behalf of 'many thousand citizens'. From the day of its publication, 7 July, 1646, we may date the entry into history of the Leveller party, though the name Leveller was not in general use before the autumn of the next year. By a brilliant inspiration the authors of this pamphlet appealed to the eyes and imaginations of their fellow-citizens by reproducing the engraved portrait of John Lilburne, which originally appeared with the story of his flogging in *The Christian Man's Trial*, but across it they got the engraver to delineate the bars of his prison. From behind these bars the young man looks out, patient but not afraid, under an ironical inscription: *The Liberty of the Freeborn Englishman, Conferred on him by the House of Lords, June* 1646. On the title-page the authors proclaimed the sovereignty of the people. On their fourth page they rejected monarchy: on their fifth they called for an end to the House of Lords and its veto. All this, even in the sixth year of a revolutionary struggle, was still so novel and so startling that some of their phrases deserve to be quoted:

A Remonstrance of many thousand citizens . . . to their own House of Commons . . . calling these their commissioners in Parliament to an account, how they . . . have discharged their duties to the universality of the people, their sovereign

LORD, from whom their power and strength is derived, and by whom (*ad bene placitum*) it is continued.

We do expect . . . that ye should . . . set forth King Charles his wickedness openly before the world and withal to show the intolerable inconveniences of having a kingly government . . . and to publish your resolution . . . to acquit us of so great a charge and trouble forever; . . . and until this be done, we shall not think ourselves well dealt withal in this original of all oppressions, to wit kings.

Ye must also deal better with us concerning the Lords. . . . Ye only are chosen by us the people; and therefore in you only is the power of binding the whole nation by making, altering or abolishing of laws. . . . [The Lords are] but as intruders . . . thrust upon us by kings. . . . We desire you to free us from their negative voice, or else tell us that it is reasonable we should be slaves.

It would be easy for any student of the political literature of this period to discover in a pamphlet by one of the Independent thinkers, John Parker or John Goodwin, or even in a speech by Pym, passages that imply the sovereignty of the people; but as yet the leaders and even the theorists shrank from drawing the practical consequences. To be sure, Henry Marten did so, when in the Commons in 1641 he defended John Saltmarsh (who as the years went on backed the Levellers boldly) for his anti-monarchical utterances; for this he was expelled from the House and sent to the Tower. But Marten, always a close ally of the Levellers, was pretty certainly one of the three authors of the *Remonstrance*; the others were Overton and Walwyn.[1]

Again at the critical moment in 1642 when the Commons were claiming for Parliament the control of the militia and the Lords hesitated to join them, they threatened, if necessary, to act alone. This, if they meant it seriously, might be taken to imply the sovereignty of the elected House. But as the years went on, the Commons grew more conservative and gave the King the best of reasons for cherishing his fatal illusion that England could not dispense with him. The more complete their victory, the more marked was their determination to get back to the old traditional muddle, the doctrine which settled sovereignty in King, Lords and Commons. Shortly before it was evicted by Colonel Pride, the majority of the Long Parliament had even swallowed the King's boast that he was responsible to none save God.[2] It may be still more to the point to remind ourselves that as late as 20 October, 1647, Cromwell made his famous speech in the Commons, three hours long, in favour of monarchy as an institution.

Against this background of conservatism the daring and originality of the advance which the Levellers made in this manifesto stand out in high relief. In less than three years the heresy of these pioneers became the accepted doctrine of the Revolution. In words that read like an echo of the *Remonstrance*, the Commons at the bidding of the Army passed on 4 January, 1649, their famous resolution: 'that the people are under God the original of all just power: that the Commons of England in Parliament assembled being chosen by and representing the people, have the supreme power in this nation. . . .' A month later, on 6 and 7 February, came the equally trenchant resolutions, that 'the House of Peers in Parliament is useless and dangerous', and again 'the office of a king in this nation . . . is unnecessary, burdensome and dangerous' and that both of them 'ought to be abolished'.

We shall see, as we go along, with what a sure political instinct the Levellers maintained the initiative they snatched in midsummer 1646. It would be tempting, though it would be untrue, to say that the young man behind those prison bars dictated those resolutions in which the Revolution culminated. Unquestionably they were repugnant to Oliver Cromwell's personal instincts. To the Presbyterian upper bourgeoisie they were hardly less horrifying than to the Cavalier. It was from the sectaries, the craftsmen and the peasants under Leveller guidance, that the drive came which carried them to realisation, and only then because these young men had swords in their hands.

The *Remonstrance* is in effect a manifesto from the opposition in the country (to use modern terminology) addressed for the sake of dramatic effect to the party in power in the House. It criticises their whole record during the past six years—their failure to prevent the outbreak of Civil War, their half-hearted conduct of it up to 1645, their surrenders to Presbyterian intolerance. It summons this perpetual Parliament to a dissolution, and calls (as the English left went on calling down to the days of the Chartists) for annual parliaments. All this, the commonplace procedure of party politics in our own day, was an unheard of innovation in 1646. An opposition was not yet a recognised part of the English constitution. With an amusing audacity which recalls Overton in his moments of high spirits, the authors in the name of the 'many thousand citizens' insist that politics and government are their concern. 'The work ye must note is ours.' This was a new way of addressing the governing class. From the crowns of their beavers to the points of their swords, Peers and Commons must have trembled with rage as they read this tract.

Walwyn, Overton and Marten were not so sanguine as to suppose that the Long Parliament would dissolve itself at their bidding. The real purpose of this manifesto was to win more thousands to swell the vanguard of 'many thousands' who already supported them. Accordingly they did for the first time what the Levellers went on doing as long as they remained an organised and articulate party: they added several planks dealing with social and economic grievances to their political platform. At the start and for some time to come, it was mainly the 'middle sort of people' in the towns whom they were addressing, together with the craftsmen and small tradesmen. Their appeal to the peasants came later.

First among the social demands of the *Remonstrance* is, of course, freedom of conscience. This is defined as a right inhering in the individual citizen, which he cannot part with or make over to any civil authority, whether Parliament or King. The Commons may 'propose what form [of worship] ye conceive best' (which in fact they had already done) but 'compel ye cannot justly, for ye have no power from us so to do'. This claim, as we should expect from these three authors, is made without exceptions, so as to include Episcopalians and Catholics, though they are not expressly mentioned. '[Ye ought] to protect and defend all that live peaceably in the commonwealth, of what judgment or way of worship whatsoever.' The broader social case for toleration—that truth can be reached only by free discussion—is implied in the repeated demand that the Commons shall set 'the imprisoned presses' free.

Next comes the demand for equality before the law, which figures in all Leveller programmes. The modern reader finds it difficult to grasp its importance because the privileges it assails have long ago vanished without a vestige. Selden wrote:

> The Parliament-men are as great princes as any in the world, when whatever they please is privilege of Parliament; no man must know the number of their privileges and whatsoever they dislike is breach of privilege.

He went on to compare Parliament to the Venetian Senate, who 'exercise the greatest tyranny that is anywhere'.[3] Among these privileges were those of the peers—'why,' asks the *Remonstrance*, 'should any of them assault, strike or beat any and not be liable to the law, as other men are?' Neither they nor the members of the Commons could be summoned to appear in court or be sued for debt, nor were they subject to direct taxes. They had, moreover, ways by which they managed to extend these privileges to their 'servants' (including their stewards and secretaries) also. That unscrupulous men did make a shocking use of these privileges there is no doubt. To take an extreme example, we read of the presentation of a petition to the Commons asking them to direct a well-known member, Sir Peter Temple, to pay his debts, estimated at £20,000.[4] No order was made against him though he was said to be the owner of an estate worth £4,000 per annum and of valuable woods. Among the privileges which the *Remonstrance* singles out for the strongest protest were the conduct of the Commons' committees in sending men to prison 'without showing cause', and subjecting them to interrogation exactly as the Star Chamber used to do.

There is a brief mention of the oligarchical government of the City of London and of the Merchant Adventurers' monopoly—subjects with which John Lilburne, as we shall see, presently dealt fully. Then come paragraphs, evidently by Walwyn, dealing with the law, with imprisonment for debt and the press gang, so important that they must be quoted:

> Ye know the laws of this nation are unworthy a free people,

and deserve from first to last to be considered and . . . reduced to an agreement with common equity and right
reason, . . . Magna Carta itself being but a beggarly thing,
containing many marks of intolerable bondage. . . . The
Norman way for ending of controversies was much more
abusive than the English way, yet the Conqueror, contrary
to his oath, introduced the Norman laws and his litigious
and vexatious way amongst us. The like he did also for
punishment of malefactors, controversies of all natures having
before a quick and final despatch in every hundred. He
erected a trade of judges and lawyers, to sell justice and
injustice at his own unconscionable rate and in what time he
pleased, the corruption whereof is yet remaining upon us to
our continual impoverishing and molestation. . . .

Ye know also, imprisonment for debt is not from the
beginning. Yet ye think not of these many thousand persons
and families that are destroyed thereby. *Ye are rich and
abound in goods, and have need of nothing; but the afflictions of the
poor, your hunger-starved brethren, ye have no compassion of.* Your
zeal makes a noise as far as Algiers, to deliver those captived
Christians at the charge of others, but those whom your own
unjust laws hold captive in your own prisons, these are too
near you to think of. Nay you suffer poor Christians, for
whom Christ died, to kneel before you in the streets, aged,
sick and crippled, begging your half-penny charities, and ye
rustle by them in your coaches and silks daily without regard
or taking any course for their constant relief. Their sight
would melt the heart of any Christian, and yet it moves not
you nor your clergy.

We entreat you to consider what difference there is
between binding a man to an oar, as a galley-slave in Turkey
or Algiers, and pressing men to serve in your war. To surprise
a man on the sudden, force him from his calling where he
lived comfortably, from a good trade, from his dear parents,
wife or children, against inclination . . . to fight for a cause he
understands not, and in company of such as he hath no comfort to be withal, for pay that will scarce give him sustenance,
and if he live, to return to a lost trade or beggary, or not much
better. If any tyranny or cruelty exceed this, it must be
worse than that of a Turkish galley-slave. . . .

The Hollanders, our provident neighbours, have no such
cruelties . . . yet they want no men.

After an emphatic call for a dissolution in November 1647, this revolutionary manifesto ends with the cheerful prediction that if the Commons will but act on its principles, 'we shall not doubt to be made absolute freemen in time and become a just, plenteous and powerful nation'.

Were the 'many thousands' really interested in such issues as monarchy and the Lords' veto? Why did the craftsmen and apprentices of Southwark and the City stand firm behind Lilburne, when they held Brentford against the King? Why, four years later, did they read Leveller manifestoes with assent? The politics of this period, like its debates on religion, were a reflection of its social and industrial struggles. In the village what really mattered was to preserve the common fields: they were the 'birthright', the heritage of fraternity and equality which the yeoman sought to defend when he put on his scarlet coat: his real enemy was the encroaching landlord who threatened his common. In the bigger towns, but especially in London, an acute struggle of classes divided the rising merchants from the sinking small master craftsmen and the mass of the journeymen. When the Levellers for a few years made the question of manhood franchise and the sovereignty of the people the dominant issue of the day, they were not talking abstract politics. Every craft, every 'mystery' in London and its suburbs, was torn by the warfare of two factions over this very issue of democracy, and every weaver, printer and brass-founder knew that on the outcome depended his day's wage and the conditions under which he worked. Each craft was a microcosm which repeated on a modest scale the mighty battle waged at Westminster.

During the century that preceded the Civil War, a sweeping change of structure and function had transformed the traditional organisations of English industry. The wealthier masters had ceased to practise their handicrafts or even to superintend the journeymen who had once worked under them. As a national market developed with its centre in London, while international trade came directly into English hands, this bigger master became a specialised merchant, trader or shop-keeper, and lost his old sense of solidarity with the craftsmen.

The small master retreated to a back street; as the years went on his direct dealings with individual customers grew steadily fewer, until he sank into dependence on the merchant for whom he now worked. Finally, as rents rose in the City, he quitted even its dimmer alleys and migrated to Southwark, Bermondsey, or Lambeth. A class of permanent journeymen had long since come into existence—men who never would be masters, either because they could not pay the heavy fees and produce a costly masterpiece, or because they could never find the capital to start an independent business of their own.

The small masters and journeymen were still members of the Livery Companies of the City, subject to their regulation and protection, but as the so-called 'yeomanry' they had an inferior status with no direct representation, for the warden and merchant-oligarchy had usurped the right to nominate the officers who should have been their elected spokesmen. This meant that every vestige of self-government had vanished. The merchant-oligarchy which controlled the companies, fixed the wages, prices and conditions to which the journeymen and the working small masters must submit. As the printers put it, in a petition a few years later, they had been made 'perpetual bondmen to serve some few of the rich, upon such conditions and for such hire and at such times as the masters think fit'.[5]

The Civil War must have aggravated the plight of the craftsmen. A petition from the weavers declares that 'many of us and our servants engaged for the Parliament', but while they fought its battles 'the foreigners [i.e. outsiders] admitted by the company, being generally malignants, staying at home got all the trading'. The result was unemployment, which they say was widespread, and of these skilled craftsmen 'hundreds were driven to become porters, labourers, water-bearers, chimney-sweepers, saltcriers and small coalmen'.[6] Throughout this whole period of twenty years, an incessant revolt of the rank-and-file craftsman was in progress against the Livery and the merchant-oligarchy. Though it was indirectly an industrial struggle for better wages and conditions, it assumed the form, characteristic of this period, of a democratic constitutional uprising within each company. Between 1641 and 1661 pewterers, stationers, saddlers, clothworkers, weavers, founders and clockmakers, all demanded direct representation on the governing bodies of their companies. In no instance did they succeed, and any trifling concessions they did win were afterwards lost.

This, then, was the background of daily life on the southern bank of the Thames, when Lilburne set about organising its craftsmen. When printers met weavers, in the more radical taverns, they must have compared notes about their respective wardens and courts, while they passed round copies of Lilburne's latest pamphlet. When they petitioned Parliament and argued their claim to direct representation in their companies, they used the current Leveller terminology and the stock Leveller arguments about the social contract and the sovereignty of the people. In the later years of this period they lost no chance of reminding Parliament that their enemies, the merchants of the court of assistants and wardens, were 'notoriously disaffected to the present government and on all occasions have manifested their malignity in words and deeds': the clerk of the Founders' Company was 'a mocker and scoffer of all manner of godliness and holiness and goodness'.[7] Parliament under the Commonwealth may have felt a transient sympathy with such appeals, but it never took effective action. It depended on the Presbyterian City for loans. These were the last struggles of the journeymen to recover their rights within the City companies. In the latter half of the seventeenth century they began to form their own distinct class organisations, out of which trade unions evolved.

These craftsmen, who felt they were on the downgrade and that their status was in danger, turned for backing and publicity to the Levellers, and especially to Lilburne. The weavers, more especially the silk-weavers of Spitalfields, habitually looked to him for support, and got it. Weavers were the aristocrats among the skilled manual workers and must have resented their rapidly accelerating decline with peculiar bitterness. The apprentices who entered this trade were all of them sons of freeholders, who must own an annual value often of 60s. but always of 40s.: the sons, that is to say, of customary tenants and labourers were excluded, and these were five-sixths of the population. In spite of their privileged status, their economic condition was wretched. 'Many a poor weaver sits at his loom from four in the morning till eight, nine or ten at night but to get seven, eight or ten shillings a week for a livelihood.' Those were relatively high earnings. A shilling a day was usual only in the West of England; often a weaver made only 5*d*. or 6*d*. a day. Work, moreover, was irregular and unemployment frequent.[8]

Shortly after the period with which we are dealing (in January 1648) Lilburne pleaded the case of the weavers while defending himself at the bar of the Commons. Once, he said, they had 'lived in good fashion', but in that winter of anxiety and high prices, no one wanted luxuries. Their specialties were laces and ribbons. On their behalf John raised his voice against the restrictions imposed on them by the oligarchy of the City. It had been their practice that they or their wives would go round the inns, peddling their wares to countrymen visiting London. This the Lord Mayor and aldermen had forbidden, by an order which was, John argued, 'illegal'. They were now cut off from any direct dealings with their customers, and were required to sell all their wares only to shopkeepers, 'who will give them but what they pleased for them'. This, he maintained, was 'slavery'.

From this opening Lilburne went on to attack another personification of the monopolists of the City, his own personal bugbear, the Merchant Adventurers' Company, which forbade him to practise the trade for which he was trained. The cloth-workers were entitled by statute to dress one white cloth in every ten of those which this company exported as half-finished goods. This right the craftsmen had now lost, because the Adventurers had become the Commissioners who ran the Customs House, since they had lent money to the Parliament on the security of the customs. In one of his most controversial pamphlets, after a legalistic argument against the company's charter, he stated the case against its monopoly on broad economic grounds.[9] What he attacked, with good reason, was the 'stint' which it imposed on its members, who were bound by oath to submit to all its regulations. In modern terminology, it was a cartel which severely restricted the amount of cloth its members might sell at home or abroad. This enabled it to buy cheap and sell dear. 'They beat the poor clothiers down to their own rates.' They paid only half the fair rate for freight, because they had their own chartered ships. At Rotterdam, where they concentrated all their continental trade, they would keep their warehouses shut, until the scarcity of cloth allowed them to dictate their own price. In this way they could count on a profit of 50 to 60 per cent. They had in fact carried these tactics too far, for at this level the Dutch were able to compete.

The worst crime of these monopolists was that they had forced the unemployed English artisans to emigrate in search of work to Holland. They would all come back, John declared, if the monopoly were abolished. Trading in the other direction, the Adventurers behaved no better: the price level of imports into England, thanks to them, was 15 to 20 per cent above what it should be. Finally, this monopoly had made them 'the great men in the commonwealth'. In every crisis they betray its liberties, as they did in the matter of ship-money. They 'envassalise' everyone in the trade, from the merchants to the sailors, weavers and spinners. They have 'kinged it and lorded it' over the rest of their brethren, till thousands and tens of thousands are 'impoverished and undone'.

When Lilburne had something new to say it was his way to arrest the attention of the public by direct action. There lay his talent as a popular leader—or shall we call him a demagogue? He shocked the average man into listening and then he poured out his arguments in print. And so, in pursuit of his campaign against the City oligarchy, as intolerant in religion as it was grasping in business, some of Lilburne's followers on 29 September, 1646 (while he himself lay in the Tower) tried to force their way into the Guildhall and claim their right as citizens to play their part in electing the Lord Mayor. They were kept out by violence and their leader, Major Wansey, a watchmaker, was arrested. While everyone in the crowded City from aldermen to apprentices would be discussing this scandal, John brought out one of his boldest (if most chaotic) pamphlets, *London's Liberty in Chains* (October 1646).

It opens with an explanation of the row at the Guildhall, but we are soon plunged into an argument about the fundamentals of popular representation, an attack on the composition of the Long Parliament as a travesty of true democracy, and finally a demand (not yet quite as clear as it soon became) for manhood suffrage. The wrong against which the watchmaker and his friends were protesting physically was the election of the Lord Mayor and sheriffs of London by the aldermen and Common Council. The right of direct election used to lie and ought still to lie 'in the body of the commonalty', that is to say with the freemen, the citizens, 'all and every' one of them. John had been doing a good deal of research into the charters to prove his point. He carries us back to King John and even to Alfred the Great, quoting liberally as usual from Coke's *Institutes*. This oddity of his, his passion for legalistic disputation, is of small historical account. He begins to interest us when he drops his musty charters and appeals to reason. When a man does that, one can smell revolution round the corner.

From the days of the Roman Consuls onwards, 'all free cities', Lilburne argues, 'have provided that all their officers and magistrates should be elective by votes and approbation of the free people of each city and no longer to continue than a year'. This follows from the fundamental Leveller doctrine of the sovereignty of the people, which he proclaims on his second page. 'All lawful powers reside in the people, for whose good, welfare and happiness all government and just policies were ordained.' In this way John (and for that matter the whole Leveller group) is leading the weavers and other craftsmen to the conclusion that the cure for their economic ills lies in political democracy. But it must be genuine, otherwise they will gain nothing from the Civil War but 'a change of masters'.

Suddenly on the 53rd page of this chaotic pamphlet, Lilburne leaps to his attack on the Long Parliament, and begins to demonstrate a new and still more explosive thesis—that by the test of any honest definition of democracy even its House of Commons was a sham. This must have struck many of his readers as a sudden and unexpected development. In July they could swallow with gusto the attack of the *Remonstrance* on kingship and the House of Lords. After all, as one of Lilburne's comrades and defenders put it then, in an imaginary address to the Lords:

Which of ye before this Parliament minded anything so much as your pleasures? . . . If you owed any man money or

abused any man, what law was to be had against you? . . .
It must needs be remembered how the war thrived whilst
any lord was employed, and how powerful the [army] is
grown, since the New Model, wherein there is not one lord.[10]

The Lords were not popular among the craftsmen and small
tradesmen. But the Commons? Did not the *Remonstrance*
address them on behalf of the 'many thousand citizens' as
'their own House of Commons'? The modern reader, if he was
brought up in the tradition of the Liberal historians, may be
equally startled. Quitting Lilburne for a moment, let us glance
rapidly, on our own account, at the Commons of this epoch.

The upper house of Parliament was composed (speaking
broadly) of the great landowners, its lower house, in the main,
of their younger sons and dependents and of the upper squirearchy. A few merchants and lawyers were returned by the
bigger towns, but most of the numerous lawyers were in origin
and outlook landed gentry. The identification of the Commons
with the landowning class was so complete that after the Whig
Revolution both houses carried a bill which restricted membership of the Commons to gentlemen who could boast a rent-roll
or income from land of £500; this was, however, one of the
two or three bills which William III vetoed. It reflected the
prevalent opinion of the governing class throughout the
seventeenth and eighteenth centuries. An act to the same effect
was actually passed under Queen Anne, though it lowered the
qualification to £300.

A house composed in this way was an 'estate' in the old
feudal sense of the word; it reflected the views of the landed
interest and only in rhetorical flourishes could it claim to
represent the people as a whole. The freeholders who elected
it in the counties were one-fifth of the peasantry. This landowning governing class was (again speaking broadly) an
endogamous caste, which looked with some disfavour on
marriage outside its ranks, though a poor squire would fairly
often mend his fortunes by seeking a good match in the City.
Sir Simonds D'Ewes for example traced his wife's family back
five hundred years to Domesday Book and found in her pedigree
only one 'unworthy' entry, a marriage to the daughter of an

alderman of the City of London.[11] One gathers that marriages
between the squire's family and that of a well-to-do yeoman
were *tabu*, even if the girl were well educated. The result of
this exclusiveness, when one takes into account the size of
families in that century, was that the governing class was a
tangled web of relationships. Cromwell, for example, when he
looked round the benches of the Long Parliament, could count
eighteen relatives among its members; in his own Parliaments
the figure rose to twenty-nine.[12] Seats in the Commons descended like peerages from father to son, or nephew. Seldom, for
example, in the eighteen Parliaments between 1472 and 1790,
had one Verney, or it might be two, failed to sit for Amersham,
Aylesbury, Wycombe or the borough or shire of Buckingham.

The idea of representation was rudimentary. The House was
conscious of itself as a privileged body, into which it would
admit only gentlemen worthy of a seat in the ruling club. The
criterion of fitness varied from generation to generation. The
Long Parliament began under Pym's management by excluding members who had contributed to the King's forced loans,
or helped as sheriffs to levy ship-money, but a threat was often
as effective as actual expulsion in ensuring a man's obedience
to the dominant party. Clarendon quoted leading men of
Pym's party as saying that in verifying elections they should be
'guided by the fitness and worthiness of the person, whatsoever
the desire of those was in whom the right of election remained'.
What Cromwell's Parliaments expected was that members
should be 'persons of known integrity, fearing God and not
scandalous in their conversation', a definition which the
Council of State interpreted to suit its interests. The idea that
the House could impose its own standards of fitness died hard,
as the exclusion of Wilkes and Bradlaugh testified.

At the best, representation could mean little so long as the
electors were kept in ignorance of what their member had said
in debate and how he had voted. The origin of this privilege
of secrecy is intelligible enough. As Macaulay pointed out, the
conduct of members had to be kept from the scrutiny of a
hostile and vindictive king, who might punish his critics as
Charles punished Eliot. This privilege was prolonged after
kings had ceased to be dangerous, since publicity would have

interfered with the trade in votes. The same historical reasons explain why Parliament was so slow to tolerate the formation of a regular opposition. Under the Stuarts the main business of Parliament was to deal with a difficult king; it could hope to succeed only if it were more or less unanimous.

When the conservative Clement Walker, a man as shrewd as he was malicious, embodied in his *History of Independency* his reflections on the Long Paraliament as he had observed it from a seat on the back benches, what chiefly impressed him were the mischiefs that sprang from its division into two factions. He starts with an attack on 'the mystery of the two juntos' which seem to keep up a hot opposition, yet combine to divide the spoils between them. 'For,' as he argues in the second of his ironical dedications, 'when two factions shall conspire to toss and keep up the golden ball of government profit and preferment between them, neither can be innocent.'[13] So far from recognition was the traditional two-party system of the English-speaking world. One of the worst breaches of privilege an outsider could commit was to suggest that opinions on some issue of current politics were divided, as William Chillingworth discovered (see p. 94 above).

The freedom of debate was severely limited. Clarendon, both in his *History* and his *Life* complains repeatedly of the Long Parliament's habit of expelling a dissentient member, sending him to the Tower or 'obliging him to receive a reprehension upon his knees'. Sir Ralph Hopton was sent to the Tower for trying to modify the offensive language of an accusation levied against the King; to save Lord Digby from punishment for his boldness in debate, the King raised him to the peerage. Henry Marten (as we have seen) was both expelled and sent to the Tower, and on one occasion Cromwell threatened even the venerable Selden with expulsion. A member might be expelled for some deviation from the correct view about the Holy Trinity, as John Fry was in 1651.[14] Needless to say, members under this system of intimidation could not always follow their own opinions when it came to voting. Sir Dudley (later Lord) North, who sat as a Presbyterian in the Long Parliament until he incurred Colonel Pride's disapproval, recorded his evidence on this matter thus:

Often times very many members of those who sat near me in the House gave their voice the same way that I did, upon putting the question, and yet upon division of the House they were ashamed to own it, for then they associated themselves with our great managers of business in the way of opposition to his then Majesty.[15]

Save in the 'decayed' boroughs, the business of getting elected was costly even for a wealthy candidate. Mr Pickwick, if he had looked over the records with Eatanswill as his standard, would have found much that was familiar to him in the practice of the seventeenth century, but the technique of electioneering would have seemed to him casual and primitive, and he would have missed the rival local newspapers. A lively ironical pamphleteer wrote in 1648 about the 'tumultuary factions and parties bandying against each other. What canvassing, plodding, plotting, contriving by friends, letters, bribings, drinkings, feastings are commonly used and employed to obtain a burgess-ship!' He thought it would be wiser to let a child draw the name of one of the candidates from a hat.[16] The fabulously wealthy Earl of Pembroke, according to *Mercurius Pragmaticus*, after the abolition of the House of Lords, had to spend £200 on ale to get himself elected for Berkshire by a small majority against a 'levelling' tanner. In one of the most amusing of the many royalist skits devoted to this monumentally stupid peer, he is made to say: 'If my steward's bill be right, every throat that votes for me costs me £20.'[17] These figures, needless to say, are to be treated only as 'illustrations'. Aubrey speaks of the quantities of 'roast beef, wine and ale' consumed at an election in Hereford.

On the other hand, it was not thought necessary for the candidate to be present in person at a contest. Sir Ralph Verney trusted the agent of Lady Rochester to get him elected for Westbury, but the superior interest of the Marquis of Hertford prevailed against him. General Ludlow stayed in Dublin when he stood against Sir Anthony Ashley Cooper for Wiltshire in 1654. The voters, he tells us, assembled at Stonehenge and the election was decided against him by the undersheriff 'on the view', which means presumably either by show of hands or by shouting Aye and No. Many, he believed, took part who were not qualified and he speaks also of 'threats and violence'. But it is clear from the documents he prints that this contest was won by the electioneering of the Presbyterian clergy, who felt that they had to defend their tithes against the republican left.[18] There was in this county (and doubtless in others also) a ministers' association which organised the 'moderate'—i.e. in 1654 the Cromwellian—vote. A minister who was reluctant to play his part in this godly operation was threatened with ejection from his benefice.

Occasionally military pressure may have been used. Denzil Holles accuses the Independents of quartering troops for this purpose on the electors during the many by-elections of 1645,[19] and Ludlow with much greater probability states that the Major-Generals used police pressure against the republicans in the election of 1656.[20] After making allowance for bribes, debauchery, the influence of the great landlords and the intimidation, ghostly or secular, of clergy and soldiers, did any elections at this period reflect public opinion? Probably a small proportion of them did represent the views of the propertied middle classes truthfully, for the most part in the larger boroughs.

To complete this rough sketch of the Long Parliament, one cannot refrain from mentioning its habit of voting public money for the enrichment of its own members. This with its notorious corruption did more than anything else to discredit it in the eyes of the Levellers and the Army. Under the early Stuarts the king was the fountain not only of honour but also of wealth. The surest path to a great fortune lay not through trade and still less through industry, but through service at court. While Buckingham grew fabulously rich by selling peerages and bishoprics, there were less dazzling favourites who did very well by the sale of minor offices. When the Long Parliament did away with the court, Westminster succeeded St James's Palace as the market place of power. Macaulay's thesis that after the Restoration political office became 'the shortest road to boundless wealth' was true in a lesser degree of the Interregnum also. Lilburne's way of putting it was that the Long Parliament 'after robbing and polling the poor kingdom by all manner of illegal taxations' divided the proceeds among its members, 'making nothing of £50,000 at one breakfast in one morning'.[21]

It happened only once, to quote Aubrey, that a whole Parliament was bribed, as the Commons were when Edmund Waller saved his life, after the detection of his plot, by distributing £10,000 among its members; but even the average member had his opportunities. One need not take literally the statement of a contemporary journalist, less irresponsible than most of his fellows, that every seat in the Commons was worth £500 a year in bribes and preferments, but presumably such a statement would not sound absurd to his readers, and they were people who took their politics seriously.[22] The Commons voted land worth £10,000 per annum in rents to Pym's heirs on his death and a like sum to those of Essex—to the former, because he was the unflinching and unscrupulous leader who with his eyes open brought on England all the disasters of Civil War; to the latter, because he was the half-hearted and inefficient general who had to be brushed aside because he could not win it. Their intention was that these vast sums—we moderns must not forget to multiply by ten—should be paid out to the unknown descendants of these men to all eternity. To the heirs of John Hampden went £5,000 a year, though he was said to be the richest commoner in the kingdom.

Pym, Essex and Hampden with all their defects and qualities were conspicuous figures. But the Commons would vote sums of a comparable order of magnitude to nonentities. When John Blakiston, one of the members for Newcastle (an Independent) died, it was felt that he had left his family ill-provided. His widow accordingly got an income of rents of £3,000 (also for eternity), while his brother got £500 on the same terms. Clement Walker commented: 'the insatiate hunger of gold and silver survives in the very ghost of a Saint after he is dead'. (The sinners, one must add, when they got their chance, behaved no better than the Saints.) Speaker Lenthal set an example which smaller men made haste to follow. He asked for the Mastership of the Rolls, and got this 'plum' of the legal profession, an office in which he cannot have done any honest work, for then as now the duties of a Speaker demanded a man's whole strength. He was also Chancellor of the Duchy of Lancaster and is said to have made from this office £6,730 *per annum,* not to mention a grant of £6,000. As a bribe for his acquiescence in Pride's Purge and the King's execution he received a valuable grant of land at Burford. He took lesser bribes to forward the hearing of petitions, which were paid by a transparent disguise to his brother Sir John (a still more unsavoury figure) or to the latter's wife.[23] Careful though he was, scandal buzzed round his name when it was discovered that he had 'salted' away land worth £11,000 a year in the name of a servant.

Watching the Long Parliament at work, what did the poorer tradesmen feel, the unemployed craftsmen and the hob-nailed privates in the ranks of the New Model? They got no compensation as a member did if the wares in their workshops were destroyed; their homeless and maimed clamoured in vain for charity, while a member had only to name his thousands if his mansion were ruined by the enemy. A member, it might be for service far behind the front lines, could get the arrears of his extravagant pay at once in broad and everlasting acres. A private had first to stage with all his fellows an alarming mutiny and then what he got for his arrears was a scrap of paper which some Saint would discount for him at 5*s.* or perhaps 3*s.* in the pound. In these circles the Long Parliament was not widely beloved.

Nearly two hundred years later, in 1832, John Lilburne got his way; the rotten boroughs were abolished. In 1654, while he was still alive, the news of a premature victory may have reached him in his dungeon in Jersey; for in that year also the same thing happened. He had stated a case so cogent that even his gaoler, the Lord Protector, had to concede it, and in the first Parliament of his reign these 'decayed' little towns (to use the term the seventeenth century favoured) lost their right to representation—though, to be sure, they regained it while the Puritans were still in the saddle.

Lilburne was bent on proving that the Long Parliament did not represent the people. The easiest way to establish that proposition was to state the facts about this flaming abuse. Others may have done it before him, perhaps in the debates of the Windmill Tavern, for of these we have no record. What is

clear is that he was the first to make it a living political issue
and to pledge a vigorous party to its redress. There were in the
Long Parliament among its 492 members, about 265 who sat
for boroughs too small to deserve separate representation,
yet each of these sent up to two burgesses to Westminster.[24]
Many of them were of recent creation, for as Lilburne put it,
'the King makes corporations of what paltry towns he pleaseth'.
A seat might be bought for £40 or £50. Often in these little
places there were only three electors, who might happen (so
Lilburne said) to be alehouse keepers, with no scruples about
selling their votes; yet in the neighbouring villages thousands
were disfranchised because they did not own 40s. worth of
freehold land.

> It is [he exclaims] unrighteous that Cornwall should choose
> fifty members and Yorkshire twice as big and three times as
> populous and rich not half so many and my own poor
> county, the Bishopric of Durham, none at all.

Its voteless inhabitants, he went on, are 'mere vassals and slaves'
like the peasants in France or Turkey. 'I profess for my part I
would lose life and estate, lived I now in that country [Durham]
before I would pay sixpence taxation.' As a matter of course, he
argued, these decayed boroughs are the stronghold of property
and aristocracy. They will choose 'only those that either some
lord or great man writes and recommends, or else one who
bribes them for their vote'.

The remedy on which Lilburne insisted in this pamphlet
was the redistribution of seats. He proposed that the House
should consist of 500 to 600 members and that each county
should

> choose a proportionable number suitable to the rates that
> county by their books of rates are assessed to pay towards
> the defraying of the public charge of the kingdom.[25]

By this definition of the basis of representation he anticipated
the Whig doctrine that property and not heads should be
counted at elections. As we shall see, the instinct of his disciples
in the Army was sounder; they called for a redistribution based
on population.

John was always thinking aloud as he wrote. His next pages

show an understanding of the rôle of economic power in politics which was not always or indeed often in his mind. He tells us that the Merchant Adventurers, because they were the Commissioners of the Customs, could control the elections in all the ports and 'sea-towns' of England.[26] He does not explain why, but it needs no great familiarity with the ways of that century to guess. Within certain limits the customs-officer could overcharge or undercharge pretty much as he chose. This made his favour all-important to the whole community of merchants, and all who depended on them, from the drysalters and ropemakers to the sea-captains. Directly or indirectly they would be able to control the press-gang also, on which hung the freedom and happiness of every working-class family in the place.

This influence the Merchant Adventurers wielded since the troubles began, in addition to the great power they already possessed over the workers in the cloth trade. Their ascendancy may explain why the sea-ports (including the City of London) were steadily Presbyterian in their politics, and why the navy, by way of contrast to the army, showed the same tendency. Their power, absolute in the 'sea-towns', could make itself felt in the elections for inland cities and market-towns also. Lilburne was thinking, doubtless, of the many by-elections, amounting in all to a minor general election, held recently to choose 'recruiters' to fill the seats vacated by the royalist members. In these centres the good will of the Merchant Adventurers as Commissioners of Excise was all important to multitudes of traders. Lilburne's personal grievance against these monopolists may have led him into some overstatement of the case against them, but broadly what he is saying here was true. There had been a noticeable shift of power, first on the economic plane and then inevitably in politics also, from the old governing class, the lords of manors and the nobility, to the merchants and financiers. Already we hear from him the cry of indignation that became in the end an admission of defeat. 'Our blood has been shed and spent in vain.' The common man had not come into his own.

As yet, however, and for some years to come, the Levellers were still militant and hopeful. The power of these new masters must be broken by ending their monopoly. Further, the demand for manhood franchise was implicit throughout this pamphlet. Indeed, as Edwards was shrewd enough to point out in *Gangraena*, Lilburne's reasoning, if one accepted his 'anarchical' premises, ought to carry him still further, to votes for women. This was put forward as a *reductio ad absurdum*. Actually, though he never wrote about women's rights, this conclusion would not have embarrassed Lilburne seriously, for the Anabaptists went a long way in recognising the equality of men and women. Soon afterwards, in a postscript entitled *The Charters of London*, after arguing that the Lord Mayor and aldermen were merely the executive officers of the Common Council on which they had no right to sit, he makes his demand for the extension of the franchise explicit and general:

> The only and sole legislative law-making power is originally inherent in the people and derivatively in their commissions chosen by themselves by common consent and no other. In which the poorest that lives hath as true a right to give a vote, as well as the richest and greatest.[27]

After six weeks' reflection Lilburne left the Whig doctrine far behind him. He now stood for integral reform—manhood suffrage and the end of the rotten boroughs.

Like most of the thinkers of their century the Levellers accepted the theory of the social contract as the basis of their political philosophy, but in their reasoning it assumed a new and stimulating form. The clearest statement of it is to be found in one of the ablest of their pamphlets, *Regal Tyranny Discovered*—in part at least Lilburne's work.[28] In its pages also are set out their reflections on the Norman Conquest, one of the most brilliant inspirations in the long record of English political controversy. This little book is notable for another reason. It was the first of the Leveller publications that called for the execution of the King. For this culminating act of the Puritan Revolution the inspiration came as much from Lilburne as from his friend Marten.[29] He even put forward an anticipation of the wretched quibble by which Charles was eventually convicted. 'Hath not Charles Stewart committed treason against King Charles? Sure I am he hath done it against the kingdom of England.'[30]

In these days every Englishman who could read knew that death was the punishment for treason. To make the case even clearer, John argues that Charles deserved a more severe punishment than Edward II who was forced to abdicate (to say nothing of Richard II and Rehoboam). The Index makes his meaning brutally clear and fills in the missing word. 'Charles Rex', it reads, 'ought to be executed p. 57.' If we may assume that he passed this entry, then we must conclude that he changed his mind more than once, for as we shall see he stood for conciliation in the spring of 1647, and again for severity in the autumn of 1648. Finally, throughout the fatal winter that followed Pride's Purge he opposed the lawless vengeance of the Commons. If he vacillated, so did Charles and so did Cromwell. But only one of his opinions influenced the masses and set the Army marching with tight lips, and that was his sentence of death.

At the mention of the social contract our minds turn back to the speculations of Hobbes and Rousseau. But the Levellers were practical thinkers who felt no interest in prehistoric man and the origin of society; it was the present that concerned them. Nor were they arguing primarily about the contract between the nation and its kings embodied in the coronation oath, though they did maintain with some justification from history that kingship in England was traditionally elective. These were opinions they shared with several of the Independent pamphleteers. What was original in their view of the social contract was that they analysed society—present-day society— into the individuals who composed it and then enquired on what terms they conferred on their representatives the right to govern them. This strikes the modern reader as a naïvely unhistorical mode of thought. For us a mature upstanding and self-conscious individual is not the beginning of the evolutionary process, but a late product achieved with much mental labour and not a little bloodshed. It took the whole career of the Atlantic civilisation to develop him. But the Leveller approach is none the less so dynamic that it set in motion ideas which still retain their power over us.

Lilburne summed up his whole philosophy of liberal democracy in a passage which he regarded as fundamental. It appears in identical shape in two of his pamphlets, compressed into a single sentence which straggles over an entire page and a quarter. Stripped of some of its verbiage and all its Biblical quotations and punctuated as four sentences, it runs thus:

God . . . gave man . . . a rational soul or understanding and thereby created him after His own image. . . . Every particular and individual man and woman that ever breathed in the world since [Adam and Eve] are and were by nature all equal and alike in power, dignity, authority and majesty, none of them having (by nature) any authority dominion or magisterial power, one over . . . another. Neither have they or can they exercise any, but merely by institution or donation, that is to say . . . by mutual consent and agreement for the good . . . and comfort each of other and not for the . . . hurt or damage of any; it being unnatural, irrational, . . . sinful, wicked and unjust, for any man or men whatsoever, to part with so much of their power as shall enable any of their Parliament men, commissioners, trustees, deputies, viceroys, ministers, officers and servants to destroy and undo them therewith. And unnatural, irrational, . . . devilish and tyrannical it is, for any man whatsoever, spiritual or temporal, clergyman or layman to . . . assume unto himself a power . . . to rule, govern or reign over any sort of men in the world without their free consent.[31]

Under the legalistic phraseology of these four sentences there are packed many charges of social dynamite. By their proclamation of the equality of all men and women, they reject not only distinctions of class but the patriarchal family also. Quietly but unmistakably they end the subjection of women. Neither slavery nor imperialism could survive where these principles were honestly professed—applications which Walwyn made without hesitation. The doctrine of consent swept away the authoritative church as well as the autocratic state.

There is in this basic statement of the Leveller creed something more than a novel reading of the social contract. There is the affirmation of the worth and dignity of the individual. A more solemn and impressive proclamation of human equality could not be conceived than this reminder that all men—and

women—were created in the image of God. Lilburne escapes
the cruder forms of anthropomorphism by insisting that it is
by the possession of a 'rational soul or understanding' that
humanity is godlike. By taking this quasi-divine equality as the
foundation of society Lilburne is escaping from the more
dangerous implications of the Calvinism he still professed. The
basic fact about humanity for the orthodox professor of the
Genevan creed was not its equality but its division into the
elect and the damned. The next step after this assertion of
inequality followed with all the rigour of logic and the in-
evitability of pride. It was for the Saints to realise the Kingdom
of Heaven on earth.

This minority, 'the honest party', necessarily thought of
itself as an *élite* appointed by Providence to rule and confirmed
in its title by the *fiat* of the God of Battles. This theocratic view
was carried to picturesque extremes by the Fifth Monarchists
who held that the Saints were ordained to rule in the name of
King Jesus. But all the People of God held it in one form or
another. In the state of Massachusetts where the Puritan ideal
came nearest to realisation, the franchise was confined to the
members of the Independent churches—no others were
tolerated—and they were one in five of the adult male population. Cromwell achieved a similar exclusiveness by three stages.
The poor were still denied a vote under the Protectorate, by a
property qualification. Then 'malignants' were disfranchised.
Lastly, the ungodly who did contrive to get elected were
excluded; in the first of Oliver's Parliaments there were round
about one hundred of them. Lilburne started his reasoning
from God and the creation and drew all his premises from the
Scriptures; yet because he was guided by the two basic tenets
of the Anabaptists, toleration and human equality, he arrived
at the secular republic.

Once the idea of a social compact had taken shape in the
minds of the Levellers, it was only natural that they should go
one step further and propose that it should be reduced to
writing. Lilburne did not in this pamphlet call for a written
constitution, but he laid the foundation on which, before the
end of this year, his followers in the Army built the Agreement
of the People. Since the individual is supposed to enter organised

society much as a citizen may enter the Merchant Adventurers or the Eastland Company, he may, nay he must, retain certain natural rights in his own hands.

> So . . . amongst the sons of men that live in mutual society . . . there is none above or over another, against mutual consent and agreement, and all the particulars or individuals knit and joined together by mutual consent and agreement becomes a sovereign lord and king, and may . . . set apart for the execution of their laws . . . officers, which we call magistrates, and limit them by what rules they judge convenient; always provided they be consonant to the law of God, nature and reason; by the force of which it is not lawful for man to subject himself to be a slave.[32]

The chief of the natural rights a man may not surrender is of course his liberty of conscience, his freedom to think and to utter his thoughts, above all about God. Richard Overton put the same idea in a more extreme and stimulating form. What one man may not surrender to another is his 'self-propriety', his property in himself, his individuality.[33] Experience had taught Englishmen in that generation that if they retained a king at all, they must 'bound' or limit him. The originality of the Levellers lay in their discovery that all magistrates, even Parliament itself, must be 'bounded' lest they invade the inner shrine of individuality.

The 'many thousand citizens' were not peculiar in the dissatisfaction with English law which they expressed in their *Remonstrance*. Far beyond the ranks of the Levellers and the left the courts were distrusted and the legal profession disliked. It was greedy and corrupt and its technical habit of mind was even more unintelligible to the common man than it is today, for the simple reason that its official documents and its statutes were in Latin or Norman French. Barristers were still trained, as we may read in Sir Simonds D'Ewes's description of life in the Temple, to debate points of law in the latter language, and Whitelock tells us that the staff of his embassy whiled away the long winter evenings at Stockholm in this pastime. Indictments were not valid until they were read out in court in Latin. What was a farmer in a remote village to make of a summons in Latin which, as might often happen, neither he nor any of his neighbours could construe? The fees lawyers charged were generally felt to be exorbitant and some of them were shameless in protracting litigation till their clients were ruined. In 1653 it was said that 23,000 causes had been waiting for settlement in Chancery some for five, others for ten, twenty and even thirty years.[34]

It happened constantly that peasants allowed their cases against landlords who robbed them of their common land by enclosure to go by default, because they could not afford to hire a Chancery lawyer. Workers who had grievances against their employer were in the same case. Since they had no trade union, they could not face the cost of litigation at Westminster; he could. Again, in turning over the pages of Thomason's Tracts one comes upon petitions from imprisoned debtors who complain that they cannot win their freedom because they cannot afford to bring up witnesses from the country. It would be easy to compile from the memoirs of this period a long list of the fabulous fortunes made by lawyers, beginning with Sir Edward Coke who is said to have made £100,000 (worth £1m. today) in a single year; he left estates worth £11,000 *per annum*.[35] Lady Verney wrote that during her stay in England in 1647 the only prosperous person she met in her own county, Buckinghamshire, was a lawyer; 'every one is going to law, either to claim debts or to protect property'.

Between them, the lawyers and big business had pushed the centralisation of commerce, administration and the law in London far in advance of the development of transport. As in no other country of Europe at this date the capital focused the most profitable activities of the nation on itself and levied its tribute upon them. The French monarchy, with better inland communications by river, had its *parlements* in several provincial centres; in England the creation under Wentworth of a northern administrative centre at York turned out ill. The Leveller case against the Merchant Adventurers was part of a much broader protest against excessive centralisation.

Throughout the sixteenth and seventeenth centuries London came near to enjoying a monopoly of exports; with 10 per cent of the population, it had 80 per cent of the country's foreign trade. The centralisation of the cloth trade in London must have entailed great waste in transport charges. To give one example; the manufacture in Lancashire of fustian, a mixture of cotton and linen, had become so important that a few years later (under the Commonwealth) it gave employment to 20,000 of 'the poor'. The cotton was brought to the Thames from Smyrna, Cyprus or Acre. Thence it had to make the journey to Lancashire. Finally since London had the monopoly of the wholesale market, the finished cloth travelled back to the capital, whence it was distributed to the various local markets, among them Manchester.[36] The roads, as everyone knows, were execrable, fit in winter only for a well-mounted rider or a pack-horse. The cost of travel by stage coach, a shilling for five miles, was if we compare it with other contemporary charges, extremely high. The location of all the higher courts in London meant not only that the provincial client had to pay lawyers' fees at the metropolitan level; he had also to pay for the transport of himself and his witnesses to London and back over these barbarous roads at some risk to health and limb and maintain them there while the suit dragged on.

The first of the Levellers' remedies were trenchant and simple. They were for ending the monopoly of the Merchant Adventurers and the rest of the foreign trading companies, chief among them the East India Company. They stood for free trade in exports, but were for retaining some restrictions over imports. Next they would abolish that 'badge of the Norman Conquest', the use of Norman French and Latin in the courts. In this Hugh Peters, for one, was in agreement with them; indeed, in social policy there was at this stage no marked difference between Levellers and Independents, though they soon began to diverge. The lawyers, however, fought hard to retain the unfamiliar languages of their 'mystery', much as the Catholic clergy did to preserve the use of Latin for their purposes. So far, judging by petitions and resolutions passed by grand juries, on these two issues the Levellers were in line with average public opinion and might have secured approval for their remedies in a referendum.

Already, however, John Lilburne had gone far beyond this starting point. In *Regal Tyranny Discovered* what he is really advocating is a return to the simplicity of Anglo-Saxon days, when, as he supposed, men did without lawyers—for he forgot that the church supplied their lack. He calls on Parliament to sweep away all the national courts at Westminster with their elaborate technicalities, and Quarter Sessions as well. His ideal was the *Gemot* which used to decide everything once a month in every hundred. He would have every case decided in the hundred or the county before a jury of twelve men. The only appeal he would allow would be to the House of Commons. In practice this would have meant one or more of its committees. It is surprising that, after his own experience, he should have thought them fit to sit as courts of appeal. Along with these radical proposals he adopted the common-sense suggestion of Sir Edward Coke that a register should be kept in every county for all leases and conveyances of landed property, a device which would have prevented much litigation.

Every revolution which brings a new class to power adopts as a matter of course a new system of law, which embodies its own view of property and social relations. The French Revolution substituted for the clotted traditions of feudalism the *bourgeois* clarity of the Code Napoléon. The Russian Revolution in its turn broke with tradition and set up its own characteristic system of civil and criminal law, with a novel procedure. The English Revolution was the exception. Its lawyers defeated every attempt at an organic reform of the common law; there was no Code Cromwell. But, as we shall see, while Hugh Peters and the more advanced Independents went part of the way with them, the Levellers put forward a revolutionary programme. It included the codification of the common law in a brief and intelligible handbook, the abolition of barbarous punishments, and the reform of the prisons; but its keynote was decentralisation, so conceived that the common man and his neighbours should govern themselves through their juries and elected magistrates.

Lilburne thought of this programme as a return to the simplicity and freedom of Anglo-Saxon times. But there were no romantic overtones in his conception of democracy. The

Levellers did not idealise the life of the peasant and the ethics of the village as the German Anabaptists did in the previous century, and the Tolstoyans in our own. There was among them no one who resembled Luther's contemporary, the scholar Dr. Karlstadt of Wittenberg, who threw away his doctor's gown, donned a peasant's smock and earned his bread behind the plough. They were plain practical Englishmen who tried to think out a way of life for the common man that would make him his own master, and deliver him from the oppression of kings, priests and those 'canker worms and caterpillars', the lawyers.

When they thought of the iniquities of the law, the Levellers reckoned imprisonment for debt far above other wrongs. So much is clear from the moving passage already quoted from the *Remonstrance* (*supra*, p. 101). They never ceased to agitate on this subject, until the lawyers emasculated the bill which Henry Marten, hoping to abolish this stupid cruelty for ever, introduced in 1649. Property defeated him, and two centuries later Dickens, who had something of the Leveller in him, described the same detestable system in his day as only a little less crude in its brutality. It was 'not from the beginning'; in fact it came in with the Tudors, under Henry VII. On this question also Hugh Peters and the more advanced of the Independents were at one with the Levellers. To grasp its importance for the craftsmen and small tradesmen who looked to the Levellers for leadership, one has to realise how much they depended on borrowed capital to start and run their little businesses. Most of them were debtors and yet they were expected to give credit. Bacon said as much in his essay on usury: 'It is certain that the greatest part of trade is driven by young merchants upon borrowing at interest.'

Capital was scarce in England and the prevailing rates of interest were much higher than in Holland, with the natural result that much Dutch capital was imported. Even big business might have to depend on capital borrowed at fixed interest: a gun-founder under the Commonwealth paid interest on £30,000. Attempts were made to fix a maximum rate of interest by law, which failed, as a policy of mere restriction always does fail, to check usury. A bill which sought to limit interest

to 8 per cent was defeated in 1621 on the amusingly contradictory grounds (1) that religion forbids usury at any rate
whatever, and (2) that landowners would be ruined, since no
one would take up a mortgage at so low a rate. This bill was
eventually passed in 1625, with a proviso that nothing in it
should be held to reconcile usury with conscience.

The goldsmiths, who became the recognised bankers during
the Interregnum, would not lend to craftsmen or small
merchants. Some of these were able to borrow from their
guilds. Journeymen shoe-makers of Oxford could borrow from
'the common box' of their trade. Sometimes a municipality
would lend, particularly to young craftsmen; Oxford, Coventry,
Nottingham, Liverpool and Kendal did so. There were
districts, even in the seventeenth century, in which the village
community was still so much alive that it acted as a credit
bank by lending cattle, sheep and money to its members, for
which interest was charged. But one gathers that in town and
country alike it was only the fortunate few who could rely on
such kindly lenders as these. Even fairly well-to-do farmers were
usually obliged to borrow at seed-time, fairs and quarter-days
to pay for seed, livestock and rent. Poor farmers were usually in
debt both to shop-keepers and landlord. As for the craftsmen
and small tradesmen, they had usually to borrow at 10 or 12
per cent. Often they had to turn to the pawnbroker before they
could pay their journeymen's wages. Hawkers got their wares
on credit, and in the wool trade with its complicated sub-
division of processes it was usual to 'buy on time', which meant
on long credit varying from six to fifteen months.[37]

The law dealing with debt was as stupid as it was brutal.
Imprisonment was a torment to an innocent debtor and it did
the creditor no good, since it prevented the debtor from working
to pay off his debt. On the other hand, it failed to protect the
creditor against a dishonest debtor, for it often happened that a
man who had ample assets would rather go to prison than pay.
This, to a modern reader, sounds improbable, until one
realises that the jailors, who came from the governing class
and usually paid a substantial bribe or commission to get their
jobs, ran the prisons as commercial enterprises. For a debtor
who could afford to pay, prison was a comfortable hotel in

which he might hope to enjoy congenial company. For a consideration, his jailor would even let him out on parole. It was said that one notorious jailor made as much as £20,000 in this way from his rich prisoners—an unlikely sum, which one quotes only as an instance of what was widely believed in this greedy and malicious age.[38]

On the other hand, the poor but honest debtors, who would gladly have paid their debts if they could, were treated by these commercially minded jailors with a cruelty that would seem incredible if the victims' complaints and petitions were the only evidence before us. But apart from the statements of the Leveller leaders, who all knew something of prison from the inside, we have similar descriptions of the sufferings of Quakers in these same prisons a few years later; the ethics of their Society discountenanced exaggeration. One petition which claims to speak for 'many thousands imprisoned for debt' states that some of them had endured this 'slavery' for twenty, others for forty years. Clothed in rags and fed on scraps, their 'lodging was many times the cold earth'. They speak of the 'hellish tyranny' of their jailors, who robbed them, starved them and kept them manacled.[39]

A somewhat earlier group of petitions, which reveal Leveller inspiration, make even more painful reading.[40] If we pass by on the other side, stopping our ears with our fingers, we shall never grasp the realities of life in this grim century. One petition complains of the exactions of Sir John Lenthall, marshall of the King's Bench prison at the Fleet, who put prisoners in irons and starved them 'in a dog-kennel' to extort his fees. Another, addressed to Fairfax and the Army, estimates the number of prisoners for debt in England at 10,000. It declares that jailors will keep debtors in prison to exact their fees, even after the creditor begs for their release. Some have been 'kept in irons (hands and feet) till their excrements coming from their body rotted their fundaments'. Two years later another petition was addressed to Fairfax and the Army in the name of former soldiers. They 'spent their estates for this Parliament' and are its creditors for ample sums, yet they are now imprisoned for debt 'in loathsome dens and hateful dungeons amongst horrible stinks and noisome vermin'.[41]

This *Inferno* runs to many cantos scattered among Thomason's Tracts.

In the remedies they proposed the Levellers were careful to keep both these evils in mind. They insisted that the law should be so revised as to make a debtor's assets available for the payment of his debts. Imprisonment for debt they would abolish altogether and on principle. One of their doctrines which Lilburne stressed continually—it came from Coke's *Institutes*—was that prisons should never be used for punishment, but only as places of detention in which the accused are confined while awaiting trial. In their belief that imprisonment serves no useful purpose they were bolder than most modern reformers—with the odd exception of Godwin, who in spite of his agreement with them in this and, indeed, in most of their opinions, held them in deep contempt. Unfortunately they never explained in any detail what they would substitute for imprisonment, beyond insisting that the criminal should make good his wrong and compensate his victim in kind or in service.[42] They proposed further that jailors should charge only according to a recognised list of fees fixed at a low level; later, they maintained that every officer of the law from judge to jailor should receive an adequate fixed salary and that the charging of fees be prohibited—in other words that prisons must not be run for profit.

The Levellers were so bent on bringing some concern for humanity into this business of debt and imprisonment, that they had little leisure for constructive thinking about the fundamental question on which the imperilled status of their clients the craftsmen depended—the provision of capital. They did, indeed, ask that a maximum rate of 6 per cent be fixed for interest on loans, and an ordinance to this effect was eventually passed by the Commonwealth Parliament in 1651. Always in the centuries that lay between the Reformation and the industrial revolution, this problem was a matter of major concern to the progressive groups who drew their support from the craftsmen and the intellectuals. Among the urban supporters of the German peasants in their tremendous rebellion of 1525, the group which went furthest in its pioneering was that which met in Nuremberg under Hübmaier's leadership. It proposed, among much else which gave proof of its originality and enlightenment, that the funds of the Empire should be used as a stock to provide craftsmen with capital. This was in essence what Proudhon, himself of craftsman and peasant stock, had in mind when he planned his famous national bank, which was to stand behind craftsmen and peasants in the same way. Had the Levellers survived a few years longer, the pressure of the craftsmen's needs might have driven them in the same direction, though they, with their passion for decentralisation, would have called in, not the state nor the empire as the French and Germans did, but the local community.

In *Regal Tyranny Discovered* Lilburne tracked all the evils he was assailing—the oppressions of King Charles, the arrogance of the House of Lords, the greed of the lawyers, the maelstrom of Westminster—back to the Norman Conquest. In nothing was his homely genius for politics so conspicuous as in his use of this inspiring myth. All these wrongs began in the piracy of the Northmen. Our kings were the descendants of the usurper and invader, William the Bastard. The lords owed their greatness to the thief and tyrant who seized our fathers' lands and gave them to his Normans, 'whom he made dukes, earls and barons for helping him to subdue and enslave the free nation of England'. The present House of Peers were 'the lineal issue and progeny' of these 'robbers, rogues and thieves'—a theme he developed with something of the extravagance but none of the wit of *Penguin Island*. 'In those days it was a shame even among Englishmen to be an Englishman.' The Conqueror broke his oath to observe the laws of St Edward the Confessor, and presently 'the iron Norman yoke' drove the people to Westminster to plead through lawyers in Latin.

Lilburne was not the author of this stirring simplification of history.[43] It is to be found in the two widely read histories of this age, Speed's *Chronicle* and Daniel's *History*. To some of it Sir Edward Coke lent his great authority. A few scholars were already interested in Anglo-Saxon literature and that industrious antiquary, Sir Simonds D'Ewes, had a manuscript dictionary of its language copied for his own use. What the Levellers did was to draw the political and social consequences from this newly awakened interest in our past. The peers of their day were merely the descendants of the Conqueror's colonels. and the lords of manors of his captains.

There are in the recent history of Europe sevcral instances that remind us what an explosive mixture is this blending of nationalism with class feeling. It fitted the republican secularism of the Leveller movement to perfection, since it roused men's emotions without invoking religion. It meant as much to Independents as to Anabaptists and to men like Marten who cared for none of these things. And yet it stirred men's blood and quickened their pulses. It gave the craftsman and the yeoman whom the arrogance and greed of his social superiors had wounded a valid reason for carrying his resentment into action. To depose these Norman lords was a patriotic deed; Manchester and the rest of them derived their privileges from a foreign invasion.

Soon this Norman myth was repeated from the pulpits and ran with the rumours and scandals of the day round the market places. The adjective Norman was enough to blast any institution. The rural Levellers applied it to base tenures of all kinds, but especially to the copyhold tenure which made most of the peasants the timid dependants of the lords of the manor. There may have been even then a few retired scholars who knew that feudalism and the manorial structure of rural society dated from the late Roman Empire, and that villeinage (the parent of copyhold tenure) was an Anglo-Saxon institution which the Normans took over as they found it. But once the idealisation of good King Alfred's golden days had got well under way, it seemed plausible, nay inevitable that the Norman invaders must have degraded the free English yeomen into villeins—the word itself was Norman. There was no one to put a sceptical snuffer on this stimulating myth; above all, it was accepted as self-evident by the Army. Cromwell's Ironsides felt that on Marston Moor and Naseby Field they recovered what was lost at Hastings.

When the many thousand citizens told the Commons in their *Remonstrance* that they expected to be delivered from all the unreasonable laws made since the Norman Conquest, they added a warning: 'ye must expect to hear more frequently

from us than ye have done'. Eight months passed before their
next manifesto, the petition of March 1647, was drafted and
circulated for signature. The Leveller party, meanwhile, was
growing not only in London but among the peasants of the
neighbouring home counties. One has the impression that it
was drawing into its ranks the more vigorous and militant
spirits of the left. In Parliament, on domestic issues at any rate,
the Independents seldom ventured to oppose the intolerant
Presbyterian majority, and when they did, they were heavily
defeated. One might have expected them to fight the monstrous
Blasphemy Bill with every device of argument and obstruction.
They did not even oppose the second reading, which was
carried without a division. On the last day of 1646 they tried to
modify the ordinance which forbade unordained laymen to
preach, or even to expound the Scriptures. Their amendment
to omit the latter prohibition was lost in a thin House by 57 to
105, with Cromwell telling, for the minority.

Their party, if it is not premature to use that name, was
poorly organised and slack in attendance. We talk of 'the
floating voter' who is said to decide general elections by casting
his vote now for one party and again for the other. In the Long
Parliament there was an even more disconcerting and incalculable character, the floating member. He was susceptible
to pressure from the City, from big business, the Presbyterian
clergy, the mobs of apprentices and watermen and presently
from the Army—from every quarter save the legitimate
quarter, his constituents. His vote registered the forces applied
to him and when in doubt, which was often, he went home
before the division.

The chief concern of politicians during these eight months
was, of course, the intrigues that centred round the captive
King. Since the publication of the French archives, we know
exactly what Montreuil and Bellièvre were plotting in their
embassy, and can understand their exasperation with Charles's
unintelligible scruples, the obstinacy of the Scots and the
dilatory incompetence of the English Presbyterian leaders.
Contemporaries knew less and guessed more. It is clear from
Overton's brilliant pamphlet *An Unhappy Game at Scotch and
English* (30 November, 1646) that the Levellers were well

aware of some of the schemes for a second civil war; even in
the Tower Lilburne could smell the 'Scotch ale' the Lords
were brewing.[44] When the Scots marched home after handing
over the King, the chief concern of the Presbyterians was to
disband the New Model Army and get rid of Cromwell. More
important in the long run than any of these manœuvres was
the weather. The first of six successive miserable harvests was
reaped in 1646 and throughout the winter that followed it
there fell torrential rain. The price of bread rose steeply during
these years until at last it was doubled. After the failure of the
next harvest, in the winter of 1647-8, we can sense in the
unkindly atmosphere new waves of revolution and counter-
revolution.[45]

The March Petition was a less startling document than the
Remonstrance. Its purpose is rather to persuade than to excite.
Its draftsman, as he himself stated, was Walwyn, though we
may assume that the other leading Levellers were consulted.
Its good manners are characteristic of his pen. There is no step
backwards, yet this document asks the reader's assent to no
more than is necessary for practical purposes. It does not call
for the abolition of the monarchy and the House of Lords; it is
content to deprive them of their 'negative voices'. That would
suffice to ensure the supremacy of the Commons. The demand
for the dissolution of the Long Parliament is not repeated, nor
does manhood suffrage yet figure in the party programme.
Lilburne in his thinking was as usual slightly ahead of his
followers.

On the other hand, the Petition is even bolder than the
Remonstrance in its challenge to powerful interests. Once more
it assails big business by calling for the dissolution of the
Merchant Adventurers' Company; again it alarms the world of
scriveners and goldsmiths, creditors and investors, by attacking
imprisonment for debt; the lawyers would find its plea for the
reform and simplification of legal procedure no easier to
stomach than before. The demand for the toleration of all who
preach or publish their opinion in religion in a peaceable way
is made without qualification. By way of answer to a furious
expression of the City's intolerance in a petition from the Lord
Mayor and Common Council (p. 168 below), it insists that no

one shall be excluded 'from bearing office of trust in the commonwealth for non-conformity'. Its clause (No. 8) calling for humanity in the criminal law deserves to be quoted, though later manifestoes went even further and were more specific. It asks:

> That the life of no person may be taken away, under the testimony of two witnesses at least, of honest conversation; and that in an equitable way ye will proportion punishments to offences, that no man's life may be taken, his body punished nor his estate forfeited, but upon such weighty and considerable causes as justly deserve such punishments; and that all prisoners may have a speedy trial, that they be neither starved, nor their families ruined by long and lingering imprisonment; and that imprisonment may be used only for safe custody until time of trial and not as a punishment for offences.

That would have ended capital punishment for petty theft with many another barbarity which disgraced English civilisation until well into the nineteenth century.

The boldest clause (No. 10) in the Petition, perhaps the boldest word the Levellers had yet put down on paper, called for the total abolition of tithes:

> That tithes and all other enforced maintenance may be for ever abolished and nothing in place thereof imposed; but that all ministers may be paid only by those who voluntarily contribute to them or choose them and contract with them for their labours.[46]

This was to defy a body of men who vied for power with the undisguised spokesmen for property—the Merchant Adventurers, lawyers and peers. United with these they dominated all England—unless the Army should oppose them. Nine thousand clergymen, one in every parish, were now provoked to denounce the Levellers as the enemies of God and for their angry sermons they could draw on an inexhaustible armoury of scriptural texts. With rare exceptions, only the preachers of the sects could have survived without tithes, and the few Presbyterians who could have held out would have had to live much more modestly. In the poorer rural parishes only a few laymen, who taught without pay, like the Anabaptists and (presently) the Quakers, would have been left to preach the Gospel. For the possession of the pulpits a class struggle in this century was waged all the time both with purse and sword. Tithes, toleration and land tenure were the fundamental issues in this Revolution, apart from which political democracy and the sovereignty of the people meant little.

Why the propertied classes felt hotly on this subject needs little explanation. They foresaw that if tithes were swept away, rents would soon follow them. This was what Speaker Lenthall meant when he told a deputation of two thousand farmers and peasants who marched to Westminster in January 1646 from the counties of Hertford and Buckingham that they understood the laws neither of God nor man. The tenth part was due to the minister precisely as the rent was due to the landlord.

Why the peasants felt hotly is no less easy to grasp. Those of them who had come under the influence of the sectaries were indignant that they should be forced to maintain preachers with whose sermons they profoundly disagreed—'blind mouths' if one prefers Miltonic language, class enemies in modern phraseology. They paid their voluntary contribution to their chapel. Why must they give to God twice over? The more clear-headed of the sectaries taught that the Old Testament had been abrogated by the New; tithes, in short, were a Jewish, not a Christian institution.

Apart from such reasons, like all imposts in kind, tithes were a bad tax, because their amount varied with the whims and cupidity of the collector. Under the old régime in rural Turkey, the author had opportunities of watching the collection in kind of a tax which was in effect a tithe or dime. As a matter of course every tax-gatherer over-estimated the crop grossly, and every peasant had to bribe. An experienced pair of eyes in an honest head might be able to guess roughly the amount of wheat harvested as the grain lay on the threshing floor, but when it came to taxing the livestock, from chickens to colts, the scope for cheating on both sides was unlimited. During the German Peasants' War the more moderate of the popular leaders did not object to 'the great tithe' on cereal crops, but they fought 'the little tithe' on livestock with all their undisciplined might. In England to discourage delay, evasion and resistance, it was the rule that the farmer or peasant, if he were convicted of any of these offences, paid three times what was due.

A petition from Kent gives many instances of oppression, with verifiable details, parish by parish. In one case to pay a tithe of the value of £14 10s. four horses were taken, each said to be worth £24; or again for a tithe of £2 cattle worth £9 were taken.[47] Quakers, who refused to pay tithes on principle, suffered so heavily that within a generation they were all driven from their farms, and had to get their living in other trades. Their records prove that the complaints from Leveller sources are not seriously exaggerated. To give only one instance out of many; at Amersham to pay a tithe of 12s., property worth £24 10s. was seized from Thomas Ellwood, including a riding horse worth five guineas.[48]

The sufferers in the cases quoted must have been well-to-do farmers. But to grasp the feeling against tithes we have to remember the average peasant was in these days a poor man, habitually in debt. Aubrey wrote that before the Civil Wars few copyholders could afford glass for their windows. A noticeably able petition 'in the behalf of the poor of this nation' which tried to diagnose the causes of their poverty, mentions tithes among them and declares that 'often those who pay lack food'.[49] There is nothing mysterious about the anger of a smallholder, subsisting with difficulty on his £10 per annum, when the goose or the pig he had fattened for market was taken for the parson, who lived as the Anabaptists used to say 'like a cardinal' on an income of £300 or £400.

One of the complications which made a solution difficult was that a big proportion of the tithes went not to the clergy, but to 'impropriators'. These were laymen, often the descendants of the new rich who got the property of the suppressed monasteries by favour or purchase. The tithes that used to go to the monks now went to these *rentiers*, who drew their tribute from the labour of the peasants, without performing any social function whatever. It may be significant that Cromwell himself was an hereditary owner at Huntingdon, entitled to draw the tithes once paid by the tenants of a suppressed Benedictine priory. At Ely he inherited the property of a maternal uncle who farmed the tithes of the cathedral and held a lease of cathedral properties with a big tithe barn. This inheritance from both sides of his family may help to account for his ambiguous attitude towards tithes. Impressionable as he was, he must have been influenced by the attitude of the sectaries round him, from the chaplains of the New Model to the officers who were his messmates and bed-fellows. They detested tithes. Again and again the Army petitioned for their abolition. It never happened. To the end, under the Protectorate, tithes were collected for Cromwell's established Puritan church exactly as they were for Laud's high church. Even the promise of a moderate reform was never fulfilled.

When it came to devising a solution, there were among the sectaries and even among the Levellers two schools of thought. Some, as in the March Petition, were for abolition without compensation—the clean solution which the French adopted, once for all, in their Revolution. Others were for a compromise, of which several versions were current.[50] Always the hated tax in kind disappeared. In its place a moderate rent charge was to be fixed, payable in money, either to the impropriator if any, or to the county or the state. From the pooled proceeds of this charge the stipends of the clergy could be paid. One gain from such a reform might be an equalisation of the incomes of the clergy. It was true that some drew their £300 to £400 from tithes, but others had to manage, like the Vicar of Wakefield, on £40 a year, or even on £20.[51] Another version of this plan proposed that the money so raised should be used to endow education.[52] As a party the Levellers showed more of the English disposition to compromise than one might have expected from Lilburne's temperament. *Fiat justitia ruat coelum* was, as he said, his motto. Walwyn, on the other hand, though opposed to 'all enforced contributions' had an alternative plan in his head 'more certain' for the public ministers and 'less irksome to the people'.[53] When there was a chance of an agreement with the Independents, the Levellers compromised, on this and other questions. When Cromwell became their open enemy, they returned to their revolutionary solution.[54]

In spite of its persuasive tone and good manners the March Petition roused the fury of the Presbyterians even before it was presented. Paradoxically they took offence because the petition was addressed to 'the supreme authority of this nation, the Commons in Parliament assembled'. They held that sovereignty lay in King, Lords and Commons. Apart from this question of constitutional theory, it assailed too many interests; tithes were for Mr Edwards and his backers in both Houses the linchpin of the social structure. The Recorder of the City, Glynne, laid a printed copy of it before a committee of the Commons, as if it had been a seditious document, and when a group of the Levellers in the lobbies avowed it, three of them, the Baptist pastor Thomas Lamb, Nicholas Tue and Major Tulidah were imprisoned—as usual in such cases without a charge or a hearing. In the row that blazed up at these arrests, the Presbyterian leaders, Holles and Stapleton, drew their swords. The Levellers, as their habit was, made the most of these events, and appealed to the House by way of protest six times in ten weeks. Two pamphlets told the story in detail. In the end, on 20 May, 1647, the Commons ordered that the March Petition be burned by the common hangman at Westminster and the Exchange.[55]

Lilburne had lost faith in this Parliament long before these happenings, and (as we have seen) the aim of his recent pamphlets had been to remove any illusion about it still lingering in the minds of his readers. He and Overton, who now realised that the House of Commons would do nothing to uphold their rights against the Lords, had already made up their minds to appeal over its head to the sovereign people. 'We for our preservation', they wrote on the last day of February in *The Outcries of Oppressed Commons*, 'shall tread in the Parliament's steps by *appealing to the people* against them, as they did against the King.'[56] But now the Commons by burning the Leveller petition had saved them the trouble of arguing their case. If the people's representatives refused to listen to the people when they exercised their ancient, traditional right of petitioning, the trustees had betrayed their trust and broken the social contract. In plain words, as Overton presently put it, England had relapsed into 'a state of nature'.[57] Holles and Stapleton, when they drew their swords on the petitioners and consigned their petition to the flames, had made what we should call a revolutionary situation.[58]

These two men, who succeeded Pym and Hampden in the leadership of the Presbyterian majority, were dwarfs by comparison. To drive the Levellers at this moment into open revolt was an act of peculiar folly, because in these turbulent weeks their arrogance was also turning the New Model Army to mutiny. Lilburne was quick to grasp this new opportunity of leadership and he now addressed not only the craftsmen of Southwark but his fellow-soldiers of yesterday who still had swords in their hands. Once more in *Rash Oaths Unwarrantable* he proved to them that this Parliament was not the representative of the people; once more he assailed its greed and corruption; again he demanded votes 'for every free man of England, as well poor as rich'. Recalling once more the wrongs which Richard Overton with his wife and brother, and the Leveller printers Larner and Paine, had suffered from both Houses, he concluded with this characteristic defiance from his prison cell in the Tower:

I am now . . . determined to appeal to the whole kingdom and Army against them and it may be thereby come to quittance with them and measure unto them as they have measured to me. . . . They are rebels and traitors to the trust reposed in them by the free people of England, their emperors, lords and masters.

The Army had ears to hear.

NOTES TO CHAPTER VII

1. The first suggestion that Colonel Harry Marten was one of the joint authors of the *Remonstrance* came from Pease (*The Leveller Movement*, p. 153n.); D. M. Wolfe agrees (Wolfe, p. 109). Neither of them gives his reasons. I, too, think that Overton was the editor, and that he wrote a good deal of this manifesto; for one thing, he alone among these pamphleteers knew how to use short paragraphs for popular effect. He was a printer as well as a writer, and knew how to design a telling page. But only Walwyn could have written the moving paragraphs I have quoted about debt and the press-gang; he, also, had a poor opinion of Magna Carta. Here are my reasons for thinking that Marten had a share in the pamphlet. (1) It is republican on principle, and so goes slightly beyond Lilburne's view, for he would always have accepted a quasi-elective, constitutional monarchy, shorn of any veto. Marten had what the others lacked, a university training in the classics, and was, as Bishop Burnet put it, a republican 'upon Roman and Greek principles'. (2) The historical survey of the Long Parliament's

doings agrees with Marten's own record, for he was (5 December, 1642) among the earliest critics in the House of Essex's generalship and an early (if not the earliest) herald of the sovereignty of the people (1 May, 1643, as Gardiner, *Civil War*, I, p. 133, convincingly interprets D'Ewes). Again the style of this historical survey, with its irony, seems to me rather too 'high-brow' for Overton and not unlike Marten's polemic against the Scots (reproduced in John Forster's *The Statesmen of the Commonwealth of England*, III, pp. 264-83). (3) The passage about the public standing bareheaded before parliamentary committees (Wolfe, p. 126) reminds me of Marten's own characteristic behaviour in Berkshire in 1648 (p. 46 above). (4) This and one or two other scattered phrases suggest to me an inside view of Parliament. But the whole subject of Marten's relations with the Levellers calls for further research. Forster's early Victorian biography of Marten is in this respect useless. A disciple of Godwin, he knew nothing of the Levellers, save a little at second-hand about 'the notorious Lilburne'.

2. The most emphatic declaration that the government of England lay in King, Lords and Commons was passed on 6 May, 1648. The adoption by the Presbyterian majority of the doctrine of the divine right of kings is witnessed by the lengthy answer of the Commons to the Leveller petition of 11 September, 1648 (see p. 354 below.)

3. John Selden, *Table Talk*, under 'Parliament'.

4. *The Moderate*, 3-10 April, 1649.

5. George Unwin, *Industrial Organization in the 16th and 17th Centuries*, p. 210.

6. *Ibid.*, pp. 207, 209.

7. *Ibid.*, pp. 205, 208.

8. Lipson, *Economic History of England*, II, pp. 280, 286, 33-4, 56.

9. *Innocency and Truth Justified* (6 January, 1646).

10. *A Pearl in a Dunghill* (30 June, 1646). Probably, as it seems to me, by Walwyn. I have substituted 'army' (between brackets) for 'enemy', which makes no sense.

11. Sir S. D'Ewes, *Autobiography*, I, p. 329.

12. Abbott, I, p. 119.

13. C. Walker, *Relations and Observations historical and political upon the Parliament* (20 August, 1649).

14. Godwin, *History of the Commonwealth*, III, p. 508.

15. *A Narrative of Some Passages in or relating to the Long Parliament*, in *Somers Tracts* (1811), VI, p. 589.

16. *Salus Populi desperately ill of a languishing consumption* (13 December, 1648).

17. *The manner of the election of Philip Herbert*, etc. (16 April, 1649).

18. E. Ludlow, *Memoirs* (ed. Firth), I, pp. 388-90.

19. Denzil, Lord Holles, *Memoirs* (1699), p. 42.

20. Ludlow, *Memoirs*, II, p. 17.

21. *Rash Oaths Unwarrantable* (31 May, 1647), p. 50.

22. *The Moderate* (21-8 November, 1648).

23. This we learn from the experience of Lady Verney. The figures of

the Speaker's income and grant come from Clement Walker, and may not be reliable.

24. I have reached this figure by deducting the number of burgesses (133) in the first Parliament of the Protectorate from the number (398) in the Long Parliament. The figure is only approximately correct because the Protectorate departed from the rule that each borough should send up two members.

25. *London's Liberty in Chains* (18 December, 1646), pp. 53-5.

26. *Ibid.*, p. 56.

27. *Ibid.*, *The Charters of London*, p. 4.

28. 6 January, 1647. This long pamphlet of 108 pages is anonymous and discusses Lilburne and his case against the Lords as if the writer were one of his friends and admirers. 'The man is full of heroicalness and a zealous lover of his country' (p. 4). None the less the style is often unmistakably his. I have followed Pease and Wolfe in attributing it to him, but I think that someone with a more orderly mind wrote a few pages and had a hand in editing it, probably Overton. The argument (p. 9) that each of the Ten Commandments is in accordance with the law of reason recalls his unfinished book on the agreement between revelation and science (p. 52 above). This is the only Leveller pamphlet provided with an index—the last adornment Lilburne would be likely to think of. The absence of a signature is easily explained if two writers collaborated. Lilburne would never adopt anonymity from motives of prudence.

29. I assume that Marten was the author of *A Corrector of the Answerer* (26 October, 1646) which called for condign punishment of the King 'as the chief of all delinquents' and a worse traitor than Strafford or Laud. See Wolfe, p. 13n.

30. *Regal Tyranny*, pp. 56-7.

31. *The Free Man's Freedom Vindicated* (16 June, 1646), pp. 11-12. Pease prints it in its entirety (*The Leveller Movement*, p. 139). The passage also occurs in *Regal Tyranny*, p. 6.

32. *Regal Tyranny*, pp. 10-11.

33. 'To every individual in nature is given an individual property by nature, not to be invaded or usurped by any. For every one as he is himself, so he hath a self propriety, else could he not be himself . . . No man hath power over my rights and liberties and I over no man's. . . . For by natural birth all men are equally and alike born to like propriety, liberty and freedom, and as we are delivered by God, by the hand of nature, into this world, every one with a natural innate freedom and propriety (as it were writ in the table of every man's heart never to be obliterated) even so are we to live, everyone equally and alike to enjoy his birthright and privilege, even all whereof God by nature hath made him free.' *An Arrow against all Tyrants and Tyranny, shot from the prison of Newgate into the prerogative Bowels of the arbitrary House of Lords* . . . by Richard Overton, 10 October, 1646.

34. *An exact relation of the Proceedings* . . . *of the late Parliament* (i.e., the 'Barebones' Parliament), in *Somers Tracts*, VI, p. 275.

35. J. Aubrey, *Brief Lives* (ed. A. Powell), p. 198.

36. Lipson, *op. cit.*, II, pp. 249, 94.

37. *Ibid.*, III, pp. 212-48; II, p. 419.

38. *The Moderate* (6-13 March, 1649).

39. *Ibid.* (27 February–6 March, 1649).

40. *England's Doleful Lamentation* (June and August, 1647).

41. *The Prisoners' Remonstrance* (30 August, 1649). The authors complain that Speaker Lenthall helped his fellow-lawyers to obstruct Marten's bill. Another petition tells an almost incredible story of legal trickery, in which both the Speaker and his brother were involved (*A pitiful Remonstrance, or just Complaint from all the poor afflicted and miserable Prisoners for debt, etc.*, 7 July, 1648). Yet another petitioner, James Freize, complains of Sir John's lawless conduct, in *The Levellers' Vindication* (8 September, 1649).

42. The fullest statement is in the articles annexed to Richard Overton's *Appeal*; see p. 233 below.

43. Some historians trace what I have called the Norman myth to John Hare. This is a mistake, for his eccentric tract, *St Edward's Ghost or Anti-Normanism*, was not published till 17 August 1647, though he dates it October 1642. Though there were some earlier mentions of the idea, the first popular pamphlets which stressed its social and political importance were the two Leveller tracts, the *Remonstrance* (July 1646) and *Regal Tyranny* (January 1647). Hare, who writes well in a rather precious style and likes to use a Greek word in Greek type when it comes handy, would have meant little to the 'honest blades' of the New Model. He drew his facts from Daniel's *History*. He describes the Germans as 'the most illustrious and primer nation of Christendom' and the Saxons as 'their most noble tribe'. After a reference to the superiority of the Anglo-Saxon laws and language, he asks indignantly: 'Is it tolerable . . . that after such privileges conferred on us by heaven we should have our spirits so broken and un-Teutonised by one unfortunate battle as for above five hundred years together and even for eternity, not only to remain but contentedly to rest under the disgraceful title of a conquered nation and in captivity and vassalage to a foreign power? . . . Our language could be mistaken for a dialect of Gallic. . . . We cannot move but we hear the chains of our captivity rattle.' After all this eloquence, it is amazing how little will satisfy him. The king must derive his title from St. Edward's legacy. Our Norman nobles must change their names and their crests. Our laws must be 'divested of their French rags'. Our language must be purged of Norman and French words. To Latin, even to laws in Latin, he has no objection. Finally, he consoles himself with the reflection that the Normans, after all, were Teutons. Hare was a romantic pedant and anti-Normanism, as he conceived it, had no social significance whatever. His later tracts were concerned with the purging of the language.

44. *Regal Tyranny*, p. 93.

45. Parliament set aside 23 December as a day of public humiliation. In Coventry on that day John Bryan, B.D., preached a sermon which was published under the title: *A Discovery of the probable sin causing this great judgment of Rain and Waters, viz. our discontentment with our present government and inordinate desire of our King*. A royalist divine, had he been allowed to preach, would have located the sin in the hearts of the governing minority.

46. Wolfe, pp. 135-41.

47. *No Age like unto this Age* (24 June, 1653).

48. *The History of the Life of Thomas Ellwood*, p. 311.

49. *The Petition of divers Inhabitants of London* (10 March, 1649). Its

tendency is protectionist; it argues strongly against indirect taxes which fall unfairly on the poor; it would encourage the fishing industry.

50. *A new Engagement or Manifesto . . . from . . . London, Kent, Herts, Bucks and Berks* (3 August, 1648).

51. *An Exact Relation, Somers Tracts*, VI, p. 268.

52. *An Experimental Essay touching the Reformation of the Laws of England* (17 August, 1648). Cf. p. 538 below.

53. *A Whisper in the ear of Mr. Thomas Edwards*, in Haller, *Tracts on Liberty in the Puritan Revolution*, III, pp. 321-6.

54. Compare for example the moderate compromise in the Petition of 11 September, 1648, with the proposal for abolition in the third *Agreement of the People* of 1 May, 1649—though even this version proposes in some way to compensate the impropriators.

55. Walwyn in telling the story in *Walwyn's Just Defence* (H. and D., p. 358) implies that the Independents were consulted in the drafting of this Petition, yet when it was ordered to be burned most of the 'uppermost Independents stood aloof and looked on'. The rank and file, however, voted in greater strength than usual, for the Presbyterians got their way by only 94 votes to 86. The 'uppermost Independent' who 'stood aloof' may have been Cromwell, because he disliked the clause dealing with tithes. My chief reason for holding that this clause was the real cause of the anger aroused by this Petition is that, as Wildman tells us, the Levellers thought it wise to omit any reference to tithes in their next petition (of January 1648), 'in order not to disengage any considerable party and so continue our distractions' (*Truth's triumph*, p. 3).

56. *Op. cit.* (28 February, 1647), p. 14.

57. *An Appeal* (Wolfe, pp. 157-88).

58. Lilburne tells the story in *Rash Oaths Unwarrantable*, which he dated 31 May, 1647.

CHAPTER VIII

The New Model

The hardest of all tasks in reconstructing history is to understand the grosser miscalculations of contemporaries. In the
spring of 1647, from March onwards, the conservative Presbyterian majority of the Long Parliament made up its mind to
eliminate the New Model Army. The plan was to disband the
greater part of it. Its victorious generals (excepting only
Fairfax) would quietly drop back into civil life. Under other and
tamer commanders, a part of it was to be sent out of the
kingdom to reconquer Ireland. Then, in concert with the Scots,
a peace would be patched up with the King, who would at last
consent—such was the reckoning—to the settlement of religion
on a Presbyterian pattern, which would impose uniformity
alike on Episcopalians and sectaries. If the Army, dominated
by Independents and sectaries, should be troublesome, Parliament would again call in the Scots, while in London it had at its
disposal the train-bands, a numerous force, together with the
floating wreckage of deserters, ex-Royalists and unemployed
veterans from which a new army could be raised. In retrospect
the folly of this plan staggers us; the Presbyterians knew neither
their King nor their Cromwell, and least of all did they understand the temper of the ranks that had swept the old world
away at Naseby.

Everyone knows the proud boast in which the New Model
Army summed up its consciousness of itself: 'We were not a
mere mercenary army.'[1] It was not the tool of any authority;
it was an army of volunteers who fought for their own convictions, religious and political, and this held for the privates in

the ranks as well as the officers. It was an army on which—to cite Clarendon's eloquent tribute—'victory seemed entailed . . ., an army whose order and discipline, whose sobriety and manners, whose courage and success made it famous and terrible over the world'. Clarendon never met this army in person, but Bishop Burnet did, and he too, though we think of him as a typical Whig, was also bred up in a royalist and Episcopalian family, and so opposed to all that the Army stood for. Here are his impressions of it:

> I remember well three regiments coming to Aberdeen. There was an order and discipline and a face of gravity and piety among them that amazed all people. Most of them were Independents and Anabaptists. They were all gifted men and preached as they were moved. . . .[2]

Another witness who knew them well was the Presbyterian Richard Baxter, who served for some months from the summer of 1645 as chaplain to a cavalry regiment. He violently disapproved of the opinions on politics and religion that prevailed among its men, yet he wrote thus of them in their early days:

> He [Cromwell] had a special care to get religious men into his troop; these men were of greater understanding than common soldiers . . . and making not money but that which they took for public felicity to be their end, they were the more engaged to be valiant.

The many petitions and declarations that still survive from the pens of rankers confirm Baxter's estimate of their level of intelligence: some of them could write in a style that still moves us across the centuries. These testimonials from opponents and critics might tempt us to ascribe to these soldiers an inhuman perfection, but they had their share of foibles and lapses. On one occasion, for example, a body of them broke into the house of their Presbyterian opponent, William Prynne, and helped themselves freely from his larder and his cellar. They hated the police duties sometimes imposed on them and if (with some allowance for exaggeration) we may believe the royalist journalists for whose 'underground' presses they had to search, they performed these odious duties roughly. When they had a commander like Monk, who was a typical soldier of fortune

with nothing of the New Model spirit in him, they could sack a
town, as they sacked Dundee in 1651, as ruthlessly as any of the
ungodly. But their ideal, as their leaders put it, was courtesy and
gentleness, to rich and poor alike. 'Whose poultry', asked a
Leveller pamphleteer, 'hath this army destroyed? Whose goods
have they spoiled, or whose sheep or calves have they stolen?'³

The cavalry set the tone of this army. As always in the
seventeenth century it was the aggressive arm; it also did the
scouting. What Cromwell looked for, when he recruited his
own regiment, was men of character, who would dare to face
'gentlemen' in the field—'such men' as he put it to his cousin
Hampden, after their disturbing experience at Edgehill, 'as
had the fear of God before them and made some conscience of
what they did'. He found them chiefly in the dissenting chapels
of East Anglia. Tradition has it, and Whitelock's recollections
bear it out, that his troopers were mostly yeomen or yeomen's
sons. In favour of this view is the fact that in these eastern
counties the ratio of freeholders to the rest of the rural population was twice as high as it was elsewhere. Farmers and
small-holders who owned their own acres were upstanding and
self-respecting, as copyhold tenants, dependent on the goodwill
of a landlord, could not be. Contemporary writers, Hobbes no
less than Clarendon and Harrington, assume this class cleavage
as a matter of course. In *Behemoth*, for example, we read that at
the outbreak of the Civil War in Yorkshire the King was 'courting the gentlemen there, the Committee [set up by Parliament
for the county] was instigating the yeomanry against him'.⁴
The troopers from Norfolk would have heard from their grandfathers how Ket and his peasants fought to defend their common
fields against landlords, graziers, lawyers and tithe-owners.

One must not draw too sharp a distinction between country
and town. The towns, even when they were walled, had their
common fields, and the apprentices who served in their craftsmen's workshops were often yeomen's sons. The ability to ride
and manage horses was, of course, widespread in that century
even among men too poor to own a horse. But historians
who stress the part played by yeomen in this army have still to
account for the predominance in it of religious radicals.
From the days of the Lollards onwards their strength lay always

F

in the urban population. Something may be learned about the composition of this army from a glance at the callings of the men promoted from the ranks. 'The plain russet-coated captain' of Cromwell's familiar phrase 'that knows what he fights for and loves what he knows', the sort of man whom the Lieutenant-General preferred to 'that which you call a gentleman and is nothing else', what had he done in civilian life before he enlisted? One of these captains of horse who was a yeoman or a yeoman's son has found his way into history, but only one. He was Captain White, the officer with whom Captain John Hotham refused to serve because he was not a gentleman. This Hotham was the son of the famous governor of Hull; both he and his father turned their coats before the war was over. We know the callings of the rankers who rose to be field officers; there was a drayman among them, a cobbler, a tailor and a maker of leather points, but no yeoman.

What is clear is that in the horse the troopers, whether they were yeomen or craftsmen, came chiefly from the lower middle class. They could not be proletarians, for they were expected to provide their own horses, saddles and arms. A horse fit for the cavalry cost in those days anything from £10 to £20; the latter figure was more than any journeyman could earn in a year. It seems that many and perhaps most of the troopers did in fact find their own horses and arms unaided, though there were cases like the famous Maiden's Troop of Norwich for which the girls of the locality collected money to equip it. Sometimes the captain of the troop would help, as Cromwell did.[5] The trooper might even have to find a second horse, if the first became a casualty. Horses were, of course, requisitioned from the stables of 'malignants' and some were captured from the defeated Cavaliers. But with all these allowances, the fact remains that the trooper had often to risk property as well as life and limb. The pay, 2s. 6d. a day (reduced for a time to 2s.) looks high, until one realises that in addition to these liabilities the trooper had to pay in his billet for his horse's keep as well as his own. But his pay was always in arrears and often for months together the men were so destitute that Lilburne, as he tells us, had to lend money to his dragoons before they could get their horses shod. Clearly Baxter judged correctly

when he said that these men served not for money but for some
disinterested end. The love of adventure may have attracted
some of these spirited lads, but in 1647 few even among the
officers were thinking as yet of the army as a career. That
came later.

The foot outnumbered the horse (if we include the dragoons
among the latter) by two to one, but theirs in the warfare of
this period was usually a defensive rôle. Their prestige was less
and they came from a more modest stratum of society. Their
pay (when they got it) was 8d. a day and one may reckon that
their expenses in billet would amount to 6d. a day. This was
the sum which Fairfax, in regulations issued in May 1646,
ordered them to pay—if they had anything to pay with.[6]
If owing to the negligence of Parliament they were penniless,
they were instructed to give 'tickets' for value received. In
assessing the value of this often imaginary pay, we have to
remember that in that negligent century there were no dependants' allowances. Rather less than half of the foot were volunteers who enlisted with the same motives that inspired the
horse. These, we may assume, set the tone in the regiment.
Some few of the men had come over from the King's army when
they were taken prisoners. About half the foot were 'pressed'
men, with whose wretched case the *Remonstrance of Many
Thousand Citizens* has made us familiar (p. 101). Only the
relatively poor were subject to this arbitrary and unequal form
of conscription; freeholders were expressly exempted from it.

Richard Baxter describes the foot soldiers as 'ignorant men
of little religion . . . who would do anything to please their
officers'. Few of them, he complains, would take the Covenant,
'because it tied them to defend the King's person and to extirpate heresy and schism'. Before this year was out the men
gave proof that they were less subservient to their officers than
this Presbyterian observer supposed. For the rest his account is
not altogether consistent. These 'ignorant' men had it seems
their definite though deplorable opinions, by which they would
stand. It may well have been their resentment against the
doings of the press-gang that made radicals of them. As for
their 'ignorance', up to a point we can measure it. As the
documents of this Army with the men's signatures appended

go to prove, only one man in five was illiterate—a low proportion in that century. Few, if any of the horse can have been
illiterate.

In this People's Army, in which any ambitious private
might hope after a few years' service to command a regiment,
there can have been no class barrier between officers and men
—albeit most of the field officers were still in 1647 gentlemen
by origin. The code of discipline, based on that of the magnificent Swedish army in the Thirty Years War, was strict; but off
duty all ranks seem to have met as equals. This they did at their
prayer-meetings in camp. It was quite usual for a corporal or a
private to preach, while his less gifted officers listened in
silence. Between politics and religion there was no sharp
division in these men's minds. The discussions of the Council
of the Army, over which Fairfax or Cromwell presided, were
punctuated by prayer meetings. It is a safe guess that men and
officers discussed politics together without much restraint. But
we may go further; off duty they mixed and shared their
pleasures with none of the aloofness imposed in class-ridden
armies. We meet for example in the records of the New Model
a certain Captain Freeman who loved music and professed a
poetical and mystical faith of his own, which his severe Colonel
thought heretical. As he rode at the head of his troop on the
march he would sing to them, and some of his songs, as his
Colonel maintained, were 'a grief to all godly Christians'.
But the really illuminating part of the Captain's story is that in
the evenings after supper he would go round to his men's
quarters and lead them in singing catches.[7] It is a picture of
complete social equality.

'With our swords in our hands'—the phrase means nothing
to our modern ears; swords are for us theatrical properties.
In the seventeenth century they were the symbol of the subjection of one class to another, the tool which ensured the
ascendancy of gentlemen over peasants and craftsmen. When
one reads the documents that came, as petitions or manifestoes,
from the rankers of this Army the phrase rings out so often
from their perorations, that it leaves its imprint on our memories. Whether they were aware of it or not, it had for the men
who used it some powerful emotional significance.[8] What

happened to the peasant or the cobbler, when first he felt a sword hanging from his belt?

Here is a story from a Leveller newspaper, *The Moderate*, that may give us the clue. It dates from December 1648, when this Army was in occupation of the City of London, but it might as well have happened earlier. Some troopers of Colonel Rich's regiment of horse were standing in Friday Street at the gate of the White Horse Tavern in which they were quartered. In the tavern in a room above the gateway some lords and Parliament men were roystering, among them the Earl of Middlesex, Lord Carre (or Kerr) and a Colonel Spencer. From the window over the gate the Earl threw the contents of a chamber-pot at the soldiers. When one of them asked 'Why so uncivil?' the Earl with an oath threw the pot at him. The soldier threw it back and the Earl threatened to pistol him. Thereupon the soldier went in to the upper room. The Earl drew, and so did the trooper; two other soldiers followed their comrade; other lords drew and the Colonel hid under the table. The affray ended in the disarming of the drunken lords by the soldiers, who took their swords.

Before they enlisted in the New Model these lads, whether they were peasants or craftsmen, would have had to endure any insolence and any grossness from so-called gentlemen, drunk or sober, without answer or redress. Now 'with swords in their hands' they were helpless no longer. The sword had won back for them what they obstinately believed to be their birthright of equality as free-born Englishmen. They meant to win it for their mates and neighbours also, in the village and the workshop. What passed in their minds as they faced gentlemen in battle and beat them we have to guess, but with the help of such scenes as this in the White Horse Tavern, it is not difficult. They were extorting respect for their class, or as they liked to put it, they were undoing the Norman Conquest.[9]

From St John's Eve in 1646 when Oxford surrendered, to May Day in 1648 when the second Civil War broke out, this Army was quit of fighting. Though it still had some marching to do, for its regiments never stayed long in any one place, lest they should become a burden to the civilian population, it had abundant leisure. It played its games; it sang its catches;

but also it prayed and preached. It debated every problem of church and state that lay within its mental range and above all it read the pamphlets that poured from the London presses, more especially the unlicensed presses.

Richard Baxter from close quarters drew the same picture of the triumph of heresy in this Army that Edwards from a distance had already drawn in *Gangraena*. Many were Independents or Anabaptists; some were Arminians and Antinomians. He tried to comfort himself with the assurance that the active heretics who led the rest astray were a small minority (not one to twenty in the Army as a whole) of 'proud, self-conceited, hot-headed sectaries', but these 'seducers', unluckily, were Cromwell's favourites. They looked on the King as 'a tyrant and an enemy'. 'They said, What were the lords of England but William the Conqueror's colonels, or the barons but his majors, or the knights but his captains?' Even in these early days they believed that 'God's providence would cast the trust of religion and the kingdom upon them as conquerors'. Sometimes they argued 'for state-democracy and sometimes for church-democracy, but their most frequent and vehement disputes were for liberty of conscience, as they called it; that is, that the civil magistrate had nothing to do to determine of anything in matters of religion by constraint or restraint, but every man might not only hold, but preach and do, in matters of religion, what he pleased'. Baxter concludes (as Edwards had done) with the statement that 'a great part of the mischief' was due to the pamphlets of Richard Overton and John Lilburne, which the men read eagerly in their quarters, 'when they had none to contradict them'. Royalist pamphleteers said the same thing in language even more extreme. The Army, as one of them put it, was 'one Lilburne throughout, and more likely to give than to receive laws'. Another declared that 'the soldier hath continually his sword in one hand and one of Lilburne's epistles in the other'.

What was in the foreground of these troopers' minds we know in some detail, for these pamphlets are all bound up for us in the chaotic treasury of Thomason's collection, and among them lie more sermons than the most industrious student is likely to read. The mental background of the men is rather harder to reconstruct. Some of the officers were classical scholars who had studied at a university and it might be at one of the Inns of Court as well. Occasionally one meets a brilliant writer among them, like the Yorkshireman who drew up a notable declaration from the officers of Hull under Colonel Robert Overton. He quotes Tacitus and Cicero aptly, and can coin some striking and imaginative phrases.[10] Some of the less puritanical of the men, if they were Londoners, may have frequented the theatre before the war broke out. For some of the countrymen there was a free grammar school in their market-town. How many of them, officers or men, had heard of Kepler or Galileo, or even of the astonishing discovery of our own Dr Harvey? All we can be sure of is that they knew their Bible, much of it by heart, and that many of them were familiar with that compendium of cruelties, Foxe's Book of Martyrs. For the rest, it is likely that most of the troopers got their culture at second hand from Hugh Peters's lively sermons, or from John Saltmarsh, who also was one of their chaplains, but above all from the Leveller pamphlets.

Every army, every regiment, evolves a collective personality peculiar to itself. That happens even in a modern army of conscripts. This collective consciousness must have had a visible expression, an audible tone of voice in an army of volunteers who came together inspired by the same ideals, the same illusions, the same fears and dislikes, an army, moreover, in which the discussion of politics went untrammelled. The countrymen who rode up to it from the remoter villages must often have been out of breath in the effort to keep pace with the most daring thinkers of their century. As the months went by, a corporate opinion was formed, a sense of the Army, which united the junior officers with the men and eventually became a tide of emotion and thought so strong that even senior officers, even Cromwell himself, were carried along in its sweep. In these months of excitement and debate, this Army marched past the milestones of several centuries, while the Levellers beckoned it towards their vision of a humane and secular republic.

NOTES TO CHAPTER VIII

1. H. and D., p. 55.

2. G. Burnet, *History of My Own Time* (ed. O. Airy), I, pp. 102-3.

3. *The English Soldiers' Standard to repair to for Wisdom and Understanding* (5 April, 1649) and *A New-Found Stratagem* (4 April, 1649).

4. Hobbes, *Behemoth*, p. 102.

5. A body of young men and maidens collected enough to buy saddles and arms for a troop. Cromwell found the eighty horses; how he does not say (Abbott, I, p. 248).

6. C. H. Firth, *Cromwell's Army*, p. 403.

7. *Ibid.*, p. 308.

8. It may be enough to cite three instances, all of them well-written documents: *The Humble Representation of the Desires of the Officers and Soldiers in the Regiment of Horse for Northumberland* (5 December, 1648); Corporal William Thomson's manifesto, *England's Standard Advanced* (6 May, 1649); and *The New-made Colonel* (30 April, 1649): 'We wear our swords to vindicate the nation from injustice.'

9. The preamble to the petition of the Northumberland horse already cited opens thus: 'The people of this nation . . . are a free-born generation; but by conquest and captivity under William, the sixth Duke of Normandy's bastard, they were made slaves. . . . Under the yoke of this Norman captivity . . . we have been held even to this day.'

10. Joseph Hemingway, *The Declaration of the Officers of the Garrison of Hull* (9 June, 1649).

CHAPTER IX

The Lieutenant-General

Each in his own way, the two commanders of the New Model knew how to win the hearts of their men. If this essay were concerned with military history, Sir Thomas Fairfax would have an important place in it. As a soldier he was not the nonentity tradition has made of him. Cromwell's military genius was so outstanding that we are apt to underestimate the talents of his senior Fairfax, and his juniors, the brilliant Lambert, the ingenious Rainsborough and the reliable Monk. Fairfax, after all, had formed the New Model and chosen its officers before a jealous Parliament allowed Cromwell to join him. Again and again in the darker hours of the struggle the legendary bravery of 'Black Tom' gave his faltering regiments the courage to fight on. After he had retired to cultivate that garden about which Andrew Marvell sang, his son-in-law Buckingham wrote this sketch of him:

> *He never knew what envy was nor hate*
> *His soul was filled with worth and honesty,*
> *And with another thing quite out of date*
> *Called modesty.*

Behind his reserve his men instinctively sensed his simple goodness, and their trust in him availed more than once to stave off mutiny. Always reticent, on quiet days he stammered. In battle, as if some dormant gland had suddenly begun to function, he was transformed, lost his stammer and performed Homeric feats of valour. Until the King was finally vanquished, he knew no hesitation and fought, as Essex and Manchester would not, to achieve a decision. But in politics his was a one-syllabled mind. So helpless was he, that when he tried to brake the pace of revolution, his moderation was pitiably ineffective. His title to our respect would stand higher had he not written, after the Restoration, the memorandum in which he excused his share in all that happened after the spring of 1647 by casting the responsibility on 'the hypocrisy and deceit' of his subordinates.[1] This gallant gentleman was as weak as he was brave.

The Lieutenant-General was a much more complicated character, though his men may well have supposed him to be simpler than he was. With his sturdy frame and his love of hawks and horses, they may have taken him for a genial country gentleman. Ludlow tells us that he would wind up a serious political argument by flinging a cushion at his visitor as he descended the stairs from his study. Richard Baxter speaks of his 'familiar rustic carriage with his soldiers in sporting'. His graver contemporaries were sometimes shocked by his lapses into horseplay, as they also were by his enjoyment of music and dancing. At the trial of the regicides the prosecution made much of the story that he and Henry Marten blacked each other's faces with their pens, when they were signing the King's death-warrant. Only malice or stupidity would fail to see in their jesting a sign of intolerable emotional tension. The phrases that bring Cromwell most vividly to life for us are Baxter's: He was 'naturally of such a vivacity, hilarity and alacrity as another man is when he hath drunken a cup of wine too much'. He was said to be 'choleric' and given to blows;[2] notoriously he had a blunt and downright way of expressing himself, nor did he cultivate the ceremonious graces and courtesies that were in fashion in his day. But though the word may sound absurd, this unusual man, with his vivacity and hilarity, must have had his own kind of charm, which he was accustomed to use consciously. For a short time his charm enabled him to manage the inert Manchester, for a much longer time the modest Fairfax. Waller's testimonial—that he was a good officer who obeyed without arguing—may mean that Waller did not perceive that he was being managed by this genial subordinate.

In later life we meet Cromwell in the records left by General Ludlow and Colonel Hutchinson, trying again and again to win over these austere republicans by a deliberate exercise of social charm. Always in dealing with the People of God he preferred to get his way by friendly persuasion, including a lavish use of patronage, rather than by force. We must dismiss from our memories Carlyle's heavy-handed hero. Cromwell's portraits also may mislead us. All of them show his face in repose: usually he wears armour and so we visualise him as the ironclad Puritan. None of these artists had the wit to paint him smiling; yet he was a rather extreme extrovert, who often wept in public but as often laughed. He delivered his inaugural speech to the Nominated Parliament as a contemporary reporter put it 'in a grave and Christian-like manner, frequently weeping'.[3] But he could also relax and spend a gay evening over a tankard of ale and a pipe of tobacco with his cronies making comic verses.

A biographer so sympathetic as John Buchan can admit Cromwell's 'duplicity' and compare him to a 'rustic horse-dealer'. A more likely explanation is that he was driven by his wish to please to go much further in meeting the desires and prejudices of those who interviewed him than a truthful man should have gone. One thinks of Lucy Hutchinson's story of how, when he was setting out from London on the road that led to the North and victory, he gave equally satisfactory assurances to Levellers and Presbyterian 'priests'.[4] In case of need he did not hesitate to lie for the greater glory of God. He may really have said what that treacherous Major Huntingdon quoted: 'that it is lawful to play the knave with a knave.' But some of his most dubious sayings admit of a slightly more charitable interpretation. When he was not really sure of the truth, he would plunge in a direction pleasing to his hearers. Thanks to the fact that he was not a 'high-brow', he had spent many years in public life before anyone accused him of excessive subtlety. A man who had cared more for his sports at Cambridge than for his books did not seem dangerous. Sir Harry Vane the younger was a much more scrupulous character, but he was feared for his 'subtlety', because he was an 'intellectual' and something of a scholar. Ireton, to take another instance, was widely distrusted in the Army because of his precise lawyer-like intellect.

His troopers had, however, sounder reasons than these for their confidence in Cromwell. Before the Civil War broke out he was known throughout the eastern counties as a tribune of the people. Again and again he fearlessly supported the cause of the peasants who shared the common fields. He did it first in his own native town of Huntingdon, then in the fens round Ely and again round St. Ives, at the cost of offending both the Earl of Manchester (the future general's father) and the Earl of Bedford. Edward Hyde (Clarendon) was shocked by the unmannerly vehemence with which he pleaded for these peasants before a committee of the Long Parliament.

In view of Cromwell's hostility in later life to the agrarian policy of the Levellers and his determination to keep 'the poor' out of politics, it may not be uncharitable to look closely into his reasons for supporting the popular cause in his early manhood. It may be that he was moved rather by hostility to these great nobles than by sympathy with the fenmen. Something of this attitude may have sprung from the family history of the Cromwells. Once in wealth and influence they were at least the equals of the Montagues (Manchester's family) in their county; in Oliver's generation they were on the down-grade. His sense of his own and his family's relative insignificance may have made him unduly self-assertive. Archbishop Williams, who was his relative, said of him that he 'loves none that are more than his equals'—in modern jargon, he suffered from an inferiority complex. It must have been in a fit of irritation during his disputes over strategy with Manchester that he said: 'it would not be well till he was but Mr Montague' and 'hoped to see never a nobleman in England'. If this was ever his sober opinion, he revised it before he was much older. In the meantime these widely publicised sayings of his would endear him to the radicals among his men, who would soon be reading Leveller tracts.

It is unlikely that on the secular plane Cromwell ever was inclined to egalitarian principles, even in his early manhood. He never forgot that he was born a gentleman and one of the governing landowning caste. But for him community of religious belief and experience could obliterate class. Among the People of God, there was neither gentle nor simple. All who had the inner assurance that they were called of God belonged to the elect. This did not make Cromwell a democrat; on the contrary, the Saints were for him a new *élite*, who drew their patents of nobility from God himself. To state such ideas in black and white may be to distort his thinking. He was neither a man of logic, nor a fanatic—though for a brief moment he and General Harrison were not far apart. His was an emotional religion and one should try to discover rather what he felt than what he thought. He felt himself at one with his fellow Puritans; he believed in the solidarity of the Saints.

It may have been this sense of fraternity that made it easy for him to promote 'plain men' to be captains of horse—perhaps the boldest and most original thing he ever did, for he had no precedents, English or continental, to encourage him—save, indeed, in the Hussite revolutionary armies. He could, to be sure, defend his choice in terms of common sense. He wished that men of 'honour and birth' would come forward, but until they did, he would choose plain men 'patient of wants, faithful and conscientious in their employment'.[5] He was not the only Puritan gentleman who acted in this way. Ludlow, as sheriff and knight of the shire of Wiltshire, would nominate 'paltry contemptible fellows, all of them sectaries', among them a godly serving-man, as commissioners for levying assessments in the county; thus, as a royalist journalist put it, 'setting up base fellows to trample down the gentry'.[6] Cromwell's familiarity with a spirited young officer like John Lilburne was not surprising, for John was his social equal: but Sexby also, who rose from the ranks, was one of his bed-fellows. Cromwell's behaviour is in sharp contrast, where class differences are concerned, with that of yet another Puritan gentleman, Colonel Hutchinson, who as his widow tells us treated his social inferiors with kindness and courtesy yet kept them at a distance.[7]

It is a fascinating exercise to imagine what service in the early months and years must have meant, first in Cromwell's own troop and then in his regiment, under a captain and a colonel who never heard or gave a word of command till he was forty-three. Solving their problems of organisation, transport and tactics by trial and error, he and his junior officers must have felt every hour and every day a sense of adventure in all they did. This is not the place to discuss his campaigns. Many of his victories, notably Dunbar, were won by his quickness to perceive a tactical opportunity and snatch it in the hour of battle. The daring of his long-range strategy accounts for his triumphs at Preston and Worcester. With every allowance for what this army may have learned from the Swedish tradition and from a few professional soldiers like Skippon, Crawford, Dalbier and Hurry, Cromwell must have been inventing and improvising all the time. One suspects that this was a brilliant army, like few others in the world, because it was never smothered in routine.

We know something of Cromwell's boldness and promptitude in the first days of the struggle, when he occupied Cambridge and saved the assets of the colleges for the Parliament, but we know little of his daily conduct. From his close and it may be excessive attention to every detail of the administration when he was Lord Protector, we may safely infer that as Captain, Colonel and Lieutenant-General he was equally conscientious. In his later life, first as the Lord General and then as Protector, he showed a concern for his maimed veterans and for the widows and orphans of his men, which they must have contrasted with the barely credible callousness of the Long Parliament. His understanding of horses must have been invaluable, for the training of cavalry horses is as necessary and not as easy as the training of willing men. His royalist opponents envied the care of their horses and their arms that he instilled into his troopers, to the point of insisting that they should be trained to lie with their chargers on the ground. After these scrupulous preparations, as much psychological as technical, he gave God the glory when victory came. He meant what he said.

The more thoughtful of the Lieutenant-General's men had yet another reason for trusting and admiring their commander. He was the tireless champion of their religious liberties. When they read the despatches he addressed to the Speaker on their victory at Naseby Field and the storming of Bristol, they must

have felt that thanks to him they were not risking their lives in
vain. (Quoted on p. 393 below.) Here was an intimation to
Parliament that this triumphant army was fighting for liberty
of conscience. 'From brethren in things of the mind we look for
no compulsion but that of light and reason.' This was a plain
yet tactful way of warning the Commons that the New Model
might have something even plainer to say, if they proceeded
with their abominable Blasphemy Bill. This the Presbyterian
majority understood, and when the two despatches were
published as official papers, these paragraphs were cut out.
Thereupon the London Independents printed the political
conclusion of the Bristol despatch as a fly-sheet and scattered it
about the streets. We may be sure that the Army knew very
well what happened to these despatches. It would also know
that Cromwell and the Independent party in the House had
managed to carry a resolution (on 13 September, 1644) which
provided for a committee to consider how the 'tender consciences' of sectaries might be respected in spite of the general
adoption of the Presbyterian system. Nothing had come of it;
the resolution was a dead letter.

So far we have surveyed the surface; can we probe a little
deeper into Cromwell's mind? This sturdy country gentleman,
accustomed to life in the open air, was described by a London
physician whom he consulted in early manhood, as *valde
melancholicus*. The words mean in modern terminology 'highly
neurotic with a depressive tendency'. His family doctor in
Huntingdon described his patient as a hypochondriac, who
would call him in the middle of the night to attend to some
imaginary ailment. It seems from a much-quoted letter of his
that he went through years of religious conflict, during which
he believed himself 'the chief of sinners'. In the end he attained
a firm assurance of his salvation. Firth, whose biography is
always revealing, dates these years of conflict from round about
1628 till 1638.[8] In 1628 Cromwell was an insignificant Puritan
back-bencher, who followed Eliot in the last Parliament that
sat before King Charles's eleven years of personal rule. In 1638
the troubles began in Scotland and the prospects of the Puritan
opposition improved. There is no reason to suppose (in spite

of royalist gossip and a notorious forgery) that Cromwell really
had much to be ashamed of in his conduct as a young man.
His crushing feeling of guilt—his guilt-complex—his sense of
insecurity in a hostile universe were presumably part of his
emotional make-up from early life, how acquired we do not
know, save that in a Puritan atmosphere the difficulty was to
escape them. Of his early relations with his parents his many
biographers can tell us nothing.

This decade of inner unrest ran parallel with the helpless
defeat of the Puritan cause. Strafford and Laud were supreme
and there was little a country gentleman could do to oppose
them. Courageous though Cromwell was, he had a good deal to
lose, and he lacked the reckless audacity of a Lilburne. He
thought of emigrating to New England, until he inherited the
lease of the tithes of Ely cathedral. The cause that was the
first of all his concerns in life seemed beyond hope, while for his
mighty energies and the love of power, of which he had at least
his normal human share, there was in his narrow provincial
world no opportunity. Hope revived when the Scots pledged
their nation to resistance. In 1640 Cromwell was back again in a
fighting Parliament in which he soon made his mark. In the
autumn of 1642 began his apprenticeship as a leader of men
and a soldier. The powers that lay dormant in him through
half a lifetime found at last their outlet, and with a sure but
unconscious instinct he steadily enlarged its scope. 'No man
goes further', as he once put it, 'than he who knows not whither
he is going.'

So a modern chronicler might tell the story of these years of
neurosis and frustration, which ended when activity and the
exercise of power restored Cromwell's mental health. We have
next to translate this story back into the language of his Puritan
generation. What happened to him in the end, as he experienced it, was that he gained the inner assurance that all his
sins were forgiven; before time was, his name was written in
the Lamb's Book of Life; he was one of the People of God, who
are the apple of His eye. What he had gained was much more
than the certainty that his own soul was saved; he knew that
the cause to which he now devoted life and fortune was God's.
As firmly as any Marxist can believe that history obeys an

immutable dialectic, so did he believe that it is shaped by God's will. Nothing could happen to a believer by chance; looking backwards after some crisis in his career he should be able to discern 'the chain of providences' that led up to it; on a grander scale one could learn to read the will of God by tracing His finger in the 'dispensations' that favoured His People. As victory after victory fell to his arms, the conviction grew in him that he and his army were 'owned of God'—untaught amateurs though they were, who had left the plough to face the gentlemen of England. What this army did at the taking of Bristol was plainly, as his despatch to the Speaker put it, 'the work of God. He must be a very atheist that doth not acknowledge it.' Three years later, with a megalomania that wore the cloak of modesty, he wrote after further victories about 'this poor Army wherein the great God has vouchsafed to appear'.[9]

His Calvinistic determinism saw the hand of God in the long-range trends of history; human wills could only mar and meddle for a time. 'What', he once asked, 'are all our histories and other traditions in former times but God manifesting Himself?' Man may seem to have some initiative, but in the end God 'hath shaken and tumbled down and trampled upon everything that He hath not planted'. There are passages in his letters and speeches in which man's part in history dwindles to nothing and human beings are seen as mere automata, into whom to suit His own ends God breathes courage or cowardice, obstinacy or enmity. According to a declaration which Cromwell's Army addressed to the Scots in 1650, it was God who 'denied' to King Charles 'a heart to assent' to the 'propositions for a safe and well-grounded peace' which were 'many times' offered him. Again it was God himself who put an 'enmity' into the heart of the Spaniard against 'whatever is of God'—a myth which justified Cromwell in levying an aggressive and predatory war upon him.[10] These lines from his peculiarly callous despatch to the Speaker recording the massacre at Drogheda might have been penned as a parody; they bring this God-drunken generation vividly before us:

> That which caused your men to storm so courageously, it was the spirit of God, who gave your men courage and took it away again; and gave the enemy courage and took it

away again; and gave your men courage again and therewith this happy success. And therefore it is good that God alone have all the glory.[11]

There is something in common between Calvinism and Marxism, but we must not carry the analogy too far. The Puritan God had no resemblance to an impersonal dialectical process; He was a person prone to jealousy and vengeance, yet capable of loving-kindness also. He could be placated or offended; His action one way or the other could be swayed by prayer. This the Puritans never forgot, least of all Cromwell. In fact they did influence the course of history by their prayers, for on their knees they were steeling their own wills and strengthening their confidence in themselves and their cause. Experience may have convinced Cromwell that he had great influence with God. The story runs that on the eve of Marston Moor a servant girl found him in a disused room on the top of a tower wrestling in prayer with his Bible before him.[12] In that Bristol despatch which revealed so much of his mind, he told the Speaker that before the assault he 'wrestled with God for a blessing'. Before the bloody sack of Basing House he spent hours in prayer. Calvinism, as he understood it, was the ideal creed for a man of action.

To our generation it is puzzling that some contemporaries and several historians, among them no less a man than David Hume, should have accused Cromwell of hypocrisy. Our material for a judgment is ampler and our knowledge of psychology, it may be, not quite so superficial. Why should we doubt that this man believed his religion with all the intensity of his passionate nature? He owed everything to his faith. It saved his mental and physical health. It gave him the self-confidence that enabled him to dominate his fellow-men, first in his troop, then in his Army and finally over three kingdoms. Moulded for him by tradition, it was the expression in his conscious, rational mind of his fundamental love of life, his will to live. Through it he escaped from his depression and hypochondria and found the place in society that belonged to him. His conversion turned the obscure Fenland squire and back-bencher into the most famous man of action Europe was destined to see between the days of Gustavus Adolphus and

Napoleon Bonaparte. That he believed his Puritan religion sincerely who that has read his letters and speeches can doubt? Whether it bore much resemblance to Christianity or stood in any close relation to social ethics—these are different questions altogether.

Amid their victories in the latter half of 1645 Richard Baxter, as we saw, found among the troopers of the New Model the conviction that 'God's providence would cast the trust of religion and the kingdom upon them as conquerors'. This army had a collective mind of its own and it did in the end succeed in imposing its corporate will upon its leaders. But however confident Cromwell and the senior officers may have been in their ability to destroy the last of the King's forces in the field, they were not at all confident about the outcome of their triangular political duel with him and the Presbyterian majority in Parliament. Round about November the Independent leaders were so pessimistic concerning their chances of securing the kind of settlement they desired, that they were negotiating with the King on the proposal that they should restore his authority at Wesminster, subject to some promise of toleration for sectaries, while they should withdraw to Ireland. After reconquest it was to become, under their rule, a second New England with an established Puritan church.[13] The natives, one supposes, would either be exterminated or driven into Connaught. In Parliament, as we have seen, the Independents during 1646 felt themselves helpless and rarely challenged Presbyterian intolerance.

Cromwell's own personal prospects, meanwhile, after the surrender of Oxford were radically changed. The extension of his command voted in January 1646 was only for six months. It was not renewed; in other words Parliament, so far as he and it could see into the future, had brought his military career to an end, though he still enjoyed the courtesy title of Lieutenant-General.[14] On the other hand, Parliament rewarded his services by a handsome grant of land with a rent-roll of £2,500 per annum. Compared with the grants that went to others whose part in winning victory was negligible, his share looks to posterity relatively small. None the less, it made him a great landowner and placed the Cromwells among England's 'three-hundred families'. He took a house in Drury Lane, as if henceforward London and not Ely were to be the centre of his activities.

But what was he to do? To the Army he owed his fame and his power. Westminster was the only battlefield on which he was ever defeated and that not once, but often. He was so tired of being constantly voted down that he ceased to attend the revolutionary executive council, the Committee of Both Kingdoms. His letters from London to Fairfax during this winter are full of complaints of the bitterness of the conservative and Presbyterian City against the Army; nor was it peculiar. 'There want not in all places men who have so much malice against the Army as besots them.' In February 1647, when the first votes for disbanding the Army were passed, he fell dangerously ill. Cromwell was liable to attacks of ague, the curse of the Fens, but it is noticeable that most if not all of his illnesses overcome him in times of grave perplexity. Even his contemporaries, who knew nothing about psycho-somatic medicine, sometimes guessed that the cause was psychological.[15] Always in the end his trust in God prevailed; it reigned in his conscious mind. But in the unconscious depths there was still instability. He saw no prospect before him in his native land, and when he recovered his health, in March or April, he had long conferences with the Elector Palatine, under whose flag he thought of serving with as many of his men as he could induce to follow him in a crusade to defend the cause of Calvinism in Germany. The resistance to the 'malice' and intolerance of the class ridden Presbyterian Parliament originated not with him nor with any of the 'grandees' of the Army, but with the troopers of its volunteer horse.

NOTES TO CHAPTER IX

1. *Short Memorials of Thomas, Lord Fairfax*, in Maseres, *Select Tracts*, I, p. 444.

2. Cromwell's roughness was by no means always genial and jocular. When his Leveller opponents irritated him he could behave very crudely. See Cornet Cheeseman's story of the Lieut.-General's conduct when this veteran ex-officer was presenting a petition to the Speaker from Captain

Bray and his disbanded troop. Cromwell, taking him violently by the shoulders, bade the halberdiers arrest him. When they struck him with their halberds, Cromwell called out to them: 'Punch him, punch on.' The whole story of the treatment of Bray and his troop makes an ugly record of injustice (Christopher Chisman, *The Lamb contending with the Lion*, 10 July, 1649). Sexby, who knew Cromwell long and intimately, wrote that 'His Highness is naturally choleric and must call men rogues and go to cuffs' (*Killing No Murder*, ed. H. Morley, 1886, p. 101).

3. Quoted by Abbott, III, p. 51.

4. Lucy Hutchinson, *Memoirs of the Life of Colonel Hutchinson* (1846), pp. 316-17. Mrs Hutchinson relates this of 1648, but she may have confused the date. It was on the way to Dunbar that Cromwell dined with his chief enemy John Lilburne, at Ware of all places (see p. 609 below).

5. Abbott, I, p. 262.

6. *Mercurius Pragmaticus*, quoted in Firth's introduction to Ludlow's *Memoirs*, I, p. xxv. Firth has restored passages reflecting on Shaftesbury which the first editor of the *Memoirs* suppressed. Were these, I wonder, the only passages he cut out? It is odd that 'levelling Ludlow', as contemporaries called him, who thrice intervened to help John Lilburne in the oppressions he suffered, makes no reference whatever to the Levellers in his *Memoirs*, or to Lilburne. Again there is no similarity of style between the *Memoirs* (secular in tone) and the pious letters to Swiss clergymen at the end of the book. I cannot help suspecting that at some stage the *Memoirs* underwent drastic editing or re-writing.

7. Lucy Hutchinson, *op. cit.*, p. 32.

8. Firth, *Oliver Cromwell*, p. 38; Abbott, I, pp. 96-7.

9. Abbott, I, pp. 374, 696.

10. *Ibid.*, III, p. 590, II, p. 283, IV, pp. 260 sqq.

11. *Ibid.*, II, p. 127.

12. John Buchan, *Oliver Cromwell*, p. 225.

13. Both Abbott (I, p. 392) and Gardiner (*Civil War*, III, pp. 12, 16) accept this curious story from the French diplomatic archives. I notice a confirmation in Clement Walker's *History of Independency*, albeit at a much later date (14 September, 1648). Walker suggests 'that Ireland may be a receptacle for the Saints against [the time when] England spews them forth'.

14. Abbott, I, pp. 405, 419, 437.

15. *Ibid.*, II, p. 419. When in May 1651 Cromwell did not know how to defeat David Leslie's Fabian tactics he called for a fast, 'that the Lord who hid His face from them might give them light what to do, and that perplexity made him unwell', as Johnston of Warriston put it—an understatement, for Cromwell was dangerously ill.

CHAPTER X

The Revolt of the Army

Not till the early spring of 1647 did it seem feasible to the ruling Presbyterian majority to disband the New Model Army. Eager though they were to do it, they dared not face the risk, so long as the Scots army remained on English soil. Their leaders, to be sure, were intimate with the Scots nobility; indeed, with the French envoys as go-betweens, they were conspiring together to restore the King on terms which the Army and the Independents would have rejected with drawn swords. But the average untravelled Englishman in those days disliked and distrusted the Scots, as he distrusted all foreigners. It was customary in the newspapers of this period to ridicule everything associated with 'Jock', from his blue bonnet to his Lowland speech and his poverty. The conduct of his troops had antagonised the northern counties, for they had been obliged to subsist on free quarter. The left had two further reasons for its hostility—the ill repute of the Scottish feudal gentry in its dealings with the peasantry and the savage intolerance of the clergy. Until these unpopular intruders had re-crossed the Tweed, the protection of Fairfax and his red-coats was indispensable.

Now they were gone, the taxpayer counted up with resentment what this ever-victorious army cost—or would have cost if it had been regularly paid. The excise, a purchase tax levied on food and the other necessaries of daily life, as well as on luxuries, was justly unpopular. Because it fell most heavily on the poor, the Levellers—pioneers in this as in so much else—argued that all taxation should be direct and proportionate to income. In their turn, the well-to-do landowners did their utmost to evade the very light monthly assessment imposed on them. What injured the Army more than its cost in taxation was the fact that the irregularity of its pay forced it also to exact free quarter much too often, even though it gave receipts for everything it took. When the men elected a 'soviet' (to borrow a contemporary word) from their own ranks, as they presently did, it exhorted its fellow-soldiers to

> eat not but from hunger which makes all things sweet . . ., to be courteous and gentle towards all you meet, whether in the streets or upon the roads; give them kind language and civil respects without jostling or brushing or bustling for the way[1]

and much more to the same effect, as wise, as homely and as terse. But for all that men and officers could do to lighten the burden, it was resented especially in this year of scarcity, while the price of bread rose steadily as the months went by and the unkindly weather threatened yet another miserable harvest.

The problem was complicated by the fact that though the unpopular Scots were gone, the hated Irish had still to be dealt with. To say that the blood of God's martyred Saints (the four thousand Protestant settlers killed when the Catholic Irish rose in 1641 to recover the ancestral lands of which they had been robbed)—to say that this blood cried out for Christian vengeance is one way of recording the facts of history. Another way of putting it is that many substantial and influential citizens of London had subscribed large sums of money for the suppression of this rebellion, in return for the promise of a further 2,500,000 acres of Irish land. Each statement is relevant. From Ulster to Armenia, robbery and massacre are never so urgent and indeed inevitable as when they have the sanction of religion. Five years had passed without an effort to redeem 'the public faith', and the City of London was growing restive. Somehow the disbanding of the New Model had to be combined with the raising of an army strong enough to re-conquer Ireland. These two purposes may seem contradictory, but the City and the Presbyterian leaders had their devices for combining them.

The initiative, doubtless by arrangement, came from the City. A petition from its Presbyterian citizens deplored the prevalence of heresy, insisted on the effective prevention of preaching by unordained persons, the suppression of all separated congregations, the exemplary punishment of heretics and the reservation of all places of public trust for whole-hearted supporters of the Covenant, or in plain words for Presbyterians. It then called for the disbanding of the Army and the pacification of Ireland, to which it added a vague but ominous demand for the condign punishment of all who had acted as 'firebrands' between England and Scotland, a phrase that pointed at most of the left from Cromwell to the Levellers.[2] The Common Council supported this petition (presented on 19 December, 1646) and underlined its demand for the disbanding of the Army. Since it asked especially for the dismissal of all officers and men who were known to be disaffected to the form of church government established by Parliament, it is obvious that its chief aim was to ensure the reliability (from the standpoint of conservative property) of all the armed forces. Economy was a pretext.

By the second week of March 1647, the Long Parliament had taken the decisions required to give effect to these petitions. As an organic force the New Model would cease to exist. The new English establishment was to include nearly as many horse and dragoons as the old, but it was to lose all its marching regiments of foot. Some 10,000 foot would still be retained, dispersed in 45 garrisoned towns. If ever the horse had to take the field again, it would have to draw the necessary complement of foot from the civilian train-bands, on which the Presbyterians thought they could rely to check any tendency to militarism or radicalism among the professional soldiers who would form the cavalry. It was hoped that the greater part of the New Model would volunteer for the new Irish army of 12,600 men. For the two armies a further 3,800 horse and dragoons would have to be recruited from men who had served in other formations. In this way a politically harmless army would be formed in England.

To make assurance doubly sure, formulae were devised which would eliminate the more dangerous officers. The

Presbyterians tried but failed to oust Fairfax from the command of the regular cavalry in England, but they laid it down that no officer above the rank of colonel should serve under him. This disposed of Cromwell, Ireton and Hammond senior. It was also provided that no member of Parliament should hold any command in England, and it was required of officers not only that they should take the Covenant but that they should conform to the government of the church by ordinance established. These two provisions, if they had been strictly enforced, would have disposed of nearly all the officers of the New Model, the juniors as well as the seniors, and of such members of Parliament as the sailor of genius whom we know as Admiral Blake, of Colonels Rainsborough and Fleetwood, Hutchinson and Ludlow, and also of Algernon Sidney. The Irish command was to go to Major-Generals Skippon and Massey, of whom the former was, like Fairfax, something of a neuter in the disputes over church government, though he was usually reckoned a Presbyterian. By this elegant solution the conservatives believed that they had got rid of the sectarian New Model and provided for two Presbyterian armies in its place.

The urgent first step was to get rid of most of the victors of Naseby Field by sending them across St George's Channel under reliable officers. Since Cromwell and the rest of the high command had, as we have seen, no thought of opposing this scheme, it might have had some success but for the parsimony of the Long Parliament. It offered six weeks' arrears of pay both to those who volunteered for Ireland and to those who were disbanded. But by 21 March the pay of the horse was 43 weeks in arrear and that of the foot 18 weeks. There was nothing unusual in this meanness; indeed, as Holles pointed out, Parliament had paid only two weeks' arrears to Essex's and Waller's men when they were disbanded.[3] Lavish as it was towards its own members, the Long Parliament had nothing to spare for its social inferiors.

For a variety of reasons the men were not keen to enlist for Ireland. Some of them had served for nearly five years and were eager to get back to their homes and their trades. Others were willing to serve in England as long as might be necessary to assure its liberties, but they were not yet what Cromwell's veterans afterwards became, professional soldiers who would go anywhere and fight for anything at the word of command. Though they may have been unduly suspicious, they feared that they were going to be 'pressed' for this service overseas, and this they resented as a break with the tradition which imposed compulsory service for defence only within each man's county but not beyond it. Again, it was remembered that English armies in Ireland had been constantly scourged by disease. So it had been under Elizabeth's Essex and so it was to be under Ireton. If Parliament forgot to pay its armies within a day's ride from Westminster, how punctual would it be when they were out of sight and mind in the wilds of Kerry and Donegal? This army loved the great soldiers who had led it to victory; it resented the slight put upon them and refused to accept Skippon and Massey as fit successors to Fairfax and Cromwell. Skippon, a sound professional soldier, was well enough liked, but he was ageing. Massey, whose manners and behaviour were those of the Thirty Years War in which he had served, was a Presbyterian only in name, but he was a conservative extremist, and his integrity even at the famous siege of Gloucester was open to question. Finally there were a few (as Mr Edwards's records show) who opposed the subjugation of the Irish people on ethical grounds.

In the end, after the case for and against enlistment for Ireland had been hotly debated by all ranks through several weeks, it turned out that only 167 officers out of the 2,320 in the New Model—a trifle over 7 per cent—would volunteer. They formed the decided Presbyterian minority in this army. Though five of them were colonels in command of regiments, they failed to induce more than a negligible number of soldiers to follow them. At one moment it looked as if nearly half of Colonel Robert Lilburne's regiment of foot had been persuaded by their Presbyterian lieut.-colonel; they even started their march towards Chester, but on discovering the deceptions he had used to win them, most of them marched back.[4]

This army would not embark for Ireland; then would it tamely disband? On the answer to this question turned the whole outcome of the Revolution. If it disappeared, leaving a body of regular cavalry under a solid corps of Presbyterian

officers in control of England, then the City and the party of
property would emerge as the real victors in the Civil War. That
spelt the end of such precarious toleration as the sectaries still
enjoyed. If they were crushed in the Presbyterian strait-jacket,
Levellers (if we may use that name prematurely) and republicans would go down with them, and such freedom as there
was for the printed and spoken word would vanish. How many
of the men in this alert and intelligent army had a clear grasp
of the political issue it would be rash to guess. Assuredly some
of the troopers grasped it as clearly as Freeborn John himself.
Most of them would have applauded a reminder that the civil
and political rights they girded on their swords to win were not
yet secured. Some guessed that a new civil war was brewing
and argued that they must keep their ranks intact while that
danger threatened. Others felt instinctively something of the
class issue at stake. Some were ready to risk everything for
freedom of conscience, and many more who were not themselves religious men would assent when those whom they
respected proclaimed this right. The Anabaptist and the
worldling were agreed in resenting the claim of Mr Edwards
and his like to control their beliefs and their morals. Finally
the collective personality of this army, proud as it was of its
record of service, resented the organised attacks of the Presbyterian clergy and the City.

These were the issues that weighed most heavily with
the thinking men in the ranks, who were steeped in the
Leveller pamphlets, but they shared the indignation of their
simpler comrades over their material grievances. Many of them,
especially in the horse, had arrears of pay due to them that
stretched back to the early years of the Civil War. The six
weeks' pay offered them would hardly suffice, after they had
paid their debts in their present billets, to carry them home, if
they lived at some distance from the headquarters at Saffron
Walden. Four of the infantryman's six week's pay would not be
quite enough to cover his fare in a carrier's wagon, if he lived
a hundred miles away, at Gloucester for example or South-
ampton. No security was offered for the rest of these arrears,
and in the absence of any arrangement for an audit, each man
would have to spend it might be weeks in hanging about an

office in London, where he might have to bribe a clerk before he could obtain so much as a paper acknowledgment of his claims.

Next the men remembered with some bitterness the case of their fallen comrades, whose widows and orphans were left to the mercy of the poor law. They thought that Parliament should provide for their needs and compensate men maimed in its service. The Army knew what Parliament did for one of its members, Colonel Thomson, who lost a leg in battle: it voted him £2,000.[5] A private who suffered the same loss might have to borrow from the pawnbroker to buy a wooden leg. Then came the angry memories of the press-gang, which had forced perhaps half the infantry into the ranks against their will. The Army wanted a very modest assurance, that men who had served as volunteers should not be 'pressed' for service beyond the kingdom. A few months later it acted on the principles laid down with such warmth of feeling by Walwyn and his colleagues in the *Remonstrance of Many Thousand Citizens*. Its final demand was for the total abolition of the press-gang and a guarantee of this immunity in a written constitution.

Lastly, the Army knew that by the letter of the law most of its acts, individual and collective, during the Civil War could be held to be criminal and punished as such. In Yorkshire where Major Henry Lilburne, John's younger brother, was organising the opposition, the men were told that fourteen soldiers had been hanged already for horse-stealing. Acting under orders they had requisitioned gentlemen's horses for the army.[6] This may be a true statement though it sounds like an exaggeration, for it is a fact that, while these discussions were going on, a former colonel was indicted and three disbanded troopers arrested in Kent on this capital charge. In their *Vindication*, a sober and cautious document, the officers of the New Model wrote that soldiers were 'frequently' indicted for such offences, and that 'divers verdicts' had been given against them at the last assizes, in spite of an order from the Commons.[7] The Army's demand was, therefore, for a fool-proof act of indemnity, passed by both Houses and accepted eventually by the King. It wanted to feel safe when he sat on his throne again, with a Presbyterian Privy Council round him.

Over its professional grievances, the Army, apart from a few Presbyterian extremists, was unanimous. The officers were in the same case as the men. Their pay also was in arrears; they too stood in need of an indemnity, and most of them were sectaries who would lose their commissions, if the Presbyterians had their way. Like the men they too would soon be exposed to the penalties of the Blasphemy Bill. But however we explain their relative passivity, the officers as a body never led the way in the Army's protest. Save for a few daring subalterns, they were content to bring up the rear behind the men.

A group of troopers went into action early in March 1647. Following the example of the civilian Levellers, their first move was to draw up a petition. In its original form it was addressed directly to Parliament; it expressed the indignation of the soldiers in plain language, and it mentioned some political questions as well as the Army's professional grievances. Before it was circulated for signature, the officers brought pressure to bear on its promoters and induced them to modify it drastically. It was now addressed to Fairfax—a procedure which contemporary military etiquette permitted; all references to politics were cut out, and, as the officers afterwards claimed, they 'removed as near as we could all occasion of distaste'.[8]

Even after it had been polished and trimmed, the men's petition was still an able and vigorous document. Its preamble declared that in spite of 'many discouragements for want of pay', the Army had 'with all cheerfulness done summer service in winter seasons' and dispersed all the Parliament's enemies. It then set forth the Army's demands in five clauses. The first asked for an indemnity fortified with the royal assent. The second called for an audit and the satisfaction, before disbanding, of all arrears since the outbreak of the war. The third was for exempting volunteers from pressing. The fourth sought equitable allowances for widows, orphans and maimed veterans, together with compensation for losses, sickness and imprisonment. Finally, the means must be provided to pay for the Army's quarters while awaiting disbandment.[9] In this form it was widely circulated with the good will of many of the senior officers and it is said to have been signed by some regiments in a body.

It is not surprising that there was some friction between officers and troopers over this petition. Exactly what happened we do not know. Some of the senior officers may perhaps have wished to suppress the petition altogether; others may then have proposed to edit it, and this compromise was eventually accepted. There is evidence of some tension in a flysheet entitled *An Apology of the Soldiers to all their Commission Officers* which must have been printed by the men for the Army towards the end of March. It uses some familiar Leveller phraseology and warns the officers of the danger of abandoning the cause of their soldiers:

> Now these and many other such like reasons being taken into your serious considerations, we hope, will be just cause for you to go along with us in this business, or at least to let us quietly alone in this our design, we desiring no more than what is just and right.[10]

There was, then, an organised group among the men before the end of March, which had the means to use the printing press for its propaganda. It resolutely took on its shoulders the leadership of the Army's revolt, and told the officers that it would go ahead with or without their help. This was the first of three warnings which in the end obliged Cromwell, Ireton and even Fairfax to fall into line at the head of an army to which these rankers gave its marching orders.

Meanwhile the two commissioners whom Parliament sent down to the Army to promote the Irish expedition had returned to Westminster. For this purpose Sir William Waller and Sir John Clotworthy (both typical Presbyterians) were not a happy choice. Some of the junior officers whom they addressed may have had in their pockets a copy of Lilburne's recent pamphlet, *Regal Tyranny Discovered*, in which he exposed with precise figures the scandalous profiteering of this same Clotworthy, one of the greediest of the land-grabbers in Ulster, as a purveyor of butter and cheese for the troops already in Ireland. They brought back with them to the Commons the news that the Army had had the audacity to draw up a petition about its grievances. Among other false tales that reached the Commons, it was said that Lieut.-Colonel Pride had forced

1,100 of his men to sign the petition by threatening to cashier them if they refused.

On 30 March the House decided to summon to its bar the senior officers who were said to be promoting the petition, Lieut.-General Hammond, his nephew Colonel Robert Hammond, Colonel Robert Lilburne and Lieut.-Colonels Pride and Grime. The angry debate went on until most of the Independents had left the House, and then, as Ludlow tells the story, Denzil Holles scribbled a declaration on his knee which the Commons at once adopted. The Lords adhered to it next day and it went down to the Army as the challenge of all Westminster.

> The two Houses of Parliament [so it ran] having received information of a dangerous petition tending to put the Army into a distemper and mutiny, to put conditions upon the Parliament and obstruct the relief of Ireland, they do declare their high dislike of that petition . . . and that . . . all those who shall continue in their distempered condition, and go on advancing and promoting that petition, shall be looked upon and proceeded against as enemies of the state and disturbers of the public peace.

Next day at the bar of the House after Pride had denied that he put any pressure on his men to sign the document, he and his fellow-officers were rebuked and sent back to their posts with directions to suppress this shocking petition.

What was in the minds of Lords and Commons as they sent this defiance to the army that had won the Civil War for them? It stands revealed to posterity in the *Memoirs* of Denzil Holles, after the Restoration Baron Holles, the draftsman of this historic declaration. The second son of the first Earl of Clare, he had estates in the West of England with a rent-roll of £2,000 a year. At a crucial moment in the early struggles of Parliament against the King, he seconded Sir John Eliot with courage and resource. Like his leader he was thrown into prison and after his release had to keep at a distance from London for many years. In the Long Parliament the King did him the honour to single him out for impeachment as one of the Five Members. On the outbreak of the war he raised a regiment of foot which fought gallantly at Edgehill and Brentford. His own military career was brief, but as an officer he incurred some financial losses and knew from experience the meaning of arrears of pay. Since his income from his lands ceased to flow while the King held the West, he had to depend for a time on his member's allowance of £4 a week. All this he set out in a memorandum addressed to the Commons only seven months before these events. His sufferings Parliament compensated with a grant of £5,000.[11] This then was the man who forbade the troopers to petition for their arrears.

As the leader of the Presbyterian Party Holles displayed a curious mixture of headstrong rashness with irresolution. He could drive the New Model to revolt with a few insolent phrases, but when it came to combining against it the forces that were ready to back him—the King and the royalist diehards, the Scots and their veteran army, the Presbyterian clergy, the City with its money-bags and its turbulent apprentices—he showed an inability to choose and follow up one of the several courses open to him which drove his fellow-conspirator, the French envoy Bellièvre, to contemptuous despair. This vacillating intriguer was at the same time a swashbuckler, who would draw his sword against a group of unarmed Leveller petitioners and wind up a debate in the Commons by challenging his opponent Ireton to a duel across the river. He makes himself in his book at once ridiculous and unsympathetic by accusing several of the Independent leaders of poltroonery, among them that 'arrant coward' Oliver Cromwell.[12] Crude though this man was in his hatreds, he was not without an occasional touch of grace or wit that reminds us of the aristocratic Whigs of the next generation. At his best he wrote well. An ability to quote neatly from the *Odyssey* and Tacitus was not uncommon; his familiarity with Chaucer was much less usual in his day. An anthology from the English prose of his century might well find room for the last page of his peroration, as dignified a statement of resignation to destiny as ever stoic penned.

Holles starts his *Memoirs* by reminding us on his first page that what was at issue between the Presbyterians and the Army was the ascendancy of his class:

The wisest of men saw it to be a great evil that servants should ride on horses and princes walk as servants on the earth; an evil now both seen and felt in our unhappy kingdom. The meanest of men, the basest and vilest of the nation, the lowest of the people, have got the power into their hands, trampled upon the crown, baffled and misused the Parliament, violated the laws, destroyed or suppressed the nobility and gentry of the kingdom . . . and now lord it over the persons and estates of all sorts and ranks of men from the King on his throne to the beggar in his cottage.

In the rapid historical sketch of his own times that follows this prelude, Holles tells us that 'the most factious, busy, beggarly men' (meaning the Independents) had insisted on prolonging the war, while their committees in the counties sequestrated the estates of the gentry. The fact was that these 'bloodsuckers' had conceived 'a mortal hatred against all *gentlemen* [Holles's italics], as those who had too great an interest and too large a stake of their own in the kingdom to engage with them in their design of perpetuating the war to an absolute confusion.'[13] He explains the Self-Denying Ordinance as a device to get rid of 'all the noblemen and gentlemen . . . who had borne the heat of the day'. Here is his description of the New Model:

> a mercenary army raised by the Parliament, all of them from the General (except what he may have in expectation after his father's death) to the meanest centinal [*sic* meaning centurion or captain?] not able to make a thousand pounds a year lands, most of the colonels and officers mean trades-men, brewers, tailors, goldsmiths, shoemakers and the like, a notable dunghill, if one would rake into it, to find out their several pedigrees: these to rebel against their masters, . . . make their will a rule that all the interests of King, Parliament and kingdom must be squared by . . .[14]

There is more to be learned from this paragraph about the structure of English society in the seventeenth century than from many chapters that chronicle events. It raises the question with which the Whig governing class also confronts us. Were they primarily plutocrats or aristocrats? Evidently for Holles the right to govern belonged to those who had at least £1,000 *per annum* in rents from land. The Whigs (it will be remembered) put the qualification for a seat in the Commons at a rather

G

lower figure. The most instructive phrase in the whole outburst is that which describes the conduct of these low-born
officers (for he treats the men as mere pawns) as a rebellion
against their masters. We shall see presently how accurately the
Levellers, both soldiers and civilians, had grasped this state of
mind in the Long Parliament. If ever its members had thought
of themselves as the representatives of the people, they had
ceased to do so long ago.

Holles briefly summarises the Army's petition, but neither
here nor elsewhere does he concede that it had any genuine
grievances or any right to ask for their redress. Its duty was to
embark for Ireland in silent obedience:

> For an army . . . to join in a petition, though but for pay,
> when their superiors (that authority which they are to obey)
> require any duty to be performed, or service to be done by
> them, as the present relieving of Ireland was, this I think,
> by the rules of war, has in all armies been held a mutiny and
> the authors at least punished with death.

He disapproves of the 'clemency' which the House showed to
'the most mutinous officers' whom it called to the bar, notably
Lieut.-Colonel Pride. He is even more plain-spoken about the
three troopers whom it called to the bar a month later (p. 181
below). He complains that the House 'let them go without
punishment'. It should have 'hanged one of them'. It would
be unprofitable to waste much more ink in quoting this man's
insults to the Army—enough that he spoke of its Council as
one chosen from the dregs of the people (*ex faece populi*) and of
the New Model as 'hired servants that had received more wages
ten times than their work deserved, and now betrayed the trust
reposed in them, rising against their masters. . . '.[15] This man
was not a rough unlettered Colonel Blimp whose life had been
spent in camps; he was a cultured aristocrat who wrote as a
devout Christian. This revealing book, written in exile immediately after these events, was not published till 1699, twenty
years after its author's death. It renders for us, none the less,
the atmosphere of 1647 and reproduces the clangour of its
class war. If Denzil Holles expressed himself thus when he
wrote for posterity, we may be sure that his language in debate

was no milder. The Army had its correspondents who frequented Westminster Hall and kept it well informed.

To the condemnation of the two Houses the Army reacted with a blend of indignation and alarm. Men and officers were agreed in feeling, much as the London Levellers did, that Parliament by denying their right to petition had robbed them of their citizenship. A news-letter sent out from Headquarters asked the question: Have the soldiers, who were 'instruments to recover the lost liberties of the nation, fought themselves into slavery'? If Parliament ventured to call them 'enemies to the state' (a phrase which meant presumably traitors and felons) when they stood together under arms, what sort of treatment had they to expect if they allowed themselves to be dispersed and disarmed?[16] The anger of the Army was still further inflamed when the Commons detained Colonel Robert Lilburne and other officers and brought up Ensign Nichol of his regiment a prisoner to London, on a charge that they obstructed the Irish expedition.

At the top, however, the behaviour of the high command was submissive and correct. Already on 30 March Fairfax had assured the Commons that the officers would 'acquiesce in whatsoever . . . you should judge reasonable to grant on their behalf'. After the vote of condemnation, the General caused a declaration to be published at the head of every regiment requiring them to desist from petitioning. The soldiers, we are told, 'such is their obedience and respect unto the General, acquiesce therein', but some of them spoke their minds, none the less, saying, 'it was a hard case with them, that they that had fought for the liberty of the subjects of England, should be denied the liberty of the subject to petition'.[17]

Parliament now sent down to the Army yet another futile delegation of Presbyterian notables, the Earl of Warwick and Lord Dacres with Waller, Massey and Clotworthy. It ignores the men (for no Presbyterian and few Independents could imagine that private soldiers were capable of any initiative) but it met some two hundred officers in the noble old church of Saffron Walden on 15 April. The outstanding fact in the debate over Ireland was that the officers were chiefly concerned with the command. They respected Skippon but did not believe that he was physically fit for such a task. 'Fairfax and Cromwell,' they shouted, 'and we all go.' The meeting agreed that though few of those present would volunteer to go, they would undertake to promote the service.

The officers, however, were still so concerned for the honour of the Army that they drew up what they originally called a 'Vindication' of its petition; for this title the timider word 'Narrative' was afterwards substituted. 'We hope,' they wrote, 'that in purchasing the freedoms of our brethren we have not lost our own.' They then argued over again, quietly but with conviction, their case over their arrears and the need of an indemnity, and concluded by asking Parliament to vindicate them from the false charges that had been made against them. This dignified and courteous document avoids any counter-attack on the Army's enemies. It is in effect a request that Parliament should cancel its vote of condemnation, but its authors did not venture to say this plainly. It was signed by Lieut.-General Hammond, 14 colonels and lieut.-colonels, 6 majors and about 130 captains and junior officers. A deputation from these officers presented it to the Commons on 27 April.[18]

So far the officers would go, but it was now clear that they would go no further. They would set out their views on paper, but no plan of action and no move for action ever came from them. Exactly how or when the Leveller group managed to organise the whole Army to resist disbandment we do not know. It is likely enough that they thought of sending a big elected deputation up to Westminster to present their petition—a common practice when civilians had anything to say to Parliament. For this purpose it is said that they meant to get two men chosen from each troop and company.[19] This may have led them to the idea of forming a representative council which could speak for the whole body of soldiers and if need be lead it to action. For these men, nurtured on Leveller tracts, the idea of representation was something novel and exciting. While the civilian Levellers argued for the election of magistrates and parish ministers, the soldiers (as we shall see) and even some of the sailors believed in the election of officers.[20]

Towards the end of April, perhaps on the 26th, the first step was taken by the cavalry, when two representatives from each troop attended a gathering of the four regiments quartered in Norfolk. When experience showed that such a conclave was too unwieldy for the transaction of business, the men lit on the device of indirect election. From the representatives of the troops each regiment chose two agents or 'agitants' to act for it, or to use the synonym most common in that generation, two 'Agitators', a word which had as yet no sinister connotation. Before the end of April the Agitators of eight regiments of horse had formed a council for action. Presently the foot followed the horse[21] and by 15 May the council could speak for all the soldiery of sixteen regiments. Last of all, but not till June, the officers imitated the men, and they also chose two Agitators for each regiment from among the captains and junior officers. It is recorded that on one occasion each soldier of the foot—the poorer arm—contributed 4d. towards the expenses of the movement; later the officers contributed.

There had been nothing like this spontaneous outbreak of democracy in any English or continental army before this year of 1647, nor was there anything like it thereafter till Workers' and Soldiers' Councils met in 1917 in Russia. We shall come across some figures among these Agitators who deserve to be remembered, but this was emphatically a demonstration of the general will of the Army. Each troop and each regiment evolved in the danger and excitement of the revolutionary crisis a collective personality, and when a question was put to the vote, the usual response was an affirmative shout of 'All! all!' More than once in the contemporary records penned by the men themselves we meet the significant phrase 'the sense of the Army'.

The first public appearance of the Agitators was as accused men, standing as many famous rebels had stood before them, at the bar of the House of Commons. On behalf of eight regiments of horse they had written an identical open letter to Fairfax, Cromwell and Skippon which three of them brought up to Westmimster in person on 29 April. The response of Skippon who had just been elected member for Barnstaple, was hostile and prompt. Next day he read it to the House as a 'dangerous' document, and the three troopers, Edward Sexby,

William Allen and Thomas Shepherd, were brought in to answer for it.

The letter, phrased in eloquent and emotional language, appealed for protection and help on behalf of the soldiery whom Parliament had so unjustly condemned to each of these three commanders who had led them through many lesser dangers to safety. 'Can we be proclaimed traitors and your honour remain secure?' After the briefest justification of the men's petition, it counter-attacked the Army's enemies. 'Can this Irish expedition', it asked, 'be anything else but a design to ruin and break this Army in pieces?' Then, couched in Leveller language, came this bold attack on the Presbyterian majority:

> But we are confident that your honour cannot but perceive that this plot is but a mere cloak for some who have lately tasted of sovereignty and being lifted beyond the ordinary sphere of servants, seek to become masters and degenerate into tyrants.

If these troopers had read Holles's *Memoirs* in which that word 'masters' sounds the key-note, they could not have described the state of mind of the ruling party more correctly. The letter ended with a defiant declaration that even if these three generals were appointed to lead it, these regiments would not volunteer for the Irish expedition until 'our just desires be granted' and 'the rights and liberties of the subjects of England vindicated and maintained'.[22]

Under cross-examination the men said that the letter was drafted at a rendezvous, that copies were distributed to every troop of the eight regiments, read aloud and unanimously adopted. Very few officers knew of its existence. When they were asked the meaning of the sentence about sovereignty, masters and tyrants, they were shrewd enough to reply that as the letter was the joint product of the eight regiments any questions should be addressed to them in writing, so that they might answer jointly.

At this point a member declared that the letter must have been promoted by Cavaliers. 'Are the troopers Cavaliers?' he asked. Then the three gave their record. All had served Parliament since the outbreak of the Civil War and one of them was wounded at Edgehill. Sexby, a Suffolk man, served first in Cromwell's horse and then in that of Fairfax. Shepherd was a Shropshire lad; taken prisoner after the relief of Gloucester he escaped and rejoined the ranks. Allen, a feltmaker from Southwark, began his service in Denzil Holles's regiment. Like John Lilburne he was taken prisoner at Brentford and sentenced to death at Oxford. Thereafter he was twice wounded, at the first battle of Newbury and again at Henley. Lying sorely stricken on the ground with five dangerous wounds, Skippon who was then his colonel, came across him and gave him 5s. to procure him some relief. Skippon had the decency to confirm his story.[23] One would like to know whether his former colonel, Holles, was in his place and heard it.

Of Thomas Shepherd nothing further is known. William Allen was, like so many Levellers, a craftsman from the South Bank and an Anabaptist, who got his education, one must suppose, from the Bible, from sermons and from revolutionary pamphlets. After his eventful service, always as a private, first in the foot and then in the horse, Cromwell, when he encountered him as an Agitator, perceived his gifts and promoted him. With the rank of Captain he was for a time Adjutant-General of the army in Ireland, but was cashiered when as a Fifth Monarchist he joined the active opposition to the Protectorate. We can read his mind, simple, modest, disinterested and on fire with an unquenchable faith in 'the good old cause of God and our country', in a pamphlet of reminiscences and exhortations written in 1659 with such sincerity that it still has the power to move us.[24]

Edward Sexby must have been the moving spirit in the group of Leveller troopers which set the petition going and got the Agitators elected. What was his trade we do not know. Probably he came from the upper stratum of craftsmen or yeomen, since he served in Cromwell's horse from the early days of the war. There were two or three free grammar schools in Suffolk and it is possible that he may have attended one of them. Clarendon's description of Sexby, whom he met in exile, is puzzling. 'The man for an illiterate person spoke very well and properly and used those words very well, the true meaning and signification whereof he could not understand.' What did

Clarendon mean by 'illiterate'? He uses it, for example, of the Earl of Arundel, famous for his collection of ancient coins and statues, and of his colleague Lord Cottington, whom he describes as 'very wise', widely read in French, Italian and Spanish literature and knowledgable about birds, beasts and agriculture. He meant, presumably, that these persons (the elder Vane was another) lacked a really scholarly familiarity with the Greek and Latin classics.

It is surprising that a man as able as Sexby should still have been only a private after four or five years' service. As we know from the historic pamphlet, *Killing No Murder*, which he wrote ten years after these events, when Cromwell seemed to him no longer a beloved leader but a tyrant fit for assassination, he was an admirable writer, even a stylist, whose rhythmical prose is remarkable for its balance and its epigrammatic strength. Something of this talent appears in two at least of the Agitators' documents, the letter to Cromwell, Fairfax and Skippon and the *Second Apology of the Soldiers*, and it is probable that Sexby wrote them.[25] A year later we shall meet him as the go-between in the dealings of the Army with the civilian Levellers, for both Lilburne and Cromwell trusted him—he became, indeed, one of Cromwell's 'bed-fellows'. How he was promoted lieut.-colonel; how he used his chances, as an intelligence officer on a mission in Bordeaux, to preach Leveller doctrines to the Huguenots; how he died, it may be after torture, a prisoner in the Tower with his wits ebbing—all this belongs to later chapters. This brilliant but unstable character ranks as one of the outstanding figures in the Leveller movement.

It looks as if the three troopers made a favourable impression on the House. Though some of the Presbyterians did speak of sending them to the Tower, so far was it from hanging one of them, as Holles in retrospect desired, that it made a feeble but unmistakable gesture of conciliation. It sent yet another delegation down to the Army, but this time it chose from its own benches four men whom the soldiers would be likely to trust—Skippon, Cromwell, Ireton and Fleetwood. They were, moreover, authorised to promise that the House would provide 'a considerable sum of money' before disbanding, that the accounts of officers and men should be audited and that an ordinance of indemnity should be promptly passed for acts done *in tempore et loco belli*. These promises, when compared with the realisation, served only to irritate the men. The House, it turned out, now offered eight instead of six weeks' pay, but in the meantime the arrears of the horse had risen from 43 to 52 weeks. Judge Jenkins, Lilburne's fellow-prisoner in the Tower, pointed out some yawning gaps in the hastily drafted ordinance.

Skippon when he and his colleagues faced a gathering of officers in Walden church—this time some men also, perhaps Agitators, were present—made the mistake of asking them to report on the 'distempers' of the men. The officers were bold enough to answer that there were no distempers and no indiscipline, but that the men had serious grievances. A committee of senior officers was appointed to report on these, and this it did systematically, consulting every troop and company within reach. These spoke their minds through their Agitators. A report, drawn up apparently by Colonel Lambert, summed up what was common to all of these 'returns'.[26] It repeated the five demands of the Petition in clear but conciliatory language. It also protested against Parliament's vote of condemnation 'which remains upon record as a memorandum of infamy upon us to posterity'. It added an additional request: that young draftsmen should be allowed to reckon their years of service in the army as part of their seven years of apprenticeship. The political demands of the men were not included in this summary. Among them, as the manuscript records show, were some of the chief points of the Leveller programme.[27] The men made an eloquent plea for liberty of conscience, insisted on their right to petition, complained of the imprisonment of freemen without a trial (meaning Lilburne and his comrades) and of the anomaly of laws in an unknown tongue. The value of this document, signed as it was by very many officers, was that in it they made the professional demands of the soldiers their own.

At the second of two meetings at Walden on 15 May, after stormy scenes caused by the Presbyterian minority, Cromwell and Fleetwood were asked to report to the Commons on the views of the Army. Cromwell's speech on that day, of which a shorthand record has survived, is the utterance of a loyal and conservative officer. Doubtless he understood the grievances of the men better than the Presbyterian leaders did, but his chief concern was to ensure the obedience of the Army to Parliament. He exhorted the officers to promote in the men 'a good opinion of that authority that is over both us and them. If that authority falls to nothing, nothing can follow but confusion'.[28] Now, as always, a dread of anarchy was one of the two or three leading motives that guided his conduct.

The Agitators, meanwhile, had been consolidating their movement and broadening its base, so as to include first of all the regiments of foot in the eastern counties and then the scattered regiments elsewhere. Though their feelings towards their officers were friendly, they meant to go on acting as an independent lever of revolt. This they made clear in *A Second Apology of all the private soldiers . . . to their Commission Officers*,[29] which was printed on 3 May. It is a stirring piece of writing, obviously from the same pen as the letter to the three generals, and even more effectively it expresses the desperation of the troopers and their determination to act—with or without their officers. It opens with what is now the typical Leveller theme; how they had expected from their victories to reap 'a plentiful crop and harvest of liberty and peace', so that 'the meanest subject should enjoy his right, liberty and properties in all things'; how Parliament had disillusioned them by its lawless oppression of its best friends, while some of their disbanded comrades had been hanged for things done in time of war.

> Therefore, brave commanders, the Lord put a spirit of courage into your hearts that you may stand fast in your integrity that you have manifested to us your soldiers, and we do declare to you that if any of you shall not, he shall be marked with a brand of infamy for ever as a traitor to his country and an enemy to this army. Read and consider. Was ever such things done by a Parliament, to proclaim us enemies to the state, as they have done about the late petition? . . . Is it not better to die like men than to be enslaved and hanged like dogs? Which must be yours and

our portion if not now looked into, even before our disbanding. . . . We have been quiet and peaceable in obeying
all orders and commands, yet now, we have a just cause to
tell you, if we be not relieved in these our grievances, we
shall be forced to that which we pray God to divert.

Reading between the lines, it is clear that by May Day 1647
the Agitators of the horse had made up their minds to resist
the disbanding of the New Model.

Thanks to the *Clarke Papers*, which include several newsletters sent out from Headquarters during the crisis and
several letters which passed between the Agitators in Walden
and one of their comrades who had ridden up to London, we
have a lively picture of what these young men were thinking and
planning. They write to each other in a tone of excitement,
taking care, none the less, by the use of a numerical cipher, to
conceal their names and some part of their meaning. Two
young subalterns are now actively engaged with the men,
Cornet George Joyce of the General's Bodyguard and Lieut.
Chillenden of Whalley's Horse; and to these we should add
Captain Francis White, a man of character and independence,
whose influence may have been decisive in the regiment which
was first put to the test, the General's foot. It can hardly be a
mere coincidence that three of the key figures in this drama had
been fellow-prisoners under sentence of death in the gaol at
Oxford, William Allen, Edmund Chillenden[30] and John
Lilburne. They went about their formidable task under Sexby's
leadership in a resourceful and businesslike way, but they were
still very young men, who enjoyed every hour of this adventure.
Always they are riding hard and exhorting each other to do the
like. 'Pray, gentlemen, ride night and day. We will act here
night and day for you.' Muffling themselves for a moment in a
cloak of cipher, they are still the bravest of the brave: 'And let
me tell you (41) and (52) in (54) are all very gallant. I pray God
keep us so too. Now, my lads, if we work like men we shall do
well and that in the hands of (53).' Appropriately this gentleman (or shall we rather call him lad?) signs himself 'yours till
death, 102'.

The most important of these documents is a programme of the
work that lay in front of the Agitators dated Walden, 4 May.

Firth ascribes it to Sexby and it reads like the minutes of decisions taken at a committee meeting. It asks for prompt action 'lest resolution languish and courage grow cold'. It begins by calling for the appointment of a council 'for the ordering the undertakings of the Army', since as yet only the horse had their representatives. Next it asks for 'a party of able pen-men at Oxford and the Army' since the presses must be used 'to undeceive the people'.[31] The meaning of this is that these young troopers were actually improvising a service of publicity to win support for the Army and the democratic cause. Since the Leveller press in London had been confiscated, they acquired a press of their own with the help of the officers, which John Harris ran for them at Oxford. Once an actor and now a printer, he wrote pamphlets over the transparent pseudonym Sirrahniho, and in 1648 edited a clever but shortlived newspaper, *Mercurius Militaris*. In the home counties and East Anglia they carried on their propaganda with marked success. They had the good sense to realise that if 'the people' were to be won over to the cause of the Army they must think of it as the champion of their own liberties. Accordingly the pen-men are to give some 'reasons for desiring reformation in civil justice', and to ask how far 'the declarations of Parliament put forth to engage us in blood' have been performed. 'For aught we yet find' it has but 'entangle[d] us in stronger chains' and 'clap[ped] upon our necks heavier yokes [of] servitude'. In fact the pen-men went a good deal further, and roused the peasants and farmers by talking about tithes and the wrongs of tenants. Then too the New Model must get in touch with the armed forces in other parts of the kingdom.

Two other objectives are indicated. The Agitators must 'prevent the removal or surprisal of the King's person'. Here is conclusive evidence that the daring expedition which Cornet Joyce led a month later originated with the men and not with Cromwell or any of the Grandees. It is known that about this time the privates in the foot round Cambridge were talking of going to Holmby 'to fetch the King'.[32]

There are vague phrases in this memorandum about calling for 'public justice and due punishment to be inflicted upon all offenders whomsoever'. This may mean that the idea of impeaching Holles and the other Presbyterian leaders had already occurred to the men.

Finally (in clause 10) the Agitators made it clear that they were still as eager to win the help of the generals as they had been when they wrote their letter of 29 April. In the meantime, it may be, they had ceased to think of Skippon as a friend (indeed, '102' wanted to tell Skippon 'to depart the Army and all other officers that are not right') but they were all the more anxious to have the countenance of Fairfax and the active support of Cromwell and Ireton. The clause runs:

> Persuade the general officers not to depart from the Army until these storms be overblown, the subject's liberty confirmed, the kingdom settled, delinquents detected and punished, the soldiers and sufferers satisfied and rewarded; in all which respects their conduct was never of more consequence, nor their interest in the Army more useful. . . .

This clause disposes of the traditional notion that the Agitators were Cromwell's puppets. On the contrary, it was they who did everything in their power to bring him back to the Army, after his command had legally come to an end.

In that century the recognised way of organising and testing public opinion was by the signing of petitions. For many months, starting in the City, the Presbyterian party had been addressing petitions to Parliament, calling for the disbanding of the Army. In East Anglia, where most of the New Model was quartered, it was the Presbyterian clergy who promoted them from their pulpits. One of these from Essex declared 'that this Army came to enslave the country and to awe the Parliament'. Another, resentful over free quarter, spoke of 'a dearth sharper than the late devouring sword'—a reminder we can hardly repeat too often that the social background of this revolutionary crisis was a scarcity that came near to famine.[33] The Agitators in reply had the original idea of getting up petitions addressed to Fairfax. Over a thousand inhabitants of Essex feared that 'we are now like to be vassalised and enslaved in the Norman laws and prerogative clutches of an ambitious party in the nation'. They complained of the burning of the Leveller petition and prayed that 'before you disband your army you would be pleased to consider the sad condition which is like to befall the freeborn people of England' and 'that you would be pleased to mediate with the Parliament in our behalf'.[34]

Similar petitions with 1400 signatures came from Norfolk and Suffolk, and these also begged the Army to 'mediate' on the people's behalf with Parliament. One would like to know the name of the 'penman' who first thought of this exquisitely tactful euphemism for dictation. A later petition from Norwich city and its neighbourhood to much the same effect claimed to speak for 'many thousands'. By far the most interesting of these petitions spoke for 1200 inhabitants of Hertfordshire, and no less than 200 'knights, gentlemen and freeholders' presented it to the General at St Albans on 16 June.[35] It spoke, however, also for the copyhold peasants, who had no political rights. It asked the Army, before it disbanded, to exact the punishment of 'the firebrands and incendiaries who maligned you' (meaning Holles and his colleagues), and then to insist on the redress of 'our grievances' also. Among these they mentioned the rotten boroughs in Cornwall, the squandering of public money more especially by members of Parliament, and the scandal of tithes. These were the commonplaces of Leveller propaganda, but one clause, whether it was the troopers or the local 'knights and gentlemen' who suggested it, struck a new note. The levelling idea had reached the villages of this county.

> That the body of the kingdom [so ran §5] consisting much of copyholders, who have for the most part been very cordial and faithful to the Parliament, may not now be left finable at the will of the lords, in regard the generality of them have been very malignant . . . and from whom they cannot but expect very severe dealing.

Themselves of the countrymen, billeted among countrymen, the Agitators must have done much more propaganda on this all-important agrarian question than our records reveal. It was this side of their activities that made the deepest impression on some of their propertied opponents. A scurrilous but amusing tract by an anonymous wit—was he the royalist Cleveland?—*The Character of an Agitator* (11 November, 1647), describes him as begotten by John Lilburne with Dick Overton's help, counselled by Mr Walwyn and patronised by Mr Marten. 'He pleads', we are told, 'for a toleration of all religions, being himself of none.' Worse still, 'he would have copyhold tenants pay no rents or fines to their landlords . . . for the earth is the Saints' and the fulness thereof'. An abler but equally malicious observer, Clement Walker, in his *History of Independency* after telling us that the Army had 'sown the cockle of heresies and schism' among the 'more beggarly sort' in city and country, went on to speak of the activities of the Agitators.

> Their plausible way of prompting the people to petition against tithes, enclosures and copyhold fines uncertain was to encourage them to side with the Army against all the nobility, gentry and clergy of the land (from whom the Army did most fear an opposition) and to destroy monarchy itself: since it is impossible for any prince to be a king only of beggars, tinkers and cobblers.[36]

In spite of the Grandees, these spirited young men were building up in the minds of the 'people' a picture of the Army as the champion of their class interests.

At Westminster, meanwhile, the Presbyterian majority made it clear that whatever minor concessions it might make to appease the men, it was still resolutely bent on breaking up the New Model. On 18 May the Commons took the decision that all of it was to be disbanded, save those who enlisted for Ireland and such of the foot as might be needed for garrison duty at home. Fairfax, who was in London for medical advice, was after some highly offensive criticisms ordered to return to his command. The details of the disbanding were left to 'Derby House'—the executive, which was at this time the Committee for Irish Affairs. News of these decisions reached the Agitators promptly in two letters, possibly from Sexby.[37] He gathered—correctly as it turned out—that the foot was to be disbanded first, and then the horse, each regiment separately at places far apart. Further, he was informed that in order to sow dissension between officers and men, the soldiers were to get all their arrears and the officers very much less. Some such discrimination was in fact contemplated. What is interesting is Sexby's prompt reaction (if the letter is his) and his advice to the Agitators: Tell the men to stick to their officers as they have stuck to us, and do not let them be abused. 'Believe it, my dear fellows, we must now be very active to send to all our several regiments of horse and foot and let them know that nothing but destruction is threatened.'

And very active they were. Next day, 19 May, there went out to all the regiments from Bury St Edmunds, whither Fairfax had moved his Headquarters, a circular letter signed by Agitators representing eight regiments of horse and five of foot. It laid stress on this sinister plan to divide officers from men, and insisted on united action. Much good would arrears of pay do the men, if they were then pressed for Ireland or hanged in England for prosecuting the petition.

> Fellow soldiers, the sum of all this is, if you do but stand and not accept of anything nor do anything without the consent of the whole Army, you will do good to yourselves, your officers and the whole kingdom. Stand with your officers and one with another you need not fear. If you divide you destroy all.

In tactical wisdom this could hardly be bettered. The men would feel magnanimous and the officers grateful. But the fears of the Agitators were exaggerated. The Long Parliament was much too mean to pay all the men's arrears.

Two days later, on 21 May, came the critical day in the Commons. Cromwell, back from Saffron Walden, made his report and after Lambert's summary (one supposes) had been read, he supported its recommendations. To that extent he was on the side of the men. He then told the House bluntly that the Army would not volunteer for Ireland, but he pledged his word that it would disband quietly. This he seems to have said on two occasions, once in March and again at this turning point in May, when he should have been better informed. Clement Walker (as biased a reporter as ever professed to be writing history) quotes him as saying (apparently in the earlier debate),

> With his hand upon his breast: In the presence of Almighty

God, before whom he stood, that he knew the Army would disband and lay down their arms at their door, whensoever they should command them.[38]

It may be that the excessive emphasis of his two assurances betrayed an inner anxiety which he tried to silence by shouting. If he failed at Walden to grasp what the men's state of mind really was, the fault lay partly with the senior officers, who exaggerated the Army's readiness in the last resort to obey Fairfax as it had always done in the past. Even when they reported on the soldiers' grievances, they mistook the strong language of the troopers for what they called 'soldiers' dialect', and toned it down to a key of polite albeit resentful submission.

The House, as resolute as ever to pursue its main purpose of destroying the New Model, and as stingy as ever in the matter of arrears, proved to be willing enough to make concessions that cost for the moment little or nothing. On this day it passed the indemnity ordinance. Defective though its drafting was, it must be said in justice to the Commons that they acted promptly and severely whenever a case was brought to their notice of the victimisation of ex-soldiers for acts done under orders during the Civil War.[39] After hearing Cromwell who spoke for all four of its commissioners, the House decided in principle that the men's accounts for arrears should be audited, 'visible security' given for the unpaid remainder on disbanding, and that the recommendations concerning apprentices, the pressing of volunteers and the maintenance of widows, orphans and disabled men should be embodied in bills.

On Tuesday, 25 May, on the motion of Denzil Holles, the fatal decision was taken fixing the times and places for disbanding all infantry regiments separately. The first on the list was Fairfax's foot, due to be disbanded in Chelmsford church in a week's time, on Tuesday, 1 June. As if to soften this heavy blow by a trifling token of amiability, the House on this day released Colonel Robert Lilburne and Major Sanderson from their burdensome attendance and Ensign Nicholls from his imprisonment. Next day, General Fairfax, loyal and correct as he always was, sent out from his new Headquarters at Bury St Edmunds a circular to the colonels of every regiment under his command, assuring them that the Army's grievances would be redressed. He went on, in effect, to forbid any further activity by Agitators:

> I do . . . require soldiers to forbear any further actings by themselves without their officers in any irregular ways. All officers are strictly to see to it . . . that there be no more such meetings or consultation of soldiers at Bury or elsewhere.

No one enforced this prohibition; no one obeyed it and no one thought any the worse of 'Black Tom' for issuing it.

The news of the decision to disband the General's foot reached the Agitators promptly, together with a contemptuous summary of Parliament's terms. What mattered most to the simplest soldier who cared nothing for godliness or democracy—and there may have been many such among the pressed men in the foot—was that after all the promises to redress his grievances only eight weeks of arrears would be paid. Some of these simple men said a few days later that they would have disbanded, if they had been given four months' pay. With this news there came from London, presumably from the leaders of the civilian Levellers, a message of approval for the tactic the Agitators had already adopted—the calling of a rendezvous of the whole Army to register a joint refusal to disband on any such terms. But the first thing to be done was to make sure of Fairfax's foot. It was the regiment most likely to obey tamely, for most of its officers from Lieut.-Colonel Jackson downwards were Presbyterians, and he, we are told, was a devout parishioner of no less a 'ghostly father' than the Rev. Mr Edwards.

On 28 May both Houses passed ordinances on behalf of the maimed veterans and soldiers' widows. A procedure was laid down for auditing the accounts of officers. It was also provided that £15,000 should be secured on the excise to cover the arrears of soldiers and non-commissioned officers. This sum, the Agitators promptly answered, was altogether inadequate; the excise was already fully mortgaged, and here finally was the discrimination they had been led to expect, for, such as it was, this so-called 'visible security' was not offered to the officers. The arrears of the horse, be it noted, now stood at 56 weeks. On this day, three months after the disbanding of the

Army first came under consideration, the Lords were visited by a startling impulse of graciousness. They suggested that a 'congratulatory declaration' should be made to the troops. The Commons did not approve. Finally, both Houses nominated a commission of six Presbyterian notables under the Earl of Warwick to go down to Chelmsford and preside over the disbanding. The extravagant sum of £500 was voted for these gentlemen's personal expenses.

As the crisis approached, Fairfax, who was evidently in great perplexity, summoned a council of war to meet at Bury on Saturday 29 May. The Agitators, however, got in their word first. They presented to the General a petition on behalf of ten regiments of horse and six of foot, among the latter the General's own. For the third time, in the plainest English, the men warned the officers that with them or without them the Army meant to act. The soldiers had not yet been vindicated against the condemnation of the two Houses, nor had their grievances been redressed. To their former demands they now added the boldest counter-offensive on which they had yet ventured. They complained that 'the intruders, contrivers and promoters of our destruction' had not yet been 'called to account'. Here was the proposal, which the Grandees soon adopted, to impeach Denzil Holles and his colleagues. The petition went on to ask the General to call a rendezvous of the whole Army and prevent its being disbanded till its grievances were redressed, failing which 'we shall be necessitated . . . to do such things ourselves'.[40]

Faced with this warning, the council of war at which Ireton and most of the senior officers were present decided with virtual unanimity to follow the lead of the Agitators. Four votes were taken in which the majority varied from 86 to 82: a minute Presbyterian minority varying from 3 to 5 held out to the end under the courageous leadership of Lieut.-Colonel Jackson. In a well-written and sober memorandum addressed to Fairfax, the council of war laid stress, as the Agitators also had done, on the insult to the Army implied in the unprecedented decision to disband it piecemeal. It asked Parliament to reconsider Tuesday's votes and redress the Army's grievances adequately. It recommended a general rendezvous because of 'the extreme earnestness and violent propensity among the soldiers' for such a meeting:

> we verily believe, [it went on] that the first attempt to disband any one regiment before equal satisfaction to all and assurance against those things they have cause to fear will occasion them all to draw together and rendezvous of themselves, as it were upon an alarm. And to prevent the inconveniences or ill consequences both to these countries [i.e. counties] and the kingdom of any such tumultuous . . . drawing to a rendezvous . . . we humbly advise your Excellency without delay after the contracting of quarters to order a general rendezvous.[41]

A vivid letter of intelligence apparently from the Agitators reported the momentous decisions of this council of war. 'It is incredible,' it commented, 'the unity of officers and soldiers.' By this it meant the radical majority, for it went on to describe how one regiment after another was driving out its unpopular Presbyterian officers. As for the General's foot which the commission was coming to disband, 'they may as well send them among so many bears to take away their whelps'. Nothing would induce it to march into Chelmsford church. It made instead with its colours, drums and baggage wagons for the village near Newmarket where quarters had been assigned to it, while the Army assembled for the general rendezvous. On the second day of its march the Parliamentary commissioners sent its lieut.-colonel and two of its Presbyterian officers after it to try what they could do to bring it to a better mind. It received them with shouts of 'There come our enemies', and when they tried to read out the details of Parliament's concessions, one of the men called out 'What do you, bringing your twopenny pamphlets to us?' With Captain Francis White, whom the men always looked on as a friend, as the officer in command, the regiment marched on to Newmarket.

In the language of '102' the Agitators had 'broken the neck' of their enemies' design: the Army was not going to disband. On 1 June a pathetic letter from Farifax was read to both Houses. He explained that he had yielded so as 'to keep the Army from disorder or worse inconveniences'. 'I intreat you,' he begged, 'that there may be ways in love and composure thought upon.' For the moment the Presbyterian majority accepted its defeat and recalled the Earl of Warwick and his fellow commissioners.

While they were organising the Army to resist disbanding, the Agitators undertook two spirited adventures that made history. They secured the King as the Army's prisoner, and they denied to the Parliament the use of the siege train and artillery which had lain at Oxford since the siege of the previous summer. Throughout 1647 the King's restoration was the settlement to which everyone—if we exclude Henry Marten and the bolder Levellers—looked forward eagerly. The only question was who should set him on his throne again, the Presbyterians who controlled Parliament, or the Independents who had the Army—if they dared to use it. There is no doubt that Denzil Holles and his friends were considering various alternative plans. Either the King should go to Scotland and take command of a Scots army which would again march south; or he should be brought to one of his palaces near London, or better still to London itself, where the Presbyterian City would rally to him. At Holmby the commissioners who had charge of his person were Presbyterians, and so were Colonel Graves and other officers of the guard which watched over him. That state of things seemed to the Agitators risky and so, as we have seen, as early as 4 May Sexby made a note among the objectives of their movement, that it should secure the person of the King. They were not yet bent on punishing 'the man of blood'; on the contrary, it was a restoration they were planning, on terms compatible with democracy and toleration.

They entrusted the daring adventure to a young officer in Fairfax's Lifeguard, Cornet George Joyce. All we know of him is that he had been a tailor in civil life. It was at first proposed that he should lead a party of 1,000 horse, but eventually the numbers were halved.[42] Where they assembled, from what regiments they came we do not know, nor whether they volunteered as individuals or as whole troops. It may be assumed that senior officers would not serve under a junior subaltern. But five hundred men could not ride through the night without becoming a mob, unless some of them had taken control. The probability is that they elected officers, or called on their

Agitators to act as such. Certainly when they paraded before the King they made a good impression on his experienced eyes.

The operations of the Agitators at Oxford make a complicated story which revolves round Colonel Thomas Rainsborough who (after Cromwell) ranks with Lambert as perhaps the ablest soldier in the New Model and the only Leveller among the field officers. His family may have been Protestant refugees who came from Regensburg in the sixteenth century and adopted its name in an English translation. His grandfather and father were sailors. The latter won fame by commanding eight ships which blockaded Sallee and freed 339 Christians from slavery under the Moors. Edmund Waller wrote verses in his honour. He refused a knighthood from King James, but accepted a gold chain and a jewel. He sat for Aldborough in the Long Parliament till his death in 1642. Thomas was a tall, powerfully built man, famous for his physical courage. He served in the Civil War first of all at sea with the rank of Vice-Admiral. Lying off Hull when it was attacked by the Earl of Newcastle, he landed for its defence 100 sailors from his ship the *Lion*, and presently raised an infantry regiment which he commanded through both civil wars. His family was connected by marriage with the Winthrops of Massachusetts and many New Englanders served under him.[43] He made some remarkable innovations in infantry tactics, but siege operations were his speciality. He won fame above all by his prowess at the savage storming of Bristol and later at Colchester, but the number of fortresses and cities he took or besieged was formidable. In the autumn of 1646 he won a seat in the Commons and became the close ally of Henry Marten.

In April Rainsborough sought and received a commission to capture the last stronghold of the Cavaliers, Jersey, an amphibious operation for which he was specially qualified. Part of his regiment had reached Portsmouth and the rest was at Petersfield, when the Agitators sent to it what they called a 'committee'. Thereupon it 'mutinied'—not perhaps the aptest word for an operation that had evidently been carefully planned—and marched inland again to Abingdon, within easy reach of the siege train at Oxford. To the Speaker Rainsborough sent a rather highly coloured account of this so-called mutiny and his own success in quelling it. Like his contemporaries, the modern reader suspects that he was telling only half the true story. Was it Rainsborough, with his professional interest in sieges, who first realised the importance of securing the heavy artillery for the Army's use, in case it came again to fighting? That he was in touch with the Agitators we know from the briefest mention of him in a letter of 28 May from one of them paving the way for Cornet Joyce's exploit—'send two horsemen [presumably as despatch-riders] to Col. Rainsborough'.[44]

Tardily as always, Denzil Holles and his colleagues at Derby House now took their measures for securing the siege train and munitions stored at Oxford in the Presbyterian—or should we say in the parliamentary?—interest. On 31 May they ordered a party of dragoons, which escorted the money destined to pay off Colonel Ingoldsby's foot quartered in Oxford, to bring back the siege train by road and river to the Tower. On 2 June the dragoons were attacked in front of All Souls' College and driven back with some casualties and the loss of their gold. It was apparently men from Rainsborough's Regiment who did the fighting, but Cornet Joyce, on behalf of the Agitators was in charge of the whole operation. Needless to say, Ingoldsby's foot, as radical as any regiment in the Army did not disband, nor did Rainsborough's. They guarded the siege train.[45]

We have now to face one of the most difficult psychological problems in English history. On his way to Oxford and Holmby House Cornet Joyce spent the evening of Whit Monday, 31 May, in Oliver Cromwell's garden in Drury Lane. Cromwell himself was present with Colonel Fleetwood and others. They discussed Joyce's plans and Cromwell not only approved them, but is said to have given him an 'order' to secure the King at Holmby. Many years later Joyce himself used this word 'order', but it cannot be accurate. Cromwell's commission in the New Model had lapsed; he could not give an order. All he could do, and doubtless did, was to promise Joyce that he would use his influence with Fairfax to make sure that the young Cornet should not suffer for the shocking act of indiscipline he was about to commit. The modern reader is apt to hurry with impatience through the controversies which have

raged from that day to this to determine exactly what it was that
Cromwell approved. By his own account and Ireton's, all they
intended and approved was that Joyce should secure the King
where Parliament had placed him, at Holmby; or, in other
words, that he should prevent the King's removal with the
connivance of Colonel Graves, a Presbyterian partisan. What
they did not foresee or approve was what Joyce actually did,
for he removed the King and made him the Army's prisoner.
The former plan could be defended as the realisation of Parliament's will. The latter was a bold defiance of Parliament.
Both Cromwell and Ireton stoutly denied the story told by
John Harris and afterwards by Joyce himself that Cromwell had
authorised the King's removal 'if occasion were'—a vague
phrase which seems to mean that the choice between the two
courses was left to the Cornet's discretion.

The dispute is interesting only because it serves to remind us
how slow Cromwell was to realise that he was playing his part
in a revolution. He kept up the fiction that the Long Parliament
was the supreme authority which the Army loyally obeyed, right
down to the day of wrath in April 1653, when he called in his
musketeers to sweep away its Rump. It was part of the strength
of this man that he could resolutely close his eyes to facts.

Between his speech in the House on 21 May and his talk
with Joyce on 31 May Cromwell's outlook must have changed.
His speech meant that he acquiesced in the disbanding of the
New Model and even professed to further it, albeit he sought a
fair deal for the men. When he backed Joyce he made the
Agitators' purpose his own, and that was to keep the New
Model in being as an organic force under its trusted officers,
with its due proportion of horse and foot and its indispensable
artillery. On the afternoon of 3 June he avowed his change of
front by riding out of London in company with Hugh Peters to
join the revolted Army at its rendezvous near Newmarket.

The simplest way of explaining the facts is the traditional
view which the older historians took over from Clement
Walker and Holles. Cromwell's assurances that the men would
disband quietly were deliberate lies. This 'masterpiece of dis-
simulation', to use Godwin's phrase, was devised to lure the
House into a humiliating defeat.[46] As for the Agitators, from

first to last they had been his tools. Truthfulness was not one of his virtues. But Cromwell was no democrat, and it is nonsense to suggest that he would spread ultra-democratic notions among soldiers from whom he expected disciplined obedience. To dispose of this fiction it is enough to cite John Lilburne's evidence. Although he was in the Tower, he could receive visitors. Through them and it may be through his wife and his brother Robert he was kept well-informed of all that was happening in the Army. In March when the movement for a petition began, he was still Cromwell's grateful and devoted admirer, but he was deeply grieved because he had heard from 'an officer from the Army' that the Lieut.-General was 'about to dash our hopes in pieces' and would not suffer the men to petition 'till they have laid down their arms', and this Cromwell did because he had 'promised the House that they shall lay down their arms'.[47] This Lilburne wrote to Cromwell himself on 25 March, and in a second letter dated 10 April he was still distressed by his old patron's conduct. This disposes of the Presbyterian theory that Cromwell said one thing in the House and used his influence in the Army in the opposite direction.

There is other evidence from Leveller sources dating from a few months later. John Wildman, who became prominent in the movement during the autumn of this year, wrote in his able but bitter pamphlet *Putney Projects* an even more definite account of the conduct of Cromwell and Ireton. They both 'in private opposed those gallant endeavours of the Army for their country's freedom'. The Presbyterians, they argued, were so powerful that any attempt to resist them could only result in 'confusion and ruin'. They tried to suppress the soldiers' petition, nor could the 'constant importunity and solicitation of many friends' prevail upon Cromwell to join the Army 'until the danger of imprisonment forced him to fly'. Wildman notes, what is so often forgotten, that Cromwell had then no commission in the Army and simply 'assumed office', since Fairfax had no power to make general officers.[48]

This is an uncharitable way of stating the essential truth. Cromwell feared that resistance to the Presbyterian majority would precipitate a second civil war. Whether his motive in quitting London was fear of imprisonment is much more doubtful. Holles believed it, but he was eccentric in rating Cromwell an 'arrant coward'. By 3 June, when he set out for Newmarket, the Commons, as we shall see, were trying at almost any cost to conciliate the Army. If they had then provoked it by sending Cromwell to the Tower, it would have marched on London and held its armed rendezvous not at Newmarket but in Hyde Park.

Rapid though Cromwell's decisions were in the field, in politics his habit of postponement was notorious. In this business of the disbanding of the Army, it took him three months to make up his mind to resist. That his friends during the latter part of this time were pressing him to do so can be demonstrated. As we have seen already, the Independents both in the House and the City had been timid and unenterprising for some months before this Army crisis. Not even the persecution of the sectaries which Edwards had provoked could rouse them into militancy. Walwyn has left a record of their refusal to support two of the Levellers' petitions against this orgy of intolerance. But round about 20 May, when the 'large' petition of March was burned by the hangman, they plucked up courage and for a time co-operated with the Levellers. The Agitators congratulated themselves on the behaviour of 'our friends' in the two Houses when the final votes for disbanding were cast on 25 May. In the Commons they walked out; in the Lords they were beaten by only one vote.[49]

It is probable too that round about this time young Sir Harry Vane learned from his Presbyterian father some details of the plot in which Holles, Bellièvre, the Queen and the Scots were engaged to remove the King from Holmby and start the civil war anew. He would doubtless carry that news to Cromwell. Then we must take account of the letter of 1656 to Cromwell, in which the Protector's close friend Sir Gilbert Pickering is quoted for the statement ascribed to Cromwell himself, that he resisted the Agitators until he received the third of three warnings, that if he would not forthwith come and head them, they would go their own way without him. And so with 'much unwillingness' he did join them at their rendezvous.[50] Of the three warnings that have come down to us, two (as we have seen) were addressed to the officers as a body and the third to Fairfax. But it is quite likely that the Agitators may also have sent similar warnings of which we have no record to Cromwell personally.[51]

Ireton was probably one of the intimate friends who at last persuaded Cromwell to overcome his hesitations. By 1647, if not earlier, he had become the adviser to whose opinion in political matters the Lieut.-General usually deferred. Ireton was still in active service, at the head of his regiment; his was a quicker and more pliable mind than that of his father-in-law, and he may have been prompter to realise that the Army would follow the lead of the Agitators, whatever the Grandees might say or do. At the council of war on 29 May which advised Fairfax to order a rendezvous, his may have been the decisive voice. But it is probable that for some little time before this Ireton may have been in friendly contact with some of the Agitators, and that he acted as go-between between them and Cromwell. When he learned of their plans to send Joyce and his five hundred to Holmby, it may well have been he who arranged that Joyce should consult Cromwell in London before he rode to his first scene of operations, Oxford. The clash of temperaments and opinions between Ireton and the Levellers later in this year may have led them, in their retrospective polemics, to do less than justice to his behaviour in this crucial month of May.[52]

Obviously Cromwell, a retired officer without a commission, could not rejoin the Army without an invitation from its general. Now Fairfax, on the eve of the council of war, was in such perplexity that he wrote to Skippon begging that not very sagacious soldier to come and advise him. If he called for Skippon's help, is it not likely that he would also turn to his far more intimate associate, his Lieut.-General? And sure enough, among the Clarke MSS there is a letter written by a soldier in London on 1 June which begins thus:

> The greatest and newest news is, our General hath declared his resolution to own the Army in their just action, and hath sent for Lt.-Gen. Cromwell down to him. I hear he is going out of town this day.[53]

In other words Fairfax invited Cromwell to join him at the

rendezvous, and among the friends of the Agitators in town, it was expected that he would start even before he did.

Lastly, we have a record of a talk in Drury Lane between Cromwell and the ablest of the Leveller leaders. Walwyn unluckily gives no date, but from the references in the context to the various petitions of his group it is pretty clear that it must have taken place during these last ten days of May. After telling us that he was often in Cromwell's house about this time, he goes on:

> And the Lt.-General also knows upon what grounds I then persuaded him to divide from that body to which he was united; that if he did not, it would be his ruin and the ruin of the General and of all those worthies that had preserved us; that if he did do it in time he should not only preserve himself and them and all conscientious people, but he should do it without spilling one drop of blood; . . . and that I would undertake to demonstrate to him that it would be so; and so through God's goodness . . . it came to pass.[54]

The only obscurity in this revealing passage is the sense of the word 'body'. Does it mean the inert group of wealthy right-wing Independents—'the silken Independents' as Lilburne called them—or does it mean the Long Parliament? Here we meet Cromwell during his days of hesitation, when he shrank from resistance to Holles and his faction, lest he should provoke bloodshed. Was it Walwyn who persuaded him, or Ireton, or the tide of events that swept him along? With his approval or without it, Cornet Joyce would ride to Oxford and Holmby and the Army would rendezvous at Newmarket.

So far we have treated the activities of the Agitators as a spontaneous movement that sprang up among the spirited volunteers of the cavalry. When young men are cheated, threatened and insulted, they will react without a Cromwell to prompt them or a Lilburne. The mental climate of their day gave their movement its democratic colour, for most of them were sectaries; some were Anabaptists reared in an egalitarian tradition, and many had learned their politics from the pamphlets of Overton and Lilburne. But as we have seen, they kept in close touch with their friends in London and they relied on the

Leveller presses, until these were confiscated, to print their propaganda—for printing was costly in those days and these lads were poor. Was that all, or did they, aware of their inexperience, rely on the advice and information of the Leveller leaders—for, as we have seen, they were always well-informed?

Lilburne, in several passages that reek of his self-centred vanity, claimed that he inspired them and organised them from the start. A reproachful letter written to Cromwell from the Tower a few weeks after these events (1 July, 1647), complains that he could get no help from any of his former friends in the Commons against his unjust imprisonment by the Lords. He therefore applied himself with 'all the interest and industry he had in the world' and with 'the expense of a great deal of money' to 'the honest blades, the private soldiers' and in spite of 'much opposition from yourself and others of your fellow-Grandees in the Army', acting 'both night and day' through their 'faithful Agitators', he formed them into 'fit . . . instruments to effect my liberty, to give a check to tyranny and settle the peace and justice of the kingdom'.[55] In two similar letters which he addressed to Fairfax somewhat later (8 September, 1647), after quoting at length from his own pamphlets, he told the General that he could obtain copies of them all from Edward Sexby, thus confirming our guess that this brilliant ranker was the organiser of the Leveller group in the Army. Lilburne then repeated his story about the pains he took to win 'the private soldiery of your Army', since the officers were selfish, timorous and over-wise.[56]

Clearly it was not from Freeborn John that the Agitators derived the adroit yet gracious tactics which persuaded the officers for a time to follow the men's lead. It may have been their own decency that inspired these generous young men. But if they had any help from an older and wiser man—for Sexby in after life was able and enterprising but very far from wise—it came, one suspects, from William Walwyn. Behind the scenes at this turning point in the Revolution one catches an occasional glimpse of this shrewd yet kindly mind, a stranger to vanity and self-seeking, 'persuading' Cromwell and counselling the Agitators—of him and of Henry Marten. Among the papers found in the latter's desk, when the prisons of the Merry

Monarch swallowed his wit and his humanity, is a key to the cipher used by the Levellers after the entry of the Army into politics in 1647. It contains numerical symbols for the names of Marten, Overton, Walwyn and Wildman, but none for Lilburne. From his cell in the Tower went out many a charge of political dynamite in the shape of pamphlets, but he may have exaggerated his personal share in the shaping of events. However that may be, enough has come to light in recent years to compel a revision of the classical story of the Revolution. Not in ideas only but in action, the initiative during this critical phase came from the Levellers. They led the struggle against clericalism and intolerance; they challenged the ascendancy of Holles and his class; they set the Army marching.

The rest of the story has been familiar to most of us since our school-days. The best account of Joyce's ride to Holmby is from the pen of the Cornet himself.[57] Arriving on Wednesday in advance of the main body, he watched the King playing bowls with Colonel Graves, the Presbyterian who commanded the guard, and the Earl of Dunfermline, the emissary of the Scots war party; and his suspicion that these two had some sinister intention was confirmed. When his men reached Holmby House, the parliamentary commissioners sent one of their officers to enquire who was in command. His answer was that 'All did command yet were under command'. Then 'with the unanimous consent of the party'—that is to say, the detachment—he went in to interview the commissioners.

He and his men came [as he explained] to secure His Majesty's person and to protect the commissioners; there being a secret design . . . to convey or steal away the King and to raise another army to suppress this under H.E. Sir Thomas Fairfax. Likewise (he said) he knew no other way to keep the kingdom from blood or another war.

Meanwhile, the private soldiers of the guard fell on the necks of his troopers and admitted them to the house. With the consent of Major-General Browne, one of the commissioners, he set his guards.

As the next day wore on there came the disturbing news that Colonel Graves had 'gone quite away', and 'some of his damning blades did say and swear they would fetch a party'. Accordingly Joyce's five hundred all 'declared unanimously that they thought it most convenient to secure the King in another place.' So at 10 p.m. the soldiers sent Joyce to tell the commissioners that he must speak to the King. After a dispute which lasted half an hour, he was admitted to the bed-chamber, where the King was already in bed. 'With as much gentleness and tenderness as he could' he explained that the Presbyterians 'had a plan to break the Army in pieces . . . and to raise another to carry on their design'. The five hundred 'did desire to secure him from being taken away, lest he should be set at the head of another army'. Thereupon the King agreed to go with Joyce next morning if he would give certain undertakings, which the soldiery must confirm. He would even go 'willingly', for he found the air of Holmby bad for him, and would never wish to return. Joyce then promised that the King should suffer no hurt, nor be forced to anything against his conscience and that his servants—under which term he included his chaplains— should attend him.

The King appeared punctually at six o'clock next morning when the soldiers were ready mounted, and asked what commission Joyce had. After trying to dodge the question, the Cornet replied, 'The soldiery of the Army, or else I should not have dared to have done what I have.' The King, persisting, then asked if he had nothing in writing from General Fairfax. The Cornet then desired the King he would not ask him such questions. Then said the King: 'I pray [you] Mr Joyce deal ingenuously with me, and tell me what commission you have?' The Cornet answered: 'Here is my commission,' 'Where?' asked the King. 'Behind me,' Joyce replied, pointing to his troopers, and desired His Majesty that that might satisfy him. Whereupon the King smiled and said, 'It is as fair a commission and as well written as he had seen a commission in his life, a company of [as] handsome, proper gentlemen as he had seen a great while.'

After that joke—did he ever make another?—Charles remembered who he was. 'I am your King,' said he, 'and you ought not to lay hands on your King, for I acknowledge none to be above me here but God.' After this formal protest, he discussed with his escort where they should go. Joyce suggested first Oxford and then Cambridge, but the King did not like the climate of either. 'The air of Newmarket agreed with him well.' Thither on Friday afternoon they set out, while the King assured the troopers that he could ride 'as far as you or any man'.

One has the impression that Charles rather enjoyed this adventure; or was it that he foresaw the chance for new intrigues? Certainly he must have found Mr Joyce's personality congenial, for two weeks after this memorable ride, he sent a messenger to Headquarters to ask that the Cornet should return to Newmarket to keep him company.[58] To the end of the chapter that young democrat went on insisting that he had acted for his fellow-soldiers, who were 'more sensible than many thousands are, how destructive another war will be'. When some of the parliamentary commissioners declared that he ought to lose his head for treason he replied that unless at the rendezvous 'three in four parts approved what he had done, he was content to be hanged at the head of the Army'.

Fairfax heard with consternation of the ride of the five hundred, and promptly sent Colonel Whalley with his regiment of horse to meet the King and escort him back to Holmby. Charles, however, was determined never to see that place again, and he insisted on riding on to Newmarket, after pausing at Hinchinbrook and Childersley. At the latter place (on 7 June) he was visited with every courtesy by Fairfax, Cromwell, Ireton, Hammond and other 'Grandees' of the Army, who assured him (as Fairfax also assured the Speaker) that his removal had taken place 'without the desire or privity of the General, the officers round him and the body of the Army'.

Meanwhile, on Friday (4 June) the Army assembled for its rendezvous on the heath not far from Newmarket. The General rode from one regiment to another, allotting them their quarters and though he made one of his usual correct and loyal speeches, each received him with 'acclamations of joy' as he went past. Yet another 'humble representation', was presented to him, unanimously subscribed by the officers and soldiers. It recited all the old complaints and added two or three more. The miserable offer of eight weeks' pay would not suffice to set the men up again in their old callings, while the arrears due for service in previous armies were forgotten. They would, moreover, receive only half this nominal amount, since abatement was to be made on the assumption that they had enjoyed free quarter. But in fact both officers and men had often paid for their quarters from their own pockets. Again, it had formerly been customary to allow a trooper to keep his horse, even if it were not his own property; this traditional favour was now omitted. Nothing had been done for the maimed or for apprentices, nor had the right to petition been acknowledged. This able and eloquent document ended, though it mentioned no names, with a counter-attack on Holles and his colleagues. Were all its grievances met, the Army could have no security for the future till those who had wronged it were 'discovered and censured'. Once disbanded and dispersed, the soldiers could not feel safe, if these incendiaries, with 'their unjust principles and desperately tyrannical spirits', were to be their judges.

What the Army feared, with some reason, was a counter-revolutionary reign of terror, directed more especially against radical ex-soldiers and officers. One has to remember that Parliament exercised judicial functions, while in the counties both justice and administration were still mainly in Presbyterian hands.

The officers and Agitators did not know, when they handed this manifesto to the General, that parts of it, though not its conclusion, had become obsolete. The events of the last few days—the refusal of Fairfax's foot to disband, the retention of the siege train at Oxford, the capture of the King by Cornet Joyce's five hundred, the rebellious rendezvous at Newmarket —these coming in breathless succession had shattered the complacency of the Long Parliament. Its reaction was as usual tardy, incompetent and contradictory, but its first impulse was on the whole to placate the Army. After a stormy sitting which ran on into the small hours of Friday, 4 June, the Commons decided by 96 votes to 79 to 'raise' from their Journal Holles's Declaration of 30 March, which put 'a band of ignominy' on the Army: they asked the Lords to 'race' it also, which was done. They decided, at last, that the privates and non-commissioned officers should receive all their arrears, subject to

H

deduction for free quarter. Commissioned officers, however, would receive their arrears for three months only (an addition of one month to the previous offer) and the rest in debentures. Here, then, was the discrimination which the Agitators had been led to expect. Where all this money was to come from was far from clear, though an additional £10,000 was voted.

Some further provisions for the benefit of officers throw a grim light on the habits of this century.[59] Officers attending the Committee of Accounts were to be protected from arrest for debt for a period not exceeding two months. Officers already in prison for debt should be the first to have their accounts audited and paid. It was not pure evangelical charity that inspired these merciful ordinances. Parliament was anxious to secure the good will of the 'reformadoes' (officers disbanded from the armies of Essex, Waller and Massey) who were clamouring round its doors for their arrears, and to induce the Presbyterian officers of the New Model to desert. Out of these it hoped to form a politically reliable army. Money and thanks were especially voted to two Presbyterian colonels, Richard Graves and Sir Robert Pye, who quitted the rebel army with a few of their men. On Friday as Captain Titus, riding hard from Holmby, brought news of the coming of a party of horse 'to remove the King', a 'more copious' and better drafted ordinance of indemnity received its second reading. A month or so earlier these ambiguous measures might have had some success. Shouting for joy in its re-union at Newmarket, the Army could neither be divided nor appeased.

Cromwell seems to have reached the rendezvous on Friday evening. He at once resumed his post as Lieut.-General—and something more. At his coming a momentous step was taken which tradition ascribes to him, though it is more likely that he and Ireton devised it together. The whole Army was bent on taking a pledge not to disband piecemeal, nor to volunteer for Ireland, until all their claims were met to the satisfaction of them all. That, indeed, was the purpose of the rendezvous. But a gathering of twenty thousand men could not deliberate; still less could they negotiate, if it should come to negotiation. The soldiers already had their representatives, the Agitators. It would seem a natural step that the regimental officers also should elect their representatives; and this was now done, evidently during the first week of June, following the pattern set by the men, first in the horse and then in the foot—two officers for each regiment. Finally, there were the general officers. They could not be left out. Men and officers during these mid-summer days were celebrating their honeymoon of 'unanimity'. No one was so pedantic as to criticise this unequal scheme of representation. Here for the first time in history was a Council of the Army, in which the men had a voice. For the moment what they and their officers wanted to say differed only by shades of emphasis. They could all shout 'No' in unison against Denzil Holles; their differences were to begin only when the Army first proposed and then imposed a settlement.

The pledge and the scheme of representation as they emerged under the influence of Ireton's subtle intellect and Cromwell's shrewd intuition are set out in *A Solemn Engagement of the Army* which the massed regiments unanimously adopted at New-market on 5 June, 1647.[60] This verbose document with its legalistic phrasing came from Ireton's pen. 'We shall not willingly disband nor divide, nor suffer ourselves to be dis-banded or divided', so ran its pledge, until the grievances of the Army shall be redressed and security obtained against such 'oppression, injury or abuse as in the premises hath been attempted and put upon us while an army, by the same men's continuance in the same credit and power (especially if as our judges)'. It then provided a Council which must reach agree-ment by majority vote concerning 'satisfaction and security'. This should be composed of 'those general officers of the Army who had concurred with the Army in the premises', together with two officers and two soldiers chosen by each regiment. It lay with the General to call the Council, and—a point im-portant in the sequel—with him alone.

The Newmarket *Engagement* dealt only with the Army's grievances and security; it did not touch on political questions. But its clumsy prose came near to revealing the sub-conscious will to power of its authors. They avowed their resolve to depose Holles and his group from 'credit and power'. But they would have denied with great vehemence any suggestion that they themselves intended to seize power. At this stage of the Revolution—the contemporary name for it was 'reformation' —what they believed they wanted and were preparing was a free election—strange as this may seem.

Sitting, contrary to all its Puritan habits, on the Lord's Day (6 June), Parliament completed its work of appeasement by ordering that its votes for the erasure from its records of its censure of the Army and its new offers of back pay should be published. What is more, it chose yet another delegation to go down to the Army in the hope of inducing it to accept the new terms; among its new commissioners was the most distinguished of the 'silken Independents', Sir Harry Vane. It was, however, buying support in other directions also. It had, to be sure, voted that extra £10,000 for the New Model, but it voted the same amount to satisfy the clamouring 'reformadoes', and yet another £10,000 for the army it was collecting at Worcester for a campaign in Ireland—or, it might be, nearer home. It made the apprentices happy by offering them a holiday on the first Tuesday of every month, to compensate them for the idolatrous festivals it had forbidden. After a riot at Smithfield it sought the good will of the average householder and his wife by exempting meat and salt from the detested excise. It even thought of placating its critics by taking into consideration a new Self-Denying Ordinance which would deprive members of most of their financial perquisites and privileges until its debts were paid.

To Parliament in its hour of need the oligarchy of the City rallied with its customary fidelity. It presented a petition from the Lord Mayor and Common Council begging the Houses so to dispose of the King that it should have free access to him, thus assuring peace to 'this tottering church and kingdom'. Further it asked for the revival of an ordinance of 1645, which empowered it to raise a force of cavalry and requisition mounts for it. On the defensive, the train-bands were an infantry not to be despised; did the City fathers imagine that they could improvise a body of horse fit to meet the Ironsides? The Commons snatched at the offer and consented.

Next Thursday (10 June) the second of the Army's historic reviews was held on the flat ground of Triploe Heath, between

Cambridge and Royston. The General with the Parliament's commissioners rode round the assembled regiments, which were for Rushworth's practised eyes 'a very gallant body'. The latest of Parliament's votes were read out first of all to Fairfax's horse and Skippon, now a Field Marshal, made a speech commending them. An officer then replied (obviously by arrangement) that the new offer should be referred to select officers and Agitators. The troopers shouted their assent—'All, all', and then (as the commissioners rode away) 'Justice, justice'. When the General asked 'Any against?' there were none to say 'No'. The Agitators would have preferred to have the question decided on the spot, but though (as we are told) the regiment would have been unanimous in rejecting the new terms, it agreed to adopt the more orderly method. The same procedure was followed with each of the assembled regiments, and so in the end the whole issue was referred to the new Council of the Army. That done, the Army marched towards Royston— on the road to London.[61]

At Royston began a new phase of its struggle for 'credit and power'. Somewhere thereabouts ran its river Rubicon. With Cromwell once more at its head, it crossed it. From Royston it issued its defiance; but with a regard for the proprieties characteristic of this very English revolution, its challenge was indirect. Its threat was addressed not to Parliament but to the City of London. Nor was it precisely a threat. It might be described as a conditional promise of safety. But only a very stupid citizen could fail to understand its meaning: 'If you go on preparing resistance, we shall sack the City.'

Carlyle, who should have known the ring of his hero's voice, ascribed this letter on grounds of style to Cromwell; in any case it spoke his mind.[62] His signature (under that of Fairfax and above those of Hammond, Ireton and nine colonels) may well have seemed a portent to the Lord Mayor, aldermen and Common Council, to whom it was addressed. It threw over the profession which the officers had first maintained, that soldiers have a right to be heard only about 'soldiers' matters'. The officers now reminded the City that though soldiers, they still were Englishmen. Having finished the war, they had as much right as any to demand a happy

settlement. This is what Sexby and the Agitators had maintained from the start. Now even Cromwell fell into line.

The Army had no desire to meddle with the Presbyterian
settlement, or to open a way to licentious liberty under pretence
of obtaining ease for tender consciences. It would submit—
so the letter declared—to whatever settlement the state may
make,

> only we could wish that every good citizen and every man
> that walks peaceably in a blameless conversation and is
> beneficial to the commonwealth may have liberty and
> encouragement.
>
> For the obtaining of these things we are drawing near your
> city. . . . If you appear not against us in these our just
> desires to assist that wicked party that would embroil us and
> the kingdom, nor we nor our soldiers shall give you the
> least offence.

As soon as a speedy settlement is in hand, it went on, the Army
would disband or enlist for Ireland. 'A rich city may seem an
enticing bait to poor, hungry soldiers', but 'if not provoked by
you', they would have to 'make their way through our blood'
to gain their ends. Most of them, however, 'value their pay'
but little 'in comparison of higher concernments to a public
good. . . .'

> It's not your wealth they seek . . . [But] if you be seduced to
> take up arms in opposition to our just undertakings, we hope
> by this brotherly premonition . . . we have freed ourselves
> from all that ruin which may befall that great and populous
> city, having thereby washed our hands thereof.

This was not a wise letter. When Cromwell, after long hesitation, did make up his mind, there was apt to be an explosion.
Characteristic also of him is the implication that what chiefly
mattered in the settlement was liberty of conscience, albeit
only for those 'beneficial to the commonwealth'. This, one
need hardly insist, was not the Levellers' concept of toleration
in a secular republic.

Happy that it had regained its unity and its trusted leaders,
the Army marched steadily on through Royston to St Albans,
confident now that it could dictate a settlement. Dreaming at

first of resistance, Parliament sat to all hours on weekdays, assembled after the afternoon sermon on Sunday, and set up a Committee of Safety empowered to raise horse and foot in co-operation with the City's militia, from whose officer corps all sectaries had already been purged. It even tried to bribe Fairfax's men to desert. Bellicose at first, the City oligarchy by beat of drum summoned every man to join his train-band on pain of death. The masses would not obey. The street boys laughed at the drummers and after some companies had counted ten men in the ranks and others none at all, the few who did assemble were dismissed.

After this experience of the temper of the citizens, the Common Council, with the approval of Parliament, sent an apologetic reply to the Army's letter, which was carried in great style in three coaches by a pompous deputation to Headquarters at St Albans. Walwyn in the short run had been right, when he told Cromwell that there would be no bloodshed if he threw in his lot with the left. The City promised that it would not raise forces against the New Model. Parliament ordered the Army not to approach within forty miles. The City was modest and begged it to keep at a distance of thirty, lest it should cause a food shortage. There was, in any case, in this unfriendly year not enough for man and beast. St Albans is 20 miles from the City's centre and there for the time being the Army meant to stay: it undertook to give notice, if it should see fit to come nearer—as it soon did. Parliament for the moment could think of nothing better than to send yet another delegation, which set out from Westminster with a haste that looks panic-stricken, at 3 a.m. on 13 June to enquire what the Army really wanted.

What did the Army want? For several days its best brains had been trying to answer that question. Posterity has the result of its reflections and debates in the *Representation of the Army*, dated 14 June. Whether it was debated by the new Council of the Army in advance at Royston, or in its final shape in the choir of the great Abbey at St Albans, we do not know.[63] The Clarke manuscripts which tell us so much about the origin of other state papers that issued from the Army are silent about this document. All we do know is that the Agitators were as active at St Albans as they had been at Saffron Walden. The new group of officer-agitators justified its existence by sending a letter to Trinity House in which it asked the navy to join the Army in its stand for justice—an appeal which failed to move the seamen, who lagged far behind the soldiers in the speed and independence of their thinking. Once more we come across the jubilant assurance that the unanimity between officers and soldiers was 'to be admired'.[64]

In this atmosphere the task of drafting the *Representation* fell to Ireton. It was, indeed, the first of three historic state papers that came from his pen—the others were the *Heads of the Proposals* (1 August, 1647) and the lengthy *Remonstrance* (16 November, 1648). How did he set about such a task? One might suppose from the pages of some of the older historians, that he sat down at his desk to compose the document and then handed it to the printer without more ado. The cult of the great man and the long shadow of the Hero lay all over the nineteenth century. Such documents spring from the social life of their time. Behind them are the 'many thousands' of craftsmen and peasants who found their spokesmen in Walwyn, Overton and Lilburne; then their employers whose ears were attuned to the pulpits of the Independent chapels, and it may be a few of the less cautious lawyers, with all the friction and suspicion that normally separated these groups and the sudden ardour of revolutionary resistance that could for a moment unite them.

If Ireton was an able draftsman (which he was), his success was due not to any literary talent (for his style was heavy and longwinded), but to his skill in devising a compromise which took account of views and interests far removed from his own and yet contrived to give to the resulting programme the shape and spirit of coherent thinking. He was not a popular, and may have been an unsociable man. The Levellers did not really dislike Cromwell, even after they began to distrust and oppose him, but they thought 'Prince Ireton' imperious and arrogant. It was his intimates like Ludlow and Hugh Peters who learned to value him for his honesty and public spirit. His political outlook was curiously similar to that of an early Victorian

Whig gentleman; while the Levellers with whom he had to reach some compromise were Chartists born before their time. His was a trained legal mind which liked to find for all human relations a basis in contract: the faith of the Levellers in reason and nature irritated and alarmed him. None the less, this man of property tried hard to reach a working agreement with his congenital opponents.

We may conjecture that if we had the records we should find that in June some such committee was at work on this *Representation* as elaborated the *Heads of the Proposals* in July. Doubtless in that century as in ours some committees were lazy and others vigilant. An alert committee first agrees on the substance of a document, and then after the draftsman has put its findings into shape, as a basis of discussion, revises his work clause by clause. The chances are that the Agitators were vigilant; they represented a movement in which 'all did command yet were under command'. Several of the officers—that unflinching idealist Harrison was one of them—had learned some law at one of the Inns of Court and would be critical even of the form of Ireton's draft. Lambert, who shared with Ireton the responsibility for drafting the *Heads of the Proposals*,[65] was interested in constitutional law and was in 1653 himself the draftsman of the first written constitution ever adopted in this island, the *Instrument of Government*.

As for the Levellers, Rainsborough, evidently an irascible character and the leader of the mutiny at Ware, was not the man to submit to dictation from Ireton or anyone else. Edward Sexby, as we shall see, was bold enough to criticise Cromwell's conduct to his face, at a public meeting in Putney church. The Leveller ideas would reach Ireton by several channels. He may have read some of the pamphlets of the movement; while at Westminster he may have listened to Henry Marten, a brilliant talker; in the field he may have disputed with Rainsborough. Finally, there was Hugh Peters, the born go-between and reconciler, himself a man of the moderate left, who was always running to and fro between the Levellers and the Grandees. We know that he was at Newmarket this June, and at Windsor with Ireton when he wrote the *Remonstrance*. In any event, however they got there, the ideas of the Levellers, phrased in their own language, stand up plain to read in the Army's *Representation*.

Unlike the earlier documents, this *Representation* is addressed without any pretences directly to Parliament. The material grievances of the Army are mentioned only in passing, but the Agitators' accusation that Holles, Waller, Massey, and the rest of the eleven leading Presbyterians were not really raising forces for Ireland, is officially adopted. After 'breaking this Army' they mean to raise 'other forces and of such a temper as might serve to some desperate and destructive designs in England'. They were named not in the *Representation* itself, but in a sort of postscript of the same date. This document, then, is frankly political. Its authors excuse their intrusion into this field by the reminder that

> We were not a mere mercenary army, hired to serve any arbitrary power of a state, but called forth and conjured by the several declarations of Parliament to the defence of our own and the people's just rights and liberties. And so we took up arms in judgment and conscience to those ends.

They justify their opposition to men who would 'put the kingdom into a new flame of war' as the Leveller pamphleteers had done, but citing arguments and precedents for rebellion drawn from Scotland and the Netherlands. 'All authority,'— Lilburne and Overton had said the same thing in similar words—'is fundamentally seated in the office and but ministerially in the persons'. This is a way of saying that members of Parliament, like all magistrates, are trustees, who should be removed if they betray their trust. Two practical conclusions follow. Firstly the House should be purged of members who on the grounds of corruption, delinquency or undue election ought not to sit there. Secondly, those members who lately wronged the Army must be 'disabled from doing the like or worse to us when disbanded . . . or to other the free-born people of England'.

The paragraph that follows strikes an entirely new note, out of tune with the Leveller music. To avoid the appearance of faction or partisanship, the Army will state its demand in general terms:

We cannot but wish that such men and such only might be preferred to the great power and trust of the commonwealth, as are approved at least for moral righteousness, and of such we cannot but in our wishes prefer those that appear acted thereunto by a principle of conscience and religion in them.

To such worthies, the authors continue, 'those beginnings of a just reformation' are due, which the Long Parliament achieved in its early days.

The modern reader will go astray if he mistakes this aspiration for a harmless commonplace. It is no doubt desirable that good rather than bad men should fill the House. What the authors of this paragraph mean, however, is that the House should be manned by Puritans, and those preferably of the 'godly' party. The next step in this reasoning is, of course, that measures should be taken to exclude the unrighteous and the ungodly. With another brief step we are in a totalitarian climate, fatal to anything but a one-party Parliament. How that was reached we need not anticipate here—purging, nomination and tests were the three means actually applied by the Army to make sure that members should all be 'persons of known integrity, fearing God and not scandalous in their conversation'. We are getting near to the enthusiasm of the Fifth Monarchists and their claim that only the Saints shall rule in the name of King Jesus.

How much of this perilous principle the Agitators or the Grandees intended to endorse one cannot be sure. The chances are that few of them would have assented to its extremer consequences—as yet. Rainsborough and Sexby would have dissented. If Levellers ever called for a purge, it was not in the name of morality and religion. Amongst the Grandees Harrison and Rich were soon to travel the whole road to Fifth Monarchism, and for a time Cromwell was arm in arm with them. (See pp. 634-7 below.)

After this vagary, the authors of the *Representation*, unconscious of any inconsistency, move on to a bold profession of democratic faith. Their aim is not to further any particular group devoted to their own opinions or principles. Their aim is rather that 'hopes of justice and righteousness' shall 'flow down equally to all in . . . its ancient channel'. Parliament must be so constituted that it offers to all the possibility that 'if they have made an ill choice at one time, they may mend it at another'. Then in a few tightly packed sentences they adopt as their own the revolutionary doctrine of the Leveller petition which the hangman had just burned—the sovereignty of the people and the supremacy of the House of Commons, entrusted as it is with the 'supreme power . . . of final judgments'. In these words they must have meant to reject the 'negative voices' and vetoes of King and House of Lords. It is, moreover, 'a mere tyranny that the same men should sit during life or at their own pleasure. . . . The people have a right to new and successive elections unto that great and supreme trust at certain periods of time.' Accordingly the Army follows the Levellers in demanding that the Long Parliament shall fix a date for its own dissolution, and a term for all future Parliaments, which must neither be dissolved at the King's pleasure, nor prolonged at their own.

In its next demand, the Army leapt over two centuries and anticipated the reforms of 1832. It called for the disfranchisement of 'decayed and inconsiderable towns' and a redistribution of seats 'proportionable to the respective rates they bear in the common charges and burdens of the kingdom'. No research is needed to determine the source of these paragraphs. They came almost word for word out of John Lilburne's *London's Liberty in Chains* which he wrote in the Tower in October 1646.[66]

Leveller influence is equally obvious in a clause that stresses the right to petition and demands justice and reparation for the prisoners irregularly condemned. The call for a check on the extravagant expenditure of Parliament and an audit of 'the vast sums that have been levied and paid' would find an echo far outside the ranks of the left. The restoration of the King is mentioned briefly, as a matter of course. 'The rights of His Majesty and his posterity' must be 'considered and settled . . . so far as may consist with the right and freedom of the subject.'

Not for the first nor the last time in history the soldiers were more generous than the politicians. The modern reader in going over the peace terms, the Nineteen Propositions which the Presbyterian majority sent to the King at Newcastle, is startled by the greed and brutality that inspired its attitude to the beaten

Royalists. What the Army wanted was conciliation and the healing of old sores. Ireton's was a shrewd and calculating brain, and he may have argued that if the Army with the help of the Levellers had to carry on a difficult struggle with the Presbyterians and the Scots, it might be wise to buy the neutrality, if not the positive good will of the Cavaliers. In this triangular or quadrangular duel several alternative combinations were possible. But this Army, even more than most armies, had an instinctive collective consciousness, a group mind, which felt in this way towards the enemy it had beaten. The old fashioned name for this state of mind was magnanimity or chivalry; we moderns with our tendency to belittle, call it sportsmanship. Cornet Joyce was not ashamed to say that he showed 'gentleness and tenderness' to the fallen King.

Aloof and introverted though he may have been, Ireton was none the less the articulate voice of the simple, hard-riding lads around him. 'When the Army was in their greatest glory and the enemy under their feet' (so Rushworth, the Army's secretary, put it a few weeeks later) 'yet we were ever humane and Christian to them, and now, being so near a reconciliation, we should not show any aversion or indisposition.'[67] It was determined that there should be no more executions or confiscations, though a few of the King's most disastrous councillors would have to remain in exile. For the rest, the *Representation* proposed that there should be a

general act of oblivion . . . whereby the seeds of future war or feuds, either to the present age or posterity, may the better be taken away, by easing that sense of present and satisfying those fears of future ruin or undoing to persons or families which may drive men into any desperate ways for self-preservation and remedy.

From the standpoint of posterity the conclusion of this document is disappointing, though it was of all its clauses the nearest to Cromwell's heart. In it, not for the first time, the Army disavows 'any design to overthrow presbytery or hinder the settlement thereof and to have the Independent [church-] government set up'. It continues in the same modest vein:

We only desire that according to the declarations promising

a privilege for tender consciences, there may be some effectual course taken, according to the intent thereof, and that such who upon conscientious grounds may differ from the established forms may not for that be debarred from the common rights, liberties or benefits belonging equally to all as men and members of the commonwealth, while they live soberly, honestly, inoffensively towards others and peacefully and faithfully towards the state.

Tactically there may once have been some prudent arguments in favour of this approach, which dated from the time when the Independents were a timid and cautious minority in the House, who did not dare to call on the Army for support. It accepts Presbyterianism as the established Church of England with its tithes and its discipline, and is content to plead that by way of exception a sectarian minority may have liberty of conscience. With the Army's support the Independents might now have ventured to say, with the Levellers, that the religious beliefs and observances of the individual or associated citizens are no concern of the magistrate. But as we shall see, Ireton in particular stubbornly refused to adopt this position. The Independents sought toleration for themselves, and in Old England for other Calvinists also, but unlike the Anabaptists, they did not proclaim it as a general principle. When in New England and more especially in Massachusetts, they were the masters, they tolerated no creed but their own, not even that of the Anabaptists or the Quakers.

Such then was the compromise by which Ireton aimed at uniting the Army and the civilian left. For a short time it succeeded. From the Levellers he boldly took over the sovereignty of the people, the supremacy of the Commons and the beginnings of parliamentary reform. Both soldiers and civilian radicals would accept his gesture of conciliation to the Cavaliers and in its substance his plea for liberty of conscience. It was not till late autumn that the dispute over manhood suffrage broke up the alliance.

The eyes of posterity turn naturally to these questions of principle, for with them the foundations of the Atlantic civilisation were well and truly laid. For contemporaries what mattered more was doubtless the decision formally taken at St Albans in mid-June to do what the Agitators first suggested in April—to purge Parliament of the ruling Presbyterian group. And that also was important, for it was the first long step in the seizure of power, which Pride's Purge completed.

With the revolt of the Army and the principles it proclaimed a new class emerged in English politics. So long as the private soldiers had swords in their hands and Agitators from their own ranks to lead them, their brothers the craftsmen and peasants counted for something in the balance of power. For it was they who made this revolt. The Grandees did, to be sure, grace it with their approval after it had succeeded; in the long run they distorted and destroyed it by the Puritan fascism at which Ireton in this manifesto was the first to hint. Lilburne lay in the Tower while the Army fixed its headquarters at St Albans. But it was he and Walwyn who led it unseen, while Fairfax and Cromwell—reluctantly as they afterwards confessed—rode at its head. The 'silken Independents' were too prosperous and too cautious—or shall we say too scrupulous? —to revolt against the Long Parliament. But for the Levellers and the Agitators and the craftsmen and peasants behind them, Denzil Holles would have achieved his counter-revolution. A Presbyterian reign of terror would have driven the Saints to New England and Charles Stuart would have returned to Whitehall with his crown precariously poised upon his comely head.

NOTES TO CHAPTER X

1. *The English Soldiers' Standard to repair to for Wisdom and Understanding* (5 April, 1649).

2. As far back as November 1644 the Scottish commissioners took counsel with their English Presbyterian friends in Essex's house, to discover a legal device by which Cromwell might be dealt with as an 'incendiary'. They had in view either his exile or his execution (Rushworth, VI, p. 2).

3. Holles, *Memoirs*, p. 81.

4. The eldest of the three Lilburne brothers, who owed his commission to John's influence, and like him was an Anabaptist, was a competent though not brilliant professional soldier, who stuck closely to Cromwell in his politics. Judging from the behaviour of his regiment at this time, and again at Ware in November, he cannot have had any great influence over his men.

5. Holles, *Memoirs*, pp. 136-7.

6. H. Cary, *Memorials of the Great Civil War*, I, p. 234.

7. Rushworth, VI, p. 470. See also the *Second Apology of all the private Soldiers* in *Declaration* (p. 10, margin), which mentions similar cases at Northampton, Warwick, Aylesbury and Salisbury.

8. *The Vindication of the Officers*, Rushworth, VI, p. 469.

9. The five clauses are in *C.P.*, I, p. xi. Firth describes it as the officers' petition, but they themselves in the passage just quoted from their *Vindication* said that 'the petition took its first rise from amongst the soldiers'. For the full text, see *Declaration* (p. 1) which describes it as a petition of the officers and soldiers, and makes it clear that they expected Fairfax to present it to Parliament.

10. The sheet reached Thomason in London on 26 March, and may have been printed a few days earlier. Professor Woodhouse was the first to call attention to it (p. 21, note).

11. Reprinted in Cary, *op. cit.*, I, p. 149. It seems from Holles's *Memoirs* that he never actually received the £5,000 because the House decided to postpone the payment of all grants to members till its debts were paid. The fact remains that Holles did put in a claim to this compensation.

12. Holles, *Memoirs*, pp. 15-17, 11.

13. *Ibid.*, pp. 1, 8.

14. *Ibid.*, pp. 30, 149.

15. *Ibid.*, pp. 77-90, 152.

16. Rushworth, VI, pp. 446-7.

17. *Ibid.*, pp. 445, 447.

18. *Ibid.*, p. 468.

19. According to a contemporary newsletter the gossip among the troopers of Ireton's horse foresaw that this deputation would probably be arrested, whereupon the Army would lay siege to London (M. James and M. Weinstock, *England during the Interregnum*, pp. 56-7).

20. The Leveller movement was never strong in the fleet, but there is a curious petition to the Commons signed by a vice-admiral, ten captains and fifteen others, printed in *The Remonstrance of the Navy* (5 February, 1649). It complains of poor victuals, low pay and the appointment of officers by 'bribery, parasitism and lordly favour'. It asks for the 'yearly election' of all officers of the fleet. Another petition in the same sheet, from Captain Richard Brooke and other sea-captains, is addressed to Fairfax and the Council of the Army. The signatories wanted closer relations between army and navy, and remarked that 'one of the sweetest flowers in the chaplet of liberty is *jus suffragii*'. Some of these officers supported Vice-Admiral Lawson when he conspired with Colonel Overton against the Protectorate.

21. Rushworth, VI, pp. 468, 485.

22. The whole letter is in Cary, *op. cit.*, I, p. 201.

23. I have combined two reports, *C.P.*, I, p. 430, and Rushworth, VI, p. 474.

24. *A Faithful Memorial*, etc., in *Somers Tracts*, VI, p. 498. Allen also wrote a brief epilogue to an edition of *Killing No Murder* published after

both Cromwell and Sexby were dead. He agrees with the case for assassinating tyrants, but adds the important qualification that you should not kill one tyrant in order to set up another—meaning presumably Charles II. In identifying Allen, I have followed Abbott (III, p. 605) rather than Carlyle (Letter CXCVII). Firth (*C.P.*, I, p. 79) shows that two more among the sixteen Agitators of the horse were rebels against the Protectorate in 1655, Brayman, then a Lieutenant, and William Prior.

25. The fact that Sexby signs first among the sixteen Agitators is no proof of authorship or of leadership. He would have precedence as a representative of the General's regiment.

26. *Declaration*, pp. 17-21.

27. Woodhouse, p. 399.

28. *C.P.*, I, p. 72.

29. *Declaration*, p. 9; Woodhouse, pp. 396-8.

30. Chillenden, however, must have been an unsteady character. He collaborated with Lilburne in smuggling prohibited pamphlets out of Holland, but, if we may believe John, he saved himself by disclosing his comrade's name. John, however (by his own account), forgave him, and in Oxford prison lent him money, which he never repaid. He seems to have abandoned the Agitators and gone over to the Grandees in the autumn of this year, for at Ware in November he acted as the military policeman who arrested some of the rebels. On leaving the Army he became the 'teacher' of a Baptist congregation. The Levellers carried on a feud with him and on one occasion attacked his chapel. But in the early days of the Agitators' movement he was an active and enthusiastic supporter of their cause.

31. *C.P.*, I, p. 22; Woodhouse, p. 398.

32. *C.P.*, I, p. 25, from a narrative dated Walden, 5 May.

33. Rushworth, VI, pp. 447, 451.

34. *Ibid.*, p. 520. This petition was presented to the General at the rendezvous on Triploe Heath.

35. *Ibid.*, pp. 552, 559, 601, 575-6.

36. C. Walker, *History of Independency*, Part I, p. 59.

37. *C.P.*, I, pp. 84-6.

38. Walker, *op. cit.*, Part I, p. 31.

39. See for example *C.P.*, I, p. 27, and Rushworth, VI, p. 479, where a high magistrate, the sheriff of Kent, guilty of a gross case of persecution of this kind, was very severely punished.

40. The text of this brief document is to be found in full with the signatures in *Declaration*, p. 16, or without the signatures in Rushworth, VI, p. 498.

41. *Declaration*, p. 12. I have given in full the evidence for the Agitators' initiative in the Army revolt, because it has been so strangely ignored by the classical historians. Gardiner was the most scrupulous of men, yet one might almost suppose that he turned away deliberately from this evidence. In his *History of the Great Civil War* (III, p. 262) he refers to the Agitators' petition to Fairfax and even quotes from it, but makes no mention of its real purpose—the warning that unless he ordered a rendezvous of the Army, they would do so themselves. Again he reports the recommendation of the council of war to call this rendezvous, with no mention of the fact that they

had the Agitators' warning before them, and based their decision on the 'propensity' of the soldiers for such a meeting. By repeated failures of this kind to notice something which clashed with his own views, Gardiner's whole story of the revolt is distorted. One notices such slips with charity and self-questioning. Am I too—are we all—in our own way equally blind?

42. *C.P.*, I, p. 106.

43. I am indebted for this and other details to Hugh Ross Williamson's able study of Rainsborough in his *Four Stuart Portraits*.

44. *C.P.*, I, pp. 106, 83.

45. Cary, *op. cit.*, I, pp. 221-2.

46. I have not thought it necessary to examine Godwin's interpretation of these events in detail, since he had neither the *Clarke Papers* nor all of the Leveller pamphlets before him. He suggests that Cromwell managed the Agitators through one of his favourites, Captain Berry, who eventually rose to be a major-general. He is described as chairman of the Agitators' Council. Colonel Wogan told a similar story, but he pitched on Captain Reynolds (also a favourite of Cromwell's who was eventually knighted) as chairman (*C.P.*, I, p. 426). There is, however, no evidence in the documents that either of these officers was active in the movement, until the officers elected agitators of their own early in June.

47. *Jonah's Cry out of the Whale's Belly* (26 July, 1647).

48. *Putney Projects*, quoted by Firth, *C.P.*, I, p. xix. Wildman was, however, certainly mistaken when he made the same statement about Ireton's as about Cromwell's commission. The Self-Denying Ordinance did not apply to Ireton, who was not a member when it was passed. He was actively engaged in the Army between March and June, as Cromwell was not.

49. *Walwyn's Just Defence*, H. and D., p. 356; *C.P.*, I, p. 112.

50. The evidence as to Vane and Pickering is quoted in Gardiner, *Great Civil War*, III, p. 264 n.

51. That the Agitators did latterly have some communication with Cromwell we know from the puzzling letter in the *Clarke Papers* (I, p. 24) dated London 5 May, which Firth ascribes to Sexby. This ascription seems to me doubtful. But the writer, whoever he was, was one of the inner Leveller and Agitator group, who used their cipher. He writes: 'I pray you tell Lt.-Gen. Cromwell that all our friends do hope the Army may be well united by this meeting (horse and foot).' Evidently Cromwell was now in touch with the group and was ready to back them in their professional demands only. Accordingly the writer advises: 'and for this time let them demand nothing but what is relating to them as soldiers'.

52. This would be even clearer if we could accept with confidence Firth's ascription to Ireton of a deeply interesting letter among the *Clarke Papers* (I, p. 101). The names both of the writer and the person he addressed are missing, and the date (25 May, 1647) cannot be correct. All that is clear is that it was written by someone of influence or authority in the Army to someone of influence in Parliament. The writer dreads the consequences of 'disobliging so faithful an Army', says that it shall be his 'endeavour to keep things as right' as he can, but doubts how long he can succeed. 'Unless you proceed upon better principles', he concludes, 'I cannot but imagine a

storm.' Firth believes that it was written on 27 May by Ireton to Cromwell. This may be one of his usually sure and brilliant guesses, but I see two difficulties. (1) Would Ireton address his father-in-law in this rather formal style, as if he were a public meeting? (2) Would he speak of the Commons with such complete detachment as 'you', as if he had forgotten that he was himself a member? Conceivably the writer may have been Hugh Peters, though I cannot prove that in the spring of 1647 he was spending most of his time with the Army. He was, as we know, with Cromwell in London on 3 June.

53. *C.P.*, I, pp. 106, xxv.

54. *Walwyn's Just Defence*, in H. and D., p. 358. This tract, which has survived only in American libraries, was not available to Firth and Gardiner.

55. *Jonah's Cry out of the Whale's Belly*, pp. 8-9.

56. *The Jugglers Discovered* (28 September, 1647).

57. Rushworth, VI, pp. 513-17; *A true impartial narration, concerning the Army's preservation of the King* (4 June, 1647). This account starts like a collective manifesto from the Agitators and then almost imperceptibly becomes a personal narrative. The two versions are not exactly identical. The conclusion also is a collective exhortation.

58. Rushworth, VI, p. 578.

59. *Ibid.*, p. 501.

60. Woodhouse, pp. 401-3.

61. Rushworth, VI, p. 556.

62. Ed. S. C. Lomas, Carlyle's *Letters and Speeches of Oliver Cromwell*, I, pp. 255-73.

63. If it were submitted first as a printed proof to the Council at Royston that might explain why the two versions of it known to us differ substantially. The version printed at Cambridge contains the important portions of paragraphs IV and V dealing with 'decayed' towns and the redistribution of seats. The version printed in London (in *Declaration*, which Rushworth reproduces) omits them. This might be due to an accidental error of the printer, but it occurs to me that someone, perhaps Fairfax, may have objected to this reform before the document was adopted at St Albans and printed in London. This is the more likely because the London version, presumably for geographical reasons the later of the two, contains (as the Cambridge edition also does) in paragraph V the phrase 'common and equal right'. The word equal has no justification apart from the omitted paragraphs. I argue therefore that they were in the first draft. Rushworth or his clerk when sending them to the London printer forgot to delete this consequential phrase (see Woodhouse, pp. 403-9 and Rushworth, VI, pp. 564-70.)

64. Cary, *op. cit.*, I, p. 237; Rushworth, VI, p. 578.

65. *C.P.*, I, p. 197 n.

66. During the Putney Debates Ireton claimed with justice that no one in the Army had been before him in advocating the reform of Parliament, particularly in the matter of the more equal distribution of seats; but he claimed no priority outside the Army (*C.P.*, I, p. 333; Woodhouse, p. 77).

67. *C.P.*, I, p. 216 (17 July).

CHAPTER XI

The Army's Bid for Peace

The two months that followed the march of the New Model to St Albans were spent in manœuvres which decided nothing. Army and Parliament were engaged in a serio-comic ballet with the home counties for their stage. When Headquarters were pushed forward to Uxbridge, the Presbyterians danced a sullen retreat; when Fairfax withdrew to Bedford they stepped forward in a bold and aggressive figure. The Eleven Members, lest they should cause embarrassment to their colleagues, asked for temporary leave of absence; they were neither expelled nor put on their trial. While the commissioners of the Commons negotiated laboriously with those of the Army on a wide range of disputed questions, the Presbyterian oligarchy of the City did its utmost to build up a reliable force of its own. The train-bands were purged of officers known to be sectaries, and an auxiliary contingent of 'reformadoes' and deserters was enlisted to the number of many thousands.

While the Army marched to and fro among the little towns round London, its General Council, short-lived though it was, had become one of the most interesting representative chambers that ever sat on English soil. It discussed every political question at issue between Parliament and the Army, which meant that it debated both the tactics and the principles of the Revolution. Its scope was in practice very much wider than the authors of the Engagement taken at Newmarket and Triploe Heath can have foreseen. On the other hand, the balance of numbers between the men's Agitators and the officers was heavily overweighted on the side of the Grandees. The Engagement provided that the general officers, of whom there were eight, should sit with the officers' representatives and those of the men. In fact all the higher officers, from colonels to majors were allowed to sit in their own right and join in the debate.

The few records of these discussions that have been preserved among the *Clarke Papers* rank among the priceless human documents of the revolutionary struggle. The Cromwell who argues on a footing of equality with the Agitators of the rank and file reveals to us facets of his complex personality that we might not have divined, if the only speeches of his we possessed were those he made from the Lord Protector's throne. Among his men he is always at his ease and nearly always good-natured, though he had to meet some outspoken personal criticisms. Above all, even when he is flatly opposed to the opinions of the majority, he answers them with gravity and in a tone of respect. There shone a phase of his genius that we miss in the dictator's orations. This it was that endeared him to these spirited lads. Henry Ireton was, at all events on the theoretical plane, by far the abler and the honester man of the two, but he had none of the tact and none of the intuitive understanding of other men's feelings which a good leader must possess.

The startling thing about this unique army was that privates like Sexby, Allen and Lockyer and junior subalterns like Cornet Joyce could face these glittering rows of Grandees and state a case to which only two or three eccentrics among their seniors assented. They spoke to be sure with perfect courtesy, yet with uncompromising boldness. The Army's shorthand writer was far from being a skilled reporter, and the clerk who transcribed his notes was a muddler. Worse still, while the reporter took down the speeches of the generals in full, he had only a few lines to spare for the privates whom he describes as 'Buff-coat' and 'the Bedfordshire man'. But with all their defects these reports can still reproduce for us the voices of men who have been silent for three hundred years—not merely the articulate few who had the art to immortalise themselves, but the anonymous many, who prayed and argued and fought shoulder to shoulder through these years of fear and glory, but never won so much as a corporal's stripes or left behind them a name to distinguish their uniforms.

The first of these debates of which we have a full report took place on 16 July, 1647, at Reading.[1] The influence of the Agitators was never greater, and there was still something near to unanimity between officers and men. The men's emissaries had just scored a great success by winning over the Army of the North, eight regiments strong. Under Colonel-General Poyntz, one of the few experienced professional soldiers who served the Parliament, it might conceivably have backed an invasion from Scotland, for he was a decided Presbyterian. But his men declared their solidarity with the New Model and elected Agitators, who then deposed their general at York and carried him, a prisoner, first to Pontefract and then to Reading, where Fairfax set him free.

The debate of 16 July was provoked by a memorandum addressed by the representatives of men and officers alike to the General. In this they argued that the peace of 'this poor and bleeding kingdom' and the cause of the Army had been gravely imperilled by its withdrawal to a distance from the capital. They proposed, therefore, that it should march at once to London or near it. They then drew up a list of five demands, which Parliament must be required to grant without delay. It must (1) disable the Eleven Members from sitting, (2) restore the old governing committee of the London militia, (3) place all the armed forces of the kingdom under the command of Sir Thomas Fairfax, (4) set at liberty and compensate all prisoners illegally committed, especially John Lilburne and the Overtons, and finally (5) pay the Army punctually.[2]

Cromwell and Ireton, while they agreed to the presentation of these demands, were against a march on London at this stage. Ireton wished that the scheme for a settlement, known as the Heads of the Proposals, should be adopted and published before the Army took any decided political action, since he believed that this bid for peace would be received with gratitude and approval by the country as a whole. Cromwell took a hopeful view of the attitude of Parliament; it was becoming more favourable than it had been to the Army, whose friends would be embarrassed if force were used. There are passages of rare wisdom in his speeches, though for posterity they have an ironical ring. 'Whatsoever we get by a treaty,' he argued, 'it will be firm and durable', and once more, 'what we . . . gain in a free way, it is better than twice so much in a forced, and will be more truly ours and our posterity's'. On a very short view the Grandees, as things turned out, had gauged the mind of Parliament correctly, but the Agitators were better informed about what was brewing in the City. Allen, backed by Sexby and Lockyer, argued their case in the debate with stubborn pertinacity—he spoke, indeed, three times.

In the end, after a plea from Cromwell for unity—'if you be in the right and I in the wrong, if we be divided I doubt we shall all be in the wrong'—a compromise was reached without a vote. The five demands were to be sent as an ultimatum to Parliament and the march on London was postponed until its answer was received. In the meanwhile, a committee was appointed, of twelve officers, including Rainsborough and Harrison, with twelve Agitators to consider the draft of the Heads of the Proposals which Ireton and Lambert had prepared.

Four of the five demands with one or two additional details were at once presented in a peremptory form to Parliament. Under the same date (18 July) in a much less peremptory form the plea for the Leveller prisoners, redrafted and emasculated, was also presented as a postscript. Instead of demanding release and reparation for Lilburne, Overton and their comrades, it called for their speedy trial in a regular and equitable way, or else for their release on bail 'if the necessity of settling the general affairs of the kingdom admit not their present trial'. Parliament was shrewd enough to understand that over some of these demands the Grandees were in earnest, over others less so. It had already named Fairfax commander of all its forces in England, Wales and the Channel Islands. The Eleven Members now sought and received leave of absence for six months and passes to go abroad. The Commons then voted, as required, that the bringing in of foreign forces would be treason. In one day (23 July) both Houses passed through all its stages a bill restoring the old militia committee, with power to appoint officers. But in the matter of John Lilburne and his comrades neither House took any action whatever. So satisfied were the Grandees that the Headquarters of the Army were now removed from Reading to Bedford, and some of the cavalry were dispersed to places as distant as Bristol and Newark.

The unity between Agitators and Grandees, when they took counsel together at Reading, was more apparent than real. The Agitators proposed to march on London because they shared the view of the civilian Levellers that the Long Parliament had become an arbitrary tyranny bent on seeking the interests of its members and their class. It ought to be dissolved, but since a few urgent bills had to be passed before an election could be held, notably the disfranchisement of 'decayed' boroughs, it was obvious that it must either be intimidated or purged—a word that might mean a bigger operation than the elimination of the Eleven Members.

While the Army marched about, menacing at Uxbridge and complacent at Bedford, the two prisoners who incarnated the levelling idea were both writing pamphlets in their cells. Overton's *Appeal from the degenerate representative body, the Commons of England, to the body represented, the free people in general . . . and in especial, to . . . Sir Thomas Fairfax and to all the officers and soldiers under his command* came from the press on 17 July.[3] It is the ablest of his writings, remarkable for its sustained eloquence. The jester thus developed into a serious political thinker. This piece is a passionate plea for the liberation of his family, addressed primarily to the Agitators. He wrote amid the stench and vermin of Newgate; his brother was in another prison, while his wife lay among the bawds and strumpets of Bridewell. Their children were scattered in the care of neighbours. Convinced, with good reason, that his imprisonment was illegal, he writes—briefly—about these wrongs and sufferings, and manages to do it without egoism. The pamphlet, though its reasoning is one-sided, is a deeply moving appeal which can still stir us today.

Overton would not have been the typical Leveller he was, if he had been content to argue the case for political democracy illustrated by his quarrel with the Lords, that and nothing more. To his *Appeal* he added an appendix in which he summed up the wider programme of social reform for which he stood—

for it seems to be rather a personal utterance than an official party manifesto. It includes, of course, the usual demands for the abolition of the Lords' veto, for simpler and humaner laws, the cleaning up of prisons and the ending of tithes and imprisonment for debt. But in this version, even more clearly than elsewhere, one realises that the democracy on which the Levellers were bent meant primarily de-centralisation. Their movement was a revolt against government from Westminster. [4]

Again, more consciously than some of his comrades, he aimed at what we call the welfare state, organised, however, rather with the county as unit than on a national basis. He stresses the need for an adequate number of free schools, maintained at the public charge of the counties, so that 'few or none of the free men of England may for the future be ignorant of reading and writing'. Again, he insists that an adequate number of 'hospitals' (meaning both infirmaries and alms-houses) be erected at the public charge of the counties, for the benefit of the aged, sick and infirm and of widows and orphans. He may have had in his memory the humane provision which the Anabaptists of Amsterdam made for their needy members in their 'cake-house'. There is evidence in this programme that Overton, like Winstanley, had read More's *Utopia*, for he borrowed some of its ideas. [5] He ends with a bold and unqualified demand for the undoing of all enclosures of common land.

The *Appeal* itself is a set of variations on the Leveller theme of the sovereignty of the people. Overton admits, indeed he boasts, that he can cite no precedents for his appeal from Parliament to the electorate: it is enough that reason, 'the fountain of all justice and mercy to the creature', justifies him. From the law of self-preservation engraved by the finger of God in the tables of the heart of every living thing, he derives the right to resist such oppression as he and his have suffered —the right which Parliament invoked against the King, and the Army in its turn against the Parliament. After repeating the familiar argument that the Commons are the trustees of the people, he vehemently maintains that in their neglect of his wrongs and Lilburne's they have betrayed their trust, as they did in their dealings with the Army. He argues that orders and ordinances passed by such traitors to their trust as Holles and his group are invalid and void of all parliamentary authority

> for it is not their sitting upon the benches or standing within the walls of that House which makes them Parliament men or their orders or ordinances parliamentary, authoritative and binding, but the discharging of their trust in moving and acting only for the weal and safety of the people.

After mentioning the stopping of the presses and the burning of petitions, he declares that 'he that oppresseth for complaining of oppression must needs be a tyrant in the highest measure'. He calls on all lovers of freedom and justice to brand as traitors not merely the Eleven Members but 'all such as are coactors and voters with them'. For treason, he insists, is something more than levying war against the King; treasonable are any actions that tend to the destruction of human society, 'the overthrow of public safety, co-habitation and peace, or to the vassalage, bondage and thraldom of a people'. His call for action rings out clear:

> Now is no time to sit thrumming of caps. If they will not give us leave to use our tongues and our pens to present and make known our grievances, we must take leave to make use of our hands and swords for the defence and redemption of our lives, our laws and our liberties from the hand of the destroyer, for our safety must be maintained.

This vigorous pamphlet ends with an exhortation to the Agitators to preserve their power and the trust reposed in them intact. Overton is more cautious and courteous than Lilburne and will not directly accuse the officers, but he makes his suspicion clear enough that they intend to deprive the private soldiers of their right to representation. If the Agitators can be befooled of their power, then 'farewell our hopes in the Army; for I am confident that it must be the poor, the simple and mean things of this earth that must confound the mighty and the strong'.

Weary of an even longer and more costly imprisonment, Lilburne also looked to the Army for his liberation and he too feared that the influence of the Agitators was being undermined. But he felt no hesitation in naming his enemy. In the

previous chapter (p. 205 above) passages were quoted from
Jonah's Cry out of the Whale's Belly (26 July, 1647) in which
John remonstrated with Cromwell in the early days of the
Army's revolt for his opposition to the soldiers' petition and
claimed that it was he, Lilburne, who started the Agitators'
movement. If we return to this extraordinary pamphlet now,
it is because the key to Lilburne's relationship with Cromwell
is to be found in it. The reasons which always in the end
frustrated the attempts of the Levellers to compromise and
co-operate with 'the silken Independents' were broader and
more significant than any temperamental clash between their
leaders. None the less, they had common interests and common
enemies and their collaboration might have lasted rather longer
than it did, if 'Honest John' could have bridled his pen.

Jonah's Cry is a series of intimate letters which he addressed
to the Lieut.-General, and these with all their reckless indiscretions and emotional extravagance he must needs send to
the press exactly as he wrote them. He flings insults as he goes
along at several of the leading Independent statesmen and the
staff officers on whom Cromwell chiefly relied. 'Thou art led
by the nose by two unworthy covetous earthworms Vane [the
younger] and St John, whose baseness I sufficiently anatomised
unto thee in thy bed above a year ago.' 'Covetous earthworm'
is an odd phrase to apply to a man whom we know as an
exalted mystic and one of the few politicians who did not rob the
Commonwealth. But his tactics erred on the side of caution and
subtlety; it was Vane's timidity which John, with good reason,
at this crisis disliked. In the first letter, dated 25 March, 1647,
Cromwell is still his hero. He recalls his 'ardent gratitude' for his
deliverance from the Star Chamber. Cromwell he addresses as
'a sanctuary and hiding-place' for 'poor people of God' and 'the
most absolute singlehearted great man in England, untainted
or unbiased with ends of your own'.

After this preface, he delivers the message which like Jonah
he had long shrunk from uttering. In biblical language, with
texts scattered prodigally over his pages, he writes as one Saint
to another. 'The redeemed ones of Jesus Christ', he reminds
Cromwell, 'are in a low and sad condition.' 'Think not that
thou shalt escape in the Parliament House, more than all the

rest of the Lamb's poor despised, redeemed ones . . . if thou altogether holdest thy peace.' After complaining of the passivity of the 'silken Independents' in the House and of Cromwell's attitude towards the Agitators, John threatens to arraign him at 'the dreadful bar' of God for betraying those who looked to him for help into 'the clutches of Holles and Stapleton'. Jealous over Cromwell 'with the height of godly jealousy', he curses the day when the House bribed him with its grant of lands worth £2,500 *per annum.*

The tone of the letters changed to congratulation after Cromwell had put himself at the head of the Army. 'I would willingly be a pioneer with you and hazard, if I had them, a million of lives for you.' At this stage he is all for treating the King 'with candour' and dealing with him 'as becomes honest men that play above board'. He believes that the King 'will grant anything that is rational', and maintains that Parliament is the worst tyrant of the two.

By 1 July his tone had changed again. He believes that his imprisonment and all his misfortunes are due to Manchester, whose enmity he incurred by the support he gave Cromwell in 1644. 'You plucked your head out of the collar, and I was catched in the briars.' In retrospect he now feels that Cromwell and 'the rest of [his] fellow great ones . . . have bought and sold the laws, liberties and justice of the kingdom for [their] own ends and greatness'. On a rather slender basis of fact he now accuses Cromwell of 'robbing by [his] unjust subtlety and shifting tricks the honest and gallant Agitators of all their power and authority'. Finally like Overton he attacks the Commons as 'traitors to their trust' since they have allowed him to spend over a year as the Lords' prisoner in the Tower, without attending to his case.

What really was the stake for which this intrepid prisoner was playing against Cromwell appears clearly only in the Postscript, dated July 16th, addressed 'as an alarum' to the private soldiers. He was bent on controlling the Army, through the Agitators whom he regarded as his followers. The kingdom, he argues, which the majority at Westminster is bent on enslaving, is 'dissolved into the original law of nature'. The soldiers hold their swords in their hands for their own preservation, and

are acting on the principles adopted at Newmarket. 'Every
individual private soldier, whether horse or foot, ought freely
to have their vote, to choose the transactors of their affairs or
else in the sight of God and all rational men are discharged from
obeying, stooping or submitting to what is done by them.' In
short, 'they act by mutual consent or agreement'. If officers
usurp power to act without this consent, their conduct 'merits a
kicking out of the Army', if nothing worse. Had he in mind for
Cromwell the fate that befell Colonel-General Poyntz?

One can understand Lilburne's desperation when he realised
that for Cromwell and the rest of the Grandees he was nothing
more than a pawn in their political game. They cared nothing,
one way or the other, for the principle he was maintaining at
such a cost—that the House of Lords can have no jurisdiction
over a commoner. For their own political ends, they did not
wish to antagonise the Lords in general or Manchester in
particular, since the balance of forces between Independents
and Presbyterians was precarious. That is why there was no
time to settle John's case in the courts. Their suggestion that he
should apply for bail did not appeal to him, for he argued that
if he did so, he would be tacitly conceding the legitimacy of
this pretended Parliament.

But there is more than this exasperation in Lilburne's singular
relationship with Cromwell. The clue to it may lie in a grateful
and cordial letter which he addressed to the Lieut.-General
towards the end of 1645. 'I could willingly', he wrote, 'lay
down my life for you, your honour and reputation, as soon as
for my father that begot me.'[6] Emotionally then, when he
indulged in his extravagant hero-worship, Cromwell was for
John a substitute for his father. It seems likely, when we put
together the few facts known to us about Richard Lilburne, that
John as a youngster felt a warm admiration for his father in the
flesh and even in later life imitated his singular behaviour. We
recall Richard's recourse to ordeal by battle in a law suit, and
the fact that he ruined himself by obstinate litigation. That was
exactly the spirited, romantic, impractical kind of behaviour
for which his son was famous. Did he not as an apprentice in his
early twenties issue from his prison cell a challenge to Archbishop Laud to debate with him the rights and wrongs of

episcopacy before an audience of peers of the realm? How often in later life did he make offers almost as fantastic to settle his quarrels with the great by arbitration; unless, indeed, his adversary preferred a duel.

But this admired father, whose conduct made so deep an impression on his son's imagination, deserted him in his hour of need, so that he must face the Star Chamber with his family against him. But John, who still behaved like a romantic adolescent—did he ever grow up?—found a spiritual substitute father in Dr Bastwick and another in William Prynne. When both of them turned out to be intolerant Presbyterians who would not allow him to think for himself and actually became his public enemies who sought to injure him, a pattern must have formed itself in John's unconscious mind to which fathers, physical and spiritual, always conformed and would conform. Always, after a spell of happiness long or short, they turn against their son, betray him and injure him. Oliver Cromwell, the greatest and most disinterested man in England, was an even nobler father than the martyrs Bastwick and Prynne, to say nothing of Richard Lilburne, but he too was a father and therefore destined to betray his son. And this in due course, like all the others—as John read the record—Cromwell did.

A psychologist could doubtless tell us much more about this father-son relationship. It ended in a singular form of rivalry. The experience that befell Oedipus at the cross-roads to Delphi varies infinitely with temperament, social structure and religion. In this curious instance both son and substitute-father were Saints, and rivals, as John saw it, for God's favour. What he wrote on this subject is worth quoting, for it gives us a startling insight not merely into his mind but into the emotional religion of the Puritans. The passage occurs in his lengthy pamphlet, *An Impeachment of High Treason against Oliver Cromwell* (17 July, 1649). He suddenly interrupts a detailed narrative of his arrest in January 1648 and his appearance before the Commons, to recite this prayer:

> But O Thou just, righteous, powerful and compassionate God, that sensibly hath (*sic*) been my God and guide about these twice seven years, . . . that hath made my heart sing

and be merry in the midst of many deaths. . . . O Thou
glorious God that hath taken me by the arm when I have
been ready to fall . . . and by whose sweetness . . . I have
been drawn to follow Thee whithersoever Thou goest: keep
now my heart sincere and upright before Thee, that I may
stick close unto Thee . . . to the death.

He then prays to be delivered from 'Thy once seeming servant
Cromwell, . . . a fallen star, an apostate from Thee'. He describes Cromwell's 'absolute commanding power over an over-
awing mercenary Turkish army'—this was written after the
defeat of the Leveller mutiny at Burford—and 'appeals to the
sovereign creator and over-ruler of all the world, visibly before
the eyes of the present generation of men to execute impartial
judgment between us', so that 'the divisions of spirit may
cease . . . amongst our native churchmen, but especially among
Thy darlings by reason of our contestings each with other, who
both have been eminent in the eyes of many thousands of those
that truly know Thee'. After this prayer covering two closely
printed pages, Lilburne resumed his story of what happened at
Wapping.

Rivals for God's favour and for the good opinion of their
fellow Saints, Cromwell and Lilburne, as the latter saw it, were
rivals also for popularity on a merely terrestrial level. Here is a
claim which John made for himself many years later in a letter
to his friends in Hertfordshire, written like so many others
from prison:

And give me leave . . . to aver it, my interest is none of the
meanest in England, but even among the hobnails, clouted
shoes, the private soldiers, the leather and woollen aprons
and the laborious and industrious people in England, it is as
formidable, as numerous and as considerable as anyone
amongst your whole selves, not excepting your very General
(let him but lay down his sword and become disarmed as
I am).[7]

The modern reader is apt to smile at this boast; John Lilburne
has no bronze statue in Parliament Square. But no one familiar
with the contemporary 'news books' would question his claim
for a moment. With the masses John's popularity was un-
rivalled. Save in the Fen country in his early days there is no

reason to suppose that the lower classes ever thought of Cromwell as their hero; only in the Army and the Independent chapels was he beloved.

With this reminder that John Lilburne was the hero of the hobnails and leather aprons, we can now grasp the full significance of the postscript which he addressed to the privates of the New Model. That Army controlled England's destinies. It might have been defeated in the field; Presbyterians, Royalists and Scots tried and failed at Preston, Dunbar and Worcester. The other possibility was that the preaching and practice of democracy in its ranks might through 'the gallant Agitators' have advanced Rainsborough or Lilburne to its command in place of the fallen angel Cromwell. That would have meant, while it lasted, the seizure of power by the craftsmen and peasants instead of the *haute bourgeoisie*. If this never happened or came near to happening, in spite of the two attempts at Ware and Burford, part of the explanation was that Lilburne in his vanity must needs give Cromwell warning of what he meant to do.

The rest of the story of Lilburne's relations with Cromwell during the summer and autumn of 1647 can best be told on this page. A month after Jonah had published his cry from the belly of the whale, he was moved to print a still more offensive letter to the Lieut.-General. In this he challenged Cromwell to visit him for a debate before witness in the Tower within four days, failing which he would lay before the public a list of all the relatives whom Cromwell had promoted to well-paid commands in the Army. In due course, the list appeared. Cromwell, as Clarendon pointed out, was always prompt to forget the verbal injuries he suffered. Early in September he did visit his old bed-fellow in his cell. John gathered from him, as they talked, that what he feared was that the arch-Leveller, if he were free, would stir up disorder in the New Model. Lilburne replied that his sole concern was to establish the principle for which he had endured so much—that the Lords have no legal jurisdiction over a commoner. If the Commons would endorse this right by quashing the Lords' sentence, he would willingly go abroad, provided Parliament would enable him to start life again overseas by paying what it owed him as compensation for his sufferings under the Star Chamber and part at least of his arrears of pay.

Soon after Cromwell had left him with 'divers fair promises', Marten's committee reported in his favour. Cromwell, however, supported a motion that the report be re-committed, and a search for precedents carried out; lawyers who were members of the House should be invited to debate the matter *pro* and *con*. Lilburne would have been a paragon of charity, if he had failed to draw the conclusion that Cromwell was for his own ends using his political power to prolong a ruinous and illegal imprisonment. He now resolved, not for the first time, to appeal to the private soldiers for the justice which their generals denied him. He now repeated in a letter to Marten's committee the offer to go into voluntary exile which he had made verbally to the Lieut.-General. On 15 October Marten's committee again reported to the House and once more further provision was made for delay by the appointment of yet another committee on this knotty business, with Maynard the celebrated Presbyterian lawyer instead of the republican Marten as its chairman. John was, however, at last allowed a measure of liberty, for on 9 November, 1647, the House voted that to consult his lawyer and attend the committee he should be permitted to go abroad without a keeper. In effect he got bail without applying for it.[8]

No one in 1647 was prepared to do what Monk did in 1660— restore the monarchy, virtually without conditions. The Presbyterians, who ended by accepting anything the King would sign, began by dictating the vindictive and humiliating terms of the Nineteen Propositions. In contrast to these, the Army's sketch of a settlement, embodied in the Heads of the Proposals published on 2 August, shines by its generosity and wisdom. Thousands of us on reading them over and thousands of our fathers during many generations must have wished that this bid for peace had succeeded. By a restoration on these lines England would have been spared the bitterness engendered first by a totalitarian dictatorship and then by eight and twenty years of reaction under the last Stuart kings. What the Army proposed in 1647 was an incomparably more liberal solution

I

than the country got at last in the Whig Revolution. But what we have to do in this chapter is to explain why, with all its merits, it won little support and aggravated the tension between Agitators and Grandees.

This document is unusual, and perhaps unique among the political manifestoes of the Interregnum, in that it is not a statement of principles but a businesslike sketch of future legislation. It is a settlement between victors and vanquished, between Independents and Cavaliers, to which have been added the outlines of a social programme interesting chiefly to the private soldiers who won the war and to their civilian allies. Its underlying assumption is that Independents, backed by Levellers, can come to terms with Cavaliers at the expense of the Presbyterians. Now as always the basic problem for Independents was how to get religious toleration for themselves. They could not get it from the Presbyterians. Then could they get it from the two extremes, from Cavaliers and Levellers, by offering to tolerate Episcopalians and Catholics? To this every other issue was secondary. A document which every historian has discussed during three centuries need not be fully analysed here. What chiefly concerns us in this essay is to see it as the Levellers saw it. They read it with Overton's and Lilburne's pamphlets ringing in their ears.

The Heads of the Proposals began by providing that the Long Parliament should be dissolved within a year. Thenceforward Parliaments should meet biennially and sit for eight months. Government should be carried on during their lengthy vacations by a Council of State and by parliamentary committees. A redistribution of seats in the Commons should be effected proportionate to tax returns, with the result that 'decayed' boroughs would lose their representatives. For ten years the great officers of state should be chosen by the two Houses of Parliament, thereafter these should submit at each vacancy three names of which the King should choose one.

The control by Parliament of all armed forces, which the King had already conceded for ten years, was prolonged for the remainder of his reign by the provision that the King should not dispose of them without the consent of Parliament. For the control of the armed forces under future kings no express provision was made, save in so far as Parliament would have its say in choosing men to fill 'the great offices' among whom presumably the commanders of the land and sea forces would be reckoned.

The first draft of the Proposals included a highly original device for dealing with the 'negative voices' of the King and the Lords. On terms which anticipated the Parliament Act of 1911, it allowed them a suspensive veto only. If the Lords had rejected, or if the King had refused to sign, a bill passed by the Commons, it was provided that if the lower House in the next biennial Parliament passed the same bill once more, it would automatically become law. In this way, subject to a delay of something less than two years, the sovereignty of the electorate was assured—though the clause was subsequently abandoned.[9]

The clauses dealing with religion were very much more liberal than those of any set of proposals or any legislation for which Cromwell or Ireton were afterwards responsible. They never afterwards accepted the central principle of toleration— that the civil magistrate is not entitled to interfere in questions of belief or worship (see below pp. 381-99). But in these proposals, since their aim was to reach a lasting peace with the Cavaliers and King Charles, devoted as he was to episcopacy, the logic of diplomacy drove them as practical statesmen to this principle, which they afterwards felt strong enough to reject. Clause XI, which silently assumed that episcopacy would be restored with monarchy, was explicit and free from exceptions:

> An act to be passed to take away all coercive power, authority and jurisdiction of bishops and all other ecclesiastical officers whatsoever, extending to any civil penalties upon any.

Further details made the meaning of this (perhaps deliberately) ill-drafted clause clearer still. Legislation enjoining the use of the Book of Common Prayer, forbidding conventicles, and requiring the taking of the Covenant or any oaths objectionable to scrupulous consciences was to be swept away. The provision for Catholics was promising but obscure:

> some other provision to be made for discovering of Papists and Popish recusants and for disabling of them and of all Jesuits or priests from disturbing the state.

What this meant in fact was that toleration would be conceded to all Catholics who would take an oath of allegiance in a form which an assembly of English Catholic priests had already approved. But it had still to receive the assent of the Pope. If these clauses were a peace-offering to the Cavaliers, they were a mortal challenge to the Presbyterians. Their system of church government might survive, but theirs would be only one church among several and it could exercise discipline only over members who freely submitted to its yoke.

The clauses defining the status of the King's supporters after his restoration were generous when compared with the Newcastle Propositions. But if the Independents were trying to reconcile the Cavaliers, or perhaps to win them over as allies against the Presbyterians and the Scots, were they liberal enough? Only five (originally seven) persons were excepted from pardon under the general act of oblivion, as against 58 Protestant Royalists together with 14 Catholics excepted under the Newcastle terms which also enumerated another 48 who were forbidden access to the court. The penalties in the form of confiscation or 'composition' were very much less severe; none the less, they would mean for many cavalier families some years of difficulty. None of them might sit in the first or second of the biennial Parliaments or hold any public office for five (originally ten) years save with the consent of Parliament or the Council of State.

As a soldier and a realist Cromwell may well have been content with these terms, since they left the control of the armed forces in the hands of a reformed Parliament during the present reign. It was not his habit to look far into the future. If the King, with the army and Parliament against him, misused his veto, he could be deposed. As for the Lords (in spite of that irritable speech to Manchester) it is unlikely that Cromwell ever objected on principle to their functions as a second chamber; he may, indeed, have hoped at this time to take his seat among them. But for the Levellers, the 'negative voices' of King and Lords had come to figure among the chief issues in their struggle for democracy. To give way here was to throw away the fruits of victory. Their view was stated a few months later in an angry and one-sided pamphlet by John Wildman, *Putney Projects*.[10]

In spite of these heavy concessions to the King and the Lords, the twelve Agitators sitting on the committee which considered the Heads of the Proposals had won, doubtless with Rainsborough's help, the recognition by the Army of nine-tenths of the Leveller programme as it then stood.

The Levellers had got, as we have seen, the endorsement of the Army for their demands for an early dissolution, a regular succession of biennial parliaments and the disfranchisement of rotten boroughs. Toleration had been defined in terms not far short of their ideal. The provision (I.8) for liberty to record 'dissents' in the Commons (on which Marten was keen) was a first necessary step towards the reality of representative government. A long step was taken towards the acceptance of Lilburne's thesis (I.10) that the Lords have no jurisdiction over commoners. Another clause (I.11) went some way towards the Leveller ideals of decentralisation and local self-government, since grand juries, apparently elected, were given the right to appoint justices of the peace and to nominate sheriffs.

After the main constitutional chapters of the settlement, came a list of slightly less urgent reforms, which the Army desired that Parliament should 'lose no time' in passing. Among these was a vindication of the right of petition, the prompt lifting of the excise from commodities necessary to the poor, the abolition of all monopolies (a blow at the Merchant Adventurers), 'some remedy for the present unequal, troublesome and contentious way of ministers' maintenance by tithes', the simplification and cheapening of legal procedure, a reform of the present practice of imprisonment for debt and an endorsement of the principle that no man may be compelled to incriminate himself. Tithes, be it noted once again, and imprisonment for debt were issues on which property in the seventeenth century took a fighting stand. The list might have served as a table of contents for a collected edition of John Lilburne's works. From the programme of the Levellers, as it then stood, nearly every item had been adopted; only the ending of the press-gang was missing and the humanisation of the criminal law and prisons. Manhood suffrage was not yet in the party's programme, though Lilburne was advocating it.

Obviously this was an impossible agenda for one session of

Parliament: there was in those days no closure. How much, then, did such a list of desirable reforms mean? Did it balance the surrender over the veto of King and Lords? Wildman overstated his case when he argued that their 'negative voices' were the chief obstacles that confronted the reformer. No House of Commons that sat during the Interregnum, not even those which had been purged, would have felt much inclination to make this programme its own. It meant something only so long as the Army led the Revolution and preserved its unity. It meant, in plain words, a good deal so long as the Agitators retained their influence, and nothing at all if they lost it.

The career of the Heads of the Proposals was unfortunate from the start. Ireton, of whom the Levellers complained that he always went his own way with scant regard for the opinions of his colleagues, may have pushed it through the committee by arbitrary methods. If we may believe Wildman, it was never laid before the Council of the Army for their approval, nor had Ireton sought the consent of his colleagues when he showed the first draft to the King's adviser, Sir John Berkeley, and amended it on his advice. Only two months back the Army had been warmly in favour of a restoration and this, as we have seen, was also John Lilburne's mood.

But though he had enjoyed every courtesy, the King's behaviour had not endeared him either to officers or men. From the start the Proposals aroused in him nothing but hostility, for he lacked the imagination to grasp what an immense concession this Puritan army was making when it proposed to restore mitre as well as crown. Berkeley has left a memorable account of the arrogant folly of his language when the document was formally handed to him at Woburn Abbey by a deputation from the New Model. 'You cannot do without me' —so he addressed the soldiers who had destroyed his armies— 'You will fall to ruin, if I do not sustain you.' Rainsborough, already sore, it may be, because his republican principles had been voted down, was so outraged that he rode at once to Bedford and spread a report of Charles's indiscretions throughout the Army. The Agitators made a shrewd guess at the calculation which underlay the King's indifference to their concessions. He was intriguing with the Scots and perhaps with the

Presbyterians in the City also for a renewal of the war. Acting on this suspicion, the men invaded the lodging of the Scots' envoy, the Earl of Lauderdale, who was negotiating the proposed invasion, and drove him back to London before he could meet the King.

Meanwhile, in the capital, the counter-revolution had begun. With the approval of the City oligarchy, a formidable number of men, 100,000 in all, had signed a solemn 'Engagement' in which, after citing the Covenant, they pledged themselves 'in the presence of God the searcher of hearts' to bring back the King to London on his own terms, 'in honour, safety and freedom', to conclude a personal treaty with 'his' two Houses of Parliament, 'and that without the nearer approach of the Army'. The movement reflected a widespread rally of sentiment towards the King. With the cost of living still mounting, the average man resented war-time taxation after a year of peace, and looked back wistfully to the easier days when Charles was King indeed. Ship money was a trifle compared with the excise. Moreover, the lonely prisoner, separated from wife and family, made his appeal to sentiment.

The Engagement was signed by the broken, unemployed soldiers (the 'reformadoes'), by swarms of apprentices, by men of the train-bands, often under pressure, and finally by the watermen and seamen of the Thames, who like most of their kind in all the ports were apt to take their cue from the conservative and Presbyterian Merchant Adventurers. A mob drawn from these groups had on 26 July invaded both Lords and Commons and extorted from them first the restoration of the Presbyterian militia committee and then an invitation to the King to return to London. Resenting the violence they had suffered, the two Speakers (though Lenthall was a typical opportunist and Manchester a Presbyterian) with 8 peers and 57 M.Ps. had placed themselves under the protection of the Army, which now undertook from Bedford the march on London (fifty miles away) it had wisely refrained from making from Reading.

At Westminster the Presbyterian majority chose new Speakers, welcomed back the Eleven to its benches, forbade the Army to approach within thirty miles, named a Committee of

Safety and prepared to defend London. Evidently it had been driven by the mob a little further than it dared but no further than it wished to go. In St James's Fields (as the Park was then called) Major-General Massey, with Waller and Poyntz as his lieutenants, reviewed the improvised army he commanded; but the usual reckoning that he had 30,000 infantry under him and 10,000 horse is fallacious, for the train-bands had in their ranks many Independents and (especially on the South Bank) many Levellers. The reaction threw up neither a popular political figure nor a talented soldier to lead it; still less had it what distinguished the left, an organisation that sprang spontaneously from the masses. The Army assigned to Rainsborough the conduct of an encircling movement. The Levellers of Southwark opened the gates of their borough to him with a welcome and no sooner had he pointed his guns at the defences of London Bridge than the resistance of the City collapsed. The former Speakers, with their followers, took their seats as before, and on 7 August the Army, horse and foot, with laurel leaves in their hats, made a memorable march through the City, 18,000 strong. Massey, Waller, Poyntz, with Holles and others of the Eleven, escaped to the continent.

The story of the next three months is a tangled chronicle of confusion and division. The Presbyterians still had their majority in the Commons and were able to defeat two motions of the Independents to declare 'null and void' the votes which the mob had extorted and to approve the actions of the Army. This provoked the Agitators to address a petition to Fairfax in which they called for the sweeping purge for which Overton had already prepared their minds; they would expel from the Commons all who sat in 'that pretended Parliament' after the Speakers refused to preside over its sittings.[11] Four days later at Kingston the Council of the Army adopted and published a lengthy declaration, which after a survey of recent history came to the same conclusion. The Army, to be precise, was now bent on a purge of 65 Members in addition to the notorious Eleven. Cromwell shared the views of his men, and would have done then what Colonel Pride did more than a year later, had not Fairfax thwarted him by delaying day after day his signature of the necessary orders. The Lieut.-General did, however, achieve something by bluff; the posting of a regiment of horse in Hyde Park intimidated the majority into passing the 'null and void' ordinance which it had rejected a few days earlier. The initiative in the Army could still spring, be it noted, from the Levellers, though the unity between men and officers was no longer as cordial as it had been at Newmarket and St Albans.

The King, meantime, was playing a double game. While one half of his mind prepared a renewal of the Civil War, the other half strove with a perseverance that extorts our admiration to whittle down the Proposals, clause by clause. He was determined to accept nothing that would lessen the rights of his posterity or injure his church or his friends. At moments he was so far disposed to adopt the Army's scheme that he sought advice from the bishops who kept his conscience over the unpalatable prospect of tolerating Puritan dissent. One of them assured him that after giving his promise of toleration under pressure of necessity, he might with the church's blessing, break it and reduce the sectaries 'to one right and well grounded religion' so soon as he 'regained the power given him by God'.[12]

Parliament meanwhile, had not forgotten the impossible Newcastle Propositions, which with some trifling amendments it once more adopted and presented to the King. This drove him at last (9 September) to a reply in which for the first time he said plainly that he would prefer the Heads of the Proposals as the basis on which a personal treaty might be negotiated. Though this committed him to nothing, it seemed to Cromwell and Ireton to justify their militant optimism. In fact the King had as yet made no concession of any consequence save that of toleration—and this his well-trained conscience would one day feel entitled to withdraw. After seven weeks of negotiation he had accepted none of the articles that limited his prerogative, nor those which assured a regular succession of Parliaments, nor any of the social and legal reforms dear to the Levellers.[13]

Satisfied for the moment with the King's characteristic blend of acceptance with obstruction, Cromwell and Ireton were preoccupied with the opposition to the Proposals at Westminster. With this they were prepared to deal, as Ireton declared, by purging the Houses, if need were, again and again, until they would 'do his Majesty's business'. But the left, from the privates in the ranks to the republican intellectuals at Westminster, was in no mood to believe that Ireton's confidence and Cromwell's in the good faith of the King was disinterested and sincere. One has to allow much for Cromwell's extrovert temperament and his will to please, before one can understand the generous folly of his famous discovery which Berkeley recorded in his *Memoirs* that the King was 'the uprightest and most conscientious man of his three Kingdoms'. The ladies of the Cromwell family had been unwise, to use a mild word, in attending the court which Charles had begun to keep in his nominal captivity.

By September even Hugh Peters, the most loyal of Cromwell's partisans had begun to rebuke both his hero and the Grandees who followed him for playing the courtier. In the Council of the Army the debates during this month were so hot that in an altercation between Rainsborough and Cromwell, the former went so far as to say that 'one of us must not live'. The same sharp division rent the Army's friends in the House. In a debate on the King's message concerning the Propositions and Proposals on 22 September, Henry Marten, who was opposed to a restoration of the monarchy on any terms, moved that 'no further addresses' be permitted to the King. He and Rainsborough secured 34 supporters, among them Blake, Algernon Sidney, Ludlow and Colonel Hutchinson, a figure which gives us the measure of the republican party at this stage. In the majority of 84 were Cromwell and Ireton, whose speeches, as the debate in the council at Putney soon revealed, were deeply resented by the radicals in the Army. Vane, St John and Fiennes also voted with the Presbyterians. These latter, in their stupid intolerance, had their own more effectual methods of rendering any negotiation with the King abortive. The House at their prompting decided next day that, as the first steps towards a settlement, bills should forthwith be presented to the King providing for the abolition of episcopacy and the sale of the bishops' lands.

During these autumnal days a startling piece of gossip exploded in the Army. The King, it was said, had bribed Cromwell to effect his restoration with a promise of the

Earldom of Essex, the title which the other great Cromwell had borne, the garter and the Captaincy of his Guard, with the Lord Lieutenancy of Ireland for Ireton and a confidential post at court for young Henry Cromwell. The story may be rejected as a malicious invention of that arch-intriguer, the Presbyterian Countess of Carlisle. But it was not on the face of it improbable, for the King had instructed Ashburnham and Berkeley to win over the heads of the Army by appealing to their cupidity. On the other hand, the King's cynical comment is on record that he did not trust the officers of the New Model, because none of them ever asked him for anything, with the single exception of Major Huntingdon. In particular Berkeley tells us that his royal master never trusted Cromwell.

To be sure, the Lieut.-General, who promoted so many of his relatives, was certainly not indifferent to the interests of his family; at the end of his life, when he named Richard his heir, his ambition to found a dynasty ruined such chances as the Protectorate had of surviving his death. Without any preliminary bargaining, if the Army brought about a restoration, doubtless there would be peerages and honours of one grade or another for its chief officers. Even the Presbyterian Long Parliament had recommended in 1645 that the elder Fairfax should be made an earl and Cromwell a baron. But this story implied a corrupt bargain—that Cromwell sold the Good Old Cause for a garter and the prospect of becoming the King's chief minister and favourite. Cromwell's stature was above that kind of dealing. But we are not left to conjecture. Sir John Berkeley in his *Memoirs* gave a sufficiently explicit denial to the whole story. Not only (as everyone realises) did he deny Lady Carlisle's statement that she had this tale from him, he went further: 'I should have lied if I had said anything to that purpose'—meaning, 'if I had told her any story of an offer to Cromwell of an earldom and a garter'.[14] One need only add that Berkeley makes on modern readers of his deeply interesting *Memoirs* the impression of an honest and sympathetic character, and that he must have known of it, if any such offer had been made to Cromwell and Ireton.

In our efforts to interpret the complex character and devious tactics of Cromwell, the chief thing to remember is that this reluctant leader of a revolution was at bottom a conservative, who believed that the surest road to stability, the key to security for liberty and property, lay in a return to the old constitution, with some necessary changes, of which the chief was toleration for the People of God. In September he would doubtless have repeated what he told Berkeley in July—that the Army wished for no more than 'to have leave to live as subjects ought to do and to preserve their consciences'; they thought, moreover, that 'no men could enjoy their estates quietly without the King had his rights'. Round those two ideas, 'consciences' and 'estates', Cromwell's political thinking always revolved.

However posterity may judge Cromwell's motives, most of his contemporaries took the crude view of his conduct. Before the year was out, Lilburne and Wildman were telling the story of the earldom and the garter at public meetings, with the exciting addition that Henry Marten had taken a vow to play Felton to Cromwell's Buckingham. Honest John with his customary lack of humour took Marten too literally, but Cromwell, as the rift in the left grew deeper, did apparently resort to some precautions against assassination.

By the middle of October it was clear to nearly everyone save Ireton and Cromwell that the Heads of the Proposals had no future. In the Army itself the Agitators (as we shall see in the next chapter) were in revolt against them and were in the act of working out on paper a new and daring settlement of their own. Each in his own way King and Parliament were giving the chance of peace the last fatal blows. The King would say nothing; by silence he killed the Proposals after his two helpers, Berkeley and Ashburnham, believed that they had smoothed out all the remaining obstacles to his acceptance. What now absorbed his attention and beckoned all his hopes was the prospect of a Scots invasion. This the Army understood so well that what its Council discussed at its meeting on the 14th was its determination to drag the King, a protesting prisoner, with the marching regiments, if they had to tramp northwards for the defence of the kingdom.

On that same day, 14 October, Selden and Harry Marten, as brilliant a pair of speakers as they were enlightened thinkers, suffered in debate in the Commons a defeat so overwhelming when they argued for the toleration of Catholics, that no one on the left would risk a division when the Presbyterians went on to deny toleration to those who use the Book of Common Prayer. After this disaster, Cromwell had the audacity to go into action yet once again for this untrustworthy King in this intolerant House. On 20 October he spoke for three hours in defence of the institution of monarchy, vowed that his aim during the whole war had been to strengthen and not to destroy it and with all his eloquence pleaded with the Commons to re-establish the throne without delay. The more closely we study his career the less inclined shall we be to brand this speech as insincere. Whether we derive it from temperament or the experience of life, the fact is that Cromwell always came back amid the many changes of these years of trouble and splendour to his ingrained, native belief in government by 'a single person', whether King or Protector made little difference. If he failed in his purpose of restoration, the fault lay not in his breast but in the complexity of the forces with which he had to grapple.

NOTES TO CHAPTER XI

1. *C.P.*, I, p. 176; Woodhouse, p. 409.
2. *Declaration*, p. 97.
3. Wolfe, p. 154.
4. It is characteristic of Overton's thinking that he has in mind some form of autonomy for the counties, subject to the over-riding authority of Parliament. They may choose county commissioners who shall enquire and present to Parliament 'what be the just laws, customs and privileges of each county'. One may compare with this Walwyn's choice of the cantons of federal Switzerland as the nearest approach in real life to his political ideal. It is significant that in France also the federalist tradition, based on the *commune* (parish) as the political unit, was always cherished by the little man, the craftsman and peasant; centralisation was always the policy of the *haute bourgeoisie*. Cromwell's dislike of this tendency among the Levellers was true to form (pp. 531-2 below). Another function of these commissioners was that they could exercise the right of recall over any of the M.P.s of their county and might impeach a member who betrayed his trust.
5. Overton borrowed some of the least admirable details of *Utopia*, when he drew up his proposals for the punishment of theft (No. 7 of his *Articles concerning the Laws*), notably the provision that thieves working for those they had wronged should wear 'a singular habit'. More specified a

white robe. Both were for conscribing habitual criminals as soldiers—a proposal which was part of More's satirical treatment of war as an institution. Evidently *Utopia* in Robinson's translation was much read, for there are in the British Museum reprints dated 1597, 1624 and 1639. My ear detects in Walwyn's *Tyranipocrit* some echoes of More's phraseology.

6. *Jonah's Cry in the Whale's Belly*, pp. 12-13.

7. *The Upright Man's Vindication* (1 August, 1653), p. 15.

8. See *Two Letters writ by Lt. Col. John Lilburne* (13 September, 1647) and *The additional plea of Lt. Col. John Lilburne* (28 October, 1647). Godwin's is the fullest account of this curious chapter in Lilburne's record, but it is marred by his usual prejudice, and ends with a story that John and Wildman were plotting to murder Cromwell (*History of the Commonwealth*, II, Chapter XIII). Pease has dealt adequately with this product of bias and carelessness (*The Leveller Movement*, p. 192). Lilburne made a similar offer to go into voluntary exile on the eve of his first trial for treason.

9. See p. 285 below.

10. Dated 30 December, 1647; see Woodhouse, pp. 426-9. Wildman wrote as John Lawmind.

11. *The Humble Address of the Agitators* (14 August, 1647).

12. John Warner, Bishop of Rochester, in Cary, *op. cit.*, I, p. 346 (28 August, 1647).

13. With a singular lack of tact the Army's headquarters published, on 9 September, the *Twelve Proposals* which the King had up to this date accepted. They concern only toleration, the act of oblivion and matters nearly related to these two subjects (see *Declaration*, p. 147).

14. Sir John Berkeley, *Memoirs* (Maseres *Select Tracts*, I, p. 371). It is puzzling that this denial has been so generally ignored.

CHAPTER XII

The Agreement of the People

Anger and frustration seldom inspire a creative advance in political evolution. For once, in this autumn of 1647, they had this salutary effect. The unrest and distrust among the troopers of five regiments of horse in the New Model stimulated them to an invention in political thinking destined one day to give their shape to mighty communities in the New World. These young men were angry for several good reasons. Parliament was hardly more punctual than of old in doling out their pay; they had as yet no security for their arrears; their maimed comrades, orphans and widows were still thrust upon the charity of their parishes. Not one of the political reforms they set out to win had yet been secured. They felt that their officers had taken the wrong course in negotiating with the King—with 'him that intended our bondage and brought a cruel war upon us'. And so, relying on themselves, they turned their backs on King, Lords and Commons and thought out a way by which the people of England should secure their own liberties for all time by an agreement among themselves. The document they framed for this purpose was the first rough draft of a written constitution in the history of democracy. These troopers were the pioneers who blazed the trail the Founding Fathers were to follow, and after them the architects of freedom in many another land from the France of 1789 to the India of 1947.

We know enough to piece together the outlines of this story. Overton's *Appeal* made its impression most powerfully and promptly on some of the regiments of horse quartered near the capital and especially in Surrey. There they were in close touch with the civilian Levellers who seem to have perfected the organisation of their party about this time. Though Lilburne and Overton were in prison, they were not inaccessible; Walwyn was a powerful influence behind the scenes and there were others, for instance Thomas Prince and Samuel Chidley, the two treasurers of the party, who could on occasion write a leaflet or a pamphlet, and William Larner who never shrank from the risk of printing what the others wrote. The distrust which the radicals in the Army felt towards the Grandees had now infected their attitude towards some of the Agitators who had, they thought, been corrupted by their officers.

Early in October the men in five regiments of horse (Cromwell's, Ireton's, Whalley's, Fleetwood's and Rich's) recalled their original Agitators and elected new Agents or Agitators in their place. Who started this movement in the ranks we do not know, possibly Sexby. The representatives of these regiments met at Guildford, and there, perhaps in conclave with some of the civilian Levellers, they reached their new strategy. They turned the Heads of the Proposals upside down. They agreed with Marten and Rainsborough that the futile and perilous business of negotiating with Charles Stuart must be stopped. He could always tear up any treaty, by pleading that at law it was null and void, because he was under restraint when he signed it. As for the 'pretended' House of Commons, they had no use for it until it should be purged of the whole faction which at the end of July started in London what was, after all, a civil war, however feeble their effort may have been. By a train of thought that sprang directly from their experience as soldiers quartered in the villages and farmsteads of southern England they arrived, by steps we can still trace, at the profoundly original idea that the sovereign people, with its Army's help, should proclaim its own rights and secure them by an agreement which would rank as unalterable and paramount law for all time.

This train of thought began when the newly elected Agitators recalled the happy days of early June. Then the Army had been popular, and petitions flowed into St Albans even from distant counties backing its claim for justice for itself, and conjuring it not to disband until it had 'mediated' with Parliament to win reforms for the people also.[1] Now in October the affection

of the people to the Army was 'cooled and near lost'. Round
about them they heard men asking 'What good have our new
saviours done for us? What grievances have they procured to be
redressed?' These voices would go on to murmur that they were
no worse off when they were slaves to the King's will; indeed,
they would rather have one tyrant than hundreds. Today the
troopers, ashamed as they were to be living on free quarter,
had to listen to the people's reproaches. They would not
disband—ran the talk now—because they wished to live idly
on the people's labours and eat the bread out of its children's
mouths. From these dismal reflections, the Agitators went on to
ask how the good will of the people could be recovered. Their
answer was by a mutual agreement. The Army should pledge
itself to get for the people all the reforms listed in the Heads of
the Proposals including the abolition of tithes and the excise,
and two or three more as well. The people, in its turn, should
stand by the Army in its demands, above all for an indemnity
and the end of the press-gang.

These reflections were set out in a document entitled *The
Case of the Army truly stated*, which was signed by the ten Agitators
of the five regiments on 9 October, presented to General Fairfax
for the consideration of the Army Council on the 18th; it had
been published as a pamphlet on the 15th.[2] Obviously the work
of several pens, as a piece of writing it does not rank among the
better Leveller pamphlets, for it is long-winded, confused and
full of repetitions; none the less, as the bridge that leads to the
Agreement, it has its historical interest and there are pages in
it which give us a human glimpse into the minds of these young
men. Like the Proposals it insists on the merciful treatment of
the beaten enemy. The clause in which it deals with tithes is
blunter and plainer: they should simply be swept away. The
paragraph dealing with the reform of the law calls not only for
an overhaul by laymen ('conscientious persons') of its procedure
and for its decentralisation in hundreds and counties; it proposes
a codification of all the laws in a single volume in English,
intelligible to every free commoner.

But the detail which in itself makes this an historic document
is the clause that proposes to confer the franchise for the biennial Parliaments on 'all the freeborn at the age of 21 years

and upwards . . . excepting those that have or shall deprive themselves of that their freedom, either for some years or wholly by delinquency'. Lilburne as we have seen (p. 117) had already made the claim for manhood suffrage. The Levellers were at one with the Independents and the Grandees of the Army in proposing to disfranchise for a term of years all who had actively supported the royal cause. The real reason for this restriction lay in the fact that the Royalists and their dependents were numerous enough to upset at the polls all their opponents had won in the field. The moral excuse—that the Royalists had thrown away their birthright of freedom by supporting the King—was characteristic of Puritan England. Democracy, as the Atlantic civilisation understands that word, cannot be honestly applied after society has been riven by civil war or revolution. Even Lincoln, bent though he was on conciliation, would not restore it in the defeated South without disfranchising the governing class and the planter aristocracy.[3]

Lastly, it must be noted that the authors alike of this preliminary pamphlet and of the Agreement itself were not academic republicans. They assume that the King may eventually be restored. Evidently they did not regard monarchy itself as the source of all their ills, as the authors of *The Remonstrance of Many Thousands* under Harry Marten's influence did. Commonly in this century the republicans were aristocrats and intellectuals brought up on the Greek and Latin classics. What mattered to the pedestrian, practical thinking of these Agitators was chiefly that the King like the Lords should be deprived of his 'negative voice', and further that he should not have around him a costly and luxurious court. But to such matters they refer only incidentally. Their aim was to 'settle the nation in peace and freedom before the King's business be considered'.

The Case of the Army drew a distinction between 'law paramount' and ordinary legislation which is and should be alterable. And so the troopers in their train of thought went on to the conclusion that though they were keen to purge Parliament and angry with their officers for their backsliding in this matter, they could not rely on Parliament to guarantee their liberties —not even if it were purged. What one Parliament could do, another could undo. In the matter of their indemnity, for example, while their pride forbade them to ask the King's pardon for defeating him, their foresight could not be satisfied with an ordinance from Parliament. They could rely on nothing less than the word of the sovereign people. The same thing held for toleration.

More clearly than any of their contemporaries the Levellers realised that the Civil War had shattered the constitutional framework of the feudal society in which they were brought up. They had slid back, as Lilburne put it, into a state of nature. A month before these newly-elected Agitators met at Guildford, Cromwell had induced the Council of War to expel Major Francis White, one of the few radical officers whom the men always trusted, because he had dared to say in the course of debate that there was 'now no visible authority in the kingdom but the power and force of the sword'. John Lilburne had put it even better when he said that 'a righteous act performed by a troop of horse was as good law as he could now see in England'. Needless to say, neither he nor the Major contemplated this state of things with satisfaction. They dreaded it, but they believed in facing facts. How, then, does society emerge from a state of nature? The answer of their generation was already a commonplace before Hobbes and Locke elaborated it. Men struggled out of savagery and constituted civil society by concluding the social contract. After the anarchy of the Civil War they must do it over again.

But there were various ways, even then, of conceiving the social contract. The Levellers inclined to think of it on the analogy of one of the 'gathered' churches, whether Independent or Anabaptist, in which they enjoyed their deepest experience of social life.[4] Membership meant their voluntary entry into a closely knit community, and the signing of a covenant with each other for mutual aid and discipline, in which they collectively subscribed to certain beliefs. The guilds and the City companies were even older examples of communities which, although voluntary, exercised within certain limits (clearly defined in their charters) an unchallenged authority over their members. To conceive a contract of this kind, voluntarily signed yet embracing a whole nation, put no such strain on the imagination of that age as it does on ours. With one such instance, the Solemn League and Covenant of the Scots, everyone was familiar. Imposed only by public opinion and its voices, the Presbyterian clergy, virtually every Scot took it, voluntarily and very often with enthusiasm. In England, to be sure, though one big party subscribed it gladly, it had to be imposed (in a slightly revised version) on the rest by the authority of Parliament. But history, for several generations round about this time, is littered with oaths, covenants and engagements which everyone, or everyone of any consequence, was expected to take, and did in fact take, though sometimes with reluctance and a mental reservation. In short, there was nothing eccentric or unusual in this notion of the soldiers that the freeborn citizens of England—meaning all or most of them, bar the 'malignants'—should put their hands to an agreement between the people and the Army.

With the other line of approach to the social contract Lilburne and Overton had by now familiarised both the Army and the Leveller party. What was significant in their doctrine that all authority is held on trust, was that it stressed the 'bounds', the limits that restricted the power conferred by the sovereign people alike on their magistrates and their representatives. In plain words, even the House of Commons must be limited as well as the monarchy. There is a fenced field into which even it, supreme though it is, may not trespass. The usual name for this enclosure in those days was all that was covered by the dictates of each man's 'conscience'. Overton, as we saw (p. 121) had a wider, more secular view of it; he called it each man's 'self-propriety', by which he meant his 'individuality'. It was what modern liberals mean when they talk of the sacredness to human personality. In the concrete, when these young soldiers tried to be precise, two freedoms stood out for them as all-important—freedom in matters of religion and freedom from conscription and the press-gang.

We can guess with some degree of confidence what happened to *The Case of the Army* when it was presented to Fairfax for submission to the Army Council.[5] The officers to whom he may have referred it in the first instance did not like it and may not have understood it fully, for it is a tactless and rather obscure document, marred by some malicious exaggeration. They sent a reply in writing to the Agitators, in which among other objections they may have stressed their disapproval of manhood suffrage. On receipt of this, the Agitators of the five regiments of horse, who now had the approval of another four regiments of horse and seven of foot, nominated someone, or more probably a small committee, to recast *The Case of the Army* in a more acceptable form.

The result was the first of the three versions of An Agreement of the People which was read at the meeting of the Council of the Army at Putney on 29 October, 1647, and was on sale in London as a pamphlet on November 3. It is a terse and lucid composition, in which even the Grandees would find nothing offensive. Its preamble and postscripts explain the reasoning by which Agents of the five regiments arrived at it. The substance of it, cut down to the barest essentials, is a first tentative draft of the Agreement or contract itself. Oddly enough, among its proposals for Parliamentary reform it does not mention manhood suffrage, the outstanding detail in which the programme of *The Case* differed from that of the Heads of the Proposals. This daring innovation may have been omitted to appease the Grandees. It can be argued, however, that manhood suffrage was implied in its prescription for the redistribution of parliamentary constituencies according to the number of their inhabitants. For its purpose this document, so persuasive, so superior to the blundering *Case of the Army*, could hardly have been better written. One asks, with Pease, can Walwyn have been its author? It must be summarised before we discuss it further.

It provided (1) that a redistribution of constituencies, proportionate to population shall be made by the Long Parliament before it is dissolved, (2) as it must be, on September 30th, 1648.

(3) Thereafter Parliaments shall be elected in regular succession on fixed dates, every two years, and shall sit for six months only.

(4) The power of the representative body is 'inferior only to theirs who choose' it (the sovereign people) and extends without the consent of any other person or persons (i.e. of King or Lords) to all fields of legislation and administration,

including the making of war and peace and the command of the militia and 'generally to whatsoever is not reserved by the represented to themselves'. The following matters are reserved: (1) 'That matters of religion and the ways of God's worship are not to be entrusted by us to any human power, because therein we cannot remit or exceed a tittle of what our consciences dictate to be the mind of God without wilful sin, nevertheless the public way of instructing the nation (so it be not compulsive) is referred to their [i.e. Parliaments'] discretion.'

(2) Impressing 'and constraining any of us to serve in the wars is against our freedom'.

(3) A complete indemnity and amnesty covering every thing done by both sides in the Civil War shall come into force on the dissolution of this Parliament.

(4) All are equal before the law and none (meaning neither peers nor M.P.s) is exempted from the ordinary course of legal proceedings.

'These things we declare to be our native rights' and the foundations of freedom, settled unalterably by this Agreement with the People.[6]

The modern reader, familiar with such documents as the American constitution and the French Declaration of the Rights of Man is astonished that the soldiers and the Leveller party behind them were content to enumerate only four 'native rights'. One might have expected at least some reference to the 'foundations of freedom' laid in Magna Carta and the Petition of Right. One might, indeed, go on asking such questions indefinitely. The Levellers were keenly aware of the importance of freedom of the press; they do not mention it here, nor yet the exemption of the accused from interrogation.

The explanation may be found in the Postscript, where the authors give their reason for 'extracting some principles of common freedom out of those many things proposed to you in *The Case of the Army truly stated*'. The things they have stressed are those for which 'we first engaged against the King'—the right of the people to representation and of their representatives to dispose of the militia. It is natural to include toleration also among these things which are the people's 'native right and price of their blood' for that, assuredly, was a chief issue in the struggle. The ending of it by an amnesty and the abolition of some of the privileges of members of the two Houses may also be included without strain in this chapter. In short, the Agreement does not profess to be a written constitution, however rudimentary. It was, like the Newcastle Propositions and the Heads of the Proposals, a sketch of a settlement which established representative democracy on a new footing, deprived the King and the defeated aristocracy of their vetoes, ended the troubles with an amnesty, freed the common man from the class discipline of bishops or presbyteries and tore from his back the traditional burden of the press-gang. None the less, if the soldiers and Levellers had ever succeeded in persuading the mass of the English people to adopt it, it would have become the corner stone of the future constitution—as would the Heads of the Proposals, if the Grandees could have induced King and Parliament to adopt them.

The Levellers soon became aware that there were disadvantages in cutting down the contents of the Agreement to the bare necessities of a settlement. When it became under Lilburne's guidance the be-all and end-all of their movement, they expanded it in the two later versions to include many additional civil liberties. They realised also that its authors had thrown away much of its attraction for the common man when they left out what had been included boldly in *The Case* and rather more cautiously in the Proposals, the ending of tithes, imprisonment for debt, and the excise. They restored these items of their programme and many more, not as unalterable rights, but as urgent reforms to which Parliament must give priority. In the second version Lilburne even added to these familiar things the abolition of base tenures, the key to the emancipation of the peasants.

The authors of the Agreement were somewhat vague as to how it was to be adopted. The first step was to get it accepted, they hoped unanimously, by the Army, not only by the men, regiment by regiment, but by the Council, including the Grandees. Thereafter, they proposed to collect signatures from the people—a slow and difficult undertaking. On the negative side, one thing was clear; they would not ask Parliament to pass it, for it claimed an authority superior to Parliament; it was to be the direct voice of the sovereign people. Eventually, as we shall see, what they proposed was that all the voters should sign it at the first general election.

Out of the discussions on its contents and its wording, there soon emerged another pioneering notion: a representative convention must be called to frame in a final form the text of the Agreement that should be submitted to the people at large. How this convention was to be chosen, we shall see as we go along.

It is with these two refinements that the Agreement evolves unmistakably into a written constitution. It could hardly rank as a constitution if only the soldiers' agents had the drafting of it. Yet it was always something more than a settlement of the Civil War, for it aimed, above all, at permanence. Seen from that angle, its chief defect was that the Levellers made no provision for its amendment. Paradox though it may sound, no constitution can endure unless it is capable of development and revision. It would be monstrous that one generation should make the bed on which its heirs must lie without the right to smooth it or to lengthen it.

To sketch the difficulties of which the Levellers became aware as they worked out the practical applications of their theory of the social contract would be a rewarding study, but it would carry us far beyond the limits of an historical essay into the realm of philosophical speculation. What, for instance, was the status of those who refused to sign the Agreement, of the 'malignants' who were given no chance to sign it, or of the indifferent multitude which would not bother to sign it? There were fanatics of logic—a useful tribe if we care for clear thinking—who drew the monstrous conclusion that these men had forfeited all their civil rights and were, in plain words, outlaws. Theirs was, none the less, a valid inference from the premise that society can be constituted on a voluntary footing, like a 'gathered' church. The next minute these same Levellers would talk of their 'birthright' of freedom and the heritage of liberty that had come down to them from the struggles of their ancestors. They knew very well that men do not choose the society in which they must live. They are born into it and bound to it by countless ties of memory, imitation and love—unless, indeed, they should deliberately seek an asylum and home beyond the seas, as in that generation so many did.

In that century and the next, on both shores of the Atlantic, men were trying out all they could derive from the bold and simple viewpoint of individualism. It led them through the slogans of two English revolutions—the Levellers' 'government by consent' and the Whigs' 'right to choose our governors'— to the ultimate question of the one and the many in its social aspect. Who consents to a given form of government? It may be the individual citizen, an answer that would lead eventually to anarchism as Godwin, reared in the same climate of dissent as the Levellers, would one day formulate it. Is it, as the Utilitarians and most of our contemporaries would say, the numerical majority who inhabit a limited territory? Or is it the community, endowed with a life that spans the centuries, which makes its choice of a form of government, occasionally by revolution, but normally by the slower processes of adaptation? Even in this last solution which tries to view the life and respect the rights of the individual as an organ of a social organism, there is still a sense in which this individual chooses the society in which he has his being. He becomes a mature man only when he consciously wills to exercise his duties as a citizen. Instinctively primitive peoples understood this better than we moderns do. They insisted that a boy or girl, born to a given tribe, should deliberately rejoin it at puberty—should be born again of his own free will, by a solemn and difficult process of initiation with the blessing of the elder tribesmen and the ancestral spirits.

But this digression is passing all tolerable bounds. Let us return to the Agitators and the Grandees as they talked these problems out on a day in late October 1647 in the parish church of Putney, below the great common on the south bank of the Thames, where a bridge crosses the river today, as it did then.

NOTES TO CHAPTER XII

1. There is evidence from the other side that this supposed popularity of the Army was not a myth. In a letter to the Speaker, dated 8 July, 1647, Sir H. Cholmeley, a middle-of-the-fence Presbyterian who sat for Pontefract and behaved very equivocally in the second Civil War, wrote that in Yorkshire 'the Parliament hath now (I fear) far more enemies than friends, the country [county] in general looking upon Sir Thomas Fairfax's Army as that which they hope will bring them a sudden peace (which they would willingly have upon any terms).' He ends with a plea for a speedy settlement, 'for otherwise (I fear) clubs and clouted shoes will in the end be too hard

for them both' (i.e. for Parliament and the Army) (Cary, *op. cit.*, I, p. 293).

2. Wolfe, p. 216. Tradition, following a remark of Cromwell's in the Putney Debates, ascribed this pamphlet to John Wildman. Doubtless he had a large share in it: the first few pages recall his dry, prosaic manner. Some later pages are emotional as he never was in the pieces we know to be his. The description of the troopers' feelings towards the civilian population may have come from a soldier's pen; the ability to write well was not rare in the ranks of this unusual Army. Mr. Wolfe suggests that one of the political programmes embedded in it may have come from Lilburne's pen. Perhaps: but I doubt it, for at this time the question which came before every other in his mind was the jurisdiction of Lords over Commons and this is not mentioned. But several details may have been suggested by Lilburne's writings. There are echoes of Overton also such as the reference to enclosed commons and the grievances of counties in §12: two verbal echoes are audible in the Agitators' covering letter. But Overton, like Lilburne, was, I think, rather an influence than an author. It is obvious that several independent drafts were hastily stitched into a patchwork: thus §7 follows §12 (Wolfe, p. 217). To my ears the appeal on the last page for unity in the Army sounds like Sexby's writing. It has several imaginative touches—the story of the father's danger that made a dumb child speak, the description of 'this Army that God hath clothed with honour' and the metaphors which recall the ravages of the sea on the East Anglian coast. 'In case the union of the Army should be broken . . . ruin and destruction will break in upon us like a roaring sea', and again the prayer that the people may come to call the Army 'the repairers of their breaches'. Sexby was a Suffolk man who may have seen broken dykes.

3. Lincoln, I may remind the reader, vetoed the bill originally passed by Congress, which disfranchised all who had voluntarily borne arms for the Confederate government or otherwise supported it. The act which replaced it was drafted after his assassination in accordance with his views. It required from voters an oath supporting the constitution of the Union and the laws emancipating slaves, and disfranchised (a) the higher military, civil and diplomatic officers of the Confederacy, all its former judges, congressmen and military or naval officers and (b) 'all persons who have voluntarily participated in the said rebellion, and the estimated value of whose taxable property is over $20,000'. The Soviet Union, in the early days before voting had become a meaningless ritual, disfranchised priests and employers of hired labour. In Germany and Austria, where Nazi violence had split society even more cruelly than did the English and American civil wars, the Allies in the first elections refused both the active and passive franchise to former members of the Nazi party.

4. This interpretation comes from the brilliant pioneering study of Dr Charles Borgeaud, *The Rise of Modern Democracy in Old and New England*, *passim*, but especially Chapter III (English translation, 1894).

5. I am here carrying a little further a suggestion first made by Firth and underlined by Wolfe (p. 224).

6. I have omitted the fifth reservation, a commonplace to which I can give no precise meaning. Laws must be good as well as equal, and not evidently destructive to the safety and well-being of the people. This perilous clause which might be made to cover anything one feared, was not included in the later versions of the Agreement.

CHAPTER XIII

The Putney Debates

The General Council of the Army sat in Putney church to discuss the Agreement of the People from 28 October to 11 November, 1647. When one compares the reports of these debates with those of its sittings at Reading in July, it is clear that in three months the temper and outlook of the Army were changed. At Putney the atmosphere is sultry and tense. In July the Agitators were for marching faster than the Grandees but they were both moving in the same direction. In November the gravest issue of principle divides them: the Grandees take their stand squarely for property, while the Agitators champion the rights of the common man. There is no verbal discourtesy in these reports, yet one senses the antipathy between radicals and conservatives. Rainsborough at one point apologises for having spoken 'with passion'. Cromwell replies to a personal criticism with dignity and calm but evidently it rankled, for before long he assails the Agitators with a heavy bombardment of sarcasm. From time to time, however, he recovers his poise and strives with an echo of his former good nature to restore the unity of the Army. For him, one senses, something more intimate than a political principle is at stake. He is struggling against the martyr in the Tower and the Agitators who spoke for Freeborn John at Putney, to retain his control over the Army that was so largely his creation. In these reports he never threatens or tries to assert his authority over junior officers and men, but evidently he has done so in some of the earlier unreported sittings of the Council. Here his method of coercion is subtler: he gets his way in the end by offering, more than once to withdraw from the Army and resign his command. Doubtless he realised that he was indispensable. There were good soldiers among his senior officers, but no one who approached him in leadership or prestige. The mass of the rank and file still loved him; if they doubted him, they blamed the influence of the unpopular Ireton over him.

This was the theme of a brief but notable tract, *A Call to all the Soldiers of the Army by the Free People of England* which defended the Agents of the more radical regiments.[1] It was in print by 29 October, in time to reach the men when the General Council met in Putney church. It repeats the demand for a purge of the Commons: 'establish a free Parliament by expulsion of the usurpers'. It exhorts the Agitators to meet together as 'an exact council' with the help of 'the truest lovers of the people ye can find'. But its main purpose is to expose the 'hypocrisy' and 'deceit' of Cromwell and Ireton. The violence of their behaviour at the last Council meeting on 22 October is described, when they held forth to you 'the bloody flag of threats and terrors' and even talked of hanging and punishment. They are attacked for 'carrying on the King's design in the Commons', where in the name of the whole Army they threatened the House into a compliance with the King, 'your most deadly enemy'. Ireton by his 'imperious carriage' has made the General Councils 'like unto Star Chambers'. 'None but flatterers, tale-bearers and turn-coats are countenanced by him.'

> And if Cromwell instantly repent not and alter his course, let him know also that ye loved just, honest, sincere and valiant Cromwell that loved his country and the liberties of the people above his life, yea and hated the King as a man of blood, but that Cromwell ceasing to be such, he ceaseth to be the object of your love.
>
> And since there is no remedy ye must begin your work anew. Ye are as ye were at Bury. Ye are no strangers to the way; ye have already made a good beginning, wherein we rejoice. Ye have men as fit to govern as others be removed. *And with a word ye can create new officers.* Necessity hath no law and against it there is no plea.

The Levellers, to put it plainly, wanted to get rid of Cromwell. To Ireton for most of the time the Lieut.-General is content to leave the statement of the conservative case. Ireton is by far the ablest debater at Putney. His thought is clear-cut, his language precise, but he is not a sympathetic or persuasive speaker. Though he is not in words overbearing, his manner may have conveyed to his hearers the impression of an 'imperious carriage'. Certainly he spoke too often and at great length. Twice in these debates he concedes that the sense of the meeting is against him. Whether by applause or in some other way his audience must have been able to show its feelings.

On the democratic side the outstanding personality is Colonel Rainsborough. By comparison with Ireton his thought is simple and his vocabulary limited, nor does he refer to the classics or quote Latin as two of the junior officers did. He had, however, read some English history with his mind wide awake and can fish out an apt precedent from it. He can convey his strong feelings with great force and more than once he uses irony with effect. If we could watch the faces of the audience it is a probable guess that of the senior officers only Cromwell and Rainsborough knew how to touch the hearts of their hearers; Sexby also may have had this gift. Rainsborough is much too apt to take offence. His feelings were complicated by a personal grievance. Because he was a sailor by descent and ranked as vice-admiral before he joined the army, he had just been chosen (under the Earl of Warwick) to command the navy, which inclined to a blend of Presbyterianism and royalism and deeply resented the cashiering of its popular but treasonable commander, Batten. Rainsborough suspected that he was to be 'kicked out of the Army'—presumably because he was the only outspoken radical among the senior officers.[2] Evidently he hoped that his naval service would only be temporary and felt hurt because his regiment had already been offered to another officer. He vowed that he would 'live and die' with the Army and would rather be sent to prison and excluded from the House than lose his regiment. In justice to his memory one must add that his radicalism was not prompted by this grievance: it was active and vocal both in the House and in the Army long before he had any such ground of complaint.

Distrusting their own ability to argue with Ireton, the Agitators, not for the first time, brought with them as their advocates two civilian Levellers. Of one of them, Maximilian Petty, we know little; the other, John Wildman, was destined to become a key figure, 'the soul of English politics' as Disraeli, exaggerating picturesquely, described him. For fifty years and through four reigns he conspired in the republican interest. Imprisoned in turn by the Long Parliament by Cromwell and Charles II, he spent (as his biographer, Maurice Ashley, reminds us) a fifth of his active political life in jails; yet he died in his bed, aged three score years and ten, one of the richest aldermen of the City of London. His portrait by Wenceslas Hollar and his motto *nil admirari* reflect his habitual caution. He talked little, and what he said (to quote Mr Ashley again) was phrased in a sort of conspirator's cipher. The style of his few pamphlets lacks imagination or character, though it is lucid and vigorous in a forensic manner, but overloaded with precedents, as if he sought rather to crush than to persuade.

Born in 1623, probably in Berkshire, his father, if we may believe Clarendon, who knew him personally, was an Anabaptist but he himself according to Bishop Burnet was a deist. He is said to have been educated at Cambridge; if so, he left without graduating. He must have studied law, but he was never called to the bar. He may have been an attorney or solicitor, for he acted as agent to the second Duke of Buckingham. He made a fortune by speculating in the grand manner in the confiscated acres of Royalists, for in five years he bought —for himself or for others—no less than fifty estates in twenty counties.[3] The stories that Wildman, elusive in this as in everything else, ever served in the army seem to be legends, but after he had quitted the Leveller party for a time Cromwell gave him a commission with the honorary rank of major; certainly when he took part in the debates at Putney he was a civilian.

His legalistic habit of mind may have been the quality that commended 'John Lawmind' (his pseudonym as a pamphleteer) to John Lilburne, for the two can have had little else in common. They collaborated very closely in the later months of 1647 and throughout 1648. Better educated than most of its converts, Wildman was evidently valued by the party for his quick wits and orderly mind and served it as an active propagandist both on platforms and as a writer. By temperament he was not a typical Leveller; it must have been the political rather than the social and humanitarian side of the movement that appealed to him. He was not an original thinker; there is nothing in the development of the Leveller programme that can be traced to him save, indeed, what he later borrowed from Harrington. Though experience taught him to be wary, courage must have been one of his native gifts, for when he faced Ireton in debate, he had only four and twenty years behind him.

The debate opened on an ominous note. Private Sexby in the name of the Agitators had to tell Cromwell and Ireton that their 'credits and reputation had been much blasted'. In their dealings with the King and Parliament they had tried to please all men and had failed to please any. As for the King, there was no way of pleasing him, unless they were prepared to cut their own throats. What the Army, or the major part of it, resented were the speeches of Cromwell and Ireton in the debates of 22 and 23 September, when they defeated Marten and Rainsborough on the vote that 'no more addresses' be made to the King. Cromwell replied that he had spoken not in the name of the Army but in his private capacity. One may doubt whether the House was much interested in the views of the Senior Burgess for Cambridge; it listened to the Lieut.-General.[4] None the less, Rainsborough intervened to acquit Cromwell of blame. Ireton, whose answer was defiant, bore the brunt of the radicals' anger, which he further provoked by attacking the Agitators for causing disunity in the Army.

The first speech in the debate that touches our subject nearly came from Cromwell. It reminds us that the leader of the Puritan Revolution, though a 'root and branch' man in religion, was by temperament a conservative. He complains that the proposals of the Agreement are 'new to us': they involve 'very great alterations in the very government of the kingdom'. They seem 'plausible', but 'another company of men' might submit others equally plausible, and then another company. 'Would it not be confusion? Would it not be utter confusion?' It would make England like Switzerland with counties like cantons contending one against another—a shrewd point, for England in this century was not homogeneous.

We should consider rather what 'the spirits and temper of the people of this nation are prepared to receive and go on along with it' (i.e. follow public opinion). He saw 'great difficulties . . ., very great mountains in the way of this'. So he appeals for a readiness to consider amendments. There are things none the less in the Agreement which even Ireton approves, while Cromwell assures the men that he is with them in their central contention that 'the foundation and supremacy [i.e. sovereignty] is in the people, radically in them'.

It cannot have happened often to Cromwell that he should be rebuked for timidity, but Rainsborough got in his ironical protest against that vision of the 'mountains of difficulty'.

> Oh, unhappy men are we that ever began this war! If ever we had looked upon difficulties, I do not know that ever we should have looked an enemy in the face.

Speaking to the Army, as he supposed, for the last time, Rainsborough maintained that whatever the difficulties round them might be,

> have you death before you, the sea on each side of you and behind you, and are you convinced that the thing is just, . . . you are bound in conscience to carry it on. . . . At the last day it can never be answered to God that you did not do it.

Cromwell's main objection to the Agreement was, however, that it was at variance with the engagements into which the Army had already entered. He proposed to begin with a systematic review of all their commitments as they stood in the newly published *Book of Army Declarations*—a dilatory device, as Rainsborough pointed out. In the debate on 'engagements' which followed, Wildman plunged recklessly at the start by maintaining that men are under no obligation to honour an engagement which they have come to consider unjust. Ireton, who stuck to abstractions, upheld a stiff, legalistic view of the sanctity of engagements. Wildman's counter-attack was ingenious and in part successful. Evidently what Ireton and Cromwell had in mind (though they never said so plainly) was the undertaking the Army had given in its *Representation* on June 14, that after the royal assent had been given to a series of bills concerning parliamentary reform, the rights of His Majesty and his posterity may be considered of and settled in all things, so far as may consist with the right and freedom of the subject and with the security of the same for the future.

Cromwell's view was typical of his habitual combination of puritan ethics with opportunism. He argued that

it's an act of duty to break an unrighteous engagement; he that keeps it does a double sin, in that he made an unrighteous engagement and in that he goes about to keep it.

But if it should be decided (contrary to his own view) that their engagements were unrighteous, these were after all public, and if they should be broken scandal could be avoided only if 'circumstances' were considered and the thing done with 'judgment and knowledge'. He assured the Council (as Ireton also did) that he had made no personal engagement with the King. Perhaps the best sense and the best morals in this lengthy debate came from the nameless 'Bedfordshire man', who maintained that these engagements between the Army and the King were unjust and must be broken if they promised the King what rightfully belonged to the people.

Suddenly in the midst of the logic-chopping and the manœuvres to gain time, Lieut.-Colonel William Goffe, an Anabaptist, intervened with a proposal which reminds us that this Army was not as others are. He moved that there should be 'a seeking God in the things that now lie before us'. Recently, he argued, 'there hath been a withdrawing of the presence of God from us', yet he hoped that 'our strayings from God are not so great but that a conversion and true humiliation may recover us again'. By a public seeking of God he believed they could recover their unity. The prayers at the meeting which took up the whole of the next morning were not reported but some speeches have survived. There were mystics among these soldiers. When Captain John Clarke asked himself what it was that had 'eclipsed the light and glory of God from our eyes', his answer was that 'we have submitted the spirit of God unto the candle of reason', and so he exhorted his hearers and himself

to lay down our reason, lay down our goods, lay down all

K

we have at the feet of God and let God work his will in us that we may be buried with God in our spirits.

This did not mean, as such language usually does, that they should obey their clerical guides. The Anabaptists among them believed in 'the Inner Light'. Goffe was more prosaic. What had gone wrong, he thought, was that they had of late 'crossed the work of God' by 'compliance with that party' which God had engaged them to destroy, though 'we intended nothing but civility'. Ireton had no such doubts. It was because the Army had fought for 'the good and freedom and safety and happiness of God's people' that 'God hath appeared with us and led us and gone before us and honoured us and taken delight to work by us'. This He did because they had made Him 'president' in their councils and followed his guidance in many things against their own reasons.

After the prayer-meeting, Ireton on the afternoon of the 29th raised the main issue that separated the high command from the Levellers and the elected Agents of the Army. He pointed out that they asked for a redistribution of seats according to the number of inhabitants and not according to the totals paid in rates. Did this mean that 'every man . . . is to have an equal voice in the election of those represIenters'? After some sparring over the Norman Conquest came the answer that this was exactly what the soldiers did mean: 'We judge that all inhabitants that have not lost their birthright should have an equal voice in elections.' In modern terminology the Army stood for manhood suffrage.

Then, in an outburst from Rainsborough came the straightest and simplest claim for equality ever made in English history:

For really I think that the poorest he that is in England hath a life to live, as the greatest he; and therefore, truly, Sir, I think it's clear that every man that is to live under a government ought first by his own consent to put himself under that government; and I do think that the poorest man in England is not at all bound in a strict sense to that government that he hath not had a voice to put himself under; . . . insomuch that I should doubt whether he was an Englishman . . . that should doubt of these things.

Rainsborough's thinking is individualistic and coloured by

the theory of the social contract, but like all the Levellers he demands a classless political democracy. The word 'government' meant at this time 'form of government' or 'constitution' and not as we often understand it, 'party administration'.

> I do not find anything in the law of God [Rainsborough went on] that a lord shall choose twenty burgesses and a gentleman but two, or a poor man shall chose none; I find no such thing in the law of nature, nor in the law of nations.

As the debate continued, he and others reinforced this claim based on 'the law of nature' by some further arguments. Many a poor man who had fought for the Parliament had lost in the war the little estate he had. Were these veterans to be disenfranchised? Others dwelt on the caprices of the traditional qualification. A tenant might have a lease for £100 for three lives and yet have no vote. The freeholders were, perhaps, one in seven of the adult male population. Among the cultivators of the land they were only one in five. But the note that recurs in speech after speech is the angry disillusionment of soldiers who realise that they had been led to the battle to confirm a propertied oligarchy in power. Sexby, who insists that he speaks for his regiment, put it as well as any:

> There are many thousands of us soldiers that have ventured our lives; we have had little propriety in the kingdom as to our estates, yet we have had a birthright. But it seems now, except a man hath a fixed estate in this kingdom, he hath no right in this kingdom. I wonder we were so much deceived. If we had not a right to the kingdom, we were mere mercenary soldiers.

He maintains that it was 'the poor and mean . . . in their stations' who have 'preserved this kingdom', and he tells Cromwell plainly that if he had 'advertised' his views about property earlier, he would have had fewer under his command.

Ireton was as blunt and unyielding as it is possible to be. He stands by the traditional propertied qualifications:

> No person hath a right to an interest or share in the disposing of the affairs of the kingdom, and in determining or choosing those that shall determine what laws we shall be ruled by here—no person hath a right to this that hath not

a permanent fixed interest in this kingdom and those persons together are properly the represented of this kingdom and consequently are also to make up the representers of this kingdom, who taken together do comprehend whatsoever is of real or permanent interest in the kingdom.

Nothing less than freehold property will satisfy him as a proof that a man has such a 'stake in the country'. He will enfranchise only the 'persons in whom all land lies and those in corporations in whom all trading lies'. He will grant no political rights to those who are 'here today and gone to-morrow'. He concedes that the unprivileged majority have, indeed, 'a birthright'; 'we should not refuse to give them air and place and ground and the freedom of the highways and other things, to live among us'. But that is all: 'a share in that power that shall dispose of the lands here and of all things here' is no part of their inheritance. As the debate went on, Wildman drove Ireton to take up a position that was really a *reductio ad absurdum* of his main contention. Ireton will not admit that the consent of the governed is essential. Foreigners who reside and trade among us are bound by our laws, to which they have not consented. Out of 'humanity' or 'hospitality' we receive them among us, but we do not consult them about our laws. It appeared then that the unprivileged majority of Englishmen have no more rights in their native land than these alien birds of passage.

With commendable honesty Ireton states his true reason:

All the main thing that I speak for is because I would have an eye to property. I hope we do not come to contend for victory—but let every man consider with himself that he do not go that way to take away all property. For here is the case of the most fundamental part of the constitution of the kingdom, which if you take away, you take away all by that.

He presently makes his meaning even clearer. If manhood suffrage were conceded, the landless majority might combine to make an end of property itself. 'If you admit any man that hath a breath and being . . . this will destroy property. . . . Why may not those men vote against all property?' This final argument against 'reform' was repeated even in the last quarter of the nineteenth century. The crudity of Ireton's use of it should not surprise us, for property, though it made full use of the pulpit, had not yet tested all its resources or worked out all its defensive techniques. What Ireton said in the heat of debate was repeated as crudely in cold blood a generation later by Locke, when he wrote that 'the great and chief end of men's putting themselves under government . . . is the protection of their property'. The men of this age were franker in their attitude to property than we are. 'What stirs the Englishmen . . . sooner to rebellion,' Milton asked, 'than violent and heavy hands upon their goods and purses?'[5]

But it is probable that the Agitators were less startled by such remarks than a modern gathering drawn from the same social strata would be. Landed property was much more widely diffused in the England of the seventeenth century than it is today. None the less, his audience reacted sharply in this debate to Ireton's challenge. Major William Rainsborough, the Colonel's younger brother, protested tersely against this exclusive stress on property: 'The chief end of this government is to preserve persons as well as estates, and if any law shall lay hold of my person it is more dear than my estate.' In *Orinooko* by Mrs Aphra Behn, the first novel in the English language which attacks slavery and the slave trade, the younger Rainsborough is described as the only humane colonist among the white landowners in British Guiana. His reversal of a rich man's values was typical of the Levellers, who fought an incessant battle against the inhumanity of English law, which never scrupled to protect property by savage sentences. Ireton had argued that if poor men commanded a majority, they might by their votes sweep all property away. Colonel Rainsborough retorted that a minority of rich men, if they were the whole electorate, might as easily enslave the rest of the nation: 'the one part shall make hewers of wood and drawers of water of the other five'. With a flash of ironical insight, the Colonel drives home his point by a reference to the inequality of sacrifice under the press-gang:

> Sir, I see that it is impossible to have liberty but all property must be taken away. . . . If you say it, it must be so. But I would fain know what the soldier hath fought for all this while? He hath fought to enslave himself, to give power to

men of riches, men of estates, to make him a perpetual slave. We do find in all presses that go forth none must be pressed that are freehold men. When these gentlemen fall out among themselves, they shall press the poor scrubs to come and kill one another for them.

In plain words these soldiers had begun to suspect that the Civil War was merely a fratricidal struggle between two rival sections of the owning class: they had allowed themselves to be used much as the masses were used two centuries later to secure the first Reform Bill which ignored them.

Ireton's reply is interesting:

I will tell you what the soldier of the kingdom hath fought for. First the danger that we stood in was that one man's will must be a law.

The privileged few, to paraphrase his argument, felt this grievance of lawless, personal power directly. But it concerned the propertyless majority also, because the laws of England permitted any man to trade, and so he might hope one day to join the privileged minority as a landowner: 'he was capable of trading to get money to get estates by'. It was therefore also to this unprivileged man's interest to support a Parliament in which he had no share, since fixed, impersonal law is vital to trade. 'I shall know a law and have a certainty', said this man to himself, and therefore with good reason he supported the Parliament. Ireton, in his unfamiliar seventeenth-century terminology, is maintaining that in the England of his day trade opened a door into the governing class. The trader, though himself unrepresented, had every reason to support Parliament, which would legislate in the interests of the mercantile community. Already these Puritan squires are basing their claim to govern on the ground which the Whig nobility afterwards took.

Ireton's defence is so far valid that in fact, from Tudor times onwards, successful merchants had been buying their entry into the landed class. But this rather subtle and possibly unfamiliar argument made no impression on his hearers. No one answers it or refers to it. Nor is this surprising. Only a minority of these soldiers were traders: either they were craftsmen or else they were yeomen, members of a doomed class destined to disappear under the rule of the great landlords and merchants. Their ultimate fate was to sink into the proletariat. The significance of these debates at Putney was that the armed vanguard of this sinking class rejected the claim of the Puritan oligarchy to act as its uncontrolled trustee. The plutocracy claimed a monopoly of political power in order to further its own class interests.

Ireton and Cromwell found no support for their advocacy of a propertied franchise and several junior officers boldly backed the Agitators' proposal. One senior officer, Colonel Rich, took a middle of the road view. On the model of ancient Rome he would give votes to all, but with weightage for the benefit of property. A few years later Harrington adopted the same idea in *Oceana*; up to the first world war, the Prussian three-class franchise secured the ascendancy of property in the same way. Towards the end of the discussion an important and to modern minds puzzling qualification was adopted without opposition. Servants and beggars were to be excluded, because, as Petty who accepted this compromise put it, 'they depend upon the will of other men and should be afraid to displease them'. A 'servant', as the word was used in this century meant anyone employed by a single master, anyone from a nobleman's steward to a skilled journeyman or shepherd. This concession would have excluded many of the Levellers' urban adherents, though most of their following among the weavers, for example, were still small, independent craftsmen. The great gain would have come in the villages where the copyhold tenants, outnumbering the freeholders by four to one, would be enfranchised. But even in the country domestic servants, hired labourers and paupers would be excluded.

The explanation lay, of course, in the disorderly conduct of elections by show of hands or shouting, by separation into two masses or by roll-call. It is odd that with all their concern for free elections the Levellers never thought of the secret ballot. The Utopians had, however, used it, and so (presently) did the people of Oceana. Unfortunately More wrote too little on the subject and Harrington far too much, for he excelled in making a simple idea difficult. In real life this method of voting was not at this time unknown; it was practised in political elections in Massachusetts, in church elections in the Netherlands, and in company elections in England till Charles I forbade it. Lieut.-Colonel Jubbes tried but failed to get the secret ballot adopted by the General Council of the Army, since he found that officers who were 'servile' often cast their votes in public against their conviction in order to please their commanders.[6]

Another attempt at a compromise was made by Hugh Peters, Cromwell's man-of-all-work. He proposed to retain the traditional franchise, but in addition to give votes to all who had fought for the Parliament or furthered its cause with free gifts of horses, plate or money. This typical politician's dodge would have met the soldiers' personal sense of grievance, while ignoring the democratic principles for which Levellers and Agitators stood.

Finally, in this debate Ireton and his opponents reach the root of the matter: they discuss the title to property. The central issue between them was very much wider than the franchise, and both sides were perfectly conscious of it. The Agents of the Army and their Leveller spokesman, Wildman, were aware that they were taking a revolutionary stand. They had, indeed, rebelled long ago against the King, but they were now contemplating rebellion against Parliament, which might, as they feared, accomplish a counter-revolution in a few days or hours by concluding a treaty with the King. In that event the Army would have to break its 'engagement' to serve Parliament. As scrupulous and honourable men, they were uneasy about it, yet on the whole it seemed to them better to break an engagement than to act 'unjustly' and betray the people's cause. Ireton will have none of this. An engagement, as he had conceded in the first part of the debate, may, nay must be broken, if its observance involves 'sin', that is to say disobedience to God, but contracts between man and man are sacred.[7]

The Levellers justify their attitude by invoking the law of nature. This idea has a long history, which ranges from Cicero to Voltaire. Always those who relied on it tried to give it an objective meaning: as an ethical principle it was something which all mankind in all ages had acknowledged, and several of the Leveller pamphleteers sought to state it in general terms.

In our day we tend to be sceptical about it: anthropology has made us aware of the extreme variation of ethical codes. Some general principles there must be which ensure the cohesion and survival of every grade and type of society, but will they yield us detailed rules of conduct? It is on the whole the better opinion that a man should not marry his grandmother, but there have been societies in which this indulgence of the flesh was obligatory. Ireton and the Levellers have this in common, that their outlook is individualistic. He maintains that the law of nature to which they would have recourse is a subjective principle. That word did not figure in the vocabulary of the day, but his meaning is clear enough:

> And therefore when I hear men speak of laying aside all engagements to consider only that wild or vast notion of what in every man's conception is just or unjust, I am afraid and do tremble at the boundless and endless consequences of it.

What really troubles Ireton, if the law of nature is to be invoked, is not merely that it may lead to the widening of the franchise, which is anarchy, but to the abolition of property itself.

> What right hath any man to anything, if you lay not down that principle, that we are to keep covenant? If you will resort only to the law of nature, by the law of nature you have no more right to this land, or anything else, than I have.

The law of nature, in short, entitles me to ensure my own self-preservation, and therefore 'I have as much right to take hold to anything that is for my sustenance . . . as you'. He insists therefore, that the foundation of all right, above all, the right of property in land and goods, is in contract, in history, in inheritance, in civil institutions—in a word, in positive law. The two positions are for him completely antithetical: if you proclaim 'an absolute natural right', you must 'deny all civil right'. He will not depart from the letter of the laws of England which confine the franchise to freeholders, because he realises that the title to property rests on the same foundation of history and tradition. Even the law of God is no help: it lays down only general principles. As he puts it, with an unexpected touch of humour: 'there is no divine law that tells us that such a corporation must have the election of burgesses.'

Neither Rainsborough nor Wildman had thought out their revolutionary position with a clarity that approached Ireton's grasp of his conservative creed. They were aware that the law of nature is a dynamic principle, which may have 'boundless consequences': that did not alarm them. They were angry when Ireton called them anarchists. They were not prepared to throw away property altogether. When Ireton argued that manhood suffrage would be the end of all things, Rainsborough allayed his terrors by reminding him that the law of God recognised property in the prohibition *Thou shalt not steal*. This, however, was cold comfort; for some, at least, of the Levellers saw the revolutionary implications of that commandment, and were prepared to use it to defend the small man against the acquisitive rich. They had begun to suspect that 'property is theft'. If Ireton appealed to history and law, Rainsborough was ready to scrutinise the titles these bestowed.

> I am a poor man therefore I must be pressed[8] [i.e. conscripted]: if I have no interest in the kingdom, I must suffer by all their laws, be they right or wrong . . . Gentlemen with three or four lordships (God knows how they got them) can always get into Parliament and evict the poor from their homes. I would fain know whether the potency of rich men do not this, and so keep them [the poor men] under the greatest tyranny that was ever thought of in the world.

Wildman, lawyer though he was, can say bluntly 'our very laws were made by our conquerors'. The process of sapping the sanctity of property was well under way among the Levellers. They started with the Norman Conquest, and went on to the evictions involved in the enclosures of common land. Their Protestant bias seems to have forbidden them to speak on the robbery of church lands. One brief passage, but only one, condemns the slave trade, which was already the source of some great families' fortunes.[9] But in the concrete, if not yet in theory, they have begun to perceive that law can only sanction and stereotype the distribution of rights and property which results from the historical balance of class-power within a society. Rainsborough, if he had survived the raid in which he fell at Pontefract, would doubtless have gone further and stormed the steepest bastion of property, land tenure, with the impetuosity for which he was famous. He had reached the stage of asking embarrassing and far-reaching questions. 'The first thing I am unsatisfied in is how it comes about that there is such a propriety in some free-born Englishmen and not in others.' Commissary Nicholas Cowling then asked whether the younger son have not as much right to the inheritance as the eldest, and went on to suggest that the privileges of free-holders came from the fact that the commoners of England had been overpowered by the barons, who had 'abundance of vassals'.

Cromwell had ceased to be the impartial chairman who intervened in the debates chiefly to preserve unity and smooth ruffled tempers. Twice he rebuked Sexby for over-confidence. His repeated threats to resign, as Captain Audley put it, if 'we do not fetch all our waters from your wells', irritated some of the younger officers. He made it clear that Ireton spoke for him throughout these debates. He shared his son-in-law's view that to give votes to men 'that have no interest but the interest of breathing' would be anarchy, and he concludes the whole discussion by declaring that Ireton's case has not been answered, 'not in one part, to my knowledge, not in a tittle'.

Meanwhile the committee which had been set up to consider the Agreement and compare it with the Army's Declarations was producing a compromise which leaned heavily towards Cromwell's and Ireton's views. How this came about is hard to guess, for when one scans the names of its members the left should have had a majority on it.[10] The basic idea of the Agreement—that the new constitution should spring directly from the sovereign people—was silently rejected. It was, however, stipulated that several of its clauses should be unalterable, 'not to be given away or abrogated by their [the people's] representatives'. The Army's part in promoting this revised version of the Heads of the Proposals was merely to send them up as suggestions to Parliament. 'Either they are a Parliament', said Cromwell, 'or no Parliament. If they be no Parliament, they are nothing and we are nothing likewise. If they be a Parliament, we are to offer it to them.'

The new Proposals, after calling for the dissolution of the Long Parliament on 1 September, 1648, and providing for a regular succession of biennial Parliaments and the redistribution of seats, adopted Hugh Peters' elegant solution of the franchise problem, while appeasing the left with a vague recommendation to the Commons 'to give as much enlargement to common freedom as may be, with a due regard had to the equity and end of the present constitution in that point'.[11] Rainsborough persuaded the committee to reject a property qualification for members; the amount (£20 per annum) was low—unless the figure be a copyist's error for £200—but the principle was detestable. The list of unalterable fundamental rights omitted the fourth, which had abolished class privileges, in so far as equality before the law can do that.

The bold and simple demand for religious toleration was watered down, so that while it forbade positive compulsion, it did not forbid negative restriction. The magistrate, that is to say, could not force an Episcopalian or even a Catholic to attend an established Presbyterian church, but he could prevent any body of believers of whom the government dis-approved from meeting for worship in their own fashion. This was, as we shall see (Chapter XIX) the characteristic view of Cromwell, Ireton and most of the Independents in opposition to the broader view of the Levellers and sectaries. It marked a retreat also from the generous formula of the Heads of the Proposals. So too the clause forbidding 'pressing' and conscription was emasculated; these unpopular methods of raising troops were still sanctioned for the defence of England or 'keeping the peace within it' and forbidden only for wars beyond its frontiers, for example in Ireland. What happened to these recommendations when they came before the full Council we know only in part, for the reports in the *Clarke Papers* are incomplete.

One of these debates has survived more or less intact, a controversy between Ireton and Wildman, with Cromwell intervening, on the 'negative voices' of the King and the Lords. Wildman, who did not shine in this discussion, took his stand on the dubious interpretation of the coronation oath widely current on the parliamentary side since 1642. It was held that the words *leges quas vulgus elegerit corroborandas* meant that the King was obliged to confirm the laws the Commons shall choose. He argued, therefore, that the Heads of the Proposals had in effect confirmed the usurped powers of the King and the Lords, nay, that 'the foundation of slavery was riveted more strongly than before'. Though Ireton did not dispute this reading of the oath, he argued that, since the King would be required to confirm all the ordinances passed since the outbreak of the Civil War, this would amount to an acknowledgement to all posterity of the right of Parliament, when the safety of the kingdom was concerned, 'to make a law without him'.

The history of the Army's thinking about these vetoes is curious and revealing. The first draft of the Heads of the Proposals contained a clause which made the vetoes of King and Lords suspensive only. Who suggested this ingenious solution we do not know, possibly Lambert. Without consulting his colleagues, Ireton struck it out when Sir John Berkeley objected to it—to the indignation of Rainsborough and the Levellers.[12] Again when the Agreement of the People came before the committee of the Council, the first suggestion of a compromise was that the Commons, if they declared a bill essential to the safety of the kingdom, would be entitled to override the veto either of King or Lords. On further consideration this proposal was dropped in favour of a legalistic device of Ireton's, which reads like a parody of the doctrine of government by consent. It was laid down that legislation passed by the House of Commons was binding on all commoners, but that the King and the Lords, in respect of their persons and estates, were not bound by it without their express consent. This manifestly unworkable solution was unworthy of Ireton's sagacity. He argued that to take away the 'distinction' of the Lords would be 'to do them wrong'. In fact he was confirming their privileged status. One has to remember that Ireton and Cromwell were party politicians as well as soldiers. They doubtless thought it important to keep the good will of the House of Lords, in which at this moment the Independents had a bare majority.

One has the feeling in reviewing these debates that Ireton and Cromwell were stonewalling in vain against an emotional cataract. When the Council opened on 1 November Cromwell moved that everyone should declare what 'experiences' God had put into their minds in answer to their prayers. Captain Francis Allen's 'experience' was that the work before them was to take away the negative voices of the King and Lords. Captain John Carter 'found not any inclination in his heart (as formerly) to pray for the King that God make him yet a blessing to the kingdom'. Commissary Cowling read in the word of God that nothing but the sword had ever recovered the rights of the people. Lieut.-Colonel Goffe believed that it was a voice from heaven which declared that 'we have sinned against the Lord in tampering with his enemies'. Private Sexby thought they were 'going about to set up the power of kings . . . which God will destroy'. Captain Bishop was sure that the reason why they were distracted in counsel was because of their 'compliance to preserve that man of blood and those principles of tyranny which God from heaven . . . hath manifestly declared against'. After all these soldiers, Wildman for the civilian Levellers thought it 'very questionable whether there be a way left for mercy upon that person'.

To all this Cromwell had two answers. The first was that of the Genevan fatalist. If God willed the destruction of the King and the House of Lords, He would find a way in which 'the thing may be done without sin and without scandal too'. His other answer—that forms of government are of no importance—was equally characteristic of him. The Jews, he reflected, had several forms of government—under heads of families, under judges, under kings at first elective and then hereditary.

> In all these kinds of government they were happy and contented. If you make the best of it—if you should change the government to the best of it—it is but a moral thing. It is but, as Paul says, 'dross and dung in comparison of Christ' and [I ask] why we shall so far contest for temporal things, that if we cannot have this freedom [peacefully] we will venture life and livelihood for it.

If he had talked in this other-worldly strain when he was raising his first troop, one may doubt with Sexby whether he would have had so many to command.

Cromwell meant a little more than Pope did in his familiar couplet:

> *For forms of government let fools contest*
> *Whate'er is best administered is best.*

He meant that Tom, Dick and Harry—or rather, one in five of them—after voting for a godly knight of the shire, should leave politics to Parliament. 'The considering what is fit for the kingdom does belong to the Parliament.' Given this view of the limits of democracy, it should not surprise us, as the years went on, that the Lord Protector had no use for a free press.

NOTES TO CHAPTER XIII

1. Professor Woodhouse follows Firth in ascribing this tract to Wildman. The style does not to my ears recall his. To my thinking it resembles Overton's. No one else among the Leveller pamphleteers understood the value of short sentences and short paragraphs in a popular work of this kind, and the occasional use of italics (Woodhouse, p. 439). For the Putney Debates, see *C.P.*, I, pp. 226-406, or Woodhouse, pp. 1-124.

2. Col. Harrison felt strongly about the King, but he took no part in these debates. Lieut.-Colonel Jubbes was a moderate by temperament, yet he was a decided supporter of the Agreement.

3. M. Ashley, *John Wildman*, p. 72.

4. This is clear from the three contemporary reports quoted by Firth (*C.P.*, I, p. 230 n.)

5. *Of Reformation Touching Church Discipline in England* (1641), Milton's *Selected Prose* (World's Classics), p. 46.

6. See Jubbes's *Apology unto the officers of the Lord General's Army* (4 May, 1649).

7. Ireton, however, a year later, had to defend the opposite view in his embarrassed and casuistical excuses for breaking the Solemn League and Covenant (*Remonstrance* of 16 November, 1648, Woodhouse, p. 459).

8. Woodhouse, p. 59. I have stuck to the MS. text, which has 'pressed'; the editor's emendation 'oppressed' seems unnecessary.

9. In Walwyn's *Tyranipocrit* (see p. 71 above).

10. *C.P.*, I, pp. 363, 407; Woodhouse, p. 449.

11. Cromwell had in the debates made a tentative suggestion that some copyholders by inheritance might be enfranchised. The franchise under the Protectorate rested on an all-round property qualification of £200 in capital. This must have disqualified many of the poorer freeholders while admitting many well-to-do leaseholders.

12. See p. 243 above.

CHAPTER XIV

The Mutiny at Ware

What was said in Putney church during the next week we do not know, for the General's clerk grew tired of deciphering his shorthand notes. What was done we can piece together from the fragmentary records. On Thursday and Friday, 4 and 5 November, 1647, Rainsborough's party in the Council of the Army, composed of the young men elected by the officers of each regiment and the soldiers' Agitators, was at the height of its power. They made short work of the feeble compromise drafted by Hugh Peters at the committee and substituted for it this straightforward affirmation of manhood suffrage (subject to the reservations already accepted);

That all soldiers and others, if they be not servants or beggars, ought to have voices in electing those which shall represent them in Parliament, although they have not forty shillings per annum in freehold land.

This was carried against Cromwell and Ireton with only three dissentients. As in the happy old days in the eastern counties, most of the senior officers must have voted with the Agitators. Next day, the second historic 5 November in this century, a motion was carried, of which Rainsborough had given notice on 29 October, 'that the Army might be called to a rendezvous and things settled'.[1] It was to be 'a general rendezvous', as we learn from a letter addressed to their regiments by Sexby and fourteen of his fellow Agitators, like those at Newmarket and Triploe Heath which adopted the first of the Army's 'engagements'. At the head of each regiment the

Agreement of the People would be read out and adopted. The plan for this rendezvous was even more ambitious. Evidently it was to be the first symbolical fraternisation of 'the people' with the Army. The people also would 'put their hands' to the new covenant, and so it would become visibly the mutual Agreement of the People with the Army.

If everything went well, a big body of weavers—rumour swelled their numbers to 20,000—was to march from Spital-fields to the scene of the rendezvous in Corkbush Fields near Ware. These were the craftsmen whom John Lilburne befriended (*supra* pp. 102-5) in one of their struggles for survival against the City oligarchy of merchants. Woollen aprons and buff coats would come together in a great mass demonstration of 'the poor and the weak' (to use Sexby's phrase) whom God always chooses to do his work. If many of the poor and weak were well armed and well mounted, so much the better.

At this same Council meeting, from which as Firth supposes Cromwell may have been absent, the decision was taken late in the evening to send a letter to the Speaker, designed to undo the impression which Ireton made on the House by his speech of 23 September. This letter was tactfully worded and did not mention Ireton by name, but it said plainly that the Army had no wish that further addresses should be made to the King and earnestly desired that 'no such consideration may be admitted into the House's resolutions in that particular'.[2]

What was at issue here was for the soldiers specifically the question whether Parliament must seek the King's agreement to a bill of indemnity. Must they ask his pardon for defeating him? The Agitators felt that the declaration submitted to the Council defining the rights of the crown left in the King's hand powers that would enable him 'to enslave and ruin you that conquered him'. The writer of this letter, probably Wildman, knew how to play alternately on the men's sense of insecurity and on their pride. The narrative goes on to state that the Agitators asked for a free debate on the question; 'Whether it were safe either for the Army or people to suffer any power to be given to the King?' and that 'Cromwell and the rest professed as before God they would freely debate it'. For that purpose a General Council was called for Monday, 8 November.

In the meanwhile Ireton had taken mortal offence at the letter to the Speaker, which had in effect repudiated a speech of his. He withdrew from the Council and vowed he would not return to it until it contradicted the letter. Cromwell made up his mind to back his son-in-law with all the weight of his authority. There was, of course, much more at stake than this petty affair of the letter to the Speaker. During five months the Lieut.-General had worked with the Agitators in the quarrel of his party with the Presbyterian majority, courted them, humoured them, put up with them, until he began to feel that democracy in an army was destructive to discipline. Big though this man was, he was not quite big enough to persevere in the experiment of treating soldiers, for the first time in history, as citizens with minds of their own. He had to the end of his days a sense of the solidarity that should prevail among the People of God, but he could not class Levellers and Agitators among the Saints. Already in the last of the reported debates he had issued his warning. He complained that rendezvous of troops and regiments were being called without the consent of the General. He had heard Royalists say that 'if they give us rope enough we will hang ourselves'. Unless the rules of war were observed, they must expect 'destruction to the Army and to every particular man in it'.[3] Cromwell's patience was exhausted and one need not enquire what specifically it was that prompted him to assert himself—Rainsborough's scheme for a general rendezvous, the affront to Ireton or the vote for manhood suffrage.

We have two brief accounts of the decisive meeting of the Council on 8 November, one in the *Clarke Papers* and the other in the *Letter* of the fifteen Agitators. The Lieut.-General would not allow the question of the King's powers to be debated at all. Instead, he made a general attack on the Agitators and their doings, argued that manhood suffrage meant anarchy and complained of the Council's letter to the Speaker. Did he, as is likely, offer once more to resign his commission together with Ireton and perhaps with Fairfax also? Was the Council cowed by his vehemence? All we know is that one man at least stood up to him, Captain William Bray, who argued in a long speech that what Cromwell 'called anarchy was for propriety'. It was decided to send a letter to Parliament asking for six weeks' pay for the Army or at least one month's together with security for arrears and the end of free quarter.

But the chief business of the day was the adoption of a resolution proposed by Cromwell that in view of the coming rendezvous and the distempers that prevailed in several units, the officers and Agitators should return to their regiments to quiet the soldiers. Next day (9 November) when Fairfax presided, a rare happening, an abject resolution was passed to satisfy Ireton, to the effect that the Army was not against the sending of further propositions to the King. Yet another letter was despatched to the Speaker in this sense. And once again a fresh committee was set up to consider the engagements of the Army, and the Agreement of the People; it may be doubted whether it ever finished its task. Most important of all, the decision the Grandees had taken to summon not one rendezvous, but three, in different places on different days, seems to have leaked out at this Council.

It is obvious that since there had to be some sort of rendezvous, Cromwell and Ireton thought out their tactics carefully, so as to make the best use of it for their own ends. First, there was to be no repetition of Newmarket. These three rendezvous would not revive the democratic myth of the June days— when the rendezvous was for everyone who took part in it the sovereign legislative assembly, so to speak, of the Army. Secondly, they dispersed the dangerous crowd of radical young men who confirmed each other day after day at Putney in their 'wild' and 'vast' notions—the intellectuals among the junior officers who could quote Latin, the Anabaptists young and old (for several senior officers were in this category) and finally the Agitators. Scattered among their regiments they would no longer be able to meet the still more dangerous civilian Levellers in council. Then there was the question of pay, which affected everyone, even the idealists, since they knew very well that living at free quarter on the country made the Army unpopular. Could Parliament be induced, at short notice, to find four weeks' pay for everyone?

Further it was necessary to put before the Army, as an alternative to the Agreement of the People, a manifesto written from the Grandees' point of view. If the men wanted to sign something, let them sign an undertaking to be loyal and disciplined soldiers. A predominantly conservative committee was nominated to draft it. Only two Agitators sat on it, over against sixteen officers. Neither Sexby nor Colonel Rainsborough was a member. Finally, the idea was abroad in the ranks that they could elect their own officers. As the Leveller *Call to all the soldiers of the Army* (quoted in the previous chapter) put it: 'Ye have men as fit to govern as others to be removed.' Doubtless Ireton was unpopular; even Cromwell had his critics. But no one criticised Fairfax; this Olympian figure played no part either in party politics or church politics; he was the soldier incarnate, round whose name blazed a legend of invincible courage. Let them 'remove' Fairfax, if they were bent on deposing somebody. And so the manifesto began with the Lord General's offer to resign.

A brief entry in the *Clarke Papers* records the meeting of the committee of officers at Putney on 11 November, 1647.[4] On this occasion Colonel Harrison, of whose speeches at the big Council meetings we have no record, if he ever spoke at all, 'made a narration concerning some things that lay upon his spirit'. 'That the King was a man of blood and therefore the engagement taken off, and that they were to prosecute him.' Further, if as he supposed the Lords had usurped their negative voice, they should be 'debarred of that power'. A man of character and courage, Harrison was, after Ireton and Lambert the most influential of Cromwell's senior officers—and Lambert was on service in the North. Ireton and Cromwell gave their reasons, drawn from constitutional law and the scriptures respectively, why it was inexpedient to punish some men of blood.

That same Thursday evening the King, on the pretext that the Levellers intended to murder him, escaped from Hampton Court to the Isle of Wight. Of this decisive event two rival explanations have found favour among historians. Did Charles ride off in the night by his own spontaneous decision, or was he lured into this adventure by the Lieut.-General's machinations? Writing long after the event, Ludlow, a prejudiced chronicler, took the view which Cromwell's admirer Andrew Marvell had expressed in his noble elegy—that his hero 'twining subtle fears with hope' plotted the escape in order to destroy the King more surely and bring him to the block. Both writers had studied the mind of the Lord Protector at close quarters, yet we who know it only from his speeches and letters find ourselves questioning this interpretation. Cromwell was certainly capable of deceit, but his lying was instinctive, devised on the spur of the moment.[5] Both Ludlow and Marvell were familiar with the long range deceit, the strategical lying so to speak, that flourished during the Protectorate, but this was the speciality of Thurloe, a pioneer yet an accomplished master in all the techniques of the police state. Cromwell's mind did not work in that way. He was the opportunist who adjusted himself to the stream of events; when they obliged him to change his course he did it with volcanic violence and the minimum of planning and preparation. If Cromwell had devised the King's escape would he not have done it with the same wisdom that William of Orange displayed, when a similar problem faced him in the next generation?[6] He had the wit to help King James to discredit himself by seeking refuge in France. Dutch William even found a ship for him. It may be argued that if King Charles had reached the continent in safety, he would have returned one day to win back his crown. Then would things have gone better for the Cavaliers in Worcester fight, if the first Charles had led them rather than the second?

There is a simple answer to these speculations. It is possible that the King's belief that the Levellers meant to assassinate him hastened his escape from Hampton Court, but his real reason was that the Army had become suspicious of his dealings with the Scots, and would not have tolerated further negotiations with their envoys. To complete his plans for the second Civil War he had to go elsewhere. The story that the Levellers plotted the King's murder may be dismissed as an invention, but certainly they were bent on bringing him to trial.[7]

The news of the King's escape—whither no one knew as yet —must have startled the Army as nothing else had done in this eventful year since Cornet Joyce secured his person at Holmby. Armies have a way of evolving a collective mind; they think and even guess in step. No contemporary document has survived to tell us what they felt in this stirring week-end before the rendezvous at Ware, but one may venture a conjecture without much risk of mistake. What they chiefly feared, and with good reason, was that the King might take command of a Scottish army. As the despatch-rider rode off to the North to warn Lambert that the King might be on his way to Scotland, everyone from the Grandees to the Agitators must have realised that the renewal of the war they dreaded had come visibly nearer.[8] In such moments of danger and excitement men instinctively close their ranks and rally to their leaders. Few of us can feel strongly about more than one thing at a time and the regiments converging on Ware were composed of fighting men with uncomplicated minds. They might be keen on manhood suffrage, but that could wait. They would like to be rid of the 'Norman' Lords, but there was time enough for that. What mattered at the moment was to present a united front to the man of blood.

Some of their Agitators circulated in their ranks a manifesto written in 'high language' that might have stirred them to rebellion a few days back.[9] With the hot news of the King's adventure in their heads, it must have seemed irrelevant and untimely. Cromwell had his faults, but this was no moment to get rid of their one commander of genius,[10] nor of the gallant Fairfax either. It is even possible that some of their boldest leaders, Sexby for example had doubts at the last moment about the wisdom of attempting mutiny and were half-hearted, if they took any action at all.[11] It may even have occurred to them that their suspicions of Cromwell had been unjust. If he and the King were really confederates, if he had sold himself for a garter and an earldom, if he was working to restore the old tyranny with himself in the part of Strafford, would the King, who enjoyed every 'civility' at Hampton Court, have escaped from his guardianship? The King's move, in short restored discipline and brought back Cromwell's ascendancy— which is the only reason, a plausible but not a convincing reason, for suspecing that he may have prompted it.

Not all of Cromwell's plans for the rendezvous were realised. Parliament paid no heed to the General's urgent prayer for

six or at any rate four weeks pay for his penniless men. He had
nothing but promises to dole out to them at Ware, and nearly
four weeks went by before the Commons managed to scrape up
£20,000 for the Army by borrowing. Was the Presbyterian
majority so irresponsible that it had no wish to help Cromwell to
maintain discipline in the Army it detested? What it did do, on
9 November, whether from clemency or for less admirable
reasons, was to allow John Lilburne to quit his prison in the
Tower by day without his 'keeper' so that he should be free to
prepare his defence. The first noteworthy use he made of his
liberty was to ride out to Ware, where in the inn he waited for
news from Corkbush Field.

The 'Remonstrance' addressed to the Army in the name of
the General and the council of war was a dry and conventional
document. After complaining of the attacks on the General and
his officers by the Agents and others, which had led to discontents and divisions, it declared that unless these abuses were
redressed, Fairfax would lay down his command. But if discipline were restored, he would do his utmost to obtain constant
pay for the Army, security for its arrears, a full indemnity,
provision for maimed soldiers, widows and orphans and freedom
from pressing. There followed a list of the political objects he
would pursue—the setting of a period for this present Parliament, provision for the meeting, sitting and ending of future
Parliaments, and measures 'to render the House of Commons
as near as may be an equal representative of the people that are
to elect'. The Remonstrance ended by asking from all a pledge
to accept the decisions of the General and his council on these
matters and to observe discipline according to the rules of war.
The list of political objectives, as brief as it was vague, omitted
all the controversial issues. It made no mention of the King or
the House of Lords, slurred over the question of the franchise
and even omitted religious toleration. What mattered in this
manifesto was Fairfax's threat to resign and the pledge of
obedience in return for which he withdrew it.

The rendezvous of the first brigade was held in Corkbush
Field between Hertford and Ware on Monday, 15 November,
1647. To it had been summoned four regiments of horse (the
General's and those of Colonels Fleetwood, Rich and Twistleton)

and three of foot (the General's, Colonel Hammond's and Colonel Pride's). The Remonstrance was read out at the head of every regiment and thereafter the General addressed each of them in turn, 'very gallantly and faithfully' promising 'to live and die with them' for the ends it outlined. They then 'by acclamation' declared their 'affections' to the General, and as many of them as possible in the short time allowed signed an agreement to obey orders.

In the General's dealings with these seven regiments everything went smoothly. But at his first coming into the field he was approached by Colonel Rainsborough and some others, who presented him with a petition and a copy of the Agreement of the People. These he brushed aside. Meanwhile Colonel Eyres, Major Thomas Scott, M.P., and some others 'insinuated seditious principles into the soldiers, incensing them against the General and the general officers'. Eyres and Scott, with others who distributed copies of the Agreement among the soldiers, were taken into custody; Scott was sent to Westminster in charge of Lieut. Chillenden to answer to the Commons for his conduct.

Only two regiments, Harrison's horse and Robert Lilburne's foot, attempted mutiny. These insisted on attending this particular rendezvous against orders, and wore in their hats copies of the Agreement with the motto printed upon them in capital letters 'England's Freedom; Soldiers' Rights'. Fairfax addressed 'a severe reproof' to Harrison's regiment, and 'when they understood their error' they tore these papers and declared their resolution to obey His Excellency's commands.

Robert Lilburne's was 'the most mutinous regiment in the Army'. It was marching to Newcastle when at St Albans it received from the Agitators copies of *The Case of the Army*. It then refused to march further or to be divided from the rest of the Army. The men seized the colours and after some scuffling in which one officer and two men were wounded, drove off its officers with the exception of the Leveller Captain William Bray and two others of junior rank. On Corkbush Heath Bray was in command and drew up the regiment

with white papers in their hats, as if they had been going to engage with an enemy. When the General had viewed the rest of the Army he came to them, attended with his officers, who commanded them to pull their papers out of their hats, but they refused. Whereupon some officers rode in among them and plucked out the papers of some of them that were most insolent and then the rest began to submit.

The picturesque story that Cromwell himself drew his sword, rode in among the mutineers, tore the papers from their hats and awed them into submission has been generally accepted by historians. But there is no mention of it in the contemporary accounts of the rendezvous. Legends always grow up round the towering figures in history. Fairfax was the general in command at this review, and it was officers of his staff who rode in among the mutineers.[12] Thereafter the scattered officers of the regiment came up and picked out eight or nine whom they regarded as the worst offenders; Captain Bray also was arrested. For the sake of example three of the mutineers were tried on the spot by field court martial and sentenced to death. They were allowed, however, to throw dice for their lives. The man who lost, Private Richard Arnold, was shot to death at the head of the regiment.

So ended the mutiny at Ware. Between them the King by his flight and Fairfax by his threat of resignation ensured its failure. There was no march to Ware by the weavers of Spitalfields. The two other rendezvous were uneventful. Normally the New Model prided itself on its discipline; one concludes from the many collective expressions of loyalty and contrition to be found in Rushworth's pages that as a body its first reaction to this fiasco of a mutiny was regret and disapproval.[13]

During the next two months the General Council of the Army had grave non-political business to occupy its attention. The high command was determined to carry out the promise made at Ware to ensure regular pay for the men. It addressed the Commons with a new urgency, threatened to send a regiment to collect arrears of taxes from the City, and warned the complacent members on 7 December that it could not be answerable for the behaviour of the soldiers for more than another week. A day or two later the officers and men of Colonel

Thornhaugh's horse reminded Fairfax that during the previous six months they had received only a fortnight's pay. As its contribution to the insoluble problem of finance, the Army agreed to some reduction in rates of pay, cut down its own numbers to a riskily low minimum of 23,000 and agreed to the disbandment of 20,000 auxiliaries with only two months' pay in cash and the rest in debentures of doubtful value. The New Model was to be dispersed to garrison the larger towns and after 15 January, 1648, the taking of free quarter forbidden on pain of death.

While this austere programme was negotiated, courts martial were sitting to try the mutineers. Six or seven men of Lilburne's regiment suffered the brutal punishment of running the gauntlet. A corporal was sentenced to be shot, but his execution was postponed until Captain Bray and other officers could be tried since they, as Rushworth tells us, were as deserving of death as the men.[14] Bray, always spirited in adversity, defied his judges and his trial was postponed. Major John Cobbett, an officer often distinguished by his courage in the field, was sentenced to be cashiered at the head of his regiment—that is to say, disgraced as well as dismissed.

During these painful trials, John Saltmarsh, the most venerated of the Army's chaplains and one of the outstanding personalities of his time, rode, though very frail, from his home at Ilford to the Headquarters at Windsor, where with the manners of a Hebrew prophet, he took his leave of the Army. He came, he said, to acquaint it with 'something revealed to him from heaven'. 'The Lord,' he told them, 'had now forsaken them, and would not prosper them, because they had forsaken Him, their First Principle, and imprisoned Saints.' With his hat on his head, like an early Anabaptist or a Quaker, he repeated this message to General Fairfax. On the graver minds in the Army this last appearance of Saltmarsh among them made a deep impression, the more memorable because this ride in midwinter cost the old man his life.[15]

From a leader of a different school, who also had taught the Army to think, there came about this time yet another protest which also made its impression. John Lilburne was outraged by the shooting of Richard Arnold after the drumhead court

martial on Corkbush Heath. He argued that the taking of life by
martial law in time of peace, when the civil courts were open,
was an abuse that amounted to murder. As the law then stood
he had every justification for this view. Behind him was the
authority of Sir Edward Coke and the plain words of the Petition
of Right. He put his case first in a brief tract entitled *A Defence
for the honest Nounsubstantive Soldiers of the Army against the proceedings of the General Officers to punish them by Martial Law*. He
also helped Corporal William Thompson, who had escaped from
his prison at Windsor, to write over the date 14 December,
1647, his closely-reasoned pamphlet on the same lines, entitled
England's Freedom: Soldiers' Rights.[16]

Their argument is not merely that Fairfax and his council
of war are 'hedge-breakers and Levellers' who are destroying
one of the fundamental laws of England; they insist as boldly
that the Engagement taken on Newmarket Heath in June
converted the Army into a body of citizens governed 'in a
parliamentary way by the soldiers' free election'. This objection to martial law in time of peace was to be from these days
onwards one of the characteristic attitudes of the Leveller
party. Impractical it may have been, as Macaulay demonstrated in his account of the dodges to which the last Stuart
kings had to resort in order to control their standing armies
without the help of martial law. None the less, it voiced one of
the deepest instincts of the English people, their hatred of
militarism and their aversion to conscription, which survived
into our own day, above all in the working class.

Was there a perceptible revulsion of feeling in the Army as
it watched the unpleasant doings of the council of war?
Cromwell may have sensed it, for when the General Council
of the Army met in Windsor Castle on Tuesday, 21 December,
a ceremony of reconciliation was staged in that august setting.
Most of the day, as Rushworth tells us, was spent in exhortations
to unity by divers officers and motions 'for passing by offences
that had through weakness come from brethren'. Major White
led the way in expressing regret for his rash speech at Putney
and was re-admitted to the Council. Next day a solemn fast
was observed by the General and his officers, among whom
there reigned 'sweet harmony'. Cromwell, Ireton, Hugh Peters

and other officers prayed 'very fervently and pathetically' from nine in the morning to seven at night. In the evening the Council was unanimous in requesting the General to write to the Speaker on behalf of Rainsborough. He had, to be sure, 'acted some things which gave offence' but 'in regard to his present acknowledgement', they begged that 'his former service might not be forgotten', and consequently that he should take up his command of the fleet.[17] On Thursday the council of war quashed all the sentences passed on the mutineers. It could not restore Richard Arnold to life, but it released all its prisoners and sent back Major Cobbett and even Captain Bray to their posts in their regiments, in return for an undertaking to observe discipline.

Rushworth's account of the reconciliation in the Army told only half the story. Prayer and fasting gave it its characteristic emotional tinge, but something more mundane, something of the first historical importance went to the making of 'sweet harmony' among these Puritan soldiers. Major White was not the first of the penitents, Cromwell led the file. If the Levellers expressed their regret for their indiscretions at Ware, it was because he had already given way on the central issue that divided them; he had thrown over the King.

In their own minds Cromwell and Ireton must have had their doubts for some time past of the King's good faith. What forced them to take a stand in the full view of the Army was the King's move at the end of November, when he sent Sir John Berkeley to Windsor to resume negotiations with the high command. Fairfax refused to re-open discussions and with a freezing correctitude forwarded his letter of credentials to Parliament. Popular though this cavalier soldier had once been among the Ironsides—he made friends even with the Agitators —Berkeley now felt that an arctic atmosphere surrounded him. It is obvious from his vivid narrative of his mission that Cromwell and Ireton could not have defied the feeling of the Army by resuming dealings with the King's envoy, even if they had wished to do so. The decision of the loyal regiments at Ware to maintain discipline under Fairfax's command implied no change in their political opinions. The greater part of the Army was still of one mind with its representatives, the Agitators; it would have nothing to do with a King who was, as it justly suspected, planning a second Civil War. Still puzzled by the rebuff he had endured from the Grandees, Berkeley heard the explanation from his old confidant, Scoutmaster-General Leonard Watson, who met him with conspiratorial secrecy at midnight in a close behind the Garter Inn. His story was that after the rendezvous two-thirds of the New Model told Cromwell and Ireton plainly that they would go ahead in their hostility to the King even at the risk of dividing the Army.[18]

Cromwell's conclusion was that anything was better than a schism in its ranks. It must have been at the meeting of the General Council of the Army at Windsor on Saturday, 4 December, that he made his famous declaration of regret for his perseverance in negotiating too long with the King.

> The glories of the world had so dazzled his eyes that he could not discern clearly the great works the Lord was doing, and said that he was now resolved to humble himself and desire the prayers of the Saints that God would be pleased to forgive him his self-seeking.

At the same time he sent 'comfortable messages to the prisoners that he had noined at the general rendezvous . . . and by these and the like arts he perfected his reconciliation'. The date and the story of Cromwell's conversion are confirmed in a malicious but amusing letter written two days later by Evelyn the diarist.[19] None of his contemporaries has left us a better account than Berkeley's of the rule that governed Cromwell's conduct from his first breach with the Long Parliament in June 1647 down to his refusal of the crown in 1657.

> His chief dependence was on the Army which he endeavoured by all means to keep in unity, and if he could not bring it to his sense, he rather than suffer any division in it went over himself and carried his friends with him into that way which the Army did choose.[20]

In plain words the initiative still lay with the Levellers.

Ten days after the public reconciliation with Rainsborough the wheel of history swung full circle. In the Commons on 3 January, 1648, in a vehement and emotional speech Cromwell helped to carry an even stronger version of the motion that No Addresses should be made to the King which he and Ireton had defeated in September, when Marten and Rainsborough moved it. He described the King, as Clarendon informs us, as 'a man of great parts . . . but so great a dissembler and so false a man that he was not to be trusted'. He then declared for the settlement of the kingdom without further recourse to Charles. Watching him from the Presbyterian back-benches, Clement Walker noted that in his peroration, as he faced his opponents, he laid his hand on the hilt of his sword. This time the motion was carried by 141 to 92.

At the end of this same week, on Saturday, 8 January, the General Council of the Army met in Windsor Castle. The attendance was large and the debates, as Rushworth tells us, harmonious. The unanimous decision was taken to send an impressive delegation to congratulate the Commons on their vote of No Addresses. Next Tuesday a declaration was conveyed to Westminster by Sir Hardress Waller and seven colonels 'with other officers of rank and quality', in which the Army assured the Parliament that it would stand by it in 'settling . . . the kingdom without the King and against him'. This, then, was the final verdict of the Army; it now solemnly reaffirmed the opinion which Rainsborough and the Agitators first expressed in their letter of 5 November to the Speaker—the letter which Ireton and Cromwell by threats of resignation forced the Council to contradict. This time all the Grandees fell into line behind the Levellers. On that same Saturday, because it was the last gathering of the Council before the Army was dispersed into the various garrisons and great towns, the General invited all the Council to dine with him in the Castle, where they congratulated each other on the unity of the Army and took leave of one another. This was, in all probability the last occasion on which the Agitators were summoned to the Council. After this memorable meeting only the elected representatives of the regimental officers attended it, together with the Grandees. It was characteristic both of Fairfax and of Cromwell to put an end to the soldiers' 'soviet' in this genial way, with a feast in the majestic setting of Windsor Castle as the last glowing memory of its sittings.[21]

On the main issue of the day the left had won a notable

victory, but its feelings during the early weeks of 1648 were rather of insecurity than of triumph. Cromwell's opportunism, as he swung within a few months from one extreme to another, stamped him as an incalculable force, on whom no one could reckon with confidence for long together. Only nine days after the General Council of the Army had made its declaration against the King, the council of war, composed of the field officers only, was unanimous in issuing a statement couched in a very different tone. In spite of unworthy aspersions, so it ran, 'they hold themselves obliged in justice and honour to endeavour to preserve the peerage of this kingdom with the just rights belonging to the House of Peers'.[22] This was no doubt a tactical move designed to keep the Lords in line with the Commons against the King. Though it did not say in unambiguous words that the Army accepted the Lords' veto, it conveyed that impression. It must have carried its warning to the Agitators, that although Cromwell and Ireton had turned against the King, they could not be reckoned as democrats. What was even worse, the Grandees were now making political pronouncements on behalf of the Army without consulting the representatives of the men or even those of the regimental officers. As the weeks went by, it began to dawn on some of the men that Fairfax had no intention of calling their Agents to his Council again.[23]

In April 1648, in one regiment at least, Rich's horse, of which the senior Agitator had been the popular young trooper, Nicholas Lockyer, the Levellers revived the demand for representation. A pamphlet entitled *The Army's Petition*, which came from the press just as the second Civil War broke out, describes the meeting in St Albans on 24 April of the representatives of this regiment.[24] Their business was to consider how best to get signatures to a petition which they proposed to send to Parliament. This document, a catalogue of all the wrongs the Long Parliament failed to redress, is an abbreviated version of the civilian Levellers' *A New Engagement* (see below pp. 328-30) though its most arresting clause, a plan for abolishing base tenures, is given in full. Hardly had the meeting begun when a body of officers rushed in and carried off the men to prison. Thereupon the men of Rich's horse addressed a petition to

Fairfax, asking for the release of their Agents. Two messengers who carried this petition were imprisoned and threatened with death but were eventually released. The regiment then managed to release some of their Agents from prison and called on other units for help. The petition which started the trouble ended with this melancholy clause. It asked

> that we may be discharged from this present employment either to return quietly to our several callings, if we can bear the yoke of our slavery, or otherwise to depart the nation to seek our freedom in some wilderness.

Evidently the boasted unity of the Army was only on the surface. Recalling his memories of this unhappy time eleven years later, William Allen, the Agitator who rose to be Adjutant-General of the Army in Ireland, wrote of the 'great jealousy and divisions among ourselves', so that 'we were fit for little but to tear and rend one another'. Some, he went on, judged it 'a duty to lay down arms'.[25] One of these was William Dell, a chaplain dear to the radicals in the Army, who followed Saltmarsh in quitting it. Edward Sexby left it about this time, though he afterwards returned. A senior officer who withdrew, Lieut.-Colonel John Jubbes, deserves to be remembered as one of the most sympathetic of the many idealists in this Army. Though he had served for five years, he had in the depths of his mind a dread of militarism and (though he spoke it in parables) of Cromwell. A devoted disciple of Saltmarsh, he dwelt, in the *Apology* which he addressed to the Army a year later, on one of his teacher's sayings that 'all the slavery in the Christian world had come by the sword'. When with Dell 'and others' he followed Saltmarsh's example by leaving the Army, he would have gone overseas if he could have secured even £200 of the £1,200 arrears of pay due to him. He gives a moving description of his misery when first he had thoughts of laying down his commission. 'The heavens and earth were shaken in me and I was forced to enquire again what God was.' He found Him at last in 'the orderly motion of the glorious bodies of the sun, moon, earth and stars. . . . Something put and keeps them in order, which Infinite Thing is today and for ever the life, motion and being of all things.'[26]

NOTES TO CHAPTER XIV

1. There is no record of this resolution in the *Clarke Papers* or in Rush-worth, both of which are very fragmentary round about these dates. It is quoted in a businesslike *Letter from several Agitators of the Army to their respective regiments* (11 November, 1647) over the signatures of Sexby and fourteen others. Woodhouse reprints it (pp. 452-4).

2. *C.P.*, I, p. 440; Woodhouse, p. 452 n.

3. Woodhouse, p. 98.

4. *C.P.*, I, p. 417.

5. The classical instance was his reply at Edinburgh in October 1648 when he assured the Presbyterian divines 'I am for monarchical government and that in the person of this King and his posterity'; and again, 'I am altogether against toleration'. For the evidence for this contemporary report see G. M. Young, *Charles I and Cromwell*, pp. 121-2.

6. How, in this connection, are we to interpret the behaviour of Scout-master-General Watson, six weeks later, when he met Sir John Berkeley at midnight in a close behind the Garter at Windsor and implored him to hasten the King's escape overseas? (See p. 301 above.) Was Watson acting thus because he really had royalist sympathies, as he professed, or was he acting in the interests of the Army, it may be with Cromwell's approval? His was a crooked personality, if we may trust the impression he made on John Lilburne and Lucy Hutchinson, neither of them charitable witnesses. Eventually Watson was disloyal to Oliver during the Protectorate. In the light of this record it is the more probable explanation that he was acting at Windsor in the King's interest. I assume what others have argued, that he was Berkeley's informant (Clarendon, *History of the Rebellion*, IV, pp. 271, 283).

7. There is no doubt that Henry Lilburne, now a Lieut.-Colonel, was the villain of this story. One of the ardent Levellers in Yorkshire in July, he was already critical of them when he spoke in the Putney Debates (*C.P.*, I, p. 368). During the second Civil War he went over to the Royalists and betrayed Tynemouth Castle to them, apparently for money. It was he who set going the story of the conspiracy to assassinate Charles, which he got, as he pretended, from his brother. The indignant denial of eight Leveller officers and Agitators rings true (*ibid.*, p. 419). But as some of the speakers avowed in the Putney Debates, they were already bent on bringing Charles to trial. Some of them hoped for his execution. But there were moderates among them who disliked that idea. Joyce told Sir John Berkeley that he favoured a trial of the King that 'they might not bear the blame of the war', not, he insisted, 'that he would have one hair of his head to suffer' (*Memoirs of Sir John Berkeley* in Maseres, *Select Tracts*, I, p. 383). Lieut.-Colonel Jubbes advocated the singular plan of a condemnation of Charles by a purged House of Commons in order to fix on him the responsibility for the war (*C.P.*, I, p. 373); he should then be restored to his throne. It is possible that some Levellers did think of raiding Hampton Court to get the King out of Cromwell's keeping. This, as Berkeley understood it, was to be the pre-liminary not to an assassination but to a trial. What Watson spoke of was a raid by 800 men on Carisbrooke Castle for the same purpose.

8. *C.P.*, I, p. 418.

L

9. The text of this attack on the Grandees is in Woodhouse, pp. 452-4.

10. The only evidence for the story that the Levellers meant to murder Cromwell in his bed is the vague statement in *Walwyn's Wiles*, a compendium of slanders as pious and malicious as *Gangraena*, dated April 1649. What is conceivable is that some of the Levellers thought of deposing Cromwell, as their comrades in the North had deposed General Poyntz.

11. None of the three contemporary narratives of the rendezvous mentions any action by Sexby, though he must have been present with his regiment. Rushworth does not include him among those arrested, though he does mention his much less conspicuous comrade 'Mr Allen', nor was he one of the eight officers and Agitators who wrote from their prison at Windsor their challenge to Henry Lilburne. If 'Mr Allen' was really the speaker in the Putney debates who made a speech which irritated Colonel Rainsborough (Woodhouse, p. 102; *C.P.*, I, p. 376) it is odd that he got himself arrested at Ware. I suggest that the speech should be attributed to Captain Francis Allen.

12. The story of Cromwell's spirited performance at Ware comes from Ludlow's *Memoirs*. He was not present at Ware and wrote long after the event. There is, however, an earlier mention of the story, among much else that is patently false, in *Walwyn's Wiles* (H. and D., p. 304). The fullest account we have was written on the spot by William Clarke, a member of the General's secretarial staff, who was presumably an eye-witness (*A full relation of the proceedings . . . at Corkbush Field*). It was reprinted with a commentary in Maseres, *Select Tracts* (I, pp. xxxii-xlviii). The report which Fairfax sent to the two Speakers is the same narrative with slight variations (Rushworth, VII, pp. 875-6). Neither of these mentions Cromwell. I have summarised them, save in my account of the doings of Robert Lilburne's regiment, which I have taken from Captain Bray's evidence at his court martial immediately after the mutiny (*The Justice of the Army against evil doers Vindicated*, 5 June, 1649). This official tract seems to have escaped the notice of Firth and Gardiner.

13. There was another complication which may have made some of the Agitators cautious at Ware. Royalist agents may have played some part in provoking the men to mutiny. The King at this time was trying both to divide and to conciliate the Army. In the open letter written before his flight he attacked both the Grandees and the Levellers, but he promised the men liberty of conscience, an act of indemnity and the prompt payment of their arrears. Firth has collected some of the evidence concerning royalist participation (*C.P.*, I, p. 231 n.). Cromwell told the Commons on 22 September that 'there was a party in the Army labouring for the King, and a great one'. He accused Major Thomas Scott, a 'recruiter' who sat for Aldborough (Yorks), not to be confused with the regicide member for Aylesbury of the same name, of subversive activities at Headquarters and 'endeavouring to debauch the Army and seduce them from their principles'. He may be the major to whom Rushworth refers in similar terms (Rushworth, VII, p. 849). Firth (*C.P.*, I, p. 231) thought it probable that he was a royalist agent. He died in prison in January 1648. It may be significant that the Levellers, who always paid homage to their martyrs, never reckoned him among them. Shortly before the rendezvous at Ware (*Ibid.*, I, p. 410 and n.) there were signs of royalist sympathies not only in Lilburne's regiment but in the General's foot also. To this evidence I would

add Rushworth's account (VII, p. 937) of the trial at Windsor of Bartholomew Symonds of the former regiment. When Major Gregson urged its men to submit to discipline, Symonds cried out 'that the Major was against the King', whereupon some of the men threw stones and broke his head. Finally, the *Moderate Intelligencer* may be cited, which reported that Lilburne's regiment had declared for the King some days before the rendezvous, adding, however, that the real trouble was lack of pay. One has to remember that half of the infantry were pressed men, whose political ideas were usually vague, though their sense of grievance was acute. These stories must be balanced against the fact that this regiment finally took as its commander Captain Bray, an extreme Leveller.

14. Rushworth, VII, p. 922.

15. *Ibid.*, pp. 913, 904. See also Saltmarsh's letter of warning to the Army at Putney (Woodhouse, p. 438).

16. Wolfe, pp. 243-8.

17. Rushworth, VII, p. 943.

18. Gardiner's time-table of Berkeley's mission is puzzling (*Civil War*, IV, p. 33). He says that Sir John appeared before the General Council of the Army on 28 November. I have followed Rushworth, who is, I think, accurate in such matters. He prints in full the King's letter to Fairfax asking for the resumption of negotiations, with the date 29 November. This means that Berkeley can have left the Isle of Wight only on the 29th, or more probably the 30th. Rushworth reports Council meetings on 25 November and 4 December; there was none on 28 November. A council of war met on 3 December.

19. The series of letters which from December 1647 to June 1649 Evelyn addressed to his father-in-law, Sir Richard Browne, who was King Charles's ambassador in Paris, are a source hitherto neglected. On 6 December 1647 Evelyn wrote that the Agitators are said to be 'reconciled with the Army'—by which he meant presumably the Grandees—and since the last Council meeting on Saturday are 'as high and strong as ever they were'. 'You will shortly hear', he continues, 'of Cromwell's vision and how on Friday night last he, being stricken blind for the space of four hours, during which he had a conference with God, persuading him to adjust with the holy Agitators, he next day put it in execution.' The story of Cromwell's vision is of course malicious nonsense. Cromwell relied not on visions for the revelation of God's will, but on 'dispensations'. But the royalist gossips were, I think, justified in their belief that even at this date Cromwell made some approach to the Agitators. None the less, it can only have been tentative, for the trials by court martial continued after this. Rushworth's brief note on the General Council of Saturday, 4 December, mentions only its discussions on the proposed disbanding of the supernumerary forces (*op. cit.*, VII, p. 922).

20. Berkeley, *Memoirs* (Maseres, *Select Tracts*, I, p. 364). I have not thought it necessary to discuss the evidence for and against the romantic story of the visit of Cromwell and Ireton to the Blue Boar in Holborn, and their discovery there or elsewhere of correspondence between the King and the Queen which finally convinced them, round about 21 November, of Charles's perfidy. The acceptance of this story by investigators as diverse as Godwin, Gardiner and G. M. Young is impressive. None the less, I incline to the cautious verdict of the last of the classical historians who studied

Cromwell's career, Professor Abbott (I, pp. 571-2). It is unnecessary to assume that something more than the pressure of the Levellers in the Army upon him is required to explain Cromwell's change of front towards the King. The maxim of the physical sciences—that causes should not be multiplied beyond what is necessary—has its relevance to history also.

21. Rushworth's account of this Council is in VII, pp. 958-9, and of the Declaration at *ibid.*, pp. 961-2.

22. *Ibid.*, p. 967 (17 January, 1648).

23. When did the Agitators cease to sit in the General Council of the Army? Firth was of two minds about it. His first opinion (*C.P.*, I, p. viii) was that the last meeting they attended was on 8 January, 1648. I also am of this opinion. But in an appendix (*ibid.*, p. 432) Firth argues that they attended the Council throughout the spring of 1648, up to the last meeting on 26 April. This was the meeting described by Adjutant-General (Captain) William Allen, who in 1659 published *A faithful memorial of that remarkable meeting of many officers of the Army in England at Windsor Castle in the year 1648* (*Somers Tracts*, VI, p. 498). Firth, in opposition to Carlyle, is clearly right in identifying this Allen, a supporter of Ludlow in Ireland, with the Agitator. If he sat *as a private* in this Council, Firth has proved his case. But it is to be noted that he described it as a meeting of many *officers*. It seems to me possible and even likely that in order to solidify his reconciliation with the Levellers, Cromwell may have given a commission to Allen the Agitator, who obviously was a man of character and ability. But my decisive reason for rejecting Firth's second opinion is the evidence I am about to discuss, that towards the end of April 1648 some of the old Agitators started a movement for representation once more.

24. *The Army's Petition, or A new Engagement of many in the Army who are yet faithful to the people* (3 May, 1648).

25. *A faithful Memorial . . .*, in *Somers Tracts*, VI, p. 500 sqq.

26. For Jubbes, see pp. 357-8, 433-4, 453, 500 below. Dr Schenk gave a full summary of his opinions in *The Concern for Social Justice in the Puritan Revolution*, pp. 172-7, and Mr Wolfe reprints his *Proposals for an Agreement . . .* (p. 311).

CHAPTER XV

The Leveller Party

During the winter months of 1647 the civilian Levellers were building the first model of a democratically organised political party, which for good and evil on both shores of the Atlantic the generations that came after have copied and developed. Republicans and Democrats in the United States, in Europe liberals and socialists, in Asia the Indian Congress Party—all of them have followed the pattern first set by Lilburne and his comrades.[1] The soldiers had shown the way, when they formed their Council. So from the Leveller groups in each district of the capital the 'London Agents' were elected. The party had its treasury to which each member made his contributions. It had its recognised headquarters, and soon its organ among the weekly 'news-books' and its distinguishing colour, sea-green.

Though in previous chapters we anticipated events by using the name Leveller, it was only about this time that it came into general use. Doubtless as the royalist turncoat, Marchamont Nedham, put it in his weekly *Mercurius Politicus* (16 November, 1647), the King helped to give it currency, when he 'christened' the Agitators.

> by the name of Levellers, a most apt title for such a despicable and desperate knot to be known by, that endeavour to cast down and level the enclosures of nobility, gentry and propriety, to make us all even, so that every Jack shall vie with a gentleman and every gentleman be made a Jack.

The name had been applied for half a century to the peasants who tried to recover their common lands from the predatory gentry by destroying the hedges or fences of their enclosures. *Politicus* was the cleverest journalist of his day and his comments on this occasion probably reflect the mind of the class he served.

> We are like [so he wrote] to have a brave world when the saints rampant have reduced our wives, our daughters, our estates into a holy community. This design against propriety is the reason why they are such enemies against lawyers.

The nickname stuck, in spite of the repeated protests of the party, and its declarations that it had no intention of 'levelling men's estates'. The fact remained that it was bent on ending every form of legal or political privilege. One has one's doubts whether the rank and file disliked the name quite as much as their leaders professed to do. A year later, when Rainsborough was buried with all the honours the party could pay a lamented leader, the epitaph on his tomb read thus:

> *Rainsborough the just, the valiant and the true*
> *Here bids the noble Levellers adieu.*[2]

Parliament, meanwhile, suffered an access of anger and alarm when it discovered that these 'London Agents' at its very doors were actively at work organising support for the Agreement of the People. The Commons had already condemned that document as 'destructive to the being of Parliaments and the fundamental government of this kingdom'. Yet the two Houses now had before them evidence from the provinces, that Anabaptist preachers and others acting for the Agents were collecting signatures to this subversive Agreement as far afield as the counties of Nottingham and Rutland. The two Houses formed a joint committee to enquire into the doings of these Agents and they instructed Fairfax to conduct a parallel enquiry in the Army. We catch a glimpse during these debates of Harry Marten fighting single-handed against the united Independents and Presbyterians. When he was accused of attending the Agents' meetings, he made the defiant reply that if the Agents stood at that moment at the door of the House, he would go out at once and join in their deliberations. To fight in the open was always the instinctive behaviour of the Levellers. On 23 November the Agents addressed to 'the supreme authority of England, the Commons in Parliament assembled' a brief, but ably written petition in which they argued that 'there can be no liberty in any nation where the law-giving power is not solely in the people or their representatives'. They went on to demand the right to debate the Agreement freely and to enlist support for it. They ventured finally to ask the Commons 'to make inquisiton for the blood' of Private Arnold, 'shot to death near Ware'. For their audacity in presenting this petition five of the leading Levellers, Thomas Prince and Samuel Chidley, the treasurers of the party, with Captain Thomas Taylor, William Larner (the printer) and J. Ives were sent to prison, as the warrant ran, 'during the pleasure of this House'.[3]

With Dick Overton and Harry Marten in their ranks the Levellers could not lack a sense of humour. Their next move was to present a second petition on 29 November in which with affected humility they asked the House to specify 'what burdens they may pray the Honourable House may be taken off and what freedoms . . . settled', so that they might not in future suffer as transgressors.[4] But the worst was yet to come. On 17 December the two Houses passed an ordinance which bracketed the Levellers, defined as those who contrived or signed the Agreement of the People, with the King's partisans and the rioters who invaded the House in July. They deprived them of the right to vote in the election of the Common Council of the City of London, or to be elected to it or as aldermen. In plain words so formidable did the Leveller party now appear to its older rivals, that it had hardly been formed before they united to deprive its members of their political rights.

With the New Year came further evidence of the impression the Levellers had made. It was easy for Parliament, while it reigned omnipotent, to imprison their leaders and outlaw their members, but it knew very well that this upstart party voiced grievances of which 'many thousands' of citizens, most of them 'well-affected' and many of them 'godly', were becoming increasingly conscious. How many of the members grasped the fact that the prestige of Parliament had fallen very low during the wasted and turbulent year just ended we do not know, but we may feel sure that some of the abler Independents like the younger Vane and Ireton were painfully aware of it.

Casting about for ways of impressing public opinion favourably, they chose to begin with the most elementary of the demands that formed the Leveller platform. Every tradesman in London from the proudest goldsmith in the City to the humblest cobbler in Southwark resented the privilege of protection from suits for debt and other financial claims which the members of both Houses enjoyed and were entitled to extend to their dependants and servants. This privilege Parliament abolished on 4 January, 1648, though it still protected its members from imprisonment for debt.

What was no less significant, when we recall the long lists of economic grievances that figured not only in the Levellers' own petitions but also in the Proposals of the Army which they inspired, Parliament now resolved to set up a Committee of Grievances to review all undertakings given in relation to the people's burdens, freedoms and liberties, measures necessary for the reform of the courts of justice and legal procedure and 'all other things of public concernment which they should hold fit and reasonable for the good and weal of the people' and to prepare draft ordinances.[5] This wording recalls Ireton's manner. The terms of reference are so wide that one asks was this committee a device for wasting time as familiar to Parliament in those days as it is in ours? Nothing in fact came of its labours. But it may for a moment have made the desired impression on public opinion, for Parliament took the unusual course of ordering that the facts relating to it, including its power to call witnesses, should be printed and published. This move reflects the tactics of the Independents in the early months of 1648—they would have nothing more to do with Charles I, but they might accept one of his sons as King; in any case sovereignty still lay for them in King, Lords and Commons. They must therefore crush the Levellers, civilians as well as soldiers, but in doing so they realised that they must redress or seem bent on redressing the more elementary of the grievances which their agitation had made odious.

From contemporary records we can trace the origin of the party organisation. It started with the gathering of signatures to the Agreement of the People. Some of its supporters, for example Lieut.-Colonel Jubbes, aimed at getting a million names

from all over the country. That meant the printing of vast
numbers of copies and the despatch of travelling missionaries,
whose expenses would have to be paid. By the end of the year
the party was promoting yet another lengthy petition and of
this, according to John Lilburne, 30,000 copies had to be
printed, though paper in those days was dear. It went on
printing petitions until it was itself suppressed. Since it had few
wealthy adherents, it met these costs in the democratic way by
weekly subscriptions from its members, who gave as they
earned. These ranged, as John reported, from twopence or
threepence a week, through sixpence or a shilling to as much as
half a crown, which only a well-to-do tradesman could have
paid. Collectors were appointed to bring in these small sums
and it was understood that all the members would be active in
gathering signatures.

Since representation must go with taxation, the party
evolved its method of indirect election. Its model was, doubtless, the Council which the scattered regiments of the New
Model had chosen, by each electing two Agitators from the
representatives chosen by every troop or company. So in
London each ward was a unit, whose local group of Levellers
met in their own neighbourly tavern. From these ward groups
representatives were sent to the committee of the parish. Finally
from the City itself and from its suburbs and 'liberties' that
lined the Thames, twelve 'commissioners' or 'agents' were
elected, who controlled the tactics of the party, while two
treasurers kept its war-chest. This executive committee met in
the evening three days of every week at the Whalebone
Tavern in the City and on one of the other days at the recognised Leveller taverns in Southwark, Wapping and other
suburbs. The Whalebone was the party's headquarters and its
host, we are told, would always receive subscriptions to its
petitions.

A letter signed by Lilburne, Wildman and two more of the
'London Agents' has come down to us addressed to the party's
sympathisers in Kent, which invites them to create a similar
organisation in their county and to attend a meeting in
support of the petition at Dartford, which John himself would
address. The campaign was to culminate in a demonstration at

the doors of the House of Commons which their adherents from all the home counties would swell. At last the 'many thousands' were to be paraded in their visible numbers.[6]

The Leveller movement had for its genial background the local tavern where men knew one another and were welcomed as neighbours. They debated their grievances over a tankard of ale or a glass of sack and enjoyed all three. Here too on great occasions they would meet for a festive dinner, as they did two years later to celebrate John Lilburne's acquittal by a City jury at the Guildhall on a capital charge of high treason. It was their way when Leveller soldiers had suffered under the brutal punishments of the military code to carry them off in a coach for a feast at the Whalebone or the Windmill. They had their own standards of decency and good manners, as Dick Overton once discovered; for they did not admire grossness. But there was nothing in their temperaments of that Puritan sourness which never tired of condemning the pleasant sins of others. It was the custom of the stricter Independents, including the senior officers of the Army, when they had said their say in a petition about the man of blood, the purging of the Commons or what you will in the field of politics, to wind up with a clause which called for the severe punishment of swearing, drunkenness and wenching. In no Leveller petition do we ever find an acid clause inspired by this negative righteousness.

Who, then, were these Levellers? John Lilburne would describe them as 'the middle sort of people', but as we have seen, it was also his boast that the leather aprons and clouted shoes followed him in their thousands. Evidently John's 'middle sort' included many working craftsmen, cobblers, weavers, printers and lead miners, together with some well-to-do tradesmen and an occasional professional man like the celebrated Dr Chamberlen. The bolder and more thoughtful of the journeymen also were sympathisers. Some of them attended Independent chapels, but large numbers and it may be the majority were sectaries. In London, Southwark was the stronghold of these latter. In the populous region round about London they were especially numerous in Hertfordshire and Buckingham.

Among them in these green counties there must have been many copyhold tenants whose chief desire was to be rid of tithes

and base tenures on which they held their fields by a precarious
grip. Neither in town nor country did the proletariat (if we
exclude the skilled journeymen) show any inclination to rally
to the Levellers. In the seventeenth century the labourers were
so abysmally poor, and so completely at the mercy of their
'betters', that they can have felt little personal self-respect and
no sense of solidarity with their class. Most of them were
illiterate and short-lived and an astonishingly high proportion
of them were paupers, driven in winter by high prices, low
wages and unemployment to depend on the poor law for a bare
subsistence. To hold opinions of their own about politics or
religion was a luxury in which they dared not indulge. If the
tide swung violently they might swing with it and it may be
take their share of the loot when the mob went rioting. On the
whole, like their descendants who joined the church and king
mobs during the French Revolution, their inertia—if they
counted for anything at all—placed them in the right-hand
scale of the balance of power.

We should go astray if we were to see in the Leveller party a
forerunner of the socialist parties of today, though in England
some of its traditional attitudes and demands descended
through the Chartists to the Labour Party. It faced and
recognised a deep class cleavage as the fundamental fact in the
world around it. But this is true only if we interpret the word
'class' very loosely. It had no functional meaning. The basic
rift in society was not for the Levellers the division between
employers and wage earners, but that between rich and poor.
The rich were chiefly merchants, usurers and landowners, but
the party felt no hostility to the private trader unless he were a
monopolist, nor did it on principle condemn the taking of
interest or the letting of land, though some of its bolder thinkers,
notably William Walwyn, did so. The master-craftsmen
among its members worked with their hands but they might
employ a journeyman and one or two apprentices. The contrast
between rich and poor, as the Levellers felt it, is commonly
expressed in the simplest and most concrete terms. On the one
side are 'your great ones, whether the King, Lords, Parliament
men, rich citizens . . ., who live in all pleasure and delicious-
ness' and on the other 'your poor friends that depend on farms,

trades and small pay' with 'many an aching heart' among them.[7] In its outlook and social composition this party of 'the common man' resembled rather the English radical party of the nineteenth century than any of the social-democratic parties of our own time.

Though the Levellers had lost long ago any illusions about petitioning as a means of influencing Parliament, they had doubtless found by experience that it is an ideal method for reaching the individual citizen. Sometimes their petitions were read aloud in gathered churches, after the service was over; groups might discuss them in the churchyard, or the market place, and then adjourn to the friendliest tavern of the neighbourhood where they could be signed. The soldiers of some regiments were active in carrying them round. Whether the Levellers, men or women, were accustomed to canvass systematically from door to door for signatures we cannot confidently say. It seems possible that the women sometimes did so. We know, at any rate, that they had their organisation in each ward and division of the City for the purpose of collecting signatures. At the least men and women would go round to seek the signatures of their friends and neighbours. This would give them their opportunity to spread the ideas of the party in the best of all possible ways, by discussion.

Twice in 1649, as we shall see, when the lives of the leaders were in danger, the women in their own names petitioned Parliament on their behalf. The rough usage they then met with from Puritan soldiers and politicians of other views is a reminder that in their attitude to women the Levellers were ahead of their time. They encouraged women to play their part in politics side by side with their husbands and brothers, because they believed in the equality of all 'made in the image of God'. This was, indeed, an article of their religious creed, which reflected the influence of the Anabaptists among them. Everyone knows that however low the position of women sank round about them, the Quakers always preached and practised equality. But few of us remember that they were following the example which their forerunners the Anabaptists had set from the early days of the sixteenth century onward. In their community women had an equal standing, an equal right to pray and speak at its meetings. So many of the Levellers were members of this sect that it must have seemed natural to practise on weekdays what they taught on Sundays.

Among the Leveller women, Elizabeth Lilburne was respected for her own sake as well as her husband's, for her courage and strength of character were outstanding. But their recognised leader was an older woman, Mrs Katherine Chidley, the mother of Samuel, one of the party's treasurers, who had made her mark as the author of a pamphlet which advocated the Independent view of church government against the redoubtable Thomas Edwards (p. 38 above). After an earlier petition on behalf of the Leveller prisoners in the Tower had been rejected by the House on the ground that the women should cease to meddle in things they could not understand, they replied in a memorable second petition, which may have come from the practised pen of Mrs Chidley.

> Since we are assured of our creation in the image of God, of an interest in Christ equal unto men, as also of a proportionate share in the freedoms of the commonwealth, we cannot but wonder and grieve that we should appear so despicable in your eyes as to be thought unworthy to petition or represent our grievances to this honourable House. Have we not an equal interest with the men of this nation in those liberties and securities contained in the *Petition of Right*, and other the good laws of the land? Are any of our lives, limbs, liberties or goods to be taken from us, no more than from men, but by due process of law and conviction of twelve sworn men of the neighbourhood? And can you imagine us to be so sottish or stupid as not to perceive or not to be sensible when daily those strong defences of our peace and welfare are broken down and trod underfoot by force and arbitrary power?[8]

The ten thousand women who signed this petition and the thousand who carried it to the House with seagreen ribbons pinned to their breasts may be reckoned in their modest anonymity among the forerunners of Mary Wollstonecraft.

Such, then, was the first political party on either shore of the Atlantic to organise itself on a pattern of democratic self-government. Its structure was complete before the end of 1647.

How many adherents or members it had at this stage it would be risky to guess; we must content ourselves with the Levellers' own claim to 'many thousands'. By the middle of 1648 they made a big advance in the technique of propaganda, when they acquired as their mouthpiece a weekly newspaper—there were as yet no dailies—*The Moderate* (see Chapter XX).

NOTES TO CHAPTER XV

1. G. M. Trevelyan, in his *England under the Stuarts* (p. 393 n.), gave the priority to Shaftesbury and his Green Ribbon Club, formed in 1675 from the broken remnants of the republican opposition. It evolved into the Whigs. It is obvious that it must have been based on memories of the Levellers. It even inherited their colours. But its organisation was not democratic.

2. *The Moderate* (14 November, 1648).

3. Wolfe, p. 237.

4. Rushworth, VII, p. 915.

5. *Ibid.*, p. 955.

6. *A Declaration of some Proceedings*, in H. and D., pp. 102-4.

7. Walwyn, *The Bloody Project, ibid.*, p. 144.

8. This second petition was presented on 7 May, 1649 (*The Moderate*; Woodhouse, p. 367). I see no reason for supposing that Lilburne wrote it. He was too much the naïve egotist to think himself easily into a woman's skin. The most likely author was, surely, Mrs Chidley.

CHAPTER XVI

Winter of Discontent

The scanty harvest of 1647 had been reaped. Again, for the second year, as they counted their sheaves, fear darkened men's minds. For all that the ghosts of medieval regulations could do to check them, the prices of grain climbed up, until by November the people's rye like the citzens' wheat cost twice what it would have fetched in a normal year. Even the stand-by of the poor, pease-meal, was scarce and dear, for during the drought of summer 'flying lice', to use the language of those days, had ruined the crop of peas.[1] Torrential rains came with the winter, and a petition from the favoured veterans housed in the Savoy complains that they were perishing of cold. Already in London the most needy were dying of want, and the pity men felt for their orphans found a voice in rhyme:

> *Grave senators that sit on high*
> *Let not poor English children die.*

Of the many petitions that reflected the distress of this winter, one which came from influential citizens of London at last moved Parliament to action and it set up a 'Corporation of the Poor' empowered to erect houses for 'setting the poor on work'. Top heavy with officials—for the Lord Mayor presided over it, with a deputy, a treasurer and forty assistants (afterwards increased to fifty-eight)—it appears to have done nothing whatever.[2] Only too often, during the Interregnum, the poor law ceased to function altogether, for there was no vigilant Privy Council to stimulate the torpid social conscience of the new

ruling class. The result was, to quote a contemporary newspaper, that since 'the poor in most places cannot earn money
enough to buy them bread' they begin to 'mutiny and rise in
some counties'.[3]

The Levellers were deeply moved by the misery around
them. The petition on which they concentrated during this
winter is still primarily a political manifesto, inspired by an
ardent faith in representative democracy, but 'the London
Agents' knew what was in the mind of their poorer neighbours.
For the first time a Leveller petition calls for higher wages. It
was not the party's cue to blame the weather for the general
distress—it would have been simple-minded, indeed, to trace it
solely or even mainly to that cause. More important, as the
Levellers argued, was the sense of insecurity which lowered
the exchange value of sterling and which paralysed both home
and foreign trade. Dreading a renewal of the Civil War, the
well-to-do were afraid to spend and took to hoarding, while the
unemployed could no longer look with any confidence to the
poor law even for a bare subsistence. John Wildman reported
in *Truth's Triumph* (18 January, 1648) the desperation of the
textile workers of the west country. Some clothiers from Wiltshire who were staying at the Saracen's Head in Friday Street
where he lodged told him that clothiers who used to 'set at
work' a hundred men now employed a dozen or so. The poor,
they went on, gather in troops of ten, twenty or thirty, seize
corn on the way to market and 'divide it among themselves
before the owners' faces, telling them they could not starve'.
But they always returned the sacks and the cart and horses.

The *Earnest Petition* of January 1648 was John Lilburne's
work. Had he not acknowledged it, we could have guessed that
he was its draftsman. No one but he among the leaders of the
party would have argued that the sufferings of the people were
due to 'the devouring fire of the Lord's wrath'. That was why
'merciless famine is entered into our gates'. No less characteristic are the elaborate marginal references that decorate its
pages. The petition repeats most of the familiar Leveller
doctrines and demands, stressing most emphatically of all the
sovereignty of the Commons, who alone were 'betrusted by the
people to redress their grievances' which they now 'declare

by their practice' they will not do 'unless the King and the Lords will.' No mention, however, was made of tithes, because (as Wildman tells us) this subject was felt to be too contentious, nor are the sufferings of imprisoned debtors mentioned, though the general principle is re-affirmed that imprisonment should be only for safe custody before trial. On the other hand, there are several new demands. The clause (6) dealing with the reform of the courts and prisons forbids all fees to judges or jailors, and insists that they shall receive from the common treasury a regular 'pension or salary' and nothing more. The clause (14) calling for the abolition of the purchase tax (excise) substitutes for it direct taxation 'according to the proportion of men's estates'.

The clause dealing with representative government adopts on behalf of the party two demands which had so far been made only by individual pamphleteers or by the soldiers. The first is a wide extension of the franchise. 'That birthright of all Englishmen' must 'be at once restored to all which are not . . . disfranchised for some criminal cause, or are not under 21 years of age or servants or beggars'. Then comes Richard Overton's proposal for the election of all magistrates. It is urged

> that some chosen representatives of every parish proportion-ably may be the electors of the sheriffs, justices of the peace, committee-men, grand-jury-men and all ministers of justice whatsoever, in the respective counties, and that no such minister of justice may continue in his office above one whole year, without a new election.

It is arguable that this was the most important and original item in the whole Leveller programme. It meant first of all decentralisation, the self-government of every parish, hundred and county, instead of the nomination of its rulers from West-minster. More important still, it deposed the landowning ruling class, who had hitherto filled every administrative and judicial post as a matter of course—unless, indeed, the peasantry chose to elect them, for one year only. Thus the Levellers anticipated what is the normal usage of the United States, with the differ-ence that direct instead of indirect election prevails there.

A marginal note gives the clue to much of Lilburne's political thinking:

> It hath been a maxim among the wisest legislators, that whosoever means to settle good laws, must proceed in them with a sinister or evil opinion of all mankind, and suppose that whosoever is not wicked, it is for want of opportunity, and that no state can be wisely confident of any public minister continuing good longer than the rod is over him.

Did the cynicism of this passage spring from experience or from the doctrine of original sin? Frequent elections could have been justified as the system which best ensures that the will of the electors shall prevail. To this first sketch of representative democracy, the Levellers afterwards added the proposal that the parson of the parish church and the regimental officers of the militia should also be elected.

One startling innovation in each petition was not enough to satisfy John Lilburne. He suddenly springs upon us the doctrine of the separation of powers, in his day unheard of though it is a commonplace in ours. The High Court of Parliament was as much a tribunal as it was a legislature, and in the English Revolution its trials of Strafford and Laud were as decisive as the Root and Branch Bill. In this petition it is boldly invited to discard its judicial powers, so that

> henceforth no particular cause, whether criminal or other, which comes under the cognisance of the ordinary courts of justice may be determined by this House or any committee thereof, or any other than by those courts, whose duty it is to execute such laws as this honourable House shall make.

Lilburne's was an empirical mind. He advances no arguments in support of his demand, but is content to say that

> many persons, of faithful and public spirits have been and are daily molested, vexed, imprisoned by such committees, sometimes for not answering interrogatories and sometimes for other matters which are not in law criminal.

Half a century later the Whigs put the case for the separation of powers before the Commons but failed to convince them.

As important and no less original is the clause (§13) which deals with the plight of 'the poor'. It asks

that the too long continued shame of this nation, viz.
permission of any to suffer such poverty as to beg their bread
may be effectually remedied: and to that purpose that the
poor be enabled to choose their trustees to discover all stocks,
houses, lands, etc., which of right belong to them and their
use, that they may speedily receive the benefit thereof; and
that some good improvement may be made of waste grounds
for their use; and that according to the promise of this
honourable House in your first remonstrance care be taken
forthwith to advance the native commodities of this nation,
that the poor may have better wages for their labour; and
that manufactures may be improved for the best advantage
of our own mariners and the whole nation.

This clause or parts of it may have been suggested by Richard
Overton, for as we have seen he believed that many charitable foundations had been diverted from their proper purpose.
But the bold idea of empowering 'the poor' to elect trustees—
Tribunes of the Plebs, as it were—was new. One asks how 'the
poor' who were to do the choosing would be distinguished from
'the rich'? Would these trustees have executive powers, or
would they have to bring every case of misappropriation into
court? This was, perhaps, the most original application of the
Levellers' doctrine of representation. When we come to discuss
their views on the land we shall see how fully aware some of
them—as well as Dr Chamberlen and of course the Diggers—
were of the social importance of the wastes and commons. One
might even argue that the disposal of this land, a third of the
surface of England, was the central issue in English history
during this century and the next. What the brief sentence
about wages meant was, presumably, that parallel with a
general increase of production, the figures fixed by the justices
should be raised to balance the higher cost of living. This must
have been the first time that any group of politicians in England
called for a higher level of wages. In spite of the maddening
brevity of this clause, it is clear that the new party felt a deep
concern for 'the poorer and most ingenious, industrious
people' round about them. This phrase, which occurs in the
next clause, suggests a readiness to idealise the craftsman and
peasant.

While the Levellers were carrying on the big effort of

organisation and propaganda which was to bring them—so John Lilburne hoped—a hundred thousand signatures for this petition, they distributed among the soldiers a much briefer and more emotional leaflet, which came from the press round about 22 January, 1648. Its title sums up its burden—*The mournful cries of many thousand poor tradesmen, who are ready to famish through decay of trade, or the warning tears of the oppressed.*[4] Its Biblical language may seem to the modern reader hectic and rhetorical and its picture of the nation-wide distress exaggerated. But for some of its statements there is ample corroboration; that 'we sell our beds and clothes for bread' was a fact. Its indignation echoes the Hebrew prophets, as when it addresses the Commons—

> 'O you Members of Parliament and rich men in the City, that are at ease and drink wine in bowls and stretch yourselves upon beds of down, you that grind our faces and flay off our skins, will no man amongst you regard, will no man behold our faces black with sorrow and famine?

After the statement that these great men have all grown rich from the spoils of public offices, comes the question:

> What, then, are your ruffling silks and velvets and your glittering gold and silver laces? Are they not the sweat of our brows and the wants of our backs and bellies? . . . What else but your ambition and faction continue our distractions and oppressions? Is not all the controversy whose slaves the poor shall be?

The pamphleteer—or shall we call him the prophet?—appeals for peace as the only remedy for all the distress; this can be won by deciding promptly 'where the supreme power resides'. As for the costs of the war and the arrears of pay, these would be more than covered by the value of all the confiscated and sequestered estates, were it not that M.P.s, of whom two are named, together with the Speaker have robbed the till.

The leaflet ends on a revolutionary note. The soldiers are implored to join 'the perishing people' in presenting the petition to Parliament. Then comes the warning: 'Hunger will break through stone walls.' The soldiers must tell Parliament that 'the tears of the oppressed will wash away the foundations of their houses'.

This is more than one of the familiar warnings that liberals so often address to a complacent governing class. The poetical imagery conveys the intensity of the writer's emotion. This, if the soldiers can be induced to fraternise with the civilian petitioners from town and country, is a summons to revolution. If enough of these should assemble and some of the redcoats and buff coats were to mingle with them, they could impose their will on a corrupt and heedless Parliament. During this winter there was to be sure a regiment of horse in the Royal Mews (on the site of Trafalgar Square) and a regiment of foot in Whitehall. Some of them as we shall see, would listen to John Lilburne; but how many? The Levellers when they penned their defiance,—'Hunger regards no swords nor cannons'—were too sanguine, but they had their grounds for confidence.

On 17 January, 1648 a well-attended meeting was held at a gardener's house in Wapping, at which Lilburne and Wildman spoke in support of the *Earnest Petition*. In the audience was George Masterson, the minister of Shoreditch, who was so shocked by what he heard that he promptly reported to Parliament everything, or nearly everything—for there was much that a man of his cloth could not repeat. The Lords, whose prisoner John still was at law, tactfully deferred to the Commons the business of dealing with this subversive agitation. Masterson's report has come down to posterity, and albeit from a hostile angle it gives us an interesting impression of a Leveller meeting. Questions and objections were welcomed from the audience and were answered in a friendly spirit by the speakers. Some were puzzled that the Levellers should take the trouble to send up petitions to a House which had them burned by the hangman. Lilburne answered firstly that we must own some visible authority for the present, or else we shall be brought to ruin and confusion; secondly that 'when we have raised up the spirits of the people through the whole kingdom . . . we shall force them [the Commons] to grant us those things we desire'. Finally, he said that the real reason for sending agents into all the counties of the kingdom was to inform the people of their liberties and privileges; apart from this he 'would not give threepence for ten thousand hands'. Incidentally John believed that the majority of the people were 'malignants', partly because Parliament had done so little to reveal to them 'the glory and splendour of their liberties' and partly because they were grossly over-taxed.

Lilburne, in an access of garrulity, told stories of attempts by the Lords to bribe him to abandon the petition. Wildman in vain tried to stop him. The chief attack of both was aimed at the pretensions and record of the Lords. There was an exciting discussion over the reasons which led Cromwell to abandon the King and support the vote of No More Addresses. Someone in the audience told the story that Harry Marten provided himself with a pistol and dagger to play the part of Felton, because he was convinced that Cromwell had sold the people's cause for an earldom and the garter. He was, however, dissuaded by another M.P., as Wildman tells the story, or locked up by him, if we follow Masterson. Lilburne believed that it was this threat of assassination which drove the Lieut.-General to declare a day of humiliation and reconciliation, and to reverse his policy in the House. Wildman's explanation was that Cromwell guessed that the Scots had outbid him by offering the militia and the negative voice to the King in England, provided they avoided any such concessions in Scotland.

Without waiting for a warrant, Lilburne and Wildman presented themselves next day at the House of Commons. Lilburne replied at length to Masterson's charges, admitting his responsibility for the petition but exposing some of the confusions in the parson's report of what was said about Cromwell. While defending himself he counter-attacked by accusing the Lieut.-General formally of treason. The debate went on until candles were brought in, and ended in the verdict that for 'treasonable and seditious practices against the state' Lilburne was to be confined a close prisoner in the Tower and Wildman in the Fleet. Lilburne, waiting with about a hundred of his followers in the lobby, convinced the sergeant-at-arms that the Speaker's warrant was out of order as a legal document. He was then allowed to withdraw, on giving his parole.

Next morning though the warrant had been amended, Lilburne, armed as usual with a copy of Coke's *Institutes*, had no difficulty in proving that it was still out of order, for like the King's famous charge against the Five Members, it mentioned no particular act of treason for which he was to be committed. He then addressed the guard which had been ordered to arrest him. He told them that they would 'subject themselves to slavery' and prove themselves 'arrant mercenaries', if they enforced an illegal warrant. So persuasive, so magnetic was this man, that they refused, officers as well as men, to lay hands on him. Only when their colonel arrived with a fresh guard was he arrested and carried to the Tower, and only then after a struggle in which his life was saved by his wife, who flung herself between his body and the swords of the soldiers.[5]

Needless to say it was not for the niceties of legal draftsmanship, that Freeborn John risked his life. The principle he meant to assert was that a mass meeting of political partisans ought not to act as a court of justice. The House of Commons, as he told the soldiers in the language of the *Earnest Petition*, was 'chosen and betrusted to make and repeal laws, but is not in the least empowered to execute the laws'. While the Commons sent the two most troublesome Levellers to prison, Derby House (the executive drawn from both Houses) took steps to silence their party. In London and the Tower Hamlets the militia was ordered to break up all its indoor meetings and like instructions were sent to the County Committee of Kent and presumably to others also. So feeble was the concern of the Puritan Revolution for civil liberty. It suited Cromwell as well as Manchester that the gadfly who plagued them both should be caged; it was, moreover, important for the Independents to keep the good will of the House of Lords, by silencing its chief opponent.

Repression, however, was not enough. The time was past when a petition of the Levellers could be dealt with by the hangman. It was now necessary to argue with this growing party on terms of equality. The executive accordingly instructed its secretary, Walter Frost, to publish a full reply to the *Earnest Petition* and the *Mournful Cries*. He did it with commendable candour, for in his pamphlet, *A Declaration of some proceedings of Lt.-Col. John Lilburne*, he included not only his own answer and Masterson's evidence but complete reprints of the Leveller documents. He adds the assurance that the original of the letter to the branch of the party in Kent can be produced, as though this most harmless of documents, seized presumably in the post, were evidence of a deadly conspiracy, though all it did was to make arrangements for the promotion of the petition at a meeting which Lilburne was to address at Dartford. This was, in fact, during the Interregnum and for some decades after it the view most Englishmen took of an organised party, even when it worked in the open.

Frost's polemic, in its superficial way, is a not unskilful piece of work. It was easy to accuse Lilburne of rhetorical exaggeration. It was easy to ignore all the novel and daring proposals with which the petition abounded. Masterson's confused story could be twisted without effort into evidence that the Levellers projected, or at least applauded assassination. With a neatly phrased platitude about the weather, their analysis of the economic depression could be brushed aside. The suggestion that the Levellers were Catholic 'missionaries' was probably too silly to do them much harm. On the other hand the defence of the three members charged with embezzlement sounds—one cannot say more—like the truth. But the most illuminating passage of this semi-official pamphlet comes in the peroration. The Levellers are exhorted 'to study to be quiet and do your own business . . . and leave the public affairs to those to whom God and the kingdom have committed them'. So far were 'the silken Independents' from being democrats.

During the spring of 1648 the idea of an armed insurrection seems to have haunted the Leveller movement. Whether it took any practical steps towards it, by collecting arms or choosing officers, we do not know. The evidence that it did contemplate something of the kind is to be found in *A New Engagement or Manifesto* of uncertain date.[6] It professes to give the

> sense and resolution of many thousands of well-affected people in and about London and some adjacent counties . . . who seeing all present authorities to be perverted from their natural end, the people's safety, are necessitated to put themselves into a posture of defending their own and the country's liberties.

The preamble declares that 'all ordinary means' such as petitions have been of no effect; the Commons intend to go on sitting 'and dividing the public treasure among themselves', while the chief officers of the Army think only of aggrandising themselves. The familiar complaints follow about the tyranny of committees, corruption, imprisonment for debt, the excise, tithes, the vast sums paid to usurers for the public debt and the neglect of the poor of whom many are perishing of hunger. Lastly the authors see a 'danger of being embroiled again each in others' blood'. 'We invite our countrymen', so runs the moral drawn from this survey, 'to join with us in a posture of defence, while we propound some certain grounds of common right and freedom.' There follows a lucid summary of the whole Leveller programme. That the authors are contemplating the use of arms to win it is clear from the conclusion. After stating that they count on the support both of the soldiers still serving and of the disbanded supernumeraries, they undertake that when these demands are secured, 'we shall gladly and cheerfully return to our private habitations and callings'.

Within this framework of militancy the draftsman has given to the programme itself a statement remarkable for its moderation. The Agreement of the People is described as a contract to be drawn and sealed between the people and their several deputies respectively, upon the day of the election, 'wherein the bounds, limits and extent of their trust shall be clearly expressed'. In the clauses dealing with the reform of the law it is provided that 'the Chancery with all other arbitrary courts be forthwith dissolved', and that 'men's lives be more precious than formerly and that lesser punishments than death and more useful to the public be found out for small offences'. The clause concerning tithes proposes a compromise:

> That tithes be wholly taken away, the parishioner from whence they are due paying in lieu thereof to the state where they are not appropriate and to the owner where they are a moderate and certain rent charge out of his land. The ministers to be maintained either by the voluntary contribution of such as desire to hear them, or else by some settled pensions out of the public treasure.

A conciliatory clause about Ireland is the first utterance of its kind from the party, though Walwyn's pacific views were well known. It asked

> that the affairs of Ireland be taken into a more serious consideration than heretofore, and that a peaceable way of reducing that nation be once endeavoured, and in case that succeed not, the war be prosecuted with vigour and unanimity.

We reach at the end (in clause 16) the most interesting innovation in the party's programme. A sober and well thought out procedure is set forth which promises security and independence to copyhold tenants—the vast majority of the rural population (pp. 437-43 below). If the Levellers, with their remarkable talent for propaganda, had ever been able, after widening the franchise, to concentrate on this proposal for emancipating the peasantry, the history of England thereafter would have run a very different course.[7]

If they did ever contemplate an armed rising, they delayed too long about it. The King's partisans struck first.

NOTES TO CHAPTER XVI

1. *Mercurius Rusticus* (12 November, 1647) quotes wheat at 9s. or 10s. the bushel; the price in a good year was 4s.

2. Lipson, *Economic History*, III, p. 453.

3. *Mercurius Rusticus* (12 November, 1647).

4. Reprinted in H. and D., p. 126, and Wolfe, p. 273. It is usually ascribed to Lilburne, and a good deal of it is certainly from his pen. But it may have been a joint production. Some phrases—e.g. 'Is not all the controversy whose slaves the poor shall be?'—recur in almost identical words in *The Bloody Project* (H. and D., p. 145), which was Walwyn's work. The style of the remarkable last paragraph of *The Mournful Cries* does not sound to me like Lilburne's.

5. *A Whip for the present House of Lords* (27 February, 1648).

6. *The New Engagement* is in one of Thomason's volumes, 669 f. 12 (99), with his date mark 3 August, 1648. In the bound volume it follows a Dutch engraving of the King's execution. The date seems impossible, since it is clear from the preamble that the second Civil War had not yet begun. *The New Engagement* seems to have been the original of which the programme in *The Army's Petition*, described as 'A new engagement of many in the Army who are yet faithful to the people', was an abbreviated copy. To this Thomason assigned the date 3 May, 1648. The soldiers repeated the civilians' clause about base tenures *verbatim*. Again, if *The New Engagement*

had been published in August, it would have been reprinted in *The Moderate*, as all the party's public utterances were. I conclude that it was drafted some little time before May 1648. One cannot be sure when or why it was published.

7. Careful though the drafting was, there are some curious omissions. It does not mention the King, the Lords or their negative voices. Nor does it call for Lilburne's release from the Tower. That it makes no mention of manhood suffrage is less puzzling, since the emancipated copyholders would automatically acquire the right to vote.

CHAPTER XVII

The Second Civil War

At last it had come—the renewal of the war the Army had been dreading. After nearly two years of peace, the New Model, with its ranks dangerously depleted, took the field again. On May Day, 1648, the council of war in Windsor Castle took the decision that Cromwell with five regiments should march for Pembroke, to quell the revolt of the auxiliary troops and the peasantry.

How the Council of the Army spent the last days of April, while the news trickled in that the whole of South Wales was up in arms for the King, was told eleven years later by Captain William Allen, once a leading Agitator.[1] Cromwell pressed very earnestly on all present to examine their actions as an Army, 'to see if any iniquity could be found in them'. On the third day of their meeting the officers unanimously agreed that 'these cursed carnal conferences' with the King were the cause that provoked the Lord 'to depart from us'. 'Loathing ourselves for our iniquities . . . none was able hardly to speak a word . . . for bitter weeping.' We saw, he goes on, that it was

> our duty, if ever the Lord brought us back again in peace, to call Charles Stuart, that man of blood, to an account for that blood he had shed and mischief he had done against the Lord's cause and people in these poor nations.

Captain Allen can hardly mean that the Council took any binding decision to try the King; many months went by before Cromwell finally made up his mind to do it and Fairfax never did. What he helps us to understand is rather the state of mind of these officers as they faced the decision, after two years of civilian tranquillity, to ride out again to wound and kill their fellow countrymen. Their regret for a political mistake in dealing with the King would not account for the emotional disturbance Allen describes. The only ground for self reproach was that the attempt to come to terms with the King went on too long. But for this only Cromwell and Ireton were responsible. Hardened veterans these officers might be and sure that they were doing the Lord's work. But does any man go out to kill his kind without a gnawing sense of guilt in his unconscious? That, surely, is the meaning of this hectic scene. The guilt of fratricidal war oppressed them, till they could scarcely speak for weeping. And then they found the inevitable solution for their distress; they laid their guilt on the head of a scapegoat—the man of blood, Charles Stuart.

Presently the demand for the execution of the King took a religious form. In Puritan England it could not have been otherwise. As one turns the pages of the pamphlets of 1648, alike in petitions and in sermons, be the authors soldiers or divines, one comes on the argument incessantly repeated that only by the spilling of more blood can the earth be cleansed from the stain of blood. It was a man so relatively enlightened as the republican Colonel Ludlow who argued that he dare not, by sparing the guilty King, 'draw down the just vengeance of God upon us all'. Of this he was 'convinced by the express words of God's law; that blood defileth the land and the land cannot be cleansed of the blood that is shed therein but by the blood of him that shed it'. One might be listening to the blind soothsayer Tiresias talking to the elders of Thebes. But no; this primitive tradition of blood-guiltiness came straight from the Old Testament.[2]

In this atmosphere of sanctified revenge, the second Civil War was fought with a brutality to which in the first struggle the Parliament's armies rarely descended. The shameful treatment of the women at the siege of Colchester and the shooting after their surrender of the royalist commanders, Sir Charles Lucas and Sir George Lyle, were unworthy of the New Model. Incomparably worse, because it was not done in hot blood, was the systematic sale of the prisoners, Welshmen, Scots and

Englishmen, to serve as slaves in all but name in the plantations of Barbados and Virginia. Many thousands of prisoners under both Commonwealth and Protectorate were punished in this way. Some were sold, apparently as cannon-fodder, to the Venetian Republic. One lot of 2,000 Scots was offered in succession first to the Most Catholic and then to the Most Christian King, but the Spaniards had no ready cash and the French bid too little.

In those days the slave trade worked in both directions, with white merchandise as well as black. After the battle of Worcester 1,500 Scottish prisoners were granted to the Guinea merchants and set to work in the mines of Africa.[3] How long, one asks, did any of them survive? It is to the credit of Sir Harry Vane's humanity that after the royalist rising round Salisbury in 1655 he protested, though in vain, against the barbarity of sending political opponents as slaves to the Caribbean islands. Our fathers continued this practice of transporting political offenders, which they had learnt from Cromwell, well into the nineteenth century. These records which count their thousands of broken lives and broken hearts haunt us, if we have ears to hear, among the inarticulate undertones of British history.

About the King, as they marched from Windsor to Pembroke and thence to Preston, officers and men thought alike, but in the minds of the men there was a strong tinge of class feeling. We have for example, a statement from the private soldiery of Colonel Scroop's and Colonel Saunders's regiments of horse, as bitter as it is well-written.[4] Still anxious over the act of indemnity, they recollect that in the early days of the struggle their chaplains used to tell them 'that if a man died in this service, his soul was in heaven before his blood was cold in his body'. And now are they to sue the King for his pardon? The two regiments reject his claim of sovereignty. It rests only on his descent from William the Conqueror. In plain words, he was King only by the sword. The *Relation* is deeply interesting when it attacks the whole working of the law, devised as these troopers saw it to oppress 'the middling sort of people'. It singles out (much as Voltaire did on the eve of the French Revolution), with instances, the iniquities of the law of mortmain.

These troopers have a moving tale to tell when they recount some of their economic grievances. Many a man was discharged after years of service without cash enough to carry him home. The infantry had often to march barefoot, while the cavalry who had to replace a horse lost on service were often £10 or even £20 in debt. Wounded men had often to borrow money to pay a surgeon.

All Parliament does for us is to set the churchwardens of the parishes in London to beg for us at the church doors. But if any member of Parliament suffers loss, the House at once votes him thousands of pounds for his loss of hundreds.

The troopers then recall the recent vote of Parliament deducting 6d. from their former daily pay of 2s. 6d.

Out of this we must buy horse, saddle, pistol, sword and clothes with meat and drink, hay and oats. Notwithstanding our hard service this last summer past, we have marched night and day, yet they have not given us any pay at all these twenty-six weeks although they did engage in their ordinance to do it.

Had any of these M.P.s ever served as private soldiers, the troopers ask, would they have cut down our pay? These two regiments now realise that 'any rich man, however knavish or foolish' can get into Parliament. They were not mistaken, they declare, in the cause for which they fought. But they were mistaken in this Parliament. They demand, therefore, the election of a council, composed of two representatives from each county and two from each regiment, first to examine the accounts of all public expenditure, especially that of Parliament, and secondly to try those guilty of two civil wars. Finally, these troopers explain, they have spoken for themselves, because their officers cannot take up their case against Parliament, since they hold their commissions from it. In these two regiments, which were to lead the Leveller revolt next summer, it is probable that their Agitators still retained their influence.

The men of Pride's foot, as they marched on Westminster, shared some of these troopers' feelings, but they had more confidence in their officers. 'It hath pleased the Lord of Hosts, Who was called upon to decide the controversy of this nation',

—so ran the petition they addressed to Fairfax—'to write His name upon your sword in very legible characters', for they reckoned their hundred and fourteen victories in the campaign of 1645 and above thirty more in the present year. After calling for the punishment of the guilty, and the setting up of a 'godly' government, it complains that 'this regiment hath had but one month's pay since May, having marched 1,300 miles this summer'. . . . 'Sir', they conclude, 'we can die but not endure to see our mother England die before us'.[5] This sounds like officers' language. The men, when they came to do their purging, expressed themselves more bluntly. Clement Walker, who was one of the purged, has left his account of that stormy 6th of December. He heard them saying, as Hugh Peters took the names of the imprisoned members, 'These are the men who have cozened the state of our money and kept back our pay'.[6]

Yet another record has survived of the soldiers' state of mind, which may be authentic, though it comes from a royalist journalist. At Windsor, shortly before the end, a sentinel said to the King,

> You, with a pox to you, must have £15 a day allowed you for your table, but we poor soldiers that stand in the cold must not have 15d. to relieve us with. Well, Stroker (for so they termed him in relation to that gift which God had given him in curing the [King's] evil) we shall be quit of you ere long.[7]

The bitterness this man felt may have been shared by most of his comrades, though few of them one hopes would have insulted a fallen enemy as he did. A sense of guilt, a primitive fear of blood, these with class enmity all played their part in the campaign that ended on the scaffold before Whitehall.

From the second Civil War the Army emerged even surer of itself than when it marched to the front. It had had to do much of its fighting in Lancashire and South Wales, two of the regions where the Royalists were always the stronger party. At its approach the Welsh peasants took to the hills and the woods, so that not even a blacksmith was left to shoe its limping horses. While it marched hither and thither, even in the once friendly eastern counties it had to realise that the great majority of the population were now on the King's side. As revolts broke out first in Wales, next in Kent and then in Essex, it could never concentrate its forces—it had even to detach a brigade to hold Cornwall—and in each field of operations it fought outnumbered. The massive fortifications of Pembroke detained Cromwell for six weeks and Fairfax, after his lightning victory in Kent, had to sit down for eleven before Colchester.

The hopes of the Presbyterians and Royalists were fixed on the invasion of the Scots army under the Duke of Hamilton, formidable by its numbers. How Cromwell and Lambert with 8,600 men, 'so harassed' (to quote Ludlow) 'with hard service and long marches that they seemed rather fit for a hospital than a battle', put Hamilton's 21,000 to total rout at Preston is a barely credible story until one follows their movements in detail. When one adds the fact that Rainsborough failed to bring back the fleet to loyalty: and that one ship in four went over to Prince Charles, while the rest were too inert or too unreliable to risk an engagement with the royalist squadron which blockaded the Thames, the marvel is that the parliamentary cause survived at all. It not only survived but, thanks as much to the bravery and physical endurance of the men as to the brilliance of the commanders, it triumphed. By 27 August, when Colchester surrendered, it was all over save for the sieges of Scarborough and Pontefract. The Army acknowledged the power of God in this ordeal by battle. As an Independent pamphleteer put it: 'the glorious majesty, power and presence of God do most visibly appear in successes when He maketh one to chase ten and two to put a hundred to flight'.[8]

Conscious as never before that it stood apart from the people, the Army felt entitled to impose its will—God's will—on the defeated majority.

Throughout the summer of 1648, London was the prize for which the armies contended. At Westminster, however, it was the policy of the Independents not to provoke or even to oppose the Presbyterians, lest they should be driven into open alliance with the Royalists. At first with the idea of appeasing the City, but presently from sheer military necessity, Fairfax withdrew his troops from Whitehall and the Tower. The defence

M

of London and the Parliament were left to the train-bands, though under the command of Skippon whom the Independents trusted. The City oligarchy and most of the citizens had swung round to the King's side, but they were still Puritans who had not forgotten their hostility to the bishops and the cavalier nobility. There is no doubt that some of the Presbyterian magnates invited Hamilton to invade England, but they had no wish that London should be involved in the fighting. Some Londoners, to be sure, especially from among the Thames watermen, did join the Kentish insurgents, but they went out as volunteers and individuals.

The atmosphere of the City, even after the first successes of the New Model in Wales and Kent, was confidently and optimistically royalist; the Scots would soon bring victory, restore the King and impose the Covenant. The presses poured out their unlicensed 'news-books' and broad-sheets. One printed the story of an anonymous gentleman who saw Cromwell mortally wounded before Chepstow and carried into his chamber to die. Another reported that Lambert had been killed—or if not killed then 'totally routed'. A third passed on the rumour that Fairfax was dead at Colchester. There was even better news than this for sale—that Prince Charles with a considerable army had landed at Yarmouth, and again, somewhat later, in Kent. When at last Parliament published the Lieut.-General's despatch reporting the destruction of Hamilton's army at Preston, the most popular of the royalist weeklies, *Mercurius Pragmaticus* (22 August, 1648), printed a summary of 'the pretended letter of Cromwell' but refused to believe a word of it.

In this mental climate Parliament went rattling into reaction. Even before the fighting had begun, on 28 April, the House resolved by 165 to 99 not to 'alter the fundamental government of the kingdom by King, Lords and Commons'. Vane and some other leading Independents voted with the majority. On 2 May the savage Blasphemy Bill was finally passed into law. A month later (3 June) the Commons abandoned the impeachment of the eleven (now ten) excluded M.P.s; some of them soon resumed their seats; Holles, the Army's chief enemy, did so on 14 August. The strength of the extreme Presbyterian-Royalist party was revealed on 18 and

21 July, when the Lords twice rejected a resolution in which the Commons had declared that any who adhered to the Scots invaders should be proceeded against as rebels and traitors. In the Commons it seems probable that the minority which voted against this declaration numbered over ninety.[9]

The last phase began on 24 August, after Hamilton's surrender, when the vote of No More Addresses was repealed. The New Model was victorious in the field. One chance of resisting it remained, however; if the King and the Presbyterian majority could come to terms, they might at last isolate the Army and, if need were, outlaw it, with King, Lords and Commons united against it. Accordingly, on 18 September, after prolonged pressure from the City, negotiations were opened with the King at Newport. On 29 September an ordinance was passed establishing the Presbyterian system of church government throughout England; not a loophole was left for the toleration of 'tender consciences'.

Of the doings of the Levellers during this anxious summer there is not much to record. This was no time for tilting at the Army's Grandees, or criticising the 'silken Independents'. The one thing needful was to win the second Civil War. Doubtless the elder men still gathered of an evening over their tankards in the Whalebone tavern to discuss the military news, with a smile at the credulity of the Royalists. Of the younger men in the party one supposes that a good many enlisted in Skippon's militia, horse and foot—the *corps d'élite* which he raised because he could not rely on the City's train-bands. The propertied classes were alarmed as they watched the growth of this force; they even addressed a petition to Parliament, in which they complained that Skippon's purpose was 'to put the power of the sword into the hands of the servants and sectaries'.[10] The class issue in this Revolution is never far to seek.

The misery of the workers in London, which had stirred the Levellers during the winter to their outcries of compassion and alarm, was now greatly aggravated. The Prince's enterprising little navy was playing the pirate (as the Levellers put it) against shipping in the approaches to the Thames, with the result that overseas trade, slack during the winter, was now entirely stopped. The Lord Mayor and Common Council of the City were petitioning Parliament for peace at any price. Their staple commodity of wool remains (so they described their plight) unsold and London lacks corn, coal, fish, butter and cheese which normally reach it by sea. The poor, they predict 'wanting work and bread . . . will in a very short time become tumultuous in all parts of the kingdom'.[11]

The Levellers saw the facts much as the City magnates did, but they had other views about the causes of the craftsmen's misery. On 17 August (the first day of the Preston battle) one of their boldest and most original tracts appeared under the title:

> *England's Troublers Troubled, or the just resolutions of the plain men of England against the rich and mighty, by whose pride, treachery and wilfulness they are brought into extreme necessity and misery.*

Obviously it is not a manifesto for which the party as a whole was responsible. It professes to be the work of a London craftsman, but its prose is that of a practised and well educated writer. Clement Walker attributed it to Henry Marten and one may adopt this ascription with some confidence. It reflects both his known opinions, his gift for satire and his recklessness, half jocular, half serious.

The pamphlet opens with an argument that the men of property have been to blame for everything that went wrong in the Civil War down to the present day. Behind the happenings at Westminster and the Guildhall the writer can discern 'a confederacy amongst the rich and mighty to impoverish and so to enslave all the plain and mean people throughout the land'.

> Ye have [he goes on] by corruption in government, by unjust and unequal laws, by fraud, cosenage, tyranny and oppression gotten most of the land of this distressed and enslaved nation into your ravenous claws. Ye have by monopolies, usurers and combinations engrossed all the wealth, monies and houses into your possessions; yea and enclosed our commons in most counties.

Parliament (like the City and the Livery companies) is dominated by the rich and so made useless to the electors. Juries are forced to stand bareheaded and intimidated by judges and lawyers

> so that it is vain for any plain, honest man to expect any reason, equity or justice against any sort of you rich and wealthy men. . . . How excessively and unconscionably have ye advanced your land rents in the country and house and shop rents in the City within these forty years! Most rich citizens get their wealth by buying handicraft goods at less than the cost of materials. . . . Ye are so rich, fat and swollen with wealth that ye esteem less of plain men than you do of your horses and dogs, which ye feed and pamper, whilst by your means such as we are enforced to starve or beg, . . . having neither one foot of land to plough nor pasture, nor house to live in, nor shop nor stall wherein to get their daily bread but at your unconscionable and unreasonable racked, oppressive and destructive rents.

This picture of exploitation and injustice deserves our attention because it was not painted by some poor man with a grievance and an inferiority complex. Marten was the son of a rich lawyer, who inherited a great landed estate and sat, like his father, in the Commons.

He goes on, in his assumed character of an unemployed craftsman, to warn the rich that he and his friends have had more time than usual to think of such things since trade stopped. 'By divine providence it begins to come to our turn.' They cannot pay their rents, nor interest on their debts, nor is there any prospect that they will be able to do so 'until the Scots that are come in by your invitation . . . be wholly withdrawn'. At this point his indictment turns to satire, and he proposes that the tradesmen who 'by your wicked means' have been brought to this misery should billet themselves 'in your houses and barns and butteries, not by way of felony or robbery but in a just, fair and usual way of free quarter'.

Those who read Marten's tract in that anxious and unhappy summer would see in it an effective assault by a daring fencer against the rapacious plutocrats of the City, who were petitioning Parliament to bring the King to London in order to put him at the head of a new army. For us it has another interest. It reveals just how far a humane and brilliant mind, reared in the ruling caste, could go in understanding the techniques of exploitation prevalent in his day. The oligarchy of landowners, merchants and lawyers which governed England was repugnant to him—it and all its ways. For its victims he felt a sympathy that drove him to break with his class. He would help them with his wit and his sword. Advanced Leveller as he was, he would make an end of imprisonment for debt, and tithes and base tenures. He was an ardent democrat and republican: but there his vision stopped. He did not call for any fundamental change in the economic structure of society.

A day or two after sending *The Troublers Troubled* to the printer, Marten went down to his constituency, Berkshire, where we may now watch him in action. He was not only knight of the shire, but had served as colonel of horse in the parliamentary armies. He now raised a regiment of horse, whose colours bore the unusual motto *For the People*. He shared the command with the Leveller Colonel William Eyres, who had been arrested for his part in the mutiny at Ware—a veteran who started his service in Cromwell's original troop of horse. The gentlefolk of the county were furious because Marten requisitioned horses for his men from the 'well-affected' as well as the 'malignants'—a thing any modern commander would do in war-time as a matter of course. It was at this time that he told the jury to keep their hats on in the presence of the judge, to demonstrate their superiority to him. Also at a court-baron—was it on his own estate?—he forbade the tenants 'to do homage unto their lord, telling them it was a slavery and a badge of the Norman Conquest'.[12]

Marten's horse rode northwards into Leicestershire—presumably to meet the invading Scots. There, so a news-book informs us, their approach caused 'great terror to all H.M's liege people'. It was reported that 'the basest and vilest of men' resorted to them, that they robbed and plundered, boasting they would 'level all sorts of people, even from the highest to the lowest'. In fact, however, Colonel Marten gave orders 'that no soldier whatsoever shall dare to plunder or use violence against any'. The panic that broke out on their arrival at Market Harborough died down on closer acquaintance, and they 'departed peacefully'.[13] From Mansfield came the reassuring news that their 'deportment and carriage is very civil'. Eventually Marten's regiment was put 'on the strength' and he was re-imbursed for what he had spent upon it.

The clash of arms could not stop the intellectual ferment the Levellers had started, and several notable tracts appeared during this perilous summer. William Walwyn's pamphlet, *The Bloody Project*, written when the military struggle was nearing its climax, is something rather deeper and subtler than the party polemics of those days.[14] Overcome by his horror at the war raging around him, he asks himself the disturbing question: what conditions must be satisfied before mass murder can be justified? 'To shed blood for money or to support this or the other interest' is merely murder, and to do it 'for a cause not rightly stated or not thoroughly understood to be just' is no better. Neither the King nor the Parliament ever made it clear what they meant by the 'general terms' for which they professed to be fighting. Parliament, the champion of the liberties of the people, has in fact made new inroads upon them, and left too many of the old oppressions standing. As for the Presbyterians, who set out to oppose arbitrary power, they would enable 'a priest or two and a few lay elders . . . to enforce all persons within the limits of their jurisdiction to believe as they believe'.

> To be short, all the quarrel we have at this day in the kingdom is no other than a quarrel of interests and parties, a pulling down of one tyrant to set up another, and instead of liberty, heaping upon ourselves a greater slavery than that we fought against.

What, then, if anything, can justify men in resorting to arms? The first condition is that it must be done upon a 'call or invitation from the supreme authority or law-making power'. Then, more tersely and persuasively than ever before, he argues that this supreme authority can only be the House of Commons, who are chosen and trusted by the people. 'That there should be either three or two distinct estates equally supreme is an absurd nullity in government.'

To this first condition Walwyn instantly adds another of equal importance—the claim of the individual citizen to determine for himself the justice or necessity of any call to arms.

> You must note that you are a free people, and are not to be pressed to serve in wars like horses and brute beasts. . . . It is not sufficient to fight by lawful authority, but you must be sure to fight for what is just, . . . lawful authority being sometimes mistaken and many times so perverted and corrupted as to command the killing and imprisoning men for doing that which is just and commendable.

He carries these pessimistic reflections, however, to a startlingly optimistic conclusion:

> By experience you now find you may be made slaves as effectually by a Parliament as by any other kind of government. Why then persist you to divide and fall into factions, to kill and slay men for you know not what, to advance the honour and interest of you know not whom. . . . Therefore, if ye are either men or Christians, hold your hands till you know what you fight for, and be sure that you have the truth of freedom in it, or never meddle but desist and let who will both fight and pay.
>
> Certainly there is none so vile, considering what hath been said, that will again incur the guilt of murderers, and fight before the cause be plainly stated and published, and if that were done as it ought to be, possibly it may be attained without fighting and might have been all this while, the difference not being so great as was imagined.

Inspired by his faith in reason he goes on to outline briefly the chief points of the Leveller programme, including complete toleration. 'For the obtaining of these things a man may justly adventure his life, all these being for a common good.' He concludes with an eloquent appeal to

> all you soldiers and people that have your consciences alive about you . . . to prevent a further effusion of blood. . . . The King, Parliament, great men in the City and the Army have made you but the stairs by which they have mounted to honour, wealth and power. The only quarrel that hath been and at present is but this, namely whose slaves the people shall be.

Against these Grandees, then, plain men, be they soldiers or civilians, must stand up as one man, confident that 'they have no strength without you'.

As a revolutionary appeal *The Bloody Project* has its weaknesses. It is vague about the future of monarchy, and silent about 'the man of blood'. It does not mention manhood franchise or base tenures. Its belief that justice and 'the good of the whole nation' can be attained without parties and against them all is not a little naïve. Acting against the wealthy and the great, on behalf of all 'that depend on farms, trades and small pay', are not the Levellers also a party? But in spite of these defects this tract, advancing along a clear cut line of argument by a natural *crescendo* to its deeply felt conclusion, ranks, as a piece of writing, among the more notable political essays of its day.

NOTES TO CHAPTER XVII

1. *A Faithful Memorial, Somers Tracts*, VI, pp. 500-1.

2. Ludlow, *Memoirs*, I, p. 207. He quotes Numbers, xxxv, 33.

3. Gardiner, *Civil War*, IV, p. 207. Abbott (III, p. 821) reckons that by the middle of 1655 some 8,000 prisoners of war had been sent to Barbados, 4,000 to other plantations, 800 to French Guadeloupe and others elsewhere. See also *Mercurius Pragmaticus*, 3 October, 1648, which states that the Colchester prisoners are marching to Bristol, to be transported God knows whither; they are harshly driven and shot if they faint. A moving set of verses from Colchester prisoners at Woodstock prays for release, but speaks gratefully of the conduct of their warder, Captain Grimes, 'the stout and just' (*The Piteous Moans . . . of the Prisoners lately taken at Colchester*, 6 November, 1648). If it is true, as Clement Walker stated, that the Army got only 12*d*. per head for its Welsh prisoners, we can guess part of the explanation of this barbarity (*Relations and Observations*, p. 97). Kept so short of cash that its own pay was months in arrear, it could not afford to pay for the keep of thousands of prisoners. This also in part explains, though nothing can excuse, the ghastly mortality among the Scottish prisoners after the battle of Dunbar.

4. *A Moderate and Clear Relation*. Thomason's date is 15 December, 1648, but obviously it was written rather earlier.

5. *The Moderate Intelligencer* (14 December, 1648).

6. Walker, *The History of Independency*, Part II, p. 31.

7. *Mercurius Elencticus* (7 February, 1649).

8. This pamphlet, *Salus populi solus rex* (17 October, 1648), ranks among the conspicuous milestones in the history of the Revolution. It is an anonymous and I think semi-official answer to the royalist Judge Jenkins. The author, who writes well, is obviously an Independent of the Cromwellian faction. Rather bolder than Walter Frost in his thinking, he may have been a divine, conceivably Hugh Peters. He frankly admits that 'everywhere the greater party are for the King', in cities as in villages. He then throws over

democracy. 'It is not *VOX* but *salus populi* that is the supreme law. . . . If the common vote of the giddy multitude must rule the whole, how quickly would their own interest, peace and safety be dashed and broken? . . . Did Herod and Pilate do well to deliver up our Saviour to be crucified because the major voice of the people cried out "Away with Him . . . Crucify Him"?' He declares that 'the scum of the people' was always against the Parliament. Finally he relies on the argument from startling military successes, 'continued seven or eight years together' (which applies to Cromwell but not to the Presbyterian generals). 'In such cases successes are to be looked upon as clear evidence of the truth, righteousness and equity of our cause.' In them 'the glorious majesty . . . of God' doth most visibly appear. The argument points the way to a theocratic totalitarian system based on a military dictatorship.

9. Gardiner believed that this declaration was passed by the Commons without a division (*Civil War*, IV, pp. 168, 271). No division is recorded in the *Journals* of the House (V, p. 640). Godwin, however, who made a close study of the Journals in manuscript, implies that divisions were not always recorded. The chief evidence for the vote is the statement addressed to the Commons by Fairfax and the Council of Officers, justifying Pride's Purge (*The Articles and Charge of the Army*, 8 December, 1648), in which they stated that members 'to the number of ninety and odd, as upon the division of the House appeared', opposed this vote. Rushworth in the first edition of his *Collections* (VII, p. 1354) gives the same figure. In the second edition (1701), the passage has been garbled (VII, pp. 1198-9). Not only is any mention of a division omitted, but also the rejection of the Commons' Declaration by the Lords. It looks as if the Whigs wished to whitewash their fathers, the Presbyterians of 1648.

10. *The Petition of the Lord Mayor and Common Council* (22 July, 1648).

11. *The Petition of the Lord Mayor and Common Council* (8 August, 1648).

12. *Mercurius Pragmaticus* (22 August, 1648). See also p. 46 above.

13. *Terrible and Bloody News*, a news-book dealing mainly with the atrocities of the Scots. The item about Marten's movements is signed W. Turvil and dated Leicester, 7 September, 1648. Turvil also reports 'armed clashes' between Major Fiecher and Marten's men, who were at first defeated but afterwards rallied. See also *Bloody News from the Lord Byron in Wales* (12 September, 1648).

14. Published on 21 August, 1648, and reprinted in H. and D., pp. 135-46.

CHAPTER XVIII

From Preston Fight to Pride's Purge

On 1 August, 1648, the Leveller party laid before the Commons one of its many petitions for the release of John Lilburne from the Tower, which over 10,000 sympathisers had signed. On that same day, after a surprising speech from Sir John Maynard, the House voted not merely for his release but for the prompt payment of the £3,000 compensation due to him for his sufferings under the Star Chamber, Sir John—not to be confused with the Presbyterian lawyer and member of the same name knighted after the Restoration—was a Devon squire, a militant Presbyterian and one of the eleven whom the Army had impeached. After a warm eulogy of Lilburne's military career, he described the resistance of 'this brave, invincible spirit' to the jurisdiction of the Lords, and endorsed everything this arch-rebel had done, with the single exception of his refusal to uncover before them.[1] Next day the Lords cancelled their sentence and John was free.

This move was not as irrational as it looks. The Presbyterians expected that he would take his revenge against Cromwell, by supporting Major Robert Huntingdon's impeachment of his former commander for treason, which the Lords were favouring until the news from Preston imposed some degree of caution upon them. 'With Honest John got loose'—so ran the comment of *Mercurius Pragmaticus*—''twill not be long ere Mr Speaker and Nol Cromwell be both brought to the stake.' But John, with all his frailties, was an honester and a bigger personality than his meaner contemporaries could understand. 'Not loving a Scottish interest', as he put it, he would have nothing to do

with an impeachment of the general whose army was all that
stood between England and the intolerance of the kirk.

On his first day of freedom (3 August) Lilburne sent to
Cromwell, as he hurried northwards by forced marches, a
letter inspired as much by his idealism as by his vanity.

> If I . . . desired revenge for an hard and almost starving
> imprisonment, I could have had of late the choice of twenty
> opportunities to have paid you to the purpose; but I scorn
> it, especially when you are low. . . . If ever my hand be
> upon you, it shall be when you are in your full glory, if then
> you shall decline from the righteous ways of truth and justice
> —which if you will fixedly and impartially prosecute, I am
> > Yours to the last drop of my heart blood
> > (for all your late severe hand towards me)

This letter meant something more than the opening of a new
phase in the always emotional relationship between Lilburne
and Cromwell. With it went another letter from someone
whom John describes as 'my comrade'—probably Colonel
Ludlow. To carry their letters they chose Edward Sexby (now
a civilian though Carlyle calls him 'Captain'), a young man
quite capable of acting as a go-between. He reported on his
return that John's letter was 'not a little welcome'.[2] This was
evidently true, for Sexby was well received at the front, took
part in the battle round Preston and was chosen by Cromwell
(together with Major Berry) to carry his famous despatch to
Westminster, an honour which insured a gratuity to him of
£100 from the Commons.

Sexby's mission seems to have laid the foundations of a
working alliance between the Cromwellian Independents and
the Levellers. One need not suppose that in his outlook the
Lieut.-General was much nearer to the Levellers at this time
than he was in after-life, but with the crisis of the Revolution
approaching he stood desperately in need of allies. The
number of the Levellers was growing rapidly at this time in
London and the home counties, and theirs was, pretty certainly, the best organisation which any of the political groups
possessed. In the Army also their influence was still considerable. With their backing, Cromwell might hope to lead a
compact revolutionary minority. Without it, even his Army

would be infected by dissension and mistrust. Amid the fatigues and excitements of a three days' battle Cromwell could not discuss political programmes; that in any event was a task he always left to Ireton. But the despatch which Sexby carried revealed his state of mind. As usual after a victory he did what he had done at Naseby and Bristol: he drew a moral in the interest of the Saints:

> Surely, Sir, this is nothing but the hand of God . . . [Let me] pray you and all that acknowledge God, that they exalt Him and not hate His people who are as the apple of His eye, . . . that all that live quietly and peaceably may have countenance from you, and that they that are implacable and will not leave troubling the land may speedily be destroyed out of the land.[3]

This is pulpit eloquence, which is not offensively precise. Translate it, however, into the prose of daily life and it seems to run somewhat thus: 'The victors of Preston will not passively endure the persecution prepared for them in your Blasphemy Ordinance. They expect you, moreover, to get ready for the execution of Charles Stuart.' It could, of course, mean a good deal less. Now these two exhortations, thus translated, convey the substance of the two chief demands on which (as we shall see) the Levellers were insisting—toleration for all forms of religious belief, and impartial justice for all the authors of the Civil Wars. It is a plausible guess that Sexby was entrusted with a message to Lilburne and Ludlow that Cromwell did mean this and not a syllable less. The message, however, was verbal and did not commit the Lieut.-General.

Encouraged by Sexby's report, the Levellers now set to work to draw up a programme to which they reckoned that the main body of the Independents might be induced to rally. Lilburne had a hand in drafting it; Walwyn had less to do with it than usual, though there are echoes of his writings here and there. Probably the London Agents elected a committee to draw it up. Whether any of the leading Independents were consulted before it was published we do not know. It is a likely guess that Lilburne talked it over with his 'comrade' Ludlow, who then went down to Colchester, on behalf of both their groups, for discussions with Ireton.

The document, always described as 'the Large Petition of 11 September', is the least interesting and the most important of the Levellers' manifestoes. It registers no advance in the thinking of these pioneers and silently omits from its programme several of their bolder proposals. Judged by its contents it is a relatively moderate pronouncement, from which anything calculated to offend Cromwell or Ireton was excluded. In fact it made history, for it cut a channel for the main current of revolutionary opinion in the country, and swept the Army into action. Though its language is not violent, it is the most unsparing of all the Leveller attacks on the Long Parliament. The preamble reminded the Commons, once again, of their supremacy in the constitution—'there cannot be two or three supremes'—and then assailed them for having

> declared to all the world that you will not alter the ancient government, from that of King, Lords and Commons: not once mentioning in case of difference which of them is supreme, but leaving that point (which was the chiefest cause of all our public differences, disturbances, wars and miseries) as uncertain as ever.

To negotiate a settlement by personal treaty with the King is to 'put him that is but one single person and a public officer of the commonwealth in competition with the whole body of the people whom ye represent'. This King, moreover, is notorious for his 'underhand dealing', and can always plead that any concessions to which he may consent were made under duress.

After this blunt condemnation of the treaty on which Parliament and City were bent, the Petition went on to lay down the alternative programme of the left in the most imperious tone of voice. 'We have long expected things of another nature from you' is the phrase with which it introduces its twenty-seven demands.[4] Of these the more familiar can be summarised in a few words, while those round which the political struggle raged must be cited in full.

THE COMMONS SUPREME

Clauses 1, 2 and 3 assert the supremacy of the Commons, reject the negative voices of King and Lords, call for annual

Parliaments and the fixing of a date for a dissolution of this Parliament. It is assumed that the monarchy may continue, since Parliament is rebuked for failing to declare 'what the duty or business of the kingly office is and what not' (19) and equally 'what the business of the Lords is' (24).

JUSTICE

Clause 25 calls for 'Justice upon the capital authors and promoters of the former or late wars, many of them being under your power'.

Parliament (§27) should have laid to heart 'all the abundance of innocent blood that hath been spilt and the infinite spoil and havoc that hath been made of peaceable, harmless people, by express commissions from the King, and seriously . . . considered whether the justice of God be likely to be satisfied or his continuing wrath appeased by an act of oblivion'.

Finally, Parliament should have 'made (§6) both kings, queens, princes, dukes, earls, lords and all persons alike liable to every law of the land made or to be made; that so all persons, even the highest, might fear and stand in awe and neither violate the public peace nor private right of person or estate (as hath been frequent) without being liable . . . to account as other men'.

RELIGION

We expected (§4) 'that you would have exempted matters of religion and God's worship from the compulsive or restrictive power of any authority upon earth and reserved to the supreme authority an uncompulsive power only of appointing a way for the public worship, whereby abundance of misery, persecution and heart-burning would for ever be avoided'.

Clause 23 condemns the Long Parliament for following 'the example of former tyrannous and superstitious Parliaments in making orders, ordinances or laws', and 'in appointing punishments concerning opinions or things supernatural, styling some blasphemies, others heresies; when as you know yourselves easily mistaken and that divine truths need no human helps to support them: such proceedings having been generally invented to divide the people among themselves, and to affright men from that liberty of discourse by which corruption and tyranny would be soon discovered'.

The burden of tithes (16) must be removed, impropriators satisfied, and a more equal way provided for maintaining the public ministers.

NO CONSCRIPTION

We expected (5) 'that you would have disclaimed in yourselves and all future representatives a power of pressing and forcing any sort of men to serve in wars, there being nothing more opposite to freedom. . . .'

LAW REFORM

Commoners to be freed (7) from jurisdiction of Lords and all trials to be by jury. None to be examined against themselves (8) or punished for doing what no law forbids: Procedure (9) to be briefer and cheaper. Imprisonment for debt (13) to be ended. Punishments (15) to be proportioned to offences.

OTHER DEMANDS

Provide constant pay (26) and an indemnity for the Army, which deserves rather an act of perpetual remembrance than an act of oblivion. Abolish monopolist (10) companies and reform the election of officers (20) in the City and its companies. Substitute direct taxation (11) for excise. Repay (17) the state's poorer creditors first. Reparations (21) for victims of the prerogative courts. Wind up (22) County Committees. Provide means (14) to keep people from begging and beggary. Throw open recent enclosures (12) of fens and commons.

NO COMMUNISM

For the first time a new fundamental reservation is introduced (18). You should have 'bound yourselves and all future Parliaments from abolishing propriety, levelling men's estates and making all things common'. Henceforward this disclaimer of communist doctrine had to be repeated in most of the Leveller pronouncements.

Two of the many omissions from this manifesto arrest our attention at once. Though the substance of the Agreement of the People is included, its distinctive characteristic—the origin of a permanent constitution in the will of the people, registered by their individual signature of its provisions—is silently ignored, presumably to placate Cromwell. Twice, none the less, this Parliament is invited to give a pledge that will bind future Parliaments—it is not explained how. Again, there is silence over parliamentary reform, both as to the widening of the suffrage which he and Ireton opposed and the disfranchisement of 'decayed boroughs' which they approved. Nothing is said about base tenures, the decentralisation of government, the election of magistrates, the codification and simplification of the laws in English, nor about prison reform.

All this was, at the moment, of secondary importance. What mattered to 'the plain man' (a common Leveller phrase) was first 'justice' (by which he meant primarily the punishment of the King), and in the second place security for his own sectarian religion. Two voices are audible in this manifesto. The first is a statement of the civilised Leveller principle that there must be one law for high and low, for kings, lords and commoners. The other is the barbaric argument from 'God's continuing wrath'—a crudity at which Walwyn, Marten and Overton may have winced. As far as words go, deposition might have been 'justice' enough, but with blood still flowing in the North, men thought and read through a crimson haze. It is significant that the leading royalist journalist, *Mercurius Pragmaticus*, when he gave the sense of this Petition in his news (12-19 September, 1648), summed it up as a demand that 'the King may be called to account in a criminal way'.

By way of contrast, what the Leveller party wrote about toleration in this otherwise moderate Petition stands out as an historical event. It nailed its colours to the mast and there, as we shall see, they still flew during the difficult negotiations with Ireton in the months to come. The scope of toleration is defined in the fewest and plainest of words: neither by restriction nor compulsion may the state meddle with religion. What is of equal importance, this doctrine is justified on rational and secular grounds. Without religious toleration we cannot hope to enjoy that 'liberty of discourse' through which alone corruption and tyranny may be promptly discovered.

No sooner was the Petition in print than the younger generation in the Army broke out into turbulent approval, without waiting for a nod from the Grandees. On 13 September a crowd of junior officers (in London, presumably, on leave) thronged the doors of the House and insisted on presenting a second petition which demanded an answer to the first. If we may trust the ears of *Mercurius Pragmaticus* (12-19 September), they were heard to say, as they talked to friendly M.P.s, that 'they knew no use of a king or lords any longer'. 'Such distinctions,' they argued, 'are devices of men, God having made all alike.' They boasted 'that 40,000 had subscribed the petition, but they conceived five thousand horse would do more good in it.' On the other hand, the Independent divines in the City were hostile. Parliament paid the Levellers the compliment of publishing what we should call a 'white paper', setting out the reasons of its Presbyterian majority for rejecting the principles on which the Petition was based. This document deserves more attention than it has received. The reaction had gone so far that rather than admit the sovereignty of the people, these Presbyterians in their panic were ready to swallow the divine right of Kings.

> We are called by the King's writ . . . not to redress grievances but to present them. It is true that our consent to such things as the King shall please to enact is necessary. . . . All the laws of our kingdom tell us the King is accountable to none but God only. . . . You are exceedingly deceived in that you say that all authority is derived from the people, for God gives the King his authority. . . . To deny the negative of the King and Lords were robbery, . . . rebellion and disobedience . . . and a breach of our trust to the people from whom we have no such power, but only to consent to such things as shall be ordained by common council, that is by the King with the advice of the Lords. . . . There must be an end of war and God's and the King's mercy implored.[5]

To record what passed in the protracted negotiations at Newport would carry us beyond the limits of this essay. Posterity knows from the King's own letters what ample experience of his dealings had already taught the Levellers, his ingrained duplicity. He did not feel bound by such concessions as he made; indeed, he made them only to facilitate his chances of escape. Between this King bent on kindling yet another war—this time in Ireland—and his people weary of strife lay, as their only constitutional guardian, a Parliament which held him 'accountable to none but God only'. If this barely credible reply to their petition had any effect on the Levellers, it was to confirm them in their opposition to the Long Parliament and their determination to bring its sittings to an end.

Backed now by their own organ in the press, *The Moderate*, which went out by the mail every Tuesday to the provinces, the Levellers had the means of scattering their propaganda more promptly than of old and much further afield. It printed the September petition in full. Week by week it drove home the moral of that manifesto in leading articles that were always resolute and sometimes entertaining. It was by far the most readable of the licensed news-books—for the royalist sheets printed underground, reckless, scurrilous and bawdy, were in another class altogether. Week by week *The Moderate* recorded the response of progressive England; for that 'Large Petition' spawned its flock of little petitions, which came hurrying back to London by every mail-coach, from Berwick on the northern frontier to Cornwall in the far West. The voices were those of civilians and soldiers alike.

Usually the chorus was content to echo and endorse the demands of the original petition, but sometimes, like the tin-miners of Cornwall and the small farmers of the northern counties, it added a proposal of its own for the redress of a local grievance. One of the petitions from the North suggested that a comparative study should be undertaken of the constitutions of the contemporary republics, the United Provinces, Switzerland and Venice. The civilians were sometimes an imposing group who had the right to speak for a considerable community. One of the earliest of the petitions of support came from the grand jury of Somerset, for this county, which lived by weaving cloth, was always on the far left, from the first days of the Civil War down to Monmouth's rebellion. Another was signed by 84 of the leading citizens of Newcastle-on-Tyne, among them the Mayor, Aldermen, Sheriffs and members of the Common Council. Others came from Bristol, Hull, and the city and county of York, the counties of Oxford, Leicester, Berkshire and Wiltshire. Even in the Common Council of the City of London there was a party which avowed its support of the Petition. The Levellers and their allies in the counties went on organising these declarations, some of which bore the signatures of 'many thousands', up to the moment when the Army struck. The ablest document among them is the petition of the Northumberland horse dated the day before Pride's Purge.

The civilians spoke for a revolutionary minority, but the Army, if we leave the Grandees out of account, must have been solidly behind the September Petition. All the supporting petitions which came from the scattered regiments in rapid succession summarised the chief demands of the September Petition, many of them endorsed it by name; the earliest of them, which came from the Army before Berwick on 9 October, was accompanied by a congratulatory letter of thanks to its promoters. These documents, according to the new rules of discipline, were signed by the officers only on behalf of themselves and their men. Occasionally, however, one catches a glimpse of the Agitators still at work behind the scenes. Officers from each troop signed the early and emphatic petition from Ireton's horse, but murmurs of revolt are audible from the men, when we learn that they refused, in the spirit of the New-market rendezvous, to allow their regiment to be dispersed over three counties. Evidently they foresaw the possibility of action. So too from Ingoldsby's foot, always a radical regiment, came, with an endorsement of the Petition, a request that Fairfax should call a meeting of the Council of the Army.

Without exception these petitions stressed the case for 'impartial justice'. One asked for the punishment of the traitors in Parliament and the City who had invited Hamilton's invasion, while another added the warning that the punishment of other delinquents would not be 'an acceptable sacrifice to the justice of God . . . while Agag is spared'. As they marched southward, after an expedition which had led them in a cold and rainy season from Windsor to Pembroke and thence by way of Preston to Berwick, four regiments under Cromwell's command—his own horse and Harrison's, with Pride's and Deane's foot—stressed the case for retribution, 'without which, as the wrath of God will not be appeased, so neither can we expect a happy issue of all our labours'. These sentiments the Lieut.-General emphatically endorsed. From the headquarters of the Southern Army at St Albans came petitions addressed to Fairfax from Fleetwood's, Whalley's, Rich's and Barkstead's

regiments which backed all the chief items of the September
Petition, above all 'equal justice against all the fomentors,
contrivers, and actors in both wars', and then went on to stress
the claims of the New Model for constant pay and security for
arrears. It is significant that in forwarding these petitions to
the Speaker, Fairfax endorsed only their financial demands
and passed over the rest in silence.

Prompted by the Levellers, the Army had spoken. Its
commanders responded each in his own characteristic way.
Fairfax, released from the dominating influence of his great
lieutenant, had been for several months his own master. At
Colchester and St Albans (to which he moved his headquarters
on 21 September) he was within easy reach of Westminster and
may have been affected by its growing tendency to appeasement, not to say surrender, a mood which the 'silken Independents' (notably Vane, Pierrepont and Fiennes) shared in
varying degrees with the Presbyterians. After the fall of
Colchester several municipalities in Essex feasted the victor;
at these entertainments a Presbyterian atmosphere would caress
him pleasantly. To restore the King by giving an uncritical
soldier's assent to anything the politicians might arrange at
Newport may well have seemed to him the easiest and most
popular way of securing the peace his arms had won. For a few
days before and after its surrender Colchester was the hub of the
political world, for Ireton and Rainsborough were there as
well as Fairfax. Ludlow's visit we have mentioned already—
important because he came from the Levellers as well as the
republican group in the House.

Another visitor was Lieut.-Colonel John Jubbes, who came
to preach 'mercy and moderation'. He brought with him his
own version of the Agreement of the People which he had
produced together with some members of the Common
Council of the City. He had devised a naïve but well-meant
plan to save the King's life, while securing the sovereignty
of the people. Charles was to be declared guilty of causing the
two civil wars, but if he would accept the Agreement, which
deprived him of his negative voice and the right to make
any appointments without the Commons' consent, he should

be proclaimed and crowned once more. During the interval between the dissolution of the Long Parliament and the meeting of the next, a Committee of State, composed of forty-five of the leading politicians, soldiers and lawyers ranging from Lilburne, Marten and Wildman on the far left to Waller, Massey and Sir John Maynard on the extreme Right, should act as the executive. Jubbes makes the surprising statement that Rainsborough and afterwards Harrison, with many other colonels, were prepared to accept this scheme, but with Ireton 'it stuck and went no further'. Later he found Cromwell equally hostile. At St Albans Fairfax promised to give it his consideration, which may have been his courteous way of expressing his inability to make up his mind. After the Army had occupied London Ireton swept it aside as 'too late'.

The evidence does not justify us in guessing why Ireton was so resolutely bent on the King's execution, and never wavered, as Cromwell did. All we can say with certainty is that when Ludlow met him at the end of August or early September at Colchester, he had made up his mind that the Army must intervene to prevent a settlement on the basis of the Newport negotiations, though he then thought that action should be delayed until the text of the treaty was known. By 27 September, however, it seemed to him that the time for intervention had come, and he wrote a long letter to Fairfax proposing that the Army should purge the Commons. Failing to convince Fairfax, he then offered to resign his commission. Though his offer was rejected, he withdrew to Windsor. There he set to work to compose the Army's *Remonstrance*, one of the ablest and most instructive documents of the Revolution. An elaborate legal and historical argument led up to the conclusion that the King must be tried, as the chief author of two ruinous civil wars.

Meanwhile, Fairfax had summoned what he called the Council of the Army, and it met in the choir of the abbey church of St Albans on 7 November. It had no right to this name for it was composed solely of officers. Fairfax and the Grandees could of course argue that the practice of admitting the men's elected representatives to the discussion of political policy complicated their task of maintaining the Army's unity. But the men could point to the engagements which their commanders took at Newmarket and Triploe Heath and observed throughout the critical year 1647. Could such undertakings be set aside without dishonour, by one party alone? A few months later this question was to vex the New Model in a much acuter form. Doubtless Fairfax knew that if he had allowed the soldiers to send their Agitators to St Albans, they would have voted as one man for the trial of the King on a capital charge. A council of officers was easier to manage. Many, perhaps most of them, now looked on military service as their profession; bent on promotion, they spoke and voted with their eyes on their superiors. The kindly Jubbes said quietly what Lilburne said in anger, that the officers were becoming 'servile', and he proposed without success that voting at the Councils should be by secret ballot—by 'balls and a ballading box' as he put it.

The first draft of Ireton's *Remonstrance* was laid before the Council on 10 November. Its only decided supporter was Colonel Harrison. It is on record that many of the colonels expressed a 'wish that the hearts of King and kingdom might be knit together in a threefold cord of love'. Of decisive importance was Fairfax's declaration. He would stand for nothing 'tending to overthrow the government of the kingdom'; he would 'commit his stock or share of interest in this kingdom into the common bottom of Parliament'; finally, he undertook that when the King signed the treaty, he would then defend King and Parliament in that agreement.[6] For the moment this checked the possibility of action by the revolutionary left. Fairfax's personal opinion might not carry much weight (though as a man and a soldier he was liked and admired) but whatever troopers and subalterns might think, they could not set the Army in motion against the will of the General and most of the Grandees.

Meanwhile in the North, a pair of royalist gentlemen committed an outrage which raised the mental temperature of troops and Levellers to fever heat. Rainsborough, the Army's specialist in siege operations, after his success at Colchester, was sent up to Yorkshire to reduce the nearly impregnable fortress of Pontefract. Early on Sunday morning, 29 October, two disguised Royalists, who pretended that they carried a message from Cromwell to Rainsborough, were admitted to his room at his quarters in Doncaster. Finding him unarmed, they compelled him to go with them. In the street, calling in vain for help, Rainsborough with his usual audacity attacked his captors with his naked hands and went on fighting till he had been run through several times. The pair, it seems, had no wish to kill him; their purpose was to capture him alive, so that he could be exchanged for the gallant royalist prisoner, Sir Marmaduke Langdale.[7] There is no doubt that this exploit was forbidden by the laws of war as the seventeenth century understood them: so much was conceded even in the royalist press. The anger roused by this murder was at once reflected in the call for punishment, which several regiments included in their petitions.

In the long run Rainsborough's death inflicted a heavy loss on the Leveller movement. As famous for his ingenuity as a tactician as for his fabulous courage, he had the warmth of feeling and the ability to express it which are among the indispensable gifts of a popular leader. What he said at Putney echoes in English ears to this day. He ranks among the few talented soldiers of these wars, who cared passionately for a principle and nothing at all for their careers. In the short run, however, his shocking and premature end—he was still in his thirties—served the cause for which he lived and died. The Leveller party decided to honour him with a public funeral and its two organs in the press, *The Moderate* and the short-lived *Mercurius Militaris*, invited all sympathisers to meet his body at Tottenham High Cross and follow it over the five miles to the Independent chapel among the ships at Wapping.

Several records survive which agree in estimating the number of carriages filled with women at 50 or 60; the number of men who followed on horseback is put by one at 500, by another at 1,500 and by a third at 3,000. The royalist *Mercuries* insist with their customary snobbery that all the carriages and horses were hired for the occasion, which may have been near the truth. Besides these, 'Will the weaver, Tom the tapster, Kit the cobbler, Dick the door-sweeper and many more eminent apron-youths of the City' followed the mounted mourners afoot. Everyone wore ribbons of sea-green, Rainsborough's colour, which from this day onwards became the recognised Leveller badge.[8] For the first time, in an hour of crisis and deep emotion, the party made its appearance in the streets of London. Here, visible in their ordered ranks were the 'many thousands' of 'plain men' who signed its petitions.

Next day (15 November), when at Cromwell's suggestion a group of influential Independents met Lilburne and his comrades at the Nag's Head to negotiate a common line of action, the Levellers must have come to the meeting with the prestige of this remarkable demonstration behind them. When on the following day (16 November) they met Ireton at Windsor to revise his *Remonstrance*, so that it should express their views as well as his, it may have occurred to that baffled Grandee that if Fairfax cut him off from the rank-and-file of the Army, he could still find mass support among the sea-green Levellers, who had marched behind Rainsborough's remains from Tottenham Cross to Wapping. Before we record these two important meetings, however, we must try to trace what was passing in Cromwell's mind.

After writing his memorable despatch on the rout of Hamilton's forces at Preston, Cromwell had to march through the devastated county of Durham in pursuit of Monro. With great sagacity he brought about a temporary reconciliation with the Scots and even converted Argyll and the Whiggamores into allies, who entertained him hospitably during his brief stay in Edinburgh. It is said that as he was entering Scotland, that is to say at the end of September, he received a second visit from Sexby, who would bring him news of what Levellers and republicans were doing and thinking.[9] By this time the echoes of the September Petition were audible, and Ireton after his first clash with Fairfax had just tendered his resignation. What advice Sexby carried back we do not know; our royalist informant had heard that he was sent to assure the Leveller M.P.s that Cromwell would adhere to them.

Somewhat later, as Cromwell marched southwards at a very leisurely pace, he seems to have had a meeting with Marten at York and with Lilburne probably at Knottingley, close to Pontefract, where he fixed his headquarters during November, when the murder of Rainsborough (29 October) obliged him to assume responsibility for the siege. The impression he made on John was unfavourable: 'things about him . . . savoured more of intended self-exalting than . . . the advancement of the . . . liberties and freedoms of the nation'. On his return to London Lilburne and his comrades sent a message by a Mr Hunt and another person to Cromwell at Pomfret (as Pontefract was usually called). These two after debating it with him brought back his reply, addressed primarily to the leading Independents of the City, who were thus led to their meeting with the Levellers at the Nag's Head Tavern.[10]

The event that made the deepest impression on Cromwell during his stay in Scotland was the audacious action of Argyll, when with the support of the Kirk he first drove the Engagers (Hamilton's party) out of the Committee of Estates, though they were the majority, and then dissolved this quasi-Parliament. As he wrote in the first of two revealing letters to his intimate young friend and cousin Colonel Robert Hammond, 'A lesser party of a Parliament hath made it lawful to declare the greater part a faction.' It then declared the Parliament null and called a new one; and this it did by force. 'Think of the example', he went on, '. . . and let others think of it too.' Obviously he was already thinking either of a purge of the Commons, or of an enforced dissolution, or of both.[11]

Hammond, as we gather from this and the second letter, shared the opinions of Vane, Pierrepont and other aristocratic Independents who wished the Newport negotiations to succeed. Because they feared that the Levellers 'would destroy nobility', they were prepared for an understanding with the King, on the footing of moderate episcopacy combined with toleration. Cromwell rebukes their timidity:

> How easy is it to find arguments for what we would have; how easy to take offence at things called Levellers, and run into an extremity on the other hand, meddling with an accursed thing.

The second letter, after mentioning 'Robin's' fear of the Levellers, dismisses them with the curt phrase 'of whom there is no fear', and asks him how he can expect 'good by this man [the King] against whom the Lord hath witnessed'. As Hammond saw the future, only a choice of evils confronted the Army, a restoration with a Presbyterian establishment or else a compromise with episcopacy.

> Both [Cromwell commented] are a hard choice. I trust there's no necessity of either, except our base unbelief and fleshly wisdom make it so.[12]

In this state of mind, then, Cromwell was promoting an alliance with the Levellers. They did not rank with the King as 'an accursed thing' 'against whom the Lord hath witnessed'. Rather Cromwell dismissed them with contempt as 'things called Levellers', 'of whom there is no fear'. For the moment he required their alliance, but whatever he might have to concede to secure it, one need entertain no fears for 'nobility'. He had not thought it out in detail; if undesirable allies cannot be cozened, or bribed, they may have to be suppressed. When the time came, he would know how to defend the interests of his class, or as he might have put it, God would show him the way.

The second letter is the indispensable preface to the whole story of the reign of the Saints. Cromwell played no part in the events that led up to Pride's Purge. He lingered at Pomfret on his march southward, as if he wanted time for reflection, and might not have arrived when he did had not Fairfax summoned him to Windsor. In this letter, though he is answering Robin's objections, he is obviously talking to himself and finally dismissing any scruples that might have deterred him from setting up a military dictatorship.

One gathers that in the letter to which Cromwell is replying, Robin Hammond had expressed his concern because 'some good men whom he loves' hold 'that it is lawful for a lesser part, if in the right, to force' a numerical majority—as in the Scottish precedent. He went on to argue that 'God hath appointed authorities among the nations to which active or passive obedience is to be yielded— . . . in England . . . the Parliament'. Cromwell's answer was, in effect, that the duty of passive obedience is not absolute. 'All agree there are cases in which it is lawful to resist.' Is ours such a case?

He replies on his conscience before the Lord that it is. If

Parliament is allowed to conclude this treaty with the King, is not 'the whole fruit of the war like to be frustrated, and all most like to turn to what it was and worse?' So much, and in similar words, any of the troopers who applauded the September Petition might have written. In his next sentence the authentic Cromwell speaks. He asks 'Whether this Army be not a lawful power, called by God to oppose and fight against the King upon some stated grounds?' To gain those ends may it not oppose one authority as well as another—the Parliament, he means, as well as the King?

Is this, he asks, 'fleshly reasoning'? Then comes the confident reply, the appeal to God's hand visible in contemporary history.

> My dear friend, let us look into providences; surely they mean somewhat. They hang so together, have been so constant, so clear and unclouded. Malice, swollen malice against God's people . . ., to root out their name—and yet they, . . . having arms and therein blessed with defence and more! I desire he that is for a principle of suffering [i.e. passive obedience] would not too much slight this. . . .
>
> What think you of Providence disposing the hearts of so many of God's people this way, especially in this poor Army, wherein the great God has vouchsafed to appear?

In plain prose, he goes on to tell Hammond that the officers of the Northern Army are unanimously for the *Remonstrance* just presented to Parliament.

Here, as so often, Cromwell's language is confused, but his reasoning is simple. Everything is based on the description of the Army as a power 'called by God' to achieve certain ends. He used to insist, when he was opposing the Agitators at Putney, that it was called by Parliament for ends laid down at Westminster. 'Without Parliament', he would say, 'we are nothing.' Now such prosaic legalism is thrust aside. 'A chain of providences', by which he means an unbroken record of victory, culminating at Preston, has convinced him that he and his fellow-officers hold their commissions directly from God. What is more, one may assume that when the officers of this Army are of one mind, their opinions will reveal the purposes of God. So much, as experience had shown, cannot be claimed for the privates.

This is, perhaps, Cromwell's most important confession of faith, so much more honest than the speeches in which the Lord Protector laboured to convince himself that he ruled by consent of the people of England. Here he argues for the right and duty of a revolutionary minority to impose its will on the majority, and to oppose the normally legitimate authority, the Parliament. This it may do when it has proof by 'providences and dispensations' that it is itself the lawful power called by God. In short, Oliver Cromwell was a theocrat, whose only political principle was the sovereignty of God, which meant in practice the trend of history. He had no real belief in the sovereignty of the people, though he felt obliged to nod assent when the Levellers proclaimed it.

One cannot begin to understand Cromwell's part in the Revolution until one grasps his vision of man's life in the universe. The intricate pattern of events was made by the continuous intervention of God, who was weaving on the loom of destiny not merely the grand design which we call history, but countless webs of detail which make the experience of each individual soul. In the main pattern He would bring about was (as for example the second Civil War) by causing King Charles to harden his heart, and then ensuring, against all the rules of probability, the victory of His Saints, who are the apple of His eye. But if one scrutinised a corner of the colossal tapestry, the Isle of Wight and Carisbrooke Castle for example, whither Robin Hammond had just gone in search of a quiet life clear of political problems, there also one could discern 'a chain of providences'. It was to the Isle of Wight and nowhere else that God sent 'that person' (the King). In all this there must be 'some glorious and high meaning'. One catches a glimpse of the King with Berkeley and Ashburnham moved like pawns round Hammond, who was one of the elect, for the trial and perfecting of his spiritual life. At the same time, moved by the same invisible hand of God, each of them is playing his part in the drama that ended on a scaffold in Whitehall.

The mind reels as it tries to grasp the complexity of this Calvinistic pattern of providences. It stems from an earlier century than that of Bacon, Galileo and Newton. There is this to be said for it, that it taught men to look at life, however fitfully, *sub specie aeternitatis*. They might retain, as Cromwell did, all the native egoisms of family and class, and yet it seemed to shed on all they did (to use his phrase) 'some glorious and high meaning'. It could endow a man of action with a confidence and audacity which only two other faiths held by civilised men have ever prompted, Islam in its early days and Marxism. But with confidence, as its inseparable twin, went a ruthlessness that stains its records with indelible shame.

Before we return with Cromwell to the theatre of action in London, we have still to notice two letters written at his headquarters near Pomfret on 20 November. One of them, which forwards petitions from his officers to Fairfax, endorses their demands for punishment:

> I find a very great sense in the officers of the regiments of the sufferings and the ruin of this poor kingdom, and in them all a very great zeal to have impartial justice done upon offenders; and I must confess I do in all from my heart concur with them.

The other protests in the name of his officers against the too merciful treatment of a pair of Welsh rebels, one of them a turncoat.[13]

At last a summons from Fairfax brought Cromwell's stay in Yorkshire to an end. He reached London on the afternoon that followed Pride's Purge. Next day (7 December) he entered the House with Harry Marten, who moved the vote of thanks to him for his services in Wales and Lancashire.

The conference between Levellers and Independents at the Nag's Head on 15 November began with a violent explosion.[14] The Independents, who included both senior officers and several divines stated their policy bluntly—to cut off the King's head and to purge the Parliament thoroughly, if not to dissolve it. Familiar as they were with the September Petition, they must have been startled when John Lilburne opposed all this. If they got rid of King and Parliament, he argued, they would be at the mercy of 'the wills and swords' of the Army, which 'had cozened us the last year and fallen from all their promises and declarations'. It was, therefore, our interest 'to keep up one tyrant to balance another', until we saw how we were to escape a slavery which might be worse than anything in the King's time. So he pressed hard for an Agreement amongst the People as the indispensable first step before he would even consider anything else. After a 'desperately choleric' debate the Independents agreed that each side should choose four delegates to consider how an Agreement of the People should be reached.

The Independents chose Colonels Titchburn and White, the Rev. Dr Parker and the Rev. John Price, the Levellers Walwyn, Lieut.-Colonels Wetton, Wildman and Lilburne. A quarrel which followed because Price refused to serve with Walwyn was composed when both were laid aside for the sake of peace. The six were unanimous in recommending that a convention be chosen (though this name was not used) by the well-affected in every county, together with representatives of the Army. This convention, meeting at Headquarters, would exercise no legislative powers, but would draw up, as a formal contract which should be 'above law', a statement of 'the limits and extent' of the powers of the people's legislative deputies, which should be signed by the well-affected people and by their deputies on the days of their election. The matters to be settled in the Agreement should be those contained in the September Petition. Parliament should continue to sit until the date fixed for its dissolution in the Agreement. These terms should be embodied in the Army's *Remonstrance*. Not the least interesting part of this story is that when Independents and Levellers met, only the latter had anything constructive to propose, although the two divines were men of marked ability. As usual the intellectual initiative lay with the Levellers.

With the *Remonstrance* as it stood in draft the Levellers were far from being satisfied. It even contained some hostile passages with 'lashes' aimed at their group. Accordingly, delegations from the Independents and Levellers went to Windsor, to interview its author, Ireton. When he came to their inn at the Garter, attended by a whole train of officers, the Levellers had to realise after 'a large and sharp discourse' that two serious differences separated them from 'the Army's Alpha and Omega'. He went only half-way with them in the all-important issue of toleration; he was ready to deny any coercive powers to the state in matters of religion, but he would retain its restrictive powers. In effect he would tolerate neither Episcopalians nor Catholics, neither Unitarians nor Jews. Again, since he realised that Charles could not be charged with an offence against any known law of the land, he wished to arm Parliament with the right to punish 'according to their own judgment' where the public has been injured and yet no law infringed—surely, as the Levellers saw it, a most sinister and perilous proposal. This talk did nothing to reconcile these two uncongenial allies and Lilburne, who even dreamed in his first hot-headed disappointment of rousing his party to oppose the Army by force, was about to quit Windsor in a rage when Colonel Harrison, an idealist far nearer to him in temperament than the cold-blooded Ireton, persuaded him and his comrades to stay and talk things over again.

The Army's *Remonstrance*, an unwieldy memorandum addressed to the Commons, confesses Ireton's authorship on every one of its seventy long-winded pages.[15] There is not an original idea in it; none the less one feels in every paragraph the power of this disciplined intellect which had the Army, and therefore England, in its grip. His was a one-track mind. Just as he was dazzled during the greater part of 1647 by the theoretical advantages of a restoration brought about by the New Model, and could see nothing else until Charles rode off to Carisbrooke Castle, so now he could see nothing but the case for executing the author of all England's miseries. In his arguments against the Newport treaty he shows a surprising ability to forecast the future. If with the same gift of tactical imagination he had ever asked himself the question: What will be the effect on public opinion for years and generations to come of beheading the royal martyr, we might have escaped a tragic mistake—for Cromwell did fitfully guess in intuition what Ireton could not work out by reasoning.

Two long digressions in this memorable state paper reveal the man who wrote it. In one of them he ascribes the victories of the Parliament ('through the favour and presence of God') to 'the sobriety, seriousness and strictness in manners of the Saints', whereas the King's party countenanced or connived at 'profaneness, looseness of manners, vanity and luxury of life' and preferred 'such as had a mixture of ambition and vainglory with a servile spirit'. This reading of causation in history is appreciably more realistic than Cromwell's. The less admirable side of the man is evident in his embarrassed excuses for breaking the Solemn League and Covenant, whereas at Putney he took his stand on the sanctity of all contracts and engagements. Like Cromwell (in his second letter to Colonel Hammond) he bases himself, as every architect of revolution must, on the maxim *salus populi suprema lex*; but he does it with a dread of excess and a warning against the habitual resort to this principle which are peculiarly his own.

Up to a point the programme of the *Remonstrance* and the September Petition are the same. Ireton takes his stand on the sovereignty of the people and the supremacy of the elected House. It is not clear whether he contemplates the survival of a House of Lords; probably he does. After the trial of Charles, any future King must be elected, must accept the Agreement of the People, must explicitly renounce any negative voice and be content for some years with very modest revenues. Lilburne, in the antiquarian phase which characterised his early pamphlets, had argued that the monarchy was always elective. Now for a time this idea was revived. Ireton is now prepared to accept the idea of an Agreement of the People, which he appears to value chiefly or solely because it will provide for a regular succession of Parliaments, annual or biennial, and for a redistribution of seats, so as 'to render the House of Commons, as near as may be, an equal representative of the whole people electing'. For a 'competent number of years' all who fought against the Parliament or adhered to its enemies shall lose both active and passive franchise. The making of war and peace and the supreme power, legislative and administrative, in 'all civil things whatsoever'—a phrase which appears to exclude religion and God's worship—is vested in the Commons subject to two reservations only. (1) They must respect an indemnity granted to both sides for everything done in the Civil Wars, save as to penalties prescribed by this Parliament; (2) they may not 'render up or give or take away any the foundations of common right, liberty or safety contained in this settlement and agreement'. Provision is made for the recording

N

of dissents in the Commons, so that constituencies may know how their deputies vote. Some merchants should be included in the Council of State, to advise it on the advancement of trade—a most revealing provision. Finally, Parliament is to fix a date for its own dissolution, but before it breaks up it should 'consider' the grievances set out in various petitions, especially that of 11 September—a very casual way of dismissing such grave matters as tithes and imprisonment for debt.

Silent about the future of the Lords and any enlargement of the franchise, Ireton's *Remonstrance* omits the provisions made in the first Agreement against pressing and class privileges. It makes no provision for religious toleration, save in so far as something of this kind may be inferred from the granting of power to the Commons over 'civil matters'. No less serious was the fact that Ireton and Cromwell either failed to grasp, or else they grasped and rejected, the case for basing the new constitution on the direct initiative of the electorate—on a convention, that is to say, chosen *ad hoc* for the adoption of the text of the Agreement and for no other purpose. The Grandees were content to refer the final adoption of the Agreement to the Long Parliament. It was, of course, absurd to expect any Parliament to limit the powers of itself and its successors; nor, if it did, would its successors be bound by what it had done. While rejecting the idea of a convention, the Grandees did, however, propose that the Agreement, after Parliament had drawn it up, should be submitted to the electorate for signature.

Ireton's was a typically English empirical mind, to which the idea of a written constitution made no appeal, though in this emergency he could not wholly avoid it. What seemed to him important was to secure a more favourable balance of class power by disfranchising the 'decayed boroughs', and to provide for a regular succession of Parliaments chosen at intervals of one or two years. If he could obtain these reforms, he would take his chance of getting what else he wanted, content with the assurance that if he failed in one general election he might hope to succeed in the next.

Let us now return to the Garter Inn at Windsor, where Harrison, 'extreme fair and gilded' as Lilburne put it, is doing his utmost to placate the angry Levellers. He told them that Ireton and he, the strangely assorted pair who led the party of action in the Army, were resolved to destroy the King, even if they had to do it by martial law. They proposed to dissolve the Parliament before it could complete the treaty with the King. The Army would, however, invite 'the honest party' in the Commons, perhaps forty or fifty men, to take refuge with it, as in July 1647, and act as its advisers until new elections could be held. Harrison conceded that there was a strong case for electing a convention to draw up the Agreement of the People, but dare they face the delay of several months which this procedure would involve? He believed that the treaty would soon be concluded. The Presbyterians would then bring the King in triumph to London, order the Army to disband and proclaim them traitors if they refused. Could they hold out against both King and Parliament? But if they did disband, the Levellers would be destroyed with them. The conclusion was, therefore, that the Army must strike before the treaty was adopted and the King restored.

The 'imperial' Ireton had roused the fighting spirit in John Lilburne, but to the friendly Harrison he responded promptly —as it turned out, too promptly. He dropped as impracticable the proposal of a convention and substituted for it the idea of a committee representing the various sections of the 'well-affected', which could meet at once and produce the text of an Agreement acceptable to all, or to a majority. The Army, the Independents of the City, the 'honest party' in the Commons and the Levellers should each appoint four; John would have liked to add four Presbyterians, but the soldiers, it seems, were less broadminded. He laid stress on only one condition, that this conference should be the 'final and absolute judge of the matter'. John describes how readily his proposal was adopted, first by Harrison, then by the 'gentlemen Independents' and lastly by Cornelius Holland and other M.P.s who happened to be in Windsor. It remained to get Ireton's approval. He, however, was in bed with his wife in the Castle, but sent out word by Harrison that 'he did absolutely and heartily agree to the foresaid proposition'. Unfortunately, though John proclaimed on the housetops his suspicions of the Grandees' good faith, it never occurred to him to get Ireton's consent in writing to his 'proposition', which was in effect that the representatives of each group should be plenipotentiaries.

In London a very large meeting of the Agents of the Leveller party gave its approval and chose as its four delegates Walwyn, Lilburne, Wildman and Maximilian Petty. The Independent delegation was headed as before by Colonel Tichburn, the M.P.s by Harry Marten and the Army's by Ireton. At a first meeting in Windsor Castle only 'the foundations of our agreement' were discussed; of the M.P.s at this and subsequent meetings, only Marten attended. Locking themselves into their room at the Garter Inn, the four Levellers and Harry Marten sat round their table until they had completed a new draft of the Agreement of the People which they could submit to their colleagues. Later meetings were held in Whitehall. This device of a committee of sixteen (which dwindled to thirteen) would have served very well to draw up the text of an Agreement, which might be laid before a convention. But it was naïve to suppose, as John Lilburne did, that it could frame a constitution in its final shape, which the electorate would then be expected without further ado to ratify with every man's signature.

While at Windsor Ireton and Harrison were coming to terms with the Levellers and the Independents, Fairfax and his council of officers were still meeting at the Army's Headquarters in St. Albans. By way of giving concrete shape to Fairfax's declaration of loyalty, they decided on 16 November to send a new set of proposals to the King on behalf of the Army. They asked for assurances about a regular succession of Parliaments, the redistribution of seats and the dissolution of the Long Parliament. No mention was made of the King's negative voice, of a religious settlement or of toleration, but the King was asked to agree for all time that the militia should be controlled by a Council of State, and to surrender his former unqualified right to appoint the great officers of the crown. If he would accept these surprisingly moderate terms, the Army would restore the King, the Queen and their royal issue to 'a condition of safety, honour and freedom'. Here was Charles's last chance. He threw it away in an evasive answer which ignored the one issue on which the officers had laid stress—the control of the armed forces—and stipulated that he must come up to London before he could consider other concessions. This was too much even for Fairfax. With the King's reply before it, the council of officers, with a near approach to unanimity, adopted Ireton's *Remonstrance* which doomed the King to stand his trial. On 20 November, it was presented by Colonel Ewer and other officers to the Commons. They postponed consideration of it for a week, and then once again adjourned the debate till 1 December—in effect indefinitely.

The evasions of the King, the silence of the Commons, the winning of Leveller support—everything that happened strengthened the hold of Ireton's and Harrison's party of action upon the Army. In the last week of November Cromwell's letter to Fairfax supporting the demand of his officers for impartial justice would be known among the higher circle of Grandees in Windsor (whither the Headquarters were transferred on 24 November) and soon among their juniors also. What was in the minds of the soldiers we have been able to guess from that bitter outburst from Scroop's horse and the simpler language of Pride's foot (pp. 334-6 above). As the regiments which fought at Preston and Colchester drew near to London, a sense may have spread through their ranks that they were marching as much against the Parliament which forced them to live by free quarter as against the King who called in the Scottish invaders. The declaration dated from Windsor on 30 November, which bore the signature of Fairfax, spoke we may feel sure for the whole Army when, in Cromwellian language, it announced its intention of appealing 'unto the extraordinary judgment of God'. This, it seems, entitled it to dissolve the Long Parliament. It went on (as Colonel Harrison had forecast) to invite as many of the members 'as God hath kept upright' to separate themselves from those who had betrayed their trust, and assured them that, until a new Parliament could be elected, the Army would 'own them, adhere to them and be guided by them in their faithful prosecution of that trust'.

Against this threat Parliament reacted with its customary indecision. It rejected the spirited advice of William Prynne, who had recently been elected, to brand the Army as rebels; instead, it tried to buy them off by authorising the Lord Mayor to find £40,000 due from the City towards their arrears of pay. They marched on, none the less, and installed the Lord General in Whitehall Palace on 2 December. We need not record the helpless debates of the Commons over the King's concessions and his removal by the Army to the gloomy security of Hurst Castle. Once more the House rejected Prynne's downright proposal to accept the King's offers as satisfactory. But it went far enough to confirm the Army in its hostility, when on 5 December it voted by 129 to 83 that the King's answers were 'a ground for the course to proceed upon for the settlement of the peace of the kingdom'.

Next morning Colonel Pride made it the first one-party Parliament in European history. His purge excluded the stubborn Presbyterian majority, some ninety members. Of these, forty-five who resisted their exclusion were under arrest for a few days, but Sir William Waller, Sir John Clotworthy and Lionel Copley were imprisoned in the Tower for many a year, untried. Denzil Holles, Massey and Major-General Browne escaped to the continent. Colonel Pride carried out his purge without the authorisation either of Fairfax or Cromwell, but no one doubts that he acted for the whole Army, from the Lieut.-General to the most rebellious of the Agitators of yesterday.

What Colonel Pride did, none the less, was not what the Windsor Declaration had threatened to do, nor was it what Ireton and Harrison had planned. He did not dissolve the House. When the 'honest' members faced the prospect of quitting the seat of power in Westminster which they had occupied for eight years, to become unprivileged citizens once more, they one and all recoiled. They believed that their party, so long as they sat within the walls sanctified by tradition, so long as they could use the name of a Parliament and stamp its seal upon their decisions, would enjoy a prestige which no group of former members attached to the Army's Head-quarters could ever hope to acquire. A cynic may suggest that they were unwilling to surrender their perquisites and privileges, including immunity from imprisonment for debt; such con-siderations do sometimes reinforce disinterested political reasoning. In vain did Ireton and his fellow-soldiers point out to them that they could be only a mock Parliament exposed to the ridicule of their fellow-citizens. In vain did the Levellers enquire who authorised Thomas Pride to choose a Parliament for the people of England. They could govern only by the power of the naked sword in the stronger hands of other men.

But the Levellers were mistaken when they told 'the honest party' that they could only be the Army's puppets, mere school-boys under the rod of an omnipotent master. In fact the soldiers needed a screen for the dictatorship of their pikes and swords; they could find it only at Westminster. The Independent carcerists and lawyers may have been as greedy and corrupt as their Presbyterian colleagues, but the extremity of their peril called out in them a courage and a competence which Denzil Holles and his followers never attained. There were, moreover, idealists among them, like Vane and Sidney, Hutchinson and Ludlow, who retain the respect of posterity. They began in these critical December days by taking their own line against the opinion of the Army, and as time went on their sense of independence grew upon them.

To understand what happened we have to suppress our own knowledge of the sequel. Holland, Challoner and Scott, when they rejected a dissolution in those December days, may not have foreseen that the Rump would go on sitting till Cromwell broke it up in the fifth year of its existence. They probably imagined that they would be able to 'go to the country' in a few months' time. The ideal of a Venetian Senate whose members sat for life was advocated many years later by Milton; it seems likely that Vane and perhaps other republicans had come to entertain it some time before the crash in 1653, but not, so far as we know, in 1648. The 'honest party' may have been shrewder than either the soldiers or the Levellers in realising that if the Long Parliament were dissolved, the next general election would turn on the fate of Charles Stuart and nothing else. If the English electorate were asked, Shall he be beheaded or restored in safety, honour and freedom to his throne, it would have voted—even if 'malignants' were dis-qualified and 'decayed' boroughs disfranchised—by a sub-stantial majority for restoration. But if, in the meanwhile, the

Army had acted on Harrison's threat to deal with God's anointed under martial law, the adverse majority would have been overwhelming. So slowly do men emancipate themselves from the inherited mythology of our species, the archetypal idea of the God-King.

In this crisis the Army had to act; so much, for all his hatred of militarism, even John Lilburne recognised, when he sent what was in effect an offer of his alliance to Cromwell before the battle of Preston. His criticisms of Pride's Purge were sound enough; it was a clumsy device, adopted in a situation so difficult that it admitted of no good solution. The Levellers could not claim that they were opposed in practice to all purges. They supported the Army when it insisted on the expulsion from the Long Parliament of its eleven chief opponents. Again, they backed the Agitators (as pretty certainly did Cromwell also) when they called for a purge as extensive as Pride's, to remove all the Presbyterians who went on sitting after the mob had imposed its will on the Commons in July 1647.

On questions of tactics doubtless the Levellers made as many mistakes and perpetrated as many inconsistencies as any other group in this confused and puzzling revolution. What they bequeathed to posterity was something bigger and of more general application than any tactical device. When civil war has reduced society to a 'state of nature', how to restore civilisation and peace and secure the gains of the revolution in a new political framework—that was their discovery. They embodied it in their plan to call a constitutional convention to adopt a new social contract, an agreement of the people acceptable to the general will. They failed to persuade our ancestors to accept this novel idea. It crossed the Atlantic, however, and bore ripe fruit. Defeated in Europe, the English Revolution found its triumph and its culmination in America.

NOTES TO CHAPTER XVIII

1. Sir John Maynard, *A Speech in the House of Commons* (27 July, 1648).

2. This and other related facts, with the letter, are from Lilburne's *Legal Fundamental Liberties*. Lilburne there (H. and D., p. 414) refers to three M.P.s as if they were acting as a group with which he was in close touch—

Cornelius Holland, Colonel Ludlow and Thomas Challoner. From Ludlow's *Memoirs* we learn that he and perhaps the other two wrote to Cromwell to encourage him before the battle at Preston. 'By the advice of some friends' Ludlow then went to Colchester (either just before or just after its surrender) to warn the Army of its danger if the treaty with the King were completed. Fairfax was as usual vague; Ireton agreed that the Army must intervene, but not immediately (Ludlow, *Memoirs*, I, pp. 200-3).

3. Abbott, II, p. 638.

4. The full text is in both Wolfe (pp. 279-90) and H. and D. (pp. 147-55).

5. *The Answer of the Commons to a Petition* (23 October, 1648).

6. *The Representations and Consultations of the General Council of the Army at St. Albans, 7 to 11 November* (1648).

7. *Mercurius Melancholicus*. The story of Rainsborough's death was best told in *The Moderate*. Mr Hugh Ross Williamson's able study in *Four Stuart Portraits* should be consulted, though I think he exaggerates Rainsborough's importance. One asks whether Rainsborough's failure to bring back the fleet to its obedience to Parliament throws doubt on his abilities as a leader of men. He had to cope with a conspiracy to deceive him in which most of the officers of his flagship were involved. Perhaps, as the curious affair of the impersonation of Prince Charles by the adventurer Cornelius Evans suggests, Rainsborough was rather easily deceived. There can be no truth in the story that he antagonised his men by harsh discipline. After the royalist mutineers took control of his flagship, his men still treated him with consideration, because (as they put it) 'he had been a kind and good-natured commander to them'. But a man who is an able and popular leader in military matters may fail in the more complicated field of politics. Rainsborough, as I read his character, was too impulsive, too hot-headed and perhaps too simple-minded to make a successful politician.

8. On the colours see a foolish adolescent pamphlet, *The Levellers' Institutions for a Good People and a Good Parliament* (30 November, 1648).

9. *Mercurius Elencticus* (4 October), which also states that Lilburne has gone to Durham and Harry Marten to York.

10. *Legal Fundamental Liberties* (H. and D., p. 415).

11. Abbott, I, p. 676. The letter is dated Knottingley, 6 November, 1648. See also *C.P*, II, p. 49.

12. Abbott, I, p. 696, dated Knottingley, 25 November, 1648.

13. *Ibid.*, pp. 690, 692.

14. I am following the narrative in *Legal Fundamental Liberties*. It is not quite clear whether the report covers several meetings held on one day, the 15th, or whether they were spread over two or three days. Lilburne's timing is always vague.

15. *A Remonstrance of Lord Fairfax and of the General Council of Officers* (16 November, 1648). Gardiner gives a good summary of part of it (*Civil War*, IV, p. 233), and there are copious extracts from the rest in Woodhouse, pp. 456 sqq. Gardiner supposes that the final text was reached by a compromise between Ireton and the Levellers. There is no warrant for this supposition in Lilburne's narrative, though there must have been a subsequent revision of Ireton's draft, since the passages 'lashing' the Levellers were cut out. Gardiner does not realise that Ireton had the text of the

September Petition before him when he composed his own manifesto, and must then have made up his mind, perhaps in consultation with Colonel Harrison and Hugh Peters, how much of it he could adopt. The Petition, if my guess is correct, had itself been so drafted as to make it as far as possible acceptable to Cromwell and Ireton. It is a weakness in Gardiner's story of this period that he never realised the importance of the September Petition. His account of it is very slight and does not even mention the clauses defining toleration. Again, Gardiner seems to ascribe the endorsing petitions from the Army to Ireton's initiative. It escapes his notice that among the first batch of them, from the Army on the Scottish Border, was an address of thanks to the authors of the Petition of 11 September.

CHAPTER XIX

Toleration

The alliance between the Levellers and the Army was wrecked by a difference over toleration. Cromwell and Ireton held the orthodox Independent position. They renounced any claim of the state to impose on the citizen religious beliefs or forms of worship which his judgment or conscience rejected. But they would retain for the legislature and the magistrate the right to restrict the public profession of belief and the practice of worship. The distinction between compulsion and restriction will be clearer if we illustrate it by recalling the policy of the various parties towards the Catholics. The Presbyterians, standing for uniformity and rejecting toleration in any of the senses of that word, sought as the Elizabethans had done to compel 'recusant' Catholics to conform, by imposing heavy fines if they failed to attend the parish (now Presbyterian) church regularly. Further, they would take the children of Catholics from their parents, in order to bring them up as Protestants. The Independents would do neither of these things. But they agreed with the Presbyterians in forbidding the celebration of the mass as a criminal offence, for which the priest might be hanged and his flock imprisoned.

The Levellers, on the other hand, would leave the Catholics entirely free to profess and practise their religion without loss or hindrance. They reached this enlightened position by two avenues of thought. One of them was the Anabaptist tradition which condemned all coercion, and proclaimed the fraternity of all Christians. Reared in this community, Richard Overton made its tenets familiar to a wide audience, as we have seen (pp. 54-6 above), through his popular pamphlet *The Arraignment of Mr Persecution*. He was careful to extend his plea for toleration to Jews as well as Catholics. The other avenue of approach was through the secular argument, characteristic of Walwyn, that only by freedom of discussion—'liberty of discourse'—can we hope to arrive at truth or ensure our enjoyment of civil liberty. Steadily, from their first emergence as a party in the *Remonstrance of Many Thousands* down to the September Petition, the Levellers went on claiming what their pioneers had preached. Outside the Netherlands, theirs was the first organised party in the civilised world which stood without qualifications for toleration.

Bold though their demand for toleration was, the Levellers themselves regarded it as a compromise. They still left to the state, however reluctantly, a great influence over religion. They would allow Parliament to do, what indeed it had already done—to set up an established church, provided it were armed with no powers of compulsion. At this stage the Presbyterian clergy, with the City oligarchy and a considerable section of the landed gentry behind them, may have seemed to them too powerful for a frontal attack.

The Levellers would even have left to the clergy of this national church an income drawn from taxation; for while they proposed to make an end of tithes in the traditional form of a levy in kind, they would consent to a fixed rent charge as a substitute for this detested burden. The Presbyterian clergy, like their Anglican predecessors, would continue to enjoy a privileged position. Since a 'living' was still in the gift of a lay patron, usually the lord of the manor, property would keep its hold over one pulpit at least in every parish. The challenging, unorthodox voices of the unpaid 'teachers' who made their living like Thomas Lamb by boiling soap, like William Kiffin by exporting gloves, like Praise-God Barbone as a leather merchant, or like Dr Chamberlen as an obstetric surgeon, would still be heard in the conventicles of the sectaries; the professional divines of the Independent chapels would still be chosen by their congregations to speak 'as the spirit moved them'. But the national church, especially in the rural parishes, would enjoy an enormous advantage over the sects in the competition to gain an ascendancy over men's minds. Men disputed in the seventeenth century over toleration. That word is too modest, for it disguises the struggle for power, in which during this epoch religion played so great a part.

While at Westminster the 'honest party' faced the tasks of government with which Colonel Pride had entrusted it, in Whitehall the committee of sixteen (reduced in practice to thirteen) was debating the draft of an Agreement of the People, which Harry Marten and the Leveller delegation drew up for it at Windsor. As it emerged from these discussions it was a much more elaborate document than the first sketch which had satisfied the Agitators. Thus it began with a complete list of the three hundred constituencies into which England was to be divided, after the 'decayed boroughs' had been eliminated. The Rump was to be dissolved on the last day of April 1649. For the succeeding biennial Parliaments the right to vote was conferred on all householders (or 'housekeepers', to use the contemporary term) who paid poor rate, with the exception of servants and beggars. This was less than the manhood suffrage the Levellers originally proposed, but it went far beyond the narrow limits for which Ireton and Cromwell contended at Putney. This second version of the Agreement, in the form in which it has come down to us, is notable chiefly for the long list of social reforms which the first reformed Parliament was asked to pass. Among them, in a postscript of John Lilburne's, was a plea for the abolition of all base tenures.

Though, if we may believe John's account, Ireton was often 'very angry and lordly' in these debates, a formula was reached over toleration which the Levellers were prepared to accept as a reasonable compromise, if thereby they gained the support of Ireton and the Army. When, however, this agreed document came before the council of officers, Cromwell, Ireton and other Grandees tore the compromise to pieces and substituted for the clause on toleration an ambiguous and illiberal version of their own. Other clauses also were mangled, notably the reservation which forbade 'pressing' for the armed forces. When, after a violent quarrel at the meeting of the council on 15 December, Lilburne and his colleagues broke off the alliance and withdrew, he determined, with the consent of the Leveller party, to publish the Agreement which the majority of the committee had approved as it stood before the final concession to Ireton was made. Here is the clause dealing with toleration which ranks as the first reservation limiting the powers of Parliament:

> We do not empower our representatives to continue in force or make any laws, oaths and covenants, whereby to compel by penalties or otherwise any person to any thing in or about matters of faith, religion or God's worship, or to restrain any person from the professing his faith or exercise of religion according to his conscience, in any house or place (except such as are or shall be set apart for the public worship): nevertheless the instruction or directing of the nation in a public way, for the matters of faith, worship or discipline (so it be not compulsive or express Popery) is referred to their discretion.

It is reasonably probable that the words inserted to satisfy Ireton and dropped when the Levellers withdrew from the alliance, were *professing Christianity* (in the sixth line of this clause—'to restrain any person professing Christianity'). The effect of these words was to exclude from toleration Jews, atheists, deists (though this term was not in common use till the next generation) and probably Unitarians also. It is clear from the reports in the *Clarke Papers* of the debates in the council of officers that the Levellers must have had in mind both Jews and atheists, and that they intended to recognise their rights when they erased Ireton's qualification.[1]

In this chapter, since we are trying to define the opinions about toleration and the record in practice both of the Levellers and the Cromwellian Independents, we must look ahead. When it became clear in the spring of 1649 that the Rump had no intention of dissolving, while the Grandees were content that the officers' version of the Agreement of the People should lie indefinitely in its pigeon-hole, the Levellers threw over the tactics of compromise they adopted in the September Petition. The third edition of the Agreement, which went out from the Tower over the signatures of Lilburne, Walwyn, Overton and Prince on May Day, 1649, may be regarded as the definitive *credo* of the party, as frank as it is mature. A few months after

the end of the most ruinous of all the wars of religion, the
Thirty Years War, they made in one bound the advance in
thought which broke the fatal link between religion and power.
They now stood for the separation of church and state. The
complication of an established national church disappeared
from the final draft of their constitution. With it, as was only
logical, tithes also vanished, whether as a tax in kind or a fixed
rent charge. As an item in a bold measure of decentralisation, it
was provided that the voters of each parish might elect a 'minister' who would have its church at his disposal—though others
would, of course, be free to set up their own chapels or conventicles. It would, doubtless, often happen that the majority
of the parishioners would elect a Presbyterian minister in
preference to an Episcopalian or an Independent. But Parliament would have no responsibility for maintaining Presbyterian
—or any other—doctrine or discipline. What, in plain words,
the Levellers stood for was the secular republic, which the
United States, and for a few years France, were destined to
realise in the next century.

We may leave the enlightenment of this policy to speak for
itself. The Levellers were far in advance of both Milton and
Locke, for neither of them would tolerate either atheists or
Catholics. The reasonable criticism to which these pioneers
are exposed is that they went too far and too fast in advance of
public opinion. Could the nation which went crazy over the
Popish Plot in the next reign have been persuaded to tolerate
Catholic worship under the Commonwealth? But a radical
difference distinguishes these two periods. Rational Protestants
took alarm, and irrational Protestants panicked, whenever
Catholic influences were powerful at the head of affairs. Pym
could rouse the mob because Queen Henrietta dominated
Whitehall. Shaftesbury could do the same because the heir
to the throne was a frank and defiant Catholic, nor was the
King himself above suspicion. But no man in his senses, not
even William Prynne, could suspect Cromwell or Ireton,
Bradshaw or Vane, of any inclination towards Popery. The
decade of their omnipotence was, therefore, the ideal period for
the introduction of toleration. One must concede, however,
that for many years much tact would have been required from

the Catholics, for anything that attracted the attention of the mob would have been dangerous. The Netherlands were in advance of England in much that constitutes civilisation. But were our forefathers so far behind the Dutch that the toleration which ennobled Amsterdam could not have been acclimatised in London?

How in fact the Levellers behaved over a complicated question that involved the issue of toleration, we shall see when we reach the spring of the next year (Chapter XXV). They opposed the re-conquest of Ireland with equal intelligence and moral courage. Their defence of the right of the Irish to keep their own fields and practise their own faith is the earliest and not the least distinguished instance in English history of the struggle of a popular party against imperialism.

We must now turn back to the sittings of the Council of the Army at Whitehall at which the officers' version of the Agreement of the People was produced. Of some of its debates we have a shorthand report in the *Clarke Papers*.[2] They lack the drama and the human interest of the discussions at Reading and Putney. No Agitators were present to speak for the men, nor did Cromwell attend these sittings. Among the officers, whose numbers varied from thirty-five to forty, there was no one of senior rank who would stand up to Ireton, as Colonel Rainsborough did at Putney. Though Fairfax, inert and silent, was in the chair, he allowed Ireton to act for him as chairman. Even more than at Putney the Commissary-General dominated the proceedings, speaking much too often and at length. Speeches are, indeed, reported by four officers who held Leveller views—Colonel Deane, an Anabaptist, who was soon to share with Blake the command at sea, and Captains Spencer, Clarke and Joyce, but the two former spoke with excessive brevity. Three of the Leveller delegates were present, Lilburne, Overton and Wildman; but only Wildman took part in the debate, the other two intervening very briefly on points of procedure. The novelty of these debates was that a number of Independent divines had been called in to advise the officers on the question of toleration. One's interest is apt to flag in the effort to follow their theological arguments. Even Dr John Goodwin, the most famous of them, arrives at his liberal conclusions by way of conventional, scholastic reasoning.

Something, none the less, can be learned even from confused and fragmentary reports of these Whitehall debates about the mind of this army. One notes in some of the officers' speeches, and also in those of two of the divines, the growth of the belief that the millennium is at hand—the breaking of the day of God, when He will thresh the mountains and use the Army as his flail. In this crisis of the Revolution the more imaginative of the Puritans are thinking, as never before, in the metaphors of Hebrew poetry. The extreme millenarian view, as William Erbury, the Fifth Monarchist divine states it, is indifferent to the Agreement, or even hostile to it, because the time has come for the dictatorship of the Saints. He believes that 'a dozen or twenty-four may in a short time do the kingdom as much good as four hundred that sit in Parliament in seven years may do'. Parliaments in short are obsolescent. A more sober and orthodox divine, the Lord General's former chaplain, Joshua Sprigge, takes much the same view. Why labour in vain, as this Agreement does, to invent a new constitution? 'God will bring forth a New Heaven and a New Earth. . . . If we could have but patience to wait upon Him . . . He would bring us out of this labyrinth wherein we are.' When at the end of these sittings Colonel Harrison sums up his view of the Agreement as a whole, it is obvious that he does not greatly care what may become of it. It belongs to an era of human history that is almost at an end.

From this millennarian enthusiasm the Levellers stand aloof. Their way of thinking, though most of them are devout Christians, seems by contrast rationalist or humanist. Such words are misleading, yet one feels that these pioneers are the contemporaries of their Puritan fellow-countrymen only in the sense that they endured the same storms and enjoyed the same sunshine. So much is this so that one is startled by Captain Joyce's speech, since he alone manages to combine with a millennarian faith typical Leveller opinions about toleration and the Agreement; he believes that the Lord is 'about to turn some of our swords into ploughshares' and will bid us 'sit still and behold His works among men'.

These debates open on 14 December with an attempt by several of the more conservative senior officers to escape any specific commitment over toleration. They realise that on both sides feeling over this issue is strong and unyielding. They dread a split in the Army at this crisis of the Revolution. Need there be in the Agreement any clause reserving religion from the authority of Parliament and the magistrate? One suggestion, expanded from Ireton's hint, was that the Agreement should concede to the people's representative 'the highest and final judgment concerning all natural or civil things, but not concerning things spiritual or evangelical'. Hugh Peters was for postponing a decision, to allow time—a month or so—for further discussion. He would have copies of what was proposed sent to every market-town and 'hung forth'—a proposal that should naturally have led up to the calling of a convention. The Council was, however, against delay, and in favour of a clause dealing specifically with religion. It was unanimous in refusing to allow the state any power of compulsion.

The whole debate then turned on whether it should have certain powers of restriction. At once Ireton's precise, legalistic mind asserted itself. He went back to the Old Testament and maintained that in many things it is still a guide to the conduct of Christians. In matters of religion and worship God laid on the magistrates of the Jews the duty of restriction, and visited them and their people with His wrath, if they failed to perform it. Specifically what they had to enforce was the first table of the Commandments which Moses brought down from Sinai: 'Thou shalt have no other gods but Me': 'Thou shalt make no graven image': 'Thou shalt not take the name of the Lord in vain': 'Thou shalt not do any manner of work on the Sabbath day'. These things, he argued, are matters of perpetual and natural right. 'What was sin before is sin still.'

From the long debate that followed what the modern reader will pick out as significant is a speech of Wildman's and some tantalisingly brief questions of Colonel Deane's. Wildman understood that the refusal of toleration means the prevalence of incessant wars of extermination. If God really gave all magistrates a command to destroy idolatry, He was ordering the extinction of mankind. Deane punctured Ireton's Old

Testament morals, by asking whether he would destroy the
Turks, as the Jews destroyed the Canaanites. Wildman had an
easy task in showing that the first four Commandments were
very far from corresponding to 'natural' religion. By the light
of nature men may come to see that there is a god, but 'the sun
may be that god'. Here was the secular road by which the
Levellers advanced to toleration. The simple but moving little
speech of Captain Spencer followed the other line of approach,
the Anabaptist tradition. 'If we labour for liberty for ourselves,
let us give it to others that are as dear to Christ as we are.'

Our reports of these debates are, unfortunately, so fragmentary that we do not know whether at later sittings Ireton
went on to apply his general principles to particular forms of
ritual and belief. Did he explain why the celebration of the
mass must be reckoned as idolatry? Did he argue that the Book
of Common Prayer takes the name of the Lord in vain, or that
it also enjoins idolatry? A word or two of reminder would have
been enough, for such arguments had been for many a year the
commonplaces of every Puritan pulpit. The apprentices who
filled the ranks of the parliamentary regiments already knew
them by heart in the first weeks of the Civil War, when they
went about smashing the 'graven images' of the cathedrals. It
was enough that Ireton should recall the fact, as he did, that the
magistrates of the Jews

> were commanded to beat down the idols and groves and
> images of the land whither they went; they were com-
> manded that they should not suffer the stranger that was
> within the gate to work on the Sabbath, and not to suffer
> swearers or idolaters of any kind.

A little later in this debate the Independent divine Philip Nye,
a more orthodox and typical thinker than the liberal John
Goodwin, drew Ireton's conclusion in even plainer words.

> There are [he argued] sins of which God will take account
> and for which He will make miserable this commonwealth,
> those who compose it being Christians, or even if they have
> the light of nature only. By the light of nature we are able to
> say that for such things God will plague a nation and judge
> a nation.

Strange and barely comprehensible as this may seem to us, it was the essence of what Puritans believed, overshadowed as they were by the Old Testament. Liberal historians of the last century often explained by political motives and even excused the refusal of Commonwealth and Protectorate to tolerate Episcopalians or Catholics. Of course politics and, what these historians usually forgot, economics also entered into it. Men were as complex in the seventeenth century as they are today. The pretensions of the Papacy could always be paraded, if one was looking for an excuse to grab the lands of Catholics in Ireland or the West of England. To probe in this way into the unconscious of the Puritan leaders may be salutary and even necessary. But their conscious motives, the grounds they themselves advanced for their intolerant legislation, were simpler. The thunders of Sinai proclaimed in advance that the mass is sin, and in a lesser degree the Book of Common Prayer as well. And sin, on pain of God's anger, must be suppressed.

The difficulty is not to explain why Ireton, and with him Cromwell, held such views; rather we have to account for the aberration of the *Heads of the Proposals*. In these they had set out (p. 243 above) the most generous and comprehensive form of toleration which even restored episcopacy (subject to certain safeguards) and set the Catholics free, while of course assuring to the Puritan sects full liberty of conscience. We must dismiss from our minds any notion that they put forward this scheme because it represented their ideal. Their ideal was the system their party and their army established under the Protectorate, when they were for a time omnipotent. In August 1647 they proposed all-round toleration to the King, because they reckoned that an alliance of Independents, Royalists and Levellers offered them their best and perhaps their only chance of defeating the Presbyterian majority at Westminster, the Scots and the City who would be strong enough, if they came to terms with the King, to crush the sects altogether. In other words, to ensure toleration for themselves they had to offer it to Episcopalians also and even to the Catholics. The victory at Preston relieved them from this policy of submitting for the sake of life and conscience to a necessary evil. They were now strong enough to defy both King and Presbyterians and yet to

secure toleration for themselves without conceding it to
'malignants'. So much of his calculations Cromwell disclosed,
in effect, in the former of his two famous letters to Colonel
Hammond (pp. 362-3 above).

With this preface we may go on to give some account of the
officers' Agreement of the People, in so far as it differs from
the second version published by the Levellers.[3] Concerning the
redistribution of seats and the technicalities of elections it is
even more elaborate; for the first time such new industrial
towns as Manchester, Leeds and Halifax are given representation. An ominous requirement, which in effect limits the right
to sit in the Commons to the 'godly' party, was inserted to
this effect:

> And we do desire and recommend it to all men, that in all times
> the persons to be chosen for this great trust may be men of
> courage, fearing God and hating covetousness; and that our
> representatives would make the best provisions for this end.

Ireton had already inserted a similar restriction in one of the
earlier manifestoes of the Army (the *Representation* of 14 June
1647—p. 219 above). Its re-appearance makes it clear that he
had already adopted the totalitarian principles which shaped
the Parliaments of the Protectorate. Only the Saints, the god-
fearing *élite*, had the right to govern.

The clause limiting the powers of Parliament to 'things
natural or civil' has been mentioned already. It seems super-
fluous since the religious settlement was so fully defined in
Article IX, which reads:

> Concerning religion, we agree as followeth: (1) It is in-
> tended that the Christian religion be held forth and recom-
> mended as the public profession in this nation, which we
> desire may, by the grace of God, be reformed to the greatest
> purity in doctrine, worship and discipline, according to the
> word of God; the instructing the people thereunto in a
> public way, so it be not compulsive, as also the maintaining
> of able teachers for whatsoever is for that end, and for the
> confutation or discovery of heresy, error, and whatsoever is
> contrary to sound doctrine, is allowed to be provided for by
> our representatives; the maintenance of which teachers may
> be out of a public treasury, and, we desire, not by tithes;

provided that Popery or Prelacy be not held forth as the public way or profession in this nation. (2) That to the public profession so held forth, none be compelled by penalties or otherwise; but only may be endeavoured to be won by sound doctrine and the example of a good conversation. (3) That such as profess faith in God by Jesus Christ, however differing in judgment from the doctrine, worship or discipline publicly held forth as aforesaid, shall not be restrained from, but shall be protected in, the profession of their faith and exercise of religion according to their consciences, in any place except such as shall be set apart for the public worship (where we provide not for them, unless they have leave) so as they abuse not this liberty to the civil injury of others, or to actual disturbance of the public peace on their parts. Nevertheless it is not intended to be hereby provided that this liberty shall necessarily extend to Popery or Prelacy. (4) That all laws, ordinances, statutes and clauses in any law, statute or ordinance, to the contrary of the liberty herein provided for in the two particulars next preceding concerning religion, be and are hereby repealed and made void.

This long clause is so well drafted that it needs little elucidation. It provides for a state church, but without tithes. It excludes from toleration all non-Christians, meaning specifically Jews, Unitarians, atheists or deists; its authors were too insular to be interested in Muslims, Buddhists or Hindoos. It provides toleration for Christian sects outside the established church, subject to the oddly phrased qualification that it shall not 'necessarily' extend to 'Papists or Prelatists'. This meant, of course, that the Council of the Army was so sharply divided that it would not risk a split by a clear pronouncement either way. It is probable that Leveller views had a majority, but in a matter of this importance it is unlikely that Ireton would have allowed himself to be voted down by the junior officers. He knew, of course, when he sent this document up to the Rump, that if it took any notice of the Agreement at all, it would show no tenderness to 'Papists or Prelatists'. To complete the story; the Army sent up the officers' Agreement to the Rump on 20 January, 1649, with a deferential covering letter. There is nothing further to relate. The Rump took no action and the Grandees of the Army were perfectly content. Thus were the Levellers 'cozened'.

As the years went on, the attitude of the dominant party among the Independent clergy and laity and in the Army was even more sharply defined. The latter was purged of its rebellious Levellers and became a professional force, content to serve under orders without a standing representative council, though its officers did meet to express its collective opinions from time to time. By the end of 1653, when the Revolution took its definitive shape in the Protectorate, Ireton was dead, Fairfax had faded out, and Lambert had succeeded Harrison as the lieutenant on whom Cromwell chiefly relied. Though the Levellers had been crushed and silenced, some of their ideas survived. Traces of their influence are obvious in the Instrument of Government, the written constitution which Lambert drafted (16 December, 1653). It is based on the first principle of the Agreement of the People, that the foundations of the nation's laws are unalterable, and while it declares that the supreme legislative authority of the commonwealth shall 'reside in one person and the people assembled in Parliament', it goes on to set bounds and limits to its exercise. The redistribution of seats, the franchise, the provisions for a regular succession of Parliaments, these and much else have been evolved from the original Agreement of the Agitators, though they have suffered a conservative transformation, and are now imposed by the omnipotent Army.

Prominent among these unalterable foundations is the religious settlement. This provides (§35) 'that the Christian religion, as contained in the Scriptures, be held forth and recommended as the public profession of these nations', and sanctions tithes, though it holds out the expectation that a less contentious way of maintaining the ministry will be found. It provides (§36) that 'none shall be compelled by penalties or otherwise' to this public profession. Then comes the enactment of toleration (§37):

> That such as profess faith in God by Jesus Christ (though differing in judgment from the doctrine, worship or discipline publicly held forth) shall not be restrained from, but shall be protected in, the profession of the faith and exercise

of their religion; so as they abuse not this liberty to the civil injury of others and to the actual disturbance of the public peace on their parts: provided this liberty be not extended to Popery or Prelacy, nor to such as, under the profession of Christ, hold forth and practise licentiousness.

This is in substance Ireton's clause, as it stood in the officers' Agreement of five years back, save that in the interval the Quakers, who have begun to disturb 'the steeplehouses' of the more sedate 'professors', have set a unique problem. Once more non-Christians (among whom with Jews, atheists and deists, Unitarians are reckoned) are outside the pale, but this time there is no ambiguity in the exclusion of Papists and Prelatists.

How sweeping these exclusions were, we must pause for a moment to consider. The non-Christians were only a handful; for Unitarians in the middle class and deists in the upper class did not become numerous till the next century. Quakers and Catholics in England and Wales formed together about one per cent. of the population. After the Restoration Protestant dissenters (meaning Presbyterians, Independents and Baptists) according to a careful reckoning by Sir G. N. Clark were at the outside ten per cent. of the population.[4] It wanted conviction, courage and integrity to profess a nonconformist creed under the Clarendon Code. If tepid and timid believers could have done it without unpopularity or risk, the percentage would have been appreciably higher. The vast majority conformed alike to the Cromwellian state church in the sixteen-fifties and to the episcopal state church in the sixteen-sixties, probably without feeling any acute discomfort in either decade. But when every allowance had been made on this score, it can hardly be doubted that those leaders of the post-1660 Anglican church who were dubbed Prelatists in the 'fifties represented a substantial portion of the population. To them, together with the overwhelming Catholic majority in Ireland, both Commonwealth and Protectorate refused toleration.

So far our analysis of what the ruling faction of the Independents and the Grandees of the Army meant by toleration has been anonymous, or else Ireton has played the leading part in it. But it is Cromwell's record that matters to posterity.

How came it that a once dominant school of historians singled him out as a pioneer of toleration, entitled on this score to our gratitude and veneration?

Practical experience taught Cromwell the soldier that if they were to win liberty of conscience for themselves against the intolerance of the King and his bishops, the various groups of Puritans must learn the lesson of unity and co-operation. Himself a man of the centre, an Independent, he ordered his line of battle with the Presbyterians as its right and the Anabaptists as its left wing. Only because they acted together was the New Model enabled to win its astonishing victories. That was the moral he drove home in his famous despatches after Naseby fight and the storming of Bristol: to quote from the latter:

> Presbyterians, Independents, all had here the same spirit of faith and prayer. . . . They agree here, know no names of difference: pity it is it should be otherwise anywhere. . . . And from brethren, in things of the mind, we look for no compulsion but that of light and reason. In other things God hath put the sword into the Parliament's hands.[b]

In this Army, tolerant within limits though it was, there were, however, no Prelatists, still less were there any Catholics. All its officers were Puritans who had taken the Covenant. Then was this all that the Lieut.-General meant—that Puritans would win no victories if they quarrelled over the niceties of church government? Certainly he meant more than this commonplace of worldly wisdom—at any rate he felt more than this, for his was a deeply emotional nature. He felt his kinship with all the People of God, and he could express it with that imaginative warmth which was native to him when he was moved. He felt a fraternity with his fellow-believers, which levelled social distinctions and made the poorest of the Saints his equal. One could compile a chaplet of sayings from his speeches and letters that breathe a spirit of tolerance:

> The state in choosing men to serve them takes no notice of their opinions; if they be willing faithfully to serve them, that satisfies.

> I meddle not with any man's conscience.

I had rather that Mahomedanism was permitted among us, than that one of God's children should be persecuted.

To be a seeker is to be of the best sect next to a finder; and such an one shall every faithful, humble seeker be at the end.

We should be pitiful and tender towards all, though of different judgments. . . . Love all, tender all, cherish and countenance all in all things that are good. . . . And if the poorest Christian, the most mistaken Christian, shall desire to live peaceably and quietly under you, I say if any shall desire but to lead a life of godliness and honesty, let him be protected.

The more attractive side of this complex character speaks in these passages, but as so often Cromwell said a good deal more than he really meant. He certainly did not mean that 'the most mistaken Christian', if he were a Prelatist or a Catholic, might freely use the Book of Common Prayer or attend mass. If he meant anything definite by such words, it was that no man should be persecuted for the passive adherence to his own faith in his own chamber. On occasion he seemed to refuse to recognise Prelatists as his fellow-Christians, for he once referred to 'men that are of an episcopal spirit' as 'men that know not God'.[6]

Who then were the People of God? Cromwell disliked precise statements in matters of faith and brushed aside a *credo* in fifteen articles which his trusted chaplain, Dr Owen, drew up to define the minimum of Christianity which every claimant of toleration must profess. His own definition is very vague. It has nothing to say about conduct or 'works'. The 'members of Jesus Christ' who are 'the apple of His eye' are all who believe the remission of sins through His blood, and are certain that they are God's People.[7] All one can say with certainty is that the People of God include Independents, Presbyterians and Anabaptists. The toleration he fought to win as the chief fruit of ten years of war was toleration for himself, toleration for his fellow-Puritans. An honest historian must point out that this was a very limited group. That does not cancel the debt which posterity owes to the Puritans. In standing up for their own civil rights they were fulfilling one of the first duties of good citizens. All of us who come after them, even those who share none of their religious beliefs, live in safety and freedom today because they struggled for liberty of conscience with such courage and endurance. Had they gone under, the wilderness beyond the ocean would have been the only refuge for men who dared to differ from a persecuting established church. Because the Independents triumphed on the battlefield, we are apt to forget how dense was the thicket out of which they fought their way.

> God hath bestowed upon us with the Gospel, peace and rest out of ten years of war, and given us what we would desire. Nay, who could have forethought, when we were plunged into the midst of our troubles, that ever the people of God should have had liberty to worship God without fear of enemies?

This Cromwell, at last omnipotent, could still say in retrospect when he addressed the second Parliament of the Protectorate.[8]

In one instance Cromwell did go beyond this narrow conception of the People of God. In one of his revealing letters to Colonel Robert Hammond though it may be only a figure of speech—he included the Jews among 'the godly people'.[9] It cannot be too often repeated to his credit that as Lord Protector he strove hard to secure for them toleration *de jure*, but was defeated by the Puritan merchants and clergy, though he did so far protect their settlement in London as to ensure toleration for them *de facto*. Was this because the Old Testament had taught him to think of them as God's chosen people, or was it for commercial reasons and because they worked for his intelligence service? His mind moved to and fro between the City, Whitehall and the Holy Land without a sense of incongruity; the probability is that all three considerations influenced him.

The crude facts are (as we have seen) that under the Protectorate toleration was refused to Prelatists, Catholics and Unitarians. Subject to an important qualification we must add the Quakers to these groups: some of them provoked their persecutors. No one is likely to forget George Fox's story of his friendly and intimate talks with His Highness. None the less, in round figures two thousand Friends suffered imprisonment during his reign, often for long terms and many of them, women as well as men, had to suffer infamous usage.[10] Many of them provoked retaliation by brawling in churches, others by refusing to take off their hats in court. But this excuse can be pressed too far, as it is in Gardiner's misleading chapter on toleration.[11] It is clear from contemporary accounts of the Friends' 'sufferings' that many—probably most—of those who put forward their views in 'steeple-houses' did it in a decent and courteous way, after waiting for the benediction. One has to remember that in this generation discussion was welcomed by some of the churches, notably the Anabaptists. Further, there is evidence that many, perhaps most, of the Quakers were convicted not for brawling but for blasphemy. It is clear that the responsibility for this panicky and vindictive persecution lay rather with the governing class as a whole—the J.P.s—than with the central government.

Cromwell's attitude to the Society of Friends wavered from time to time, influenced it may be by his personal contacts with Friends, ranging from Fox to the Groom of his Bedchamber, Charles Harvey. His last recorded speech on this subject, to the Common Council of the City in March 1658, was hostile. He urged his hearers to make full use of 'the good law made against the Quakers . . . for . . . they were against both magistracy and ministry'.[12] As this phrase of the Lord Protector's conveys, they were regarded by the propertied class, whose constable he had become, as dangerous radicals and anarchists. Their persecutors knew, what modern writers are apt to forget, that some of them were frustrated Levellers, defeated in the political arena, who had taken to novel ways of carrying on the class struggle, primarily against the hired clergy of the established Puritan church.

Unitarians, then known as Socinians, were not yet numerous as the Quakers were. Oliver shared the view of his second Parliament that they were blasphemers, who must be punished and suppressed. But (save in Ireland) he never was a 'man of blood', and one must count it a kindly act on his part that he and his Council sent John Biddle, the Unitarian pamphleteer, to prison for six months in the Scilly Isles, and so delivered him from Parliament, which might have dealt with him much more severely. This did not mean that the Protector valued or

respected an adventurous mind. His reply to one of the Anabaptists who petitioned on Biddle's behalf betrays no trace of
sympathy: 'You curl pate boy, you, do you think I'll show
favour to a man that denies his Saviour and disturbs the
government?' Again, when Biddle had appealed to the liberty
of conscience promised in the Instrument of Government, he
declared that it

> should never, while he had any interest in the government,
> be stretched so far as to countenance them who denied the
> divinity of our Saviour, or to bolster up any blasphemous
> opinions contrary to the fundamental verities of religion.[13]

Biddle accordingly was punished, but not severely. In this
context the fact must be recalled that Cromwell was opposed to
the barbarous punishment of John Nayler, the Quaker, for
blasphemy. This was, however, rather an instance of his
dislike (save in Ireland) of needless cruelty than of his tolerance.

Prelatists were not savagely persecuted as Quakers were, but
without qualification they were denied toleration by the
Instrument of Government. The only leniency they enjoyed,
and that only for a time, was that some of their sequestered
priests did still venture to use the Prayer Book and to administer the sacraments in private houses or in the chapels of
the nobility. But such favours were few and precarious. If the
authorities sometimes connived at these idolatrous doings under
a private roof, they would on occasion order their troops to
invade these gatherings. Evelyn wrote bitterly of the spiritual
hunger Episcopalians endured when they were deprived of the
means of salvation. In his experience the Protectorate was less
lenient than the Commonwealth. Seldom have harsher prohibitions than those of Oliver's Declaration of 4 October, 1655,
been drafted in the English language. It forbade 'malignants' to
keep in their houses as chaplains or schoolmasters 'any sequestered or ejected minister . . . [or] permit any of their
children to be taught by such', nor must these keep any school,
either public or private. They must not preach even in private
meetings (save of their own family) nor baptise, marry, 'administer the Lord's Supper' or use the Book of Common
Prayer.[14]

This refusal to tolerate the 'Prelatists' and the Prayer Book, which association had endeared to their hearts and ears, was one of the most fatal of Cromwell's mistakes. It begat in the Episcopalian gentry a temper of revenge. As so often in history the right far outdid the left in severity, and after the Restoration dissenters had to suffer not only the suppression of their conventicles but the rigours of the Clarendon Code. They were, moreover, excluded (as the 'malignants' had been) from every civic or political office. The Whig Revolution brought them toleration only in the negative sense of that word. They were still second-class citizens, and many a generation had to pass before they enjoyed full equality of rights with Anglicans. Down to our own century England remained, at all events in the provinces, a country of two nations (if one may give to Disraeli's phrase another application), segregated by religion and snobbery. Its whole history would have been happier and less class-ridden if Cromwell and his officers had drafted the Instrument of Government in 1653 with the same generous tolerance that Levellers and common soldiers put into the Agreement of the People in 1647.

In Ireland Puritan intolerance wrought a tragedy which has not spent all its legacy of hatred even in our day. His admirers are fond of quoting the first part of Cromwell's reply to an appeal for toleration which reached him from one of the rebel commanders, Sir Lucas Taafe: 'For that which you mention concerning liberty of conscience, I meddle not with any man's conscience.' After this boast he went on:

> But if by liberty of conscience you mean a liberty to exercise the mass, I judge it best to use plain dealing, and to let you know where the Parliament of England hath power that will not be allowed of.[15]

Cromwell's policy in Ireland was in fact the suppression of the Catholic religion and the extermination of its priesthood. The utmost mercy any of them enjoyed was banishment from their native land. At one stage of the re-conquest, a reward of £10 was offered for the head of a priest; a wolf's head fetched £5, and that of a wolf-bitch twice as much. Englishmen of our generation who know anything of this chapter of history can hardly read without a blush the record of Oliver's negotiations with Mazarin over the persecution of the Waldenses. He did well to beg the Cardinal to use his influence with the Duke of Savoy to stop it, but he had no honest answer at his command when the ruler of France, who did himself tolerate his Huguenots, asked the Lord Protector in return to alleviate the plight of the Catholics in England. It may be true, as the liberal historians remind us, that during the Protectorate only one Catholic priest was actually hanged, drawn and quartered for saying mass in England. (An exception was made, of course, for the embassies of Catholic powers.) The fact remains that the practice of the Catholic religion was still a capital offence and that English Catholics were subjected to wholesale expropriation, for the act of 1657 robbed each of them of two-thirds of his estate. In Ireland Cromwell's policy, after massacre and famine had wiped out a third of its inhabitants, was to rob the survivors of their lands and drive the whole of the native population to the barren moors of Connaught. Milton wrote a moving sonnet against the persecution of the Waldenses. He would stand higher in the calendar of humanity's saints if he had ever protested, were it only in a few plain words of prose, against the savagery of his fellow-Puritans in Ireland.

Cromwell, to sum up, was never the pioneer of toleration. A man is tolerant in proportion as the differences he overlooks and respects in his opponents are wide and fundamental. To his opponents—save in so far as the Presbyterians, once his allies, must be reckoned during several years as opponents—Cromwell was never tolerant. What he felt, in spite of unessential differences, was a sense of fraternity for all his fellow-Puritans. The name for that state of mind is not tolerance. Rather let us say that with warmth and sincerity he believed in the solidarity of the Saints.

NOTES TO CHAPTER XIX

1. See especially *C.P.*, II, p. 98, and Woodhouse, p. 143.

2. *C.P.*, II, pp. 71-186; Woodhouse, pp. 125-78.

3. Wolfe, p. 331; Gardiner, *Constitutional Documents of the Puritan Revolution*, p. 359. Woodhouse gives both texts, pp. 355-67.

4. G. N. Clark, *The Later Stuarts*, p. 18 and Note B (p. 26).

5. Abbott, I, p. 377.

6. *Ibid.*, IV, p. 707.

7. *Ibid.*, pp. 204-5.

8. *Ibid.*, p. 706.

9. *Ibid.*, I, p. 676.

10. W. C. Braithwaite, *The Beginnings of Quakerism*, p. 451.

11. Gardiner, *Commonwealth and Protectorate*, IV, Chapter XLI.

12. Abbott, IV, p. 758.

13. *Ibid.*, III, p. 834.

14. *Ibid.*, p. 839. [For a different view of the position of Episcopalians under the Protectorate see G. F. Nuttall, *The Holy Spirit in Puritan Faith and Experience*, pp. 128-31.—Ed.]

15. Abbott, II, p. 146.

CHAPTER XX

'The Moderate'

In one of the quieter corners of the Abbey, where we remember our poets and our thinkers, a grateful country might well perpetuate the name of George Thomason the London book-seller. Between 1640 and 1660 he collected virtually everything that came from the presses of England in revolution. George III presented his treasures, which include 22,000 'tracts'—though there are books also, and newspapers among them—to the British Museum. Bound up together in sumptuous volumes, the Royalists still thunder at the regicides, and the little England of five million people comes alive with all the Babel of its conflicting voices. What dramas are played out on these silent shelves! Levellers with their lives at stake argue with the Grandees of the Army, Cavaliers sing elegies for their murdered King, while the divines with a parade of Greek and Hebrew texts argue for toleration and against it. One lives through the fears and hopes of London's citizens, as they read the weekly newspapers that poured in a spate from the presses during the second Civil War. Whom were they to believe? The unlicensed royalist 'news-books' assured them that Cromwell had been killed in the Welsh campaign. And then came his characteristic despatch reporting his staggering victory at Preston. When one tires of sermons and tracts, there is much else of interest. A pamphlet, which describes the riches of Virginia, advises 'people of all degrees, from the highest master to the meanest servant, how suddenly to raise their fortunes'. A petition on behalf of the Jews proposes that this persecuted people shall be carried in English and Dutch ships to Palestine.

o

On the other side, the former Bishop of Rochester argues that their dispersion was a just punishment for their murder of the Son of God. And then, as one turns the pages, one comes on the first English version of 'the Alkoran of Mahomet', translated from the French. But republican England was still a Christian land; the printer was taken into custody and his press seized.

Flat and smooth, within the covers of a volume of Thomason's Tracts, bound in calf and adorned with the royal arms, lies the first number of *The Moderate*. In the wintry light of the North Library, its pages have a frozen look, and face the reader silent as any fossil in its sheath of flint. But set your mental ears to listen: the torpid shape will stir and you may hear the beating of its wings. Shouting as they run, with bundles of its sheets under their arms still damp from the press, the hawkers rush up Fleet Street in a noisy tumult towards Temple Bar. Under the over-hanging eaves the faces of its wayfarers are all in shadow, yet some are radiant and others dark. To some the news conveyed in raucous shouts brings victory, security and hope, to others peril, poverty and defeat.

Already in those days journalism was what it still is, a highly competitive industry, whose pulse beat in hasty jerks. The Leveller organ, *The Moderate*, came into being as the fruit of a professional intrigue. Because John Dillingham, the 'author' (meaning editor) of the *Moderate Intelligencer*, had quoted in proofs which he submitted to the censor a French saying which favoured short parliaments—*Dieu nous donne les Parlyaments briefe, Rois de vie longue*—Gilbert Mabbott, who held that post, not only refused to license his copy but reported him to the Lords as deserving of punishment. This was at the height of the Presbyterian reaction, in June 1648. Thereafter Mabbott made his own terms with Dillingham's printer, appropriated the title and the characteristic features of his newspaper, himself assumed the editorship and as censor stamped his *imprimatur* on its pages.[1]

By modern standards such abuse of his office would seem an incredibly dirty trick. In those less scrupulous days, licensers of the periodical press, like most officials, received no salary and lived on the fees they exacted. The customary charge for passing each sheet of a periodical was one shilling. A censor,

it seems, made in this way round about £100 p.a., a good professional income. But the editor of a successful 'news-book'
might hope to make anything up to £400 p.a. In this instance
the House of Lords disapproved of Mabbott's feat; for on
appeal it ruled that the 'author', rather than the printer, owned
the copyright of a title. Dillingham, who started life as a tailor,
accordingly went on publishing the *Moderate Intelligencer* as
before, while Mabbott christened his imitation the *Moderate*.
All that we know of Mabbott is that the Royalists described
him as a cobbler's son from Nottingham, which he denied. He
had served as junior to William Clarke the shorthand writer,
his relative by marriage, on the staff of John Rushworth, the
secretary of the Army. He received his job as censor presumably
as a 'perquisite' for good service.

Commonplace though it was in other ways, the *Moderate
Intelligencer* had a speciality. It was the only news-book of those
days which printed any foreign news: indeed, it devoted half
its space to paragraphs, usually brief, dated from cities scattered
over most of the accessible earth. The majority came from such
centres as Augsburg, Hamburg, Pilsen, Venice, Rome and
Warsaw, but sometimes a short despatch from Ceylon or
Brazil, or even from China, would figure among them. The
contents turn as a rule either on power politics or court intrigues, but occasionally one lights on some such story as that
of the luckless adventurer who undertook to fly—with mechanical wings—for the King of Poland and came to grief in the
attempt. The best performance of this newspaper was a serial
history of the Thirty Years War continued over several weeks.
At first one may be simple enough to admire the enterprise of
Mr. Dillingham, who must have had, one supposes, his
correspondents in all these remote places. The truth is less
flattering to our forefathers, who were far behind both the
French and the Dutch as pioneers in journalism. In fact he
employed a bi-lingual sub-editor, a Mr John Cotgrave, son
of the compiler of the first Anglo-French dictionary, who made
translations for him from the French press and at the same time
edited for him a miniature news-sheet of four pages in French,
Le Mercure Anglois, which summarised the English news of the
week. For the rest, Dillingham's few leading articles, obscure

and ill-written though they were, deserve notice for the humanity and good sense with which he discussed the problems of
famine and unemployment that darkened these years of
crisis.

The first five numbers of the *Moderate* are dreary and feature-
less specimens of a drab and undistinguished species. No idea
illumined its pages; it published no verses; it made no jokes.
It was in short a Puritan newspaper. In the press the two sides
lived up to the characters Ireton ascribed to them: the parliamentarian sheets were sober, all too sober, those of the Royalists
were lively and licentious. The Parliamentarians had to
submit to a preventive censorship. It was their habit to grovel
when the Lords found fault with them. The Royalists on the
other hand laughed at danger, defied the victors and worked
'underground'. Sometimes the former opened with a short
leading article of no literary pretensions: the rest was a collection of news paragraphs, flung together without headlines
or any concern for the art of display. The Royalist struck his
lyre at once with a prelude in verse, three or four quatrains of
it, printed in italics. Its quality varied greatly. Often it was
little better than doggerel composed for the sake of the malicious or bawdy suggestion in the last stanza. It is amazing how
many rhymes a royalist scribbler can find for 'whore'; the
modern reader can supply yet another; it begins with b. But
there were one or two poets among these versifiers, who even
in the hurry of going to press could dash off lines like these:

> *Thou art the glory of this ball*
> *Great Charles, so wise, so just,*
> *As if that heaven had said, 'Here's all*
> *That can be made of dust.'*
>
> *The Saints do dread thee and throw down*
> *Their cudgels for to treat,*
> *And those that would have sought thy crown*
> *Couch at thy royal feet.*

Written as the Newport negotiations opened, these verses, in
spite of their sanguine exaggeration, do express genuine
feeling.[2] In darker hours *Mercurius Melancholicus* laments in the
last week of 1648 the desecration of St Paul's, where Cromwell's

troopers stabled their horses and made bonfires of the wood-
work to keep themselves warm:

> ... *Thy arched roof*
> *Is lined with smoke and soot; the horse's hoof*
> *Beats on thy holy pavements; and we weep*
> *To think where men should watch and pray, they*
> *sleep.*

These royalist weeklies were conceived on the model of a
news-letter from a well-informed Londoner to friends in the
country. He writes in the first person and expresses a point of
view of his own in a lively, gossiping style, with none of the
solemnity of a leading article. Always his news is coloured, and
sometimes fantastically mistaken, but it is surprising how often
the abler of these journalists discover something about the
views or intentions of the leaders on the other side, which could
have been known only to their intimates. The gossip, as one
would expect in an atmosphere of civil war, is so malicious that
one need believe little or nothing of it. It may have been fun
to accuse the Saints who led the Rump of habitual lechery, but
to print the names and on occasion even the addresses of their
mistresses showed a total disregard of the decencies. When we
are told that the stolid, middle-aged matron Mrs Oliver
Cromwell is conducting an intrigue with her husband's
secretary, the only adequate comment is Queen Victoria's
characteristic phrase: 'We are not amused.'

A common stock of jokes served all the cavalier weeklies. It
was obligatory that every issue should jeer at Cromwell's red
nose ('Oh! ever refulgent nose'), at Black Tom's gout and at
Henry Marten—'a legislative Priapus'—for his defiance of
Puritan morals. The Levellers were accused of a design to
nationalise women. 'The Saints rampant' aim at 'community
in all things, their wives not excepted'. The versifiers can do
rather better, as for instance when they assail the unlucky
Duke of Hamilton:

> *How did the royal workman botch*
> *This Duke, half English and half Scotch . . .*
> *'Twas he patched up the new divine*
> *Part Calvin and part Catiline.*

The snobbery of these royalist gentlemen pervades every number. They delight in describing Cromwell as 'the brewer of Ely', and commonly refer to the General Council of officers as 'the mechanics' council'. Each side had its official astrologer, but all their predictions went wrong. 'The heavens' did not 'combine to relieve our distressed sovereign', as Wharton predicted they would; nor was the parliamentarian Lilly's warning justified that Cromwell would be killed in Ireland. It is pleasant to put it on record that when Wharton got caught and was in danger of the gallows, Lilly used his influence to obtain for his fellow watcher of the stars his pardon and release.

Evidently the lively royalist weeklies were in great demand, for they sold for 2d., while the sober parliamentarian newsbooks fetched only 1d., though even at the latter price they were not cheap, at a time when a modest dinner in a tavern might cost no more than 3d. Some of the royalist journalists were mercenaries, like the notorious Marchamont Nedham, one of the editors of *Mercurius Pragmaticus*, who turned his coat twice. But others—Sir George Wharton, John Cleveland, Samuel Sheppard and the ballad-writer Martin Parker—must have felt a genuine devotion to the King's cause, for if they failed to dodge the Parliament's 'beagles' who hunted their secret presses incessantly in the slums of 'Alsatia', they had to face its noisome prisons and the risk, if they were caught too often, of the noose at Tyburn. Even the women who sold their Mercuries were liable to a whipping. Wharton's *Mercurius Elencticus* was from a literary standpoint the best of the royalist weeklies, and it carried on its controversies with marked ability. *Mercurius Pragmaticus* seems to have been the most popular of them.

There is no reason to suppose that Mabbott when he founded the *Moderate* had anything more in mind than a commercial speculation. Evidently it did not prosper, for by his third number (18 July, 1648) he found it necessary to economise. He cut down the twelve pages with which he started to eight, printed on paper of miserable quality. The mails went out from London twice a week. To prevent competition with the *Moderate Intelligencer* the Lords had ordered him to change his day of publication to Tuesday. Week by week his foreign news dwindled and finally vanished. At last in the issue of 8 August,

1648, one senses that a new hand has grasped the editorial pen.
His style is livelier. He recounts picturesque anecdotes from the
daily life of the City, to show how royalist it has become. There
is a militancy in his tone. He dares to publish intercepted
letters which reveal the intrigues of City and Lords against the
Commons. He comments freely, as if he were writing a leading
article, upon Major Huntingdon's impeachment of Cromwell.
Most significant of all, he quotes John Lilburne's saying: 'A
coward lies upon advantage.'

What had happened? In the previous week John was released from the Tower and resumed his political activity. It is
a plausible guess that he may have helped Mabbott to find
some additional capital for the embarrassed *Moderate* and
suggested what it needed even more than capital, a new
editorial writer.[3] However that may be, it became each week
a little bolder than before. On 5 September we are told that
threats have been uttered to suppress it, because it alone dares
to expose designs about which all other 'weekly pens' are
silent. It boasts that it alone writes to undeceive the kingdom
and not for particular advantage as all other writers do. There
follows a leader on the folly of concluding a personal treaty
with a King addicted to duplicity and perfidy. The writer is
obviously echoing the preamble to the Levellers' 'Large Petition' of 11 September, of which he must have had an advance
copy in front of him. The next issue (12 September) devoted
more than half its space to a *verbatim* reprint of that lengthy
petition. At this stage, if not earlier, the *Moderate* was avowedly
the organ of the Leveller party. The clever, ironical leader
of this same issue jested in a fashion that was a novelty in the
Parliamentary press. Colonel Poyer, it tells us, the defender of
Pembroke and its stubborn fortress, 'swore by his god Bacchus'.

Whose then was the new pen that transformed the dull
pages of the early *Moderate*? The leader in the next issue may
help us to guess. Though it ran to an inordinate length,
(3,300 words, more than two pages of a modern weekly of the
New Statesman's format) there is not a dull line in it, and in spite
of the small type and yellow paper one is still carried away by
it today. It opens with a brilliant ironical attack on the proposed treaty, as deadly for the King as for the Presbyterians.

Then, lest we should grow tired of his reasoning, the writer breaks off and gives us a discussion among some of the Army's royalist prisoners. Each speaks in character, the timid Duke of Hamilton and the reckless Goring (the father of the more famous general of the West). To Hamilton, who fears punishment for his invasion, Goring replies: 'Fear not that, my Lord, for most of the members in both Houses and the chiefest men in the City are as deeply engaged herein as any of us.' This unique leading article follows up the dialogue with some polished mockery over the victories won by so few over so many. It ends abruptly with the phrase: 'But to intelligence. . . .' Then comes the news of the week.

There was one man among the Leveller pamphleteers who certainly could have turned his pen to journalism and done it brilliantly. Richard Overton may have been a frequent contributor to the *Moderate* and may even have brought out some numbers of it.[4] There is no doubt, however, that Mabbott remained the responsible editor, but judging from the early numbers he cannot have been much of a writer, and may have employed several helpers in the course of the paper's brief existence. The news-books of those days were of very modest dimensions, eight or twelve octavo pages, which resembled a thin pamphlet rather than a modern newspaper. One man in a week, even if he spent some time in gathering or verifying news, could write and sub-edit the whole production with ease, and enjoy his full share of leisure as well.

During the last quarter of 1648 the 'authors' of the *Moderate* evidently felt that there was only one subject to discuss. Week after week they are preparing their readers' minds for the trial of the King. At the same time, by frequent exposures of the venality of M.P.s and the greed of lawyers, they are clearing the way for the forcible dissolution of the Long Parliament by the Army, or else for a large-scale purge. There is nothing original in these articles, but most of them are competent, argumentative essays justifying the party's line. The order of the day was unity and there is no hint of any difference of outlook between Levellers and Independents. In one issue Cromwell is referred to as 'Old Noll', the affectionate nickname of his troopers.

There is nothing uncompromising in the *Moderate's* republicanism. 'For any monarch or prince', it wrote on 28 November, 'to claim the crown by succession, or propinquity, or priority of blood, is against the law of God, nature or reason.' This leaves the door open to elective, constitutional monarchy. In the next two numbers it argues in general terms, with precedents both from sacred and secular history, that kings may be deposed for misgovernment, and that the next heir to the crown may be passed over in the order of succession. Evidently it was thinking, like some of the Army's Grandees, of the Duke of York or the Duke of Gloucester as the next king, though it did not mention their names. Tuesday, 30 January, 1649, was the last day Charles Stuart spent on earth. It was also the day of the *Moderate's* publication for on that morning, as usual, the mails went out to the provinces. It printed a grave, brief leader, in effect a sermon on the theme: God and the law are no respecters of persons. Did it publish next week its account of what happened in Whitehall? We do not know, for it so happens that this number of the *Moderate*, and this number only, is missing from Thomason's collection.

The policy of a newspaper is disclosed as much by what it omits as by what it includes. It is a remarkable fact that during the weeks when the Agreement of the People and the difficult issue of toleration were under discussion in the Whitehall Debates, the *Moderate* published no account of these proceedings. It is possible that secrecy was enjoined on the large number of persons present, but leakage there was, for some brief and scrappy reports appeared in the royalist press. Mr Mabbott's readers would assuredly have valued reliable reports. For a time, while negotiations were going on, silence may have been praiseworthy, but only for a time. It may be significant that the *Moderate* never discussed toleration in a leading article, and never on this issue sided with the Levellers against Ireton and Cromwell.

Thanks, doubtless, to its leading articles (the best in the parliamentary press) and still more (it may be) to the growth of the Leveller party, the *Moderate* must have thrived. In the issue of 21 November it appeared once more with twelve pages, of which five were devoted to foreign news. Henceforward the number of pages was never reduced; it even rose on one occasion to sixteen. The foreign news, drawn apparently from the same French sources, filled more often four pages than five. Evidently the pressure on space was severe, for the unpleasantly small type was retained. While most of the home news revolved round Westminster, the paper had its correspondents in Chester, Derby, York, Bristol and other provincial centres. There were Leveller groups in most of these places; that of Newcastle-on-Tyne was particularly vocal. Often these local reports are painful accounts of the dearth that came near to famine.

Two other newspapers favoured the Leveller cause for a time, the *Perfect Occurrences* of Henry Walker and the *Mercurius Militaris* of John Harris. Walker's publication, which ran from the beginning of 1647 to the destruction of the free press in the autumn of 1649, was for domestic happenings by far the best newspaper of its day. It printed no foreign news, and its leaders were few, brief and pedestrian. Printed on a slightly larger sheet, it had therefore more space than its rivals for the home news, which it arranged with competence. One may infer that it had a big circulation from the fact that its 'author' had a house in the fashionable King Street. It was generally regarded as a Leveller organ, as *Walwyn's Wiles* tells us, until it broke with Lilburne towards the end of 1648. Thereafter Walker, an ordained minister who made a great display of his knowledge of Hebrew, stuck closely to Cromwell, who rewarded him with three Independent chapels in succession. He ratted with indecent enthusiasm at the Restoration.

To this dull but efficient newspaper the *Mercurius Militaris or the Army's Scout* formed a sharp contrast. Its author was no Saint. John Harris (or Harries), an actor turned printer, was the craftsman on whom the Agitators relied, during the revolt of 1647, when their 'able penmen' got to work with their fly-sheets, tracts and petitions. Thereafter he was for a time the Army's official printer, who marched with his press in the wake of Headquarters. He evidently had the spirited purpose of producing an uncensored Leveller newspaper. If ever he applied for a licence, he never got it. Mabbott would not welcome a rival to the *Moderate* which came out on the same day, Tuesday. Harris's *Mercury* followed the royalist pattern and even started with verses, most of them pretty bad. He wrote well in a lively, popular style. His leaders, if one reads with one's ears, often drop into blank verse, and embody in the texture of their prose Shakespearian fragments. He prints his news from Scotland in broad Scots, laughs at the pretensions of the Kirk, and writes in a tone of jocular sympathy about 'poor Jocky and Jimmee' the Army's prisoners.

His news includes several items reporting with approval acts of independence, not to say indiscipline, in several regiments of horse. Starting on Tuesday, 10 October, he laughs in an amusing, ironical style not only at the proposed Treaty of Newport but at the institution of monarchy itself. In his second number, to which Edward Sexby may have been a contributor, he warns 'Noll' against the designs of Argyll, and seems to be writing as his partisan against Fairfax, who is supposed to be keeping him out of the way at the sieges of Pontefract and Scarborough. He makes a savage attack on 'that sneaking sycophant Staines, who now makes a monopoly of the General's favour'. Quartermaster-General Staines was also one of Lilburne's numerous bugbears.

One can often, in reading over the few numbers of this *Mercury* which Harris was allowed to print, catch the authentic tone of voice in which the Agitators would address the men of the New Model. Here are the *clichés*, the epigrams, the jokes which formed the common stock of their speeches. 'The children of kings are all born with crowns upon their heads and the people with saddles on their backs.' Kings were anointed by God; who ever saw it done? or again, Why 'pay any kind of tax to His Majesty? What work of the people doth he for his wages?' Or this on the King's responsibility for the civil wars: 'Is it reason that a poor man shall be hanged for stealing 14*d.*, and that a great man shall confess he sent his compeers to break houses, plunder and murder . . . and yet not so much as some reparation to be given them [the suffering people] out of his lands?' The Norman Conquest is another of Harris's favourite themes. He was, as it turned out, in the right when he criticised (31 October) the General's order to disband all above 80 in every troop and company. 'Your peevish officers,' he predicted, 'will disband and enlist until their whole troops are their slaves'

—which was what happened, albeit gradually, from 1649 onwards.

These young men had their heroes; Rainsborough was one of them, John Lilburne the other. *Mercurius Militaris* of 8 November tells the story of Rainsborough's end and eulogises his 'transcendant gallantry for his country's freedom'. Some of its verses on him may help us to understand the impression he made on his fellow-soldiers.

> *. . . Who shall henceforth stand*
> *A pure example to inform the land*
> *Of her true freedom? Who shall counter-check*
> *The wanton pride of greatness, and direct*
> *The soldiers in the true magnifick way?*

More than ever, after this event, the Army was out for revenge, and Harris's newspaper asks why the King should not be tried for murder and felony. 'Does any statute exempt him? Is he above the law?'

To the legend of 'honest Jack Lilburne' the *Mercurius Militaris* of 21 November added a popular story, which had the merit of being true, to illustrate his moral (and technical) superiority over those caterpillars the lawyers. A 'company of honest lads of Wiltshire' were like to be baffled by a priest's audacious counsel in appearing before the Committee of Plundered Ministers. John quixotically offered to plead for them for 'any small piece of silver as fee'. William Prynne, however, objected, because John had never been called to the bar. In reply he was able to quote a statute of Edward I, which recognised 'every man's right to say what he can for himself or to choose whom he please to speak for him'. He won his case, defeated Prynne and broke the monopoly of the lawyers. From his clients for five days' work he took a fee of 8*d*.[5] This was the last number of his *Mercury* which Harris managed to print. The 'beagles', he tells us, who had already prevented the appearance of his previous number, were determined to hunt him down.

Lack of space and the cost of paper were the chief problems with which these pioneer journalists had to contend. Luckily for them their public did not expect them to serve up news of sport. Horse-racing still went on—indeed, it was forbidden, for reasons of policy, only under the Major-Generals in the grimmest phase of the Protectorate. The Thames water-men had their boat-races. The lead-miners of Derbyshire would strip to the skin and race naked, like Greek athletes, before big crowds. The famous Cornish wrestlers would on occasion even give a display of their skill in St James's Fields. But these were local events in a little England which still thought of the hundred, or at most the county, as the units of its social life.

We can trace in the *Moderate* the first step towards reviewing. It would sometimes print as an item of the week's news the title, author's and bookseller's names of some new book or pamphlet which had just appeared, followed by a word or two of recommendation. Occasionally one comes across a notice of the loss of something of value, usually a horse, for which a reward is offered. It is possible that Mabbott, a keen man of business, made a charge for his rudimentary book-reviews. One may feel reasonably sure that the notices of lost property were paid for. Here, then, were the barely perceptible beginnings of advertising, the source of revenue which eventually solved the newspaper's problems of finance. Another technical invention of the *Moderate's* happily died with it. It took to mixing editorial comments with the substance of its news, distinguishing the one from the other by printing the comment at first within square brackets and latterly in italics. This was not a device that made for objective reporting, but it did lend itself admirably to propaganda, for these comments were terse, pointed and occasionally witty. This cramped and undistinguished little paper with its small type never managed to look attractive, but it did contrive to be readable. How the *Moderate* faced the long crisis that followed the King's death and how it ended shall be described in a later chapter (pp. 569-71 below).

Turning Thomason's pages, a reader with an antiquarian eye will notice the development of yet another technical innovation. In September 1648 at the bottom of the last page of one of the *Moderate's* parliamentarian rivals, the *Kingdom's Weekly Intelligencer*, there appeared in rather large italics a summary of three lines in which one could take in at a glance the contents of the paper, or in other words the week's news. Headlines these news-books had none; an octavo page does not lend itself readily to the art of display. But here were footlines, so to speak. Eight months later it occurred to the author of yet another parliamentarian weekly, the *Mercurius Brittanicus* (*sic*), to imitate this device. He too condensed the outstanding items of the week's news into three lines of rather bold italics. But he placed them under his title and date-line at the top of his first page. In miniature he had made the first modern newspaper. As time went on the italics were discarded in favour of something blacker and more arresting. But that lay still in the future. No journalist of the Interregnum felt the need to shout or gesticulate in that way.

Shorthand was just coming into use and it became a favourite sport to take down the speeches of one's opponents *verbatim*. A Royalist composed a rollicking sermon for the Rev. Hugh Peters, the Army chaplain. But the favourite butt was Philip, the fourth Earl of Pembroke. As a comely youth he was one of the favourites of James I, who poured offices and lands upon him. With £30,000 a year, he may have been the richest man in England. He knew all about horses and dogs, packed an oath into every other sentence and boasted of his ignorance in politics. Listen to his last speech in the doomed House of Lords:

> My Lords, damme, I mistake your titles. I may call you as well spades, down-diddles or anything. For down you must, that's flat, levelled, all fellows now. By God, 'tis but just with us if the Army would pull down our breeches and whip us. We have sat seven years to pull down the King (with a pox) and now we must be pulled down ourselves by a pocky General (Army, I should say). . . . Damme, our soldiers are now our kings, dukes, lords, preachers, nay and cash-keepers too. 'Zblood, we are like to have a thorough reformation indeed. . . . I thank God I am neither soldier nor scholar, but an upright Commonwealth's man. 'Tis confessed I have been a Privy Councillor, but damme, I scorn to be an evil councillor though I have unjustly given sentence in the Star Chamber. . . . Evil be to them that evil think, and I thank God I can justify my innocence by my ignorance. . . . Damme, you ought to submit when you cannot otherwise help it, and if you will still remain obstinate, then take what follows. . . . Sirs, I am never

tedious in my impressions, and therefore include my speech, and desire you seriously to consider the scope and syrup of what I have said.

Mrs Malaprop could hardly have bettered this oration.

It is for the raw materials of human history that one goes to these old news-books. But the natural historian also may have something to learn from them. In the spring that followed the King's death, the *Moderate Intelligencer* reported that the keeper of one of the late King's parks in Sussex, while walking his rounds with a gun,

> espied a stork, which he knew not to be so. The stork did not seem to shun him, but came up towards him, which made him think it was a devil. Presently, he shot and killed it, and thereupon saw four or five more. Since which unkind usage, they all fled and were never seen since. It is preserved and may be seen at Lewes in Sussex. 'Tis said in history that these birds never come but into republics, as in Holland. The same man killed an eagle in the same park two years since.

So that is why we have no storks in England. One curses that keeper, but it is only fair to remember that we should have lost the storks in any event at the Restoration.

NOTES TO CHAPTER XX

1. For some of the facts about Mabbott and Dillingham I am indebted to a book indispensable for the study of this period—*A History of English Journalism to the foundation of the* GAZETTE by J. B. Muddiman (*né* Williams), 1908. He gives the necessary references (pp. 104-5). To his research we owe most of the little that is known about the anonymous journalists of this period. The opinions expressed in this chapter about the various newspapers and the guesses about writers are however mine and not his, and the quotations are of my gathering. Mr Muddiman's book must be used with caution, for his bias is strongly royalist. He reached some surprising opinions, e.g. (p. 141n.) that Lady Fairfax was an Anabaptist, and he inclined to accept as truthful any statement, however malicious, by Cavaliers about their opponents.

2. *Mercurius Elencticus* (4 October, 1648).

3. There is another possibility—that the *Moderate* was financed from the funds of the Independents. This suggestion comes from Clement Walker (as untrustworthy as he was well informed) who wrote that it had 'a large share in the £500 or £600 a year allowed to these pamphleteers

for divulging state-lies and slanders amongst the people' (*History of Independency*, Part II, p. 24.) If true, this statement would not rule out some influence by Lilburne, since he was, round about this time, on very friendly terms with Cornelius Holland, perhaps the most active of the Independent M.Ps. With Holland and his family Mabbott claimed a life-long acquaintance (*The Moderate*, 26 September–3 October, 1648).

4. Walwyn in a mood of high spirits might conceivably have written some of the later articles in the same vein, which are inferior and cheaper stuff. The well-to-do Walwyn might possibly have written an occasional contribution to help the party organ, but he would not have done the work of a sub-editor, which the impecunious Overton, a printer by trade, may well have undertaken for a time. The device of introducing comments, distinguished by square brackets or italics, into the news looks to me like an invention of his. The difficulty in attributing to Overton any considerable share in producing the *Moderate* is that someone of like calibre, at his best a brilliant writer who showed great ingenuity in dodging the censor, was at work upon it while Overton was in the Tower. Stone walls could never defeat the Levellers. Newspapers have been edited from prison as late as the nineteenth century. This was supposed to be a particularly rigorous confinement. But if these prisoners could smuggle out tracts and manifestoes, as they did, then why not newspaper copy? The difficulty would be to get it to the printer punctually. It is, however, possible that a third hand was called in; if so, he was a very clever journalist. I think I detect yet another editorial hand round about 21 November, 1648, when the publication was resumed of foreign news, translated presumably by John Cotgrave. Two or three leaders reveal a familiarity with French history and contemporary French controversies, e.g. 19 December and 26 December, 1648, 2 January and 26 June, 1649. I venture the guess, then, that we can distinguish four hands in the pages of the *Moderate*: (1) Mabbott or a hack substitute in the first five numbers, (2) Overton, (3) Cotgrave, (4) the brilliant unknown of the last months. Can he have been John Harris?

5. See also the *Moderate* of 14 November.

CHAPTER XXI

The Levellers and the Land

A familiar passage from the speech with which Oliver Cromwell opened the first Parliament of the Protectorate explains why he crushed the Levellers.

> What was the face that was upon our affairs as to the interest of the nation, to the authority in the nation, to the magistracy, to the ranks and orders of men, whereby England hath been known for hundreds of years? A nobleman, a gentleman, a yeoman—that is a good interest of the nation and a great one. The magistracy of the nation, was it not almost trampled under foot, under despite and contempt by men of levelling principles? I beseech you, for the orders of men and ranks of men, did not that levelling principle tend to the reducing all to an equality? . . . What was the design but to make the tenant as liberal a fortune as the landlord? Which I think, if obtained, would not have lasted long. . . . That this thing did extend far is manifest, because it was a pleasing voice to all poor men and truly not unwelcome to all bad men.[1]

Clumsy though its phrasing is, the meaning of this passage is clear. It reveals the Lord Protector as the conservative dictator, who has brought the Revolution to a standstill and rescued England from radicals bent on upsetting the venerable social pyramid, 'the ranks and orders of men', which had endured for centuries. This, with its three strata, nobility, squirearchy and yeomanry, the Levellers threatened with their anarchical principle of equality. Their aim was, in concrete terms, to raise the tenant's 'fortune'—or did Oliver really mean 'status'?— to a level with the squire's.

This reading of the Levellers' 'design' is a simplification as unexpected as it is revealing. Casting our minds back over their 'remonstrances' and petitions, if we were asked to name their central purposes, we might single out unlimited toleration, democracy in its most generous scope including the effective sovereignty of the people, the election of all officers and magistrates, the decentralisation and simplification of the law together with the end of tithes, the press gang, and imprisonment for debt. But about agrarian questions the party as yet had said very little. Cromwell, however, was not the only one of its opponents who believed that it was courting popularity by promising the redress of the peasants' grievances. There were Royalists and Presbyterians who shared that impression. Assuredly, if ever it had won power, the most fateful question it would have had to face would have been the emancipation of the copyhold tenants. Until their status was so secure that they would dare to vote against the squire, democracy had no future in our island. What is equally clear, the party stood no chance of enlisting the active support of the copyholders and tenants at will. In the green England of those days they formed a big majority of the population. To Cromwell, though they strung up his carcase at Tyburn, the squires owed their survival as the ruling class for two centuries to come.[2]

Throughout the formative twenty years that lay between the meeting of the Long Parliament and the Restoration, Englishmen debated, often with subtlety and eloquence, a great range of subjects, theological and political. But the ownership of land was not widely discussed until the last years of the Protectorate, when all the intellectuals fell to debating the economic interpretation of history which Harrington put forward in *Oceana*. In this matter the Saints acted with a minimum of talk. Amid this silence a change in the ownership of property was carried through on a scale and at a pace to which there is only one parallel in our history—the secularisation of the monastic lands a century earlier. The records are incomplete, but it is known that the estates of 1,677 Royalists were confiscated outright, while in many hundreds of cases they were sold or alienated in whole or part, when the owners were allowed to 'compound' for their malignancy. A crew of speculators dealt in these estates: one man alone disposed of twenty-three manors, another of thirteen and a third of twelve.[3]

This shift in the ownership of English land during the Civil War came as the catastrophic climax to a slow process of evolution which had been going on for a century. Like every other class in the England of Tudors and Stuarts the aristocracy and the gentry had to adapt itself to the slow process of inflation which began early in the sixteenth century and came to a stop shortly before the Long Parliament met. During these hundred years prices rose more than threefold. In the first phase of this process the tenants throve, for their rents stood still while the yield of their produce soared. Their landlords were forbidden to raise rents or fines, save at fixed intervals of years, as tenancies expired. Even then, some of the more decent of them, reared in another tradition, hesitated to adopt a commercial code of behaviour. Nor for reasons of prestige was it easy for them to economise. Fashion prescribed a certain 'port' for a gentleman. Lavish display was expected of him; he must be served by crowds of attendants and escorted by platoons of retainers. He must keep open house for all his neighbours, great and small, and provide in his stables for a whole troop of cavalry. The court, if he had entry to it, imposed lavish expenditure upon him, and he had often to maintain a town house. He might by bribery or favour get a job, or he might marry money in the City; but failing these expedients, he was apt to run into debt and the next stage was the sale of his lands in whole or part.

Steadily during these three generations the old-world gentry, who would not or could not adapt themselves to the new commercial epoch, were eliminated. Thus we learn that nearly two-thirds of the gentry who owned land in 1620 in Bedfordshire had sold it and left the county by 1668, or again that half the estates in Staffordshire changed hands in sixty years.[4] The new men who came in were usually merchants or lawyers, for the law was at this time the surest way of getting rich quickly. The gentry who did survive, and the newcomers who bought their way into the squirearchy, had their choice of several ways by which to turn their land into a secure invest-ment. They might themselves on their home-farm raise grain, wool or livestock for the market or exploit the timber of their estate and the minerals, if any there were, of its subsoil. More often, after evicting customary tenants and buying out small freeholders, they let the land so won in big units on lease. Leasehold rents, according to Thorold Rogers, rose sixfold in half a century. Only too often the new techniques involved the kind of enclosure that led to depopulation.

Swiftly or gradually, this change was destined to break up the common fields. The process of enclosure was continuous, and spread over four centuries. It first attracted the hostile notice of Parliament towards the end of the fifteenth century, and it was still proceeding on a considerable scale in the early decades of the nineteenth. But it went so slowly that in 1685, on the eve of the Whig Revolution, it was estimated that three-fifths of England was still 'champion' and unenclosed.[5] The decisive rôle of cavalry in the Civil War becomes intelligible only when we realise that most of its battles were fought over waste land and open fields.

It was my good fortune, during the second world war, to see the last English village that still retains its open fields. Laxton in Nottinghamshire is ten miles due north of Newark, where the Scots had their headquarters at the close of the first Civil War. Earlier forms of the name Laxton—Lessington and Lexington —remind us that the 'town' of the Lessings must have sent its settlers to New England. The village lies in rolling country amid what is left of Sherwood Forest, with its glades of mingled oak and birch. Its centre is a graceful Gothic church, which records the styles and tastes of several centuries; under a mound outside it are the ruins of a Norman keep. Its peasant farmers still cultivate the soil much as their forefathers did, who first made a clearing in the woodlands. The village, in which the barns, stables and homesteads are all clustered together, with the traditional pound for stray cattle, wears an unmistakable air of prosperity and the sturdy plough-horses convey the same impression.

All Laxton's arable land lies in three big 'open fields'. The

arable total shrank from 800 to 500 acres during the re-
organisation of the manor carried out in 1904, but this is the
only significant change since the illuminated survey, with its
handsome baroque ornamentation and its amusing sketches of
daily life in the fields, was made in 1635 for the merchant-
prince, Sir William Courteen of the City of London, who bought
the manor from the Buckingham estates.[6] Not a hedge nor a
fence breaks the continuity of their surface. Almost invisibly
they are divided into long, narrow, parallel 'lands', several
yards wide. A furrow ploughed deep to serve as drainage for
the heavy soil is the only boundary between one 'land' and the
next. Two or more 'lands' make up a 'strip'. This is each man's
share and is repeated in each of the three great fields. A stake
at either end is the only landmark needed. A ploughman
laughed when I wondered how he could recognise his own,
where all looked alike. He had helped to till these fields from
boyhood. Since the consolidation of the strips arranged half a
century back, it is now possible to use some machinery. But the
older farmers still scatter the seed broadcast, and everyone
ploughs with horses.

The essence of the 'open fields' system is that each man must
follow a recognised routine of cultivation, sowing and reaping
the same crops on the same date. After the harvests of hay and
corn, the pastures and stubble fields are thrown open to be
grazed by every villager's beasts. True to the traditional rotation, one field of the three lies fallow for a year. Of the others,
one grows the main crop, winter wheat. The second, known at
Laxton as 'the beanfield', may grow spring corn, peas, beans,
vetches, and clover. The rotation could be varied and new
crops introduced only after the tenants, meeting in the manor
court, had sanctioned the change by a favourable vote.

The strip system of cultivation had its origin in the distant
century when the great wooden plough, an enormously weighty
instrument, first reached our shores. So unwieldy was it that on
heavy soil eight of the little oxen of those days were required to
draw it. The poor villeins, each of whom might own perhaps
one, perhaps two of these beasts, could till the soil only if they
formed a co-operative group which pooled its resources and
worked as a team. It might be able to plough as much as an

acre in a hard day's work if the soil were light; this area, which
might measure as much as 220 yards in length by 22 in breadth
went to the first man of the team. To the second went the next
'land', and so on, until they started again. The longer the strip
the less often would they have to face the troublesome business
of turning the plough.

The first of the open fields I came across was the West Field,
measuring 200 acres, which that year lay fallow. It was far from
flat, nor did its strips form a regular pattern. One thought of the
gay patchwork quilts which our grandmothers used to make
from fragments of silk of every conceivable shape and colour.
The 'patches' in the great field were adapted to the contour
and slope of the undulating ground so that, for the purpose of
drainage, their furrows should always point downwards. Here
and there among the ploughed patches were stretches of grass-
land, some triangular, others more or less straight. The latter
were grass roads which gave the farmer access to his strips.
Others of irregular shape were left unploughed where the
patches met at an awkward angle. Even these had their use;
sheep were grazing on them. The open fields were never
planned, they evolved as the needs and nature of the plough
dictated, to feed a growing population. No better system could
have been devised by peasants who farmed without modern
machines to raise food for their own families.

As I walked across to the 'beanfield', with its various crops
of every colour in nature and its idle windmill against the
skyline on the ridge, my memory went on its travels. I recalled
talks in India with old men in the Pathan borderland, and in
central Russia with peasants round Vladimir, who were familiar
in their younger days with the village community of the one
and the *mir* of the other. In both there was to the last a lively
sense of community and fellowship, which sprang from the
collective ownership of the open fields. These were redistributed
every few years, so that all should share by turns the more
fertile and the poorer strips. That practice survived down
to quite recent times in Scotland, but not, so far as is known,
in England. If we may trust such authoritative interpreters as
Vinogradoff, the feudal organisation of the manor, derived as it
was from the late Roman Empire, overlaid but never quite

obliterated the communal structure of primitive Teutonic society. It was a closely knit group, which only occasionally admitted strangers as squatters and labourers. It protected the customary rights of its members against encroachment. In some cases it would even help them in times of need with loans of money or cattle. In return, it exacted punctual obedience to its traditional rules of good husbandry. Steadily, to be sure, through the centuries, economic pressure reinforced by the law courts was at work to turn the feudal lord of the manor into a commercial landowner. But even he was bound by immemorial custom—until he enclosed.

The Levellers were not inventing out of nothing when they published their schemes for creating (or as they said 'restoring') an advanced democracy, operating through elected officers in every hundred or county. They had only to look around them to discover in every still vital manor an organisation of this kind on a smaller scale. Such a functional democracy survives at Laxton to this day. The pompous names of court leet and court baron should not disguise from us the fact that these manorial courts were primarily meetings of all the tenants, who elected from among themselves the various officers of the year, though the lord or his steward presided over them. The duty of these officers and the twelve jurymen was to see that the manor's many rules of good husbandry and neighbourly conduct were obeyed, and to punish, by a fine, those who transgressed them. Each man must do his part in cleaning the ditches into which his furrows drained; he must not exceed the number of animals he might pasture on the common; he must cut down any thistles on the waste land before they seeded. It appears from the Laxton records that the jury even ventured to fine the lord of the manor himself for the breach of some such rule. These records were kept (by the steward) during the Interregnum *in English*; from 1660 to 1732 they reverted to Latin. It is worth noting that during three centuries very few of these jurymen were illiterate. This jury could investigate and punish any cases of violent disorderly behaviour that disturbed the village or its fields, and it could attack the property of debtors. When historians tell us that the peasantry in the seventeenth century was not fit for the democracy the Levellers advocated, they forget that in countless villages it had learned for many a generation to govern itself.

The lord of the manor might rank in law as the owner of the waste lands round the village, but for the peasants these were a common in which each had his rights of pasturage. Custom prescribed the number of beasts, from cows to geese, which everyone might graze upon it. In the woodlands attached to the manor, though the timber was the lord's to fell and sell, the peasants had the right to gather firewood and pasture their swine. Meadows were situated for choice, like the 130 acres at Laxton, beside a stream which flooded them in winter. These were allocated in sections, known as 'doles', to the tenants for mowing.

Round Laxton one could see at a glance the whole historical problem of the waste lands. Nature was the only husbandman they had known, since first the forest was cleared. Until a few months before my visit, a sparse growth of poor grass covered them, varied here and there by clumps of bramble and whin. Even in this uncultivated state these 88 acres of 'waste' had a far from negligible value as rough pasture. But during the emergency of war-time the county authority stepped in, ripped up the turf of a score or more of acres, and ploughed in the accumulated fertility of a millennium. Out of this virgin soil there sprang as noble a crop of wheat as one could wish to see.

Stimulated by this happy sight my mind went back to the years of civil war in the seventeenth century. The sparse population of those days endured six years of near famine, while all around it in every manor there lay great stretches of barely utilised land, which could have produced under the plough for man and beast many times the value of the food they furnished under the traditional pattern of agriculture. Awakening, round about this time, to the exciting possibilities of this problem, men reckoned that one-third of the cultivable area of England lay in such waste lands. Under their turf was buried the key to the social and economic future of England for two centuries to come. Who would find the capital and the labour, animal and human, for this immense operation? Who would develop—and, it may be, appropriate—the latent riches of these acres? Not Cromwell's legions, nor Monk's, nor even Dutch William's were as decisive a force in shaping the class structure of our island as the landlords and their lawyers who enclosed these commons. There were, as we shall see, a few far-sighted men, both Levellers and Diggers, who perceived that the operation might be organised by collective effort for the common good. In fact the thing was done by capitalist enterprise, roughly, and with a minimum of concern for the peasants, whom it degraded to the level of a landless proletariat.

After this digression let us return to Laxton. Even there the defects of the open-field system were obvious enough. The fallow like the waste was an uneconomic device. Because there were no fenced fields, it was not easy to arrange the breeding of livestock from better strains. The pace of improvement was slow, since the more enterprising peasants had to drag their conservative neighbours after them before an innovation could be adopted. If a farmer's aim was to produce, not what his family needed, but what he could market at a profit, then 'severalty' and individual management would suit him better. Undoubtedly, when open fields were broken up and enclosed, the land produced more wealth, measured in terms of cash. Whether the process of enclosure brought an equal gain in happiness and self-respect to the rural population is a question on which economic science can throw no light. The ploughmen with whom I talked at Laxton were proud that they alone in all England had been strong enough to preserve their ancient peasant way of life. Nothing, they assured me, would induce them to abandon it.

At Laxton I had seen at their best the open fields and the 'communitive happiness' (to use a phrase of Walwyn's) that went with them. But as I left its busy acres with regret, I had to remind myself that its case was unique. In defiance of all the rules of probability, during the fifteen generations that passed between Bosworth Field and the occupation of Berlin, it never happened that any lord of Laxton was driven by debt or tempted by gain to run the manor on commercial principles. Not one of them tried to infringe the customary rights of his tenants: not one of them tried to appropriate the common or enclose the open fields. Sooner or later everywhere else the motive of gain prevailed, and rode roughshod over the fragile customs that were the peasant's sole defence.

There are moments in the long process of enclosure which mark the opening of a new chapter. Up to the reign of the first Charles the crown sought by legislation and penalties to arrest it, and did in some degree lessen the pace. From the middle of the eighteenth century Parliament actively promoted it by enclosure acts. The turning point can be precisely dated. It fell in 1656, under the Protectorate, when for the first time Parliament threw out a bill which proposed to check enclosure.

The change in the attitude of the governing class to enclosure must have taken place in the generation that preceded the Civil War. The new Dutch technique in farming hastened it on. This mercantile age found the argument from profit conclusive, and beyond a doubt enclosure was profitable—to the owners. King Charles, indeed, during his eleven years of autocratic rule, did something by administrative severity to check it, and Laud earned the hostility of the gentry, for as Clarendon said of him, 'he did a little too much countenance the Commission for Depopulation'. How far this policy was dictated by a concern for the peasantry is, however, doubtful; the royal family did a good deal of enclosing on its own lands, while the fines imposed on enclosing landlords (who did not restore the common fields they had taken) were a far from negligible source of revenue.

The shift in opinion occurred only in the upper strata of English society. Down below, in the villages, among the peasants, nothing was changed, nor did the countryman lose his attachment to his common fields for two centuries to come. He felt during the Civil War what his grandfather had felt when he defended them under Ket's leadership against Warwick's foreign mercenaries on Mousehold Heath. Indifferent, for the most part, to the issues for which gentry and tradesmen fought at Edgehill and Marston Moor, peasants were still ready to take a risk to tear down fences. There was no national movement; no leader emerged who could make his voice heard beyond his parish; as usual these unlettered men left no articulate record behind them. Yet in district after district, throughout the years of struggle and Civil War, the villagers rose to

break down the enclosures and win back their common fields.
The *Journals* of both Houses are full of records of these riots
during the years from 1640 to 1644. They started on the royal
estates in Cornwall and thereafter few counties were immune.
Three or four hundred rioters are mentioned in one case, and
in another one hundred and fifty who had arms. Usually the
train-bands could deal with them, but occasionally the Parliament's troops had to be called in.[7]

It requires no difficult exercise of the imagination to guess
what was in the minds of those men. They rebelled, as their
fathers or their sons would have rebelled, to recover their
common fields at any moment throughout this period of
centuries, because they supposed that the family feud among the
gentry had given them their chance—which, indeed, was what
the men actually said who broke down the Earl of Suffolk's
fences in Essex in April 1643, 'alleging that if they took not
advantage of the time they shall never have the opportunity
again'. Ten years later, under the Saints' Parliament, Cromwell's Council gave orders for the suppression of the countrymen in Staffordshire who had pulled up the fences of enclosures
and returned the land to the common fields.[8] In England there
simmered a perpetual peasants' war, latent and undeclared.

It is evident that the widespread change in the ownership
of manors hastened in some degree the process of enclosure
and altered the condition of the customary tenants for the
worse. Parliament acted for a time through commissioners, as
lord of the manor of the confiscated estates, until they found
purchasers. Itself in desperate straits for ready money, it was
often a grasping landlord and its tendency was to raise fines and
rackrent its tenants. The royalist gentry, who had often been
ruined, first of all by their lavish gifts to the King's war-chest
and their outlay in raising troops for his service, and then by the
penalties imposed on them for 'delinquency', in their turn
passed on their losses to their tenants. The oppressions of the
new speculative landowners who bought their estates in whole
or part were notorious. Only too often, either by raising fines
and rents to a level which their tenants could not bear, or by
flatly refusing to renew tenancies, they cleared the land for
enclosure. In some cases the new men were guilty of fraud on a

bold and impressive scale. In the meanest of several recorded
instances, the successful criminal was a Colonel Thomas Wayte.
This Saint had sat in the Long Parliament. The villagers of
Humbledon in Rutlandshire, who had had from him a formal
promise that he would not enclose, described his oppressions in
a petition. They included the loss of one-third of each man's
share in the open fields, all their cow pastures and their water-
supply. They were living under a threat that the process of
enclosure would eventually lead to the eviction of about eighty
tenant families and thirty families of labourers.[9] It is not known
whether they secured any measure of redress.

As a rule, the Long Parliament turned a deaf ear to petitions
from the peasants ·for the redress of their grievances. This
ceases to surprise us, when we discover that half the members
returned for the five midland counties had been fined for
depopulation or belonged to families which had been recently
fined.[10] Again, when the new lords of the manor came to
scrutinise the titles by which the customary tenants held their
land, it was on occasion discovered that a quarter or even half
of them could produce no evidence which would satisfy a
court of law. These ruthless measures of extortion resulted in an
inordinate increase in the value of land, and Thorold Rogers
cites as typical the case of Ruislip manor, worth £66 13s. 4d.
per annum in 1607, which was valued at £320 per annum in
1664.[11]

It has been argued on good evidence that the making of
sheepwalks was no longer the chief purpose of enclosure in the
seventeenth century. Wheat rather than wool was now the
rising commodity in the market. But the picture is patchy, and
in some counties, chiefly in the Midlands, it is clear that much
enclosure was still effected in this century at the expense of
arable farming, and that it was still causing depopulation and
widespread misery. Early in the century, after the outbreak of
the original Diggers and Levellers in 1607, when their leader
had been duly hanged, a *post mortem* was held in the customary
English way to inquire into the dead man's wrongs. The
commission, which then investigated the progress of enclosure
in seven Midland counties, reported that there was not much
complaint of the loss of common rights over pasture and waste

lands; the grievance bitterly felt was the loss of the common fields. It was of depopulation for the sake of pasture that the men's own manifesto spoke. The offending landlords were summoned before the Privy Council and ordered to rebuild the dwellings they had demolished. It is not recorded that they restored the fields.

Again in 1630 the Council sent a circular letter to the justices of the midland counties ordering the restoration of all enclosures carried out in the two previous years. It is doubtful whether this drastic injunction was obeyed. During the two years 1630 and 1631 ten thousand acres were enclosed for pasture in Leicestershire, and as many in Northamptonshire. Between 1635 and 1638 the Privy Council fined no less than six hundred persons for enclosures resulting in depopulation.[12] In these cases no redress followed: what the crown wanted was the offenders' money. But, indeed, the visible evidence of what happened in this big midland region survives to this day. Every observant traveller has noticed, again and again, beside road or railway, a curious regular formation of arched ridges in many of the endless fields of green pasture. It is particularly noticeable after heavy rain, when the water lies in what were once the furrows of the open fields.

Again, from another region, one may cite as a witness the antiquarian Aubrey, who left us a valuable description of Stonehenge as he knew it. In his *History of Wiltshire* he says that the whole county was once a lovely 'campania', meaning that at the end of the sixteenth century it was still unenclosed. There were then no rates for the poor; 'the church ale at Whitsuntide did their business'. In his day everything was changed: 'Since the Reformation and enclosures aforesaid, these parts have swarmed with poor people. Enclosures are for the private not for the public good. For a shepherd and his dog or a milkmaid can manage that land that upon arable employed the hands of several scores of labourers.'[13] Aubrey began to write in 1656, though his preface bears a much later date (1685).

During the Commonwealth and the Protectorate, enclosure for pasture was still depopulating the midlands. Under the administration of the Major-Generals, who had ample powers in such matters, it would have been easy to check enclosure, if that had been the policy of the ruling party. So far as we know, only one of them acted. During the critical year 1647, Colonel Whalley, as he then was, gave no sign that he himself held radical opinions, though his regiment was one of the most daring of the New Model in its devotion to the Leveller cause. Its commander was, throughout his military career, first of all a loyal member of the Cromwell family. He had, however, a more sensitive social conscience than most of the Grandees, and it is on record that he stood for mercy and leniency in Ireland (see p. 494 below). In the Midlands and particularly at Leicester he met with a wrong that moved him to action. A petition dating from about 1653 speaks bitterly of depopulation thereabouts. 'Tillage doth daily decay, whereby many of the inhabitants are constrained either through want of work or through cruelty of landlords to fly to other places and especially to market towns.' In April 1656 Whalley reported that the grand juries of Leicestershire and Warwickshire had raised this issue with no prompting from him. He believes that the other counties under his charge, especially Nottinghamshire and Lincolnshire, were of the same opinion. He briefly describes the solution he imposed. It was that 'two parts in three of their arable land should for ever be kept in tillage', and 'the poor amply provided for. . . . Upon these terms I hope God will not be provoked, the poor not wronged, depopulation prevented and the state not damnified.'[14]

In the same year, 1656, Whalley tried to induce Parliament to legislate against enclosure. His bill stands out as the last of the long series which sought to preserve the common fields. When in the next century Parliament returned to the subject, it was to facilitate their destruction. To Whalley belongs the distinction, rare in this or any century, that he proposed to legislate to his own hurt, for, as he told the House, all the commons on the estates conferred on him for his services were enclosed; but, as he put it, 'it is for the general good to prevent depopulation'. His bill was more than an empty prohibition; it set up administrative machinery under three commissioners, who were to act with a jury. In the debate, the Master of the Rolls, the ex-Speaker Lenthall, remarked that 'he never liked any bill that touched upon property', and a Mr Fowell called it 'the most mischievous bill that ever was offered to this House'. It was thrown out at the first reading.[15]

Whalley made no further attempt to save the common fields. He lost his estates as a regicide at the Restoration, but saved his life by fleeing to New England. There a legendary tradition surrounds his last days. With Goffe he lived, thanks to the sympathy of the colonists, hidden in a cave. When the aged Roger Williams, who had been the Indians' best friend, had to lead the train-band of Rhode Island in defence against a powerful body of them during King Philip's war, it is said that Whalley and Goffe suddenly appeared in their faded New Model uniforms, ordered its ranks, and led it to victory. The Twin Helpers then vanished as suddenly as they had arrived.

Ireton had told the Levellers that property derives from history. They proposed to apply this maxim with a difference. The unending tragedy of the enclosures was still the background of the countryman's outlook on society. The victims of it sank for the most part out of sight into the helpless proletariat. They were voteless, and if they carried arms during the Civil War, it was usually in the militia, or as pressed men in the infantry, which played only a minor part in politics. Articulate leaders they had none. The English lower class in this century could breed genius, but in Bunyan and Fox it turned not to politics but to introspective religion. The Army, however, and its Agitators were deeply concerned with this problem. The Leveller leaders, whatever their origin, were men busied in the city. In its early phases, until it permeated the New Model, the movement showed little interest in the land. But as it radiated outwards from London it was reminded of this fundamental grievance of the enclosures. As the champions of the common man, the Levellers could respond only in one way.

The first of their spokesmen who gave much thought to the matter was Richard Overton, and it may be significant that when he put his ideas about the land on paper, he addressed them to Fairfax and the Army in his *Appeal from the degenerate representative body of the Commons*.[16] After insisting that all charitable donations for education and the relief of the poor

which had been misappropriated must be restored to their
proper use, he went on to provide that 'all grounds which
anciently lay in common for the poor', and are now enclosed,
be 'laid open again to the free and common use and benefit of
the poor'. In *The Case of the Army truly Stated* the Agitators
repeated this demand in almost identical words. The next
document, the petition from the civilian Levellers of January
1648, included as we saw two new proposals (1) that trustees
be chosen by the poor, with wide powers, and (2) 'that some
good improvement may be made of waste grounds for their
use' (p. 323 above). The last statement in this series, that of the
epoch-making Petition of 11 September, 1648, though the
briefest and vaguest of them all, is important, because it was an
item in a moderate programme common to the Levellers,
the London Independents and the Army. It declared that
Parliament should have 'laid open all late inclosures of fens
and other commons, or have enclosed them only or chiefly
to the benefit of the poor'.[17] The word 'late', meaning 'recent'
should be noted; the previous demands were subject to no
limitation of time.

It is not easy to determine the exact scope of these four
demands, nor do they necessarily mean the same thing. The
Levellers were not drafting a statute; they were framing a
popular programme. What Richard Overton and the Agitators
proposed was in its audacity and scope the perfect prescription
for a social revolution. To undo all enclosures without time
limit was to reverse all that the new owning class had achieved
since the Wars of the Roses. Property meant to the new squirearchy the power to exploit the land within their own hedges as
they thought fit.

What Lilburne and the organised Leveller party proposed
in 1648 was of a much more modest scope, but for that very
reason, it may have been a more dangerous threat to vested
interests. It was a workable programme, not of revolution but of
reform. The demand for the restitution of charitable bequests
and donations sounds uncontroversial. No one would defend
the robbery of the poor on principle; but the lawyers of the
Long Parliament knew very well how to obstruct such reforms
in the committee stage. The reversal of recent enclosures of

fens and commons was no more than Cromwell himself had
furthered in the marshy land below Ely. The Levellers aimed
at redressing the wrongs which 'the poor' had suffered by
enclosure. (By the vague word 'poor' they usually meant the
squatters and cottagers—the landless labourers—who were
allowed to use the waste land.) One may safely assume that they
had no intention of undoing the harmless or beneficial enclosures which had been arranged among the tenants themselves
by the exchange and consolidation of strips in the open fields.
Voluntary enclosure of this kind had all but abolished the open
fields in Kent, Essex and Devon. What they meant to undo
were the enclosures carried out by force or fraud on a large
scale for pasture—the enclosures which led to eviction and
depopulation, and only the more recent of these.

The first instinct of the peasants, from Ket's rising onwards,
as they watched the advance of the new capitalism, was always
to cry 'Halt!' in a nostalgic and reactionary mood. But under
the stimulus of Leveller thinking two positive and progressive
ideas made their appearance. With the more prosaic and practical of the two, the conversion of 'base tenures' into freehold,
we shall deal presently. The other was the enclosure of some
of the waste land for the benefit of the poor themselves. To settle
landless labourers upon it as cultivators sounds to the modern
reader deceptively easy, because we are familiar with the use of
public credit to provide the capital required for such schemes,
with easy terms of repayment. Not even in Holland, where
money was abundant and cheap, had seventeenth-century
statesmen yet discovered how to conduct such operations. The
pioneers of the radical movement, such men as the sober
Lieut.-Colonel Jubbes and the dashing Dr Chamberlen, who
tried to solve the agrarian problem with the primitive economic
techniques of their day, were attempting a barely possible feat.
One cannot but admire their intellectual courage.

Jubbes's plan was embodied in his amended version of the
Agreement. The most important of its new provisions was an
ingenious scheme which combined a solution of the agrarian
problem with a new way of paying the Army's arrears. Hitherto Parliament's only resource for the payment of its debts was

to squander the nation's capital heritage by selling the lands of
church and crown. Jubbes proposed rather to use the rental
from public lands to pay a pension or annuity to the troops. All
the marsh lands, fens and common pastures within the kingdom
were to be enclosed and so divided that one part in four should
go to the tenants, another quarter to 'the poor', and the
remaining half towards the payment of the Army's arrears. A
trooper would receive for every year of his service £4 *per
annum* during his life—a substantial sum, since many had
served for five or six years. He writes with tantalising brevity
and obscurity, so that one perceives only a dim outline of the
immense and prolonged operation on which he proposes to
embark. Are the fens to be drained, and if so who finds the
capital? What is novel and interesting is the assumption on
which he proceeds that the waste lands and fens are morally the
nation's property, though certain local interests have to be
satisfied. Jubbes offered to bring sixty members of the Common
Council of the City to testify that the plan (meaning the
agrarian proposals) was workable and that the City was ready
to further it.[18] What the Lieut.-General may have disapproved
even more than the scheme for the Army's arrears was the
preceding clause which provided for the conversion of all 'enslaving tenures' into freehold. This would have given the tenant
if not a 'fortune', at any rate a status equal to the squire's.

In 1637 an influential syndicate sought from the King a
patent which would authorise it to 'improve' the many
thousands of acres of heath and barren commons on the crown
lands 'not annually worth 6*d.* an acre', which might be made to
yield 'plenty of provision' and to 'enrich many thousands'.[19]
Dr Peter Chamberlen, one of the few professional men in the
radical movement, had this plan before him and doubtless
that of Lieut.-Colonel Jubbes as well, when he wrote *The Poor
Man's Advocate*. He may also have had in mind the military
colonies of Rome. From these materials his sanguine imagination devised a project for paying not merely the arrears of the
Army, but all the debts and most of the current expenditure of
the Commonwealth as well.[20] Unrealistic though the doctor's
plan may be, it has its interest for the modern reader, since it
shows that some of the more active minds among the radicals

were turning in a socialist direction. Chamberlen was a graduate of Cambridge and Padua; to these two schools an unkind critic might add the Academy of Laputa. As the fashionable surgeon-accoucheur of his day, he served both Charles I and that prolific father of his people, Charles II. His family kept as its profitable secret for four generations its invention of a short obstetrical forceps—conduct unusual in the profession of healing. Far in advance of his age, he advocated the incorporation of midwives and for hygienic reasons the public provision of baths. A leading Anabaptist, he acted as 'teacher' to one of the meetings of this radical sect.

In spite of the motto he chose for his pamphlet—*bonum quo communius est melius*—one cannot reckon him a consistent socialist, for he argued that 'men are entrusted with riches that (as God's stewards) they might reward the laborious industries of the poor'. On a later page, however, he confesses that 'most become rich through dishonesty'. The syndicate which he proposed to form would advance money at 5 per cent. to set 'the poor' to work—no less than 200,000 of them at cultivating all commons, wastes, forests, heaths, moors, fens, chases, bogs and mountains, as well as the deans' and chapters' lands. Each, he was optimist enough to believe, could produce a surplus of £20 in addition to his keep. The syndicate would take over new engines and inventions and bring them into use. For good measure it would also run a national bank. Based on public faith and the security of public lands, this unprecedented institution would get the busines of 'all nations'. The profits of a herring fleet run by the syndicate would suffice to maintain the navy.

The poor would have the choice between working as tenants on as much land as they personally could cultivate, or else 'in common'. For those who chose to work in teams under discipline, chambers would be provided in 'public houses'. The disused palaces of the King and the bishops would serve for this purpose. The women would do all the indoor work, cooking, baking, brewing, weaving and repairing linen; the men would do all the outdoor work, repairing buildings, and milking as well as ploughing. Superficially these 'public houses' resemble the communal farms (*kibbutzim*) of contemporary Israel, with the all-important difference that they would not be self-governing. When not engaged in military duties, the army also would till the soil.

Though Chamberlen compiled a fairly detailed budget showing an expenditure of £3 millions against a revenue of £7 millions, he is often so confused that one can only guess what his proposals really are. Was the syndicate to own the commons and fens, the bank, the herring fleet, the mines and the new inventions which it ran? Or were these to be national property? Probably that is what he meant when he said they were 'to be as a public treasure of the land for all public designs in one common stock'. He nowhere tells us how much capital his syndicate would have to raise, nor what compensation, if any, it would pay to vested interests. Apparently, the nation was to leave this vast enterprise to be conducted, without any form of public control, by trustees elected annually by the shareholders (adventurers or 'undertakers'). He holds out the hope that these will soon be content with 3 per cent. and, indeed, thanks to the nationalised bank, that the general level of interest will fall to this modest rate. His plan for reforming the Customs need not detain us.

Incidentally Peter Chamberlen has much that is enlightened to say about 'the poor'. He shares the usual Anabaptist disapproval of prisons, and maintains that houses of correction only turn the poor into vagabonds and beggars, by taking away their 'repute for honesty', so that no one will employ them. His purpose in inventing this whole elaborate project was evidently as much to find happy work for 'the poor', as to pay off the nation's debts. Nothing came of his project. The 'adventurers' of his generation wanted something more remunerative than socialism at 3 per cent.; they preferred to speculate on their own account in forfeited royalist estates going dirt cheap at ten or twelve years' purchase. But the doctor's scheme found one belated admirer, as we shall see (pp. 613-14 below). Four years after its publication, John Lilburne made its theme his own in his last excursion into active politics, before Cromwell's dungeon in Jersey engulfed him in silence.

The less speculative of the two Leveller solutions for the

agrarian problem was, of course, to convert 'base tenures' into freehold. Base or servile tenures were those which evolved out of villeinage. The most onerous of the villein's services, those which made him in economic fact a half-slave or serf—the three (or it might be two) days of unpaid labour which he had to render to the lord of the manor on the demesne or home-farm in each week throughout the year—had begun to be commuted for a fixed rent in kind or cash even before they were swept away in the fourteenth century in the catastrophe of the Black Death. But the lesser burdens of villeinage lingered through many generations. These were chiefly the days of 'boon-work' which had to be performed at the busier seasons of the year. Remnants of such services, can be traced even into the seventeenth century, as for instance on a Lancashire manor in 1628 where four days of ploughing were exacted in the year.[21] The more hateful and humiliating marks of a servile status had not wholly vanished in the more backward regions of England. Even 'merchet', the fine paid on the marriage of a tenant's daughter, was occasionally exacted. But it is none the less broadly true that the personal status of bondage had ceased to be enforceable. The distinction between 'bond' and 'free' now applied to the land, and no longer to the man. Certain acres were still held by 'a base or servile tenure' and to its conditions the tenant had to conform, even if he were by birth a freeholder or a baronet.

A freeholder was still by the theory of feudal law a tenant, and not an owner in the modern sense of that word. If he held, as the vast majority did, by 'socage' he owed 'homage' and an oath of 'fealty' and might have to offer the lord of the manor some token of it—a pound of pepper, for example, with a gilly-flower or a red rose. His fixed money rent had become, since the inflation in the sixteenth century, so trifling, that few stewards troubled to collect it. By contrast with other tenants (if we treat him, as what he technically was, a tenant) his lot was enviable, because he enjoyed complete security. A land-lord bent on enclosure might oppress him by infringing on his share in the waste, the woods and even the water common to the village, but could not dispossess him of his strips of arable land, save by buying them. The freeholders, however, were by no means, always or even usually, the wealthiest of the tenants. Occasionally they might farm a hundred or even two hundred acres, but commonly they held no more than ten and in the eastern counties their average seems to have been three or four acres. Their numbers varied greatly in the different regions of England. In the early seventeenth century they were 36 per cent. of the whole body of tenants in Norfolk and Suffolk. Over England as a whole the freeholders were, in rough figures, 20 per cent. of the tenants.

Over against the freeholders stood two main classes of tenants, the leaseholders and the customary tenants. Leasehold is the modern form of tenancy, at first adopted when the lord, lacking labour, farmed out the demesne to one or more tenants, who paid him a competitive rent, fixed only for a term of years. Such men were often graziers, who possessed some capital and belonged to the new age of commercial agriculture. At the other end of the scale of prosperity were the squatters, permitted for a small consideration to settle on the waste. By far the more numerous in our period were the 'customary tenants', embracing in varying proportions the copyholders and tenants at will. A copyholder was the successor and descendant of the former villein, who held the same strips, in the same open fields. His tenancy depended on his possession of a copy of the relevant entry in the court roll of the manor, and was subject to its customs. Sometimes, with dire results if the manor changed hands, these tenants had in fact no documentary proof of their rights.

The customs of the manor varied widely. The tenancy might run for a term of years or for life. The rents on customary holdings had in fact often remained unchanged from the fourteenth to the seventeenth century. But where custom was weaker, rents could be abruptly raised when the term of a tenancy was up, and might be doubled or even multiplied tenfold. The usual practice, however, was for the landlord to leave the rent at the low figure fixed by custom, but to levy a 'fine' on the renewal of a tenancy. These arbitrary fines might in our period amount to many years', on occasion to twenty years' rent, though the ancient traditional practice had been to charge only one or at most two years' rent at renewal, or as the so-called 'heriot' on inheritance. There was, however, no obligation to renew, and copyholders, as their term fell in, could usually be evicted. The power of custom to bind a lord of the manor steadily weakened as the commercial age set in. On the other hand, a grasping lord could still, on occasion, even in the seventeenth century, impose on his tenants irregular and occasional exactions based on the ugliest feudal models. Thus on a manor in Cheshire, the landlord, who had just bought a neighbouring estate, called his tenants together and demanded from each of them a gift equal to three years' rent to help him pay for it; he threatened that should they refuse, their tenancies would not be renewed when they fell in.[22] It will be realised that the objection to 'base and servile tenures' rested on something more than sentiment.

If these were the economic consequences of 'base and servile tenures', we need not waste many words on their political effects. The tenant who was liable at recurring intervals to eviction at the will of his lord dared not indulge in the luxury of a political opinion. In quiet times, since he had no vote, it was easy for him to play for safety by indifference. But when it came to civil war, his squire expected his unflinching support. Ludlow in his *Memoirs* (under the date December 1641) reports a frank outburst against the Parliament by a Royalist who was his fellow-student at the Inns of Court. 'What!' this young gentleman exclaimed, 'shall we suffer these fellows at Westminster to domineer thus? Let us go into the country and bring up our tenants to pull them out.'

It happened, none the less, in counties which were solid for the Parliament, that many of the copyholders who had a royalist landlord did venture to back the popular cause. What would happen to them when the cavalier squire, defeated and impoverished, got back to the manor house again? That was the problem raised in the petition already mentioned, presented to the Army by many of the country folk of Hertfordshire at St Albans in June 1647.[23] It asked

that the body of the kingdom, consisting much of copy-holders, who have for the most part been very cordial and faithful to the Parliament, may not now be left finable at the will of the lords, in regard the generality of them have been very malignant . . . and from whom they cannot but expect very severe dealing.

The lesson of experience, then, was clear. If the Levellers meant to get political democracy, they must begin to face the economic problems of ownership—at the least they must sweep away those relics of the Norman Conquest, 'the base and servile tenures'. The votes which they proposed to confer on the copyholders would be useless, unless the tenants were first of all emancipated from the pressure to which their landlord could subject them. Unless this were done, the squire would march his tenants to the poll much as he had marched them to Edgehill. The Levellers, during these dizzy years, had many lessons to learn.

· The obvious solution was to turn the copyholder into a peasant owner, a yeoman in the proper sense of that word. The clearest statement of it is to be found in *A New Engagement or Manifesto*, claiming to speak for 'many thousands' in London and the counties round about which seems (like the similar soldiers' engagement *The Army's Petition* of 3 May, 1648) to have been drafted just as the second Civil War was breaking out. It proposed (§16) :

> that the ancient and almost antiquated badge of slavery, viz. all base tenures by copies, oaths of fealty, homage, fines at the will of the lord, etc. (being the Conqueror's marks upon the people) may be taken away; and to that end that a certain valuable rate be set, at which all possessors of lands so holden may purchase themselves freeholders, and in case any shall not be willing or able, that there be a prefixed period of time after which all services, fines, customs, etc. shall be changed into and become a certain rent, that so persons disaffected to the freedom and welfare of the nation may not have the advantage upon the people to draw them into a war against themselves upon any occasion by virtue of an awe upon them in such dependent tenures.

The status of the tenant who is to pay a fixed rent and no more is not defined as clearly as one could wish. Obviously he is secure for life against eviction. To encourage him to improve his holding he should also have the right to pass it on to whom he will.

In this sober policy there is no hint of revolution. It recognises without qualification all the rights in landed property which the common-law courts enforced, and though it implies an ethical condemnation of them as 'slavery' and traces them back to the violence and usurpation of the Conquest, it does not dispute their validity and proposes to compensate the owners of these anti-social claims. The curiosity of the modern reader is aroused by what is, none the less, a bold and comprehensive scheme for an immense social change. But he may feel doubtful, as the Levellers themselves evidently did, whether any large proportion of the copyholders would in fact have been able to raise the funds with which to compensate their landlords. There is no means of guessing how much—how many years' rent—they would have had to pay on a valuation for the freehold of their acres.[24] Money in those days was scarce and dear, and—failing any public provision of credit to facilitate payment by instalments on the model of the Irish Land Purchase Acts—it is doubtful whether the poorer copyholders could have risen into this envied class. The reformers accordingly fell back on an alternative plan, less attractive perhaps, but none the less far-reaching. This was that all fines and uncertain services should be abolished, and the tenant freed from every burden save a fixed rent.

This was, in either of its forms, a very moderate compromise. It left the lord still drawing his unearned tribute from the land, which owed its fertility to the painful labour of generations of villeins and copyholders, who made its tilth with plough, harrow and hoe through the centuries and often enriched it with loads of laboriously carted marl. But this reform, moderate though it was, would have changed the face of England. A fixed tribute is compatible with mental, social and political independence and with a hopeful spirit of enterprise. The peasant's improvements would have been his own. The insecurity and the fear of rackrent and exploitation, which bent him into a posture of cautious servility, would have vanished. The Levellers, in short, would have peopled the English countryside with an enfranchised peasantry, so securely planted on the soil that it would have dared to stand erect. This, needless to say, was not a communistic policy: it was in its inspiration individualistic, though something of the traditional communism of the open fields would have survived through several generations. But it would have broken the power of the great landed families which ruled England through the next two centuries, by adding immeasurably to the capacity of the villages for resistance. It would have made of rural England what rural France became after the Revolution, a land of small peasant owners. But to say this is to point out that the Levellers and the troopers of the New Model were naïvely proposing to reverse history. The Great Rebellion had other ends in view.

That the abolition of base tenures would break the ascendancy of the squirearchy was not the secret of the Levellers. The Cromwellians understood it at least as well. When they did want to break the power of a hostile land-owing class, they carried out this plan with scientific ruthlessness. Because the royalist nobility and gentry of Scotland, after twice invading the soil of England, still persisted in backing Middleton's guerilla operations in the Highlands, Oliver and his soldiers made up their minds to end the rule of this governing class for ever. The Act of Union of 1654 abolished the Parliament of Scotland, but it contained provisions even more far-reaching which provided that Scottish tenants and their heirs 'shall be from henceforth for ever discharged of all fealty, homage, vassalage and servitude . . . and from all military service and personal attendance upon any their lords or superiors . . . and from all manner of services personal or real'. After sweeping away base tenures with all the degrading lumber of the feudal system, the Act laid it down that the fine levied on inheritance or a change of tenancy should be limited to one year's rent. When he had liberated the peasantry from all its arbitrary and humiliating burdens, the Lord Protector went on to deprive twenty-four great landowners of their estates and to impose crippling fines on another seventy-five.

If the landed gentry in England had been solidly 'malignant', the Civil War might well have ended, there also, in the abolition of base tenures. But of the lords of the manor not a few were reckoned among the People of God. Cromwell himself was born in the squirearchy and so were all his clan, Ireton, Whalley, Claypole, Desborough and Fleetwood; into it were clambering all the Grandees of the Army, even the Hewsons and the Prides. To free the tenant from his servitude and to make him 'as liberal a fortune as the landlord' was not the reward they expected for their perilous service. To be sure, a bill was drafted which abolished oaths of fealty and another which limited fines on inheritance to one year's rent; but though four Parliaments came and went, these bills never found their way to the statute book.[25] It was not to reform base tenures that the gentlemen of England drew their swords against their King.

During the second Civil War the attention of the Levellers was absorbed in questions more urgent than land tenure. On the day before Pride's Purge (5 December, 1648) two reminders of what their peasant adherents expected reached them from counties separated by several centuries as well as by many hundreds of miles. In those days the men of Buckinghamshire rode in the van of the democratic army, while the borderers of Northumberland, many of them still true to the old religion, trudged in the rear. Those fourteenth-century pioneers of the peasants' cause and the Protestant Reformation, the Lollards, setting out under Wycliffe's inspiration from Oxford, met with a warm welcome from the charcoal burners and woodworkers of the Chiltern beechwoods. From under the whitewash that used to mask the stone walls of the lovely old church at Bledlow, a fresco has been recently uncovered which shows a peasant in the costume of Wat Tyler's generation digging, while a woman spins beside him. 'When Adam delved and Eve span', we repeat automatically as we look up at it, 'Who was then the gentleman?' These Lollards knew how to die for their radical creed; two of them were burned alive at Amersham. From the villages of the fertile plain of Aylesbury, not yet enclosed, a thousand mounted yeomen are said to have escorted John Hampden when he rode to Westminster to take his seat in the Long Parliament. Into Buckinghamshire the Anabaptists penetrated early in the Interregnum. Here too William Penn and Thomas Elwood were at home and Quaker quietism spread as the militant Puritan left, overcome by disillusion, awaited its final defeat. In this county it was to be expected that the Levellers would pioneer and in point of fact they were able by May 1649 to hold a gathering at Aylesbury which was attended by representatives from three of the Chiltern Hundreds.

At the height of the constitutional crisis in the last month of 1648 there came from these groups a pamphlet that bore the intriguing title *Light shining in Buckinghamshire*. It has been mistakenly ascribed to Gerrard Winstanley, but he may have been a member of one of the groups that produced it.[26] Of the anonymous author all we can say with certainty is that his thinking was moulded by the Anabaptist tradition. From the same pen four months later came a sequel, *More Light shining in Buckinghamshire*. In the interval the King had gone to the block, the Commonwealth had been proclaimed and the Grandees of the Army had incurred the bitter hostility of the Levellers in Aylesbury as in London, but the same light shone undimmed in the Chilterns. In literary skill these two pamphlets rank far below the writings of the Leveller leaders, while their clownish jokes and their lengthy excursions into Old Testament history are likely to irritate the modern reader. They have, none the less, things of the utmost moment to say, and these they say with passion and conviction.

Here for the first time, from the pen of a Leveller who claims to speak for many of his comrades, is a confession of faith which we can only describe as ethical socialism or communism, in spite of the Biblical language in which it is thought out—for there are many echoes in both these tracts of the Epistle of St James, which in its turn reflects the radicalism of the early church and it may be of the Essenes also. But if we shrink from using contemporary political names, the fact remains that these pamphlets preach a rule of complete equality, economic as well as political. They also express, with an explosive violence, the revolt of the more radical countrymen against all the clotted relics of feudalism that clung round the manorial system. For the rest, these rural converts professed the entire Leveller creed, which they derived from the myth of the Norman Conquest. Infuriated by the buying and selling of justice, they call on the soldiers to pull the judges out of Westminster Hall. Attacking tithes, they make the surprising statement (which John Lilburne repeated) that the impropriators carry off a third part of what each peasant produces.[27]

They would withdraw their charters from the incorporated towns, with their patents, monopolies and tolls—a proposal peculiar to this Chiltern group.

The passionate advocacy of equality in property and income is the main theme of both pamphlets. The first proclamation of the principle is based on the statement in Genesis (i.26) that when God had created man in His own image, He gave men 'dominion over the fish of the sea and over the fowl of the air and over the cattle and over all the earth and over every creeping thing that creepeth upon the earth'. If God gave the earth and the creatures alike to men, it follows that all enclosure is criminal. Nay, it is the source of all the slavery in the world. To get rid of kings will be useless, unless we realise that commonwealth means equality. It must ensure to each man a just portion wherewith to live.

> It is God's command that all work . . . and if all work alike, is it not fit for all to eat alike, have alike and enjoy alike privileges and freedoms? . . .
> And therefore weep and howl, ye rich men. . . . God will visit you for all your oppressions. You live on other men's labours, and give them their bran to eat, extorting extreme rents and taxes on your fellow-creatures. But now what will you do? For the people will no longer be enslaved by you.'[2]

The second pamphlet opens with an attack on the idle rich, who live by owning. 'They are rebels against God's command, for saith He, "*In the sweat of thy face, thou shalt eat bread*." By *thou* is meant all mankind, none exempted.' The next step in the argument is again a Scriptural quotation, '*Those that will not work, let them not eat*'. And so we arrive at the conclusion—Proudhon's paradox—that property is theft. 'Now the other that sweats not at all [the idle owner] yet makes this man [who has worked for his bread] to pay him tribute out of his labour by rates, taxes, rents, etc., it is theft.' Then comes the bold assertion, 'all men are equals', and our author again repeats his doctrine that 'for man to enclose all lands and creatures from his kind is utterly unnatural, wicked and treacherous; for if man shall eat bread by his sweat, then he must needs have ground to sow corn; therefore to enclose all grounds from him is to starve him, for if no corn, no bread, and if no ground, no corn; then this is theft in the highest degree'. He turns with angry contempt upon the owning and governing class:

> Mark this, you great curmudgeons, you hang a man for stealing for his wants, when you yourselves have stole from your fellow brethren all land, creatures, etc. . . . So first go hang yourselves for your great thefts and then . . . afterwards . . . you can go hang your poor brethren for petty thefts, as for a sheep, corn, etc.[29]

Thomas More had said much the same thing in *Utopia* and shortly after him, Thomas Münzer—the scholar who turned Anabaptist and was the most radical leader of the German peasants in the nation-wide revolt of 1525—said it in almost identical words in a much quoted sermon, which this persecuted sect seems to have cherished as part of its tradition for more than a hundred years. Under the guidance of this vital and persistent sect these Chiltern peasants found in the infallible Scriptures the confirmation of what they already believed upon instinct. It was their experience of the manorial system in its predatory commercial decadence that distilled from their feelings of indignation and shame this passionate faith in equality.

The lord of the manor is, of course, the chief encloser and tyrant, since he snatches the land without which other men cannot raise corn for bread. He and his lawyers appropriate as 'gentleman's game' the beasts, birds and fishes over which God gave 'dominion' to all mankind. It follows that the lord of the manor must be deprived of his power to exact at his pleasure fines and heriots from his tenants. Copyhold tenure must be abolished—precisely how is not explained. There must be no more privileges for hunting and hawking. As for the manorial courts, these are a degradation to free men, who ought not to be required to swear fealty to the lord. Even 'socage' tenure is shameful, because it obliges the freeholders to pay homage and acknowledge themselves slaves to this tyrant, who exacts a quit-rent from them. The author does not pause to tell us how the open fields are to be managed. His only hint at a constructive policy is to urge that the bishops' and crown lands must not be 'swallowed up', nor commons, parks, woods and forests which 'your great ones gape for to enclose, but let them be for the poor'. Evidently he is thinking of settling 'the poor' upon them.

The *Declaration* which reported the conclusions of the Levellers who met in conference at Aylesbury went appreciably further. Speaking for 'all the middle sort and poor people' against 'all slavish and base tenures', tithes, Westminster terms and martial law, it declared their readiness to 'further' the doings of any of the poor who may 'join a community in God's way . . . and desire to manure, dig and plant in the waste grounds and commons'.[30] Thus did these rural Levellers give their blessing to Winstanley and the Diggers (see Chapter XXXIV).

The second of the two reminders which their rural adherents addressed to the Leveller leaders and the Army came from the officers and troopers of the Northumberland horse. The fathers of these men grew up before the union of the crowns in the troubled borderland between two kingdoms. The customary tenure, by which they held their strips of land for a trifling rent, required them at the summons of the lord of their manor to attend a muster with 'horse and harness'. Twice, in the Pilgrimage of Grace and the revolt of the Northern Earls, their forebears rose against the schismatic Tudor monarchy. At one with their aristocratic leaders in loyalty to the despoiled and persecuted church, they none the less resolved to use their arms for their own ends, to redress the wrongs of the peasantry. The petition which this regiment addressed on the eve of Pride's Purge to Lord Fairfax is the ablest and the widest in its scope of the many that came from the Army in support of the Levellers' Large Petition of 11 September. In several particulars it went further, notably by calling for a convention to draw up the Agreement of the People.[31]

This petition, which the troopers say they adopted 'with our swords in our hands', begins with a preamble that reflects the light that shone in Buckinghamshire and includes a clause dealing specifically with the grievances of the peasantry in the northern counties. Repeating the usual Leveller myth of the Norman conquest, the preamble lays stress on the enslavement of the British natives. Their properties, which they had held by fee simple, were converted 'into strange tenures by knight, homage, villein and other services to the conqueror and his Norman earls, lords and knights'. The sixth clause made the customary claim that enclosed commons and ancient donations be restored to their proper use for the good of the commonalty. The seventh packs so much of peasant history into a few words that it deserves to be quoted. It asks:

> that the ancient tenures of lands in the county of Northumberland, Cumberland, etc. which have been destroyed by several earls and lords of late times to the undoing of the commonalty in those parts, and utterly disabling them from all good nurture in learning or trades, and forcing them from generation to generation to be hinds, half hinds, quarter hinds, shepherds and herdsmen, be now enquired into; and if no better that the ancient right of the old rents (for the good of those counties and commonwealth) be restored again.

The meaning seems to be that when the old nominal rent of the 'horse and harness' tenure was raised to a commercial level, the copyholder could find money to pay it only by hiring out himself or his sons as labourers or shepherds, with the result that his boys got little education and could not be apprenticed to a trade. The remedy, however, was not to be found by going backwards. It lay with the Leveller leaders to find the way forwards.

If the peasants looked to London for leadership they were doomed to disappointment. The Leveller party was absorbed in the political crisis that ended in the King's execution. All its thoughts were bent on the achievement of the democratic ideal enshrined in the Agreement of the People. It was about to live through one of the great moments in the history of the English speaking nations. Can we wonder if its attention was diverted from the little despots of the village, while it watched the throne of three kingdoms toppling to its fall? Their business would soon be settled—so the average Leveller may have reasoned—when the House of Commons was 'bounded' and the Lords lost their negative voice. Fitfully and in rare moments of insight the party did realise that as a citizen the peasant would not dare to oppose the lord of his manor so long as he held his strips of land under a servile tenure. But this perception never induced it to give priority in its programme to the reform of land tenure. It never again attained the prominence it won in those two militant manifestoes which reflected the revolutionary mood of the party and some of the troops in the spring of 1648.

The second version of the Agreement which John Lilburne sent to the printer on 15 December, 1648, contained a list of reforms, not included among the unalterable fundamentals of the constitution, but none the less so urgent and important, that the electorate should give the next Parliament a mandate to pass them at once. Over eleven of these reforms the whole delegation, composed of London Independents as well as Levellers, was agreed. But there were four others which Lilburne added on his own account, obviously because they were too extreme for his Independent allies. Of these No. IV runs thus: 'That the next representative be earnestly desired to abolish all base tenures.' The brevity and simplicity of this demand may have been deliberate; it would cover either a moderate measure such as we have been considering, or a revolutionary act of abolition without compensation.

The third version of the Agreement, published over the signatures of Lilburne, Walwyn, Prince and Overton on May Day, 1649, ranks as the classical statement of the Leveller programme. Its thirty articles ignore the agrarian question altogether and make no mention of base tenures.[32] There is no reason to suppose that Lilburne or his colleagues changed their minds about land reform, but it is clear that they no longer regarded it as urgent. Its importance may have been better understood by younger militants of the party. In 1653, when it survived only as an underground organisation, without known leaders, it published a fourth version of the Agreement which contained this brief but trenchant article (No. 18):

All servile tenures of lands, as by copyholds and the like, to be abolished and holden for naught.[33]

'Peaceable' though the Levellers claimed to be who drafted this manifesto, they had got beyond compromise and compensation.

To explain the leaders' lack of interest in this question is not easy. None of them wrote anything about the land question, with the exception of Overton, and even he did not touch on base tenures. One would have expected that an alert democratic party would have sent out its missionaries and its organisers into the villages to talk to the peasants about the questions which touched them most nearly. Servile tenures, predatory enclosures, tithes and conscription—these were the things that the least literate of them understood, and of these it was the issue of enclosures that roused them to fighting pitch. But when missionaries were sent into the counties, as they were in the autumn of 1647, it was to expound the Agreement, a novel idea, not at all easy to grasp, though the 'middle sort of people' in London and the craftsmen came to believe in it as fervently as their descendants believed in the Charter.

In their taverns and chapels how often did the Levellers recollect that the peasants and among them the copyholders —on whom they were bent on bestowing the vote—formed the great majority of the English people? With them lay the key to the future, if ever the masses took their stand against the governing class, the landed gentry. That was equally true whether it was of a 'peaceable' victory at the polls that the Levellers were thinking, or of a victory won in a 'posture of defence' (as the manifesto of the stormy spring of 1648 put it). By impulse (as we have seen), without national leaders or the clarion of propaganda, the peasants all the way from Cornwall to Durham took up such arms as they possessed, each village at its own moment, without concert, to level the hedges and fences in the early years of the Civil War. Roused and led by a party which understood organisation, their numbers and the intensity of their feelings would have counted for something in a revolutionary struggle.

Looking backwards, we moderns can perceive how grave was the plight of the peasantry and how urgently it called for a remedy. The failure of the Levellers to perceive it betimes was the real reason for their own defeat. They did enough for the tenants' cause to provoke Cromwell and the gentry to crush them, but not enough to mobilise the villages as their resolute allies.

Nothing came of the clamour for land reform audible throughout the Interregnum. Copyhold tenancies dwindled rapidly in numbers and the typical holding came to be the tenancy at will, which lacked even the frail protection of the custom of the manor. Towards the end of the seventeenth century Richard Baxter wrote his elegy on the peasantry which his fellow-Puritans had helped to destroy:

> The husbandmen are the stamen of the commonwealth. All the rest do live by them . . . and yet whose case is so hard as theirs? Gentlemen say our land is our own, and he that will give most for it shall be our tenant. The custom used to be to let lands for periods of lives or a long term of years, but now in most counties yearly rack rents predominate. Poor husbandmen are little better than slaves, for none are so servilely dependent . . . as they are on their landlords. They dare not displease them lest they turn them out of their houses, or increase their rents. I believe that their great landlords have more command of them than the King hath.[34]

This age saw tendencies but it rarely measured them in numbers. None the less, from an occasional writer we do get an attempt at a statistical estimate which enables us to form some idea of the shift in wealth and power which occurred at this period. At the end of this century Davenant estimates the annual income of England at £43 millions, and the yearly rent of land alone at £10 millions—an enormous tribute concentrated in relatively few hands. A century after our period, Arthur Young made an interesting reckoning which Thorold Rogers threw into high relief.[35] In Young's day, round about 1770, the rent of agricultural land averaged 10s. an acre. In the Middle Ages and up to the debasement of the currency under Henry VIII it stood pretty steadily at 6d. an acre. Wheat had risen from 6s. to 40s. a quarter. The farm-labourer's wage had risen from 2s. to 7s. 1d. weekly. That is to say:

> Rent rose 20 times
> Wheat rose 6½ times
> Wages rose 3½ times

In other words, if we compare the rewards the two classes

drew from the land, the share of the owners multiplied nearly six times in comparison with that of the workers. In Young's day the more enterprising of the owners were just beginning to make by capital outlay and intelligent management a positive and considerable contribution to the yield of the land. But this, save in such great enterprises as the drainage of the fens, was a recent development. They had also, for good and evil, sunk money in fences and lawyer's fees. With these exceptions, it is broadly true that throughout the period that ran from the loot of the church and the great inflation to the Whig Revolution, they were the passive receivers of an unearned tribute levied on the toil of tenants and labourers. Their swollen rents are in epitome the history of this epoch.

The revolution that really happened was not the enlargement of English freedom. What in fact it accomplished was to bring the land under the new capitalistic system. It favoured the great owner: it made the balance of class power under which the process of enclosure was completed by a Parliament of landlords. In the Act of Settlement of 1662 it virtually revived serfdom by tying the labourer to his parish, and with uncanny prescience made ready a proletariat for the mills of the industrial revolution. The King, indeed, was beaten at Marston Moor and Naseby, but the vanquished party in the Civil War were the peasants who charged behind Fairfax and Cromwell.

NOTES TO CHAPTER XXI

1. Abbott, III, pp. 435-6 (4 September, 1654).

2. The reader may remind me that the reformed franchise under the Instrument of Government conferred the vote on all occupiers in the county, including copyholders and leaseholders who satisfied a fairly high property qualification (which must have excluded many of the poorer freeholders). But, subject as they still were to the insecurity of their 'base tenures', copyholders would not venture to vote against the will of the lord of the manor. In all essentials their liberation was as far off as ever.

3. Margaret James, *Social Policy During the Puritan Revolution*, pp. 85-7.

4. R. H. Tawney, 'The Rise of the Gentry', *Economic History Review*, XI, p. 21.

5. W. H. R. Curtler, *The Enclosure and Redistribution of our Land*, p. 139.

6. Maps, sketches and statistics are reproduced in *The Open Fields*, by C. S. and C. S. Orwin.

7. James, *op. cit.*, pp. 90-3.

8. B. Whitelock, *Memorials of the English Affairs* (1853), IV, p. 34 (30 August, 1653).

9. James, *op. cit.*, p. 391.

10. Tawney, 'Rise of the Gentry', p. 34.

11. T. Rogers, *A History of Agriculture and Prices in England*, V, p. 809.

12. E. C. K. Gonner, *Common Land and Inclosure*, p. 167.

13. Quoted by Curtler, *op. cit.*, p. 104.

14. James, *op. cit.*, pp. 123, 392.

15. Ed. J. T. Rutt, *Parliamentary Diary of Thomas Burton*, I, pp. 175-6.

16. Wolfe, p. 194.

17. *Ibid.*, pp. 216, 270, 288.

18. *Several Proposals for Peace and Freedom by an Agreement of the People* (22 December, 1648). See also Jubbes's *Apology* of 4 May, 1649. *Several Proposals* is reprinted in Wolfe, pp. 311 sqq. Dr Schenk summarises Jubbes's opinions in *The Concern for Social Justice in the Puritan Revolution*, p. 172.

19. Tawney, *The Agrarian Problem in the Sixteenth Century*, pp. 394-5.

20. P. Chamberlen, *The Poor Man's Advocate* (25 April, 1649), esp. pp. 49 sqq.

21. Tawney, *The Agrarian Problem*, p. 53.

22. *Ibid.*, pp. 118, 54.

23. Rushworth, VI, p. 575. See p. 190 above.

24. Two authors on the fringes of the Leveller party were discussing this question about this time. The author of *An Experimental Essay touching the reformation of the laws of England* (17 August, 1648) quotes Coke and Bacon, and may have had a legal training, in spite of his hostility to the legal profession. He wants to codify the laws in a 'little book . . . and then all might have leisure to study the mysteries of art and nature'. He would abolish the death penalty save for murder and treason, and has a plan for enclosing waste lands and using the rent 'for the good of the town'. He wants all base tenures to be bought out and states that 'some manors have been extinguished by selling all the lands free to the copyhold tenants belonging to them for 30 years' purchase, because of the fines at death and alienations'. He means that the high figure of 30 years is explained by the fact that it allows for fines as well as rent.

The amended version of *The Agreement of the People* by Lieut.-Colonel Jubbes (p. 357 above) contains this clause (15): 'That all inslaving tenures upon record by oaths of fealty, villeinage, homage and fines at will of the lords, may all be bought in at such rates as shall not exceed twenty years' purchase to the lord, upon a conscientious computation of profits made according to the reign of King James.' Jubbes's figure means 20 years' purchase of all fines as well as rents levied in the reign of James I. Rents would usually be much lower in that reign than they were during the Interregnum. This mode of reckoning seems therefore to favour the tenant.

25. See p. 652 below. There was some concern, expressed in several petitions, lest malignant landlords should penalise their well-affected tenants for their opinions. From Whitelock (*op. cit.*, III, p. 158, 5 March,

1650) we learn that a debate took place concerning a bill for their protection. Four years later he reports (IV, p. 132, 30 August) that the Council of State issued an order for the relief of such tenants in Cheshire and Lancashire.

26. It is reprinted in Sabine's edition of *The Works of Gerrard Winstanley*. Prof. Sabine's reasons for rejecting Winstanley's authorship are conclusive. I would add to them considerations of style. The author of *Light Shining* knew neither how to build a sentence nor how to construct a coherent essay. Winstanley had these skills. But some of the atrocious punning etymologies in *Light Shining* and *More Light* are like Winstanley at his worst. He may have collaborated with its author (see p. 660 below).

27. Sabine, *op. cit.*, p. 628.

28. *Ibid.*, pp. 615-16.

29. *Ibid.*, pp. 633-4.

30. *Ibid.*, p. 643. Thomason dates the *Declaration* 10 May, 1649.

31. *The Humble Representation of the Desires of the Officers and Soldiers in the Regiment of Horse for Northumberland* (5 December, 1648).

32. Wolfe, pp. 397-410.

33. *The fundamental laws and liberties of England, claimed, asserted and agreed unto by several peaceable persons of the City of London, Westminster, Southwark, Hamlets and places adjacent, commonly called Levellers. . . . July the 9, 1653.* An earlier petition from 'many thousands', which endorsed most of the usual Leveller demands, asks that 'copyholds and the like . . . may be taken away' (Whitelock, *op. cit.*, III, pp. 433-5, 29 June, 1652).

34. I owe this quotation from *The Poor Husbandman's Advocate to Rich Racking Landlords*, with much else in this chapter, to Miss Margaret James, *op. cit.*, p. 129.

35. T. Rogers, *Six Centuries of Work and Wages*, II, p. 479.

CHAPTER XXII

The Commonwealth Emerges

It was not the revolutionary tribunal over which Bradshaw presided that condemned King Charles to death. What it did was to put into legal language the verdict the Army had pronounced as it trudged, counting its scars, over the miry roads that led from victory to victory. Historians have pieced together the record of all that went on at Westminster during the last month of 1648 and the first of 1649. They tell us how Cromwell hesitated, while Ireton and Harrison drove implacably forwards. Fairfax stammered and young Vane argued for mercy, backed by the Dutch republic which tried to save the life of a king who had never been its friend. All this is as interesting as it is irrelevant. This thing did not come to pass as the fruit of balanced arguments in rational debate. It came to pass because a resolute minority which understood organisation canalised the passions of 30,000 men of action who had swords in their hands. Was it revenge for their maimed comrades and their dead that chiefly moved them? Was it the primitive belief that only blood can wash out the stains of blood upon the earth? Or was it that these men, veterans though they were, were oppressed by remorse for the blood they had shed, and sought to lay their guilt on the head of a royal scapegoat?

To these instincts and passions the Levellers knew how to appeal with their democratic principle that one law must govern noble and simple alike. The reader will remember that the first plain demand in print for the deposition, trial and execution of King Charles came from John Lilburne in January 1647, in his memorable pamphlet *Regal Tyranny*

Discovered. Based in sober language on rational grounds it was the most urgent of the proposals that made the Levellers' Large Petition of 11 September, 1648, one of the decisive documents of the English Revolution. By a notable feat of organisation it then rained petitions from all the regiments of the Army scattered between Berwick and Land's End. These echoed the Large Petition and more especially its call for justice on the capital authors of the civil wars. With this evidence of the Army's mind in front of him Cromwell declared his solidarity with his officers and men. All that then remained to be done was to purge the Parliament, so that it should carry out the Army's will.

It is the Levellers, then, who must bear before history the responsibility for this act of retributive justice—or shall we call it in plain words revenge? It was an act of distinguished courage, not merely because this minority of Levellers, soldiers and Independents defied the immense majority of its fellow countrymen—the neutral apolitical masses, the Presbyterians and the Scots, as well as the Cavaliers; it was an act of signal courage because it challenged the archetypal idea of the King's divinity, an idea that may be co-eval with the first crop of wheat neolithic men reaped with flint sickles.

On a short view, it was a ruinous and unnecessary mistake. It blotted out from the national memory the record of the disastrous reign of an infatuated prince, to set in its place the gracious image of the royal martyr. It dug deeper still the chasm of hate between sectaries and churchmen, unbridgeable through many generations. It wrecked the Leveller plan for democracy, because in the teeth of this outraged majority it was now impossible to risk a free election. The worst of these consequences could have been avoided, had the victorious minority been satisfied with the deposition of King Charles, whom it might then have banished, or better still permitted to escape to the continent. But these are the trite moralisings of posterity after the fears and angers of revolution have had three hundred years in which to cool. In the long run something was achieved by our ancestors' audacity; the enslaving dogma of divine right could never be revived.

For the tragedy in Whitehall, as for so much else in this

Revolution, the initiative sprang, then, from the Levellers. The story of their share in it is, however, complicated and by no means easy to unravel. Though Lilburne's narrative in *Legal Fundamental Liberties* assures us more than once that, for every critical step he and his colleagues took, they had the approval of the party's respresentative council, it is not so clear that the leaders themselves were always in agreement over tactics. At Windsor, on the eve of Pride's Purge, while the Leveller delegation was negotiating with Ireton and Harrison over the Agreement of the People, it seems that Walwyn was strongly opposed to the march of the Army on London.[1] How he would have acted in face of the determination of the Presbyterian majority at Westminster to conclude the 'personal treaty' with King Charles and bring him back to power—this we do not know. Musing, some months later, in the quiet of the Tower, on the events of that winter, he made the most civilised of all the contemporary comments on the end of Charles's reign. He approved the action of the Commons in bringing his 'usurpation' to an end, but he was 'sorry' that they killed him, since his was an 'hereditary tyranny'. Walwyn remembered what most of his contemporaries forgot, that Charles learned from his father the doctrines on which he acted with obstinate, nay with heroic fidelity; it was, therefore, an injustice 'to take away his life for his parents' sin'. Like Andrew Marvell, this sensitive spectator was impressed by the King's dignity; he suffered 'patiently and cheerfully . . . which was a token of a good conscience and a noble mind'. None the less, Walwyn believed that this 'tyrant's' end would serve as 'a *caveat* for princes'. 'By this example other kings may know that they are not lords but subjects to the law.'[2] Overton alone among the leaders approved the execution of the King without criticisms or reservations; he called it 'the supremest piece of justice that ever was in England'.[3]

Lilburne had no objection in principle to the trial of the King, or to his execution, if found guilty. But he held that neither the Long Parliament, which had exhausted its mandate, nor that 'mock Parliament' the Rump was entitled to try the King or send him to trial. That was an act which only a truly representative House of Commons was fit to undertake.

He wished, therefore, to postpone all action against King Charles until the Agreement of the People had been adopted and signed by the 'well-affected' electorate, and a new Parliament chosen on the model it prescribed. Holding these views he was bound to condemn any action the Rump took against any of the capital authors of the Civil War, the King among them, as an arbitrary abuse of the power of the sword. He had further objections, and these of the gravest, against the course actually taken. The High Court of Justice was an 'extraordinary' tribunal, an invention devised for a political emergency and packed with partisans who could only caricature the forms of impartial justice. The charge brought against the King was open to the fatal criticism that it was based on no known law; Parliament, the Levellers maintained, has no right to punish 'where no law provides'.[4] This principle, enshrined in the constitution of the United States, they were the first among English parties to proclaim. It ranks among the precarious gains of the pioneers which constitute civilisation.

The King, John Lilburne argued, was entitled like every Englishman to be tried in one of the regular courts of the land, before twelve jurymen subject to challenge. The charge to which he stood exposed was that he had counselled and commissioned murder—that is to say in battle. Apart from the difficulty that no jury of the King's peers could be found, this positive proposal, typical of John's legalistic mind at its worst, was as unhelpful as his negative criticisms were sound. He rejected an invitation to sit as one of the judges of the High Court and was absent in Durham during the trial. On his return to London his outraged sense of justice moved him to offer his practical help to three leading Royalists in their defence —Hamilton, Holland and that attractive personality 'stout Capel'. He had no sympathy with what they had done, but he held that they were entitled to trial before a regular court. Henceforward it became a principle with the Leveller party to follow their leader's example in such cases. Militants though they were, they were also liberals, who kept an ideal of objective thinking and disinterested conduct alive while the totalitarian darkness closed in around them.

In this last phase of the long struggle against monarchy, the

Levellers felt none of the exhilaration of victory. Ireton had shattered their alliance with the Independents. Scots, Cavaliers and Presbyterians were all defeated, but of the two surviving powers who faced them, the remnant of the Parliament and the Grandees of the Army, they could trust neither. In their darker moments the fear haunted them that all their struggles for liberty and democracy might be ending in a military dictatorship. The Army, none the less, had adopted their programme, or most of it; they had nothing further to propose. For several weeks, at the turn of the year, as if its work were done, the party went out of action. Lilburne travelled up to County Durham to collect from the estates of delinquents the compensation Parliament had awarded him for his sufferings under the Star Chamber. Out of the £3,000 due to him, he never managed to collect more than £600. About this time John Wildman quitted his Leveller comrades and devoted his great abilities to the pursuit of his own career. Overton commented on his desertion with whimsical malice, and John Lilburne must needs say in print that this 'bosom friend and zealous and bold asserter of England's freedom' had

> not only lost all his zeal, but I am afraid his honesty and his principles and is closed with familiarity and design with Cromwell, although no one knows his knavery better than he.[5]

John's wrath, however, cooled rapidly and in the following year he was again collaborating with Major Wildman.

Sexby also was attracted back to the Army and was for several years in high favour with Cromwell, who promoted him rapidly. Still a ranker in 1648, he was by 1651 a Lieut.-Colonel. Henry Marten, so far as we know, was never elected to any position in the Leveller party; none the less he was a collaborator so close and influential that one inclines to rank him among its leaders. When Marten the regicide became one of the leaders of the Rump and the Council of State, this co-operation came to an end, though his personal friendship with John Lilburne survived. Even Walwyn stood for a time aloof. For 'several months' in the early part of 1649 he ceased to attend the meetings of the party. The tactical problem that faced it may well have baffled him, and since he did not know what to do, like a wise man he did nothing. The radical activity of some of the soldiers soon brought the party to life again, with Lilburne and Overton to sound the reveille.

This depressing picture of slackness and desertion may be accurate in its details, yet it conveys an entirely false impression. If Wildman and Sexby dropped out of the ranks, they could plead that the objectives for which they enlisted had been won. Had the Levellers been given to complacency they might have lit their bonfires on every hill-top when the Commons proclaimed the sovereignty of the people in their resolutions of 4 January, 1649. Here they are *verbatim*:

> That the people are under God the original of all just power; that the Commons of England in Parliament assembled, being chosen by and representing the people, have the supreme power in this nation; that whatsoever is enacted or declared for law by the Commons in Parliament assembled hath the force of law, and all the people of this nation are concluded thereby, although the consent and concurrence of King or House of Peers be not had thereunto.

Could anything be more familiar? Here is a terse summary of the political doctrine that inspired all the Leveller tracts from the *Remonstrance of Many Thousand Citizens* of 7 July, 1646, down to the Large Petition of 11 September, 1648. One might say much the same of the Act abolishing the office of King (17 March, 1649). With its appeal to experience to prove that regal power has always oppressed and enslaved the subject, it echoes the *Remonstrance* of 1646, which argued that monarchy is 'the original of all oppression'.

The argument from experience of the Act abolishing the House of Lords (19 March, 1649) which describes that House as 'useless and dangerous' was Leveller doctrine from the beginning. These opinions were not a native growth from the brains of Cromwell and Ireton, nor were they congenial to most of the Grandees of the New Model. As recently as October 1647 the Commons had to listen for three hours to Cromwell's defence of the institution of monarchy; as recently as January 1648 the Grandees sent their delegation to assure the Lords that they had nothing to fear from the Army. Throughout the two crucial years of opposition to the Long Parliament and the traditions for which it stood, always the initiative came from the Levellers, sometimes from the civilians and sometimes from the representatives of the soldiers. Even when Ireton became the draftsman and manager of the opposition, it was still the ideas of the Levellers that he put down on paper though often in a devitalised form. This is, indeed, an understatement. Had not the rankers of the Army, inspired by the Levellers, with their elected Agitators to lead them, resisted the disbanding of the New Model, no opposition could have survived. In the everlasting Parliament, when it did venture to make a stand, it suffered monotonous defeat. The Blasphemy Act, bristling with penalties as savage as any that Laud imposed, would have silenced Independents, Anabaptists and Seekers alike, or driven the bolder of them to look for freedom in the wilderness.

Here lay the core and motive of this opposition. The democracy for which Levellers and Agitators argued and fought was a means to an end. The sovereignty of the people, the republican constitution, the single-chambered Parliament, the redistribution of seats, household franchise, the election of magistrates, parsons, and officers—all this elaborate framework was constructed as the answer to a simple question of self-preservation. How were 'the middle sort of people and the poor'—in other words the tradesmen, craftsmen and peasants—how were they to survive, against the regimentation of the Presbyterians, if they were bent on doing their thinking for themselves? Thinking in those days was dominated by religion. 'The poor' were organised not in trade unions, but in 'gathered' churches or conventicles, under 'mechanic preachers' who had never learned to translate at sight from Hebrew into Latin. Step by step in eager debates among themselves, under the stimulus of events, the Levellers reached their answer. The right to think aloud, the right to be oneself in association with one's equals, survival with self-respect—these could be secured only in a democratic and secular republic. One can distinguish three basic ideas in the web of the Levellers' thought; all the rest is machinery.

First comes the realm of individuality, 'self-propriety' as they called it, which they fenced off from the intrusion of the state. This they never defined exactly, but two things they stressed. It included everything concerned with God and His worship—speculation about Him, contemplation, ritual and prayer. No less certainly did it include provinces of conduct where the 'inner voice' or conscience spoke with imperious clarity. Here what experience singled out and emphasised was the right of the individual to decide for himself whether to fight or stay at home—freedom, in short, from the press-gang and conscription.

The second basic idea affirmed the individual's right of association with his fellows. Though never clearly defined, this meant in practice chiefly the right to form 'gathered' churches, and to use the press freely without censorship. It also included the right of combination for political ends, chiefly (according to the usage of their century) by presenting petitions, with the meetings and publicity this involved.

The third of these basic ideas was the equality before the law of rich and poor, noble and simple, and (an even more daring innovation) their equality in political power. This meant in the concrete the ending of all class privileges and vetoes, with the cheapening and simplification of legal procedure. It meant also manhood or at any rate household suffrage. The party as a unanimous group had got no further than this. But some of its abler members, notably Walwyn, had come to realise that equality in political power would be unattainable without equality in education and some approach to equality in income. At moments the party understood that economic power vested in a landowning class could render its claim to equal political power of no effect, and it had its plan for abolishing base tenures. But this it never pursued wholeheartedly and in the long run that may well be the explanation of its failure to shape and direct the English Revolution.

By the turn of the year, 1648-9, the Levellers had achieved the chief of their negative aims; the obstructions of monarchy and the Lords' veto were swept away. Their positive aims of equality and humanity were still to win. Whether they could be won depended on the omnipotent Army. The Levellers had saved it from disbanding, but they had lost their footing in its councils. Could they recover it?

NOTES TO CHAPTER XXII

1. *Legal Fundamental Liberties*, H. and D., p. 421.

2. *Tyranipocrit*, pp. 54-6. For Walwyn's authorship of this tract, see p. 71 above.

3. *The Moderate*, 6-13 March, 1649. For Overton and *The Moderate* see Chapter XX above.

4. *Legal Fundamental Liberties*, H. and D., p. 422.

5. *An Impeachment of High Treason against Oliver Cromwell* (10 August, 1649).

CHAPTER XXIII

Lilburne's Challenge

No sooner had the axe fallen on the platform before Whitehall than the testing time for the new government began. Abroad, from Hague to Kremlin, through republics as well as monarchies, ran a shudder of horror and anger. In Ireland for the first time a united nation came into sight to resist re-conquest, as the southern Protestant gentry rallied to the confederate Catholic majority. Beyond the Tweed another outraged nation, furious because an English Parliament had done the King of Scotland to death, acknowledged Prince Charles as his heir and prepared for action by depriving of political rights all who seemed to its Presbyterian clergy unworthy of God's blessing in the struggle that lay ahead—all given to swearing, whoring or drunkenness, and all who neglected family prayer. At home half the common-law judges refused to serve the new order. Even with the help of its military police, it could not stop the re-printing by the underground presses of *Eikon Basilike*, which most of our ancestors accepted as the authentic self-portrait of the royal martyr. In many counties the greater part of the middle and upper class, women as well as men, went into mourning for him. Even the Presbyterian clergy, as a royalist scribbler put it, were now 'snivelling out a little loyalty'. In some provincial cities, notably Exeter, Northampton and Lincoln, the judges of the regicide Commonwealth were boycotted by the mayor and all the local gentry when they came to open the assizes with the traditional pageantry.

It was not the upper classes alone who stood aloof. In villages and cities alike this was a winter of acute suffering for the poorer classes, and for this they were beginning to blame the powers above them at Westminster. Nature for the third year running had been unkind; by reason of incessant rain the harvest of 1648 had been once more a partial failure. But the unemployment that was the curse of 1649 was something far graver than the scarcity of work which always afflicted the agricultural labourers in winter. The industrial workers suffered as heavily, and the distress continued after the coming of spring. It is not difficult to guess some of the causes. There was, doubtless, a crisis of confidence, for after the King's execution property was frightened and pessimistic. Because of their fears, as a Puritan journalist put it, many of the nobles and gentry bent all their thoughts on scraping up a little money 'to fly with', instead of using it 'to employ either the poor labourers or handicraftsmen'.[1] Then, during the orgy of speculation in land which followed the confiscation, in whole or part, of the cavalier estates, vast sums of money were withdrawn for long or short periods from circulation. Again, there must have been an appreciable drain of wealth, in the form of jewellery or gold, to meet the needs of the exiled Royalists. But the chief cause of the widespread unemployment may well have been the failure of wages to rise, so as to balance the monstrous increase in the cost of food. It was not yet realised in that century that 'the poor' rank high among the employers of 'the poor'; they were now poorer than ever.

One looks in vain for any precise figures to measure the distress, but a good deal can be learned from the newspapers. A petition from London, which shows the influence of Leveller thinking, estimates that all over England four times as many persons as usual were in need of relief, yet the total amount of relief distributed did not exceed the customary figure.[2] How inadequate this relief was may be gleaned from some statements in the *Moderate Intelligencer*. Though flax and hemp were being imported in some cities 'to set the poor on work', many of them were employed in this way only for two days a week. The same journalist, a humane and intelligent man, declared that 'a third part of the people in most parishes' stood in need of relief, but they got it only 'under some heavy affliction of sickness or loss'. Many hundreds of thousands, he reminds his readers, 'have food in summer and little or none in winter'. Even those who have work, he goes on, are so ill paid that they can hardly buy bread enough with their wages, and nothing more. He predicts (in March) that before the next harvest many are 'like . . . to be at death's door or dead'.³ A week later a tantalisingly brief account of a debate in the Commons confirms these impressions. The House was concerned over the prices of food, at least double what they were wont to be, 'while the labour of the poor is cheaper'. A bill to enforce three meatless days in each week was introduced. Two days later an order was sent out to Justices of the Peace reminding them of their duty to fix the wages of servants and artificers.⁴

The details of this general picture are filled in by the correspondents in the provinces who send local news to the Leveller *Moderate* and its more conservative contemporary. Typical is a paragraph from Poole.

> Many country people . . . cry out that they have no trade, their families ready to starve. . . . They desire the Army or Parliament would take some speedy course to set all sorts of poor people to work.⁵

Two of these reports are from industrial areas. From Somerset, which made the famous West-country broadcloth, came news that 'the poor' were in 'a sad condition' with 'no employment or little' and 'all things dear and labour cheap'. To this (after mentioning with astonishment the levelling opinions of the soldiers quartered in this county) the correspondent adds his prediction that 'the poor' will soon turn as radical as the troopers.⁶ From Colchester, which specialised in 'baize' cloth, we learn that in May 'the poorer sort were mostly unemployed'. A number of spinners and weavers, in their desperation, seized some timber that had been felled and sold it 'to get bread'.⁷ This was unusual; the English poor starved as a rule with patience, but at Colchester there was a strong infusion of Dutch blood among the cloth workers.

The correspondent of the *Moderate* in Lancaster reports on 13 April: 'we have not bread to put in our mouths. . . . The poor are almost famished'. He quotes the local prices: wheat

20s. a bushel, peas and beans 16s. or 17s., oats 12s. The normal price of wheat was round about 5s. In next week's issue we learn that in Westmorland the Justices of the Peace certify that no less than 16,000 families—a high figure for this thinly peopled county—have neither bread nor money to buy it. In Lancashire rioting is likely unless help arrives betimes. Help was on its way, but Prince Rupert's fleet of privateers cruising in St George's Channel captured the ship laden with corn for Westmorland. A petition from Kendal asks for a convoy for the next cargo which was expected from Hamburg. The convoy was promised. 'Alas!' comments the *Moderate*'s correspondent, 'they have no seed corn to sow their grounds and what bread corn is imported they have no money to buy it; and before any corn can come from Hamburg, they are like to be famished.'

In a despatch from Newcastle, we learn that the Justices of Cumberland, who certified that there were 30,000 families in their county who lacked seed and bread corn or money to buy either, had appealed for help to Northumberland. A collection was made, but not enough was raised to feed so many. The belief that there were generous hearts and corn to spare on the east coast was the last hope that kept the poor of the Lake District alive, though many 'died in the highways for lack of bread'. 'Most of the meaner sort in Cumberland,' this Northumbrian Leveller writes, 'have left their habitations and travel with their wives and children into these parts to get relief, but few are able to help them.' After this picture of the trek of starving thousands across the moors, it is pleasant to read at the end of May that in Preston famine was relieved by the arrival of grain from overseas, but, adds this ruthless chronicler, plague and pestilence followed in its wake.[8]

Faced with danger abroad and unpopularity at home, the Rump kept up its courage, while it played for safety. It dared not reduce the Army if it was bent on re-conquering Ireland, and it was the high cost of the Army which obliged it to impose on an impoverished people its detested system of indirect taxation, the excise or purchase tax. If it had listened to Leveller advice and relied on direct taxation, it would have antagonised the propertied groups on whose support it depended. The same calculation forbade it to take action against the corruption and graft that stained its record, alike at Westminster and in the counties. On the contrary, because it was unpopular and its prospects looked precarious, it had to distribute perquisites and *pourboires* with a lavish hand to the lawyers, soldiers and politicians who backed it, in order to buy their loyalty or refresh it. It had nothing to offer the groaning taxpayers and the ribald worldlings who found the group of godly politicians as greedy and acquisitive as their rivals. One thing was changed in its domestic outlook and only one. The Saints were freed from the fear that the Blasphemy Act would be set in motion against them.

There was, after all, no noticeable difference in social composition between the Rump and the evicted Presbyterians. The majority of its members were country gentry and the rest were lawyers or merchants. The two latter groups rarely came from a separate class. Many of the men of business were, like the barristers, the younger sons of a landowning family; they inter-married with the squirearchy and most of them invested their gains in land. There seems to be no warrant for the belief which the Levellers held that the lawyers were numerically the dominant group in the Rump,[9] though it may well be that their skill in using and abusing the procedure of the House gave them an influence out of proportion to their numbers.

When it came to choosing an executive the Rump elected a highly respectable team with plenty of 'blue blood' in its veins. Only one of them, Major-General Skippon, was born outside the propertied class, and he was a conservative. Two could be described as Levellers, but they were Colonel Henry Marten, a big landowner, and Lord Grey of Groby. The list began with four earls, of whom two, Pembroke and Salisbury, had sat as judges in the Star Chamber. Of peers, eldest sons of peers, baronets and knights there were (including the earls) no less than seventeen. Six were senior lawyers or judges. Two were aldermen of the city. Only eleven were regicides. But twenty-two disapproved of the King's execution, or at all events refused to approve it. The *Moderate* found the last of these facts disturbing; it should have gone some way towards reassuring conservative opinion.

This Council of State was armed with formidable powers; like one of the prerogative courts of the monarchy, it could summon, question and imprison whom it would. Several of the political prisoners under its control, notably Sir William Waller, lay in the Tower for many years untried; one, Judge Jenkins, was released only at the Restoration. It took the place of the old Privy Council, but with this important difference, that instead of being nominated by the King it was elected annually by the Commons. It did not exercise power over life and death; that was the function of the High Court of Justice, a revolutionary tribunal composed of sixty persons, most of them laymen and all of them partisans, who sat as judges and jury at once. Like all the major revolutions in European history, the English Revolution had to resort to extraordinary tribunals armed with exceptional powers, but it made only a sparing use of them. If there never was anything that could fairly be called a reign of terror (ugly though life became under the Protectorate in 1655) two facts stand out as the explanation. Thanks to the Channel and the navy, the English revolutionary government was never attacked, as those of France and Russia were, by the armies of the neighbouring powers in alliance with native reactionaries—unless, indeed, one reckons the Scots as foreigners. If geography counts for much, ethics may count for even more. The steady appeal of the Levellers, pedantic though it sometimes was, to legal tradition and an ideal of impartial justice, stopped the soldiers from resorting too crudely or too often to naked force.

For the rest, in its domestic policy the Rump seems to have acted on the calculation that the Saints were obliged to support it anyhow, while nothing would avail to win over the sinners. What impressed the Levellers was the lack of imagination the revolutionary government showed in devising means to win over the masses. It may be that it did not greatly value their support or fear their indifference. The consequence was that the Puritan Revolution failed, because the Saints never managed to rally to their cause any public wider than the sects who shared their religious outlook.

What John Lilburne would have done in their place he set out in the address he was allowed to deliver from the bar of the

House on 26 February, 1649. The climax of his proposals was that tithes should be abolished forthwith. This he singled out by way of illustrating the new attitude to life in the rulers of England which would, if they were to adopt it, 'so fasten you in the affections of the people and of the honest officers and soldiers, as that you should not need to fear any opposite power whatsoever'.[10] That was a step the Commonwealth never so much as attempted, nor the Protectorate after it. How Henry Marten's bill to make an end of imprisonment for debt was rendered worthless by the ingenuity of the lawyers we shall see in Chapter XXXIII. To give yet another illustration, hardly had the Council of State assumed control of the fleet than it set the press-gang in motion. 'The plain man' (to use the Leveller phrase) was soon murmuring that though the King was beheaded, nothing in his own daily round was changed.

Hardly had the first year of freedom dawned when the Rump began to silence criticism by intimidating the press. On 5 January it revived the brutal ordinance of September 1647 in order to suppress unlicensed pamphlets. This imposed fines or imprisonment on author, printer and bookseller, but the really deterrent penalty was that the offending press was to be seized and broken in pieces. Any peddler who sold unlicensed pamphlets was to be whipped as a common rogue. Fairfax was instructed to make full use of his military police to enforce this ordinance. This use of the Army for police purposes made it unpopular among Londoners and was detested by the soldiers themselves, who performed their unpleasant tasks (as both Levellers and Royalists testified) very roughly and very ill.

To this threat of suppression, the Levellers, who had always relied for most of their propaganda on the daring unlicensed printers in their own ranks, amongst them Richard Overton, replied with the petition addressed to the Commons which was published on 19 January. It is a bold and unqualified vindication of unlicensed printing, well argued and well written, though it lacks the verbal magic of Milton's immortal tract. It reminded the Commons that they would never have dared to proclaim the sovereignty of the people, as they had just done, had not the Levellers prepared the way by their unlicensed pamphlets. It protested against the punishment of whipping, 'fit only for slaves or bondmen'. But what afflicted the petitioners above measure was the setting up of 'a military jurisdiction', which above anything in this world they desired for ever to avoid.[11] Henceforward all their energies were concentrated on the struggle against the threat of military dictatorship, which they identified with Cromwell's ascendancy. Lilburne's was a one-track mind. Once it had set out in this direction, it had eyes and ears for nothing else, not even for the doings of the Scots.

As for the Independents, they had no wish as yet to throw over their troublesome allies. Offers of well-paid jobs were made to John himself and to several of his colleagues. In the rambling, garrulous pages of *Legal Fundamental Liberties*—what a lovable character this friendly egotist was, with all his foibles!—he explains why he had to refuse these tempting offers, in spite of the fact that he was living on his capital and saw no way open to him to gain an honest living by trade. He could not in conscience serve a 'mock-Parliament' (which is all that the Rump was) nor could he bring himself to draw his salary out of 'the bowels and pining bellies of the overtaxed poor'.[12]

Lilburne's political instinct told him that he could counteract Cromwell's influence only by sapping his control over the Army. The first move of the Levellers was to set going in the ranks a petition which voiced the soldiers' feelings about martial law. They drew their inspiration from John's saying that it is immoral to 'imbase the hearts of the people'. The discipline of the New Model, in other words, was felt to be degrading. They ask

> that the articles of war now may be renewed and mitigated as being too severe and tyrannous for an army of freeborn Englishmen, and that martial law may not be so frequently exercised in such a cruel manner.

They ask, further, that the Army may no longer be used for police duties, such as 'seizing upon unlicensed books or printing presses'.[13] It was a brilliant device of the Levellers to use the soldiers themselves for their attack on militarism.

This petition roused all the defensive instincts of the high command. That civilians should meddle with the discipline of the Army was felt to be intolerable. After a debate at the general council of officers on 22 February, an order of the day was drawn up in the name of Lord Fairfax which set severe limits to the soldiers' right to petition.[14] The holding of meetings to promote petitions was forbidden. If any troop or company should feel aggrieved, it may still petition, but only if the petition is approved first by its captain, and then by the commander of the regiment, who must hand it over to the General to be by him presented to Parliament—if he sees fit. The mood of the Grandees was expressed even more clearly in a further request addressed to Cromwell and Ireton that they should promote legislation for the infliction upon civilians who 'breed division in the Army' of the punishment they would suffer if they were soldiers. Some of the Grandees even proposed that they should be empowered to try such civilians by court-martial. A saying of Colonel Hewson, who always figures in contemporary records as the toughest of the tough, was quoted to the effect that they could hang twenty while the civil magistrate was hanging one.

These threats from the Army's Grandees convinced John Lilburne that he must appeal to Parliament and public opinion while he was still a free man. He rapidly completed a pamphlet addressed to the House of Commons under the title of *England's New Chains Discovered*. This (or rather what came to be known as the first part of it) he and other Levellers presented to the House on 26 February; the soldiers' petition about martial law reached it on the same day. The startling event of this day was that John was called to the bar of the House and allowed to address it. This was not his first appearance at the bar; he had stood there as a prisoner to answer for his life. But on this occasion, for the first time in his turbulent career and the last, he stood there as the leader of a friendly party on whose alliance his hearers depended. The explanation may lie in the fact that the Leveller party was growing rapidly, though we need not take too literally John's boast that for every adherent of a year ago, it now had hundreds.[15]

The Levellers still cherished the illusion that the Grandees of the Army were in earnest when they adopted the Agreement of the People. Lilburne, therefore, devoted much of his space to an able criticism of the officers' version of this charter. He stresses chiefly the danger latent in the provisions for a bi-ennial Parliament, which is to sit only for six months, while the Council of State, armed with the most far-reaching powers, is to reign supreme for the other eighteen. What he has to say about the ambiguities and omissions in the officers' draft shows the same good sense, but it need not detain us, since no one seriously intended to base the constitution upon this document. John's fear of what a Council of State might do, if it sat so long unchecked by the people's representatives, was reasonable. But his suspicion of all authority now carried him to the other extreme, when he proposed that Parliament should dispense with any standing executive or cabinet, and manage its affairs 'by committees of short continuance'. What he had to say about toleration and tithes, press-gang and censorship, might have impressed the House more favourably had he not called for the dissolution of this Council which it had just elected.

The Levellers carried to the point of morbid extravagance the characteristic belief of their century and the next that government is an evil, albeit a necessary evil. The state whose constitution they drafted would have been barely capable of coherent action. Only by accident could its foreign policy have shown any consistency. In the state as power the Levellers took no interest; indeed, the quasi-pacifist Walwyn came near to rejecting the whole idea of power as uncivilised and un-christian. The practical conclusion from Lilburne's criticsm of the officers' draft of the Agreement was that Parliament must be not biennial but annual. The revival of this antiquated idea is intelligible only in its historical setting, as a protest against the everlasting Long Parliament; yet it became the Levellers' legacy for many generations to the English left. Monmouth had to promise it to the weavers and coal-miners of Somerset; Charles James Fox kept it alive and the Chartists found it still so dynamic that they embodied it in a programme which contained only one point that would have seemed strange to their forerunners—the secrecy of the ballot. In the final draft of the Agreement, the Levellers carried their fear of authority and their indifference to continuity a step further still.

Not only was the life of a Parliament limited to one year, but its members might not be re-elected until another year had elapsed.

The real purpose of this pamphlet was, however, to awaken civilian vigilance against the peril from the Army. Lilburne dwelt on the power its commanders possessed, through the selection and promotion of officers, to mould it to their purposes. By exercising martial law with much cruelty they debased the men's spirits and made them subservient to their own wills and pleasures. This audacious pamphlet wound up by beseeching the House to consider 'how dangerous it is for one and the same persons to be continued long in the highest commands of a military power . . . which was the original of most regalities and tyrannies in the world'. Here though it named no names was a demand for the dismissal of Cromwell and doubtless of Ireton and Fairfax also. To ask the House which Colonel Pride elected to perform this feat was a masterpiece of unconscious irony.

The Levellers' challenge to the Army's Grandees found its echo promptly from the ranks. On 1 March a petition was addressed by eight troopers to Fairfax, which was a bold and brilliantly written criticism of his order of the day concerning petitions. There was nothing treasonable in it, but it was a deadly little essay in polemics.[16] There is no doubt that Richard Overton wrote it for the soldiers and saw to its publication. It went back to the stirring days of 1647, when the Army was unanimous in claiming for the soldier against the harsh ruling of Holles and Stapleton the elementary right to petition Parliament. Once again these troopers proudly declared that they were 'English soldiers engaged for the freedoms of England and not outlandish mercenaries to butcher the people for pay'. They reminded Fairfax that he had formerly backed them in asserting that 'our being soldiers hath not deprived us of our right as commoners'. Nothing worth preserving of that right was left, if their petitions must pass through 'a vexatious labyrinth of thraldom' and run the gauntlet of the negative voices of captain, colonel and general. They went on to argue that the officer is nothing without 'the soldier that endureth the heat and burden of the day and performeth that work whereof the officers bear the glory and name'. They criticised the High Court of Justice and the Council of State, 'entrusted with little less than unlimited power' and composed of 'the most pernicious interests of our rotten state, lords, lawyers, Star Chamber judges and dissenters from the proceedings against the King'. They wound up by declaring their agreement with Lilburne's *England's New Chains Discovered.*

These daring troopers were at once arrested, and court-martialled on 3 March. Three of them apologised and were pardoned, but the other five (Robert Ward, Simon Grant, Thomas Watson, George Jelles and William Sawyer) faced their judges with courage. They were told that for their letter 'tending to breed mutiny in the Army' they deserved to be punished with death, but 'in mercy' they were sentenced to be cashiered the Army after riding 'at the head of their regiments with their faces towards the horses' tails, their faults written upon their breasts and their swords broken over their heads'. After this degrading punishment, the five troopers found coaches waiting for them which carried them off to one of the Leveller taverns, where they were entertained to a 'plentiful dinner' as the party's guests of honour [17]

The Leveller plan of campaign went, however, far beyond the printing of petitions, risky though these were for those who signed them. In one district at least the troopers quartered in the market town were inciting the people to civil disobedience. A report in the sober *Moderate Intelligencer* (8-15 March) describes what went on at Hitchin in Hertfordshire. Troopers came into the market-place, fixed up John Lilburne's petitions on posts, read them aloud and made speeches, in which they exhorted the people

> to join with them, dissuading them from paying excise, advising them not to give free quarter, it being against all law and conscience. . . . They tell the people they will live and die with them in their deliverance from such like slaveries and from this new tyranny, naming the most eminent of the Army to the people. . . . Some of the militia . . . do abet them.

This narrative reads like a truthful record by a local reporter, perhaps an eye-witness. One conjectures that leaflets by John

Lilburne may have been printed which went further in their incitement to resistance than any of the pamphlets of this date that have come down to us—something pithy and brief, suitable for fixing on posts. These troopers were risking the firing squad. To advocate tax-resistance was mutiny.

On page after page of the *Moderate* for the following week (13-20 March) one notes the revolutionary tone. The background to all the appeals and reproaches addressed to Parliament is the misery and starvation in the counties. The leading article warns the government that the poor may revolt, 'Hunger breaks stone walls and famine cries out with a loud voice'. The affections of the poor, it argues as John Lilburne had done, could be won, but now they fear 'perpetual slavery'. 'Provoke not too much, for fear it be too late to repent; and ease the poor nation of the burden, for fear they shake it off and lay it upon their backs that are better able to bear it.'

That startling scene in the market-place of Hitchin may have been repeated elsewhere. The royalist newspaper *Mercurius Pragmaticus* of this same week reported that John Lilburne, seeing his Agreement of the People violated and himself in danger of prison, had gone over to the offensive. Together with his confederate 'that pernicious Catiline' Harry Marten, he has sent out some of his followers into many counties such as Hertfordshire, Berkshire and Hampshire. These messengers have posted up John's addresses in several market towns and called on the people to refuse excise and other unreasonable taxes. This the people are doing, since they argue that the money derived from the bishops' lands, compositions, confiscated woods, parks and forests should suffice, 'without . . . the cruel racking and extorting from the poor their livelihoods'. As so often, *Pragmaticus* was doubtless well-informed, though it is most unlikely that Marten, himself a member of the Council of State, would join in this enterprise. 'The poor', then, were actually in revolt, though only here and there as yet. The significant fact about this bloodless rebellion was that its organisers were not Royalists, but the shock-troops of the revolution itself.

It was never the Levellers' way when they rebelled to do it

silently. From Overton and Lilburne on the 21 and 24 March came pamphlets which completed their breach with the Cromwellian Independents. The first of them bore the fanciful title *The Hunting of the Foxes from Newmarket and Triploe Heaths to Whitehall, by five small Beagles (late of the Army)*. Like Overton's early anti-clerical tracts, it was 'printed in a corner of freedom, right opposite to the council of war'. It was, of course, a defence of the five troopers who were cashiered for petitioning: like good cavalry-men they defend themselves by attacking. Once more, at full length, with chapter and verse, they prove that the Grandees had run away from all the proud principles to which they pledged their loyalty at Newmarket in the summer of 1647. To require from soldiers abstention from political activity is a reasonable rule, but only if the same discretion is expected from officers. But the officers of the New Model were the leading figures in the political life of the Commonwealth, active, vocal, conspicuous. That they should exact silence from their men was an odious example of class discrimination. The men, writes Overton, might as well allow their officers to bore holes through their ears and become their slaves for ever. 'What,' he asks the men, 'are you now? Your mouths are stopped, you may be abused and enslaved, but you may not complain, you may not petition for redress.' It seems that this tightening of discipline went far beyond a ban on political activity. It was now all but impossible for a soldier to demand redress for any wrong an officer may have done him. At this point Overton does some muck-raking at the expense of the New Model. There were officers, he declares, who enriched themselves by Falstaff's device of 'false musters'. 'Daily,' he tells us, 'honest men are cashiered for complaining against their officers.' Any institution which understands discipline in this sense is bound to degenerate.

This clever, hard-hitting pamphlet has left its mark on the traditional reading of Cromwell's character and the ways of the Saints.

Was there ever [Overton asks] a generation of men so apostate, so false and so perjured as these? Did ever men pretend an higher degree of holiness, religion and zeal to God and their country than these? These preach, these fast,

these pray, these have nothing more frequent than the
sentences of sacred scripture, the name of God and of Christ
in their mouths. You shall scarce speak to Cromwell about
anything, but he will lay his hand on his breast, elevate his
eyes and call God to record, he will weep, howl and repent,
even while he doth smite you under the fifth rib.[18]

Overton tells the story—pretty certainly a myth—of the bargain
struck by Cromwell with King Charles, to restore him in
return for an earldom and the garter. He predicts, as Lilburne
also does, that the usurpation of the Council of State will end
in some form of monarchy—'a new regality'. During the
Whitehall debates both of them had heard some of Cromwell's
officers contending 'that this nation must have one prime
magistrate or ruler'. John supposed that the 'single person'
would be Fairfax, with Cromwell as the real dictator under
him. Their evidence that the Protectorate had been thought of
five years before it was set up is interesting.[19]

Lilburne's pamphlet, which appeared as *The Second Part of
England's New Chains Discovered*, is as biased as Overton's and
much less readable, yet it makes an impression of clumsy
sincerity.[20] In a somewhat confused narrative it traces Cromwell's record from the spring of 1647 onwards. For the baffling
inconsistencies and contradictions of his dealings with the
Agitators and the King, it admits only one explanation—
that he and his fellow-Grandees were opportunists who aimed
throughout at power and domination for themselves. It then
describes the means by which they were turning the Army into
their subservient tool. The psychology is crude, none the less it
was an important factor in the history of the Revolution that
Cromwell made this impression on most of his contemporaries,
not merely on Royalists who disliked his religious outlook, but
on many who were reared in the same nursery of radical
Puritanism, and on some like Lilburne who knew him intimately.
What they had come to dread, however, was something more
formidable than one ambitious soldier, it was the New Model,
now evolving under his direction into 'a company of bloody
and inhuman butchers of men, that had served seven years'
apprenticeship to that bloody and wicked trade of cutting
men's throats for money and nothing else'.[21] These were the

words not of a pacifist but of the man who commanded the dragoons on Marston Moor.

In this pamphlet Lilburne refrained from any direct attack on the House of Commons, but he did say that it had become 'the channel through which is conveyed all the decrees and determinations of a private council of officers'. Once more he called attention to the stopping of the press whose freedom, he declared, is 'the most essential part' of the nation's liberty. Once more he dwelt on the intolerable burden of taxation. But he will not give way to pessimism. He is sure that there are some members who will be loyal to their trust, and if they should fail he is confident that the response of the people and of 'a conscionable number of the soldiery' to the Levellers' appeal will suffice to defeat this 'faction of officers'. There were, he was sure, only two means of saving England from militarism, and he appealed to the Commons to further them both. The first fundamental was to adopt the Agreement of the People, which would, of course, involve the election of a new Parliament. But it was no less necessary that the Army should submit to a truly representative council, chosen according to the pattern laid down at Newmarket, by men as well as officers. In democracy Freeborn John still had unshaken faith.

NOTES TO CHAPTER XXIII

1. *Moderate Intelligencer* (8-15 March, 1649).

2. *The Petition of divers Inhabitants of London in the behalf of the poor of this Nation* (10 March, 1649).

3. *Moderate Intelligencer* (1-8 and 22-9 March, 1649).

4. *The Moderate* (3-10 April).

5. *Ibid.*

6. *Ibid.* (24 April–1 May).

7. *Ibid.* (22-29 May).

8. *Ibid.* (17-24 April; 24 April–1 May; 15-22 May).

9. Messrs Brunton and Pennington reckon the total members of the Rump at the high figure of 209, of whom only 33 were lawyers (*Members of the Long Parliament*). It should be noted, however, that by 'lawyers' they mean practising barristers only, and do not so reckon either those members like Commissary-General Ireton who had had a legal training, or the attorneys. But the maximum number who actually attended the House never exceeded 80. A statement that out of 80 members in the Rump 57 were lawyers will

be found in *The Levellers' Vindication* (8 September, 1649), by James Freize. Freize, a Muscovy merchant imprisoned for debt, who could spin a good yarn about Boris Godunov, was not a highly educated man, but he was no fool. Would his figures be gravely mistaken if a wider definition of 'lawyer' were adopted?

10. *England's New Chains Discovered*, H. and D., p. 167.

11. *The Petition of firm friends to the Parliament*, Wolfe, pp. 322-30.

12. H. and D., pp. 434-5.

13. *Moderate Intelligencer* (15-22 February, 1649), and *The Moderate* (20-7 February, 1649).

14. *C.P.*, II, pp. 191-2.

15. *England's New Chains*, H. and D., p. 166.

16. Wolfe, p. 372.

17. *The Moderate* (6-13 March, 1649).

18. Wolfe, pp. 370-1.

19. *Ibid.*, p. 366; H. and D., pp. 187, 443.

20. H. and D., pp. 171-89.

21. *Legal Fundamental Liberties*, H. and D., p. 447.

CHAPTER XXIV

Cromwell's Counterstroke

To personal criticism Cromwell was throughout his life indifferent; he took it without resentment, as he would have taken a thrust in fencing. But the second part of *England's New Chains* was much more than a personal attack. It struck not only at the source of his power, his control over the Army; by making a division in its ranks between his followers and 'the uncorrupted part of the soldiery', it threatened the safety of the Commonwealth and the stability of the Revolution. It was not, like Overton's *Hunting of the Foxes*, the personal utterance of a brilliant *frondeur*; it went out into the world as a manifesto of the Leveller party. Though everyone knew who wrote it, the title page of the first edition bore no author's signature, but invited the sympathetic reader to send his name to the promoters of the Large Petition of 11 September, 1648.

On the afternoon of Tuesday, 27 March, 1649, in the Commons Cromwell struck back. Yet in the morning of that very day, while John Lilburne was in the lobby, he received from one of the Lieut.-General's men of business for the last time the offer of a well-paid post. He made it clear, once for all, that he was not for sale.[1] Thereupon in the House a resolution was moved and carried, which ran thus:

> The House being informed of a scandalous and seditious book printed, entitled *The Second Part of England's New Chains Discovered*, the said book was this day read. Resolved ... that this printed paper ... doth contain most false, scandalous and reproachful matter, and is highly seditious and destructive to the present government, as it is now declared

and settled by Parliament, tends to division and mutiny in the Army, and the raising of a new war in the Commonwealth, and to hinder the present relief of Ireland and to the continuing of free quarter. And this House doth further declare, That the authors, contrivers and framers of the said papers are guilty of high treason and shall be proceeded against as traitors; And that all persons whatsoever that shall join with and adhere unto and hereafter voluntarily aid or assist the authors, framers and contrivers of the aforesaid paper, in the prosecution thereof, shall be esteemed as traitors to the Commonwealth and be proceeded against accordingly.

The debate, as we learn from *Pragmaticus* (27 March-3 April, 1649), ran for three hours. For the resolution spoke Cromwell and Sir Arthur Haslerig, who attacked not only John but the Lilburnes in general. A local feud had set these two Durham families at enmity. Sir Arthur is not an attractive figure; gruff and notoriously acquisitive, few of his contemporaries (save, indeed, the kindly and charitable Ludlow) had a good word for him. Which of the Levellers' friends opposed we do not know—perhaps Marten, perhaps Ludlow; there is no record of a division. Though the authors of the pamphlet are not named in the resolution, evidently there was no such reticence in the debate. In effect, then, the House, without hearing their defence, passed a sentence of death on John and certain of his colleagues—for treason was a capital offence. The part of the charge that really mattered was, of course, the accusation that their pamphlet tended towards mutiny in the Army. The House then instructed the Council of State to discover the authors. In its last sentence, vaguely worded though it was, it threatened the whole Leveller party, if it continued its activities, with this same charge of treason. This threat was meant to be taken seriously, for on the following day the Rump's resolution was read aloud in the streets of London, to the accompaniment of drums and trumpets, at the head of a troop of horse.[2]

In the early hours of Wednesday, 28 March, between four and six, four detachments of horse and foot numbering each between one and two hundred men, marched to the homes of Lilburne, Walwyn, Overton and Thomas Prince (the treasurer of the Leveller party, by trade a wholesale cheese merchant).

They roused the four sleeping households, alarmed the be-
wildered neighbours, arrested the four Leveller leaders on a
warrant for treason and set off with their prisoners in military
order through the silent streets. Without warrant or reason the
officer who arrested Lilburne insisted on taking also the two
young sons of his landlord, whose house he shared. Three of
the detachments converged on St Paul's, where Lilburne,
Walwyn and Prince met as fellows in misfortune. After they
had managed between them to persuade the senior officer to
release the two young men, John, who was always genial on such
occasions, invited him and his two less experienced comrades to
a neighbouring tavern for their 'morning draught'. Restored
to his humanity by this treatment, the officer was now content
to leave his little army behind in the City, while he escorted his
three prisoners by boat to Whitehall.

Richard Overton was less fortunate in his officer. Lieut.-
Colonel Axtell (noted in after years for his merciless conduct in
Ireland) took it into his head that the crowded lodgings in Alders-
gate in which Overton lived were a bawdy-house. He insulted
several of the women in it as well as Overton and the landlord,
and arrested a trooper, who was in bed with his wife, for
fornication. The manuscript of an unfinished book of Overton's
was appropriated and lost. At length, with a soldier holding his
arm, and two hundred horse and foot to guard his diminutive
person, he was marched through London to Whitehall.

The Council of State did not sit till five in the afternoon,
when it met at Derby House with Bradshaw in the chair. The
prisoners were shown in to it one by one for examination;
Bradshaw, who knew some of them personally, treated them
with courtesy and allowed them to speak without interruption.
John Lilburne, whose spirits always rose to such occasions,
addressed it in a blend of irony and indignation. What sort of
fire-breathing monster was he that two hundred cavalry and
infantry were required to arrest him? He congratulated the
victors in a hundred battles on their conquest of four unarmed
men. He understood, of course, perfectly well that these forces
and the choice of the uncanny early hour were a tribute to the
popularity of the Levellers and a precaution against rescue. He
then argued that the Commons did wrong to act as a court of

justice which could condemn men for treason. Far ahead of his
time, in accordance with Leveller principles, he called for the
separation of legislative and judicial powers. Overton also
made good use of his opportunity. He proposed that the
Levellers and the Army should make one more effort to reach
unity by reconciling their two versions of the Agreement of the
People. Walwyn was not in the same case as his comrades.
For three or four months he had ceased to attend the meetings
of the Leveller party and he had no responsibility for its
recent pamphlets. He and Prince were not old gaol-birds like
the other two, nor could they as merchants forget that these
doings might ruin their credit in the City.

The four prisoners were called in one by one a second time
before the Council. Bradshaw asked them whether they were
the authors of the pamphlet. Each of them refused on principle
to incriminate himself or his comrades. Bradshaw explained,
however, that the Council did not propose to try them.

While they sat in an ante-room, the Council debated their
case. Lilburne laid his ear to the door and heard

> Lt. Gen. Cromwell (I am sure of it) very loud, thumping
> his fist upon the Council table, till it rang again, and heard
> him speak in these very words or to this effect; I tell you, Sir,
> you have no other way to deal with these men, but to break
> them in pieces; and thumping upon the Council table again,
> he said, Sir, let me tell you that which is true, if you do not
> break them, they will break you; yea and bring all the guilt
> of the blood and treasure shed and spent in this kingdom
> upon your heads and shoulders; and frustrate and make void
> all that work, that with so many years' industry, toil and
> pains you have done, and so render you to all rational men
> in the world as the most contemptiblest generation of silly,
> low spirited men in the earth, to be broken and routed by
> such a despicable, contemptible generation of men as they
> are; and therefore, Sir, I tell you again, you are necessitated
> to break them.

Cromwell's motion was to commit all four prisoners to the
Tower. Ludlow proposed that they should be released on bail.
He was defeated, but only by one vote.

Midnight was striking before the Council broke up, and so a

friendly officer allowed his prisoners to spend the rest of the night at home on parole. Next morning the gates of the Tower closed upon them. The story of that last day of liberty, as they have told it, had its vein of comedy but they were well aware that they might be going to their deaths after a trial, without a jury, before the revolutionary High Court of Justice. Even Overton, who seldom spoke in a tone of solemnity, felt moved to write

> For my part, I had rather die in the just vindication of the cause of the poor oppressed people of this Commonwealth than to die in my bed.[3]

John Lilburne, too, may have felt that he was composing his own epitaph when he described himself as one 'that never feared the rich nor mighty, nor never despised the poor nor needy'. Regretting nothing and retracting nothing, he sounded 'an eternal trumpet of defiance to all the men and devils in earth and hell'. Since his conversion twelve years ago, he had always felt able 'to lay down his life at a quarter of an hour's warning', and now 'clothed with the glorious righteousness of Jesus Christ' he will 'sing and be merry'.[4]

Cromwell, however, was in no hurry to make martyrs of his popular prisoners. So he sent an Anabaptist preacher named Richardson to the Tower on an errand of mediation. The four were willing enough to discuss a reconciliation. They repeated therefore the offer Overton had already made to the Council. If they could reach a compromise between their version of the Agreement of the People and that of the officers, there need be no further differences between them, though they would still ask for an audit of public accounts. Let Cromwell, Ireton and two of their nominees meet the four prisoners and discuss the differences of the two texts. If they failed to reach agreement, let each side name two arbitrators and agree to abide by their majority proposal.

In their new quarters in the Tower three of the prisoners sat down at once to write a narrative of their experiences. Walwyn told his story separately somewhat later in the *Fountain of Slander Discovered*. *The Picture of the Council of State* appeared promptly on 11 April, so ineffectual, as yet, was the work of the military police in silencing the unlicensed press. The tactics, of course, are Lilburne's. Always he knew how, by assuming the reader's sympathy, to put his oppressors in the wrong. The use of force is always ugly, and in this instance the behaviour if not of the Council of State then of its agents was at once ridiculous and brutal. From the moment those forces of horse and foot wakened the first of the four sleeping households in the dark hour before dawn, our sympathies are with their civilian victims, and our instinctive dread of militarism, once aroused, remains with us while Cromwell thumps the table and talks of breaking the Levellers in pieces.

One may suppose that this brilliant piece of propaganda told in the prisoners' favour as the weeks went on. But their danger, as their friends believed, might be immediate, for anything seemed possible, even recourse to martial law. The first of several petitions for a fair trial was presented to the House by 'eighty gentlemen' in person on behalf of the 10,000 Londoners who signed it. When one recollects how primitive were the means of communication, the collection of so large a number of signatures during four days, of which one must have been spent in drafting and printing the document, was a remarkable feat of organisation. It seems likely that the Leveller party must have had on its books in the City of London, not reckoning the suburbs, round about 10,000 members or adherents on whom it could call for support at short notice. Many would sign on Sunday at chapel. This petition wound up by demanding that 'our worthily esteemed friends' be either enlarged or tried 'in some ordinary court of justice'.[5]

A second petition, signed chiefly in Westminster and presented on 18 April, was more aggressive. After asking for bail for Lilburne and his friends, it declared that the real crime for which they were molested was their endeavour to 'reduce the military power to a real subordination to the civil authority'. In a passionate rebuke the Speaker told the petitioners that they were no better than the prisoners, but he promised a fair trial before the King's Bench (now known as the Upper Bench). Petitions came also from Southwark, from Essex and from a group of apprentices, but the most novel of these demonstrations was the presentation on 23 April by several hundred women of a petition which about ten thousand women had signed. Women had been appointed in every ward and division to receive signatures. They declared that they could not eat, drink or sleep in peace through fear for the safety of their sons and husbands. They went on to speak of their distress because famine was now causing several deaths every week in London. They wound up by entreating the House to favour the Agreement of the People.

A royalist newspaper describes the 'uncivil' behaviour of the troops guarding the House. Some pointed their pistols ready cocked at the women's breasts, others threw squibs among them. Twenty, however, were admitted to the lobby. One of the members who found them there told them to go home and wash their dishes. 'Sir,' answered the gentlewoman who led them, 'we have scarce any dishes left to wash.' When another member told her that it was strange that women should petition, she answered that what was strange was not therefore unlawful. 'It was strange that you cut off the King's head, yet I suppose you will justify it.' Cromwell, as he passed through the lobby, assured them that there would be 'law' for the prisoners. 'Sir,' said this gentlewoman, 'if you take away their lives or the lives of any, contrary to law, nothing shall satisfy us, but the lives of them that do it, and Sir, we will have your life if you take away theirs.' Finally, the sergeant-at-arms came out to the women.

> Mr Speaker (he said) by direction of the House, hath commanded me to tell you that the matter you petition about is of an higher concernment than you understand; that the House gave an answer to your husbands, and therefore that you are desired to go home and look after your own business and meddle with your housewifery.

With what dignity and spirit the Leveller women, in a second petition, replied to this insult we have seen already.[6]

By these petitions the Levellers achieved their first objective —the promise of a fair trial before a jury. They had their successes in mobilising public opinion, but they also had their losses. Hitherto they could reckon on the support of the growing Anabaptist community, always in the van of the Good

Old Cause. Some of its teachers and preachers were among their most devoted adherents. But when, in accordance with their usual practice, the Levellers brought the *Second Part of England's New Chains Discovered* to the Baptist meeting houses for signature and expected support from the pulpit, they met in several of them with a rebuff. This happened not only in seven of the leading chapels in London, but in Newcastle also. On 2 April, a petition was presented to the Commons by that wealthy and influential Saint, William Kiffin, from 'several churches of God in London, commonly, though falsely, called Anabaptists'. The seven preachers regretted that Lilburne's pamphlet was read aloud in several of their meetings and disclaimed any share in abetting it. They went on to assure the House that their meetings would not 'intermeddle with the ordering or altering civil government', which they left submissively to Parliament. They wound up by asking it to pass laws against whoring, drunkenness, cheating and such like abominations.[7] This Baptist manifesto marks a date of some importance in the history of the Puritans. A part of their left wing rallied to the *haute bourgeoisie* and ceased to function as an opposition. As the years went on a sharp division cleft their ranks, for General Harrison and most of the Millennarians were in chronic rebellion against the Protectorate.

Besides the 'middle sort of people' and the sectaries, yet another stratum of society was listening to John Lilburne. The impact of Leveller propaganda on the Royalists can be followed in the pages of *Mercurius Pragmaticus* and its rivals. 'Is not this brave sport,' *Mercurius Pragmaticus* writes (24 February–3 March), 'when rebels impeach each other?' He gives a summary of the first part of *England's New Chains*, predicts that its author will be imprisoned, and then claps John on the back. By 20-27 March *Pragmaticus* is rejoicing at great length over the quarrel between the Levellers and the Cromwellians. 'Be not baffled, bold Levellers,' he exclaims, 'be constant and prosecute your claims of justice against the perjured traitor Fairfax to the death.' He backs the five small beagles and praises Overton's *The Hunting of the Foxes*, 'a very rational piece and well-penned'. From the fact that 'the

Westminster cannibals' are issuing writs to fill some of the vacant seats, he infers that the usurpers dare not dissolve Parliament.

> These traitors intend to sit for aught you know their lifetime and make their sons their heirs after them. Then, for shame, stand up all you that desire either monarchy or freedom, rouse yourselves and help to destroy them who will else devour both you and yours.

Thus from the royalist side there began the overtures for an alliance with the Levellers, which soon became one of the main themes in the discordant pattern of the Interregnum. Three weeks later *Pragmaticus* (17-24 April) is labouring to remove any prejudices his readers may feel against the Levellers.

> But that you may not be scared with the Levellers hereafter, I tell you they are such as stand for an equal interest in freedom against the present tyranny and are so much the more tolerable in that a little experience will teach them that a just monarch is the best guardian of public liberty.

Other royalist journalists were prompt to follow Nedham's lead. Incidentally they were helping to make 'honest John', as they often called him, the most popular figure in the public life of their time. At the end of April (23-30) a new 'underground' royalist weekly, the most reckless, the most amusing and the most bawdy of them all, *The Man in the Moon, discovering a World of Knavery under the Sun*, told at length, with the customary exaggeration, the story of John's rejection of Cromwell's 'bribes' and how he 'bade their money perish with them'. After a sneer at Kiffin and his snivelling flock who 'fawn on tyrants', the *Man in the Moon* broke into doggerel verse: 'Stand to them, John, our champion thou shalt be.' If John had been as wise as he was brave, the flattery of the Royalists should have warned him that there were perils in the policy he had chosen.

Cromwell, unfortunately, wrote no pamphlets. If we seek to penetrate his thinking during these crucial months, there are no letters of any political bearing to guide us, and only one speech. Events had forced him to play the politician from Pride's Purge to the beheading of the King. By the end of

March, when he accepted the command of the army in Ireland, he became once more first and foremost the soldier. Busy with his preparations for a difficult campaign, he must have resented the interruption due to Lilburne's challenge. If he had to turn aside to crush the Levellers, his first and most pressing reason was, of course, that they threatened the unity of the Army at the very moment when its good temper and trust in its officers were all-important. The prospect of fighting in Ireland had never been congenial to the men of the New Model, as we saw when they had to face it in the spring of 1647. If Lilburne and Overton were allowed to go on corrupting its discipline, it would soon be unfit to cross St George's Channel. Angry as Cromwell may well have been with Lilburne when the Council of State sent him to the Tower, he felt, as yet, no irreconcilable ill-will against that headstrong young man. He would gladly have come to terms with him, if Mr Richardson could have found a basis for compromise. But where was it?

The Levellers would have dropped or postponed all their other demands if they could have got from Cromwell a promise that he and his Independents would actively further a version of the Agreement of the People rather nearer to their own original draft than to that of Ireton and the officers. But Cromwell, at bottom a conservative, from the first sight of the Agreement at Putney in the autumn of 1647 had always disliked it, as a rash innovation which had no place in the English political tradition. The squire in him dreaded the consequences of manhood or even of household suffrage, nor was he prepared to tolerate Catholics, Prelatists or Socinians. He thought that it carried decentralisation dangerously far. It might have suited a land of peasants, Switzerland for instance, but not the imperial England of his ambitions.

For Cromwell was an Elizabethan in his outlook on world affairs. The romance of the feud with Spain at sea and in the Indies was in his blood. His idealism was that of a Protestant crusader, who aspired to lead the Calvinist and Lutheran hosts against the Whore of Babylon. The England of his dreams, a great power with a base on European soil and omnipotent at sea—the dream he realised during the Protectorate—could not be reconciled with the England of the Agreement, which had no executive capable of pursuing a consistent foreign policy. The England of Lilburne and Walwyn would have been at the best a loose federation of parishes, hundreds and counties. No great power could be built on this plan, and still less a great empire. How soon they supposed they could disband the New Model is not clear. But there was no place for a standing army in the final draft of the Agreement. They relied for defence on a citizen militia, commanded by elected officers. It is significant that in all their planning they made no mention of a navy, so little were they thinking in terms of power.

Their outlook was that of the tradesmen, craftsmen and peasants who formed their membership. The little man, the 'middle sort' of citizen, can realise himself only within the narrow boundaries of his parish or hundred, where he can exert some influence and even wield some power by sitting on a jury and by electing his officers, pastor and magistrates— where too, he stands some chance of being elected himself. He dreads the centre, the metropolis, with its ruinously costly law courts, its predatory lawyers and at Westminster— to borrow Walt Whitman's phrase—'the never-ending audacity of elected persons', who can be safely trusted with a little 'bounded' authority only for a year at a time.

The England of the Agreement, if ever it had come into existence, would never have grown rich by the slave trade, nor could it have conquered India. But on the homely scale of county and parish it might have had some success in combating ignorance and poverty. Inspired by a new respect for the life and personality of the individual citizen, free to think and free to debate, it might have developed a culture as civilised as that of neutral Switzerland. But its parliamentary 'committee of short continuance' that dealt with defence would have had some awkward questions to answer. If ever it had talked things over with the 'Generals-at-Sea', Blake and Deane, or even with the Leveller Vice-Admiral Lawson, these sailors would have told it that in the hour of need a fleet cannot be improvised.

Cromwell, on the other hand, can never have forgotten that he was born into the ruling class of a great power. For several generations a Cromwell had always sat in the Commons.

Though during two reigns the Puritans had turned their backs on the court, which they regarded as vicious and extravagant, they still thought of England as a European power and had their own characteristic views on foreign policy. Cromwell was linked by blood and friendship with the Providence Island group, which kept alive the Elizabethan traditions of piracy and trade on the Spanish Main, and was at the same time the focus from which the Puritan opposition to the court was organised.

It can be argued that since Cromwell's views on church government were those of the Independents, his tendency also and the leanings of his supporters must have been towards de-centralisation. That certainly was their original stand, for they represented the extreme reaction against Laud and the authoritarian church. But as time went on, under the Protectorate, Cromwell created a national organisation in which Presbyterians, Independents and even Baptists played their parts. This settlement of religion can only be described as a Puritan established church and it was for Oliver (with the conquest of Ireland) the proudest achievement of his reign. With its 'single person' (the Lord Protector) and its nominated and self-perpetuating Council of State the Protectorate meant centralisation. In practice, the efficient police state which Thurloe constructed was as highly centralised as any of the totalitarian régimes of our own century.

The reasons then were deep-seated—whether one refers them to class outlook or to temperament—why Cromwell and the Levellers could not come to terms over the Agreement of the People. Another reason, more prosaic and superficial, stood in the way. The Agreement prescribed an early dissolution—by the last day of April 1649. But while a great part of the population was still mourning for Charles the Martyr, anything like a free election would have been fatal to the regicides and Independents, even if 'malignants' had been disfranchised. The Presbyterians, with most of the pulpits to back them, would doubtless have polled well, and so, if the franchise had been widened, would the Levellers—we need not try to guess in what proportions. The date could, of course, have been postponed. But it was not till the late summer of

1654, in a vastly different political context, that the Cromwellians did venture to go to the polls, after raising the property qualification. With the press in chains and the leaders of the opposition in prison or effectively silenced, the contest bore not even a distant resemblance to a free election. The Levellers might have agreed to wait a few months for a dissolution, but hardly for five years, since the Rump had no valid claim to represent the supreme people. With the most original of the Levellers' ideas—that since society had relapsed during the troubles into a state of nature, a new start could be made only by seeking directly from the sovereign electors their assent to a new constitution drawn up by a convention chosen for this purpose—with this idea Ireton and Cromwell were never in sympathy, if indeed they ever grasped it.

But Cromwell's mind was busy with something more concrete than political subtleties. In an address to his officers at Whitehall on 23 March, he surveyed the military outlook. What he chiefly dreaded was 'disunion among ourselves'. He observed among the Scots 'a very angry hateful spirit . . . against this Army as an army of sectaries'. In Ireland he believed that the Papists and the apostate Protestants were together so strong that failing prompt action 'our interest' there may be rooted out and

> they will in a very short time be able to land forces in England. . . . I had rather be over-run with a cavalierish interest than a Scotch interest; I had rather be over-run with a Scotch interest than an Irish interest, and I think of all this is the most dangerous. If they shall be able to carry on their work, they will make this the most miserable people on the earth, for all the world knows their barbarism.[8]

It is one of the basic rules of politics that a war of conquest—or re-conquest—must always be masked as a war of defence. God's nominee as C-in-C would sail for Dublin to repel the descent of these barbarians on the shores of England. The nightmare of an Irish invasion had been invoked by Pym to destroy Strafford, and now Cromwell was using it to put the Levellers in the wrong. If they went on causing disunion at home, these savages would soon be upon us.

The Lieut.-General wound up by asking the council to

consider what regiments should go to Ireland and what financial inducements should be offered them. A committee of officers was appointed to study these questions. It met at Whitehall on 24 March and began by spending a whole day in fasting and prayer—so much still remained of the old Puritan spirit in this veteran professional army. In the mood which these spiritual exercises would induce, Colonel Whalley raised, at the start, a fundamental question of ethics. Of all the 'Grandees' belonging to the Cromwell family, he seems to have been the one who possessed the most sensitive social conscience, as we saw from his action against land-enclosure and depopulation. He now proposed and carried a motion for

> the impowering the C.-in-C. that goes over so to capitulate with the enemy as to conclude a peace, and that no ill terms be imposed upon him as either to eradicate the natives or to divest them of their estates.

The officers decided, that is to say, against a policy of 'unconditional surrender'; the new C.-in-C. should be authorised to negotiate with the Irish and to offer them tolerable conditions of peace. Evidently Whalley knew that powerful interests in the City reckoned on the acquisition of 2,500,000 acres of Irish land and were prepared to 'eradicate the natives' in order to get this property. Already there may have been soldiers also who saw in Irish acres the best 'visible security' for their arrears of pay.

Whalley, evidently, was the decent, middle-of-the-road Englishman who was prepared to go to war armed with muskets, pikes and good intentions. For this campaign, in addition to humane phrases, four regiments of horse and four of foot would be required, together with five troops of dragoons. They were to be chosen by lot. The Levellers were radicals for whom humane phrases were not enough to sanctify a war of conquest. They opposed it on principle. The search, then, for unity had failed. No basis of compromise could be discovered. The Cromwellians had no use for the Agreement of the People and the Levellers did not wish to re-conquer Ireland.

NOTES TO CHAPTER XXIV

1. *Legal Fundamental Liberties*, H. and D., p. 448.

2. *The Moderate* (27 March—3 April, 1649).

3. *The Picture of the Council of State*, H. and D., p. 225.

4. *Ibid.*, pp. 212-13.

5. *A Perfect Weekly Account* (28 March-4 April) and *The Moderate* (27 March-3 April). Gardiner, by what looks like a slip of the pen, speaks of 80,000 signatures (*Commonwealth and Protectorate*, I, p. 42).

6. *The humble Petition of divers well-affected Women* (24 April, 1649); *The Moderate* (17-24 April); *Mercurius Pragmaticus* (17-24 April). See p. 317 above.

7. *The humble Petition and Representation of several Churches of God in London, commonly, though falsely, called Anabaptists* (3 April, 1649); see also *A Perfect Weekly Account* (28 March-4 April, 1649).

8. Abbott, II, p. 38.

CHAPTER XXV

For a free Ireland

As the time for the Irish expedition drew near, the memories of all whom it concerned travelled back to the Army's revolt and the election of the first Agitators. Cromwell set to work to remove the material causes that made campaigning across St George's Channel unpopular. He saw to it that ample supplies of good food should be available. He must have known that the ragged battalions fighting against heavy odds under Colonel Michael Jones round Dublin had faced the winter half-naked. In those days the men had to find their own clothes; none the less Parliament was induced to vote for the infantry that soon would be going over, 2,000 cassocks and breeches and 2,000 cassocks extra, on the plea that their pay was small.[1] Cromwell may have recollected that English armies in Ireland were always decimated by disease. That doubtless was his reason for including the radical Dr. Chamberlen in his staff. The royalist wits cracked their jokes on the assumption that the Saints would employ him in his usual capacity as surgeon accoucheur; they chose to forget that he had novel ideas about fighting epidemics by preventive hygiene.

But the main grievance of the men in 1647 had been over their arrears of pay. The Independents were too wise to repeat the meanness of the Presbyterians. They voted three months' pay for those who obeyed the call to Ireland, together with debentures covering their arrears since the New Model was enlisted in 1645. The raising of all this money was a slow and difficult task. To complete our account of Cromwell's prepara-tions we must add that this considerate treatment was only for

those who could be induced to embark for Ireland. Those who
chose to stay in England were promptly cashiered as men unfit
for further service, and sent home with barely enough cash in
hand to pay for the journey. Colonel Hewson even stripped
these men of the coats on their backs before he would let them
go.[2] In spite of this treatment—or perhaps because of it—three
hundred soldiers of his regiment did lay down their arms. They
left the Army without so much as an IOU for their arrears
of pay.

Some of the men could be satisfied with cassocks, breeches
and money, but there were others, in some regiments a majority,
who recalled the concerns for which they struck in 1647. They
then swore that they would not allow themselves to be disbanded or divided, and therefore would not enlist for Ireland
save on terms approved by the elected representatives of the
whole Army.

As week followed week in the spring of 1649 the cry for the
election of Agitators and the calling of a genuine General
Council grew steadily more articulate and imperious. The men
always believed in the good faith of Fairfax, though they might
not pay that compliment to Cromwell, whom they admired but
seldom trusted.

Did the Lord General fail to carry out an obligation of
honour? If the 1647 Engagement was still valid, then his duty was
clear; he ought to call a truly representative Council. He could
have pleaded, if ever he had cared to defend his conduct, that
the conditions out of which the Engagement arose had been
transformed. Parliament was no longer a hostile institution,
which insulted and exploited the New Model with the avowed
intention of destroying it; it was now the ally of the Army, or as
some would say, its tool. There was now no thought of placing
the Irish expedition under second-rate and politically unreliable commanders; it was to serve under Cromwell. He,
moreover, had done all that could be expected of him to satisfy
the material interests of his men—those, that is to say, who
obeyed his call. Up to a point this would have been a good
defence. But it ignored the men's right to be consulted. We
moderns, broken in to compulsory military service, must
remind ourselves that these men were not conscripts; they were

R

volunteers who took up arms to defend the Parliament at home; they could not be sent overseas save with their free consent. To extort it through financial loss and disgrace was not the honest dealing fame ascribes to Fairfax.

For the civilian Levellers the Irish expedition raised deeper and wider issues than these. They watched with horror the transformation of the New Model into a mercenary, professional army which would murder at the word of command. Their code of ethics stopped short no longer at the frontiers of their own country. They saw in the Catholic Irish their fellow men, whose claim to liberty was as valid as their own. This novel conception of international morality—a startling advance in civilisation—found expression in the pamphlets of this spring. The first of them was *The English Soldier's Standard, to repair to for Wisdom and Understanding, in these doleful, back-sliding Times: to be read by every honest officer to his soldiers and by the soldiers to one another.* Its style as well as its arguments have convinced me that it came from Walwyn's pen; it applies to fighting in Ireland the ethical principles which he had worked out in *The Bloody Project.*[3] A vigorous introduction set out the familiar reasoning based on the 1647 Engagement and wound up with an appeal 'to choose out from amongst yourselves such faithful men, whether officers or soldiers, as in these doubtful, staggering times have stood firm to their first principles'. Then, turning to the Irish question, Walwyn administered a shock to his readers by calling up a vision of the *dies irae.* 'It will be,' he declared, 'no satisfaction to God's justice to plead that you murdered men in obedience to your general.' They would not be able to answer, as they might have done hitherto, that they had taken life 'for those just ends, the rights and liberties of the people'. 'Is there such haste?' he asks,

> If you are wise stay a little. . . . Certainly before you go, it will be good for you to see those rights and liberties of the people, for which you took up arms in judgment and conscience, cleared and secured by Agreement of the People, and not to leave them at the mere arbitrary mercy of a Council of State or a packed Parliament.

Their first step must be to establish a new representative of the Army by free election from every regiment.

For consider, as things now stand, to what end you should hazard your lives against the Irish. Will you go on still to kill, slay and murder in order to make them [your officers] as absolute lords and masters over Ireland as you have made them over England? Or is it your ambition to reduce the Irish to the happiness of tithes upon treble damages, to excise, customs and monopolies in trades? Or to fill their prisons with poor, disabled persons, to fill their land with swarms of beggars, . . . to take down monarchical tyranny and set up an aristocratical tyranny. . . . Before you go . . . see those evils reformed here, that when occasion shall justly invite you thither, you may carry a good platform in your hands, such a one as possibly they will never fight against. And it would be much more to be wished that you might overcome them by just and equal offers than by strength and force. . . .

It has come to a pretty pass with most of your great officers. They would have you to obey their commands, though to the killing and slaying of men, without asking a reason; and as the church of Rome holds the poor ignorant Papists in blind obedience . . . so would they have it with you, to be led this way and that way (as men lead horses) into Ireland or Scotland or any whither. . . . [But] he that runs to kill men merely upon authority or others' judgments or for money is condemned of himself in his conscience as a murderer, be the cause what it will, and first or last shall not escape the judgments of God.

The argument recalls Tolstoy's formidable attack on military oaths of obedience. Though Walwyn was not what the Russian prophet was, a Christian anarchist, he rated the sovereignty of the individual conscience in matters of personal conduct high above the jurisdiction of the state, even when it stood on a democratic footing, and this the English Commonwealth lacked.

For the rest, this pamphlet reminds us of the report in *Gangraena* that Walwyn and others among the Levellers, both soldiers and civilians, sympathised with the rebels in Ireland and were opposed on principle to its reconquest (p. 41 above). In the savage attack on him entitled *Walwyn's Wiles*, published some three weeks after *The English Soldier's Standard*, the same charge was repeated. He had been heard to say 'that it is an

unlawful war, a cruel and bloody work to go to destroy the
Irish natives for their consciences . . . and to drive them from
their proper natural and native rights'.[4] That the Leveller party
as a whole shrank from a war of re-conquest is obvious from the
New Engagement or Manifesto of August 1648 which called for a
re-consideration of the affairs of Ireland so as to reach a peaceable settlement (pp. 329-30 above). True to his motto, 'mercy and
moderation', Lieut.-Colonel Jubbes, towards the close of
1648, begged his fellow Puritans 'not to execute cruelty for
cruelty'.[5]

In the pitiless struggle waged without quarter since the Irish
peasants rose in 1641 and butchered the settlers who had
robbed them of their ancestral lands, there had been nothing
to choose in savagery between the two sides; in the navy it was
the rule, when Irish prisoners were taken, to tie them back to
back and throw them into the sea. Writing from the Tower
three months after his fellow-prisoner Walwyn, Thomas
Prince enlarged with characteristic simplicity on the belief
of the Levellers that if the Agreement of the People were in
force in England, the Irish would be so impressed by 'the goodness of the government' that they would make haste (if conscientious negotiators were sent over) 'to change their condition of bondage for freedom'; he even anticipated that they
would willingly surrender up to justice the chief authors of the
massacre.[6] This ignorance of social conditions in Ireland and
the mental outlook of its people should not surprise us; it was
universal among our ancestors in those days. The two peoples
inhabited different centuries. No contemporary Englishman
had ever caught so much as a glimpse of the traditional culture
of the other island, nor did anyone grasp the ties that bound the
clansmen of Ulster to their nobles and chiefs. The Cromwellians
erred more grossly when they mistook the Irish for savages
than did the Levellers who supposed that they would be
attracted by the democratic perfection of the Agreement.

While Walwyn's pamphlet was circulating in the Army,
lots were cast at headquarters to decide which regiments
should be selected for the Irish expedition. Four regiments
of horse were chosen (Ireton's, Lambert's, Scroop's and

Horton's), four regiments of foot (Deane's, Hewson's, Ewer's and Cooke's), together with five troops of dragoons. While the men in these regiments were balancing the alternative prospects that faced them—for they could at a heavy financial sacrifice step out of the ranks—the Levellers published yet another leaflet addressed to the troops. It was composed of eighteen queries, which asked the most searching questions about the right of our ancestors to conquer Ireland, and of their descendants to re-conquer it. In the disguise of questions it called upon the men to oppose the expedition, and outlined a plan for creating a friendly and independent Irish free state. No copy has survived of this leaflet, the boldest of all the Leveller publications, since it defied the inflamed Protestant sentiment of the day and incurred the capital penalty for treason by seducing the Army from its obedience. It is, however, easy to reconstruct it. The Cromwellians were evidently disturbed by the impression it made upon the troops, for an elaborate answer was produced, which the *Moderate Intelligencer* published by instalments. Fortunately with the antidote it gave the poison also, for it quoted the queries, one by one, before it demolished them.[7] Here, very slightly abbreviated —for there was some repetition—are the more important of them;

(1) Whether the land or inheritance that any nation hath for so many hundreds of years enjoyed . . . be not their right which God and nature has given them?

(3) Have we the right to deprive a people of the land God and nature has given them and impose laws without their consent?

(5) How can the conquered be accounted rebels, if at any time they seek to free themselves and recover their own?

(6) Whether Julius Caesar, Alexander the Great, William Duke of Normandy or any other great conqueror of the world were any other than great lawless thieves, and whether it be not as unjust to take laws and liberties from our neighbours as to take goods one from another of the same nation?

(9) Whether it be not the duty of every honest man to divert, what he can, the intended expedition?

(10) Whether those who pretend for freedom (as the English now) shall not make themselves altogether inexcusable in entrenching upon others' freedoms, and whether it be not the character of a true patriot to endeavour the just freedom of all as well as his own?

(12) Whether the English would not do as the Irish have, if the Irish should dispossess and tyrannise over them?

(13) Whether it be not England's duty to repent of the oppressions and usurpations over the Irish nation by their kings and forefathers?

(14) If the war against the Irish be continued, whether it will not be lasting and over-chargeable to England, . . . render the [English] nation no lovers of peace but domination, give occasion to the enemy to blaspheme, make our religion odious, spoil the English trade by piracy, be at last England's ruin, and whether a perfect conquest over them will equipoise the charge and blood that will be spent, . . . especially considering their eternal loss who die in so unjust a quarrel.

(16) Whether if the state of England, now in their full strength, should send and proclaim Ireland a free state, repenting of all the evil themselves have acted and intended, and that our kings have formerly acted against that nation, and that they will not further act to their prejudice: but only sit down by them as a neighbour state, as Holland doth: desire only to be in mutual league as friends, to seek the peace and welfare of each other, not countenance or assist or protect each other's enemies, nor any that shall disturb the peace of nations, only require some considerable seaports or towns for security and bond to tie the Irish to performance of covenants, whether this may not be every way as advantageous to the state and people of England as a conquest of them, the charge considered.

The answers to the *Eighteen Queries* can be summarised in a few lines. They repeat over and over again that the Irish are murderers and must be punished. They are 'more brutish than Indians' (meaning, presumably, the Redskins); it is, therefore, the duty of the English to 'tame such wild beasts' (an early version of the White Man's Burden). Not even if they had grievances should they have rebelled; they might have peti-

tioned. It is argued that the Irish forfeited the right of prior
possession by misconduct, but in any case the sixty years of
quiet possession, which the English enjoyed, bar more ancient
claims. More weight is conceded to the warning in the 14th
query that the conquest will be chargeable, but if this should
happen, it will be the fault of the management; if Ireland were
left unconquered, it would become the jumping-off ground for
the Pope's forces.

Those of us who can recall Easter Week, the defence of the
Four Courts and the doings of the Black and Tans will allow
that the author of the *Eighteen Queries* saw rather further into
the future than his Cromwellian opponent. None the less, the
latter wielded the more practised pen of the two, and behind
the slickness of his conventional reasoning one divines a legal
training. But this Leveller pioneer saw truths hidden from his
generation, on which in our perilous times the life of civilisation
will depend. His definition of the true patriot—he who endeavours the just freedom of all as well as his own—might
serve as a motto for world-government, if mankind survives
to create it. His rejection of the right of conquest, his respect for
the right of 'distinct' nationalities to retain their own lands
and liberties, and, above all, his perception that the society of
nations must be governed by the code of morals that unites
individuals within a national state—these thoughts of his place
him far in advance of his contemporaries. Not even the learned
Grotius, struggling to bring the rudiments of law into the
jungle of international relations, saw all that this layman
perceived. In the next generation the Quaker, William Penn,
profiting by the same tradition, sketched in the institutions that
might be built on this new vision of international ethics.

For yet another reason the *Eighteen Queries* are memorable.
They lay down the moral foundations for the opposition
of the Levellers to Cromwellian imperialism. These men are
the spiritual ancestors of a long line of descendants,—philo-
sophic radicals, Gladstonian liberals, socialists—who battled
for the liberties of Irishmen and Boers, Africans and Indians.
Always they risked unpopularity; often they suffered loss; a
few of them went to prison, but it was the four Leveller leaders
who had the courage to face the hangman's rope in order to

spare Ireland the suffering and England the disgrace of a perennial reconquest.

This Leveller, however, was no visionary but a practical Englishman who had a shrewd constructive policy to propose as an alternative to the punitive expedition. The official case for military action was that if the Irish could unite (as in fact they were doing) they would soon be able under royalist leadership to raise an army for the invasion of England and the restoration of the monarchy. To this there were several good replies. In her impoverished and distracted condition, Ireland could not pay and often could not feed her ill-disciplined forces. If she had managed to land them anywhere in England, the whole population, Cavaliers, Presbyterians, Independents and Levellers, would have united to resist an invasion of Papists. But the sufficient answer was that (apart from lucky raids on a miniature scale) no invasion in force could be carried out or maintained while the English fleet held the command of the seas. The best precaution against invasion was to give Blake and Deane the ships and men they needed. This the Commonwealth did. But what if Prince Rupert found a base for his piracies in an Irish port, as in fact he did? To deny him, or any other enemy of the Commonwealth, a base or a friendly footing on the coasts of Ireland was plainly, then and for all time to come, one of the essentials of English defensive strategy dictated by geography. In order to attain this, was it necessary to re-conquer Ireland and hold her down?

The Leveller reply is contained in Query 16. It would suffice that Ireland should become a friendly neighbour, bound by treaty to refuse all aid to any enemy of England—to benevolent neutrality in modern terminology. For an idealist the draftsman of this clause had a remarkably shrewd notion of a diplomatic bargain. He proposed that England should ask from Ireland, as security for the observance of the treaty, some considerable sea-ports—which would of course serve her as naval bases. There was a provision of this kind in the first form of the settlement in our own day (1921), which set up Eire as an independent state, but gave Great Britain the use of Queenstown (Cóbh) and other ports as naval bases. The author of the *Queries* believed that England, negotiating from strength,

could secure such terms as these, if she would recognise Ireland
as a free state. The Commonwealth had, he argued in the next
Query, more to offer than Prince Charles or Prince Rupert or
'such like forlorn soldiers'.

It is, indeed, probable that the main body of the Catholic
Irish, who felt no attachment to the Stuarts or the English
connection, would have welcomed such terms as these. What
their gentry chiefly valued was security, for their lands and
their religion. There is evidence about the readiness of one of
their leaders to come to terms in the communications that went
on during the summer of this year between the Council of State
and Father Crelly, an envoy from Owen Roe O'Neill, the
paramount chief of Ulster, who was a man of great influence
and outstanding ability. We need not discuss in detail the
'cessation' (armistice) for three months which he had concluded with Colonel Monk, and wished to prolong as the
basis of a lasting peace. The Council of State disapproved o
Monk's action, wanted no peace with Papists and would not
even receive Fr. Crelly. It did, however, appoint a committee
to confer with him, of which Colonel Ludlow was a member.[8]
The O'Neill asked for an act of oblivion or amnesty, the
restoration of his ancestral estates and the toleration of the
Catholic religion. Abbot Crelly said he would not approach
Prince Charles, because experience of the late King had taught
the Irish distrust; they had, moreover, reason to believe that
the present government favoured liberty of conscience. They
held out a promise that if such liberty were granted them,
they would be as zealous for a Commonwealth as any other
party and gave instances from other countries where Catholics
had behaved in this way. It seems from Fr. Crelly's own report
that he was asking for the toleration of the Catholic faith in all
the territories of the Commonwealth and not merely in Ireland.[9] The Confederate Catholics with whom the O'Neill was
at feud might have been more exacting over political questions,
but they would hardly have asked for more than the Levellers
were prepared to grant. But the Council of State would concede neither an amnesty nor toleration. So things went forward
to the massacres of Drogheda and Wexford, the predatory
Cromwellian land settlement, the attempt to destroy the

Catholic church and three centuries of agrarian exploitation enforced by coercion.

The atmosphere in the Army had become so tense that it was bound to break in tragedy. A trivial dispute over pay sufficed to provoke it. One of the troops of Whalley's horse billeted at the Bull Inn at Bishopsgate was ordered to a rendezvous in Essex. The men refused to stir until they received some of their arrears, since they had to pay for their quarters. They were offered a month's pay on account, but this, they said, would not cover what they owed, and they were angry because other troops got more. Thirty of the men seized the colours and took up positions with their arms in the gallery of the inn. Their colonel could do nothing with them and they yielded only when Fairfax and Cromwell arrived. At the court martial two days later (26 April) six troopers were sentenced to death and five to be cashiered after suffering the painful and humiliating punishment of riding the wooden horse. On Cromwell's intercession those sentenced to death were pardoned with one exception, Robert Lockyer.

Whether he was the ringleader may be disputed, but he certainly had been the political leader of the troop in 1647. This was his first offence against discipline. His friends dwelt upon his courtesy at all times and his valour in the field. He was only twenty-three years of age, yet he had served seven years. The Cromwellian *Moderate Intelligencer* described him as 'a pious man, of excellent parts and much beloved'.[10] The Levellers with a hastily improvised petition and a formidable letter signed by Lilburne and Overton did their utmost to save this promising young life, but in vain. Lockyer was troubled only because 'so small a thing as contention for his pay should give his enemies occasion to take away his life'. Refusing to wear the usual bandage over his eyes, he faced without fear the firing squad which shot him to death in front of St Paul's. Before he fell, he told the men who composed it that their obedience to superior orders did not acquit them of murder.

On the following Sunday, 29 April, through silent streets lined with respectful crowds, his friends carried his body to a

grave in Westminster. First came six trumpeters sounding the
last post followed by many hundreds of troopers and other
soldiers marching slowly in step. Then, though he was but a
common trooper, his horse, draped in black, was led by friends
in mourning cloaks, an honour usually reserved for high
commanders. On his coffin, borne by six soldiers in mourning,
his naked sword lay upon sprigs of rosemary dipped in his
blood. His kinsmen followed and after them many hundreds of
citizens. At the end of the long procession walked a contingent
of women. Everyone wore ribbons of the Leveller colour, sea-
green, and also of black. A great body of citizens ('some
thousands', according to one report), who also wore these
colours, awaited the coffin at the grave. 'Liberty,' commented
a royalist journalist who described the scene, 'lies in lavender
for the next generation.'[11]

While these mourners made their protest against militarism,
the Leveller opposition to the Irish expedition inspired yet
another leaflet.[12] Printed on one side only of a single sheet of
paper, it was 'cast abroad' in the streets on the Saturday before
Lockyer's funeral. It was a brief version of Walwyn's tract
addressed to the soldiers. It reminded them of all the Grandees
were doing to 'reduce the Army to a servile and base temper'
Once that was achieved, they could 'enslave the Commonwealth' to their arbitrary wills. Repeated purges, sometimes of
twenty men at a time in a troop, were eliminating all who 'desire
to be satisfied in their consciences of the justice of the cause
before they engage in the killing and slaying of men any more'.
Their places were filled, as was notoriously the case in Hewson's
regiment, with the unemployed—'such ignorant, needy and
servile men as these miserable times through loss of trade hath
begotten'. The leaflet concluded with an appeal to the soldiers
to 'keep every man his place and post and stir not, but immediately choose you out a Council of Agitators once more'.

This summons was promptly obeyed. Round about May Day
several regiments of horse elected Agitators once again.
Scroop's, Ireton's and Harrison's were among the first to do so.
Quartered round Bristol under an ambitious colonel troubled
with few scruples, Reynolds's horse was divided; some troops
like that of the Leveller, Captain Bray, were among the most

radical in the Army, while others are said to have been packed with royalist prisoners from Colchester. Scroop's horse had already begun its march towards a port of embarkation. By May Day it had reached Salisbury. There it stood still. No further in the direction of Ireland would its men consent to go.

Hitherto the tracts and leaflets that have come our way set forth the exhortations and questions which the civilian Levellers addressed to the soldiery. From Bristol comes a tract, *The Soldier's Demand*, unique in its kind.[13] In the over-centralised realm of England there were then only two printing presses outside London and the universities. A generation later, William of Orange was amazed to find that the busy city of Exeter could not print his proclamations. Bristol had one of the two presses. Even more unusual was it that this tract came from the ranks, and gave the response of the men to the appeals of the leaders in London. The writer was probably the trooper in Scroop's horse who wrote the remarkable petition that came from this regiment in the autumn of 1648 (pp. 334-5 above). There is in both outbursts the same bitterness over the men's economic grievances. If their wages are unpaid and their backs bare of clothes, the reason may be that their pay has stuck in their officers' fingers. The widows of their dead must be content with a 'pension of half-a-crown a week (and that not paid them neither), and the poor cripple which hath lost his legs or arms [with] some ten groats or a noble [3/4 or 6/8] to carry him where he was born. . . . The money he had will scarcely buy him a pair of crutches.' For all this, he argues, the General and the Grandees are now responsible, since they control Parliament. Are soldiers, he asks, to 'come at their beck and go where they call' on pain of being cashiered and their arrears confiscated? It would be an 'infamy' if, to enforce obedience to these officers, soldiers 'should be hangmen or executioners of one another'.

In complaints of this kind there is nothing new. But a new note startles our ears in the first paragraph of this tract:

> Fellow soldiers. . . . Oh! the ocean of blood that we are guilty of! Oh! the intolerable oppression that we have laid upon our brethren of England! Oh! how these deadly sins of ours do torment our consciences! Oh! how are we able

to answer these pestilent acts of ours at the dreadful bar of God's divine justice?

Veterans though they were, these men shrank from the call to shed more blood in Ireland. Here is this soldier's conclusion:

What have we to do in Ireland, to fight and murder a people and nation (for indeed they [the Grandees] are set upon cruelty and murdering poor people, which is all they glory in) which have done us no harm . . .? We have waded too far in that crimson stream already of innocent and Christian blood.

Such, then, were these troopers' thoughts as they halted their westward march at Salisbury on May Day.

NOTES TO CHAPTER XXV

1. *The Kingdom's Weekly Intelligencer* (27 March–3 April, 1649).

2. Hewson's behaviour is described in *Sea-Green and Blue* (6 June, 1649). As to arrears see also Gardiner (*Commonwealth and Protectorate*, I, p. 44). After the outbreak of open mutiny Fairfax and Cromwell undertook that this grievance should be redressed. This promise was kept, but in a very grudging style.

3. Dated by Thomason 3 April, 1649. See p. 167 above. Its prose, terse, lucid and rhythmical, is in Walwyn's best popular manner and it is free from personalities and abuse. It quotes many proverbs, as he so often did, and uses irony with skill. Its vocabulary is predominantly Anglo-Saxon—as I reckoned from a passage chosen at random—82 per cent. Finally it mentions the Anabaptists of Münster, who make their appearance in his writings like the white horse in the paintings of Wouwerman, without which none is genuine.

4. H. and D., p. 288.

5. Wolfe, p. 318.

6. *The Silken Independents' Snare Broken* (20 June, 1649.)

7. These Queries are taken from the *Moderate Intelligencer* of 3 May, 1649, and the five following issues. The total number of Queries is given in one issue as 18, but in the last as 17. The answers to these 'very cunning and pernicious Queries' were probably supplied to the editor by the Secretariat of the Council of State. Three months later (27 September, 1649), as the date of John Lilburne's trial approached, the government published a lengthy, polemical 'white paper' directed against the Levellers, *A Declaration of the Parliament of England*. It describes their efforts to prevent the sending of forces to Ireland. After summarising the Queries, it concludes: 'What effect this had and how long the relief of Ireland was hindered . . . is very well known' (p. 26). The Queries must have had in some form the approval of the party, otherwise the leaflet could not have been distributed on a

large scale in the Army, as it evidently was. Its contents would be discussed by the four leaders in the Tower, but who the draftsman was we do not know.

8. Ludlow, *Memoirs*, I, pp. 227-9.

9. Gardiner, *op. cit.*, I, p. 93.

10. 26 April–2 May, 1649.

11. See *The Army's Martyr* and the official *A True Narrative of the late mutiny* (1 May, 1649). For the funeral see *Mercurius Pragmaticus* (24 April–1 May), and *The Moderate* (24 April–1 May). Of the two men who actually endured the punishment of the wooden horse, according to *The Moderate*, one during seven years' service had spent £80 in replacing horses, while for his arrears Parliament owed him £140. The patience of these troopers under habitual injustice is more astonishing than their occasional recourse to mutiny.

12. It begins 'All worthy officers and soldiers, who are yet mindful that you are engaged not as a mere mercenary Army', and is dated by Thomason 25 April, 1649.

13. Thomason's date is 18 May, but it may have been printed a week or two earlier.

CHAPTER XXVI

News from Burford[1]

Mutiny is a crime that admits of several degrees. The troopers of Scroop's horse, who refused at Salisbury on May Day 1649 to march any further in the direction of Ireland, had no wish to upset the government and would have been horrified if anyone had accused them of starting a third civil war. They thought that the pledge of the high command to call a General Council before the Army was divided should be duly honoured, and for this purpose they chose their Agitators. They were indignant also because those who did not choose to serve in Ireland were to be deprived of their arrears. It is, as they put it, in a series of resolutions,

> as if a man should owe a servant £20, and then tell him he will give them £5 of the same, upon condition that he will do another service for him (which is greater) in another place.[2]

They were ready to serve in Ireland but only if their grievances were met and the General Council approved. Their spirits would, doubtless, rise when four troops of Ireton's horse joined them and confirmed their mood of opposition. Their colonel seems to have handled them tactlessly. He used too many threats, talked too soon of mutiny and separated the troops from each other. The preachers whom he used to foster loyalty irritated the men by telling each troop (falsely) that all the others had submitted. His last mistake was to order the removal of the men's horses (their own property) to a field two miles from their quarters.

When the officers realised that the men would no longer obey them, Colonel Scroop and nearly eighty of his subordinates quitted the regiment; only a few subalterns remained with the men, who now chose officers to replace those they had lost. It was a fundamental tenet of Leveller democracy that officers should be elected by the men. The mutineers had no commander-in-chief. Their movements were directed by their Council of Agitators, drawn from the six regiments in revolt— four of horse (Scroop's, Ireton's, Harrison's and Horton's) and two of foot (Skippon's and Ingoldsby's)—an unwieldy committee. One senior officer rallied to them, Lieut.-Colonel Eyres. He had served in the first troop that Captain Cromwell raised; we have since met him twice, at Corkbush Field near Ware, where he was arrested, and in Berkshire, where he helped Colonel Henry Marten to raise and command his own regiment of horse. But it does not seem to have occurred to the men or their Council to offer the command to this experienced officer, though he had given ample proof of his loyalty to the Leveller cause. Conspicuous among the few junior officers who stood by the men was their chaplain, Cornet Henry Denne, who spurred them on to the boldest courses. The humane heresies of this popular Anabaptist were exposed (as we saw) in *Gangraena*. But the mutiny was an adventure without a hero. This gifted preacher turned out to be an unstable character.

During the twelve days the mutineers spent in Salisbury, they got into touch with the other regiments of the same way of thinking quartered in the West of England. The first plan that commended itself to their Agitators was apparently to assemble for a rendezvous near Britsol. This was, of course, a phase of mutiny a good deal more serious than the election of Agitators, or the calling of a Council. If several regiments came together, they were an army in the field capable of imposing its will. After this long delay a declaration signed by all their Agitators was read out on 11 May to the two regiments at Salisbury, who consented to it unanimously 'with joy and acclamation'. This document keeps clear of politics, save that it calls for 'the restitution of our shaking freedom' and its redemption 'out of the hands of tyrants'. It mentions neither the Agreement of the People nor the case of the four prisoners in the Tower. The casting of lots to send them to Ireland without their consent deprived them, it argues, of their native liberties in a way 'no age can parallel'. After dwelling on their financial grievances, it demands the calling, in accordance with the Engagement of 1647, of a Council consisting of two officers and two men chosen by each regiment, together with the general officers. This General Council they promise to obey. Finally, since the news had evidently reached them that Fairfax and Cromwell were marching against them, the men appeal to their 'dear fellow-soldiers' not to draw their swords against them. They wind up with an apology for exacting free quarter and an assurance that they have no thought of levelling men's estates.[3]

Meanwhile, another body of Levellers, armed and mounted, was assembling in Oxfordshire under the conduct of an unusual character commonly known as 'Captain' William Thompson —though he had never risen above corporal's rank in the New Model. Most of them were troopers from Reynolds's horse; a few were from Marten's horse and a local Oxfordshire formation, while others were civilians from London, in all perhaps some three hundred men. The little we know of Thompson comes from the Army's publicity service. Authority did not like him. He was a hot-tempered man, self-confident, aggressive and much too quick to draw his sword. His physical courage was legendary. But apart from his romantic daring, he must have had other qualities that endeared him not only to his fellow-troopers but to John Lilburne also, who stood by him more than once in his differences with the law.[4] He published on 6 May at Banbury, over his own signature, a spirited and eloquent manifesto, *England's Standard Advanced*. If he wrote it, he had abilities that never found their full scope; but much of it reads like the work of Freeborn John. Unlike the declaration from Salisbury it is concerned chiefly with politics and only incidentally with soldiers' grievances. It is a summons rather to rebellion than to mutiny. The cries and groans of the poor, the breaking in upon them of beggary and famine like a mighty torrent, the barbarous taxes, the setting up of bloody and tyrannical courts—these things, as well as the dissolution of the Council of Agitators and the iniquities of martial law, have forced him and his men to betake themselves with their swords in their hands to the law of nature. They are bent, therefore, on settling the Commonwealth according to the Agreement of the People and they attach a copy of the latest version of it to their declaration—probably they displayed their paper on their hats. If a hair of the heads of the prisoners in the Tower is touched, they will avenge it seventy times sevenfold. They are resolved to stop the payment of all taxes and wind up by declaring their solidarity with the mutineers at Salisbury.

When it came to the test of fighting, Thompson's men turned out to be half-hearted. These troopers would applaud a spirited page of radical rhetoric when a popular leader read it aloud to them, but to thrust their swords into the ribs of old comrades—that was another matter altogether. Colonel Reynolds, who could rely on about half his regiment, set out from Banbury to deal with the rebels. When he came up with them on 11 May, he demanded in a parley that they should deliver their colours and their leader. Thompson, obedient to the democratic tradition of the Levellers, then called a council. The majority were for surrender; some went over to Reynolds; others, being ill-armed, dispersed; only a few followed their captain when he rode off. Reynolds then sent a detachment in pursuit. Wheeling about, Thompson faced his pursuers and with his own hand shot their officer dead, wounded another, dismounted a third, and so made good his escape with a score of his faithful partisans.[5]

The news of the Leveller mutiny was the signal for panic in London. A new garrison, picked for its reliability from tough Hewson's regiment, was put in charge of the Tower and its prisoners. The formidable four were now closely confined in their cells, cut off from visitors and forbidden to meet one another. They were deprived of their weapons—ink, paper and pens—and no allowance was paid to them to cover the heavy cost of living and tips in the City's fortress. It was something worse than political change that the prosperous citizens feared. To that by now they were broken in. They were convinced that if the 'sea-green blades' should win the day they would be forced to behave like primitive Christians and fling their wealth into the common stock. No denial ever

overtook this legend, not even when the mutineers themselves
repeated the reasoned refutation of the leaders. The fear of
communism that haunted the wealthier Puritans was doubtless
an expression of the unconscious guilt they felt when they
contrasted their own prosperity with the hunger of the poor
around them. What if there were, after all, a God who would
avenge the widows and the fatherless?

It was the belief of the party in power that all the prestige
of Fairfax and Cromwell would be needed to subdue the
mutineers. Before setting out for the West the two generals
held a review of their forces in Hyde Park. Many of the men
even in their own crack regiments of horse came to the rendezvous on 9 May with sea-green ribbons in their hats. One of
them even had the audacity to ask questions. Cromwell made
a persuasive speech at the head of each regiment, while Fairfax,
as a royalist chronicler observed, nodded his head. In the five
months since the Army entered London, Parliament had
performed that great work of justice, which cleansed the land
from the stain of innocent blood; it had made an end both of
the monarchy and the House of Lords, raised the navy to its
greatest strength in history and brought about the revival of
trade. Then with his customary facility Cromwell gave the
two promises for which the men were waiting. 'Those who
thought martial law to be a burden should have liberty to
lay down their arms and receive tickets for the payment of
their arrears, which should as punctually be discharged as
the arrears of those that stayed.' The programme of the officers'
version of the Agreement would be carried out, including
'putting a period to this present Parliament'. A declaration
addressed to the mutineers, over Fairfax's signature, repeated
the substance of Cromwell's speech, with some additions. It
warned them that they were tempting the Cavaliers to fly to
arms. It told them that they would be defying God if they
disobeyed the clear call He had given them, when the lot fell
on them for the service of Ireland. In concluding, Fairfax
assured the men: 'If you submit, I am ready and willing to
pass by and pardon', if not 'I shall endeavour by force to
reduce you'.[6]

Marching northwards from Salisbury to Marlborough and

then by way of Wantage to Abingdon, the aim of the Levellers was to join first their comrades of Harrison's horse who were quartered in Buckinghamshire, and then those of Horton's horse in and around Gloucester. At Abingdon two troops of Harrison's regiment joined them. Advancing westwards by rapid stages from London, the aim of Fairfax and Cromwell was to overtake the mutineers before they could double their forces by uniting all four regiments. The infantry were not involved in these movements on either side.

During these complicated manœuvres the Generals and the Agitators were never out of touch. Fairfax chose two 'messengers' as his commissioners, Colonel Scroop and Major Francis White. Scroop had no success in bringing the men to submission. But White was one of the few senior officers whom the Levellers regarded as one of themselves. He had boldly taken their part during the Army's revolt in 1647. A man who thought for himself—he had, for instance, opposed the trial and execution of the King, while advocating his deposition— the Major never enjoyed the favour of the Grandees, who denied him the promotion that seemed to be his due.[7] No one would question this man's integrity. We have his own narrative of these events. The instructions of Fairfax were that he should try to 'procure a union' with the revolted regiments; to which Cromwell added, as he rode off: 'Let them know that though we have sent messengers to them, we will not follow with force at their heels.' These words 'my Lord General confirmed'. Here was an explicit assurance that the generals were prepared to negotiate. This is borne out by their correspondence. The first letter from the Agitators of Scroop's and Ireton's regiments set out their financial grievances, and their reliance on the Engagement of June 1647. It wound up by asking Fairfax to hear them patiently and take them under his protection. 'All we require is the performance of our Engagement at Triploe Heath.'

In his reply, dated 13 May, Fairfax assured the men that they would not be disbanded without sufficient pay and rebuked them for their 'disorderly precipitancy'.

However, since you now desire to be heard and taken under my protection, I have given way to Colonel Scroop to receive you under protection and am ready to hear you in anything concerning the Engagement by you mentioned.

The last phrase should be noted. It would convey to the Levellers that Fairfax was prepared to negotiate, not merely over pay, but over the real issue in dispute—the calling of a General Council that represented men as well as officers. Did he honestly mean this?

A further letter from the men's Council thanked Fairfax for his 'clemency' and then went on to stress in the bluntest of plain English their views of the Engagement. 'You kept not covenant with us.' In conclusion, it told him that if he refused to call a General Council, at his door would lie 'all the misery, bloodshed and ruin which will follow'.

The Levellers meanwhile had begun to suspect that the Generals were doing precisely what Fairfax as well as Cromwell undertook that they would not do—following their messengers 'with force at their heels'. Some of them, as their narrative puts it, then reproached Major White

> that he came to betray us. To which he replied: That the General and Lieut.-General had engaged their honours not to engage against us in any hostile manner till they had received our answer—no, not so much as to follow their messengers or commissioners with force. And being too credulous to the General's words, knowing that he never broke engagement with the Cavaliers in that kind, we gave the more credit to the Major, who seemed extreme forward and hasty to make the composure [i.e. agreement].

White and the Agitators were so fully in sympathy that they entrusted him with the task of drafting a suitable reply to Fairfax. In this, while they repeated their demand for the calling of a General Council, they added an undertaking to abide by its decisions and vowed that they would not 'harbour any evil thought or prejudice' against him on account of these differences.

Turning sharply westwards from Abingdon the Levellers came upon a party of Reynolds's horse which fell back towards Newbridge and held that crossing over the Thames against them. They felt no scruple about attacking these men, 'a mercenary, damme crew' largely recruited from the royalist prisoners taken at Colchester. When, with Lieut.-Colonel Eyres at their head, their 'forlorn hope' (i.e. vanguard) had 'tied up their cloaks' and 'ridden a career' with the intention of charging and forcing the bridge, Major White interposed and persuaded them to cross the Thames by an inconvenient ford higher up the valley, so as to avoid shedding blood. Thus on the evening of the 14th they came to Burford, where and in two neighbouring villages their twelve troops were quartered. Only the slightest guard was posted, for they trusted the Major's assurances. He vowed that if the forces of the generals should fall upon them, he would stand between them and the bullets.

During that day, 14 May, Cromwell, to whom Fairfax entrusted the operation, covered with his cavalry and dragoons by forced marches some forty-five miles. At midnight, weary though they were, with greatly superior numbers they fell upon Burford from both ends of its main street and took the slumbering Levellers completely by surprise. Shots were fired in the darkness from the door and windows of the inn where some of the troopers, among them Lieut.-Colonel Eyres, were quartered; and that was all. When the news reached Major White that Fairfax and Cromwell were at the town's end with two thousand horse and dragoons, he did what he could to prevent bloodshed. He rushed out in his slippers to look for the Lord General. Pistols were firing 'very thick' and in the confusion he was taken prisoner. When at length he was released, he had to return to his own quarters and only thereafter managed to find Fairfax, to whom he handed the mutineers' letter. One man was killed on either side and three or four wounded, among them Colonel Okey. Three hundred and forty prisoners were taken and placed under guard in the church. The rest of the mutineers, some five hundred men, escaped but without their horses, which fell as booty to the loyalists. These leaderless men never rallied, but made their way, embittered, to their homes. Cromwell's victory over the Levellers was complete and it was nearly bloodless. But still there rings in our ears the blunt verdict of those too credulous troopers: 'You kept not covenant with us.' After the lapse of three centuries we can find nothing better to say.[8]

Next day in the church the prisoners were relieved of the
threat of decimation that hung over them, but they had to
listen to reproachful sermons from Cromwell and others of the
Grandees. Some of the men, we are told, were still resolute,
but most of them 'did melt into a noble and Christian sorrow
and abundance of tears for their offence'. The court martial
chose four victims from among them whom it sentenced to
death, Cornet Denne the chaplain, Cornet Thompson the
younger brother of the 'Captain' and Corporals Church and
Perkins. Lieut.-Colonel Eyres, since he had been cashiered from
the Army, was committed to be tried as a civilian for treason.
Denne, who must have been a talented exhibitionist, made great
play with a winding sheet which he had bought for this occasion.
He 'rejoiced to suffer with willingness under so righteous a
sentence'. His penitence was so impressive that the General
pardoned him and set him soon afterwards to preach to the
prisoners. They, meanwhile, were lined up on the leads of
the church to witness the shooting to death of their three comrades. These kept their self-respect, more especially the
two corporals, who 'died like Romans'.

With a dozen troopers 'Captain' William Thompson made
his way to Northampton, where he played his part as the
romantic rebel for the last time. He released three Levellers
who had been imprisoned for circulating the mutineers' leaflet.
He then took their money out of the excisemen's tills and
scattered it in the streets among the poor. At Wellingborough
he was overtaken by a troop of the Oxfordshire horse. Retreat-
ing to a wood he 'scorned to take quarter' and sold his life
dearly. Charging three times though wounded, he killed one
officer and wounded another, before he fell himself. When she
heard of his end, his wife, who was with child, miscarried and
died.[9]

The relief with which Puritan England heard of the defeat
of the Levellers at Burford is a measure of its fears. The officer
who brought the news to the Commons was rewarded with a
gratuity of £150. At Oxford the victors were received with
great pomp. Magdalen College entertained them 'nobly'
at a feast; thereafter in the Schools 'with great respect' Fairfax

and Cromwell, those twin sons of Mars—*alteri Martis gemelli* as the Public Orator put it—were clad in the scarlet gowns of Doctors of Civil Law, while Harrison, Hewson and Okey graduated as Masters.

Three weeks after the victory, property was still rejoicing over its escape from levelling. Parliament consecrated 7 June as Thanksgiving Day. The most distinguished of the Independent divines, Drs Owen and Goodwin, preached at Christ Church, and the City invited the two generals with their chief officers and the Council of State to a banquet at Grocers' Hall. Trainbands lined the streets and the Lord Mayor observed the ancient ritual of presenting his sword, no longer to the King, but to Speaker Lenthall, who duly handed it back again. By a singular coincidence, in this same week, Parliament made a gift of a great landed estate at Burford to Lenthall and his heirs for ever. On the wines and dishes they consumed that afternoon the City oligarchy spent £3,500, a sum that would have kept twelve thousand ploughmen and their families for a week. A further £1,500 was spent on the plate and purse they gave to the five generals.[10] The City could well spare a trifle for Fairfax; thanks to him it now felt secure. The monopoly of the Merchant Adventurers would go untouched; its debtors would still languish in gaol; tithes would keep the right sort of parson in nine thousand pulpits; the burden of taxation would still fall most heavily on the victuals and clothing of the poor; the nightmare of elected magistrates could be dismissed and landowners could laugh at the threat of abolishing base tenures. All this was worth a basin and ewer of beaten gold.

Dick Overton has left us a whimsical picture of the dejection and paralysis that came upon the civilian Levellers as they sat in the Whalebone Tavern, digesting the news from Burford.[11] No one in London was responsible for the course events had taken. The incompetence of the men's leaders, the readiness of Major White to believe and of Lieut.-General Cromwell to promise—no one could have forecast it all. None the less, the fact was that the Levellers had challenged the revolutionary government to a decision by arms and suffered an overwhelming and pitiful defeat. It was to the soldiers that all their arguments had latterly been addressed—over martial law, the right to petition, the Engagement of Triploe Heath, the iniquity and unwisdom of re-conquering Ireland. To make an end of the rule of the sword they had—unsheathed their swords. The battle was over: the side with the longer sword and the fewer scruples had won. Here, one suspects, was the first of the experiences that presently turned so many of the Levellers to the Quaker way of peace.

In the Tower, however, John Lilburne, as yet undaunted, retained his faith in reason and himself. The regiments that marched from Salisbury to Burford had not been following his tactics. On the day after the government's thanksgiving he penned his criticism of the mutineers:

> The business of Scroop's men is wrongfully fathered upon me, who never will incite soldiers, nor others, to declare upon anything else but our printed Agreement of the 1 May 1649.

'When they do draw their swords', he went on, 'against their General, etc.' they should

> throw away their scabbards and rather fight with him than treat with him, without either resolving to give or take quarter.[12]

John Lilburne's formula for rebellion was followed in every particular by 'Captain' William Thompson. He inscribed the Agreement on his standard; he gave and took no quarter. With him perished his brother, his wife and their unborn child.

NOTES TO CHAPTER XXVI

1. The chief sources for the story of the mutiny are (1) the official despatches of Fairfax, published as *A Full Narrative of the proceedings between Lord Fairfax and the Mutineers* (10 May, 1649); (2) a further narrative, also official, published as *A Declaration of the Proceedings of the Lord General* (23 May); (3) the first of the Leveller narratives, a somewhat confused anonymous polemic against Denne, *Sea-Green and Blue* (6 June, 1649); (4) an able and well-written narrative which six former Agitators of Scroop's, Ireton's and Harrison's regiments had the courage to sign, *The Levellers, falsely so called, Vindicated* (14 August, 1649); and (5) Major White's apologia, *A True Relation of the proceedings in the business of Burford* (17 September, 1649). The newspapers printed many wild rumours and are rarely of much use, save for events in London.

2. *The Resolutions of the Private Soldiery of Col. Scroop's Regiment of Horse* (dated Salisbury, 1 May, 1649).

3. *The unanimous Declaration of Col. Scroop's and Gen. Ireton's Regiments at Old Sarum* (11 May, 1649).

4. The official exposure of him is in *The Justice of the Army against Evil-Doers vindicated* (5 June, 1649), p. 7. He was cashiered in 1647 after a drunken brawl in a tavern during which he assaulted the servants, because he believed he had been robbed of £20. But the men took up his cause and he managed to remain for a full six weeks in his regiment (Whalley's horse). Accused of rousing Fleetwood's horse to sedition, he was eventually sentenced to death, but managed to escape twice from prison. He was then for a time an outlaw who played the part of Robin Hood at the head of a troop of mutineers in Essex. On another occasion he stabbed one of the Army's spies who was in the act of seizing unlicensed pamphlets at an underground press; the man died a month later, from a neglected wound. Lilburne stood bail for Thompson, and helped him to write his pamphlet against martial law (p. 299 above). One has the impression that this exposure exaggerates his misconduct in the tavern and understates his political activity, which was his chief offence. See also *The same Hand again* (25 July, 1649).

5. The clearest of several accounts of this skirmish is in *The Kingdom's Weekly Intelligencer* (8-15 May, 1649).

6. *A Declaration from His Excellency* (12 May, 1649).

7. See *The Copies of Several Letters* (White to Fairfax, 22 January, 1649), (20 March, 1649.)

8. The conduct of Fairfax in failing to keep his engagement has been discussed already (pp. 358-9 above). Chaplain Denne after his pardon published a novel defence of the Lord General in *The Levellers' Design Discovered* (24 May, 1649), to the effect that most of the regiments of the Army had petitioned him to dismiss the Agitators, dissolve the Council and summon it again only when he saw fit. This seems to be a muddled version of what happened on the eve of the Ware rendezvous. There is no trace of any such petition in Rushworth or Thomason. If one accepts Major White's narrative as truthful, there is no escaping the conclusion that the surprise attack at Burford was, as the Levellers argued, 'treacherous'. The weak point of their case is that, if they were expecting negotiations, they should have stopped their march to join the other mutinous regiments. Both sides should have stood still. It is odd that neither Gardiner, Firth nor Abbott discuss Cromwell's conduct in this affair.

9. *A Moderate Intelligence Impartially communicating Martial Affairs to the Kingdom of England* (24-31 May, 1649).

10. *The Kingdom's Weekly Intelligencer* (5-12 June, 1649); *A Modest Narrative of Intelligence* (2-9 June, 1649); *Mercurius Elencticus* (4-9 June, 1649).

11. *The Baiting of the Great Bull of Bashan* (16 July, 1649).

12. *Legal Fundamental Liberties*, H. and D., p. 448.

CHAPTER XXVII

The Levellers' Platform

What happened at Burford in the Cotswolds settled the allegiance of the New Model. For the rest of Cromwell's lifetime it was his to command. Meanwhile, the four prisoners in the Tower, who did not foresee the defeat of their followers in the field, were preparing in its final form their appeal to Christian charity and reason. The third version of the Agreement of the People was the last collective testament of the Leveller leaders, to the English nation and to history. In it their political programme stands mature and complete. As a team they never spoke again with a united voice, though as individual thinkers both Lilburne and Walwyn still had something of importance to say. The last edition of the Agreement was sent to the press on May Day 1649. But before we discuss it, we must consider the preface, *A Manifestation*, which Walwyn drafted and the four prisoners signed on behalf of themselves and 'others commonly (though unjustly) styled Levellers' on 14 April.[1]

Written with charity and good manners in William Walwyn's most persuasive style, the *Manifestation* is an *eirenicon* that aims at calming the tempers Overton and Lilburne had ruffled with so much talent and success. 'Peace and freedom is our design; by war we were never gainers, nor ever wish to be. . . . We desire that what is past may be forgotten.' Such is the keynote of this composition. Its soothing influence would, unluckily, be cancelled when the news of the Levellers' mutiny and defeat reached the ears of its leaders. It is not the defeated who can at will blot out the past. Walwyn's chief purpose in this preface is to dispel the prejudices that clung to the authors of the Agreement and hampered their work as peacemakers. They are, he protests, neither atheists nor Jesuits; because they value above all things the practical part of religion they are not strict upon its formal and ceremonial side. Neither are they anarchists. It is strange reasoning to argue that 'because we have laboured so earnestly for a good government, therefore we would have none at all'. As little are they Royalists. For 'though we have not been any way violent against the persons of the King or Queen or their party, yet . . . those principles and maxims of government which are most fundamentally opposite to . . . the King's interest take their first rise and original from us'.

The last of the 'aspersions' which Walwyn has to deny in the name of himself and his colleagues is that they were 'communists'—the only one of these charges which interests us today as much as it interested the Levellers' contemporaries. We must beware, however, of a verbal confusion. In the course of three centuries the words 'community' and 'communism' have radically changed their meaning. To the men of the seventeenth century what they recalled was the 'all things in common' of the first generation of Christians, the quasi-monastic way of life which the church of Jerusalem may have borrowed from the Essenes. This was the ethical ideal which appealed to the early Anabaptists of Switzerland, the Rhineland and Moravia. This was the light that shone in Buckinghamshire—a smoking candle, it may be—against the English background of the common fields. And this was the inspiration which prompted Everard, Winstanley and their companions to dig and manure the waste land on St George's Hill in Surrey. The suspicion Walwyn had to meet was that the four prisoners and their followers shared the principles of 'the true Levellers' and would, if they could, make an end of private property. When once their opponents set out on this alarming train of thought, they found it easy to see in Freeborn John a reincarnation of Jan of Leyden, the revolutionary prophet of Münster.

Never was there among all the multifarious dishonesties of party politics a cruder invention than this. John Lilburne was an

aggressive individualist who felt no sympathy whatever for any
school of egalitarian or communistic thought. If it had fallen
to him to draft the *Manifestation* he would have disavowed the
Diggers roughly, and with frank contempt. A few years later
he did, in one of his autobiographical tracts, explicitly reject
'the erroneous tenents of the poor Diggers at George-hill in
Surrey'.

> In my opinion and judgment [he wrote] this conceit of
> levelling propriety and magistracy is so ridiculous and foolish
> an opinion as no man of brains, reason or ingenuity can be
> imagined such a sot as to maintain such a principle, because
> it would, if practised, destroy not only any industry in the
> world, but raze the very foundation of generation and of
> subsistence. . . . As for industry and valour, by which the
> societies of mankind are maintained and preserved, who will
> take pains for that which when he hath gotten [it] is not his
> own but must equally be shared in by every lazy, simple,
> dronish sot?[2]

Walwyn, on the other hand, was a decided egalitarian, who
pleaded for equality in education for all men and for a near
approach to equality in incomes. The communistic ideal
attracted him, though he may have been unable to think out
the means by which it might be realised in the world of his day.
What he had to say, on behalf of the whole body of Levellers,
was that neither communism nor the equalisation by law of
men's estates figured among the aims of their party. He did it
without a word of disapproval of the Diggers, or of disloyalty
to his own personal creed. Indeed, in the first sentence of the
Manifestation he began (with an echo of Cicero's *Non nobis
solum nati sumus*) by affirming a social conception of morals.
'No man is born for himself only': we are 'obliged by the laws
of nature, . . . Christianity . . . and public society . . . to employ
our endeavours for the advancement of a communitive happiness.' He admires the 'charity and heavenly-mindedness' of the
first Christians, but he insists that they were never commanded
by the Apostles to bring all their goods into the common stock;
the community among them was voluntary. He reminds his
readers that the Leveller party is already pledged against 'an
equalling of men's estates', notably in the Petition of 11

September, 1648. To attempt anything of the kind would be wrong, 'unless there did precede an universal assent thereunto from all and every one of the people'. Why the Levellers, whose principle it normally was that the will of a majority of the electorate should prevail, should in this case insist on unanimity, he does not explain.

By reckoning this prohibition of levelling as one of the inalienable fundamentals, guaranteed by the constitution, the party gave the impression that for it the ownership of property was a sacred right, comparable to the immunity of the citizen from dictation in matters of conscience. This may have been a shrewd move in the party tactics of the day, but that is all it was. It served to distinguish the Levellers from the Diggers. In practice this prohibition tied their hands much less than one might suppose. It would not have forbidden them to do anything that any modern socialist party has ever proposed to do— not even to nationalise the land. Not even today in Russia are 'all things in common', forty years after the Revolution, nor is there yet equality or a distant approach to it in men's incomes or estates. One may doubt whether this repudiation of levelling did much to appease property. The City knew very well that the Levellers were still in favour of manhood suffrage and in that they saw, as did Whigs and Tories alike until the nineteenth century, a dire threat to their ascendancy. A party which would make an end of tithes, base tenures and indirect taxation, was for every man of property his deadly enemy.

Walwyn went on to explain why he and his colleagues were about to publish a revised version of the Agreement, 'cast into a model and platform, . . . as the standard and ultimate scope of our design'. Faulty though the officers' version is in some respects, it contains so much that is good that they would have accepted it 'had it been put in execution'. But the time proposed for carrying it into effect is already past. The Levellers will therefore send out copies of their own final version for signature by the electors. They do not propose to present it to Parliament, since such an Agreement should 'take its rise from the people'. In sending it out, they 'rely . . . solely upon that inbred and persuasive power that is [in] all good and just things to make their own way in the hearts of men and so to procure their own establishments'. These words came from four prisoners, who lay in the Tower of London awaiting their trial as traitors.[3]

The four prisoners spent two weeks in composing the third Agreement of the People, but behind it lay many years of danger, suffering and struggle. To read it as a student who lacks historical vision and reads a legal textbook would be to miss most of its meaning. It should be read, so to speak, in depth. Seen in perspective, these provisions for a democratic franchise recall the debates at Putney, where Rainsborough and Sexby invoked the claims of universal humanity against Ireton's concern for property. The clauses which define toleration within a secular republic are the outcome of a passionate and perilous struggle for power—first against Laud and the King's Star Chamber, then against the Presbyterians, the City and the Scots, and finally against the narrowness of the Independents. The juridical principles are not impersonal formulae; John Lilburne, as daring a pioneer in legal thinking as Coke or Grotius, won them with a bleeding back and fettered ankles. In the humanity of the sections dealing with debt, the press-gang, and the gallows, we hear the voices of Walwyn the practical Christian and Overton the sceptical Anabaptist.

Behind the four prisoners who drafted this amateur sketch of a written constitution, a group hitherto inarticulate and unorganised is forcing its way for the first time into history— the middle sort of people, the craftsmen, the tradesmen and the peasants. Here voiced with startling clarity are their aspirations, here are the measures they demand, for the protection of their interests against the squirearchy, the lawyers and the merchants of the City churches for whom Cromwell played the constable and dictator. Economic motives will go some way towards explaining this programme. But amid the struggles of opposing groups there were moments when the more far-sighted of the Levellers could rise above the battle, and define a principle that must hold good within any human society worthy of that name.

The text of the third Agreement can be found in two accessible modern collections.[4] A full analytical summary of it may serve our purpose better than a literal reprint of its thirty articles. While the title-page and preamble stressed once again the intention of its authors to tender 'a peace-offering to this distressed nation', in point of fact this final version of the Leveller platform discarded the compromises of the historic petition of 11 September and the second Agreement of 15 December, 1648. Here are its chief provisions:

THE ELECTORATE

All men of twenty-one years and upwards enjoy the Parliamentary franchise, active and passive, with the exception of (1) servants and (2) those receiving alms, while (3) active Royalists who fought for the King or served him with voluntary contributions are disqualified for ten years.

No property qualification survives. The chief effect is to enfranchise the great mass of the rural population, the copyholders and tenants at will, together with the independent craftsmen and the tradesmen in the towns. The term 'servants' covers all who are employed by a single master, from the chaplain, bailiff or secretary of a great nobleman down to domestics and hired labourers. Many journeymen in skilled crafts would thus be denied the franchise on the ground that (in the absence of a secret ballot) they would not dare to vote against their employer's wishes. Those disqualified for receiving alms would include the many unemployed proletarians, who were driven in winter to seek relief under the poor law. Among them, failing provision to the contrary, would be classed the maimed veterans of the Civil Wars. Distressing though these exceptions seem to us, on the balance the gain to democracy from this advance was revolutionary.

THE CENTRAL GOVERNMENT

The supreme authority is 'the representative' chosen by this electorate, i.e. the House of Commons. No mention is made of King or House of Lords, nor would it be possible to include either without extensive amendments, which are forbidden. The representative consists of four hundred members elected by constituencies distributed according to population. The rotten boroughs accordingly disappear. Parliament (i.e. the Rump) is asked to draw up a list of constituencies for use in the first election of the new régime, and to prescribe the method of voting.

Members are to be paid and Parliament is asked to fix their salary.

The Long Parliament is to be dissolved on the first Wednesday in August (1649): thereafter the life of a representative is limited to one year, during which it must sit for at least four months. It is forbidden to set up a Council of State, nor is there any provision for a standing executive to act throughout the year in the place of the old Privy Council or the modern Cabinet. If the representative adjourns (as for a maximum of eight months it may) a committee chosen from and by its members will act for it under its instructions.

Starting with the election to be held in the autumn of 1649, no member of the previous Parliament may sit in its immediate successor. Experience had taught the Levellers that power corrupts. The same provision had ruinous consequences during the French Revolution.

No salaried military officer and no official of the revenue may be elected, nor may any lawyer, if elected, practise in the courts.

The representative is empowered to deal with foreign relations, defence, finance, the regulation of commerce, the preservation of freedom, internal security and the redress of grievances, subject to the following reservations.

RESERVATIONS

Toleration in matters of religion is thus defined (article 10):

We do not empower or entrust our said representatives to continue in force or to make any laws, oaths or covenants, whereby to compel by penalties or otherwise any person to anything in or about matters of faith, religion or God's worship, or to restrain any person from the profession of his faith or exercise of religion according to his conscience, nothing having caused more distractions and heart burning in all ages than persecution and molestation for matters of conscience in and about religion.

Tithes must be wholly abolished, nor may anyone be compelled to pay towards the maintenance of any minister; but

s

impropriators (lay owners of tithes) must be compensated.

Each parish shall elect its own minister and may provide for him, by voluntary contract. No minister may be imposed on a parish, i.e. there shall be no state church. In addition to the parish church with its minister thus chosen by the parliamentary electors, other churches or chapels may of course be set up without restriction.

Catholics (i.e. such as maintain the Pope's or other foreign supremacy) may not hold any public office. This prohibition (which did not infringe on the toleration Catholics would enjoy) might be justified as a compromise, designed to ease tension and suspicion during a limited period of transition. As a permanent restriction it is a blot on the Agreement.

Pressing or conscription to serve in war by sea or land is forbidden: 'every man's conscience being to be satisfied in the justness of that cause wherein he hazards his own life or may destroy another's'.

An amnesty is proclaimed covering everything done in the civil wars.

CIVIL RIGHTS

All are equal before the law: privileges and exemptions are abolished, even those of M.Ps.

The Petition of Right and Magna Carta must be observed. Together these provide that no man may suffer in his person or estate save by due process of law, nor may any financial burden be imposed save by common consent in Parliament. The Petition forbids billeting and the resort to martial law in time of peace.

JURIDICAL PRINCIPLES

No man may be condemned 'where no law hath been before provided', i.e. under a law passed after the commission of the offence: 'where there is no law, there is no transgression'.

The separation of legislative and executive powers is decreed. Parliament may not 'intermeddle with the execution of any law whatsoever', consequently it may not function as a court of law—as in fact it did down to the trial of Warren Hastings and the affair of Queen Caroline.

No one may be required to incriminate himself by answering questions in a criminal case—the principle of the Fourth Amendment to the American constitution. The effect of this is that pressure cannot lawfully be used to extort confessions.

All proceedings in law must be terminated within six months.

All laws and legal proceedings must be in English.

Any man may plead his own cause or call in whom he will to plead for him; thus the lawyers' monopoly is broken, and those accused of felony are entitled to employ counsel.

Any man tried for life, liberty or estate has the right to call witnesses (a right denied to those accused of felony even after the Whig Revolution).

Imprisonment for debt is forbidden as unchristian and of no advantage to the creditors, but neither may a man's real or personal estate be exempted from payment of his debts.

Capital punishment is abolished save for murder and 'other the like heinous offences destructive to human society', or for 'endeavouring by force to destroy this our Agreement', an offence which was thus equated to treason. Thus the Levellers proposed to do what was at last accomplished only in the nineteenth century, thanks to Samuel Romilly. There is nothing in other writings of the Levellers to suggest that the 'other the like heinous offences' included anything more than treason. Further, Parliament was instructed to revise the whole scale of punishments 'that so men's lives, limbs, liberties and estates may not be liable to be taken away upon trivial or slight occasions, as they have been'.

DECENTRALISATION

In future all trials, civil and criminal alike, shall be 'by twelve sworn men of the neighborhood to be chosen in some free way by the people and not picked or imposed' as so often in the past. The word 'neighborhood' covers parish, hundred and county. What the Levellers proposed was a return to Anglo-Saxon traditions, with the hundred as the chief unit of self-government. All the costly professional law courts at Westminster, including Chancery and the King's Bench, would be swept away, nor would judges appointed by the central government go round on circuit.

No public officer may be imposed on any county, hundred, city or borough. The people enfranchised by this Agreement shall 'choose all their public officers, that are in any kind to administer the law, for one whole year and no longer',—sheriffs, Justices of the Peace, and the rest.

DEFENCE

The same principles of decentralisation and democracy apply also to defence. Parliament alone may decide what total force must be raised, and upon what service it may be employed. It appoints the general and all general officers. It assigns to each county, city, town and borough in due proportion the number of men it must enlist, equip and pay.

In each of these units of local government the electors choose the officers who command regiments, troops and companies and may remove them, if they see cause.

In plain words, there shall never again be a standing professional army, or a New Model. The general directs operations in the field, but cannot dominate his officers in the old way since he has lost the power to promote, nor can he intimidate and degrade officers or men, in time of peace, by martial law.

ECONOMICS

All monopolies in foreign trade, e.g. those of the Merchant Adventurers and the East India Company, are abolished.

Within four months all indirect taxation of commodities, whether by customs or excise, shall come to an end and all revenue shall be raised thereafter 'only by an equal rate in the pound upon every real and personal estate in the nation'. The objections urged against indirect taxation are that it is burdensome to trade and relatively costly in collection; what may have influenced the Levellers even more decidedly: it weighs with disproportionate severity on the poor.

The second version of the Agreement exempted from all taxation persons 'not worth above £30' (meaning capital, not annual value) though they would still pay poor and other local rates. It seems unlikely that the failure to repeat this exception was deliberate.

Here for the first time the Levellers proposed to abolish customs as well as excise. This would have amounted in effect to free trade in the modern sense of those words. Parliament could still forbid the export or import of certain goods, but to enforce such prohibitions would be difficult if the customs service were disbanded. One must not suppose, however, that Lilburne and his colleagues shared the economic outlook of the Manchester school. They were not advocates of *laissez faire*, nor was it their chief aim to capture the world market with cheap exports; far beyond their range was the thinking of the more idealistic Liberals who argued that the labour of mankind would be lightened, if each people specialised in producing only such goods as its traditions, resources and climate fitted it to place on a free international market with the utmost efficiency and cheapness. It is, however, likely that the familiarity of Lilburne and Overton with life in prosperous Holland, where a near approach to free trade prevailed, may have influenced them.

In this economic chapter must be included the prohibition to 'level men's estates, destroy propriety or make all things common'.

All the above provisions of the Agreement were fundamenta and valid for all time. Not only was there no provision for its amendment, but any member who shared the guilt of a Parliament which transgressed any of its provisions would incur the penalties for treason. Why certain of these articles, important though they were, for example the declaration of an amnesty, should have been classified as fundamentals of the constitution is puzzling.

FURTHER REFORMS

To the second version of the Agreement was added a list of urgent reforms, outside the framework of the constitution, which Parliament was asked to carry in the first session of the new order. Some of these are embodied in the third Agreement; others are omitted. There were, moreover, proposals set out in earlier Leveller documents which find no place in either edition of the Agreement, presumably because they were regarded rather as 'circumstantials' than as 'fundamentals'. It is unlikely that the party had changed its mind about any of the following reforms, which should therefore be regarded as part of its 'platform'.

(1) Its agrarian programme, including the plan for the conversion of base tenures into freehold, with vaguer suggestions for the restoration to the poor of some enclosed commons and the utilisation of waste land.

(2) The codification of the civil and criminal law. A revision of the latter is implied in the clause dealing with punishment. It was the soldiers who sounded the bugle call for codification in *The Case of the Army*, which asked 'that all the laws might be reduced to a smaller number to be comprised in one volume in the English tongue, that every free commoner might understand his own proceedings'.[5]

(3) Free primary education for all—or at any rate for boys —as outlined by Richard Overton in his *Appeal*.[6]

(Walwyn went much beyond this in *Tyranipocrit*, but gave no details. Of detailed plans the most humane and liberal came from that incalculable genius, Harrington. Though he was neither a democrat nor a Leveller, he proposed free schools for all from the ages of nine to fifteen, followed either by apprenticeship or education for a profession. The 'needy' were to be eased of the 'charge of their children' while at school, which must have meant that they should be maintained by the republic.[7])

(4) The provision in every county at the public charge of hospitals for the nurture, maintenance or relief of orphans, widows, the aged, the sick and the lame, as proposed in the same *Appeal* by Overton.

(5) The freedom of the press as defined in the petition for unlicensed printing.[8]

(6) Prison reform. The exaction of fees was forbidden either in prisons or courts of law and it was proposed that the gaoler, who used to run his prison for profit, should become a salaried public servant.

(7) The election by the poor of a trustee, or tribune of the people, who acts for them in recovering lost endowments or common lands.

(8) The setting up in every county of a land register in

which all conveyances, bills, bonds and the like must be entered, as proposed by John Lilburne in his postscript to the second Agreement. Designed to minimise litigation, this proposal was obstructed by the lawyers, though it had originated with Sir Edward Coke.

(9) The limitation of interest to 6 per cent.

This, with the adoption of English as the language of the law and the setting up of a land register, were the only items of this entire programme enacted by the Commonwealth. An emasculated version of the article forbidding imprisonment for debt tricked the Levellers' hopes.

Together with the third Agreement of the People these nine proposals made up the Levellers' platform—a sketch of a written constitution to which must be added the reforms they regarded as urgent.

When the Levellers composed the third Agreement it was not only to their former allies, the Independents, that they tendered it 'as a peace offering', but to 'this distracted nation' as a whole. England, as John Lilburne saw it, had relapsed into a 'state of nature'. She could recover only by the creative act of all her people, who must renew the social contract by signing an agreement to entrust their Representative with an authority which they limited and defined. This was a pregnant exaggeration. England never sank into the primeval chaos of Hobbes's imagination, when man was a wolf to his fellows. What had happened was rather that her national unity had been shattered. One could even draw on the map a line which reflected the schism in men's thoughts and the distrust in their hearts. How to restore the national unity was, therefore, the problem the Levellers had to solve. They never framed a definition of nationality; the epoch of Herder and Mazzini lay far ahead. But in half-conscious groping they had reached their own notion of it. They cherished with passion the heritage of freedom won for them by their ancestors. They justified the disfranchisement of the Royalists for a time on the ground that these men, by their indifference to this heritage, had excluded themselves from the national community.

When they thought of the Norman Conquest, a blend of

race-consciousness with class-consciousness entered into their idea of nationality. In everything that galled them in their daily round, from the burdens of land tenure to the brutalities of the criminal law, they saw the badges and reminders of the Conquest. The restoration of national unity involved therefore the ending of all the vetoes and privileges which an intruding aristocracy had usurped. It meant, above all, a recognition of the civil and political equality of all the strata of this recon- stituted and re-united nation, which would regain the right to use its native English once again in its courts of law, as it had not done for some six hundred years. Thanks to this political myth, when the Levellers invited the liberated descendants of the Anglo-Saxons to claim the proud status of equal citizens in a commonwealth, it was not to a perilous journey towards a remote and unhomely Utopia that they summoned their fellow- countrymen. They invited them to resume their 'native rights'.

To stamp the defeated Royalists as 'Normans' and foreigners was not a happy prelude to reconciliation. In any event the royalist aristocracy must surrender its privileges. But to them also this peace offering had much to promise. The amnesty would protect them from further spoliation. Inspired by the same liberalism which led John Lilburne, a few months back, to stand up for the rights of such unpopular Cavaliers as Hamilton and Holland, the new charter of civil rights guaran- teed them against the lawless vengeance of their political opponents. Above all, the offer of toleration meant that they could enjoy for choir and pulpit, altar and font, without fear or concealment, the comforts of their Episcopalian confession —nay more, in many parishes, as time went on, they might count on electing their priest to minister to them in their ancestral parish church. Was this enough to reconcile them to the new order? The memory of King Charles forbade it, and for that the Levellers were heavily to blame. Overbold in that tragedy, they were timid in delaying the exercise of political rights by the defeated Cavaliers for a full ten years. But only one man among the republicans had the audacious wisdom to propose their immediate enfranchisement, and in this eccen- tricity Harrington failed to carry with him even his most faithful disciples.

As a peace-offering, then, the Levellers' Agreement, liberal though most of its clauses were, fell far short of its aim. How generous it was, none the less, judged by the temper of that age, we can estimate by comparing it with the rival version of the officers. That left the whole apparatus of Independent domination intact—the New Model Army, the Council of State, the High Court of Justice. It would give to Prelatists no promise of toleration. It proposed to tax them for the support of the Puritan clergy. It excluded active Royalists from election to Parliament not for ten but for fourteen years. Finally, it erected in their path Ireton's totalitarian wicket gate. His formula, which would admit only 'men of courage, fearing God and hating covetousness', of which qualifications the parliamentary majority would be the judge, ensured to the godly élite for the foreseeable future a monopoly of representation and power.

Seen in retrospect from the angle of our own time, the Leveller programme presents a baffling juxtaposition of forward-looking and backward-looking proposals. The secular republic resting on a generous franchise and a single chamber, the end of the entanglement of the state with religion which went back to Constantine's day, the enlightenment of the newly defined civil rights, the humanity of the clauses that all but ended the cruelties of gallows and dungeon—all this anticipated something of what we have achieved in three centuries and much that we have not yet achieved. But what are we to say about the lengths to which the Levellers carried their revolt against all centralised authority? It is intelligible that insular Englishmen, face to face for the first time with militarism efficient and triumphant, should respond with these extravagant precautions. After a few years of trial and error these excesses might have been corrected, but for the worst mistake of all—the clause that forbids amendment.

Before 'the troubles', national unity had been preserved not only by the supervision of the local administration from the watch-tower of the Privy Council, by its prerogative courts and by the judges sent out to preside over assizes in the counties, but also by the authority and prestige of Chancery and the higher courts of common law at Westminster. Under these latter, though inland transport was still primitive, England was becoming a single national market, dominated by a system of law that favoured the creditor, while Chancery upheld views of landed property that favoured the lord of the manor. Under the third Agreement this whole central apparatus of supervision and appeal was swept away. It could be foreseen that 'the twelve sworn men' of each neighbourhood, who according to Leveller doctrine were judges of law as well as fact, would soon begin to render sharply divergent judgments. Royalist Cornwall and Presbyterian Essex had in that century very little in common—not even language and religion. Given the wide differences in culture and economic structure between the backward, agrarian West and North with its Celtic fringe on the one hand and the more advanced East and South with its industrial salients on the other, such national unity as England and Wales had attained would soon have vanished. To such a forecast the prisoners in the Tower might have replied that they had their own expedient for preserving national unity— the drafting of a simple and intelligible code of English law, by which they meant a code that would reflect their own principles of humanity.

The attempts of the Levellers to reverse the movement of history came to nothing, for it was only the poorer strata of society that backed them. The tide of events, after the proclamation of the Protectorate at the close of 1653, made irrevocably for centralisation. Nor had their party and its allies any success in advocating the codification of the law. This idea found able advocates among the pamphleteers of the left,[9] but the legal profession was solid in opposing it. In the Revolution which the Puritans began and the Whigs completed the victor was the upper middle class. It overthrew the prerogative courts which administered law on the Roman model, and in their stead confirmed the authority of the courts which administered the common law.

Based on innumerable and sometimes conflicting precedents, the common law could be understood and applied to particular cases only by a skilled body of professional lawyers, who levied a heavy toll on the rest of the nation and made a resort to the courts so costly that only the rather rich or the very rash would venture on litigation. In every rank of society below the upper layer to which the legal oligarchy belonged, a dread of the law courts and a detestation of lawyers were widespread. John Lilburne when he talked of 'ridding this kingdom of those vermin and caterpillars the lawyers, the chief bane of this poor nation' was singular only in his use of a highly picturesque vocabulary. Nearly everyone on the parliamentary side of politics wished or professed to wish for a cheaper and less dilatory legal procedure. But what the Levellers found amiss in the legal system of their day was something worse than its expense. In a tract that dates from the first months of the Civil War, William Walwyn, who never talked at random, drew a scorching impeachment of the society around him in which 'lawless judges grew rich and potent', and a wise man would 'let go his right or inheritance' rather than be 'eaten to the bare bones by griping judges and avaricious lawyers', a society 'wherein a poor man was hanged for stealing food for his necessities and a luxurious courtier . . . could be pardoned after killing the second or third man',[10]

Looking back on the seventeenth century the author of the classical *History of Criminal Law in England*, Sir James Fitzjames Stephen, who was far from being a humanitarian, confirms from his own standpoint as an expert on procedure this contemporary verdict. Denied the help of a solicitor or counsel, with no right to see his own witnesses so as to put their evidence in order, the accused man had to fight for his life when he came into court with absolutely no knowledge of the evidence to be produced against him. The result was that 'an amount of injustice frightful to think of must have been inflicted at the assizes and sessions on obscure persons of whom no one has ever heard'.[11]

For these obscure persons the Levellers spoke.

NOTES TO CHAPTER XXVII

1. Wolfe, p. 388.
2. *Lt. Colonel John Lilburne his Apologetical Narration* (April 1652).
3. The third Agreement enjoyed a distinction almost unique among the Levellers' tracts; it went to the press with an official *imprimatur*. For this

indiscretion Gilbert Mabbot was dismissed from his post as censor. Mabbot was an opportunist who liked to pose as an idealist—a type that throve under the Saints. After his dismissal he pretended that he had resigned his post of censor at the prompting of his conscience. That elastic organ permitted him to resume this profitable employment under the Protectorate. As a protégé of General Monk he was rewarded after the Restoration with a valuable sinecure.

4 In full in Wolfe, pp. 400-10; in part in Woodhouse, pp. 355-67.

5. Wolfe, p. 216.

6. *Ibid.*, p. 194; Woodhouse, p. 377.

7. J. Harrington, *Oceana* (Morley's Universal Library), p. 203-4, 210.

8. Wolfe, p. 326.

9. See the anonymous *Experimental Essay touching the Reformation of the Laws of England*, and L.D.'s *An Exact Relation of the Proceedings . . . of the Late Parliament, Somers Tracts*, VI, pp. 266-84, esp. pp. 276-8.

10. *Some Considerations tending to the undeceiving those whose judgments are misinformed by Politic Protestations, Declarations, etc.* (10 November, 1642). The description in the last clause fits Sir Thomas Lunsford.

11. Sir J. F. Stephen, *History of Criminal Law in England*, I, pp. 389-402.

CHAPTER XXVIII

'Walwyn's Wiles'[1]

The Levellers' peace-offering evoked a perverse response. A week after the appearance on the book-stalls of their *Manifestation*, a pamphlet was licensed under the singular title of *Walwyn's Wiles, or the Manifestators manifested, . . . declaring the subtle and crafty wiles, the atheistical, blasphemous soul-murdering principles and practices of Mr William Walwyn. . . .* In a preface of inflated pulpit eloquence it was dedicated to the Army, while it carries on 'the transparent work of God in the world'. Its main purpose was to counter-mine the Levellers in their opposition to the re-conquest of Ireland. Unless this expedition were undertaken, 'the rebels would descend upon this nation like a mighty torrent sweeping all before them'. There followed this tempting question addressed to the Army: 'Are you unwilling to be possessed of that good land, that land that floweth with milk and honey?' Their attack, the authors explain, is directed against Walwyn the Jesuit, who misled his 'simple-hearted and simple-headed' companions, Lilburne and Prince. The signatures follow of seven of the leading divines of the day, both Baptists and Independents, with William Kiffin at their head. The breach with these Baptists is startling, because the Leveller doctrine is a rendering in secular terms of the traditional Anabaptist gospel of toleration and equality.

Kiffin stands out as one of the typical Puritans of his age. Left an orphan by the plague, he climbed from modest beginnings, acting for a time as clerk to John Lilburne in his brewery. He soon rose to be simultaneously the 'teacher' of the chief Baptist meeting in the City, and one of its most prosperous merchants. He made his money at the start by exporting leather gloves to the continent and importing tar, hemp and ropes. From an outlay of some scores of pounds, as he tells us in his memoirs, he made as many thousands.[2] He served in the City militia, and rose to be lieut.-colonel. Always a supporter of Cromwell, he sat in both Parliaments of the Protectorate. After the Restoration, though he was prosecuted more than once for nonconformity, he managed at considerable expense to keep his chapel going. Charles II asked him for a 'loan' of £40,000; he thought it wiser to give the King £10,000 outright, whereby, as he reckoned, he saved £30,000. Thanks to this *pourboire* and other political investments of the kind, he enjoyed some influence with Clarendon, which he used to ease the lot of persecuted Baptists. It was through his mediation that the lives of the twelve condemned to death at Aylesbury were spared. A cautious and far from heroic character, he survived and enjoyed, as he put it, 'what estate God hath blessed me withal', while the bolder idealists of his creed, the Bunyans and Harrisons, languished in prison or perished on the gallows.

Among the seven divines the most conspicuous of the Independents is John Price, co-pastor with Dr John Goodwin of the most influential of their congregations, which met at Coleman Street in the City. Price, who had practised his pen in several hard-hitting polemics against the Presbyterians, was evidently the writer both of the preface and the lengthy pamphlet it introduced. His portrait of Walwyn is not without merit as a work of imagination. His Walwyn is what Iago might have become if he had taken to politics. This 'past apprentice and journeyman to the Prince of Darkness' had evolved a technique for corrupting all who came within his reach that Mephistopheles might have envied. His purpose was to undermine their faith in God and the Bible, and to ruin the commonwealth. In page after page of lurid exposition his devices are described. Mr Price understood the use of innuendo. He will not say in plain English that Walwyn was a member of the Society of Jesus, but he hints at it again and again. After repeating a yarn about a plot of the Agitators to murder Cromwell in his bed, he conveys the impression that Walwyn was mixed up in it.

But some of his slanders lack nothing in precision. He tells a painful story of what befell a citizen's wife well known for her abilities and her piety. Walwyn sapped her faith in the Holy Scriptures and when the doubts he implanted drove her to intolerable 'anguish and perplexity', he persuaded her that 'the honourable and valiant' way of escape was by taking her own life. After two or three attempts she succeeded in strangling herself. The truth was, as her physician and Walwyn's son-in-law Dr Humphrey Brooke put it on record, that she suffered from pains in the head so severe as to be well-nigh unendurable. Walwyn, as an intimate friend of the family, went out of his way to entertain her and keep her cheerful, and for a time had some success in dissuading her from suicide. The best answer to these clerical scandal-mongers is that the dead woman's sons and sister were among those who had the moral courage to visit Walwyn in prison.

As far back as 1646 Dr Goodwin's congregation appointed a committee to examine Walwyn's record. In spite of some slanders and some absurdities, its report was substantially truthful. His sympathies were with the Irish rebels, and he never disputed the statements about them attributed to him now by Mr Price as formerly by Mr Edwards in *Gangraena*. He would not explicitly deny nor would he accept the communistic and egalitarian sentiments ascribed to him. They do not clash with the colour of his mind. Thinking aloud, he may well have said something of the kind to a friend whom he trusted, without intending that his words should go beyond the walls of his library. Here is Mr Price's record:

This Mr. Walwyn, to work upon the indigent and poorer sort of people and to raise up their spirits in discontents and clamours, etc., did one time profess he could wish with all his heart that there was neither pale, hedge nor ditch in the whole nation, and that it was an unconscionable thing that one man should have ten thousand pounds and another more deserving and useful to the commonwealth should not be worth twopence—or to that purpose.

At another time, discoursing of the inequality and disproportion of the estates and conditions of men in the world, had words to this purpose, That it was a sad and miserable thing that it should so continue and that it would never be well until all things were common; and it being replied, Will that be ever? answered, We must endeavour it. It being said, That this would destroy all government; answered, That then there would be less need of government, for then there would be no thieves, no covetous persons, no deceiving and abusing of one another, and so no need of government, etc. But if in such a case they have a form and rule of government to determine cases, as may fall out, yet there will be no need of standing officers in a commonwealth, no need of judges, etc., but if any difference fall out, or any criminal fact be committed, take a cobbler from his seat or a butcher from his shop or any other tradesman that is an honest and just man and let him hear the case and determine the same and then betake himself to his work again.[3]

The last part of these musings is not far removed from the plans for the decentralisation of the law in the final version of the Agreement of the People.

But Walwyn's own comment on these stories in his *Just Defence* deserves to be quoted:

Where you charge me, that I find fault that some abound whilst others want bread, truly I think it a sad thing in so fruitful a land as through God's blessing this is; and I do think it one main end of government to provide that those who refuse not labour should eat comfortably.[4]

He then denies that he ever intended, as Price had alleged, 'to turn the world upside down', and begs the courteous reader to turn to the Agreement; 'so far as that is am I for plucking up of all the pales and hedges in the nation; so far for all things common'. Here, brief though it is, is an outline of policy far in advance of the times. Until the Labour Party laid down the principle in 1918, it never entered the minds of British statesmen that it is any part of the duty of government to assure to the working class a minimum standard of life worthy of a civilised community. Walwyn proclaimed this principle in 1649.

Again and again Mr Price stresses the iniquity of Walwyn's views about 'the disproportion and inequality of the distribution of the things of this life', and quotes him as saying:

What an inequitable thing it is for one man to have thousands and another want bread, and that the pleasure of God is that all men should have enough.

The modern reader grasps the attitude of these Puritan divines with difficulty. They believed that inequality is part of God's ordering of society; wealth is His reward for virtue and poverty His punishment for idleness and vice. The upper middle class borrowed this justification of its privileged position from Calvinism. So, logically enough, these pastors and teachers were shocked because Walwyn inveighed against 'the unworthiness of our times in making riches . . . the characteristical token of men's fitness for government'. To the delight of 'the shallow and injudicious' he would argue that 'it will not be well until such time as men shall be eligible into places of trust that are virtuous and able, though poor and low in this world'. From this he would go on 'to foment jealousies against the most active, prosperous and successful persons of the nation'. In plain words he was an incendiary who was for upsetting the providential order under which the Kiffins, the Prices and their congregations had thriven.

What was worse by far, this Walwyn was no mere babbler; he knew how to organise. The exposure goes on to describe how the Levellers had got hold of the press, which publishes their manifestoes with good will. In the country, more especially the home counties, they have their agents in every parish who see to the distribution of their pamphlets, and the same thing goes on in the Army, where every troop and every company is infected. Indeed, they can now boast that thousands and tens of thousands are behind them.[5] One notices that contemporaries never dismissed the Levellers, as our classical historians do, as a negligible minority group; on the contrary they are always treated, even in official polemics, as a power as formidable as it was sinister.

Mr Price goes on to describe the most dangerous of all Walwyn's devices—the new use he has found for petitions as instruments of subversion designed to kindle dissensions and discontents. In these he enlists the rude, ignorant and vicious part of the nation, first against magistrates (who may not use the press-gang), then against ministers (who are to be robbed of their tithes), next against the lawyers and finally (in the name of free trade) against the merchants. While stubbornly defending this unpopular upper middle class, Mr Price knows very well that the evils against which the Levellers direct their petitions are widely resented. He falls back, therefore, on pulpit opiates to reconcile the masses to things as they are. There are passages in the Gospels which warn us not to 'expect perfect freedom here below'. They tell us 'that in the world we shall have tribulation; that through many afflictions we must enter into the Kingdom of God; that here we have no continuing city, but we look for one that is to come'.

In our day we have lost the skill to recognise an emissary of Satan when the tempter stands before us, but it must be admitted that Mr Price had some provocation. He divined correctly that Walwyn would have upset, if he could, the class-structure that endowed 'the silken Independents' with riches, prestige and power. He assailed the clergy with merciless insight and wit. Though he never stooped to personalities, he did describe the orthodox Puritan divines as mercenaries who 'make a trade in religion'. He annoyed Dr Goodwin's admiring congregation by his ironical praise of that learned preacher's art in making simple things difficult. He went so far as to doubt the use of 'preaching or long set speeches' altogether. In their place he preferred 'conferences and mutual debates one with another' as the best way of arriving at truth. He even had the audacity to write—after commenting on the use which tyrannical statesmen make of the pulpit:

> Neither will men ever live in peace and quietness one with another so long as this veil of false counterfeit preaching remaineth before their eyes, nor until the mock churches are overturned and laid flat.[6]

When, some time before the end of February 1649, he came to write these last passages (taken from the *Vanity of the Present Churches*), he had left behind him the ironic playfulness of his replies to Mr Edwards; his hopes of a happy outcome to the Revolution have dwindled and he utters his thoughts with a pessimistic plainness of speech.

As a companion picture to Mr Price's sketch of Walwyn as Mephistopheles, his victim now painted a collective portrait of the Independents as he had observed them in Dr Goodwin's congregation. After 1646 the numbers of this sect had increased rapidly, and it was from the upper ranks of the middle class that the new recruits were drawn. 'They have, as it were' (so Walwyn put it), 'scummed the parish congregations of most of their wealthy and zealous members.' Some of them 'contrary to all example of the Apostles', were usurers; others had large investments in the excise. Not for the first or the last time, he comments on the luxurious life of these Saints.

> View them well in their apparel, . . . their diet and . . . their furniture . . . , even in these sad and miserable times, and then say whether their silks, their fine and delicate linen, their laces, beavers, plushes, their fancies, plate, rings and jewels do not demonstrate from what root they are, that they are mere worldlings indeed, and Christians only in name and tongue.

These people had almost come to believe that 'prosperity is a mark of the true Church'.[7]

Once separated from their parish churches in close and exclusive societies, they went on to 'asperse' those who would not join them with an intolerance and an assumption of infallibility worthy of 'the man in Peter's chair'. 'These seeming saints, . . . so solemn in their countenances, so frequent and so formal in their devotions', so watchful over others' tripping, have their scruples over 'the lawfulness of playing at cards or the like recreation as being a vain expense of time'. In the daily round of business they are so closely 'confederated together' that they will always support one another on the exchange and even in courts of law, by oath if need be.

> Touch one, touch all; all have one purse for a common end, offensive and defensive. And, if they should by these courses grow so odious as that no body else would trust them, their confederacy is so large that, by buying and selling and purchasing and lending, they are able to enrich one another, so as they grow to a mighty interest, as distinct almost as the Jews in Amsterdam, and much to the same ends of gain, but have greater aims of power and dominion.[8]

Walwyn's sketch came from the pen of a deeply injured man,

who felt himself as he lay in the Tower on a charge of treason, literally these men's prisoner. But no attentive reader of the cruel libel to which the seven divines affixed their names will think his sketch seriously exaggerated. On a first reading what strikes us in this series of pamphlets is the spectacle of a powerful and original personality at bay before these conventional minds. But on further reflection, beyond this clash of personalities one perceives a far more significant shock between diametrically opposite attitudes and ideas. The Independents were what their vanquished enemies King Charles and Archbishop Laud had also been, firm believers in theocracy. Their political ideal was such a commonwealth as their emigrants established in New England. There only members of its Independent churches enjoyed the right to vote; no other churches were tolerated, and heresies such as those of the Quakers were punished by exile or death.

The Independent ministers, Dr Goodwin, Dr Owen, Hugh Peters, John Price, were not for their hearers what they are for us, fallible thinkers and stumbling rhetoricians. They were prophets, who believed that the Holy Ghost inspired them as they mounted their pulpits to address a hushed congregation which shared this belief. Their churches were for the Independents the only social units that rallied all their emotional loyalties, for the guilds were dead and the city companies degenerate. There was never an Independent party in the modern sense of that word, but there was a collection of Independent churches, each of them the chief focus of its members' social life, subject to discipline and inspired by unquestioning faith. The peculiarity of these churches was, as Walwyn pointed out, that their members formed an acquisitive 'confederacy', with a common purse and a habit of mutual aid for purposes of gain. Drawing their leading adherents from the upper middle class, these churches would attract the ambitious younger men, the industrious apprentices, since membership meant admittance to this formidable conspiracy which held in its hands the keys to office, wealth and power. Once they had made an end, under pressure from the Levellers, of the monarchy and the House of Lords, the Independents became the most reliable buttresses of the existing social order, conservatives who could invoke God's Word for the patient acceptance of things as they are.

The realistic historian is apt to think of the government of England, from Pride's Purge to the Restoration, as a military dictatorship. That phrase is too crude. Always the Army believed that it was acting as the sword of God. Translated into the prose of daily life this meant that it was carrying out the will of the Saints, the *élite* who came together in the 'gathered' churches. Without the prayers and approval of its pastors and chaplains, some of whom had blessed its ranks as they charged to victory, it would not have dared to do what it did. Was it ever sincere in its professions of loyalty to the Parliament it first purged and then dissolved with a gesture of contempt? The 'honest party', the active, revolutionary minority, the public opinion to which ('under God') the Army held itself responsible, was to be found in the congregations assembled on Sabbaths and fast days in Independent chapels and Baptist meetings. The most characteristic of all the New Model's doings during the whole fifteen years of its existence, the most genuine expression of its political outlook, was the calling of the Saints' Parliament in 1653, which the officers' Council chose from the nominees of the 'gathered' churches. So close was the connection that in the last chaotic year of the Commonwealth's life the Independent churches of the City offered to raise three regiments for its defence.[9]

Mirrored in these pamphlets is the drama that made this phase of the Revolution so decisive: the theocrats of yesterday confront the democrats of tomorrow. The seven divines do not mention among the Levellers' crimes their advocacy of manhood suffrage; what horrifies them is the prospect that if Walwyn and his dupes won power, they would introduce the election of magistrates and officers. They themselves would have to submit to government by the common man, by craftsmen, even perhaps by cobblers.

It is a mistake to think of the Levellers as the left wing of the Independents. They were not theocrats; nor were they Puritans. What they refrained from saying in their petitions and pamphlets is as important as what they said. They never wished to charge the state with the duty of enforcing a rigid code of morals. No Leveller petition ever included among the reforms it demanded the repression of swearing and drinking. No Leveller ever called for the stricter observance of the Sabbath, or the banishment of fiddlers from the taverns. The typical Independent programme, even when it came from the officers of the New Model, would emphasise these negative aspects of sainthood. It is, moreover, important to remember that the Levellers were the first Englishmen to conceive the idea of a political party as a secular organisation, whose affairs were managed on a democratic model. The Levellers made the final breach with theocracy, when they advanced from a plea for religious toleration to a complete divorce between religion and the state. Theirs is the distinction that they were the first party in the modern world to call for a secular republic. That does not mean that they were inclined to agnosticism or unbelief. John Lilburne had nothing of the sceptic in his ardent nature; he was a Calvinistic Baptist until he quitted politics and turned Quaker. Walwyn's religion was a glowing love of his neighbour; though he cared nothing for dogmas or ritual taboos, he had a warm, emotional belief in Christ's sacrifice of himself for mankind and it was in words from the New Testament that he summed up his revolutionary ethics. So strong was his dislike of the institutional religion which dominated the England of his day that (as we have seen) he dared to write and even to print his hope that 'the mock churches' might one day be 'overturned and laid flat'.

These may seem external facts of no great significance, but there are signs that a profound cultural change was beginning in the minds of the Leveller leaders. They had to face the conviction of the Independents that success is a proof of God's favour. When the Prices and the Kiffins boasted that their wealth was bestowed on them by God with his blessing, Walwyn answered, in effect, 'No, it is due to the unscrupulous techniques of your financial confederacy.' When they argued with an almost Islamic assurance that the unbroken victories of the New Model were a miracle which only God's intervention could explain, the Levellers invited them to study history. The victories of Julius Caesar, who destroyed Rome's liberties, were even more remarkable than Cromwell's. Was he likewise God's commissioned officer? Did God own and appear for him? The simple-minded Thomas Prince was the first who asked that uncomfortable question in print.[10]

The Levellers never explicitly challenged the assumption common to most of the great preachers of their age, Catholics as well as Protestants, Bossuet as well as Hugh Peters, that the finger of God manipulates men on the chequer-board of destiny to fulfil His purposes. Flashes of creative insight they did enjoy, but they had no master-key to unlock the book of history with its seven seals. They were not philosophers but empirical Englishmen, busied with the urgent political problems of the hour. It was not they but their contemporary Harrington who evolved, a few years later, in his *Oceana*, the book which ranked him among the great European intellects of his time, the first pioneering essay towards an economic interpretation of history. But if we could put to Walwyn, Overton and Prince the simple question: Is history a divine puppet play, or are events interlinked in a chain of causality? there can be no doubt about their answer. They would reject the myth and accept the scientific explanation. They were freemen of the century of Galileo, Harvey and Newton.

NOTES TO CHAPTER XXVIII

1. This chapter is based on a series of pamphlets reprinted in H. and D., pp. 252-398. These are, in chronological order: (*a*) *The Vanity of the Present Churches*, (*b*) *Walwyn's Wiles*, (*c*) *The Charity of Churchmen*, (*d*) *Walwyn's Just Defence*. The first of these pamphlets, which is certainly by Walwyn, was written and published by him before the appearance in print of *Walwyn's Wiles*. He had, however, a shrewd idea of what it would contain, and was defending himself in advance by an attack on the Independent churches. Here, by a contemporary observer, is an analysis of the connection between Calvinism and the development of capitalism which anticipates much of what first Weber and then Tawney (in *Religion and the Rise of Capitalism*) wrote on this subject in our own day. The first reply to the slanders of *Walwyn's Wiles* came from Humphrey Brooke, M.D., Walwyn's son-in-law. Walwyn's own defence, which he wrote with reluctance, is not among his best pamphlets. It has none of the wit of his replies to Edwards and goes into tedious detail to expose the treachery of his Puritan assailants. As a postscript to *The Vanity of the Present Churches* it completes his sketch of the rise of capitalism in the Independent churches.

2. *Remarkable Passages in the Life of William Kiffin* (ed. W. Orme).

3. H. and D., pp. 302-3.

4. *Ibid.*, p. 384.
5. *Ibid.*, pp. 306, 314.
6. *Ibid.*, p. 271.
7. *Ibid.*, pp. 264, 372.
8. *Ibid.*, pp. 394-5.
9. Whitelock, *Memorials*, IV, p. 357 (10 August, 1659).
10. *The Silken Independents' Snare Broken* (20 June, 1649).

CHAPTER XXIX

Towards a bounded monarchy

One afternoon towards the end of May in 'the first year of freedom' (1649), while John Lilburne in his room in the Tower was dining with his wife, two visitors were shown in— Hugh Peters, who often acted as Cromwell's confidential man of business, and his friend Dr Robert Massey. John did not welcome this intrusion. He refused to believe that the two had dropped in out of mere friendliness. With his usual bluntness he assailed Peters as 'the setting dog or stalking horse of the great men of the Army', and went on to complain of the treatment he had to endure in his unjust imprisonment. Presently he and Peters fell into debate on the nature of law itself. Hugh Peters (as John reports him) maintained that 'there is no law in this nation but the sword, . . . neither any law or government in the world but what the sword gave and set up'.[1] One is reminded of the crude doctrine of Thrasymachus, that might is right, which Socrates demolished in the *Republic*. John's reply was a question embedded in half a page of scriptural quotations:

> Was it not on behalf of the laws, then, above all for Magna Carta and the Petition of Right that the Parliament took up arms? . . . If the Grandees of the Army repudiate the Petition of Right, I would rather live under the Grand Turk.

Hugh deprecated all this heat and tried to reassure his angry host; his life was not really in danger. With a jest at John's habitual legalism, Peters argued that, from the days of the Norman Conquest, order in England had always been imposed by the power of the sword. He then fell back on his favourite maxim: 'Good men, not good laws, must save kingdoms.'

If good men administered affairs in obedience to the only perfect and absolute law, the word of God, we should have no need for Magna Carta and the Petition of Right. Coke and Littleton would vanish, with all the other relics of heathenism, popery and tyranny.

In spite of his superficial likeness to the sophist Thrasymachus, Peters the divine was not a raucous materialist. With all the force of his emotional personality he believed in theocracy, in the divine government of the universe, in God as the motive power of history. The Puritan God chose the saintly few as an *élite* to rule the earth. If any questioned the title of these 'good men' to govern, the answer lay in the miraculous victories God wrought through their Army.

But John had still something of practical importance to say before his uninvited guests departed. It was a prediction that the people would soon be turning to Prince Charles—not merely to cry him up but to fight for him and bring him into his father's throne—if the 'bloody tyranny' of the Cromwellians with its insupportable burdens went on much longer.

> Yea, and for my particular, [he went on] I must aver unto you, I had rather by many degrees choose to live under a regulated and well-bounded King without tyranny than under any government with tyranny.

He ended with a characteristic jibe at the Independents for their love of money. Had not Cromwell just got 'at one clap' land worth £3,000 to £4,000 *per annum* with £20,000 worth of timber upon it?

It was, one suspects, chiefly for the sake of this last passage about the Prince that John published this dialogue in the Tower. Was it a warning to the Commonwealth, or was it an invitation to the Royalists to discuss with the Levellers the conditions under which they would fight for a restoration?

Lilburne was an unflinching democrat, but he was never what Marten, Vane and Ludlow were, a republican on theoretical grounds. Of the outstanding Leveller manifestoes, only the *Remonstrance of Many Thousand Citizens* of July 1646 opposed monarchical government in principle, but though it pleaded the cause of Freeborn John, he had no hand in it; it was the

work of Overton, Walwyn and Marten. Sometimes he argued
for an elected king. His preference was decidedly for a Commonwealth, but he could adjust himself without difficulty to the
idea of a 'bounded' or constitutional monarchy. How early and
through what channels the Cavaliers first got into touch with
him, we do not know. But there is evidence in a curious letter
from Evelyn the diarist to the Prince's headquarters in Paris
that some of the Royalists were in contact with some of the
Levellers during the mutiny which ended at Burford. He
reported that the Levellers were considering as one of the
courses open to them the acceptance of 'monarchy strictly
regulated', but he added the cautious comment: all is not gold
that glitters.[2]

The disaster in the Cotswolds flung the party into deep
depression. In two letters from the Tower to his 'brethren of the
sea-green order' who met at the Whalebone Tavern, Dick
Overton described with humorous exaggeration 'the dumps'
into which they had fallen and incited them to renewed
activity on behalf of 'our persecuted, wounded, forsaken and
almost murdered cause'.[3] In this mood the more sober of them
may have realised that they could not hope to defeat the
'tyranny' of the Independents unaided. The Royalists were the
only possible allies in sight, for the Diggers were only a handful.
The underground cavalier press went on flirting in almost every
issue of its *Mercuries* with 'the honest Levellers', 'the brave
blades', 'the free-born boys'. Some of Prince Charles's counsellors
were well-disposed towards them. The ablest of them, Edward
Hyde, who lives in the nation's memory as Lord Clarendon,
argued in an official despatch that the Levellers were to be
preferred as allies to the Presbyterians. They had 'little of
ambition, pride or covetousness in them' and though their
notions of reform were extravagant, he thought they might be
content with a good deal less—toleration, the reform of legal
procedure, some improvement in the condition of the poor,
respect for the fundamental laws and frequent meetings of
Parliament.[4] But Hyde knew nothing of the Levellers at first
hand, nor was he well-informed—he described John Lilburne
in his *History* as a book-binder—and evidently he had no conception of their passionate faith in democracy, which blazed,

even in these days of dejection, undimmed. John had not lost his fighting spirit, nor had the young men in the City's workshops deserted their beloved leader.

The Levellers felt that they were facing a 'bloody tyranny'. The phrase strikes us as exaggerated. Save in fair fight at Preston and Colchester, the victorious Independents had shed little blood—a few royalist aristocrats and a few radical mutineers—for the Irish massacres were still to come. But what sort of 'tyranny' was it that Colonel Pride's Parliament exercised? Here is a rough definition: the rule of a single party which maintains itself in power by coercion qualified by propaganda and a monopoly of the means of mass expression. The classical liberal historians failed to recognise it. In our day painful experience has familiarised us with this social phenomenon; we have invented an ugly name for an ugly thing and learned to label it when we see it. But in the seventeenth century the despotism of a party which claimed to be an *élite* was something new, and down to our own day it remained the unique specimen of its kind. No less novel was the combination of propaganda with coercion. We shall watch it evolve rapidly during the summer and autumn of 1649, but it was only when Thurloe organised his police state under the Protectorate that the totalitarian tyranny of the Saints came near perfection.

In May the Levellers could still meet freely in the Whalebone, and occasionally their *Moderate* printed a rather risky leading article. But in the middle of this month the Rump passed the act that was to serve it as its chief instrument of coercion. Its Treason Act brought in a new definition of this capital crime. Hitherto it had been confined to deeds, the murder or attempted murder of the King or the waging of war against him. It was now extended to words and the expression of opinions calculated to undermine the prestige and authority of the party in power. Here it is, stripped of its legal verbiage. It began with a reminder that 'the Parliament hath abolished the kingly office . . . and settled the government in the way of a Commonwealth . . . without King or House of Lords'. It went on to declare it high treason: Maliciously to affirm the present government to be tyrannical, usurped or unlawful; or that the

Commons in Parliament are not the supreme authority; or to endeavour to alter the government. Or to affirm the Parliament or Council of State to be tyrannical or unlawful, or to endeavour to subvert them or stir up sedition against them. Or for any person to stir up mutiny in the Army.

It had come, then, to this: that no opposition would be tolerated which contradicted the correct opinion—that of the minority—on the main political issues of the day. This act struck equally at Cavaliers, Presbyterians and Levellers, who would henceforward risk the gallows if they dared to speak their minds.

After coercion, propaganda. Evidently it was the Levellers whom the keepers of the liberties of England most dreaded. Against them was directed a pamphlet, as clever as it was dishonest, entitled *The Discoverer*, which was 'published by authority' at the beginning of June.[5] One of its authors was probably a Baptist preacher, John Canne of Bow. It directs against the four prisoners in the Tower (whom on its title-page it accuses, by name, of sedition) the same charges that the seven divines brought against one of these prisoners in *Walwyn's Wiles*. They were atheists and communists. These were in the seventeenth century the deadliest names with which any man's reputation could be blasted. The authors had too much skill to rely on abuse, which they employ sparingly. They prove all their charges by ample quotations and for these they give chapter and verse in the margin.

These citations are perfectly genuine. The man who wrote most of them was a brave and outspoken communist. Though he was no more of an atheist than was George Fox, he too was violently anti-clerical. It is true that like the Quakers he had no use for sermons or sacraments, and he did identify reason with God. He was, in short, as unorthodox as it is possible for a Christian mystic to be. But this man was not a Leveller, still less was he one of the four in the Tower. He was Gerrard Winstanley, the Digger. His little band of pioneers called themselves 'The True Levellers', by which title they clearly meant to distinguish themselves from the organised party, whose creed was set forth in the Agreement. Its leaders, on the other hand, always disclaimed the nickname, and referred to themselves as 'the Levellers (falsely so called)'. (See Chapter XXXIV.) The authors of *The Discoverer* are dishonest enough to ignore the unequivocal repudiation of economic levelling, which appeared first in the Petition of 11 September, 1648, and again in the Agreement. They go on to identify the Levellers with the revolutionary Anabaptists of Münster whose doings were still, after more than a century, a legend that caused the teeth of men of property to chatter. This trick of loading on to English shoulders the excesses of others—first of Jacobins and then of Bolsheviks—has since been practised with equal lack of scruple by the meaner sort of partisans. But they did not do it 'by authority'.

In this offensive of the godly against the Levellers there is only one thrust that finds its mark. 'That they are atheists . . . or little better . . . may be clearly seen by the Agreement of the People.' Its proposal that each parish shall elect its minister 'opens the way for the choice of atheists and blasphemers, who may teach Alkoran or Talmud'. The real fear of these prosperous Puritans was rather, one suspects, that an elected minister might preach social radicalism. This dread of an elected ministry shows how far the City churches under the Kiffins, Prices and Cannes had swung to the right. The election of the parish priest by his flock was one of the basic ideas of the Reformation. It was one of the German peasants' twelve demands; that gracious liberal, Erasmus, was one of its supporters.[6]

The latter part of this pamphlet, probably by another hand, carries on the attack from a humdrum, secular standpoint. It ignores all the constructive pioneering of the Levellers for democratic and humanitarian reform, and singles out for censure some of John Lilburne's verbal extravagances. But was it tactful in those days, when Foxe's Book of Martyrs ranked second to the Bible, to justify the suppression of dangerous pamphlets by citing the Act of Philip and Mary?

> If any by books, rhymes, ballads, letters or writing shall publish false, seditious or slanderous things against the King or Queen, his right hand is to be stricken off for it.

Apart from some clumsy passages defending the censorship,

the press-gang and court martial, *The Discoverer* is a brilliant essay in propaganda, as able as it is unscrupulous. It may have done incalculable harm to the cause of the Levellers. Addressed to educated readers (for it is packed with Latin quotations) it would furnish to many a preacher all over England material for thrilling sermons, in which these atheists were damned in this world and the next.

The government had, of course, a censorship of the press, though it worked none too well. But over the pulpit, the mass medium which in that generation was even more powerful than the press, its control left much to be desired. The more obstinate of the royalist clergy who went on using the Book of Common Prayer had been eliminated long ago; they lost their livings and were turned adrift. But now the Presbyterian ministers who had inherited their tithes and parsonages, together with the old incumbents who conformed outwardly in order to keep a roof over their heads, presented a difficult problem. They detested their rivals of the 'gathered' churches, the Independents and Baptists. Violently opposed to toleration, they heard with alarm the clamour against tithes that came from the victorious Army as well as the Levellers. For these, and for less interested reasons, they too were royalists, and after the King's execution the bolder of them took to praying and even preaching for the princes in exile. Their flocks looked up to them (if they led decent lives) as spokesmen for Jehovah. What was to be done with them? They could hardly be tried as traitors for an impromptu prayer. Besides, there were eight or nine thousand of them.

The government's solution was a mixture of conciliation and coercion. The Parliament of the Commonwealth reassured its Presbyterian opponents in a binding declaration that their tithes would not be taken away until another way of mainten-ance was provided no less large and honourable—an under-taking which successive Puritan Parliaments went on repeating down to the eve of the Restoration.[7] The established church was to be Presbyterian, though all churches that tend to godliness should enjoy freedom. But the Rump resolved that a bill should be drafted forbidding ministers to meddle in affairs of state. This was passed on 9 July, 1649. It provided that if any ministers shall (1) directly or indirectly preach or publicly pray against the power, authority or proceedings of this present Parliament, or against the present government established by authority thereof, or (2) mention Charles and James Stuart save as enemies, or (3) fail to observe days of humiliation or thanksgiving, or to publish acts, orders and declarations when directed, they shall be deemed delinquents liable to sequestration.

This method of muzzling the pulpit had the advantage that it could be enforced by administrative action through a partisan committee, without the scandal of a public trial for treason. It is noteworthy that Cromwell and Ireton, who were always keener than some of their colleagues to win Presbyterian support for the Commonwealth, divided the House against the third reading of this bill.

Three days later, Cromwell set out for Ireland 'in that state and equipage as the like hath hardly been seen'.[8] He drove in a magnificent coach drawn by six horses, escorted by a Lifeguard of eighty troopers, who were all officers or esquires. They wore flaunting feathers in their hats, and their colours were a dazzling white. Near Bristol, as they rode westwards towards Ireland, a shepherd's boy was overheard to say, 'They will be dyed red enough before they return from thence.' He was apprehended and taken into safe custody.[9]

England's new chains were tightening round her limbs. It was not usually John Lilburne's way to delay his answer to a challenge, but he had been sorely stricken this summer where he was most vulernable. While he lay in the Tower his family was visited by smallpox, and the news reached him that the elder of his two boys was praying for a sight of his father before he died. Parliament, which could on occasion show a surprising humanity, passed on 18 June, thanks to Henry Marten, an order for John's release during the hours of daylight. Both his sons perished in this epidemic, while his wife and daughter only just escaped with their lives. This affliction so chastened him that he began to hope for a 'composure' with his 'unrighteous adversaries'; he delayed the publication of a pamphlet which was already in the printer's hands; he had even been on the point of burning the whole edition.

However, the financial injuries he suffered, meanwhile, in County Durham from Sir Arthur Haslerig (see p. 578 below) revived his militancy, and early in August there appeared one of the most controversial of his tracts, *An Impeachment of High Treason against Oliver Cromwell and his son-in-law Henry Ireton* (10 August, 1649). This chaotic composition reveals the character of the impulsive and emotional man who wrote it, torn between pious resignation to the will of God, and the most unregenerate of human passions. As a contribution to the politics of the Revolution it has something both definite and novel to say. Addressed in warm, comradely language to the Levellers who met at the Whalebone, it urges them to rally the masses round the Agreement of the People. To begin with, John recorded his belief that Cromwell meant to make himself king. He went on to propose the meeting of a national convention (though he did not use that word) to settle the principles of the Agreement. The Leveller party in each county was to choose two representatives and send them up to London, 'with money in their pockets' to meet 'the culled and chosen agents' of the metropolis.

When once the Agreement had been adopted as its 'standard and banner', the convention should take a unanimous decision to support no one— neither 'the present men in power' nor the Prince—who failed to give good security for the steady observance of its principles.

Upon such terms I do not see but you may justifiably . . . join with the Prince himself. . . . If we must have a King, I for my part had rather have the Prince than any man in the world, because of his large pretence of right, . . . if he come not in by conquest by the hands of foreigners (the bare attempting of which may apparently hazard him the loss of all at once, by glueing together the now divided people to join as one man against him) but by the hands of Englishmen, by contract, upon the principles aforesaid. . . . The people will easily see that presently thereupon they will enjoy this transcendent benefit (he being at peace with all foreign nations and having no regal pretended competitor), viz. the immediate disbanding of all armies and garrisons, saving the old Cinque Ports, and so those three grand plagues of the people will cease, viz. free quarter, taxations and excise, by

T

means of which the people may once again really say, they enjoy something they can in good earnest call their own. Whereas for the present Army to set up the pretended false Saint Oliver (or any other) as their elected King, there will be nothing thereby, from the beginning of the chapter to the end thereof, but wars and the cutting of throats year after year; yea and the absolute keeping up of a perpetual and everlasting Army, under which the people are absolute and perfect slaves and vassals. . . . And therefore rouse up your spirits before it be too late to a vigorous promotion of the aforesaid Agreement.

In these tangled and ungrammatical sentences John Lilburne had something to say of the first importance. He took a long step forward in the development of political techniques within the Atlantic civilisation when he proposed the meeting of this convention. The Levellers were the first democratic party which thought of calling an elected national conference to formulate its demands. In 1794, the London Corresponding Society alarmed William Pitt by calling just such a convention to claim manhood suffrage, and in the next century first the Owenites and then the Chartists followed where the Levellers had led the way.

Next, John Lilburne conveyed to the Royalists who were courting him what his party's terms for supporting a restoration would be. The Prince must give his whole-hearted assent to the Agreement of the People.

Lastly, he warned the Royalists that they would ruin their cause if they brought in foreigners to set the Prince on his father's throne by force. 'Foreigners' meant above all the Scots, but during this summer the underground press of the Cavaliers was keeping up the courage of its readers by bragging of the formidable levies of Danes and Swedes who would soon be landing on our shores. If there was to be a restoration, it must come, after negotiation, by consent. This Lilburne would favour; for the alternative, the kingship of Saint Oliver, meant servitude and financial ruin under a military dictatorship which would never establish an enduring peace.

John saw further into the future than most of his contemporaries, whether Royalists or Independents. Everything he predicted came to pass. But did he seriously suppose that the Prince could endorse the Agreement as it stood? Or if the Prince did sign it, would he scruple in the hour of triumph to tear it up? To satisfy the Scots he signed the Solemn League and Covenant. A year after his glorious entry into London, it was publicly burned in divers places in the City by the common hangman.

Two notable documents were printed in this month of August which adopted the new strategy. The first of them, *The Levellers Vindicated*, signed by six troopers on behalf of their comrades, was (as we saw) chiefly a defence of the rebellion that ended at Burford (p. 521 above). They wound up their narrative with an appeal for the election of Agents by every regiment to join the convention in London. Rather than be vassals to the 'martial monarchy' set up by 'the ruling swords- men', they would even prefer to be the Prince's subjects. The only escape from slavery under either lay in a settlement by the Agreement of the People. 'Conquest', they declared, 'will never allay the feuds among us; for the sword . . . begetteth no love but fomenteth and engendreth hatred and revenge; for blood thirsteth after blood and vengeance rageth after vengeance.' So much these veterans had learned from seven years of civil war.

The second of these tracts, *An Outcry of the Young Men and Apprentices of London* (29 August, 1649), bore the signatures of ten 'Agents' chosen by those of them in the City who approved the Agreement and the *Vindication*. Addressed to the private soldiery of the Army, it exhorted them to elect their Agents to the convention, while in every ward of the City and every county of England the people were doing the same thing. The six troopers may have had Walwyn's help in writing their *Vindication* but Lilburne was, manifestly, the author of the *Outcry*. It repeated his opinion that King Charles was 'illegally put to death'. It took a big step towards the Royalists by criticising the Independents for 'extirpating' instead of 'rectify- ing' monarchy. For this, the tract argues, they had no mandate from the people, which engaged in the Civil War with no thought of 'destroying kingship' but in order to 'regulate' it. One of three estates, as he had argued elsewhere, cannot rightfully destroy the other two 'without the authority of a higher power, . . . which is the people, the fountain and original of all just power, which they never did in their lives'.[10] But John and the apprentices have some plain things to say about Prince Charles:

> There is no way to obtain the true love of the understanding English people (without which he will never obtain his desired crown), but by a cheerful, hearty and real promotion of such principles therein contained [i.e. in the Agreement] as do sufficiently tie his hands from cutting the people's throats at his will and pleasure, the endeavouring of which exposed his father to that fatal end that befell him.

With these three pamphlets the Levellers hurled their challenge at the Cromwellians and defied 'the raging lawless sword' of the Army. As defined by the new totalitarian act, they were deliberately committing treason many times over.

Some action followed, but on a small scale. Only one regiment elected Agents (the name 'Agitator' had fallen out of use), but it went much further. Ingoldsby's foot, part of which was stationed at Oxford, came under the influence of Colonel Eyres, who was awaiting trial there for his share in the Burford mutiny. Its officers tried for several days to reach agreement with the men's Agents. The men were pliable, but their Agents stood out firmly for the restoration, on the lines laid down at Newmarket, of the General Council of the Army; and made extravagant demands about arrears of pay. On 8 September these negotiations broke down and the officers were disarmed and imprisoned in New College, where the Army's stores were kept. According to a later report, the Oxford mutineers, who, of course, supported the Agreement of the People, were also 'for the bringing in of Prince Charles'. They believed that they would soon be joined by thousands of their fellow-soldiers from neighbouring counties, from whom an 'offensive field army' would be formed. Someone, it is said, had a fund of £5,000 ready for the purposes of the mutiny. Many civilian Levellers are said to have rallied to them, but not one troop or company of any other regiment.

In haste and alarm Lambert, who was acting as Cromwell's

under-study during his absence in Ireland, set out from London with a regiment of horse and some dragoons to suppress the mutiny. By the 11th, before he reached Oxford, it was all over. An enterprising young officer, Captain Wagstaff, who happened to be in the neighbourhood, slipped past the men's sentries into the town and persuaded a few soldiers to join him. Meanwhile, the major of the regiment and five or six of his officers half-forced, half-argued, their way to freedom, got swords in a cutler's shop, released their colonel and with Captain Wagstaff's help arrested all the men's Agents. In the brief struggle only one man was killed. The court martial, on which sat Major-General Lambert with Colonels Ingoldsby, Robert Lilburne and Pride, sentenced three men to be shot (of whom one was pardoned) and six to run the gauntlet, while three officers were cashiered. A royalist newspaper printed a story that the Levellers had planned a rebellion on a nation-wide scale, which broke out prematurely at Oxford. They had a genius for propaganda—in the better senses of that word—but for conspiracy no talent whatever.[11]

During this eventful summer a fierce industrial dispute turned the lead miners of Derbyshire into militant Levellers, for even in the remoter counties the atmosphere was sultry with the threat of revolution. Of these miners there were about four thousand and a population of some twenty thousand dependent on this industry, which was then the most important in the county. They were knit together in a venerable organisa-tion, at the head of which stood a tribunal known as the Bar-mote with its master and twenty-four jurymen. It kept alive the traditional rules, measures and customs of their craft. To defray the costs of litigation—for sometimes the miners had to defend their interests in a court of law or before Parliament—the men kept a fighting fund going from a levy on their earnings. For the best part of two centuries they fought the church over the tithe it exacted from all the ore they raised.

They were their own masters and, like the weavers, ranked among the aristocrats of the working class. They worked in teams and were paid as a gang, according to the quantity of ore they got, at long intervals that varied from six weeks to six months.

When times were good, they were relatively prosperous; many of them owned horses, and they had some leisure for the enjoyment of sport. But during this century a period of decline set in. Like the weavers, many of them were sinking to the level of day-labourers directly employed by the wealthy mine-owners of the new capitalist era. Chief among these was the Manners family of Haddon Hall, whose head was the Earl of Rutland. Some mines, however, were nearing exhaustion and work in them was more perilous than before. It is not easy from the partisan accounts in the London news-books to form a clear picture of the plight of the miners in the summer of 1649. They still had considerable resources, but there may have been a good deal of unemployment among them. It was fear that nerved them to fight. The correspondent of *The Moderate* in Derby wrote that 'the poor' were living on what they could 'glean from the harvest-fields'. He must have meant, not perhaps the skilled miners, but the labourers who worked with them. At this season of the year the agricultural population would not be in want.

For some years the miners had been at feud with the Earl of Rutland, whom they described in a petition as their 'implacable enemy'. His agent replied by boasting of his charities. The immediate issue turned on a custom which according to the men's organisation had prevailed from time out of mind in Derbyshire, and had been honoured even in the days of the King. It gave the men the right to sink their mines wherever ore was to be found. This the Earl would not permit in his demesne, where (as his agent and the conservative *Moderate Intelligencer* argued) it would render his house uninhabitable. The men (backed by the Levellers' organ, *The Moderate*) replied that Rutland was 'opposing his single interest against the interest of the nation', and this at a time when 'many thousands were ready to perish for bread'. Their moral case was clear; they were fighting for the right to work. As to their legal case, they insisted that the only issue at stake was the existence of the custom to which they appealed. They wished to carry this question to arbitration or to the court of the Duchy of Cornwall, which had jurisdiction in all disputes over the mining of tin and lead. But the Rump, always eager to enhance its own authority as a court of law, kept the matter in its own hands.

Meanwhile, the Levellers in Derby had made common cause with the miners. From Derby *The Moderate's* correspondent reported (8 September) that the miners, who were 'very numerous' and had 'arms sufficient and hearts answerable to their resolutions', were issuing a declaration of their rights, which they 'will maintain with their lives and fortunes and likewise the Agreement of the People and the Petition of 11 September 1648'. A fortnight later *The Moderate* carried the news from Westminster that the committee of the House had reported against the miners. Till far into October the underground cavalier press went on announcing that the miners were 'in a posture of war to purchase their freedom'. Its news was out of date when it was printed. It was a fact that on the pretext of attending a horse-race or, when the sheriff forbade horse-racing, a foot race, or a bowling match, the miners to the number of five or six thousand were gathering in a rebellious mood, half of them on horseback, armed with pistols and swords. But the Council of State was vigilant. Fearing the beginning of an insurrection, on 10 October it ordered Colonel Saunders to disperse these tumultuous gatherings, which his cavalry proceeded to do, disarming the miners and taking from them horses as well as swords. Resolute they may have been, but they could not face veteran troops.[12]

After Freeborn John and the ten apprentices had published their *Outcry* there was a brief pause in the warfare between Levellers and Independents. Its printer, to be sure, was flung into Newgate and his press seized, but for the moment that was the only reprisal. It occurred to someone in governing circles that yet another effort should be made to close the rift between the two parties, so recently comrades in arms, before the Levellers came to terms with the Royalists. Accordingly, in the first week of September several conferences 'for procuring a right understanding' were held on the model of 1648 between four of the House, four of the Army and four of 'those called Levellers'. Some compromise must have been proposed which was not rejected out of hand by the agents of the Levellers, for

to the government it seemed worth while to carry the negotiations a stage further, by bringing in the imprisoned leaders.
Walwyn, Overton and Prince, 'by desire of the Council of
State' were given 'the liberty of the Tower' in order to carry on
'the tripartite treaty'.[13] Lilburne already was at large in the
hours of daylight; a few days earlier indeed he had performed
one of his characteristic feats. A file of musketeers, to the
alarm of his wife, came to his home in his absence to arrest him.
When he arrived on the scene, he forced them to realise that
their warrant gave them no such powers, and they departed
shame-faced with a few of his pamphlets as their only booty.[14]
The discussions among the four prisoners were spread over
two days (7 and 8 September) and then broke down. It was,
if we may trust the royalist press, the Levellers who rejected
the compromise offered them. John threatened to kick one of
the mediators downstairs.[15]

Since conciliation had failed, the Independents resumed the
offensive. The Commons on 11 September condemned the
Outcry as seditious and its 'contrivers' as traitors who must be
tried for high treason by a special commission of Oyer and
Terminer—before an extraordinary tribunal, that is to say,
chosen for the occasion, a procedure traditionally reserved for
offences peculiarly destructive to the Commonwealth. Everyone
understood that John Lilburne was the only one of the 'contrivers' who mattered. At the same time the Commons instructed
the Council of State to prepare a polemical 'Declaration'
against the Levellers. Propaganda was as important as coercion.

The next blow was struck at the press. The licensing laws
were already stringent, but the act passed on 14 September
strangled the entire parliamentary press in less than two weeks
after it came into force. It set up no less than three censors, one
who acted for Parliament, another for the Council of State
and a third for the Army. To these the authors, publishers and
printers of all books, pamphlets and newspapers were subject.
If a newspaper contained news or opinions bearing on the
doings of Parliament, the Council and the Army, as virtually
every issue of every newspaper necessarily did, then it must
receive the *imprimatur* of all three censors. Printers were

intimidated by the clause which required them to find two sureties of £300 that they would print nothing scandalous or treasonable. To the monopolist Stationers' Company large powers were given to seize and break up the presses of the printers of unlicensed matter. The circulation of newspapers was penalised by the clause that threatened with fines or imprisonment all purchasers of unlicensed printed matter, and all hawkers, 'mercuries' (the women who sold newspapers in the streets) and ballad singers with arrest, a whipping and the loss of their stock. There were penalties also for dispersing unlicensed matter by post or carrier. The manufacture of presses and types was controlled. No printing was permitted save in London, Oxford, Cambridge and York. The act came into force on 1 October.

In the massacre of the entire licensed press that followed, the last survivor was *Perfect Occurrences*, whose editor, Henry Walker, a close friend of Hugh Peters and like him an Independent minister, was a loyal follower of Cromwell; but it too vanished for ever after 12 October. The only remnants of a free press were the underground newspapers of the Royalists, two of which managed to dodge all the beagles employed to track them down till the early summer of 1650. The last issue of the *Man in the Moon*, as bawdy and cynical as ever, was dated 5 June, 1650. What the Council of State offered, to replace the entire parliamentary press, was a couple of official gazettes—*A Brief Relation* and *Several Proceedings*—as meagre as they were dreary, which printed as much of the week's news as it was good for the public to know. But this is not the place to tell the story of the totalitarian official press. It became more readable, if not more honest, when the turncoat Nedham was appointed to edit the *Mercurius Politicus* under the supervision of the author of *Areopagitica*.

Here let us erect a humble gravestone to the *Moderate*. The last issue of the Leveller organ was dated 25 September, 1649. For many a month it had lived dangerously, dodging the censor and contriving to hint at some of its opinions in parables which the more quick-witted of its readers would decipher more easily than we can do, as we blink over the faded type of its yellow pages. On 5 June, 1649, two days before the official

day of the thanksgiving for the crushing of the Levellers at
Burford, it printed as a leading article a web of scriptural
texts. 'But (saith the Lord) the feasts or rejoicings of the wicked
My Soul hateth . . . and though you make many prayers, I
will not hear you . . . for your hands are full of blood . . .'
and so on for the better part of a page. No censor could object
to this; it was all in the Bible.

Rather harder to decipher is the elaborate story in the following issue of a race between three horses, Policy, Integrity and
Royalty:

> Policy pursued close by Integrity, . . . being almost overtaken,
> entreats speedily a treacherous reconcilement. . . . The
> overture . . . begs a positive rejectment. This unexpected
> response diverting the great design, Royalty claps in afresh
> . . . and makes the race disputable; . . . yet that Integrity
> wins the race, we'll lay you 6 to 3.

Integrity is Honest John; Royalty is Prince Charles and Policy
the Cromwellian government or Council of State. The story of
the race assures us that the attempts of Hugh Peters and others
to corrupt the prisoner in the Tower will fail. The Prince is
in sight of the winning post, but whatever happens, the odds
are two to one on John. No censor would bother to blot out this
nonsense, but over their tankards in the Whalebone the
Levellers (falsely so called) would spell out the message.

Again, in the week when Cromwell drove in almost regal
state through London on his way to Ireland escorted by Life-
guards arrayed in white, the *Moderate's* leader was a little essay
on Alexander the Great, who used to wear a garment 'white
without but lined with treacherous purple within'. What
censor could object to the *Moderate's* denunciation of the
Macedonian soldier for 'ambition and hypocrisy'?

In the last months of its short existence—it ran for sixty-three
weeks—the *Moderate* ceased to print the Leveller manifestoes,
as it once had done. There is not in its pages even a brief quotation from the *Impeachment* or the *Outcry*, nor any support for the
convention to ratify the Agreement. Mabbot in his managerial
or editorial chair grew more cautious with each issue. But the
last of his leader-writers—was he John Harris?—had his say

from time to time. Obviously he belonged to the left wing of the party, and his favourite gambit was to warn the government that by its deafness to the complaints of 'the poor and meaner sort' it was provoking their wrath (20 March, 1649):

> Provoke not too much, for fear it be too late to repent; and ease the poor nation of the burden, for fear they shake it off and lay it upon their backs that are better able to bear it. . . .

Again, in the issue of 11 September which carried the alarming news from Oxford and Derby, he reflected that though the people were rid of the King's tyranny, the covetousness and ambition of the propertied victors, swimming in the golden ocean at Westminster, had so increased the people's burdens that they were now beginning to rage and cry out for a new Parliament. 'The fire breaks out, the wind rises and if the fuel be dry and some speedy remedy be not taken', he saw ahead what a modern journalist would label social revolution.

The *Moderate* might have spared its pains; there was no need (in Burke's phrase) to 'ingeminate terror'. By the middle of September panic gripped both the country and its rulers. It was the general belief that the Levellers were about to rise in armed revolt. Their phantom armies had been seen now in this county and again in that. Once more the harvest had failed, and we read the barely credible news that the shilling wheaten loaf was selling at half a crown; it is not surprising that here and there 'most of the meaner sort were forced to pawn their bedding'.[16] A dread of these starving poor, and of those who might organise their suffering into rebellion, seized the propertied Puritans and began to distort their Revolution. One is reminded of the panic that took England by the throat after the French Terror of 1793, when Pitt and Dundas suspended the *habeas corpus* act, turned the Privy Council into a Star Chamber and called out the militia to quell insurrections that never had been planned.

From the Council of State at its meeting on 17 September, 1649, went out a notification to the military governor of Windsor that the Levellers were planning the seizure of the castle; similar warnings were sent to all garrisons in the North, and to J.P.s and county committees throughout the country.[17] At a joint meeting of the Council with the Rump on 18 September, according to a royalist journalist who was often well-informed, Thomas Scott, one of the members for Newcastle, was particularly violent against the Levellers. 'Unless,' said he, 'Lilburne and his confederates be cut off we shall have all our throats cut.' The idea was that the Levellers were planning a massacre of the leading Independents. Several of the regicides, this chronicler tells us, changed their lodgings, and Bradshaw's guard was doubled. A parliamentary newspaper laughed at the story of 'the white army' which marched through Hertfordshire about a week before, and are 'ever since invisible'.[18] At Birmingham, as we read in the last issue of the *Moderate*, the rumour ran round that the Levellers of the county had raised a force of six hundred horse. Scouts reported in alarm that four strangers who 'must needs be Levellers' had put up in the inn. Two of them, it turned out, were messengers of the Council of State. Of the many stories of armed revolt that found their way into print, only two are perhaps authentic. Bands of countrymen, who had some arms, under Leveller leaders, fell on the excisemen at Stourbridge in Worcestershire and at Nantwich, surprised their escorts of soldiers and carried off what money they had collected.[19]

There was no Leveller rebellion, but doubtless in 1649 as in 1794 the spies and the *agents provocateurs* were busy. The government was none the less in peril, and it knew it. Save against the press, it did not dare to make a bold use of the formidable totalitarian weapons with which it had armed itself. Month after month it put off the crucial test of its authority, the trial of Lilburne for treason; again and again it sought to come to terms with him and even to bribe him. In face of the unanimous hostility of the Presbyterian clergy its act for muzzling the pulpit was little more than a dead letter. In Devon and Dorset the ministers of that church—the established Church—even called a conference to organise defiance of the government; they declared themselves supporters of the King, the House of Lords and the secluded Commons and pledged themselves to ignore official fasts and thanksgivings.[20] Nor were other

counties more docile. Under the Commonwealth the Presbyterian clergy never were tamed.

The next move came from the Levellers. On 21 September
they published a manifesto which ranks among all their
utterances as the most reckless and the most revolutionary. It
was also the most popular, for close on a hundred thousand
persons approved it with their signatures. The party's record
was blotted with failure after failure; its leaders were prisoners
in the Tower; yet in the autumn of 1649 it reached the height
of its influence and prestige.

The Remonstrance of many Thousands of the Free People of England
is a declaration of war hurled at 'all those tyrants and usurpers
now sitting at Westminster'.[21] 'Our burdens', it declares, 'become so insupportable, that we are . . . compelled to make use
of that means nature teacheth us for our own preservation.'
It calls for disobedience to all the acts and orders of these
usurpers, and especially for a refusal to pay all taxes, assessments and tithes.

It then enumerates the Levellers' aims. (1) They will bring
to justice all who murdered their friends at Ware, London,
Burford and Oxford. (2) They will secure their debentures for
the soldiers. (3) They will force all M.P.s and members of
administrative committees to disgorge their ill-gotten gains
and surrender the surplus of their estates over and above what
they owned at the beginning of this Parliament. (4) Then come
some of the chief planks of the Agreement—laws in English,
the prompt trial by jury of all cases in each county, no monopolies, the annual election of officers and magistrates, manhood
suffrage, and complete religious toleration. (5) Among these
planks is now included an affirmation of the right to work:
'That every free commoner shall be put into a way and enabled
with means for his natural subsistence . . .' (6) After a settlement according to the Agreement of the People they undertake
to make good to all who join them any damage they may suffer
by so doing. (7) They promise, when victorious, to refer to the
counties the question whether this commonwealth can be at
peace only if it has 'one head or king to reign' over it: 'that if
we must have a king, the crown of England may return to the

right owner, or if most appear against that government, it may be governed as free estates and not otherwise. . . .' (8) The peroration makes it clear that the Levellers were proposing not merely 'civil disobedience' or tax resistance (as in contemporary France) but an armed rebellion. 'For the attainment of all these ends we have drawn our swords and are resolved not to put them up again till we have obtained the things before specified, not doubting of the aid and assistance of all honest and well-meaning men.' A postscript made the claim that:

> This is already signed with 98,064 hands, and more to be added daily, so soon as we can give notice hereof to our afflicted brethren in all the counties of England and Wales.

This is, with a single dubious exception, the only instance during the Interregnum of a 'remonstrance' or petition that carried a number of signatures anywhere near this total. The petition from Londoners calling for 'justice' on Strafford made a record in its day (1641), but it mustered only 20,000 signatures; the same number signed the famous petition from the City for a personal treaty with Charles I in July 1648.[22] Leveller petitions usually carried about 10,000 names, though one of them, on not very good authority, is said to have had about 40,000 signatures. This figure, ascribed to the Large Petition of 11 September, 1648, the signatures to which were drawn from Greater London and 'places adjacent', would be most impressive, if we could be sure of it.[23] The population of the City and its suburbs in this period may have been some 450,000 persons, which might mean about 100,000 households.

In the case of the *Remonstrance* we have not a round but an exact figure which we must accept, unless we like to call it a deliberate lie. Whether the signatures were gathered honestly we do not know, but that reservation has to be made about all these petitions. Neither do we know from how wide an area they came—doubtless from the home counties as well as from Greater London; in some of the small towns of this region, Aylesbury, St Albans, Deptford, Watford and Wycombe we know that the Levellers were active and numerous. It is, therefore, likely that a respectable proportion of the householders signed the *Remonstrance*. How far they understood and approved the Leveller programme, or whether their motive was chiefly hostility to the 'usurpers' at Westminster—that is more than we can say. But it is a reasonable guess that at this moment, in this area, in a general election the Levellers, thanks to their admirable organisation, would have outvoted the unpopular Independents; in the country as a whole the Presbyterians, because of their control of the pulpits, would easily have headed the poll, since the Royalists could not have competed openly.

The longer one pores over this startling manifesto, the more puzzling does it appear. Gone is the pacifist mood of *The Vindication*. The plan of holding a convention in London to adopt or amend the Agreement is abandoned. Instead of the proposal to support Prince Charles on terms after negotiation, the new strategy is to overthrow the tyrants at Westminster by military action combined with tax-refusal, on the understanding that after their fall the people shall decide by some sort of referendum whether it prefers monarchy or republic. But if it should decide for a monarchy, it will still be committed to an extreme form of democracy with elected magistrates and manhood suffrage. This was not a mere improvisation. Some details, especially the demagogic baits, had been thought out clearly, for instance the proposal to strip the Saints of their booty. Had as much care been given to the military side of this adventure? Had a commander been chosen, or a staff? What stores or munitions had they for the volunteers? Had they any funds?

Why, then, was no attempt made to 'draw the sword' on a nation-wide scale, during Cromwell's absence in Ireland? There are several possible explanations. (1) The appeal to the Army to elect Agents may have failed, save in Ingoldsby's foot. The other regiments on which the Levellers had counted were purged too thoroughly in the spring. (2) The Royalists whose alliance the Levellers were courting may have drawn back when they realised that their partners in the proposed rebellion were in earnest over democracy. The restoration to which the Cavaliers looked forward would bring back the House of Lords as well as the King, while parsons and magistrates would be chosen by and from the gentry from above and not by election from below. In its issue that appeared on 19 September, two

days before the *Remonstrance*, the *Man in the Moon* had made up
its mind to oppose this alliance.

> The Levellers [it wrote], if they could but unite, are able
> and fully bent to fetch them [the Independent 'usurpers']
> down with a vengeance . . . [But they are] implacable
> enemies to monarchy, . . . whatever they pretend to the
> contrary. . . . The Levellers, . . . no whit daunted, . . . have
> yet a powerful design a-working, but I hope the loyalists
> are more wise than to join them.

(3) According to this shrewd observer, then, the Levellers
as well as the Cavaliers were divided over this 'powerful
design'. It could, indeed, hardly be otherwise. One cannot
imagine Walwyn approving it. Lilburne, whose mental
processes were rapid, had travelled during the summer all the
way towards this alliance, but devoted though his party was
to him, would they all troop after him in this 'deviation to the
right'? When it came to the point of drawing swords, how
many Levellers would face a third civil war for the sake of
crowning yet another Stuart? The undertaking to refer the
question of a restoration to a referendum looks like a device to
re-unite John's divided following. (4) To these explanations we
must add another which the rival royalist newspaper, *Mercurius
Pragmaticus*, suggested. The rebellion came to grief because it
broke out prematurely at Oxford. Colonel Eyres, who may
have been chosen to command it, was then removed to Warwick Castle and the stores in New College, on which the
Levellers may have reckoned, would no longer be available.
Worst of all, the plans that had been worked out for the formation at Oxford of an 'offensive field army' and for surprise
attacks on Windsor Castle, Plymouth and Leicester, were
unearthed when the defeated mutineers were examined; and
these plans were transmitted, of course, to the Council of State.
There were, then, some solid grounds for the panic that
gripped our forefathers in the fall of 1649. By good staff work
and prompt preventive action the rebellion was staved off, and
nothing remained of the challenge but a rather foolish tract.
The task that now faced the government was to try the most
popular man in England for treason. It prepared public

opinion for the shock by methods with which contemporary totalitarian régimes have made us familiar. It calumniated him and his party. Once more it charged the Levellers with atheism. In order to dramatise this accusation the Army endured a day of humiliation for the growth of atheism.[24] While buff coats fasted and prayed to order, black gowns in the pulpit would, we may be sure, embroider distorted extracts from Winstanley's mystical speculations.

Round about this date was published *A Declaration of the Parliament of England*, the polemic against the Levellers which the Rump instructed the Council of State to prepare.[25] This tedious, long-winded pamphlet began by praising God for 'the series of miracles and wonders' He wrought 'on behalf of a sinful and undeserving people'—meaning the victories of the New Model. After attacking the 'wild principles' of the Levellers who called for universal toleration, and wanted 'liberty without property', it declared that they were 'turning to atheism and licentiousness'. That they had 'now espoused the interest of Charles Stuart' was clear from an intercepted letter taken two or three days before the Oxford mutiny. Written on 6 September, by a royalist prisoner in the Fleet to an exile in Paris, it said that 'all our hopes here depends upon His Majesty's seeming compliance with Lilburne and the Levelling party'. While the writer could not refrain from jesting about 'the simple-hearted Levellers', he was frank enough to admit that though the King's friends increase daily, they cannot 'embody unless the Levellers lead the way . . ., which will be, I hope, suddenly put in execution'. The next charge against the Levellers was that they were aiming at the dissolution of Parliament,

> though they very well know that as the present distemper of the people was . . . either these elections could not be free, or the people must have lost their liberty by it, which was the things they had in design and prosecution.

In a passage quoted already the *Declaration* then accused the Levellers of delaying the re-conquest of Ireland. After some account of the three mutinies, it called for justice upon 'the chief of those who laid and carried on those dangerous designs'.

From that day forward John Lilburne engrossed the attention of the Levellers. There was no more thought of drawing
swords or resisting taxation. All who admired him postponed
their revolt till his trial should be over. If he should be condemned to death, they would rise, of course, to rescue him. He
was in his element, conscious that the eyes of the nation were
fixed upon him, the people's champion, who was about to
defend the common cause by single combat. As always in
seasons of heightened vitality his pen was busy. He had already
published his furious attack on Sir Arthur Haslerig.[26] That
acquisitive Saint, if we may believe John, confiscated, without
due process of law, nearly £2,500 worth of landed property
bought with the grant the latter received from Parliament as
compensation for his martyrdom in the days of the bishops. The
pretext for this robbery was that the Council of State had since
condemned him as a traitor. This, Lilburne declared, was
worse than anything Strafford ever did; Haslerig was therefore an outlaw, who deserved to be knocked on the head like a
polecat. This shrill vituperation was Lilburne at his worst.

In *Strength out of Weakness* on the other hand, he is the lovable
egoist, lucid though garrulous, and sure of himself. This
pamphlet gives an account of a discussion at the Inner Temple
between himself and Edmund Prideaux, the Attorney-General.[27]
John refused to recognise him in his official capacity, but they
discoursed none the less, 'with great civility with their hats on'.
John told the story of his negotiations at Windsor in 1648 with
Ireton and Harrison. The two talked repeatedly of 'the mock
Parliament', which was all that was left after Pride had purged
it. 'If Ireton or Harrison deny it, I will make it good, as a
soldier, with my sword in my hand.' When Prideaux questioned
him about his attitude to monarchy, he declared that he would
still prefer a commonwealth, 'provided it be limited and all
its magistrates annually elective and accountable'. He wound
up this characteristic pamphlet with a memorable epigram;
'No man can be a slave but he that is afraid to die.'

> I bless God [he went on] I have already learned to die,
> having ever since my first contest with the bishops always
> carried my life in my hand, ready at a quarter of an hour's
> warning to lay it down.

After 27 September, Lilburne was once again a close prisoner in the Tower. On 13 October the Council of State at last fixed the date of his trial; it would begin before the grand jury on 24 October. As he lived through the blank days, his spirits would rise and fall. At one moment he challenged Cromwell and Haslerig to submit their case against him to arbitration; in the next he proposed banishment—on his own terms. Since he and the principles he professes are a burden to the rulers of England, he offers to emigrate to the West Indies, if others may go with him, with their arrears paid and allowance for the poor among them, for he will not go into the desert alone. Was it to please his 'half-distracted' wife and his devoted brother Robert that he made these 'proffers', or had the brave man his fleeting hours of weakness?[28]

From the petitions that still came in on John's behalf, and from the few surviving newspapers, one gains the impression that in both camps Englishmen awaited the day of his trial in breathless anxiety and suspense.

NOTES TO CHAPTER XXIX

1. *A Discourse betwixt John Lilburne, close prisoner in the Tower of London, and Mr Hugh Peters, upon May 25, 1649.* . . . Gardiner (*Commonwealth and Protectorate*, I, p. 50n.) denies that the meeting ever took place, and dismisses this tract as a fabrication by some forger unknown. Evidently he had never come across Dr Robert Massey's pamphlet: *The Examination and Correction . . . of the Discourses between Mr Hugh Peters and Lt.-Col. John Lilburne* (1649), which Mr Stearns summaries in *The Strenuous Puritan*, pp. 347-9.

2. In this letter, dated 14 May, 1649, Evelyn says that he has it 'as a very great secret from persons of very great moderation' that the Levellers' mutiny means more than appears on the surface. They had debated among themselves several alternative courses, one of which was 'to incline to monarchy strictly regulated'. He added two interesting details. The mutineers were convinced that they could elect from the ranks officers as capable as any then in commission. There were, however, serious disagreements among them, since some were for universal toleration and others 'for English freedom only' (whatever that may mean). In conclusion he would not have his readers 'believe *omne hoc micans aurum esse*. Any accommodation could be only temporary.' The next letter, which is missing, would presumably report the defeat at Burford. This bit of evidence, which has hitherto escaped attention, is confirmed by a news-sheet entitled *The Declaration of the Levellers concerning Prince Charles* (17 May, 1649). In a statement dated Gloucester, 14 May, we are told that the country-people were much impressed by their 'fair pretence for Charles II'.

3. *Overton's Defiance* (2 July, 1649) and *The Baiting of the Great Bull of Bashan* (16 July).

4. *Nicholas Papers*, I, p. 139.

5. *The Discoverer*, Part I (2 June, 1649), p. 48; Part II, on similar lines, but much less effective, appeared on 13 July.

6. In a letter to the Calixtine church of Bohemia.

7. See *A Modest Narrative of Intelligence* (7 April, 1649). The last of these Parliamentary declarations was passed by the restored Rump on 27 June, 1659.

8. *Moderate Intelligencer* (5-12 July, 1649).

9. From *A Bloody Fight in Hertfordshire* (17 July, 1649).

10. *Legal Fundamental Liberties* (8 June, 1649), p. 57, a passage omitted from H. and D.

11. This account of the mutiny is based on the newspapers of the fortnight 11-25 September, especially the two *Moderates*. Captain Wagstaff's story is in *A Modest Narrative of Intelligence* (8-15 September). For the court martial see also *Mercurius Elencticus* (17-24 September), and for the story of the general revolt *Mercurius Pragmaticus* (18-25 September).

12. For the episode of the lead-miners, see the newspapers of 11-25 September cited in the preceding note; *A Brief Relation* (16 October, 1649), and *Mercurius Elencticus* of 22 October; also *C.S.P. (Domestic), 1649-50*, pp. 335-8. For the background see *History and Gazeteer of the County of Derby*, by S. Glover and T. Noble, and *The Victoria County History of Derbyshire*, II, pp. 132, 183, 331, esp. chapters by Mrs J. H. Lander.

13. *The Moderate* (11 September).

14. This, the most commonplace version of the story, is from *The Moderate* (21-8 August). For more romantic variants, see *Great Britain's Painful Intelligencer* (17-24 August) and *A Modest Narrative of Intelligence* (18-25 August). In these three newsbooks one can watch a legend growing.

15. *Mercurius Elencticus* (17-24 September).

16. *The Moderate* (10-17 July, 25 July—1 August).

17. *C.S.P.D. (Domestic), 1649-50*, pp. 303, 312-15.

18. *Mercurius Elencticus* (17-24 September); *The Kingdom's Weekly Intelligencer* (18-25 September).

19. For the story of Stourbridge see *A Perfect Weekly Account* (3-10 October) and *Mercurius Pragmaticus* (2-9 October). The Levellers, who numbered 300, armed with muskets, swords, bills and pitch-forks, were led by Nicholas Denne, 'condemned and freed at Burford'. This is presumably a mistake; for the name of Cornet and Chaplain Denne was Henry. Other details, the name of the exciseman, etc., may be authentic. For the Nantwich affair see *The Man in the Moon* (26 September–10 October). I can find no confirmation for the wildly improbable story told in a news-sheet, *Prince Charles His Message to the Levellers in the West* (13 September), that three troops of Sir Hardress Waller's horse fell on a body of 1,500 Levellers, who had hoped to surprise Plymouth, killed 13, took many prisoners and dispersed the rest. Had there been any truth in this tale the Council of State would have published it with a loud trumpet blast.

20. *Great Britain's Painful Messenger* (16 August, 1649).

21. 21 September, 1649. Godwin and Gardiner make no mention of the *Remonstrance*.

22. *A Petition to Parliament* (17 July, 1648). The 'engagement' of July 1647 for the King was said to have been signed by 100,000 apprentices, watermen and members of London train-bands, an impossible figure equivalent to about one person for every household in London (Godwin, *History of the Commonwealth*, II, p. 365).

23. The statement was made by a number of junior officers who were supporting the petition at the House (*Mercurius Pragmaticus*, 12-19 September, 1648).

24. *A Perfect Weekly Account* (3 October).

25. Dated 27 September; Thomason's date is 3 October. See p. 509 above.

26. *A Preparative to a Hue and Cry after Sir Arthur Hasᶦerig* (18 August, 1649). Cf. also pp. 610-11 below.

27. Dated 30 September; Thomason's date is 10 October. In another brief tract, *A Salva Libertate* (14 September, 1649) Lilburne justified his refusal to recognise Prideaux.

28. *The Innocent Man's First Proffer* (20 October) and *The Innocent Man's Second Proffer* (22 October). At the time John ascribed these 'proffers' to the suggestions of his wife and brother. In retrospect he offered another explanation—that he was trying to confuse his adversaries; by alternate defiance and compromise he left them without a clue to his future behaviour when he came to the bar (*Lt. Col. John Lilburne Revived*, 27 March, 1653, p. 4). His last suggestion of all—that the trial might be postponed, so that he might have time to convince himself of the lawfulness of the Commonwealth government—carried tactics to indecent lengths. Actually his conduct followed a pattern familiar throughout his life story. He challenged Archbishop Laud to arbitration when he faced the Star Chamber in his youth. He vacillated between defiance and submission while awaiting his last trial in 1653. But always this labile, mercurial temperament rose to the height of his manhood when the hour of combat struck.

CHAPTER XXX

The Jury of Life and Death[1]

The Guildhall in the seventeenth century was a medieval building. Tradition echoed from its stones; tradition shaped its fretted rafters; tradition spoke in the symbols of its radiant windows. In the ranks of the chiselled figures on its reredos survived the City's memories from distant generations. How many of the kings of England had smiled at the grotesque idols, Gog and Magog, who broke the dignity of its Gothic grace? How often had judges made precedents and citizens appealed to Magna Carta within its walls? Into this great hall in the early hours of Thursday, 25 October, 1649, walked in due hierarchical order the forty dignitaries who composed the Extraordinary Commission of Oyer and Terminer formed to try Lieut.-Colonel John Lilburne.

First, in his magnificent attire, glittering with tradition, would come the Lord Mayor, and then, at the head of a majestic file of seven justices and barons of all the courts of common law, in their scarlet robes and hoods, Richard Keble, one of the Keepers of the Great Seal. Seven knights who held various legal offices would follow the judges, and then in their particoloured robes of purple and scarlet three serjeants-at-law. The Recorder of the City would come next and after him in their venerable splendour nine aldermen. One at least of them, Robert Tichborne, may have worn under his robes his colonel's uniform. The Common Serjeant and ten distinguished citizens would bring up the rear. Blazing with scarlet, ermine and gold, blending with sombre purple and black, the dais would sparkle like a bed of autumnal flowers. Here were the riches and learning of England, here were the traditions of six hundred years gathered to overawe the prisoner and his friends. A voice from the distant past arrested the attention of the multitude that thronged the hall, as the Cryer recited in Norman French the traditional formula *Oyez, Oyez.* Then across the civilian brilliance of the dais flashed a glitter of military steel as the Lieutenant of the Tower and a special guard of soldiers led their prisoner to the bar and handed him over to the sheriffs.

We can still see John Lilburne at the bar in Wenceslas Hollar's engraving—a slight and rather elegant figure, tense and alert. The spurs on his boots like his scarlet coat would remind his audience that he commanded the dragoons on Marston Moor. Gradually as it listened to him, it may have guessed what he was trying to do. He was going to strip from the august shoulders of that dazzling tribunal the robes of tradition they wore, till they shivered like exposed usurpers.

The cryer summoned him to hold up his hand. Instead of doing so, he addressed to Mr Justice Keble, as the president of the court, a plea not for mercy but for his right as a freeborn Englishman to be heard:

Mercy [he added] I crave from God alone . . . whom I hope to meet with joy when this fading and uncertain life shall have an end, to live with him in glory and blessedness for evermore.

Other courts which had tried him for treason had granted him this right, even the arbitrary House of Lords and the royalist Lord Chief Justice Heath who presided over a Special Commission of Oyer and Terminer at Oxford in 1642. Captain Lilburne (as he then was) was taken in open hostility against the King:

Yea, Sir, and I must now tell you, in such open hostility that we were but about seven hundred men at Brentford that withstood the King's whole army in the field about five hours together and fought it out to the very sword's point and to the butt end of the musket, and thereby hindered the King from his then possessing the Parliament's train of artillery and by consequence of the City of London.

This reminiscence sprang from something better than garrulity; it was a calculated appeal to the younger men in the Hall, some of whom may have served under him in their apprentice days, and to their employers who sat among his judges. Notwithstanding this flagrant act of hostility, Heath promised him 'the utmost privileges of the law of England, which is a law of mercy'.

> And accordingly he gave me liberty to plead to the errors of my indictment, before ever I pleaded Not Guilty, yea and also became willing to assign me what counsel I pleased to nominate, freely to come to prison to me and to consult and advise with me and help me in point of law. This last he did immediately upon my pleading to the indictment before any fact was proved—all which is consonant to the declared judgment of Sir Edward Coke, that great oracle of the laws of England, whose books are published by special orders and authority of Parliament for good law.

After quoting this precedent for his right to have counsel, the prisoner complained that as he came in, he found the gates shut and guarded by armed men, 'which is contrary both to law and justice', for no man should be tried 'in holes or corners' but in courts open and accessible to all. While John quoted a precedent for this also, from his own ample experience, the presiding judge must have sent an order to the sentries, for presently he interjected: 'Mr Lilburne, look behind you and see whether the door stands open or no.'

The next point Lilburne raised was substantial. He argued that trials by Special Commission of Oyer and Terminer of 'an individual person or persons for a pretended extraordinary crime' are contrary to the Petition of Right and to the act of 1641 which abolished all such extraordinary tribunals, among them the Star Chamber. The powers of all courts, he maintained, must be 'universal . . . to administer the law to all the people of England indefinitely, who are all born free alike, and not to two or three particular persons solely'. In support of this doctrine he was able to quote a speech by no less a person than Edward Hyde (afterwards Lord Clarendon) which he made to the Lords on behalf of the Commons in April 1641, 'when they were in the virginity of their glory and splendour'.

Rambling on he protested against his arrest by hundreds of armed mercenary soldiers, his interrogation by the Council of State, the delay of several months in bringing him to trial, the severity of his close imprisonment and the confiscation of his property in Durham. He maintained that he should have been tried, not in the City of London, but in Surrey since it was at his home in Southwark that his alleged offences were committed. He then complained that he could not read the illegible parchment of his summons, writ in an unusual, strange hand and in Latin, of which he understood only some ordinary words. (This, by the way, was an excess of modesty, for a few years later we find him reading the *Defensio Secunda*, though Milton's Latin style was not of the simplest.) Vowing that he had done nothing unbecoming 'a man that does believe the resurrection of the dead and life eternal, nay that does believe that I myself shall arise and go to the Lord of Glory', he wound up by desiring to see and hear the extraordinary commission of his judges, so that he might consider whether it were 'consonant to the Petition of Right and other the good old laws of England'.

At the close of this prefatory harangue, Judge Keble remarked drily: 'Mr Lilburne, you are fully heard.' In the briefest of replies Prideaux, the Attorney-General, failed to answer any of John Lilburne's objections and was content to assert that the Commission for his trial was 'unquestionably legal and used for these many hundred years together'. He stressed the fact that the prisoner would be tried by 'a jury of good and legal men of the neighbourhood, by men that . . . understood what is fact, what is law, and to do justice indifferently between both'— an obscure saying which cannot have meant what John took it to mean, that a jury is judge of law as well as of fact. Judge Keble also dismissed all John's objections, 'although,' as he put it, 'you have spoken fair words, and happily more than your friends expected from you'. Judge Philip Jermyn, second in seniority to Judge Keble, undertook that the judges would act as counsel for the prisoner. He too said that Commissions of Oyer and Terminer were usual for 'high offences and such as tend to the destruction of the nation'. He reminded Lilburne that he had been found guilty of treason by the grand jury, 'able men, men of religion, men of estate, men of conscience, men of quality. It is they not we that proceeds against you.' The grand jury was not yet the useless formality it afterwards became.[2]

Next, John Lilburne went back to the first act of conformity required of him. He had been asked to hold up his hand, but he did not know the significance of this gesture and feared that because of his ignorance of the practical part of the law in Latin and French, he might throw away his life upon some punctilio. Judge Keble replied that it meant only that he acknowledged himself to be the person called upon and charged. Judge Jermyn after declaring that 'the law of England is the law of God, . . . no written law but the law that hath been maintained by our ancestors by the tried rules of reason and the prime laws of nature . . . uncorrupted and unpolluted by human humours, wits or wills' added that by holding up his hand he would declare the innocence of his heart. The prisoner, who still abstained from holding up his hand, then declared that he was John Lilburne, son of Richard Lilburne of County Durham, a freeman of the City of London and sometime Lieut.-Colonel in the Parliament's army.

After some more sparring over 'punctilios' the real business of the trial was reached and the indictment, a document of interminable length, was read aloud.

Hold up thy hand, John Lilburne [so it began], thou standest here indicted of high treason . . . for that thou as a false traitor, not having the fear of God before thine eyes, but being stirred up and moved by the instigation of the devil, didst endeavour not only to disturb the peace and tranquility of this nation but also the government thereof to subvert.

It went on to accuse him of bringing the House of Commons 'into hatred and infamy' by writing and printing sundry 'scandalous, poisonous and traitorous books' in which he asserted that 'the government aforesaid is tyrannical, usurped and unlawful'. Finally, it charged him with endeavouring on divers days and in divers places 'maliciously, advisedly and traitorously . . . to stir up a dangerous mutinous and traitorous distemper, mutiny and rebellion in the Army'. He was, in short, accused of doing precisely what the two acts of 14 May and 17 July, 1649, declared to be high treason. Amid the verbiage and tautology of these antique legal formulae were inserted by way of proof quotations from all the recent Leveller pamphlets. Most of them from John's pen, racy, familiar and picturesque in their wording, they must have rung out under the Gothic rafters of the Guildhall like a voice from another century in another language.

The reading of the indictment ended, the clerk invited the prisoner to plead 'guilty' or 'not guilty'. Once again, John Lilburne demurred. He insisted that by the laws of England, and in particular according to the Petition of Right, he could not be compelled to answer questions against or concerning himself. (There is, however, nothing in the Petition of Right that bears on this subject.) Because of his ignorance of legal formalities, he begged to be allowed counsel, a copy of the indictment so that he might ground his plea upon it, and a reasonable period of time, say eight or nine days, in which to prepare his defence. All these requests Judge Keble refused but he gave his undertaking to take no advantage of the prisoner's ignorance of the law. 'Upon that engagement' John pleaded Not Guilty.

Then, following the traditional procedure, the clerk put the routine question of those days, 'By whom wilt thou be tried?' To this John replied: 'By the known law of England and a legal jury of my equals.' To this answer one of the clerks objected, 'You must say "By God and your country", that's the form of the law'. 'Why,' John asked, 'must I say so?' Modern research has traced this sacramental form of words back to the days when a prisoner had to choose whether he would be tried by ordeal (that is to say, by God) or (not and) by a jury of his neighbours.[3] Judge Jermyn's explanation was that God is everywhere present, 'yea in all courts of justice', while by country is meant a jury of the neighbourhood.

Here is the formula as John eventually paraphrased it:

I desire to be tried in the presence of that God . . . that beholds all the actions that are done upon the earth and sees and knows whether any of your hearts be possessed with a premeditated malice against me . . . and by my country, that is to say by a jury of my equals, according to the good old laws of the land.

This drew from Judge Keble the commendation: 'You have done like an Englishman so far as you have gone.'

There now began between the prisoner and his judges one of the most amazing dialogues ever recorded in a court of law. John Lilburne was bent on securing a copy of the indictment, the help of counsel and a week's delay. Again and again the judges refused his request; again and again, he repeated it with fresh arguments. The indictment was very long; no one could possibly carry it all in his memory. Moreover, he must have subpoenas for his witness since some of them were M.P.s or soldiers, who would not come unless they were obliged. Others lived eighty or a hundred miles away: how could he reach them in time? The Bench repeated, over and over again, the same reply. The facts of the treasons of which he stood accused must first be established: for that he needed no help. If any disputed question of law should arise, for that he should have counsel. That, John replied, would be too late; he wanted counsel before any evidence was taken, to advise him in making exceptions to the indictment itself. The real question at issue was one of law and it arose at once. Before the prosecution tried to prove that the words attributed to him were his, it must first show that they were in their nature treasonable. Again it is a question of law whether the pretended treasons said to have been committed in several counties can properly be included in a single indictment. He had heard all the proceedings when Strafford was tried for treason. Strafford, as John saw with his own eyes, had counsel continuously with him at the bar, and they had free access to him in the Tower.

Then John went back to the romantic story of his own experiences as a prisoner of war at Oxford and told it with fresh details. He had been in irons, a close prisoner to whom pen and ink were denied. Chief Justice Heath, Cavalier though he was, had his irons struck off, allowed him pen, ink and paper, and assigned him a lawyer to help him before any evidence was taken, with a whole week for consultation. The bench dismissed the Strafford precedent as inapplicable, since he was impeached by the Commons and tried by the Lords. But at Oxford, as John replied at once, the tribunal was the same, a Special Commission of Oyer and Terminer. He offered to call one distinguished witness after another to confirm his statements about that trial. Judge Nicholas swept the whole argument away with a blunt: 'We are not to walk by Oxford precedents.' John's comment was even blunter:

> Then you for whom I fought will be more cruel to me than the Cavaliers against whom I fought. . . . Oh Lord! Was there ever such a pack of unjust and unrighteous judges in the world?

By turns John would behave with scrupulous politeness and play to the gallery. He would drive home his pleadings with the reminder, repeated rather too often, that his life was in the balance: to which Judge Keble replied: 'Our souls' too 'are at stake, if we do you any wrong'. At one moment John sharply rebuked one of the judges, because he was talking to the Attorney-General, not openly but 'in a hugger-mugger' and in whispers.

Skilfully, by question and answer, John Lilburne managed to put his judges on the defensive, as he exposed the arbitrary and lawless procedure under which he had suffered. He was arrested and locked in the Tower in March, seven months ago. Yet the treasons of which he was now accused were dated the first of October, 'and divers other days and times as well before as after'. By what right, then, was he imprisoned without charge or trial through the previous six months? He could not prepare his defence, for he did not know with what crimes he would be charged. His wife had heard from Parliament men that he would be accused of corresponding with Prince Charles. To that charge he got his answer ready.

It seems that forged letters were circulating among members of Parliament, which John Lilburne was supposed to have addressed to the Prince in Jersey. In these he promised to act for the Prince as his agent 'and to embroil the nation again in blood'. Cornelius Holland, one of John's best friends among the Independent M.Ps., told his wife that he had seen these letters and that the handwriting was her husband's. The forger may have been Tom Verney, who acted in the Tower for Thomas Scott (then the head of the political police) as his spy and *agent provocateur*. If the letters had been genuine, they would have been produced at the Guildhall as the most damning evidence of treason. The prosecution was too intelligent to do this, but the letters were none the less used to discredit the Leveller leader at Westminster. The once friendly General Harrison supposed them to be genuine, and so did Desborough. The Saints were dirty fighters.[4]

But now (to resume our summary of John's defence) for the first time when he heard the indictment read out, a few minutes ago, he discovered that his pretended offence was the printing of books said to be treasonable. How could he improvise his defence and gather his witnesses at a moment's notice? But the prosecution had had ample time in which to devise their traps for him. As far back as four or five months ago, Prideaux the Attorney-General began to consult most of the judges who were now trying him, at meetings in Serjeants' Inn, about the charges on which he should be indicted. This Judge Jermyn admitted and even defended conduct which in our own day would be regarded as a scarcely conceivable scandal. John's comment was not extravagant:

> I bless God I have . . . always carried my life in my hand, ready to lay it down, for above this twelve years together, having lived in the favour and bosom of God.

Prideaux's reply was characteristic of the spirit of the criminal law in that century. Chief Justice Heath, for his own reasons, may have granted Captain Lilburne a special privilege at Oxford, but the settled practice in cases of treason, murder and other felonies was to refuse the prisoner either counsel or a copy of the indictment. If counsel were granted, trials in criminal cases would never come to an end. Then, with that complacency which reigns so often on the bench, Judge Keble sought to re-assure his angry and desperate prisoner: 'The law of England is,' he declared, 'the tenderest law in the world of a man's life. I say again that no such trials for life is to be found in the world as in England.'

At last, after yet another plea for a week's delay, Judge Keble declared that the court would allow him an afternoon's respite, but no more. That was a favour never yet granted to any prisoner in the like case, for by the law of England treason

must be tried without delay—he might, indeed, have put it
even more strongly, for the accepted rule was that the trial of
such cases must be finished in a single day.[5] 'But because all
the world shall know with what candour and justice the court
do proceed against you, you have till tomorrow morning,
which is the court's extraordinary favour, and the doors are
wide open that all the world may know it.'

John Lilburne made good use of the brief respite he had won
by his importunity. Among the friends he consulted was John
Maynard, better known to posterity as Sir John; for this
cautious Presbyterian lawyer, whom Colonel Pride had purged
from the Long Parliament, was knighted at the Restoration. To him Lilburne evidently owed some valuable hints on
'punctilios' and procedure.

When the court met again at seven o'clock in the dim
Guildhall a minute before sunrise on Friday, 26 October,
the prisoner at the bar begged for leave to speak but one word.
He had discovered yet another precedent for the granting of
counsel in a case of treason on the very threshold of the proceedings. When at the Hampshire assize in August 1648, Major
Rolfe of the New Model was accused of conspiring to poison
and pistol the late King, which was by definition the highest of
treasons, his judge, now Chief Baron Wilde, because of his
ignorance of the law, assigned to him as counsel Mr Maynard
of the Temple and Mr Nicholas now sitting as one of the judges
on the dais. At the hearing by the grand jury, thanks to
Maynard, the indictment was annulled on a point of law. Two
witnesses swore to the Major's two pretended treasons, one of
them to each; but, as Maynard argued successfully, the classical
statutes of Edward VI, which define treason, require two
sufficient witnesses to each fact of treason.

Relying on this precedent John once more humbly craved
for counsel to detect the many errors as to matter, time and
place in his own indictment which would render it illegal.
Judge Nicholas sat silent. Judge Keble talked impressively
about his conscience and his immortal soul, but as to granting
counsel he still refused to budge; indeed, he made it clear that
when he offered to grant counsel after the facts had been

proved, should any question of law arise, all he meant was that he and his fellow judges would act as counsel to the prisoner.

The jury was now sworn, after the prisoner had successfully challenged four names. Then for the second time, in all its amplitude, the immense indictment was read aloud. Ever since the end of February 1649, when he published the first part of *England's Liberties in Chains*, John Lilburne had been the uncompromising critic of the military dictatorship of the Independents and of the sham parliamentary institutions with which they sought to disguise it. But political criticism, by word of mouth or printed page, had never been held by English law to be treason. In order to silence the Levellers effectively the Rump had to pass the typically totalitarian Treason Act of 14 May. The more reckless of the leading Independents may have intended at first to treat it as retro-active but the agitation of the growing Leveller movement among citizens, soldiers, countrymen and women was so formidable that these crude tactics were abandoned. With one curious exception the pamphlets on which the prosecution relied were all published after the Treason Act came into force —*Legal Fundamental Liberties*, *The Impeachment of High Treason against Oliver Cromwell*, *The Levellers Vindicated*, *The Preparative to a Hue and Cry after Sir Arthur Haslerig*, and most important of all, *The Outcry of the Young Men and Apprentices*. That 'peace-offering to the nation', the final version of the Agreement of the People, was also cited as 'a false, scandalous and traitorous book', although, as John Lilburne pointed out, it was published on the first of May with the censor's *imprimatur*. Stranger still, the in-dictment took no notice of the latest and by far the most revolu-tionary of the Leveller tracts, *The Remonstrance*, which was a defiant summons to armed rebellion against the Commonwealth.

The audience may have been mildly interested when the clerk began to read out the verbose jargon of this long-winded document. But as he turned page after page, it fell to talking until the noise rose to such a pitch that the prisoner had to complain because he could no longer hear the indictment. Then, turning to the people, he addressed them: 'Pray hold your peace, gentlemen, I beseech you be quiet.' John's assump-tion that he could control the audience nettled Judge Keble, who rapped out: 'Quiet you yourself, we will quiet them for you.'

The first task of the prosecution was to fix on the prisoner responsibility for the books mentioned in the indictment. That done, it would have to show that their contents fell under the new definition of treason. Mr Prideaux's job looked easy. Never in his life had John practised concealment, least of all about himself. Unlike most of the pamphleteers of the day, he signed nearly everything he wrote. It could be proved that he and a friend went openly with the manuscript of the *Outcry* to a printer's workshop. He had given another of the tracts, *A Salva Libertate*, in his own handwriting to his gaoler, the Lieutenant of the Tower. In the hearing of two clerks in the service of the Attorney-General he had boldly avowed his authorship of yet another—'saving the errata'. Cross-references in the margin of this pamphlet confirmed his responsibility for several of the rest. One of them he gave in his innocence to a supposed friend to carry to Colonel Eyres in Warwick gaol, where of course it was seized. Over a cup of beer, he gave the most dangerous of all the tracts, the *Outcry*, to a soldier who turned out to be an *agent provocateur*. Handicapped by his own reckless frankness and his genius for publicity, he had now to defend himself without the help of counsel.

His first expedient was the obstinate, stone-walling passive resistance which won him fame when as a mere stripling he defied the Star Chamber. He would answer no questions that could incriminate himself. He would not help the prosecution by avowing his own handwriting nor would he admit his authorship even of books that bore his name on the title-page. Prideaux, of course, had his taunt ready on each occasion: 'My Lord, you may see the valiantness of this champion for the people's liberties that will not own his own hand.' Stung by these jibes, John Lilburne risked a retort, that would seem to his hearers less startling than it does to us:

I have answered once for all, I am upon Christ's terms. When Pilate asked Him whether He was the Son of God, and adjured Him to tell him whether He was or no, He replied: Thou sayest it. So say I: thou, Mr Prideaux, sayest it, they are my books, but prove it; and when that is done

U

I have a life to lay down to justify whatever can be proved mine.

He would deny nothing that was his, neither would he avow it.

When the opportunity came, he used his chances of cross-examination skilfully. He made it clear that nothing in the printer's evidence suggested his authorship of the *Outcry*. It was his friend Captain Jones who fixed the price for the work, handed over the manuscript and corrected the proof: John Lilburne was present as an onlooker only. Again, though the indictment charged him with going among the soldiers to seduce them from their allegiance, he showed from the soldiers' evidence that it was Private Lewis who went up to him and addressed him first, then spoke of his eagerness to buy a copy of the *Outcry* and finally, after John had given him one that he happened to have in his pocket, asked where he could get more.

Since the bench had refused the prisoner's pleas for counsel to scrutinise the validity of the indictment, he had to do his layman's best unaided. In this game of wits an amateur was pitted against a professional champion and the amateur's life was the stake for which they played. This was no fencing match but a duel in which one of the combatants wielded a bated foil and the other a naked blade. To us 'the punctilios and niceties' in which the lawyers of the seventeenth century exhibited their hired skill are so unfamiliar that we grasp with difficulty the state of mind of an audience like that of the Guildhall. It would watch a bout between two professional antagonists with malicious pleasure and the more absurd and recondite their arguments were, the better pleased it would be, since their quibbling served to mitigate the severity of the law by reducing it to a farce. But in this case one of the opponents was their fellow-citizen and neighbour and they would watch the movements of his rapier with the sympathy of seconds.

John's first thrust was well directed. He pointed out that the treasonable acts with which he was charged were performed (if they happened at all) in three several counties. He trusted the City of London jury absolutely, but was it in law the appropriate body to enquire into what went on in Surrey and Middlesex? About his own home, where one of these supposed treasons was enacted, there could be no question. It was in

Southwark and therefore in Surrey. What he did in the Tower
happened in a part of its grounds that ranked as a detached
portion of Middlesex. For this bit of antiquarian lore he quoted
the opinion of its Lieutenant himself, as well as the precedent
of a trial for treason in Tudor times. The rule that limited the
jurisdiction of a jury to its own county was still good law in his
day. It led to endless complications in which lawyers revelled
right down to the reign of George IV.[6]

The second of John's points of law vexed English political
history for a century and a half, until it was finally decided in
his sense. Must two witnesses be produced, as the famous
statues of Edward VI provided, before anyone could be
indicted for treason or convicted of it? Or was this provision
implicitly—though not as Prideaux argued, formally—repealed by an act of Philip and Mary? When Sir Walter
Raleigh stood at the bar he appealed to this rule and failed. In
Strafford's case, however, Parliament conceded the need for
two witnesses. During the debates on the Popish Plot it was
universally admitted, and accordingly Bedloe had to repeat
Oates's perjuries. Finally, in 1695 the Whig Parliament made it
a statutory requirement in every trial for treason. Broadly,
then, the tendency of the law was what John Lilburne believed
it to be, though it wavered during the Interregnum.[7]

The last of John's punctilios looks to us like a clever parody
of contemporary quibbling but his seconds in the Guildhall may
have thought it a palpable hit. When he avowed his authorship
of the *Hue and Cry* he excepted the errata and these, he had
insisted, 'were many'. It could not be assumed that the treasonable passages were free from printer's errors. Two at least of
John's contentions raised substantial issues of law. Had he
succeeded on these not much would have been left of the
indictment.

The second of the prosecutor's tasks looked even easier. To
prove that the contents of these pamphlets came under the new
definition of treason, it was only necessary to quote their
notorious indiscretions. 'Tyrants', 'usurpers', meaning 'those
at Westminster'—this was treason in the very words of the act.
With a confident air Mr Prideaux directed the clerk to read
out the marked passage on page so and so in the first of the

tracts. But as one select passage followed another it soon
became obvious that something was going wrong. After the
dreary legal verbiage of the indictment these audacious
paragraphs from John's writings, phrased in the homely
language of every day, must have burst on the ears of the
audience in that venerable hall with the force of an explosion.
Whether they ridiculed 'that pretended false Saint Oliver', or
dismissed the Parliament as the puppets of the Army elected by
Colonel Pride, whether they denounced militarism or spoke in
tolerant, open-minded terms of the exiled Prince Charles, each
man who listened may have felt that these were exactly his own
sentiments. Something in these City tradesmen, weary of the
economic misery the Revolution brought with it, exasperated
by free quarter and impoverished by the excise, would respond
as they listened to the *Outcry* of their desperate apprentices:

> Our masters possess nothing (to buy themselves or us bread
> to keep us alive) that they can call their own, therefore its
> no boot for to serve out our times and continue in our
> drudging and toiling trades, whilst these oppressions,
> cruelties and inhumanities are upon us and the rest of the
> people.

It must have been fun to hear these forbidden opinions read
out by the clerk of the court himself, robed as he was in ceremonial dignity. What did it sound like when this solemn
official read out John's comparison of some of the Independent
magnates and particularly Sir Arthur Haslerig to 'polecats
and weasels'? The reading of passages from these plainspoken
books 'pleased the people as well', a contemporary tells us, 'as
if one of Ben Jonson's plays had been acted before them.'[8]
Was their laughter audible? However that may be, the Attorney-General may have sensed their hostility, for his speech in
winding up the case for the prosecution was brief and his
eloquence somewhat deflated. He dwelt on the iniquity of
incitement to mutiny against a 'noble general whose fame rings
through the world', and ended by invoking 'the honour of the
Army'. But the prisoner had punctured this peroration in
advance by reminding the audience that Mr Prideaux once
stood in the Army's black books. It was only recently that this
careerist rallied to the victors.

The climax of the trial came with John Lilburne's speech in his own defence. With the instinctive sagacity of his emotional nature he knew from the start how to win the attention and sympathy of the jury whom he always addressed as his fellow-citizens and neighbours. After a brief reminder of the objections he had raised to the validity of the indictment he asked once more that counsel be assigned him, but this time it was to the jury 'who have as men the issues of my life and death in their hands' that he made his appeal. His strength, moreover, was far spent; he had been wrestling against this charge for more than five hours already. His body was not made of steel. Must he lose his life for lack of physical strength to make his defence? Judge Keble then pulled him up sharply because the court had heard all his arguments for counsel already and answered them. Never before, he added, had a man of the prisoner's condition had a court to try him of 'so many grave judges of the law'. When John replied that he would rather have faced a legal and ordinary assizes or sessions, the judge retorted that if he had had a less imposing court to deal with, he would have out-talked them.

Truly, Sir [answered the indomitable prisoner], I am not daunted at the multitude of my judges, neither at the glittering of your scarlet robes, nor the majesty of your presence and harsh, austere deportment towards me; I bless my God for it, who gives me courage and boldness.

After yet another reminder that he was weary from many hours' standing, John pleaded once more for a week's delay, or if that were too much 'till tomorrow morning'. Finally he begged for an hour in a private room in which to peruse his notes and refresh his spirits. When this also was refused he appealed, 'with a mighty voice', as the report puts it, to the righteous God of heaven and earth to judge betwixt him and the Bench. Immediately thereafter, a temporary scaffolding fell down and some of the people on it were hurt. Amid the noise and confusion John used the opportunity to arrange his papers and books. There followed this incident:

Sir [said the prisoner] if you will be so cruel as not to give me leave to withdraw to ease and refresh my body, I pray you, let me do it in the court. Officer, I entreat you to help me to a chamber pot; which whilst it was fetching Mr Lilburne followeth his papers and books close, and when the pot came, made water and gave it to the foreman.

After this brief respite, Judge Keble ordered the removal of the prisoner's chair and bade him plead 'for it grows very late'.

After drinking a glass of canary, John Lilburne started with a question that disclosed his daring strategy. When he had dealt with matters of fact, would he be allowed to address the jury, his countrymen upon whose integrity depended the lives and liberties of all the honest men of the nation, since the jury are the judges not only of fact but of law. When Judge Keble repudiated this heretical doctrine, John burst out with:

You that call yourselves judges of the law are no more but Norman intruders; and indeed and in truth, if the jury please, are no more but ciphers to pronounce their verdict.

He then tried to justify this 'blasphemy' (as Judge Jermyn called it) by quoting some doubtfully relevant passages from Coke's *Institutes*, to which he referred, by a slip of the tongue, as *Coke upon Plowden* instead of *Coke upon Littleton*. The Bench made the most of this mistake, the one lapse of a tired brain in all the long day's proceedings.

After this skirmish, John Lilburne analysed the evidence, soberly and ably. The printer did not allege his responsibility for the *Outcry*, nor did the soldiers suggest that he incited them to mutiny. Some of the supposed treasons were perpetrated in another county; for some only one witness was produced, for others not even one. Finally the dates of the pamphlets ascribed to him were not established: the jury had no proof that they were published after the Act of Treason. One of them—the Agreement of the People—antedated it by a fortnight. But as St Paul said: 'where there is no law, there can be no transgression'. He ended this calm dissection of the evidence with a solemn appeal to the jury as men 'who believe that they shall have a portion in the resurrection of the dead and stand before the tribunal of the Lord Almighty', to see right done between him and his adversaries.

John Lilburne concluded his defence on a more personal

note. He quoted the classical legal maxim: *actus non facit reum nisi mens sit rea*; which he took to mean that it is not the act but the intention which establishes guilt. But he had never meditated any mischief to his country, 'unless it be a mischief to oppose great men's wills'. Again and again he had offered to refer all his differences with the ruling party to arbitration. Tens of thousands had proved their trust in his patriotism by signing petitions on his behalf. Never in the field had he turned his back to the enemy. For the benefit of the jury, who had not heard it, he repeated the story of his stand at Brentford and his refusal of the Cavaliers' bribes during his imprisonment at Oxford. When Judge Keble stopped him, because the story of his life was not relevant to his defence, he appealed to the jury to take notice of the court's unjust dealings with him, when his life was at stake. He wound up with a defiant repetition of his battle-cry, that the jury are the sole judges of law as well as fact; 'you judges that sit there, being no more, if they please but ciphers to pronounce the sentence, or their clerks to say Amen'.

Thereupon, as the report has it:

> The people with a loud voice cried 'Amen, Amen' and gave an extraordinary great hum, which made the judges look something untowardly about them, and caused Major-General Skippon to send for three more fresh companies of foot soldiers.

Mr. Prideaux still had the right to the last word, but he may have been rattled by the behaviour of the audience, for he made a poor use of his opportunity and did himself no good by his patent distortion of some of the evidence. In one breathless and casual interruption, as the Attorney-General sat down, the prisoner at last blurted out what was the real issue in this trial. He argued from certain statutes passed in the reigns of both the Tudor queens, that Parliament in their day 'abhorred and detested the making of words or writing to be treason'. He said no more, for it would have been fatal in that court to question the Commonwealth's act. But the quicker wits among the jury may well have understood him.

There was no summing up in the modern sense of that term,

but Judge Keble and Judge Jermyn both had some last words to say. The former argued persuasively against the traditional rule that two witnesses are necessary for each fact of treason. He then dwelt on the enormity of the prisoner's crimes; 'never was the like treason hatched in England'. Judge Jermyn would have it that his guilty intention was demonstrated by his poisonous words. After the jury had asked in vain for a quart of sack to refresh themselves, the court adjourned for an hour till six o'clock.

While the jury are considering their verdict, we may busy ourselves with our own reflections. To the modern onlooker the behaviour of the judges in this historic trial presents a puzzling contrast. On the one hand, for all their imposing grandeur as an Extraordinary Commission of Oyer and Terminer, they showed curiously little concern for the dignity of the court, or for the orderly conduct of the proceedings. They allowed the prisoner to talk at large and at great length and tolerated a violence of language from him that no ordinary magistrate would endure, then or now. On the other hand, they stiffly refused him a copy of the indictment and the help of counsel. The explanation of their tolerance may well be sheer timidity. For several months before this trial began, they and the ruling group of Independents had been anticipating it with anxiety, since they were well aware of John Lilburne's popularity. Their military precautions betrayed their fears, and when the judges faced the packed audience in the Guildhall, they may have sensed its hostility. John was the people's idol and the court did not venture to treat him roughly. But their rulings concerning counsel and the like were a relatively impersonal matter. Here they followed the well-established practice of that generation, for there can be no doubt that, in spite of John Lilburne's precedents, it was usual to refuse the prisoner in cases of treason, murder or felony any such facilities for his defence. He had to improvise it as best he could, after one hearing of the indictment, and with no previous knowledge of the evidence that would be brought against him. Against this habitual iniquity John Lilburne and the Levellers took their stand, as they did against so much else in the barbarous legal system of their day. John's struggle for counsel was one of the memorable engagements in the long campaign for reform. The Whigs failed in 1691 when they made their first attempt to civilise criminal procedure. They won a notable victory with the act of 1695, but for its logical completion our fathers had to wait till 1702.[9]

John Lilburne's doctrine that the jury are judges of law as well as fact presents another interesting problem. Emotionally it must have been linked with the hatred of lawyers and distrust of the law characteristic of John himself, the Levellers and 'the middle sort of people' in the seventeenth century. This John made clear when he spoke of the judges as Norman intruders. That phrase made its appeal to the class antipathies of his hearers. Leveller mythology (which here reversed the facts of history) regarded juries as an Anglo-Saxon and therefore a popular institution. It is unlikely that John improvised this 'blasphemous' doctrine in the heat of his duel with Judge Keble. However that may be, it was still alive a generation later. In 1688 at the trial of the Seven Bishops the jury were allowed to decide the question whether these popular heroes had correctly interpreted the legal question of the King's dispensing power. That juries are not the judges of law was finally settled, if we may trust the legal historians, only in 1731.[10]

But one suspects that the Levellers meant more even than this by their revolutionary doctrine. They meant that juries had the right to reject any law of which the people strongly disapproved —in this case, the Commonwealth's totalitarian Treason Act. Juries, John Lilburne was maintaining, are the custodians of English popular liberties, of 'the good old laws' our forefathers won for us. Usurpers and mock Parliaments come and go, but juries speak for the immortal nation. They voice what Rousseau called the general will—*la volonté générale*. John trusted the jury to grasp—if only by instinct—the real issue of this trial: that words or writings cannot constitute treason, which must be revealed in overt acts. Here he was, against the infidelities of Cromwell, Bradshaw and the Independents, the champion of the sovereign principle of free speech which shaped our civil liberties, in a series of definitions of treason, from the classical act of Edward III down to that of 1848.

It was not first principles and rebellious doctrines alone that made the people in the Guildhall John Lilburne's partisans and moved them to shout 'Amen'. Many of them were his followers already and all of them were bitter over free quarter and the excise. But even the political illiterates would be stirred by the drama of his defiance. The slight little figure at the bar challenged not merely the scarlet robes on the dais but the ever-victorious Army behind them. Only a churl could be indifferent to the courage and endurance of this solitary fighter or refuse its sympathy to a man who had to stand from dawn to dusk ten hours upon his feet and think out his defence while he stood.

But how faithfully would the jury reflect the feelings of the people?

Before the hour was up, the jury were back in the hall. Between them the clerk and the cryer asked the questions prescribed by ritual. Were the jury agreed on their verdict? They were. Who should speak for them? Their foreman. Then, after a command to John Lilburne to hold up his hand.

Is he guilty of the treasons charged upon him or any of them? Not guilty of all of them, nor of any one of them.

Did he fly for the same? No.

Which No being pronounced with a loud voice [the report goes on] immediately the whole multitude of people in the hall, for joy of the prisoner's acquittal, gave such a loud and unanimous shout, as is believed was never heard in Guildhall, which lasted for about half an hour without intermission.

The jury were then discharged, and through the cheering multitudes Major-General Skippon escorted the prisoner back to the Tower. The very soldiers who guarded him shouted for joy as they rode through the streets, let off their pistols and in spite of their officers made their trumpeters sound *Victoria*. At the Fleet Bridge the people lit bonfires, and neither the judges nor their officers could prevail on them to put them out. As the evening wore on, the church bells rang out and bonfires sprang up all over the City, while the people in their thousands shouted and drank and feasted in the streets. The judges, one chronicler tells us, hurried home 'like so many gadarenes . . . mocked and derided by men, women and children'.[11]

John Lilburne's release was unaccountably delayed till the people began to grumble. According to the letter of the law, it seems, he was not entitled to immediate discharge.[12] Clarendon tells us that amid his victories in Ireland Cromwell was enraged and perplexed by the news of the acquittal and looked upon it as 'a greater defeat than the loss of a battle'. Some hotheads talked of trying John again, by court martial. In the end, on 8 November, Bradshaw signed the warrant for his discharge. His fellow-prisoners in the Tower, Walwyn, Overton and Prince, were also released, after they had signed the new Engagement—'to be faithful to the Commonwealth as the same is now established without a king or House of Lords' —which, as a cynical Leveller chronicler assures us, they promised to keep as faithfully as Bradshaw, Vane or Prideaux kept the Covenant.[13]

The Leveller party, needless to say, shared in the general rejoicing. Shortly after John's release, to quote his own words, 'abundance of the middle sort of people of London' appointed a day of thanksgiving. At their meeting

> six or seven persons spake and prayed and praised God publicly for my deliverance from death. . . . And from the place where it was performed, we marched in great troops and companies to a great feast to the King's Head Tavern in Fish Street, . . . so considerable that the stewards had to pay £12 or £14 for the fouling of his [the host's] linen.[14]

While they feasted and marched the Levellers did not forget 'the jury of life and death' to whom they owed their leader's deliverance. The twelve had taken a risk, for in those day juries might be punished for verdicts that displeased their rulers.[15] In their honour the party caused a medal to be struck. On one side it bore the names of the jurymen, on the other a portrait of the prisoner, with this defiant inscription:

> John Lilburne, saved by the power of the Lord and the integrity of his jury, who are judge of law as well as fact. Oct. 26, 1649.

We owe the news of John Lilburne's acquittal and release to

the underground cavalier press. The parliamentary newspapers had already been closed down. Not a mention of the
trial appeared in the official organs of the Commonwealth.

NOTES TO CHAPTER XXX

1. This chapter is based on the nearly *verbatim* report published a month
after the trial under the editorship of Clement Walker: *The Trial of Lt. Col.
John Lilburne By an Extraordinary or special commission of Oyer and Terminer at
the Guildhall of London the 24, 25, 26 of October 1649. Being as exactly penned and
taken in shorthand, as it was possible to be done in such a crowd and noise, . . . with
an appendix.* Published by Theodorus Verax. A note by John Lilburne,
Southwark, this 28 Nov., 1649, states that 'the penman hath done it with a
very indifferent [i.e. impartial] hand'. The appendix contains his two proffers. A second edition included the woodcut showing John Lilburne at the
bar. My own copy (151 pages), which I owe to Mrs Frida Laski, seems to
be an earlier edition. It lacks the title-page, the engraving and the appendix.

Also useful are three royalist newspapers: *Mercurius Elencticus* (22-9
October), *Mercurius Pragmaticus* (23-30 October) and *The Man in the Moon*
(24-31 October, 1649).

In describing the Guildhall I had before me a photostat of a drawing by
the architect who restored it in the last century. It shows no dais, but I
assume that one would be erected for a trial of this importance—as the
scaffold for spectators was.

2. The grand jury met on 24 October. Its proceedings are reported in
The Second Part of the Trial of Lt. Col. John Lilburne (22 April, 1650), pp. 31
sqq. Judge Keble's charge explained what treason meant in terms of the
Rump's two acts. According to this report, confirmed by *Mercurius Elencticus*
(29 October, 1649), John challenged Judge Jermyn's statement that the
grand jury found him guily of high treason. 'Let me see this jury', he cried.
When they were brought in, they explained their verdict. 'No, my Lord,
we have only found him guilty of writing some part of those books he is
charged with in the indictment, but not of high treason.'

3. Stephen, *History of Criminal Law*, I, pp. 298-301.

4. See *A Defensive Declaration of Lt. Col. John Lilburne* (22 June, 1653). The
Prince was in Jersey from 17 September, 1649 to 13 February. 1650.

5. Stephen, *op. cit.*, I, p. 403.

6. On venue, *ibid.*, I, p. 277; II, p. 371.

7. *Ibid.*, I, pp. 334-6, 362.

8. *Truth's Victory over Tyrants* (16 November, 1649).

9. Stephen, *op. cit.*, I, pp. 398-414.

10. *Ibid.*, pp. 316, 322.

11. *Truth's Victory over Tyrants.*

12. Stephen, *op. cit.*, I, p. 457.

13. *Truth's Victory over Tyrants.*

14. *The Upright Man's Vindication* (1 August, 1653).

15. Stephen, *op. cit.*, I, pp. 329, 375. The last jury to be punished in this
way acquitted William Penn in 1670.

CHAPTER XXXI

After Victory Eclipse

From John Lilburne's triumph at the Guildhall dates the decline of the Leveller party. A revolutionary movement cannot stand still. If it marks time, if it has no plans for future action, it will lose, one after the other, its hope, its cohesion, its courage. But what was this party to do? The Army would blow its trumpets to celebrate Freeborn John's acquittal, but it would not defy its generals by electing Agitators. That disposed of the Idea of calling a representative convention to adopt and promote the Agreement of the People. The spokesmen of the omnipotent Army would not attend it, and there were loyal regiments that could be trusted to disperse it. Tax resistance might be tried on a larger scale than before, but was the nation in a hurry to bring down 'those at Westminster'? They had a duty to perform before they relinquished the powers they had usurped, a task which no one else could carry out so well. By the end of the year 1649 it was obvious to everyone that only the New Model stood between the English people and yet another invasion by the Scots, bent on imposing their Covenant and the discipline of their kirk.

On grounds both of principle and expediency the Levellers opposed the re-conquest of Ireland. They could not oppose a war to fend off the Scots; on the contrary, since most of them were sectaries as well as radicals, they had even stronger grounds than the majority of their countrymen for resisting the Presbyterian yoke. In October the Army may still have looked to them like 'janissaries' who threatened the freedom of the English people; by the New Year the Ironsides had become its only sure defence. Throughout the summer of 1649, in a series of pamphlets, John Lilburne had looked forward cautiously to the restoration of a constitutional monarchy. But he had always insisted that the King must regain his throne by 'contract' and 'not by conquest'. He had predicted that if Prince Charles were to rely on the swords of foreigners he would 'glue' the whole people together to resist him. This was precisely what the 'King of Scots' was preparing to do. A Scottish army was still for our forefathers a foreign army.

As if the massing of David Leslie's forces were not provocation enough, this inexperienced young prince went on angling month after month for German or Danish mercenaries who were to land in Kent, while yet another body of invaders was to disembark in Torbay. When he failed to get money from the Pope, he tried to pawn the Scilly Isles to a syndicate of Dutch bankers. All that went on at the exile's court was promptly carried to Whitehall and figured among the sifted news in the Commonwealth's official journals. So alarming was the prospect of invasion that in the early days of the New Year (8 January, 1650) Parliament recalled Cromwell from Ireland, though he had recovered only a fraction of the territory he set out to conquer. It was not till May that he actually returned, but in the meantime Prince Charles completed at Breda the negotiations by which he bought the support of the Scots for the recovery of his English crown. Early in June, on his way to Scotland, as his ship lay at anchor off Heligoland, he signed the ominous treaty which subjected King and kingdom alike to the Solemn League and Covenant.

By its own characteristic methods the Rump prepared for the inevitable struggle. It tried to impose loyalty on the whole population by ordering everyone on pain of outlawry to take the Engagement of fidelity to the Commonwealth. It had then to learn with a shock that its own Captain-General, Lord Fairfax, was among the first who refused. It tried to make sure of London by expelling from it malignants, Papists and soldiers of fortune. It erected yet another High Court of Justice which sat without a jury. Finally to secure the favour of the God of Battles this Puritan Parliament passed a series of acts which enforced the stricter observance of the Sabbath, imposed fines for swearing and punished adultery by death. The news of Cromwell's astonishing victory in September at Dunbar did little to relieve the tension. The well-affected were kept informed of the perils that encompassed them around. The Cavaliers were ready to rise in the West; the Presbyterian merchants of the City would provide them with funds and when the hour of destiny struck from the crowded City, at the call of the Presbyterian clergy, a multitude of its young men and apprentices would surge westward to overwhelm the Parliament.

To such a prospect the Levellers could not be indifferent. Once the battle is joined in a civil war there is no room for a third party. The younger Levellers would do their duty in the train-bands; their seniors would applaud the successes of Cromwell, Lambert and Blake, while they kept the Sabbath and paid their taxes, but their party had no function to perform in a belligerent Commonwealth. Its voice, moreover, had been silenced when the *Moderate* was closed down. The Leveller party reached the height of its influence in the autumn of 1649, when it gathered those 98,064 signatures to its revolutionary *Remonstrance*, and again when it lit its bonfires after the Guildhall verdict. Thereafter it was neither defeated nor suppressed. It faded out because it had nothing to do. After Worcester a grateful people would not have tolerated a revival of the opposition to Cromwell on the old lines, while for the time being the Scots had made the young prince impossible. In 1652 the Dutch war had broken out. This was no time for dividing the nation.

After John Lilburne's narrow escape from death, his wife and brother used all their influence to induce him to abandon politics. He moved from Southwark to the City. His new neighbours thereupon nominated the hero of the Guildhall to represent them in the Common Council, and John accepted the honour. This was an odd way of avoiding politics, for throughout the Interregnum the City was a whirlpool of party strife second only to Westminster in importance. All its doings followed a single pattern. In the Common Council as in the Livery Companies the commonalty was struggling against the oligarchy at the top for the right to elect its officers. Lilburne had opened this campaign in 1646 and Wildman carried it on in 1650. After the second Civil War the radicals had the upper hand. They had to struggle not only for the election by the citizens of the Lord Mayor, sheriffs and burgesses, but also for the removal of the veto which the Lord Mayor and aldermen claimed over all the decisions and legislation of the Common Council. We know enough of these democrats to feel reasonably sure that most of them were Levellers. They had, for example, the audacity to sit covered in the presence of the Lord Mayor. Again, we find him rebuking them because they adopted a resolution to the effect that taxation should be proportionate to income, whereas, in fact, 'poor people of small estates were over-rated', while the rich got off cheaply.[1] No less characteristic was their concern for the sufferings of poor prisoners; thus we find them asking Parliament to check 'the oppression of gaolers' by appointing inspectors in every county to visit the prisons.[2] Many of them gave their support to Lieut.-Colonel Jubbes's scheme of land reform and his version of the Agreement of the People.

With Freeborn John to lead them, these Cockney radicals would have gone far. The Rump had, however, its device for excluding him. It passed an act which disabled from holding office in the City those who refused to sign the new Engagement. Duly elected on 21 December, he surprised everyone by taking this pledge, but promptly added the reservation that by the Commonwealth to which he promised fidelity, he meant 'all the good and legal people of England' and not 'the present Parliament, Council of State or Council of the Army'. This was too much for the Lord Mayor and the aldermen. They flung the Leveller leader's two chief supporters into prison and referred the scandal of his election to Parliament, which quashed it on the 26th. For the first time in his life John endured hard usage in silence. Early in 1650, since he had a family to support, he took up the useful but not very interesting trade of soap-boiling.

During the month that Cromwell spent in London after his recall from Ireland, he was reconciled to his old bed-fellow, John Lilburne. The Lord General (as he now became after the withdrawal of Fairfax) stood in need of all the moral support he could get for his preventive war against the Scots. Lilburne had in the meanwhile applied to Parliament for the payment of the compensation still due to him for his sufferings under the Star Chamber. On the last day of his stay in London, Cromwell spoke strongly in John's favour at a meeting of the Council of State. It was, then, as much personal gratitude as political good will that induced the leader of the Levellers to ride on 28 June in the General's train five and twenty miles along the Great North Road, to speed him on his way towards Dunbar. John Lilburne even dined with his old adversary in a tavern at Ware, where three years earlier he had waited—was it the same tavern?—to learn the outcome of the mutiny that failed. Next day, he followed up that public gesture with an extravagant letter of thanks for 'your Excellency's most obliging and noble favours manifested unto myself after so many high and unfortunate misunderstandings betwixt us'. Finally he pledged the Lord General his support:

> No man in England shall be more forward and ready to hazard his life with you and for you, in the face of ready-to-be-discharged cannons and muskets and all the dangers of the world.

This man could never do anything by halves. If he was not impeaching Saint Oliver for high treason, he was laying down his life for the Lord General at the cannon's mouth. Cromwell was always for him the substitute for a father, and in that emotional relationship the son may swing violently from attraction to repulsion. But to interpret these vagaries is not easy, and John's contemporaries may be excused if they adopted a cruder explanation. A fortnight later, on the initiative of Henry Marten, the Rump voted him a grant of £1,500 to be raised from dean and chapter lands. It was easy after this to accuse him of apostasy. His conduct must have robbed him of the confidence of thousands who had hitherto looked up to him as their leader. He had, none the less, good reasons at this crisis for lending his support to the Commonwealth. Confronted by an ambitious soldier who would defend his religious beliefs and a prince who had sworn to extirpate them, he chose the lesser evil.

Finding the manufacture of soap an unprofitable venture, Lilburne made up his mind to study law in earnest.[3] After his brilliant performance at the Guildhall a career at the bar seemed to beckon him. But when he applied for admission to the Temple, his adversary of yesterday, Prideaux, forbade his entrance. There was, however, still work he could do as an amateur counsel to petitioners who had cases before parliamentary committees. Two of these affairs which trenched on politics soon brought him into danger again.

In partnership with Major Wildman he undertook in 1650 to back the commoners of Epworth Manor in their claim for the restoration of 7,400 acres appropriated by the Company of Adventurers, though it had been their common land 'time out of mind'. In the long run the draining of the fens, which it financed and Vermuyden engineered, added vast agricultural riches to the eastern counties, but in the short run the peasants suffered much injustice. Incited (so it was said) by Lilburne and Wildman, the men of Epworth tore down a village built for the Adventurers' Dutch workmen on the fen-men's ancestral soil. If their Leveller champions succeeded in recovering this land for the commoners they were each to receive a thousand acres as their reward. One does not recognise in this deal the John Lilburne who used to charge only a few shillings when he pleaded a poor man's cause. He did, however, serve these clients with conspicuous ability; the petition he wrote for them is a most persuasive document.[4] In spite of it, the verdict of Parliament went against them. The feud of these turbulent peasants against the landed gentry was still raging in the next generation, when they burned down Epworth parsonage and the child John Wesley had to be snatched from the flames.

The second of these affairs was John Lilburne's undoing. He acted for his uncle George in a complicated dispute with his powerful neighbour, Sir Arthur Haslerig, the Governor of Newcastle. Harraton colliery near Durham belonged to a Catholic royalist, but Josiah Primate claimed that he had leased it from this man long before the Civil War. In 1647 George Lilburne and George Grey took over Primate's interests and began to pump out the water from the neglected mine, which would yield, they reckoned, an annual income of £5,000, an immense stake in those days. But in 1649, Haslerig, ignoring their rights, sequestered the colliery as the property of a delinquent, and disposed of it to a third party. The Committee at Haberdashers' Hall in the City to which the case was referred decided by a majority against Primate and Lilburne, but its chairman, Samuel Moyer, dissented.[5] John thereupon rushed into print with *A Just Reproof to Haberdashers' Hall* (30 July, 1651), in which he made a savage personal attack on his old adversary Haslerig.

After this reverse Primate appealed to Parliament in a petition which accused Haslerig of 'over-awing' the Committee. John was not the author of this petition, but he was one of those who signed it and he distributed copies of it among M.P.s On 15 January, 1652, the House voted this petition false and scandalous, condemned it to be burned by the hangman, fined Primate £7,000 and committed him to prison until this should be paid. With John Lilburne it dealt even more severely. On him it imposed a fine of £3,000 together with damages of £4,000, and condemned him to die as a felon, if he were found in England at the end of thirty days. On 30 January in execution of this 'judgment' the House passed 'an act . . . for the banishment of Lieut.-Colonel John Lilburne' which shortened the period of grace to twenty days. Henry Marten forced a division but was defeated. No specific charge, be it noted, was brought against John Lilburne, nor was he heard in his defence.

By this arbitrary procedure the Rump was defending the privileges of an influential member. But if John's accusations were false, Haslerig had his appropriate remedy in a case for slander. Evidently the Independent Grandees had made up their minds to get rid of a truculent critic for ever. Was it only these two affairs that changed the friendly feelings Cromwell professed at Ware, and once again shortly after the battle of Worcester?[6]

In the Low Countries, first in Amsterdam, and then in Bruges, John found the life of an exile hard. Because Haslerig had seized his land in County Durham, he had to borrow to get his bread. He sorely missed his wife's company and in London she too had her money troubles. He knew no Dutch and thought himself too old to learn it. Surrounded by royalist exiles, he found himself in a crazy world of espionage and intrigue. Some of the Cavaliers, among them Secretary Nicholas, believed that Cromwell had sent 'that rogue Lilburne' to spy upon them, and that his banishment was only a blind. Others recognised his honesty. With Hopton, Percy, Culpepper and that 'wise and shrewd blunt man' the Bishop of Londonderry he was soon on friendly terms. The Duke of Buckingham, who always prized originality in the human specimens round him, sought his advice, since he was eager to return to England. John on his side was overcome by the Villiers charm.

Among these middle-of-the-road Cavaliers, as his *Defensive Declaration* tells us, he 'always maintained his own principles', and he vows that there was never any 'contract or confederacy' between him and them to advance the Prince's interests. His principles, however, were now decidedly in favour of constitutional monarchy. After re-reading John Speed's *History* he came to the conclusion that

> of all the governments now extant in the whole world . . . our government in England . . . under the establishment of kings, . . . with all the imperfections in the constitution of it, was the best, rationalest and most securest.

The change to 'a nominal free state' was, he thought, 'as yet only for the worse'.[7] Since Charles had ceased to be dependent on the Scots and bound by the Covenant, John Lilburne's chief reason for opposing a restoration no longer held good. It is, therefore, likely that he discussed with his royalist acquaintances the prospects of a restoration with Leveller support on the footing of 'a new and rational contract and agreement of the people of England'. (See Appendix A at end of chapter.) These discussions came to nothing because of the opposition of Hyde and Nicholas.

In this unfamiliar environment John's mind had leisure to grow. He was meeting Cavaliers for the first time face to face. To his surprise, he found that some of them were rational and sympathetic human beings. He had time to read. Machiavelli stimulated his thinking as much through the *Discourses on*

Livy as through *The Prince*. The world of the ancients came alive for him in the pages of Plutarch. In a letter to Henry Marten he describes his excitement as he sat up all night reading the *Lives* for the first time. The story of the martyrdom of the Gracchi for their *Lex Agraria* made a particularly vivid impression on him.[8] Hitherto he had been so busy with political questions that he had all but ignored economics. Now with naïve enthusiasm he leaps into the midst of problems of credit and land tenure, as confident and assured as he was in his adolescence over questions of theology.

In a letter to the Levellers of Hertfordshire he tells them that he used his time abroad to think out a plan which will make his native country 'honoured, courted and respected by all the neighbouring princes and commonwealths round about her, even by Holland itself'.[9] He undertakes that if he is allowed to come home to expound this programme, 'the trade and traffic' of England will flourish again within one year or two 'more than before the late wars and more than Amsterdam and Holland in its greatest glory'. In a glittering perspective of promises he is confident that population will increase and that 'thousands and tens of thousands of watermen' will be added to 'the bulwarks of England', her sailors and fishermen. The burden of debt which 'at the present is like to break the poor husbandman' will be eased and three-quarters at least of the load of taxes and excise lifted. The middle sort of people stand to gain most of all. He hints in a few confused but glowing words at the central idea of the plan, the settlement on waste land and commons of veterans and landless labourers. The plan, he writes, will give

> to every soldier now in arms in England, etc., and settle upon him and his heirs for ever, without alienation, so many acres of land as shall be worth £10 or £15 stg a year; and upon every poor, decayed housekeeper (like the Law Agraria among the Romans) shall settle for ever so many acres of land as shall be worth after the first year's husbandry, to him and his heirs for ever, £5 or £6 stg. per year; and shall also provide for all the old and lame people in England that are past their work, and for all orphans and children that have no estate nor parents, that so in a very short time their shall not be a beggar in England, nor any idle person

that hath hand or eyes, by means of all which the whole nation shall really and truly in its militia be ten times stronger, formidabler and powerfuller than now it is.

In this preliminary prospectus he does not expressly mention the nationalised herring fleet whose profits were to finance the navy, nor the Bank of England and the chartered Company of Adventurers which were to reduce the general level of interest to 3 per cent, but they must have been in his thoughts. This daring plan of his was borrowed (without acknowledgment), from Dr Chamberlen's *The Poor Man's Advocate*.[10] It seems to have been John's reading of Plutarch in the watches of the night that awakened his interest in it. He saw himself as the Caius Gracchus who would win fame and it may be martyrdom through this modern *Lex Agraria*. At last, in this all too romantic form, his interest in the land question and the rural proletariat was aroused. What would have happened, one is tempted to speculate, if he had been allowed to campaign for the colonisation of the commons and wastes? Would the veterans of the New Model have followed him? Would he have won the labourers in the villages, as he had already won the craftsmen in the towns? Could his sober friends of the Common Council and the Whalebone Tavern have helped him to re-shape his soaring project in a more practical form? It is not often that a demagogue of genius shows this imaginative ability to think afresh. From the standpoint of the possessing classes men who dream such disturbing visitions should not only be banished; they should stay banished.

On 3 May, 1653, Elizabeth Lilburne rejoined her husband at Bruges, bringing with her the news that Cromwell had dissolved the Rump. In the happy glow of their reunion the pair took a hopeful view of their prospects. Since Cromwell had broken with the Parliament, he should be willing to repair its injustices. Elizabeth accordingly returned to London to seek a pass that would authorise John's return. It was refused. Like so many exiles in his day and ours he seems to have lost the ability to interpret what was happening at home. On second thoughts he abandoned the cheerful theory that Cromwell and his officers were tired of the Rump's tyrannies. He now supposed that what they wanted was a more servile tool. He foresaw that Cromwell, like Julius Caesar, would adopt 'a new name, but with a power in reality far above a king, as perpetual dictator'. In this mood he penned a deplorable letter to Cromwell in which he wrote:

> it hath been your constant design to pursue my life like a partridge upon the mountains for these six or seven years together. . . . You were the chief man who got me banished.

He had even persuaded himself that Cromwell was the cause of the death of three of his children.[11] The strain of these days of uncertainty after a year of exile was too much for his unstable emotional nature.

After some weeks of hesitation, John Lilburne made up his mind to end his banishment, even if it cost him his life. It had never been his way to shrink from risks. 'Perhaps, after all,' he may have reasoned, 'Cromwell will relent when I appeal to him; if not, the new Parliament may set me free. Failing that, all London will rally to my side, as it did during the Guildhall trial. Once more a jury of my fellow-citizens will acquit me. If not, "I bless God for it, it is no more dreadful to me at present to die than to go to sleep".'

The newspapers reported his arrival in London on 14 June. The petition was now published in which he threw himself on the Lord General's protection,

> resolved to live as quietly and submissively to the present government as any man, having no other . . . intentions . . . than to live godly and peaceably with my poor distressed family and to study to serve the commonwealth, if those trusted with the government thereof should at any time conceive me fit for their service; or otherwise to confine myself to the most private life.[12]

In plain English, he was asking for a job. This letter was out of character; he wrote it, as he afterwards explained, to please his wife. Cromwell, however, was not appeased. The City authorities were instructed to arrest him and on the 16th he was imprisoned in Newgate, awaiting trial for felony. His next move was to petition the nominated Saints' Parliament for his release. It would not reverse the government's decision, and after the grand jury had found a true bill, his trial began on 13 July at the Old Bailey before a bench on which sat Chief Baron Wilde, Judge Keble, his old adversary Prideaux and two others.

During the month that passed since John Lilburne landed at Dover the drama of his challenge to the Army mobilised all London for him or against him. The government sought to prejudice Parliament, the Army and public opinion, by publishing the reports of its spies about his intimacy with the Royalists in the Low Countries. He kept the presses busy printing a whole series of pamphlets, in which he re-told the story of his banishment, denied the charges of the spies and outlined the grounds of his defence against the arbitrary sentence of the Rump. His old lieutenants, Overton, Prince and Chidley, rallied to his support and so did his father, uncle and cousins. Walwyn, whom the government evidently thought too dangerous to be left at large, was thrown into the Tower.[13] Three reliable regiments were kept in constant readiness round St James's to crush any attempt at rescue. Prayers were offered on John's behalf in the chapels of Southwark, always a Leveller stronghold. In the streets of London papers were scattered at night on which were printed the lines:

> And what, shall then honest John Lilburne die?
> Threescore thousand will know the reason why.

It rained petitions in his favour. No less than three came from groups of women. There were others from the young men and apprentices and from the well-affected in the City, Buckinghamshire, Hertfordshire, Bedfordshire and Kent. The petitions of the soldiers were, of course, suppressed.

In many ways this trial resembled the first. Fighting for his life, the prisoner showed the same indomitable courage, the same presence of mind, the same sure touch in appealing to the emotions of his hearers. Once more he made a skilful use of 'punctilios' and technicalities, yet in spite of these trivialities the real issue emerged sharply: a citizen, convicted of no crime, had been sentenced to banishment or death, without due process of law. In the end it was the Rump Parliament that

stood at the bar, rather than John Lilburne. This time, however, the proceedings were long drawn out for, with protracted
interruptions, they dragged on from 13 July till 20 August.

As at the Guildhall, so at the Old Bailey, John's first aim
was to obtain a copy of the indictment and counsel. Until these
were granted, he refused to plead guilty or not guilty. This
time he succeeded and so, as Sir James Stephen commented,

> he performed the feat which no one else ever achieved, of
> extorting from the court a copy of his indictment, in order
> that he might put it before counsel and be instructed as to
> the objections he might take against it.[14]

This did not mean that he had a barrister to conduct his case
for him in court. That, like every prisoner accused of treason,
murder or felony, he still had to do himself. But he had professional advice, notably from his old helper, John Maynard,
in framing his objections. Some of these were technical. The
John Lilburne, gentleman, of the indictment was not formally
identified with the Lieut.-Colonel John Lilburne of the act.
There were discrepancies, as to time and place, in defining the
felony, between the judgment of the Commons and their act.
But the chief objection was one of substance. The act was based
on an invalid judgment, since Lilburne had never been indicted or charged with a specific crime or brought into court
or permitted to plead in his own defence before he was banished for life.

John's arguments, and his 'subtle wit', as the Venetian
diplomatic records tell us, 'drew immense crowds' to the Old
Bailey and 'plentiful sympathy'.[15] Backed by this popular
support Lilburne faced the bench with startling audacity. At
one point in the lengthy debate he threatened his judges that
he would 'cry out and appeal to the people' against them.
Amid these 'furious hurley burleys' the clerk of the court
proposed that he should be gagged, and some troops of horse
were sent for to keep order. In the end the court brought these
interminable preliminaries to a close by forcing him to plead.
This it did by threatening him with the barbaric medieval
penalty of pressing to death. At last, on 20 August, he pleaded
'not guilty' and the jury was impanelled.

The case of the prosecution was simple. All the jury had to do was to satisfy itself that the prisoner at the bar was the person mentioned in the act. Since he was visibly in England, he would then be convicted automatically of felony—and that meant death. In his defence John Lilburne presented the court with an awkward dilemma. Either the Rump which banished him was a lawful Parliament, or it was not. If it was a lawful Parliament, then Cromwell, who broke it up by force, was the real criminal. But if it was not a lawful Parliament, then the judgment it passed on him was null and void.

At the Guildhall John Lilburne had argued that the jury are judges of law as well as of fact. At the Old Bailey he disclosed the foundations on which this novel doctrine rests. Law, he argued, must conform to certain general principles which constitute 'common right, common equity and common reason'. If it violates these principles it cannot claim the obedience of the people. The mere fact that a Parliament had passed this iniquitous act of banishment did not suffice to make it good law. For this basic principle John could invoke the authority of Coke's *Institutes*: 'Where reason ceaseth, the law ceaseth', and again

> All customs and prescriptions (Acts of Parliament, laws and judgments) that be against reason are void and null in themselves.

If these premises were granted—and Coke was in those days an oracle whom all acknowledged—it was easy to show that this particular act violated all the dictates of reason. Parliament, when it condemned him unheard, broke a rule as old as civilisation. It was characteristic both of John and his times that he proved his point by quoting Genesis, Deuteronomy and the Acts of the Apostles. Second only to the Scriptures came Magna Carta and the Petition of Right, and from them he drew the conclusion that only in the courts of common law could a free Englishman be judged, and nowhere else. This was, he maintained, one of the 'old native fundamental rights and liberties' for which he and his comrades fought in the Civil Wars.[16] It was, of course, the jury that gave these courts their high place in the Leveller scheme of values. A jury, the

Levellers held, was capable of deciding by the light of nature when an act of Parliament violated the dictates of reason. Parliament in their view was, after all, only the servant of the sovereign people, entrusted for a limited time with limited powers. In the moving appeal to the jury that wound up his defence, John Lilburne reminded them that he had been charged with no crime. By defending his rights, they would be defending their own. 'If I die on Monday, may not the Parliament on Tuesday pass such a sentence against every one of you twelve, and upon your wives and children?'

The jury were absent for several hours. While they deliberated, 'many soldiers marched up and down the town . . . to prevent insurrections'.[17] There were rumours that six or seven hundred armed Levellers were waiting to rescue their leader, if he should be condemned. But the jury found him 'Not guilty of any crime worthy of death'. Once more, as in 1649, 'the shouts of joy and applause were universal'. Once more the soldiers blew their trumpets and beat their drums.

But this time the too popular hero was not released. On 27 August the Saints' Parliament instructed the Council of State to 'take some course for the further securing of Lieut. Colonel John Lilburne for the peace of the nation'. By night on the 28th he was removed from Newgate to the Tower. Its Lieutenant had orders from the Council to pay no attention to any writ of *habeas corpus* his prisoner might procure. The precaution was unnecessary. He failed to get his writ.

The jury, meanwhile, were summoned before the Council of State to explain their misconduct in acquitting an arch-rebel. Most of them were craftsmen or small tradesmen—one was a book-binder, another a tallow chandler, two or three were drapers and one a brewer. Most of them would say no more than that they gave their verdict in accordance with the dictates of conscience. Three of them declared that what they heard out of the law-books convinced them that they were judges of law as well as of fact. The Council inflicted no penalty upon them, but henceforward when it had political offenders to try relied on the High Court of Justice which sat without a jury.

As the weeks went by and John Lilburne though acquitted was not released, his friends began to bestir themselves. The

Levellers of Hertfordshire presented no less than three petitions on his behalf. They went up to Westminster a hundred strong, and many hundred hands signed their appeal. On the way they met men from Bedfordshire who went up to town on the same errand. All their appeals for their leader's release were slighted. 'No men in power before them', they commented, 'did ever pretend to such a degree of holiness and piety', yet 'we must submit to them like Turkish slaves'.[18]

Throughout the next winter John Lilburne lay in the Tower, a close prisoner. No printed page came from his cell to remind his countrymen of his existence. But Cromwell, now reigning as Lord Protector without a Parliament, was not yet satisfied that the arch-rebel had been silenced. On 16 March the decision was taken to banish him. On the 22nd the Governor of Jersey was informed that the Protector and Council thought fit 'for the public peace' to transfer him from the Tower to Mount Orgueil Castle in that island. 'Within the compass' of that gloomy fortress, built by the Normans on a rocky promontory, Freeborn John, as this *lettre de cachet* put it, must henceforth be 'confined'. This method of disposing of inconvenient persons by sending them to one of the remoter islands—*relegatio ad insulas*—was the invention of Imperial Rome. The Puritan Caesar found it equally convenient. It was revived in our own day by Mussolini.

Out of Jersey, two months later, came the last political utterance of the Leveller leader.[19] It is very brief—five pages of large type. The work of a tired and despondent man, there is no trace in this *Declaration* of his old turbulence and militancy. Though his title-page promises 'the freeborn people of England' that he has something to say 'concerning the government of the Commonwealth', what it amounts to is a confession of frustration and disillusionment. Lilburne now realises that 'a true and perfect freedom cannot in this world be attained to'. The best to hope for is a relative freedom. We may escape the curse pronounced upon Canaan by Noah, that he should be 'the servant of servants'. To check the decline from servitude to actual slavery is the duty of governments. But looking round the world he perceives that 'all mankind at this day is near that curse of being the servant of servants'. He may be thinking of

France after the Fronde and of Spain under Philip IV, but 'the servants of servants' whom he has chiefly in mind are doubtless the people of England, governed by Cromwell's disciplined officers and his complacent judges. Yet he does not name them. He attacks no one nor does he criticise the constitution of the Protectorate. But he has begun to reflect on the inevitable evils of revolution. When change in the state 'begins with violence', the many who are wronged will not rest 'until they find an opportunity of revenge'.

His purpose in writing this little tract was to appeal for his own release from a lawless imprisonment. He had applied for a write of *habeas corpus* addressed to Colonel Haynes, the Governor of Jersey, but he must have known that such writs did not run in the Channel Islands.[20] He kept his faith, none the less, in the rule of law: 'where just law ruleth there God may be said to rule'. He rejects the delusion that an arbitrary government is a strong government: 'those commonwealths are weakest where injuries may be daily offered to the people by those in government'.

Such is John Lilburne's plea for 'water of life to revive a free Englishman from the death of imprisonment'. One realises in reading this moving appeal for liberty that he will never fight again. He is facing the fact of defeat. It is not yet the harsh conditions of his captivity on Mont Orgueil that have broken his will, for he has spent only a few weeks in Jersey. He is brooding over the past and (it may be) questioning the wisdom of much that he and his comrades in arms have done. When next he sends a manuscript to the printer, two years later, it will be to announce 'the resurrection of John Lilburne' through his conversion to Quaker quietism.

NOTES TO CHAPTER XXXI

1. *A Declaration of the well-affected Common Council men of London* (13 April, 1649).
2. *Several Proceedings* (7 December, 1649).
3. *The Just Defence of John Lilburne*, H. and D., p. 461.
4. *The Case of the Tenants of the Manor of Epworth* (18 November, 1651)

See also M. James, *op. cit.*, pp. 127, 186, and M. Ashley, *John Wildman*, pp. 77-81.

5. *A Juryman's Judgment upon the case of Lt. Col. John Lilburne* (22 June, 1653), p. 4. Moyer, a wealthy financier and an alderman of the City, was a Baptist and a radical in politics.

6. *A Defensive Declaration of Lt. Col. John Lilburne* (22 June, 1653).

7. *The Upright Man's Vindication* (1 August, 1653), p. 12.

8. *Lt. Col. John Lilburne Revived* (27 March, 1653).

9. *The Upright Man's Vindication*, p. 21.

10. I found the clue to John Lilburne's borrowing in *The Humble Petition of Officers and Soldiers, citizens and Countrymen, poor and rich and all sorts, etc.* which was printed in a Leveller publication dated 14 February, 1652. The same tract contains *A Declaration of the Army concerning Lt. Col. John Lilburne.* The latter document reports the meeting of a council of officers and soldiers, at which 'after a large dispute, many declared their ardent affection to stand and fall with so great and faithful an assertor of England's liberties; others resolved to submit their wills to the will of the power that imposed the sentence'. The Army, in other words, was too much divided to take any action on John's behalf. The Levellers who called this soldiers' meeting were, presumably, the same people who drafted the Humble Petition. It is an exact summary of *The Poor Man's Advocate*, which was published on 25 April, 1649. It begins by asking Parliament 'to grant to your petitioners . . . and to all the poor of England . . . all or so much of the commons, forests, chases, etc., as is due unto the poor' together with mines not in use, drowned lands, etc. The petitioners will put in sufficient security for various purposes, including the setting up of 'a public bank'. 'This is the way', it concludes, 'to gain the love of the people.' This document, published just before John left London, must have been in his hands. One cannot be sure that he ever saw the pamphlet it summarised. See also p. 436 above.

11. *The Upright Man's Vindication*, p. 25.

12. *The Weekly Intelligencer* (21 June, 1653).

13. I found this surprising detail in Thurloe. [Not traced—Ed.]

14. Stephen, *op. cit.*, I, p. 367.

15. *C.S.P., Venetian*, 1653-4, p. 119.

16. The quotations are from a pamphlet which was almost certainly from Lilburne's pen: *Lt. Col. John Lilburne's Plea in Law* (2 July, 1653).

17. *Thurloe State Papers*, I, p. 429.

18. *A Letter from the North* (19 September, 1653).

19. *A Declaration to the freeborn people of England* (23 May, 1654). This tract seems to have escaped the notice of historians because John Lilburne's name does not appear on the title-page. It is, however, signed at the end. It is missing from Wolfe's list of his pamphlets.

20. Whitelock, *op. cit.*, IV, p. 109, under date 29 May, 1654, reported that John Lilburne's counsel had moved for a writ of *habeas corpus*. It was not granted, since he was a prisoner in Jersey, 'where the government is distinct from the laws of England'.

APPENDIX A

DID LILBURNE CONSPIRE WITH THE ROYALISTS?

Godwin (*History of the Commonwealth*, III, p. 551), Gardiner (*Commonwealth and Protectorate*, II, p. 293), Pease (*The Leveller Movement*, p. 334) and Miss Gibb (*John Lilburne*, p. 304) all discuss the charge brought by the Commonwealth's spies that Lilburne conspired with the Royalists while abroad; and also his vehement denials. Gardiner accuses him of telling 'a direct falsehood'; Godwin thinks he was not 'a man of very delicate veracity'; Miss Gibb accepts his word, while Pease conjectures, as I do, that some abortive discussions were held. The most reliable evidence may be that of Secretary Nicholas, an honest though prejudiced onlooker (*Nicholas Papers* I, pp. 291, 301, 321). He had heard that Lilburne, while in Amsterdam, subject to certain conditions, undertook to make Charles King, 'having, as he saith, above 40,000 men that will upon such conditions rise for the King'. 'I am told,' Nicholas adds, 'that Lord Percy and some others here are of opinion that Lilburne is more able to set the crown on the King's head than ever Scotland was, if his Majesty will follow his advice.' This is, however only hearsay, for Nicholas had not met Percy and the other moderate Royalists since their talks with 'the infamous John Lilburne'. The other evidence came from a tainted source, spies and turncoats (Isaac Birkenhead, Captain John Titus, Captain John Bartlett and Richard Foot). It was that if he were furnished with £10,000 Lilburne would undertake to destroy Cromwell, the Parliament and the Council of State within six months. The money was to be spent on printing in Amsterdam propaganda from his pen, which would be dispersed throughout England (*Several informations . . . taken concerning Lt. Col. John Lilburne['s] . . . apostasy to the party of Charles Stuart*, 13 July, 1653). John's denials in *A Defensive Declaration* (22 June, 1653) are absolute, unless we suppose that he is quibbling with words. 'Never such words [as the spies alleged] passed from my mouth nor such thoughts entered my heart.' Again in *The Prisoner's Most Mournful Cry* (1 July, 1653) he wrote, 'I had rather be boiled alive in hot lead than have the least finger in bringing Charles Stuart to England to embroil the nation in blood.' His denial that he contemplated military action may have been sincere, for he and many Levellers were already turning towards pacifism. But to suppose that Cromwell could be brought down by propaganda alone would be impossibly naïve. I do not find it easy to follow his thinking at this time, but I should be slow to suspect him of conscious falsehood. What he had in mind may have been the bloodless insurrection under the guise of an armed general election, which some of the Levellers planned for 16 October, 1653 (pp. 630-1 below).

APPENDIX B

THE SUBSEQUENT FATE OF THE LEVELLER LEADERS

From 1655 onwards, when Lilburne was in prison, Overton, Sexby and Wildman were conducting conspiratorial discussions with the Royalists. Whether they represented anybody but themselves is not clear. Descriptions of these negotiations, and further references, can be found in M. Ashley's *John Wildman* [or D. E. Underdown's *Royalist Conspiracy in England, 1649-60*—Ed.]. Sexby died in jail in 1658. Wildman made a fortune by land speculation, and with Overton was suspected of acting as a government spy in the sixteen-fifties. But after the Restoration Wildman still had before him thirty years of dogged political activity in the republican cause, underground and in exile; and the last we hear of Overton is when he was arrested in 1663 for printing an attack on Charles II's government. Henry Marten spent the last 20 years of his life in prison, dying in 1680. Walwyn and Winstanley, so far as we know retired into private life. Of Jubbes we know nothing. Most artistically satisfying was the end of Richard Rumbold, former Agitator. After taking part in the Rye House Plot in 1683, he sailed from the Netherlands with Argyll's invasion of Scotland in 1685. He was condemned to a traitor's death, and on the scaffold gave posthumous fame to a Leveller commonplace by his last words: 'I am sure there was no man born marked of God above another; for none comes into the world with a saddle on his back, neither any booted and spurred to ride him.'

CHAPTER XXXII

What became of the Party

During the years that lay between his two trials John Lilburne swung from one heady extreme to another in his relations with Cromwell and his attitude to Prince Charles. By turns he renounced all political activity and embarked on new adventures. In the end, as a hopeless prisoner, he faced the irrevocable fact of defeat and sought consolation in religion. How far was this career typical of what went on in the minds of those he used to lead? This man with his pioneering intelligence, his zest for danger, his reckless angers, could never be typical of the average citizen of the middle sort, whose hard life was spent at his loom or his printing press on six long days of the week, and at his chapel on the seventh. But the mass of mankind choose a leader because he reflects in more resolute deeds, in more eloquent gestures, their own reactions to the events of their time. With more courage than they could muster, he did what they should have done: with a quicker wit than theirs, he said what they were just about to say: with sharper eyes than theirs, he saw what was amiss in the life of debt and insecurity that plagued them; he dared to shout in blazing words the truth about their oppressors, which they could only mutter under their breath. But during the greater part of these four eventful years John Lilburne was silent, save when he was fighting for his life. Walwyn wrote nothing but a brief tract about juries, and Overton nothing at all that we can identify. Wildman was busy making money. The *Moderate* had been suppressed, and the lively, irresponsible royalist newspapers had vanished. The news that reached the Leveller rank and file was

w

what 'those at Westminster' thought fit that they should read.

It is unlikely that the party's elaborate democratic organisation, with its elected executive and its weekly membership fee,
continued to exist as it did between 1647 and 1649. There was
nothing for it to do while the war against the Scots was the
focus of public life, and it would atrophy as unused organs will.
But Levellers would still no doubt meet in the sectarian congregations, where free discussion was encouraged. Only the
more conservative preachers drew any line between politics
and religion. Then there were the taverns, for in Southwark,
Aylesbury and St Albans doubtless the radicals of the suburbs
and market towns had their haunts, where they felt at home and
free to talk as those of the City did at the Whalebone. Because
they had these social centres they could on occasion improvise
activities that called for a good deal of organisation. The
array of petitions on Lilburne's behalf in the summer of 1653
is impressive. Some enthusiasts, among them women, gave up
their scanty leisure to collect signatures. We hear again in
1653, as we did in 1649, of leaflets or broadsheets scattered at
night in the streets of London. For this purpose money would
have to be collected, for paper was costly in those days.

This activity was dangerous and the volunteers who engaged
in it, presumably youngsters, risked prison and a whipping.
Five of the young men who presented the apprentices' petition
for John's release to the Nominated Parliament were sent to
hard labour in the noisome gaol of Bridewell, because they
were 'something stiff' at the bar and refused to answer questions.
Their petition, it must be conceded, was highly provocative,
for they told the Saints that they had no right to call themselves
a Parliament. But most of those who signed these petitions
would be mature men and women. In 1649 the Levellers of the
City could collect ten thousand signatures for such a purpose
at short notice. In 1653 no comparable figures are recorded,
but the Levellers of Hertfordshire, always in the van of the
movement, speak of 'several hundred hands'. Evidently the
scale of what the movement can achieve is dwindling. Its
manifestoes appear with diminishing frequency and rarely does
one meet in them a new idea. After 1653 the mass of the
Levellers is merged in a republican opposition which blends the

most incongruous elements—Grandees like Sir Harry Vane and Sir Arthur Haslerig, a group of Anabaptist colonels, and the intellectuals whom Harrington inspired. Others, down the crooked lanes of conspiracy, seek an alliance with the Royalists.

It is possible to trace the thinking of the Leveller movement and what is even more important, its collective emotions, in the few public documents that came from its members during these years. In the summer of 1650 they organised a petition on behalf of the royalist conspirator, Eusebius Andrews, who had been condemned to the gallows by the High Court of Justice as a traitor.[1] Though he was charged with a share in 'plots and confederacies which we utterly detest', they argue that he is entitled to a trial by jury. In so doing they kept alive the generous, liberal tradition of which Lilburne was a pioneer when he tried to help Capel and Holland in their defence before the same unconstitutional court.

A little later in a grave and well-written address to Parliament, in which they describe themselves as 'approvers of the petition of 11 September, 1648', they set out their repugnance to the totalitarian devices of the Commonwealth, its treason acts, its press act and above all its High Court of Justice. For good measure they also attack their older aversions, tithes and the excise. What is distinctive in this petition is its humanitarian feeling. It enters its protest against cruel punishments, whipping, gagging, the pillory and above all the use of the gallows against minor offenders. One notes the growing alienation of the Levellers from the once popular Army; they now associate it with militarism and dictatorship. They speak of the grief of fathers and mothers that so many of their sons are joining the Army. In this revealing document we meet with an early complaint about the stifling atmosphere which the new police state was creating. So many 'officers' were employed—the word was used of civilians as well as soldiers—that 'men can hardly say anything or discourse together for fear of being ensnared in their words by some of them'.[2]

During the twelve months that lay between the battles of Dunbar and Worcester, and throughout 1652, the year of Lilburne's exile, the Levellers had nothing distinctive to say about politics. They were not in active opposition to the

Commonwealth. One has the impression that their thoughts were busied chiefly with the reform of the law and with such questions as the abolition of tithes. Here they might hope for a measure of success, since they could count on some support both from the officers of the omnipotent Army and from the left wing of the Independents who looked to Hugh Peters for inspiration. The elaborate petition of 'many thousands' sent up to the Commons in June 1652 illustrates the tactics of the Levellers at this time. It is silent on the political issues that separated them most sharply from the Cromwellians—the sovereignty of the people, the Agreement, the suffrage. But it includes in its thirteen clauses most of the social and legal reforms catalogued in the third Agreement and two which it omitted—the ending of base tenures and the recognition of the freedom of the press.[3] The party, in so far as it still had a corporate personality, was bent on achieving something tangible —something for the debtors, something for the gaolers' victims, something for the peasants ruined by arbitrary fines and tithes. It was in this year that Samuel Chidley, one of the party's treasurers, started his campaign against the hanging of poor men for petty theft.

In the following year, 1653, the Levellers faced a new political landscape. The Army dislodged the Rump and set up its own parliament of nominees. John Lilburne was back from the Low Countries, where his dealings with the Royalists raised once more the perplexing issue of a restoration on terms. It looked as if one had to choose between a military dictatorship disguised to look like a republic, and a monarchy which, in return for Leveller support, might be induced to accept a democratic constitution. So far as we know, only Wildman among those who once led the party was inclined towards the latter alternative. We have neither memoirs nor newspapers to guide us, and have to interpret the few relevant documents as best we can. A likely guess is that this difficult choice split the Levellers into two factions and destroyed, with its unity, whatever was still left of the party's organisation.

The first of the two documents we have to interpret bears the title:

The Fundamental Laws and Liberties of England claimed . . . by several peaceable persons of the City of London, Westminster, Southwark, Hamlets and places adjacent, commonly called Levellers. Presented to the serious consideration of all the free people of this Commonwealth, July the 9, 1653.

Written in the week when the Nominated Parliament met, it protests against the despotism of Cromwell and the Army. 'We cannot look upon ourselves as a conquered people to receive our laws and government at the hand of a conqueror.' It cannot be a crime to claim 'our fundamental liberties'. And so it asks 'the gentlemen convened in council'—it will not call them a Parliament—'to restore us to the full fruition thereof'. It then enumerates them in 28 articles. Its catalogue follows the third Agreement pretty closely, though there are some omissions and some additions. Of the latter the most important, as we have already noted, is the peremptory demand for the abolition of all servile tenures (p. 449 above). Another new clause declares that juries are judges of law as well as of fact. But the real purpose of this manifesto is disclosed at the end:

As for the claims of kings, lords or priests, though they challenge great antiquity in this nation, yet are they no other than the fundamentals of bondage and tyranny. . . . The people cannot be a free people, while the supreme power or authority is wrested out of their hands into the hands of one particular or some few. . . . The prime badge and principle of their freedom is their own election; while that is wanting, they are mere slaves at will and discretion.

The same thing is said more briefly in the second clause:

The supreme authority cannot be devolved upon any person or persons, but by election of the free people.

In concrete terms what these peaceable Levellers are saying is (1) that they will not accept the Lord General as the self-appointed head of the Commonwealth; (2) that the Saints' Parliament can claim no lawful authority; (3) that, for all its antiquity, monarchy is and always will be bondage and tyranny. In short, they will have nothing to do with John Lilburne's idea of a constitutional monarchy. Their principles, if one construes their words literally, could perhaps be reconciled with an elective monarchy, but if that had been in their minds, would they not have said so plainly? Naturally while their beloved leader is fighting for his life at the Old Bailey they will not repudiate him by name, but the practical conclusion from their premises, that they want no flirtation with the Royalists, would be grasped at once by contemporary readers. By describing themselves as 'peaceable' they may have meant to convey the warning that any attempt at restoration must involve the nation in bloodshed.

The second document is a call for action, a revolutionary manifesto. It was scattered by night in the streets of London, while the trial of John Lilburne was still going on. He must have approved and may have written it. In its style it recalls the equally belligerent manifesto of September 1649. Entitled *A Charge of High Treason exhibited against Oliver Cromwell Esq.*, it is addressed to 'the Lords the people of England' whose 'hired servant' he was. His crime was not that he dissolved the Rump, which was trying to make itself perpetual, but that he failed to restore the people's right to elect their supreme authority. They can never recover their liberty, it argues, while he is master of their strongholds, their army and their navy.[4]

The manifesto went on to propose what Pym originally suggested in the triennial act of February 1641 as a device for overcoming the propensity of King Charles for personal rule— a spontaneous general election in which the nation would dispense with the formality of writs. The same idea was embodied in the final version of the Agreement of the People. On 16 October, 1653, 'all the people of England . . . as well masters, sons, as servants' are invited 'as one man' to repair armed to their county towns, there to elect the number of persons who usually represent the counties and boroughs in Parliament. These shall be

> conducted to London with such forces of the several counties as then shall appear. . . . If you the Lords the people of England will be unanimous in this the recovering of your liberties, it will cost no blood. . . . Such of the Army as shall join shall be . . . continued in their trusts of arms.[5]

What was the point of insisting that all the people of England, as well servants as masters, should take part in this spontaneous election? This was not the definition of a popular franchise on which Levellers and Agitators had agreed; servants were excluded because (for lack of a secret ballot) they would have to vote as their masters bade them. That 'malignants' were not excluded may be equally significant. What the authors of this manifesto had in mind may have been that the royalist gentry in the country should bring up their armed retainers and tenants to the poll, while in the towns the Levellers did the same with their young men and apprentices. The militia in the counties and those of the regular Army who were still loyal to the Good Old Cause were encouraged to join by the promise that their commissions should be renewed. The scruples of the 'peaceable' Levellers were answered by the not very plausible prediction that this armed general election would be bloodless. If everything had gone according to plan the Parliament elected on 16 October, 1653 would have carried out the restoration that had to wait till 1660. But if the Levellers instead of the Presbyterians had brought it about, they believed they were strong enough to impose their terms. This proposal for a free general election may have been the scheme John Lilburne laid before the more 'rational' royalist exiles in the Low Countries, though it was then his intention to pave the way for its success by drenching England with propaganda.

Like the insurrection timed to break out in September 1649, the plan came to nothing. So far as we know, the Levellers made no attempt to carry it out, not even in such strongholds as Southwark. Cromwell had ample notice of their bloodless insurrection and he seems to have taken his precautions against it by tightening discipline in the Army. He cashiered the one radical officer whose fame and popularity might have made him a dangerous adversary, Lieut.-Colonel Joyce, the captor of King Charles.[6] With the Levellers in the navy, who were well organised under Vice-Admiral Lawson and three captains, he did not venture to interfere.

When one brave scheme after another ended in pitiable failure, where were the ardent young men and women of the Leveller movement to turn? Some who began by questioning the wisdom of their temperamental leader ended by rejecting the democratic principles in which he trusted. They did not need to go over to the enemy. There was, after 1653, yet another legion of idealists in whose ranks they could still wage war on both fronts, against Cromwellians and Royalists alike. Many of them found an outlet for their disappointed hopes in the millennarian movement. They kept what evidently was for them the dearest aim of the Leveller party, its cry for justice for the peasant and the artisan.

At this date and for long afterwards, the majority of pro-testant Christians, according to each man's capacity for belief, held the doctrine of Christ's Second Coming. Few, that is to say, allowed it to influence their conduct or their politics. It gave, however, an unearthly splendour to the contemporary scene and inspired some majestic pages of rhetoric. The Reformation they completed in religion, the freedom they embodied in the Commonwealth, the empire they won for England on the waves—in all this the victorious Puritans saw the breaking of the Day of God. The reign of the Saints was beginning. So much, in its more exalted moments, even a disciplined legal mind like Ireton's could feel.

But there was in the Puritan party a powerful group which believed with literal faith in the Second Coming, and based their political conduct and tactics upon it. They felt themselves able to apply to contemporary history, without faltering and in minute detail, the prophecies of the Book of Daniel and the blood-stained visions of the Apocalpyse. Through the past, four empires had moved in procession—those of the Assyrians, Persians, Greeks and Romans. The last of them, the Holy Roman Empire, was even now visibly staggering to its doom. When the House of Habsburg should fall, then would the Scripture be fulfilled and the Fifth Monarchy would begin. The Saints would prepare the earth, until Christ should descend in glory from the clouds to reign a thousand years.

Within the political movement and far beyond it, the intellectuals lost their way when they tried to interpret the times and seasons and to identify the Little Horn. In vain did some of the greatest mathematicians of that century devote their genius to the study of the prophetic books, from Napier of Murchiston, who invented logarithms to ease his reckonings with the number of the Beast which is 666, all the way to Sir Isaac Newton. They never reached agreement. Famous among the pioneers was Hanserd Knollys, a popular Baptist preacher. Like Hugh Peters he was a Cambridge man, and like him a settler in New England who returned to the old country to play his part in the struggle for liberty. In a sermon preached in 1641 he argued that the millennium would begin in 1650, though another forty-five years would pass 'before it comes to full head'.[7] Another Baptist preacher, perhaps the ablest and most scholarly of them all, John Rogers, fixed on 1666, the *annus mirabilis* of the next generation.[8] Over these calculations learned men once sweated, on their knees in prayer.

The simple man did not calculate. He felt. What he knew in his heart was this: that the Kingdom of God would overthrow the kingdoms of this world and bring the poor to power. His pulse beat faster to the rhythm of the *Magnificat*: 'He hath put down the mighty from their seats and hath exalted them of low degree.' The millennarian faith was through all the centuries a call to revolution. That is why it appealed to the slaves of the early Empire, the Poor Men of Lyons, the Czech peasants who sat round a common table on Mount Tabor, and the Anabaptist journeymen of Münster. Christ at his Second Coming would make all things new, but before this could happen, old things must pass away, broken in pieces like a potter's vessel. There is a passage in the book of the prophet Ezekiel (xxi. 26, 27) which the common man, as he trod the streets of London during the years of civil war, began to repeat with growing confidence that it applied to his own case:

> Thus saith the Lord God: Remove the diadem and take off the crown. . . . Exalt him that is low and abase him that is high. I will overturn, overturn, overturn it and it shall be no more, until he come whose right it is.

Amid the clash of arms, the unhappy and the oppressed heard with joy and assent the word of the God of Battles: 'overturn, overturn, overturn'.

The millennarian idea permeated all the Puritan churches, but it was the Independents and still more the Baptists who submitted most readily to its influence. Through their preachers it reached the New Model. Among the soldiers it was a popular opinion that Christ had already appeared—in the Army. 'God is now rising', wrote one of its most influential chaplains, William Erbury, 'as a man of war in the Saints, by whom He will destroy all oppressors and oppressions of men. Do not expect Him,' he went on, 'to come in the clouds; God comes when he appears in glory in us.'[9] This was a doctrine that made for activity and daring. These militant Saints did not wait patiently on God; they carved a throne for Christ with their swords. What this meant in political terms was first set out in February 1649 in a document which the Puritan churches in and around Norwich addressed to the General Council of War. In a series of searching questions, it discusses how the Fifth Monarchy, which it envisages as a dictatorship of the godly, can best be inaugurated. One of its queries makes its position sufficiently clear. 'How can the Kingdom be the Saints', when the ungodly are electors and elected to govern?' The question is answered by a programme of theocracy. The church 'shall put down all worldly rule' and exercise dominion on earth, through 'such officers of Christ and representatives of the churches as they shall choose and delegate, which they shall do till Christ come in person'.[10]

This prescription was carried out to the letter in April 1653, when Major-General Harrison, the leader of the Fifth Monarchists, helped the Speaker of the Rump Parliament out of the Chair. When Christ first came to earth, so Mr Knollys pointed out, 'God used the common people and the multitude to proclaim that the Lord Omnipotent reigneth. . . . Not many wise, not many noble, not many rich, but the poor' were the first to receive the Gospel. But 'though the multitude may begin a thing', this preacher (who was in private life a high-up civil servant) went on, 'it is not for them to bring it to perfection', for what they do is commonly mixed with confusion and disorder, like 'the voice of many waters' which John heard on Patmos. Thereafter

> God moves the heart of great ones, of noble, of learned ones, and they come into the work, and their voice is as the voice of mighty thundering, a voice that strikes terror and hath a majesty in it to prevail.[11]

The great ones did come into the work in the persons of
Cromwell and the Grandees of the Army. The Lord General, as
he himself admitted, was at this time in pretty close agreement
with the millennarian preachers.[12] Certainly it was the Fifth
Monarchy myth that dictated the procedure of the Army in
calling the Nominated Parliament. It represented the victorious
Saints, for the Army picked its members from persons chosen
by the Independent and Baptist congregations of England and
Wales. It went to work with a will during its brief five months
of life on a bold programme of social change. Amid cries of
rage and alarm from the propertied classes, led by the lawyers
and the clergy, it broke up before it could complete any of its
dangerous projects. Its collapse, followed by the proclamation
of the Protectorate, marked the transition to counter-revolution.

Henceforward the Fifth Monarchy men were in opposition.
They had no popular hero to rival John Lilburne, no writers
to compare with Walwyn and Overton, nor did they ever
display the talent of the Levellers for organisation and propaganda. But they had courageous adherents among the senior
officers of the Army and some eloquent spokesmen in the
pulpits of the 'gathered churches', while in Major-General
Harrison they had a leader whose moral courage and integrity
was as conspicuous as his gallantry in the field. In their political
outlook they were poles apart from the Levellers. They identified church and state, which their rivals in opposition were bent
on keeping separate. They rejected the sovereignty of the
people. They would have nothing to do with parliaments
elected by the carnal multitude or with Agreements signed
by ungodly hands. Only to the sanctified would they give
political rights. Yet in their criticisms of the class-ridden society
around them, and even in their social programme, they were
at one with the Levellers. John Rogers, though he aimed at
what he called a 'theocratic government' set out in 1653 a
social programme which hardly differed from that of the
Levellers.[13] 'The purpose of law', he maintained, 'is to curb
great men and the rich.' He even called for 'the abolition of
manorial lords'.

When in 1657 the Fifth Monarchists composed a collective
manifesto, which William Medley, the son-in-law of Thomas

Venner signed as their 'scribe' on behalf of their party, it echoed the Leveller tracts on page after page. In this pamphlet, *A Standard Set Up*, they insist that the Sanhedrin, their substitute for a Parliament, which would represent 'the Lord's freemen', must be elected annually. Though it is customary to describe them as fanatics, they were ready to tolerate all forms of worship. They struck their blow at the detested lawyers by providing that every man might plead his own cause before the judges of the county courts, who were henceforth to be elected. Like Parliament in the Agreement of the People, the Sanhedrin would be bound to observe certain foundations of common right and freedom, which it must not violate, surrender or enervate. All should be equal before the law. Pressing for military service would be illegal. Customs as well as excise were to go, and direct taxation (assessments) could be levied only by consent. Tithes were to disappear, and ministers would have to support themselves or rely on voluntary contributions. Finally, all copyholds and customary tenures, together with all heriots, fines and services were to be abolished. These millennarians forgot what they had learned from the Levellers only when they were expounding their tenet that the law must be modelled on the Mosaic code. The researches of the American scholar Perez Zagorin have now established the fact that though it can be traced back to the early years of the Interregnum, Fifth Monarchism became a mass movement only after the failure of the Levellers. 'In an age still religious', as he argues, 'it was an inevitable product of the failure of the left-democratic revolution to consummate itself.'

How did it end? The picture of Venner's rising that leaps from the memory in answer to that question can only mislead us, as it misled the contemporaries of that magnificent rebel. He and his men were no more typical of the Fifth Monarchists than of the Quakers and republicans who suffered with them in the panic-stricken reprisals that followed their outbreak. The followers of Thomas Venner, the wine-cooper from New England, were troopers cashiered from the New Model, and there was not an officer among them. The fifty men who twice swept through the streets of the City in the first year of the Restoration, a tornado of valour and faith so furious that only

overwhelming numbers could check them, left behind them a
record that tells us of what human nature is capable when it
does whole-heartedly believe. They were sure when they hurled
themselves on the kingdom of Charles II that King Jesus would
appear in person to lead their assaults.

The typical Fifth Monarchist had perished before they
sprang to arms. General Harrison made his first appearance in
history as the dashing cavalry officer whose rule in warfare
was audacity and attack. He it was among the Army's Grandees
who first proposed the execution of King Charles, and then, in
step with Ireton, followed this course implacably. Again it was
he who insisted on the dissolution of the Rump and the calling
of the Saints' Parliament; the Lord General followed where he
led. But when history swung to the right, and Cromwell made
himself the Lord Protector of property in the three kingdoms,
a change came over Harrison's millennarian tactics. Fearless as
ever, he would not bend, but neither would he resist. When
Oliver sent him, an untried prisoner, first to Portland and then
to Carisbrooke Castle, he submitted without a word. He would
join in no plans or plots to hasten the fall of Antichrist and
prepare the way for the Messiah's coming. He waited patiently
on God, confident that He would intervene when the hour
should strike. So serene was his fatalism that when the day of
the Restoration came, though he had ample time for action, he
disdained to hide as some regicides did, or to flee abroad. Sure
that whatever happened was God's will, he stood erect before
his judges, and awaited with a smile the hangman's noose.

While some of the Levellers were attracted by the millennarian
movement, others joined the Society of Friends. This was a
natural development. The Levellers' programme was, as we
saw, a translation into political terms of the Anabaptist gospel.
From this deep spring they drew their principle of tolerance,
their passion for equality, their dislike of the idea of punishment, their anti-clericalism and their insistence on a secular
state. In this creed the minds of John Lilburne and Richard
Overton were formed, and it is likely that many, perhaps most,
of the members of their party attended Baptist meetings. In
their turn the Quakers, if the reader will pardon the repetition,

carried the creed, the ethics and the congregational discipline of the Anabaptists to their final perfection, though they went even further in their quest of simplicity by abandoning the sacraments and discarding the last traces of a Calvinistic outlook. In the North, George Fox's mission dates from 1647, but it was only in 1654 that two of his young converts, Francis Howgill and Edward Burrough, began to preach his doctrines in London. The latter was a magnetic and emotional speaker, 'a son of thunder', capable of dominating and winning crowds and even mobs. The records that have come down to us show that in the early days they drew many, perhaps most of their converts from the Baptist meetings, which were thrown open to them for discussion, according to the salutary practice of that sect. In 1654, after Burrough and Howgill had addressed one of the Anabaptist meetings in Southwark, a part of its congregation seceded and formed a Friends' meeting. Something similar happened in East Anglia, where we are told that it was particularly the Arminian (or 'General') Baptists who suffered by desertions to the Friends.[14] When these Baptists were 'convinced' by a Quaker missionary, they would not abandon their Leveller principles.

Under the Protectorate, the Quaker message, which was not yet decidedly or consistently pacifist, spread to the Army. General Monk was disturbed by the large number of Quakers, both officers and men, in his forces. He described them in 1657 as 'a very dangerous people . . ., neither fit to command nor obey, but ready to make a distraction in the Army and a mutiny upon every slight occasion'. In a report addressed to him, Colonel Daniel said that they kept alive 'that factious temper of the Army about the time the Levellers appeared at the first, whose disciples they are'.[15] This was not an exaggeration, for some of those who were active among the Agitators reappear among the early Quakers, notably that attractive personality, Captain George Bishop, one of the young officers who had the courage to oppose Ireton.

Up to the Restoration there are in the writings of most of the early Friends legible traces of their social radicalism. These Dr Schenk has collected and interpreted with insight and sympathy.[16] As these pamphleteers watched the Puritan dictator-

ship at work, they shared the disillusionment of the Levellers
and their disgust at the greed and ambition of Cromwell and
his followers. The little that George Fox and his disciples have
to say about politics is casual and vague, but one gathers that
they approved the Leveller plans for decentralising the administration and the law, for ending servile tenures, for widening
the franchise and, of course, for abolishing tithes. One of them
said of John Lilburne that 'God owned him in opposing many
of the unjust powers of the nation'.

There was, however, one of these early Quaker writers who
had had some training in political thinking, which he manifestly owed to the Levellers. Edward Billing, who fought at
Dunbar, was 'convinced' by George Fox at Leith in 1657,
when he was a cornet in one of Monk's regiments of horse.[17]
Though he was not a pacifist, for he described himself as 'an
owner of the sword in its place', he left the Army and was in
1658 a brewer and a leading Friend at Westminster. He published in 1659 a tract entitled *A Mite of Affection, manifested in
31 Proposals*. Most of these were drawn straight out of the
Leveller programme. They include demands for annual parliaments, equal constituencies, the decentralisation of the law, a
land register, the recognition of certain unalterable fundamental
laws, the annual election of magistrates, direct taxation proportionate to estates, the reform of prisons, the poor law and the
law as to debtors and even the abolition of 'all servile tenures or
copyholds . . ., being the badge or yoke of the Conquest'.

He departed from the Levellers' position only in two respects.
He modified their demand for religious toleration in that he
proposed to forbid idolatry and images in public, and he
wished to prohibit gaming and other profane pastimes. The
interest of this political programme lies in the fact that he had
hoped to issue it with the endorsement of the Society of
Friends.[18] When he laid it before them some objected, either
because they disagreed with certain of his proposals, or more
probably because they thought it unwise that the Society should
sponsor them. Friends act only when their meeting can reach
agreement without voting. Evidently Edward Billing believed,
when he sat down to write, that all the leading Friends held
levelling opinions, which they would be ready to avow. His

assumption, mistaken though it was, confirms the guess that many of the Levellers found a spiritual refuge in the Society of Friends. This cautious decision to refrain from a rather elaborate political pronouncement may have been the first symptom of the change that came over the Society after the Restoration, when it turned its back abruptly, not only on political action but on political thinking also.

What was England's loss was America's gain. When in the next generation West New Jersey was colonised by Quakers it fell to Billing, who in the meantime had suffered savage persecution, to draft its constitution and its first code of laws. The constitution was signed by a hundred and fifty persons. Edward Billing's name is the first of them, William Penn's the fourth. Many similarities between this document and the proposals in Billing's pamphlet reveal his authorship. The massing of all these signatures suggests that this was in effect an Agreement of the People, which every citizen of the colony ought to sign. As in the Agreement its provisions were unalterable.[19] In this way the Quakers passed on the Leveller torch to the New World.

NOTES TO CHAPTER XXXII

1. *The Petition of divers Inhabitants of London* (21 August, 1650).

2. *The Petition of divers well-affected people inhabiting London* (31 August, 1650).

3. Whitelock, *op. cit.*, III, p. 433, under 29 June, 1652.

4. Thomason gives the date of its dispersal as Wednesday night, 14 August, 1653. Gardiner argues that the correct date was 14 September (*Commonwealth and Protectorate*, II, p. 303); Abbott dates it 11 October (III, p. 104). Abbott is mistaken in supposing that the Lords were being summoned as well as the Commons. Neither Gardiner nor Abbott notices that this document is a plan for restoration of the Stuarts.

5. Wolfe, p. 404.

6. The suggestion is Gardiner's (*op. cit.*, II, p. 306).

7. *A glimpse of Zion's glory* (Woodhouse, p. 233).

8. See *The Life and Opinions of a Fifth-Monarchy Man, John Rogers*, by E. Rogers (1867).

9. *The Lord of Hosts; or God guarding the Camp of the Saints* (24 December, 1648).

10. *Certain Queries presented by many Christian people* (19 February, 1649) (Woodhouse, p. 241).

11 Woodhouse, pp. 234-5.

12. In February 1655 the Lord Protector conducted an examination of John Rogers, who was at this time an untried prisoner in Lambeth Palace. Rogers with great courage attacked the Protector and the Army for breaking their promises, and demanded a legal trial. Cromwell's reply was: 'The time was there was no great difference betwixt you and me. I had you in my eye and did think of you for employment (and preferment); you know it well enough' (Abbott, III, pp. 607-12).

13. I owe these references to Fifth Monarchist writings to Mr Perez Zagorin's *History of Political Thought in the English Revolution*, esp. pp. 102-5. The quotations from Rogers are from his *Sagrir* (1653), pp. 52-9.

14. *The London Friends' Meetings*, showing the rise of the Society of Friends in London, by William Beck and T. Frederick Ball (1869), pp. 12, 137, 15.

15. *Thurloe State Papers*, VI, pp. 136, 167.

16. Schenk, *The Concern for Social Justice in the Puritan Revolution*, Chapter VII, *passim*.

17. I am indebted for these facts to the kindness of John L. Nickalls, Librarian of Friends' House. His *Children of Light* contains a chapter devoted to 'The Problem of Edward Byllinge'.

18. *Ibid.*, pp. 120-3.

19. *Ibid.*, p. 124. The persecution followed Billing's refusal in November 1662 to promise not to take up arms against Charles II. The constitution is dated November 1681. Billing, who was then 50 years of age, never himself went to New Jersey.

CHAPTER XXXIII

Rival Reformers

As social reformers the Levellers had to face the competition of Hugh Peters. By turns their ally and their rival, he ended by supplanting them, after the disaster at Burford, in the affections of the New Model. Among the Independents who followed Cromwell and Ireton, he was the only man who could compete in popularity (though far behind him) with John Lilburne. He was one of the favourite preachers of his day, famous for his gift of humour. Though he had never been what John was, a daring combatant and an enterprising officer, he belonged heart and soul to the Army, whose perils and hardships he shared for many years as a chaplain in the field. In many an anxious moment before a cavalry charge or the storming of a fortress, his eloquence had spurred the men to victory. He was always the champion and never the critic of this army—least of all did he oppose it, as the Levellers did, when it undertook the conquest of Ireland. During all the years of difficulty and crisis, from the rendezvous on Newmarket Heath to the 'crowning mercy' at Worcester, he rode at Cromwell's side, his admirer, his counsellor and his devoted man of business. So it came about that he reaped what the Levellers had sown. It was they by their ceaseless and audacious propaganda who made it inevitable that any revolutionary government must at least make a show of carrying out some social reforms. But when the time came to draft a programme of reform, it was Peters's version and not Lilburne's that Parliament adopted. But a draft it remained and a forgotten scrap of paper. Hugh Peters had no party behind him to insist on legislation, nor was he the man to embarrass the Lord Protector.

In many ways Hugh Peters was typical of the Puritan Revolution. Born at Fowey in 1598 in a well-to-do family of ship-owners, he may have inherited from them both his acquisitive instinct and his love of adventure. Educated at Cambridge, he was scholar enough to write an elegy on Ireton's death in Latin verse. He cared little for Greek or for literature, but had some interest in Bacon and physical science. Under the patronage of the Earl of Warwick he secured a living in Essex, became a popular 'lecturer' and busied himself, in close touch with the heads of the Massachusetts Bay Company, in raising money to buy livings for Puritans. At the age of 27 he married a wealthy widow of 50. After his bishop had revoked his preaching license, he fled to the Netherlands in 1627. There he spent seven years as an Independent pastor, chiefly at Rotterdam, where he enjoyed the favour both of the Merchant Adventurers and of the municipality. Here in 1630 he published his famous Calvinistic catechism, *Milk for Babes and Meat for Men*. In this he stressed the arbitrary authority of God, who is above all law and does 'whatsoever pleaseth Him'. His Providence 'reacheth to all things, even the smallest'. At the right hand of God, Christ makes intercession for us, but only for the elect. Sanctification is God's gift. 'We can no more convert ourselves than we can beget ourselves.'

He served for a time as chaplain to the English troops in the service of the Dutch, and visited the army of Gustavus Adolphus at Nuremberg. After pressure from King Charles's government had made the plight of the English refugees in Holland difficult, he migrated in 1635 to Massachusetts, where he became pastor of Salem, in succession to the exiled Roger Williams. He played a leading part in the trial, excommunication and exile of Mrs Anne Hutchinson for heresy. Neither at this time nor later did his conduct follow the lessons of tolerance which he claimed to have learned in Holland. It was as a shrewd man of business that he rendered the best service to New England. He promptly organised the fisheries and later promoted ship-building and started an iron foundry. Sent to London in 1641 as agent for Massachusetts he secured for it free trade in both directions with the mother country, appeased its creditors and raised money for the foundation of Harvard University. From the grateful colony he received 1,025 acres of land and acquired also three houses, three farms and a mill.

Back in England he served the cause of Parliament, first in the pulpit and then in the field. He joined the New Model on its formation, as chaplain to its siege train. Great though his influence was at headquarters, happily it did not always prevail. He urged Fairfax to delay his westward march into Somerset, so that the Army might demolish 'the monuments of heathenism at Stonehenge'. Of the two duties, its commander thought the raising of the siege of Taunton the more urgent. In March 1646 Fairfax chose him to give at the bar of the Commons a narrative of the brilliant campaign in the South West. For this the House voted a grant of land worth £250 *per annum*, to Peters and his heirs for ever. To him also fell the honour of preaching the thanksgiving sermon before both Houses of Parliament, the Westminster Assembly and the Lord Mayor and aldermen of the City.[1] In this he had the moral courage to make on behalf of the victorious Army his first suggestions of social reform. He pleaded for the maimed veterans, asked the lawyers to hasten the course of justice and get rid of 'that badge of conquest, . . . the laws in French', and went on to attack imprisonment for debt. He was in 1649 the chief advocate in the pulpit of the King's execution. So impressed was Cromwell by the practical ability of this ship-owner's son that he put him in charge of the transport between Milford Haven and Ireland with the rank of Colonel. In two pamphlets he carried on his advocacy of social reform. They reveal a restless mind which drew its inspiration by turns from the Pentateuch and from *New Atlantis*. He starts by basing his reformed legal code on the laws of Moses; after a few pages comes the recommendation that magistrates shall be instructed to further 'the new experimental philosophy'. His private life was darkened by the insanity of his second wife, but his relations with their daughter were happy. In his later years he was afflicted by prolonged attacks of suicidal melancholy. It is pleasant to remember that he repaid the hospitality of the Dutch, at grave risk to himself, by his efforts to avert war. He paid with his life in 1660 for his regicide sermons.

Like the Levellers, Hugh Peters was concerned for the welfare of his poorer fellow countrymen. But his pamphlets of October 1647 and June 1651 make it clear that he was no democrat.[2]

He stressed in both the need for a strict censorship and the licensing of the press. As was the practice in New England, he was for making membership of a reformed church a qualification which electors as well as magistrates must possess. He advocated a system of indirect election to Parliament (for which he cited the authority of Moses), since he doubted whether the majority of the electors were fit to choose a member. He would tolerate any church that professed 'the fundamental doctrines of the Reformation'—a phrase which excluded Prelatists as well as Unitarians. At first, as the Dutch did, he was prepared to welcome Jews; but at the critical moment of decision in 1655 he angered Cromwell by opposing Menasseh ben Israel's petition for their recognition as a tolerated community. He advocated a plan by which tithes, or something analogous, should be paid into a common stock, from which preachers should draw salaries at the rate of £150 to £200 in towns and £100 in the country. Of the ministers under this scheme he wrote bluntly: 'the state pays them and thus they have dependence upon the state'. He also stipulated that the covenants of all individual churches must conform to a pattern laid down at the centre by the state.

Clearly, in spite of his borrowings from the Levellers, he was not an advocate of decentralisation. He realised, however, that by capturing the state the Puritans had taken only the first step in establishing their Revolution. 'What you have gotten by the sword must be maintained by the word.' He called, therefore, again and again, for the despatch by the state and the universities of itinerant preachers to proclaim the message of the Revolution in the provinces, more especially in the backward West and North. It was this that he had chiefly in mind when he proposed that university colleges 'to train godly ministers' should be set up in Cornwall, Wales and Yorkshire.

His programme of social reform reveals a humane mind, which drew its inspiration first from the Dutch and then from the Levellers. He felt by instinct what was amiss, but he had no interest in general principles, while his detailed proposals were often vague and sometimes contradictory. He drew up a plan of a New Model for the navy, which dispensed with the press-gang save in times of impending disaster, such as the

Spanish Armada: sailors could always be attracted by regular and punctual pay. He condemned imprisonment for debt, but did not absolutely forbid it: he stipulated, however, that the creditor must pay for the keep of the imprisoned debtor. It horrified him that thieves should be hanged for 13*d*. and he argued that the gallows did not act as a deterrent. He would send thieves to the galleys. He wrote with indignation about the 'loathsome prisons', in which the innocent as well as the guilty so often lost their health. He called for 'the total absence of all forms of torture' and insisted that prisoners must be well-fed and kindly treated in sanitary gaols.

As we have seen, he was a critic of the common law, for which he would have substituted a code inspired by Moses. He called for laws in English and for a county register to record all wills, transfers of property, leases and mortgages. He aimed at speeding-up the course of justice and would have employed lawyers as little as possible and at fixed low fees. His model was Holland where 'you may get justice as often and as naturally as their cows give milk'. The expedient borrowed from the Dutch on which he chiefly relied was the appointment in every parish and ward of three lay arbitrators, whom he called 'friend-makers', to decide all small cases, criminal and civil, without appeal, while in graver cases he would allow an appeal to the county courts but no higher. Only the latter might try a man for his life. Like the Levellers, he wanted to dispense with the Westminster law courts and as far as possible with professional lawyers, but his 'peace-makers' (his later name) were not to be elected, as all jurors, magistrates and officers were in the Leveller schemes of reform.

Hugh Peters borrowed from the Levellers his proposals for a single direct tax and for free trade (save in certain imported luxuries). He went rather further than they did in proposing to exempt altogether from taxation artisans with incomes (varying according to the size of their families) from £20 to £40. He proposed luxury taxes on gold and silver lace, coaches and 'fancy' weddings, feasts and burials—a programme inspired rather by Puritan morality than by economics.

Peters stood for civil marriage and was deeply interested in all questions that concerned the inheritance of property, entail

and primogeniture (of which last, like Harrington, he disapproved). On such questions the Leveller leaders never
touched: the propertied classes were not their *clientèle*.[3] He had
much more to propose which he drew from his Dutch experience. 'Holland,' as he wrote, 'seems to get the start of us.' Each
town should have its municipal bank to lend at reasonable rates
to reliable persons 'upon their pawn'. He wrote also about
marine insurance and drafted plans for a great commercial
bank, a clearing house and bank of deposit, which would lend
to the state. The profits of all these institutions should be used
for the common good. On the model of the Dutch towns he
wished to rebuild London of stone or brick instead of timber,
to set up a fire brigade in every ward and to clean its 'most
beastly, dirty streets'. He was, in short, the practical reformer,
who felt little of the passion for ideas that inspired the Levellers.

The Independent leaders understood very well that they
could not ignore the demand for social reform to which the
Levellers in their petitions gave an articulate voice. That was
the explanation of the committee which the Long Parliament
set up- it may be at Ireton's suggestion- in the autumn of
1647 to review proposals for reform that had come before it.
Nothing came, however, of this concession to public opinion,
and it was not until Parliament had completed the political
revolution in the spring of 1649 that it had leisure to consider
social reform once more. Its output of legislation was modest.
Only one bill passed through all its stages—an act for the
relief of prisoners committed for debt. Introduced in the first
week of March, it was not till 4 September that it was finally
carried. During the endless and complicated debates one loses
track of all its adventures as it is tossed to and fro between the
whole House and the committee stage. When a rumour reached
the debtors imprisoned in the King's Bench gaol that the bill
had been dropped, they revolted (if we may believe a royalist
newspaper) and tried to break out. After a troop of horse and
a train-band company had been called out, a 'silly woman was
mortally wounded' by musket fire and others hurt 'to teach
them what it is to rebel against the keepers of their liberties'.[4]
The bill was not dropped, but it was so drastically amended

that in its final form it bore little resemblance to its first draft. Its promoters, of whom Henry Marten was the chief, had intended to make an end of imprisonment for debt for all time, save in cases of contumacy or fraud. At the last moment the spokesmen of property managed to add this fatal qualification, 'provided that this act . . . shall not extend to any person or persons than such as are now in prison'. All it did was to clear the gaols for the time being of the poorest of the imprisoned debtors (those not worth £5) and even then they were still liable to distraint for the old debt. From these mercies all who had fought against the Parliament were excluded. As the years went on the prisons were once more peopled with debtors, and when a somewhat similar act was passed by the Saints' Parliament on 5 October, 1653, three hundred 'poor starving souls' were freed thereby in and around London alone.[5]

While the Rump was still dawdling over the bill for the release of poor debtors, a petition was presented to it on 10 July, 1649, from the senior officers commanding the regiments on the point of sailing for Ireland. Couched in the most loyal terms, it laid before Parliament seven requests that amounted to a programme of reforms on which the field officers were agreed. After approval by the House it was printed by the Parliament's printer with beautiful type on the best of paper, a startling contrast to the shabby pamphlets of the Levellers. These Puritan soldiers began (1) by exhorting the Commons not to tolerate swearing, drunkenness, uncleanness and Sabbath-breaking. They went on (2) to call for cheap and speedy justice and for legal proceedings in English. No suit should be started until three honest men chosen annually in each hundred have heard the difference without charging fees. Only if these 'peace-makers' fail to settle the dispute should it be carried to the courts. (3) 'How sadly doth this nation groan under law quarrels!' From this premise the officers went on to recommend the keeping in every county of a register of all lands and houses as a means of lessening litigation. (4) For tithes they would substitute a tax of 2s. in the £ on land and 1s. 6d. on houses; from the revenue so raised in each county the stipends of preachers should be paid. This fund should also be available for the relief of the poor and many other uses.

(5) Public debts must be paid before gratuities are voted to particular friends. (6) All accounts of public funds should be audited. Finally (7) they asked for the speedy relief of prisoners for debt. This petition bore the signature of thirteen of the Army's 'Grandees', Colonels or Lieut.-Colonels. Among them one notes the names of Colonel Hewson, who was for trying the Leveller leaders by court martial, and Lieut.-Colonel Axtell, who used Dick Overton so roughly.[6]

Though several of these officers had risen from the ranks, among them Hewson and Axtell, one must suppose that the democratic doctrines of the Leveller party did not attract them, nor did its idealism appeal to them—besides, these troublesome fellows were always interfering with discipline. Evidently they were not interested in manhood suffrage or in the enfranchisement of base tenures and least of all in toleration for Catholics. But the more pedestrian of the Levellers' themes did mean something to them—the squandering of the taxpayers' money, the iniquity of imprisonment for debt, the scandal of tithes and above all the exploitation of the plain man by the lawyers. While they assembled at Milford Haven they would be likely to meet Colonel Hugh Peters, and he may well have had a hand in drafting this petition. The reader will have noticed how closely the suggestion in the second clause for the nomination of lay arbitrators corresponds to his plan for 'peace-makers' in its earlier form. It was, moreover, his substitute for tithes that the officers adopted. This endorsement of his programme of reform by these tough gladiators as they set out for the arena in Ireland may have made a lasting impression on the minds alike of Cromwell and of the legislators at Westminster. Caesar may have heard in its loyal dedication their *morituri te salutant*.

One cannot doubt that Cromwell at this time and for some years hereafter intended to carry a genuine programme of social reform, though he was well aware of the opposition to be expected from the clergy and the lawyers as the spokesmen of property. One may suppose that Hugh Peters would remind him from time to time of the expectations of the Saints. The evidence of General Ludlow on this subject, familiar though it is, deserves to be quoted. In a long heart to heart talk with

Ludlow in London in June 1650, just before he set out on the road to Dunbar, Cromwell said that he meant to make a thorough reformation of the clergy and the law, but

> 'the sons of Zeruiah are yet too strong for us'. . . . We cannot mention the reformation of the law but they presently cry out we design to destroy propriety: whereas the law as it is now constituted serves only to maintain the lawyers and to encourage the rich to oppress the poor.[7]

A few months later, on the day after his startling victory at Dunbar, here is the exhortation Cromwell addressed to the Speaker on 4 September, 1650, in the name of the Army:

> Relieve the oppressed, hear the groans of poor prisoners in England; be pleased to reform the abuses of all professions; and if there be any one that makes many poor to make a few rich, that suits not a Commonwealth.[8]

The mention of 'the groans of poor prisoners' might have served as a rebuke to the Commons for their wretched act for the relief of debtors. As was his custom in such utterances Cromwell was speaking for the officers around him. The army in Scotland shared with the army in Ireland its detestation of lawyers. It knew what use it meant to make of its victories. It is on record that after Dunbar Colonel Pride declared that he hoped to hang up the lawyers' red gowns with the colours taken from the Scots as spoils of war in Westminster Hall.

A few weeks later the Revolution scored its one indisputable victory over the lawyers. After a long and sharp debate in which, as Whitelock tells us, 'some spake in derogation and dishonour of the laws of England' the Rump carried *nem. con.* 'an act for putting all the books of law and the process and proceedings in courts of justice into the English tongue'. As the head of his unpopular profession, Whitelock himself delivered an elaborate lecture to the House, in which with impressive antiquarian scholarship he assailed the anti-Norman mythology of the Levellers, but even he did not venture to cast a negative vote.[9] On this subject lay opinion was unanimous. For ten years not a word of Norman French was heard in the land. As a symbol of the triumphant reaction it came back with

crown and mitre at the Restoration, and fell out of use only
gradually in the course of the eighteenth century.

With the long spell of peace that followed the triumph at
Worcester, the Army felt that the time had come to insist on
the fulfilment of its hopes of reform. After some prodding by
the Lord General the House on 20 December, 1651, appointed
an additional or 'subsidiary' committee of 21 (later 23)
persons, none of whom was an M.P., to report to it on 'the
inconveniences of the law'. The chairman was the most famous
lawyer of his day, Matthew Hale, and he was backed by other
notable members of his profession, among them Steele the
Recorder of London and Cooke of the regicide High Court.
Hale was no liberal: he had a shocking record for the persecution of witches. Among the soldiers, headed by Major-General
Desborough, were Colonel Tomlinson and Major Packer; of
the civilian laymen the most distinguished were Sir Anthony
Ashley Cooper, who was to be the first Lord Shaftesbury, and
Hugh Peters.

> None of them (wrote Bulstrode Whitelock) was more active
> in this business than Mr Hugh Peters the minister, who
> understood little of the law, but was very opiniative and
> would frequently mention some proceedings of law in
> Holland, wherein he was altogether mistaken.[10]

Whitelock, was, after Selden, the most learned lawyer of his
day and he did not suffer laymen gladly.

The appointment of the committee awakened keen interest
throughout the country and some notable petitions were sent
up to town to speed it on its way. One, which betrays Leveller
influence, came from divers counties; another from the northern
counties may reflect Peters's influence. It attacks 'the swarms of
lawyers, . . . nourished with the bread of oppression' and prays
for 'justice given not bought', by which it means the hearing
of suits free under a written code, so 'that justice everywhere
may come down like a mighty stream, free for the poorest to
resort unto, too strong for the richest to divert'. Both petitions
assail tithes.[11] The committee went to work with a will and
produced in several draft bills (the last of them January 1653)
a series of reforms impressive if only by their range and volume.

The result is an astonishing mixture, in which the amateurish suggestions of the humanitarian Hugh Peters are blended with the medieval barbarities of the legal tradition.[12] Much that was salutary did, none the less emerge, with the help one supposes of the soldiers, for Desborough, though he was slow-witted, had a mind of his own.

Of all these proposals the agrarian reforms were much the most important. They began, like those included in the Scottish Act of Union, by sweeping away oaths of fealty and homage, those relics of feudalism which the yeomanry were beginning to detest. They went on to limit to one year's rent the fines due from copyholders upon every descent or alienation. This did not abolish 'base tenures' altogether, but it did promise the mass of the peasants a measure of security and independence they never had enjoyed or were destined to enjoy. These projects of reform were due to Leveller pressure, for at no time in any of his writings did Hugh Peters show any interest in agrarian questions.[13] As a sop to the lords of the manor, these proposals were balanced by stiffer provisions for the speedy recovery of rent. In this chapter, together with suggestions about the law of entail, may be included the draft ordinance for setting up in every county a register for all transfers of land, wills and mortgages. This was a reform dear both to Levellers and to Hugh Peters's followers, which only the more conservative lawyers openly opposed. Ludlow put it on record that some of them obstructed it at the committee's sittings for three months, until the term 'encumbrances' was defined to their satisfaction.

Next in importance were the committee's proposals for the reform of legal procedure. What stands out from its elaborate but far from radical plan for the reconstruction of Chancery is the use it proposes to make of the land register and its reduction of barristers' fees to relatively modest figures—for advice 10s.: for a pleading £1. Members of Parliament (as the Levellers insisted) were forbidden to plead as barristers. Similar plans were offered for the speeding up and cheapening of procedure in the common law courts.

Hugh Peters got his way in a set of proposals for creating 'peace-makers'. Every year in every county the Justices of the

Peace were to appoint five commissioners who were to decide by summary arbitration every case of debt, trespass, damage, disputed contracts and the like up to £4 (equivalent in today's values to at least £40). They should have power to distrain goods, or to require the debtor to work for the creditor, and might send him, if recalcitrant, to the workhouse. No solicitor or attorney might plead before them.

The same policy of reducing the rôle of professional lawyers to a minimum re-appears in some curious provisions for creating a national court entitled to hear appeals in all cases both civil and criminal. From a panel of twenty persons, to be named by Parliament or the Council of State, none of whom might be judges, barristers or practising lawyers, seven should be chosen by lot to hear each appeal together with two professional judges. The appellant (unless too poor) was to deposit £10 which he would forfeit if he lost his appeal. A poor suitor who lost his case would be sent for a month to the workhouse and whipped. No appeal was allowed in capital cases.

Thanks to Hugh Peters a bill was drafted providing for the civil celebration of marriages before Justices of the Peace. John Lilburne's agitation was doubtless responsible for the proposal that a prisoner should always be entitled to call on counsel, for matters of fact as well as law, and also to summon witnesses to testify on oath. This was a reform which the Whigs failed to carry even in the heyday of their glorious Revolution. With two victories for humanity we end the happier pages of this programme of reform. It would have abolished the ghastly penalty of pressing to death (*la peine forte et dure*) inflicted on prisoners who were 'mute of malice', or in plain words refused to plead. Two prisoners were crushed to death for this reason at Oxford in 1650.[14] The committee was also for ending the burning alive of wives who murdered their husbands.

We now have to note that informers were to be rewarded who reported cases of drunkenness, swearing and Sabbath-breaking. Duelling was to be punished by the loss of the offender's right hand, as well as banishment and the forfeiture of all his property. Death was to be the penalty for adultery and bigamy. For assaulting or resisting a sheriff or constable, the culprit's right hand was to be cut off. For perjury the penalty was to be the cutting off of both ears, the slitting of both nostrils which were then to be seared with a hot iron, a stance in the pillory and six months in the workhouse. It was proposed that hanging should no longer be the punishment for theft nor should it be inflicted on the first offence as the punishment for horse stealing, picking pockets and cutting purses; instead, the criminal was to be branded on the left hand, to perform hard labour in chains in the workhouse for two years, to be whipped once a month, and to restore before his release three times the value of what he stole. Thereafter a visible collar of iron was to be riveted round his neck for the rest of his life; if he were found without, he should be hanged.

The most instructive sections in this programme are those which deal with debt. The passionate protests of the Levellers backed by Hugh Peters and many of the Army's Grandees were so far successful that debtors would seldom be sent to prison; but property saw to it that they should not gain too much by this concession. If the distrained goods of the debtor— only his necessary clothes were exempted from distraint—do not suffice to pay his debt, he should be sent to the workhouse, whence half the proceeds of his labour go to the creditor. If the debtor cannot work, he must go to prison, where his creditor shall pay sixpence a day for his keep. After a year the judges may pronounce him 'miserably poor' and release him. The workhouse was under the control of the gaoler and was obviously regarded as a wing of the prison. The debtor, if allowed to work outside the workhouse, must wear a bonnet of yellow cloth. Should he omit to do so, a collar of iron must be riveted round his neck. No trace is to be found in these recommendations of the pleas for prison reform that came from Hugh Peters as well as the Leveller pioneers, unless, indeed, one reckons as an alleviation of hard labour in chains the appointment to every prison of 'a godly and painful preacher'.

Of all these draft projects of reform only two found their way to the statute book while the Rump still sat. It made adultery a capital crime and it set up the county register for deeds, mortgages and wills. It paid Hugh Peters the compliment of appointing him one of a commission for the probate of wills. In this capacity he was lodged in the chambers at Whitehall once occupied by Archbishop Laud. Under the Protectorate a reform of Chancery on somewhat different lines was imposed on the protesting judges. Whitelock pronounced it unworkable and was dismissed, but Lenthall found it both workable and profitable. It was allowed to lapse after 1657. Oliver's Parliaments like their predecessors went on tinkering with imprisonment for debt. With what result? When the brief reign of Richard Cromwell came to an end, his Parliament found it necessary to pass a vote to exempt 'Tumble-down Dick' 'from all arrest for debts'.[15] *Finis coronat opus.*

NOTES TO CHAPTER XXXIII

1. *God's Doings and Man's Duty* (2 April, 1646).

2. *A word for the Army and two words to the Kingdom* (11 October, 1647); *Good Work for a Good Magistrate* (17 June, 1651).

3. I know of only one Leveller document, a petition of June 1652, which opposes primogeniture as a relic of the Norman Conquest (Whitelock, *op. cit.*, III, p. 433).

4. *Mercurius Elencticus* (6 August 1649). Whitelock confirms the story (*op. cit.*, III, p. 76).

5. *An exact relation of the proceedings . . . of the late Parliament, Somers Tracts*, VI, pp. 266-84.

6. A similar but less radical petition was presented to the Commons by Colonels Goffe and Pride on behalf of Fairfax and his Council of Officers on 13 August, 1649. It too attacked the lawyers (Whitelock, *op. cit.*, III, p. 87).

7. Ludlow, *Memoirs*, I, p. 246.

8. Abbott, II, p. 325.

9. Whitelock *op. cit.*, III, pp. 260-73 (22 November, 1650).

10. *Ibid.*, p. 388 (31 January, 1652).

11. *Ibid.*, pp. 374-5 (11 December, 1651), 395-6 (24 February, 1652).

12. Reprinted in *Somers Tracts*, VI, pp. 177-245.

13. There is, however, a very curious petition from Norwich which reflects many of Hugh Peters's ideas (Whitelock, *op. cit.*, II, pp. 553-4), addressed on 12 March, 1649, to Fairfax, 'Lord General of the forces raised for the defence of the Gospel of Jesus Christ and the enlargement of the liberty of the well-affected English'. It reproduces Peters's views about tithes, law courts and taxation, but it also asks 'that who will may purchase lands to be freehold in socage for a reasonable fine, and that the base oath of fealty and homage may make no more perjured souls in the kingdom'.

14. Whitelock, *op. cit.*, III, p. 140 (15 January, 1649). Pressing to death remained in force till 1772. Cases of its use occurred in 1658 and 1726.

15. Whitelock, *op. cit.*, IV, p. 353 (4 July, 1659). Twelve days later an order for £29,640 was passed to pay his debts and provide him with a comfortable maintenance (*ibid.*, p. 354).

CHAPTER XXXIV

The True Levellers[1]

On Sunday, 1 April, 1649, a band of a dozen landless men with their families camped on St George's Hill, near Walton-on-Thames, and proceeded to dig and manure the common. Their leader, William Everard, had served in the New Model Army, until his radicalism caused him to be cashiered: but this was to be for him and his comrades a peaceful, albeit revolutionary act. The 'True Levellers', as they called themselves, had lost their faith alike in the men of property who dominated the Long Parliament, and in the Grandees who commanded the Army. But with unflagging courage they meant with their spades to open yet another campaign for freedom. They would by direct action make good their natural right to use the earth and enjoy its fruits: they would undo the Norman Conquest and challenge the slavery of property, which had oppressed Englishmen through six centuries. They sang, as they dug in company, a naïve chorus:

> *You noble Diggers all, stand up now, stand up now,*
> *You noble Diggers all, stand up now,*
> *The waste land to maintain, seeing Cavaliers by name*
> *Your digging does disdain and persons all defame.*

The song, of which the tune may have been better than the verse, went on to defy by turns the gentry, the lawyers and the clergy. 'The club is all their law . . . but they no vision saw.' The Diggers meant 'to conquer them by love' for 'freedom is not won neither by sword nor gun'. A century had passed since the Saints had used those weapons at Münster in vain.

Once more, this time in England, the broken bodies of peasants manured the fields that others owned. The Diggers, with a faith that no disillusionment could quench, would attempt a new way to establish 'community'. They were the pioneers: presently, as they believed, five thousand of their proletarian comrades would join them in digging the waste lands. But their movement was also the culmination of the long guerrilla struggle against enclosure (see Chapter XXI). The True Levellers fought the last bloodless battle in this war, which differed from the obscure skirmishes that preceded it in this— that these rebels were inspired by a simple but clear-cut communist theory and had worked out a tactic by which they believed they could end the usurpations of property and establish a classless society. For the first time they made articulate the instinctive belief of every peasantry that God gave the earth to his children (to use the Diggers' phraseology) as their 'common treasury'.

The story of this spirited enterprise is soon told. The Diggers were men of courage, whose faith gave them a stubborn perseverance against impossible odds. First at St George's Hill, and afterwards at Cobham, they challenged the rights of two lords of the manor, not merely by squatting on the commons and cultivating them, but also by defiantly felling timber. They succeeded in causing considerable alarm to the Council of State, and troops of horse were twice sent to repress them. Twice their doings brought them into court. Fairfax, with his usual courtesy, listened to what they had to say, but the lords of the manor were less tolerant and twice their hired men, helped by the troopers, broke up the Diggers' settlement, destroyed the cottages they had built and turned the cattle into the growing corn. Their numbers grew, none the less, from twelve men to fifty: they managed to raise corn on eleven acres of waste land, not to mention other crops, and they kept up their defiance of the landlords, the Army and the law for rather more than a year. Their missionaries, meanwhile, were touring England in carts and preaching their gospel as they went. They had some success. Their example was followed at Cox Hall, in Kent, and at Wellingborough, Northamptonshire. There, as a broadsheet published for the Diggers in 1650 tells

x

us, there were, in one parish alone, 1,169 persons dependent on alms. They had petitioned the Justices in vain to be set to work, but nothing was done for them. The itinerant Diggers organised them and they set to work 'to dig up, manure and sow corn upon the common and waste ground called Bareshank, belonging to the inhabitants of Wellingborough'. They evidently met with a good deal of sympathy in the town and some farmers gave them seed, but they, too, were suppressed; which is not surprising since their broadsheet, which their leaders had the courage to sign, boldly proclaimed the right of all to the use and enjoyment of the land.

Fortunately for posterity, there was among the Diggers a man of rare talent and originality, Gerrard Winstanley, who has left behind him in his voluminous writings a record of the faith and beliefs with which he inspired this movement. Though Everard may have been its leader in the early days of its adventure, it is probable that Winstanley inspired it from the start and certain that he soon took over the leadership. During its hectic year of activity he poured forth pamphlets in which he addressed by turns the Army, the City of London and the Parliament. In these, in simple but vigorous English, in the language of the Bible and of daily life, he gave a straightforward narrative of what the Diggers had done and suffered and set forth the principles on which they acted. Of his life very little is known. He was born at Wigan in 1609 and doubtless had a grammar school education and no more. He then went up to London, where he was in business in some branch of the cloth or linen trade. Like many others, he was ruined in the Civil War and withdrew to the country, somewhere in the Thames Valley, where friends gave him a lodging: in return, he took charge of their cattle. Here he had leisure to think, and during 1648 he published no less than four pamphlets in which, without touching on politics, he set forth his daring theological opinions, which evolved rapidly through a pantheistic mysticism to a position that can only be described, if we may use modern terms, as agnostic and secularist. He bravely signed his name to them, though the least unorthodox of them exposed him to the grim penalties of the Long Parliament's Blasphemy Act. They went into several editions, but he escaped the fate that overtook some less audacious heretics even under Crom-well's relatively tolerant rule.

Suddenly, in this year, his interest turned to politics and he wrote the most characteristic of his books, *The New Law of Righteousness*, which is in reality a Communist Manifesto written in the dialect of its day. Throughout the next year, 1649-50, he was the life and pen of the Diggers' adventure. When that failed, after writing *Fire in the Bush*, a defence of his ideas addressed to the churches, he published in 1652 the most mature of his books, *The Law of Freedom in a Platform*. It was dedicated, in an eloquent and plain-spoken address, to Cromwell, whom it summoned to lay the foundations of a communist commonwealth. The sketch of a classless society that follows is a deeply interesting blend of the radical demo-cracy professed by the main body of the Levellers with the communism of More's *Utopia* and a secularism that was Winstanley's own. Like More, he advocated an economy with-out money, organised round public storehouses. To these each should carry the products of his work and from them each should satisfy his needs. Though the book lacks the literary and imaginative grace of More's work, it is in the history of socialist thought the more significant of the two, since it sprang from a proletarian movement and proposed a strate-gical plan by which communism could actually be realised. This was the last of Winstanley's writings, and all that we know of the rest of his life is that in 1660 he was living at Cobham and had evidently become more prosperous, since he was able to file a suit in Chancery to clear up his financial affairs. The traditional belief that he joined the Quakers is mistaken, though he had much in common with them. Of his death we have no record.

How did Winstanley come by his ideas? There is nothing to suggest that he read widely. He quotes no book except the Bible and never mentions *Utopia*, though he must have read it carefully. Once he exclaims 'England is a prison', which may be an echo of Hamlet. Once, and only once, he quotes a Latin line. He tells us that in his early years he listened attentively to sermons and was 'dipped' as a Baptist. There we have the first important clue. Communist thought in the sixteenth century had two chief sources, the persecuted left wing of the Bohemian Hussites and the Anabaptist movement, whose doctrines were preached underground in England by the persecuted Family of Love (see Chapter II). This tradition, of which the main stream was pacifist, filtered through most of the more radical sects of the Commonwealth period, kept alive by word of mouth. There is one outstanding passage in Winstanley which echoes almost *verbatim* a revolutionary sermon by Münzer, the German peasants' leader—though it is unlikely that Winstanley had ever heard of him.

The other decisive formative influence was the controversial literature of the Leveller movement, though Winstanley never refers to it. It is probable that he came in contact with the Levellers of the Chilterns and the Thames Valley, who published *Light Shining in Buckinghamshire* and *More Light Shining in Buckinghamshire*. Winstanley cannot have been the author, for the crude style of the pamphlets is not his; but he may well have had a share in drafting them (see pp. 444, 454 above).

Winstanley, then, was no lonely theorist, but if we could have asked him where he got his communism he would have mentioned neither the Anabaptist tradition nor the Leveller movement. It came to him by direct revelation from God. Three times, as he tells us, in trance and out of trance, he heard a Voice which uttered these three commands:

Work together; eat bread together; declare this all abroad.

Israel shall neither take hire, nor give hire.

Whosoever labours the earth for any person or persons, that are lifted up to rule over others, and doth not look upon themselves as equal to others in the creation: the hand of the Lord shall be upon that labourer: I the Lord have spoken it and I will do it.

In obedience to this Voice he went to work with the first pioneers on St George's Hill. For the benefit of others, who had not yet learned in silence and patience to listen to the Voice of the Spirit within, Winstanley would argue his case, if need be from Scripture, but preferably from history and experience. Fundamentally, his argument was ethical. He assumes throughout, as men have done from the earliest days of the cult of ancestors, that mankind is naturally, was originally, or was by God's ordinance and promise, a family of equals.

This was the commonplace of every peasant movement from the days of John Ball downwards. But Winstanley saw much more than this and he contrives to analyse the society round him with a shrewdness unusual in mystics. The only difficulty in understanding him comes from the simplicity of his language. He has no technical terms and it is only when we translate his Biblical idiom into modern phraseology that we realise how much he understood. More clearly than any of the instinctive communists who preceded him, he saw the source of all exploitation and of most of the misery round him in the private appropriation of the means of life, which, in the green England of his day, meant the land. When men take to 'buying and selling the earth', as he puts it, 'saying *This is mine* . . . [they] restrain other fellow-creatures from seeking nourishment from their mother earth. . . . So that he that had no land was to work for those, for small wages, that called the land theirs; and thereby some are lifted up into the chair of tyranny and others trod under the foot-stool of misery, as if the earth were made for a few; not for all men.' Again and again he declares that labour is the source of all wealth and that no man ever grew rich save by appropriating the fruits of others' work. 'No man can be rich, but he must be rich either by his own labours, or by the labours of other men helping him. If a man have no help from his neighbour, he shall never gather an estate of hundreds and thousands a year. If other men help him to work, then are those riches his neighbours' as well as his; for they be the fruits of other men's labours as well as his own.'

Winstanley perceived that this institution of 'particular propriety' was inevitably the source of all oppressions and all wars. 'All the strivings,' he writes, 'that is in mankind is for the earth', and again of those who own land he says 'that they or their fathers got it by the sword'. Property can be maintained only by the sword, or by the law which originally sanctioned the feudal claims of 'the Norman bastard's' officers. He saw, too, and said plainly, that economic inequality degrades those who must submit to it and infects them with a consciousness of their predestined inferiority. The enslaved worker, as he puts it, 'looks upon himself as imperfect, and so is dejected in his spirit'.

Winstanley's revolutionary strategy was prescribed by 'the Voice of the Spirit within him'—or, as we should say, by his sub-conscious self, clarifying, it may be, the confused discussions he had held with the Levellers of the Chilterns. In one passage he says, as Rousseau did, that no man should retain more land than he can till with his own hands. But his ideal was not peasant ownership. He aimed at 'community', which meant for him both team work and eating at a common table. He saw two ways of reaching this. Landless men were to join together to dig the waste lands. But even more emphatically he insisted on making an end of all hired service. In plain words, he summoned the workers to withdraw their labour from employment on the land. This was, as he saw it, more than a general strike: the strikers would find permanent work in cultivating the commons for themselves. This may sound to our ears more simple-minded than it was. Did he really forget that the Council of State had Fairfax and his dragoons behind it? But he believed, as well he might, that revolution was on the march, and he knew that many a troop of these same dragoons was on the verge of mutiny. But to grasp Winstanley's approach to communism we must try to understand his whole *Weltanschauung*.

The difficulty in grasping Winstanley's view of the universe and human society is that his thought was in flux and underwent a rapid development. His voluminous writing was all done, much of it rapidly, in four years: he had little sense for form or order in his compositions and often seems to be thinking aloud. His was an intuitive mind rather than a trained intellect, and his ideas reach us most clearly in single phrases or sentences which often have a poetical colour. In his early religious pamphlets he had not yet reached his own distinctive position, which may have come to him in his talks with William Everard. In the first of these he argues for 'universalism', at that date a most dangerous heresy: he will not believe that any soul can be eternally damned: there will be a final delivery, by God's mercy, even of the wicked from hell. In his later writings he abandoned any belief in hell. It was in the daring pamphlet *Truth Lifting Up Its head Above Scandals* (1648) that he first outlined his theological opinions by way of defending Everard, who had been thrown into gaol at Kingston for blasphemy. In this, as in all his subsequent works, Winstanley throws over the idea of a personal God, reduces to very narrow limits the significance of an historical Christ, and offers us in their stead the pantheistic conception of an ordered cosmos. These, needless to say, were not his words—he rarely used an abstract term—but they render his meaning fairly in modern phraseology.

Let us try, first of all, to reach his positive beliefs. He first startles us by telling us that he proposes 'to use the word Reason instead of the word God' in his writings. He objects that when men tell him that 'God is the chief Maker and Governor, and that the chief Maker and Governor is God', he is 'lost in this wheel that turns round'. This seems to mean that he cannot distinguish God from the universe. For him Reason is 'that living power of light that is in all things'. The Spirit Reason 'lies in the bottom of love, of justice, of wisdom'; 'it doth govern and preserve all things . . . for Reason guides them in order and leads them to their end, which is not to preserve a part, but the whole creation'. Again, he tells us that Reason 'hath a regard to the whole creation and knits every creature into a oneness'.

This, it may be, is poetry rather than metaphysics. So, too, are many of his happier sayings. Thus he tells us that 'the whole creation is the clothing of God'. But what he is trying to say is quite clear. In flashes of insight, before Newton wrote his *Principia*, he had grasped the idea of the order and unity of the universe. God for him was this order and 'the incomprehensible spirit Reason', of which he might have said what Wordsworth said of Duty: 'Thou dost preserve the stars from wrong.'

How much did he mean by this identification of God with the cosmos? The test must be sought in the negative side of his thinking. There he did not flinch. 'What other knowledge have you of God,' he asks, 'but what you have within the circle of the creation?' In one passage he even speaks of 'The law of nature (or God)', as Spinoza used to write '*Deus sive Natura*'. To these must be added the many passages that amount to a denial of a personal God. 'Neither are you to look for God in a place of glory beyond the sun, but within yourself and in every man . . . He that looks for a God outside himself and worships a God at a distance worships he knows not what.'

This did not prevent him from using the word God fairly often, for he did not stick to his resolution to use only the word Reason. Even more often he uses the name Christ, and declares more than once that Christ is 'the true and faithful Leveller'. Elsewhere he speaks of 'Christ, or the spreading power of light'. He gives this name, with no thought of its historical connotations, to the spirit of love, order and reason that dwells in the heart of all men—and even, as he expressly insists, of the beasts. Again and again he repeats that men cannot be 'saved by believing that a man lived and died long ago at Jerusalem'— and he insists that Christ is 'not a man at a distance, but the wisdom of the Father'. Always he rejects from his theology any 'outward Christ'—a word we may fairly translate by 'historical'. He defines Him as 'a meek spirit drawn up to live in the light of Reason', which is his way of sublimating the story of the Resurrection. The passage implies quite clearly that any man may become such a 'meek spirit'. He goes on to deny the physical resurrection and ascension pretty bluntly: the Apostles cannot have seen Christ 'arise and ascend' to God in heaven, for God is in no 'particular place' but 'in every place and in every creature'. Again and again, in one phrase or another, in all his books he declares that 'heaven is not a local place of glory at a distance': a good man has 'heaven within himself'. Neither are we bound to believe that there is 'a local place of hell': 'as yet none ever came from the dead to tell men on earth, and till then men ought to speak no more than they know'. In his last book his agnosticism about the after-life is even more outspoken: he is not sure of man's personal survival after death. 'After the man is dead' he may be scattered 'into his essences of fire, water, earth and air of which he is compounded'. He recommends to us the example of 'wise-hearted Thomas', who believed nothing but what he saw reason for. Elsewhere he sweeps away the whole body of Hebrew and Christian mythology as 'the deceit of imagination and fleshly wisdom and learning; it teaches you to look altogether upon a history without you of things that were done 6,000 years ago and of things that were done 1,649 years ago'. He is never weary of tilting at the Bibliolatry of the Puritan divines, and likes to remind them that they have no better ground than 'tradition' for trusting the 'copies of the Scriptures in their universities' and that there are 'many translations and interpretations, which differ much one from another'. He could, none the less, quote these Scriptures copiously when they suited his purpose.

It is proper to stress this negative side of Winstanley's thought, since in the Puritan England of the seventeenth century it was all but unique. None the less, in his own individual way, his was a deeply religious mind. One belief he retained with intense conviction, which he shared with the whole of the Puritan left—the Second Coming of Christ. It is true that he sublimates it almost beyond recognition. It is no sudden miracle that he means. He was as far as possible from expecting, as General Harrison and the Fifth Monarchy sect did, that the Saints will conquer the earth, with the Lord of Hosts ordering their ranks. What he did believe was that 'Christ, or the spreading power of light', will penetrate men's minds so that they will cease to covet and oppress, and 'community' will be realised without recourse to the sword. When that happens 'the whole creation will laugh in righteousness' and even the waste commons will blossom. It will make an end of government as we have known it in the past: 'the state', as Marx put it, 'will wither away.' 'You soldiers may see the end of your trade.' With his sharp consciousness of class, he loves to quote the Biblical prophecies which assure this triumph to 'the despised ones of the earth' and bid the rich men 'weep and howl'. He predicts that this revolution will be accomplished 'ere many years wheel about'. It is a law of human nature that every revolution must attain this certainty before it risks its all. Men got it in that century from the Book of Revelation as they get it in ours from the Marxist interpretation of history. If we could delve into the deeper strata of Winstanley's consciousness we might discover that he got it as much from observation as from prophecy. He had seen the mighty hurled from their seats. A king's head had fallen in Whitehall before he flung his challenge at property. The revolution he desired was to come through a change wrought by 'the Spirit Reason' in men's hearts. But that in no way deterred him from devising a shrewd tactic to hasten the process of conversion.

The positive side of Winstanley's creed was an unshaken faith in the 'inner light', which he shared with the Anabaptists before him and his contemporaries, the first Quakers. Like them, he held that the spirit of Reason and Love will reveal itself to a mind that waits in patience and silence. To dismiss this conviction of his as a pre-scientific way of saying that the mind has its sub-conscious processes would be a superficial misunderstanding. He meant much more than this. The self-discipline he prescribed consisted of 'righteous actions and patient silence'. The mind must cease to dwell on outward objects; it must strip itself of covetousness and acquisitiveness, which lead inevitably to oppression; it must practise the golden rule towards its fellow-men and also towards the cattle; it must aim at universal love, which is for him the whole basis of 'community' (i.e. communism). In a long definition of prayer he dismisses words as unimportant and stresses only conduct and the rule of 'waiting with a meek and quiet spirit'. A man who lives thus will discover that he has 'a teacher within himself', for he is brought 'into community with the globe'. To grasp his meaning we have only to remember that it is Reason, or God, that 'knits every creature into a oneness'. By right conduct and patient waiting we overcome our finitude and become conscious of our part in the cosmos: then, and then only, it will reveal itself to us and speak to us. This doctrine of the 'inner light' is often interpreted as the extremest expression of Protestant individualism. As Winstanley understands it, it is, on the contrary, an inference from his mystical pantheism. The ordered whole of the universe becomes conscious and vocal in a mind that lives according to Reason.

From this doctrine of the inner light, Winstanley drew the extremest consequences without flinching. The Scriptures may be useful, but the inner light is a superior authority, and it alone can interpret them. He boldly sweeps away all organised religion, churches, Independent meetings, and all the sacraments, including marriage, baptism and funeral rites. 'What is

the end of all this but to get money?' He will not use what the
Puritans called the means of grace. 'That which you call means
doth harden your hearts.' He pours his scorn on the universities
which claim 'to own the writings of the Apostles'. He despises
the hired clergy: 'you go on selling words for money to blind
people you have deceived'. 'Men must leave off teaching one
another' and speak only from 'the original light within'. A
strong consciousness of class colours all he writes about the
universities and the clergy. 'A ploughman that was never bred
in their universities' may know more of the truth: the first
prophets and apostles were shepherds and fishermen.

This contempt for the hired clergy was a common attitude
among the Levellers and far outside their ranks: Milton shared
it. But Winstanley, in his anti-clericalism, went much deeper.
He compares the 'imaginary' science of the 'divines'—their
'divining doctrine', as he calls it—to witchcraft, and broadens his
assault into an attack on all supernatural religion, with its by-
products of melancholia and hysteria. What is even more
important, he saw that organised religion had become the
instrument of the owning class. One outstanding passage from
The Law of Freedom deserves to be quoted in full:

'There is a threefold discovery of falsehood in this doctrine.

For first it is a doctrine of a sickly and weak spirit, who hath
lost his understanding in the knowledge of the creation . . .
and so runs into fancies either of joy or sorrow.

And if the passion of joy predominate, then he fancies to
himself a personal God, personal angels and a local place of
glory, which, he saith, he and all who believe what he saith
shall go to after they are dead.

And if sorrow predominate, then he fancies to himself a
personal devil and a local place of torment that he shall go
to after he is dead, and this he speaks with great confidence.

Or, secondly, this is the doctrine of a subtle running spirit
to make an ungrounded wise man mad. . . . For many
times when a wise understanding heart is assaulted with this
doctrine of a God, a devil, a heaven and a hell, salvation and
damnation after a man is dead, his spirit being not strongly
grounded in the knowledge of the creation nor in the temper
of his own heart, he strives and stretches his brains to find
out the depth of that doctrine and cannot attain to it. For,

indeed, it is not knowledge but imagination. And so, by poring and puzzling himself in it, loses that wisdom he had, and becomes distracted and mad. And if the passion of joy predominate, then he is merry and sings and laughs, and is ripe in the expression of his words, and will speak strange things; but all by imagination. But if the passion of sorrow predominate, then he is heavy and sad, crying out, He is damned; God had forsaken him and he must go to hell when he die; he cannot make his calling and election sure. And in that distemper many times a man doth hang, kill or drown himself. So that this divining doctrine which you call spiritual and heavenly things, torments people always when they are weak, sickly and under any distemper. . . .

Or, thirdly, this doctrine is made a cloak of policy by the subtle elder brother to cheat his simple younger brother of the freedoms of the earth. For saith the elder brother, 'The earth is mine, and not yours, brother; and you must not work upon it, unless you will hire it of me: and you must not take the fruits of it, unless you will buy them of me, by that which I pay you for your labour: for if you should do other-wise, God will not love you, and you shall not go to heaven when you die, but the devil will have you and you must be damned in hell. . . . You must believe what is written and what is told you; and if you will not believe, your damnation will be the greater'. . . .

Well, the younger brother being weak in spirit, and having not a grounded knowledge of the creation, nor of himself, is terrified, and lets go his hold in the earth, and submits himself to be a slave to his brother for fear of damnation in hell after death, and in hopes to get heaven thereby after he is dead; and so his eyes are put out, and his reason is blinded.

So that this divining spiritual doctrine is a cheat; for while men are gazing up to heaven, imagining after a happiness, or fearing a hell after they are dead, their eyes are put out that they see not what is their birthrights, and what is to be done by them here on earth while they are living: This is the filthy dreamer, and the cloud without rain.

And indeed the subtle clergy do know, that if they can but charm the people by this their divining doctrine, to look after riches, heaven and glory when they are dead, that then they shall easily be the inheritors of the earth, and have the deceived people to be their servants.

Thus, two centuries before Marx, Winstanley, in the simplest of plain English, dared to say that 'religion is the opium of the people', and not only did he write it, he thrust it under Cromwell's eyes.

In this last book of his, though he was sketching an ideal community, Winstanley has his feet firmly on the earth. His mood of exaltation has passed and the long internal conflict in his mind between the tradition in which he was reared and the rationalism he won by wrestling, ends in the complete victory of his new outlook. He was, after all, the contemporary of the pioneers who were soon to found the Royal Society, but it may have been from More that he derived the enthusiasm for experimental science that glows on so many pages of *The Law of Freedom*. He was impatient with universities because, as he said, they were busy only with words and traditions. He now proposes to organise research into all the secrets of nature, largely with a practical purpose. The only titles of honour he would bestow are to go to inventors. He suggests that the postmaster of his commonwealth shall conduct a weekly gazette, to which correspondents in every district shall contribute not merely news of local happenings, especially where help or relief is needed, but, above all, reports of the discovery of 'any secret in nature, or new invention in any art or trade, or in the tillage of the earth'.

The most significant detail in his picture of an ideal community is his sketch of Sunday, for it is entirely his own. It is 'very rational and good,' he writes, that 'one day in seven be still set apart' for fellowship and rest. Under the charge of a 'minister' (a layman, of course) elected annually, each parish is to hold its meetings. For these he will have no ritual of any kind. The minister may read aloud the laws of the commonwealth, which are to be few, simple and brief, and also the reports on 'the affairs of the whole land' contained in the postmaster's gazette. Then are to follow 'speeches' or 'discourses' on history and the sciences, among which he mentions especially botany and astronomy:

'Likewise men may come to see into the nature of the fixed and wandering stars, those great powers of God in the heavens above; and hereby men will come to know the secrets of nature and creation, within which all true knowledge is wrapped up.'

Other lectures may deal with the nature of man. He stipulates that others, beside the minister, shall speak, as the latter may arrange: but 'everyone who speaks of any herb, plant, art or nature of mankind is required to speak nothing by imagination, but what he hath found out by his own industry and observation in trial'. In plain words, experimental science was Winstanley's substitute for the dogmatism of the chapels and churches. Another touch is significant: he suggests that some of the lectures should be given in foreign languages: from the days of the Hussites downwards, communists had always an inter-national outlook. 'By this means,' he sums up, 'in time men shall attain to the practical knowledge of God truly; that they may serve him in spirit and truth, and this knowledge will not deceive a man.'

Truly, we are an ungrateful and forgetful nation. Never, though its population counted less than five millions, has England produced in thought and action so many daring pioneers as in these days of the Commonwealth, when men staked their all for an idea, and lived with an intensity their descendants have never touched. Among them, buried though he is in oblivion, Gerrard Winstanley ranks high, as much by his startling courage as by the clarity of his intellectual vision.

NOTE TO CHAPTER XXXIV

1. [As explained in the Editorial Note, this chapter was not written by Brailsford for this book. It is reprinted from an article which he wrote for *The Plain View* (July 1945), published by The Ethical Union. This article has been slightly abbreviated, in order to avoid repetitions; the first two paragraphs were extracted from Brailsford's original Chapter II.—Ed.]

CHAPTER XXXV

The Red Flag at Bordeaux[1]

There grew up in our fathers' minds during the Interregnum
the belief that the English Revolution would set going a
world wide reformation. What they felt about their rank among
mankind was something more than national pride; it was an
exalted mystical patriotism. Who, even in our sophisticated
age, can repress a glow of excitement on reading over in
Areopagitica the pages in which Milton set out this conviction?
Once already, in the days of Wyclif, God chose out this nation
'before any other that out of her, as out of Sion, should be
proclaimed and sounded forth the first tidings and trumpet of
reformation to all Europe'. And now, bent on reforming
reformation itself, what does God do, but 'reveal Himself to
His servants, and as His manner is, first to His Englishmen'?
To this 'nation of prophets, of sages, of worthies' came the
revelation in its capital, 'the mansion-house of liberty', while
the hammers and anvils fashioned out 'the instruments of
armed justice in defence of beleaguered truth'. What a great
poet said with lyrical eloquence scores of his contemporaries
repeated in the prose of daily life from their pulpits and the
benches of St Stephen's.

Hardly had the Independents triumphed when the more
imaginative of them proposed to act on Milton's vision.
Charles Stuart was still an untried prisoner when the idea of
exporting the revolution to the continent was proclaimed by
the chosen spokesman of the victors at Westminster. Preaching
at St Margaret's before the Lords and Commons on a fast day

in December 1648, Hugh Peters said that 'the Army was resolved to end monarchy' not only in England but in France and other kingdoms, 'the Lord having a great work to finish throughout Christendom'.[2] Some time passed before the Army could turn its attention to France; monarchy had first to be abolished in Ireland and Scotland. But the idea was not forgotten. On this occasion we must not suppose that Peters spoke for his patron the Lieut.-General. It was never the republican idea that inflamed Cromwell's mind. By instinct he was always a believer in 'government by a single person'. When he was ready for action in France, it was his solidarity with the French Protestants that inspired him.

Even before Cromwell's arrival in power, French politics had begun to reflect the movement of thought in England. So keen was the interest of the intellectuals in our troubles that throughout the greater part of the Interregnum a weekly paper devoted solely to English news was printed in French for their benefit. The *Parlement* of Paris—though it was the organ of the legal profession, the magistracy and the higher bureaucracy—began to ape the English Parliament, and to act as if it were a representative legislative assembly, a function that belonged, of course, to the States-General. It even drafted the outlines of a constitution, which included a *habeas corpus* clause and an article recalling the Petition of Right that deprived the crown of the power to impose taxation by its arbitrary will.

It may be well here to glance briefly at the series of conspiracies, revolts and civil wars that ran parallel to our own troubles during the decade which ended in 1653. Richelieu's death in 1642 brought to an end twenty years of efficient despotism. A formidable centralised administration had been built up under the crown; the political power of the great nobles had been broken and the influence of the *Parlement* of Paris diminished; the Huguenots had been deprived of the political and military rights, which made them a state within the state, though they still retained their civil and religious liberties; rich territories had been added to France, yet this brilliant government was detested by the people, crushed as they were by a brutal system of taxation. The feeble Louis XIII survived the great Cardinal only by a few months; his heir was a boy of five. With a Spanish Queen-mother as Regent and a Sicilian Cardinal as her chief minister, the feudal nobility and the *Parlement* of Paris saw the chance of throwing off the yoke Richelieu had imposed. They could do it, moreover, in the name of French patriotism, for Mazarin, though he had long been the favourite pupil of his great predecessor, spoke—and acted—with a pronounced Italian accent to the end of his days. Ten years of strife and confusion, of hunger and poverty, were to pass before the French discovered that this supple southerner, with his patience and his tact, was a governing man hardly less capable than his strenuous northern master.

Save that they marked a reaction of the old ruling classes against twenty years of strong, centralised government, it is impossible to discover any idea that accounts for the troubles that began in 1643 with the conspiracy of the Grandees (*les Importants*) and went on through the civil wars of the Fronde. The *Parlement* of Paris had, to be sure, some concern for civil liberty, but its chief aims were to supplant the *États-Généraux*, and to protect the financial interests of the hereditary caste of lawyers who composed it. In the end the *Parlement*, when it realised that the aristocracy aimed at anything rather than civil liberties, made its peace with the crown.

But the great feudal princes and nobles counted for much more than this imposing tribunal. Their grandfathers in the sixteenth century massacred one another and laid waste the fields of France in the name of religion; the aristocrats of the Fronde and the rival beauties who ruled their salons fought for power, pelf and fun. With rare exceptions each of them had his price, and when it was paid in cash, offices and titles they would change sides without a scruple or a blush. As frivolous as they were greedy, there was nothing to be said for these noble egoists save that when in their memoirs they set forth their views of life, they could do it, like La Rochefoucauld, with cynical wit in polished epigrams. As for the people, its part in these civil wars was to endure, while the contending armies trampled its crops and slaughtered its oxen. Only on rare occasions did it play an active part, as on the famous day of the barricades in Paris when it rose to rescue a beloved leader, 'Bonhomme'

Broussel, and forced the Queen and Mazarin to flee into the provinces.

Less well known, but for English readers much more interesting, is the part the people played during the Fronde in the South, but above all in Bordeaux. Linked with our history since the Middle Ages, this great city was the political capital of the province of Guienne and for the purposes of commerce and culture the centre of the whole South-West. In its *Parlement* sat a numerous and learned body of magistrates and officials. From its port on the Gironde its shipping carried the wines of its region to a thirsty London. It boasted two famous centres of learning, the ancient college of Guienne and a modern Jesuit college. It kept three firms of printers busy. Calvinism made its first converts among the dons of the Collège de Guienne, then among the wealthy merchants, and finally spread among the artisans. Not only in the city but in the whole region round it the Huguenots formed a powerful and well-organised minority, which dominated several of the small towns in its neighbourhood. But, indeed, from the Albigenses down to the Girondins and the Marseillais, the South and South-West of France was always the stronghold of her radical pioneers.

How deep in the social strata of the South-West did this radicalism penetrate? Far down, for the misery caused first by the wars of religion, then by the feudal exactions of the nobles, and finally by Richelieu's savage taxation, made rebels of the peasants in two successive generations. In 1594 a revolt of countrymen whom their lords and masters nicknamed the Clodhoppers (*les Croquants*) broke out in Périgord and spread to Guienne. In it men of both religions united against the nobles, who 'treated them', as they put it, 'like slaves'. To the number, it is said, of 200,000 they assembled round Bergerac, hoisted their hats on their weapons and cried '*Vive le tiers état! Liberté! Liberté!*' Henri IV appeased them by cancelling their arrears of taxes, but next year they rose again. The nobles accused them of trying to found a democracy in imitation of the Swiss. In spite of the heavy slaughter of these rebels, the *Croquants* rose again in the next generation to resist Richelieu's taxation. Such was the background to the radicalism of Bordeaux during the Fronde.[3]

Throughout the last five years of the civil wars the Bordelais were intermittently under arms and always on the side of the rebels. The *Parlement* raised a volunteer army and fleet to defy the detested royalist governor of Guienne, the Duc d'Épernon, and though his professional troops could defeat their militia in the field, they were still strong enough to drive him out of the city. Among their leaders was a militant radical priest, the Abbé Bonnet, famous both for his virtues and his learning.

From 1650, if not earlier, the Bordelais were listening to republican manifestoes from the pulpit. A sermon has come down to us in which the people were exhorted to create a republic, 'not only to escape a repetition of the scourges their kings inflicted on them in the past, but also . . . for the glorious end of setting up a free and independent government which all the princes and potentates of Europe would court and respect'.[4] Only those who forget how far ahead of the rest of France in its political thinking was this south-western region will be startled by such an utterance. A century had passed since Montaigne's friend, Etienne de la Boétie, wrote one of the great classics of the humanist Renaissance, the *Discours de la Servitude Volontaire, ou Le Contr' Un,* the boldest attack on monarchy until Tom Paine challenged the hangman with his *Rights of Man.*

The orator who predicted that Bordeaux would be courted by the potentates of Europe if she proclaimed a republic was thinking, of course, of the Commonwealth. The sailors of the Gironde knew the way to the Thames and so did its radicals and its Huguenots. So much we may learn from the chronicle in doggerel verse, which appeared in Paris as a weekly newspaper during the Fronde:

> *La bordelaise nation*
> *Maintenant bien et beau se pique—*
> *De s'ériger en république.*

After this statement that the people of Bordeaux were bent on establishing a republic, the rhymester went on to say that they were declaring their sympathy not only with the Independents but even with the Levellers (*les Niveleurs*).[5] This may imply that as early as the summer of 1650 they were in communication with the republicans in England. Among the leaders of the left we know of two who had a good knowledge of French, because they received part of their education across the Channel, Sir Harry Vane and Henry Marten. In the bundles of papers which the latter left behind when he was arrested as a regicide at the Restoration there are several that suggest an active interest in the politics of France. Thus he was receiving newsletters in June 1650 both from Bordeaux and Paris. A letter of the same month from a merchant in Bordeaux to his brother in London gives news of the doings of the royal army. Again, there are letters from Paris and Saumur running to the end of 1651 from a correspondent who uses a numerical cipher for all the names in his bulletins of news.[6] Can Marten have been the member of the Council of State specially entrusted with French affairs? Vane went to Paris, probably in 1651, to test the ground, and had a talk that led to nothing with the arch-frondeur, Cardinal de Retz.

After Worcester Cromwell's hands were free and we find him sitting with Thomas Scott and Whitelock on the committee of the Council of State that dealt with French affairs. They had to face the danger that France, which recognised Prince Charles as King of England, might, when the distractions of the Fronde were over, lend him active assistance to recover his throne. Would it, then, be politic to aid the rebels in her civil war, in order to keep her preoccupied and weak? Cromwell's ideas of European policy always had as their foundation his great design of an alliance of the Protestant powers. To play a part on the continent it seemed to him essential that England should possess somewhere on its western shores a port that could be used as a base for operations on land. In the end he got Dunkirk. La Rochelle attracted him for sentimental reasons. Like most of the Puritans he felt a deep sense of shame because the Huguenots lost this famous fortress through the incompetence of Buckingham and the duplicity of King Charles. The third candidate for his interest was the magnificent port on the Gironde, now the centre of the rebellion in the South-West.

To Bordeaux, accordingly, in the autumn of 1651 the Council

of State sent a mission of five persons, whose chief was the
ex-Agitator, now Colonel, Edward Sexby. He must have been
Cromwell's choice. After quitting the Army in 1647, he re-
entered it two years later as governor of Portland, with the
rank of captain. He then raised a regiment of foot which he
commanded for a time in Scotland. In June 1651 he was
cashiered by court martial for using undue pressure to induce
some soldiers to re-enlist in his regiment. Since he had acted
'for the public service', though with too much zeal, his offence
did not debar him from further employment. From a petition
for expenses which was duly honoured after his return, we learn
that he spent twenty-three months in France. From La Rochelle
and Bordeaux he sent back reports twice a week. His instructions were 'to give an account of the state of that country
[France] and the affections of the people'.[7] One of his four
colleagues whom he sent among the Protestants of Languedoc
was put on the rack and tortured to death. Another, of whom
we know only his name, Arundel, returned to England about
the same time as Sexby. Of the other two we know nothing.
Were they soldiers or divines, Englishmen or Frenchmen?
The mission, at all events, was not unsuccessful.

Evidently from 1650, and perhaps earlier, there was a
republican movement in Bordeaux. It had, as we shall see, a
formidable organisation characteristic of that epoch. The
Parlement of Guienne led the opposition in the early years of
the Fronde, but it had no republican tendencies. It was
composed of lawyers who had bought their judicial posts and
were bent on passing them on to their sons; they did not cease
to be conservatives when they sided with the princes against
the upstart foreigner, Mazarin. At the Hôtel de Ville the
municipal administration had fallen into the grip of a plutocracy even more exclusive than that of the City of London,
which managed to evade the election of its councillors (*jurats*)
by the citizens and any scrutiny of their handling of the city's
finances. The guilds (*corporations de métiers*) had degenerated like
our own livery companies into jealous oligarchies dominated
by a hereditary master-class.

The vital organisations of that day, within which the artisans felt happy and preserved their self-respect, were the brother-hoods of the *compagnons*. These were secret societies which protected the craftsman's interests and taught him to feel pride in the service he rendered to society. They grew up among the workers whose creative genius built the cathedrals of medieval France. Like the free masons of the Rhineland they traced their origin to the erection of Solomon's Temple. Since every ambitious artisan spent many years of his youth in going the round of most of the cities of France to learn the secrets of his craft, a brotherhood that provided homes for him as he journeyed from one strange region to another could count on his devotion. At each stage of his pilgrimage he could reckon on finding a hostel that would welcome him, if he knew the pass words. Elaborate rites of baptism and initiation celebrated his entry into the grades of apprentice and *compagnon*. Senior craftsmen taught the lads their trade and schools were pro-vided at which they learned drawing and geometry. In every town an elected officer ran what was in effect a labour exchange. Each *devoir* (as the local organisation was called) had its common purse which would maintain a member who was sick or unemployed. The discipline was strict; on pain of expulsion members were required to pay their debts and carry out their duties towards their employers. If they got into trouble with the law for a peccadillo the brotherhood gave them every help, but if their offence was disgraceful, as for example theft, they were ruthlessly expelled.

There was no lack of gaiety among the 'companions'. They had their traditional songs and their friendly convoys to speed a wanderer on his way, while on the feast of their patron saint they would march in procession to church, decked out with coloured ribbons behind a symbolic square and compasses. Occasionally they resorted to a strike, as the printers of Lyons and Paris did in 1539, but usually they imposed their standards of pay and conditions by boycotting any master who stood on their black list. Though these organisations were too powerful and too independent to enjoy the smiles of authority, they survived every attempt to suppress them—even the edict which the Sorbonne published in 1655, that to belong to any of them was deadly sin.

Out of such brotherhoods grew the republican party of Bordeaux, for its rules reproduce something of their spirit. It came to be known as *l'Ormée*, because it held its public meetings under the elms (*ormes*) on a plateau just outside the town. Like the Levellers it drew its support from 'the middle sort of people' (*la bourgeoisie moyenne*). It had an inner core of five hundred active members, but under its wing it had in addition an organised body of adherents, said to number twelve thousand. There were among them few, if any, of the big merchants of the port. Most of its adherents must have been artisans, many of whom would be past or present *compagnons*. But its most influential members seem to have been master craftsmen and tradesmen who had their own workshops—shoe-makers, jewellers, apothecaries, confectioners, pewterers and the like—the sort of people who made the Revolution at the end of the next century. Their rules mention peasants also. Though they cried out like the Levellers for a drastic reform of the law, they had several lawyers among them, who rose by their eloquence and audacity to positions of leadership.

Some writers have supposed that *l'Ormée* was a Calvinist organisation. This is an obvious mistake, for their most famous leader, de Villars, was a practising Catholic, but there doubtless were a good many Protestants among them. It was class rather than religion that made the dividing line between royalists and republicans in Guienne. The big Protestant merchants of the Atlantic ports were already inclining to conservatism. The truth seems to be that the Ormistes, though like the Levellers they had kept their religious beliefs, were like them anti-clericals, who were violently opposed, not so much to the secular clergy, as to the monastic orders which were at Bordeaux, as a recent writer has put it, 'so numerous, so wealthy, and often so insolent'.[8] The most conspicuous leader of the brotherhood was an eloquent advocate, de Villars, whom Professor Jullian in the standard history of Bordeaux describes as clever, ambitious and greedy. But the leader whom his followers revered and even his enemies respected was Duretête, who started life as a butcher.[9] An organiser rather than an orator, his democratic convictions were as ardent and sincere as his conduct was disinterested. The government of the party was in the hands of an elected committee known as '*la Chambre de l'Ormée*', whose decisions every member was pledged to obey whether they dealt with questions of policy or disputes between individuals.

Whatever their more distant objects may have been, the first step, as the Ormistes saw it, was to win power in Bordeaux. They aimed therefore, according to their constitution, at securing for the great majority of the people of the city a full deliberative voice in its municipal assemblies. They also meant to exact from the councillors (*jurats*) an account of their management of its finances. By these democratic reforms—in effect by the widening of the franchise—they reckoned that power would pass from the ruling oligarchy to the main body of the citizens. *Vox populi vox dei* was their favourite slogan. Further, like the Levellers, the Ormistes were bent on the reform of the legal profession. They meant to abolish the practice of buying and selling the posts of judges and magistrates, and to render legal procedure less dilatory and costly.

Their 'articles of union' enjoined on their adherents the virtues of fraternity and Christian charity. The *Ormée* promised help to any of its members who got into trouble with the law; it would lend money free of interest to those who were in debt and it promised its help and protection to its members' widows and orphans. Should a member fall into poverty, it would try to find suitable work for him; should it fail in this, it would give him material help in such a way that only those responsible for its provision should know of it. Strangers (*étrangers*) settling in Bordeaux should enjoy the same privileges within it as natives of the city. Finally any member who led a scandalous life or failed to observe these articles should be expelled as a traitor. For the rest, like the *compagnons*, the *Ormée* had its mystical side. Its arms were an elm with a serpent round it. It venerated the Holy Ghost, and cherished the symbols of the dove, the heart in flames and the lily in flower.[10]

The third and last phase of the Fronde broke out in the summer of 1651 under the leadership of the Prince de Condé. 'Le grand Condé', as he was called to distinguish him from his ancestors, ranked with Cromwell and Turenne among the great captains of his age; his speciality lay in surprise and rapidity of movement. Though the arrogance and egoism of this prince of the blood royal were notorious, his dashing presence and spirited conduct won him a measure of popularity. Since he was the Governor of Guienne, he decided to establish his power first of all in the South-West. Arriving in Bordeaux in September, he was welcomed by all parties from the conservatives of the *Parlement* to the radicals of the *Ormée*. Because he was not strong enough to stand alone against the forces of the crown, he sought foreign aid, first from Spain and then from England. From Madrid in November the ablest of his civilian lieutenants, Pierre Lenet, brought back a treaty of alliance. But the Spaniards, as it turned out, though willing to give enough military help to keep France distracted, would never give enough to ensure Condé's victory. A Spanish fleet did, however, sail into the Gironde and a Spanish garrison occupied Bourg on its shores. There was nothing incompatible in this double approach, since Spain and the Commonwealth were on good terms and both were opposed to the French monarchy.

Throughout the winter Condé struggled with indifferent success to secure his hold over Guienne. Apart from some half-armed levies of peasants, his seasoned troops were outnumbered by those of the crown by nearly ten to one. Hoping for better fortune in the North, he made in March 1652 a sudden, reckless dash with a handful of men through the enemy's lines to take command of the forces of the Fronde on the Loire. He left behind him as vice-governor his younger brother, the Prince de Conti, a vain and capricious weakling, assisted by a council on which sat his spirited sister the Duchess of Longueville and his two trusted lieutenants, the civilian Lenet and the soldier Marsin.

The members of the council took to quarrelling violently among themselves, while the *Parlement* believed that it was strong enough to crush *l'Ormée*. It forbade any more of these meetings under the elms to which some of the radicals used to go armed. It then took the decision to arrest de Villars and Duretête and to hang them. The *Ormée*, thereupon, mobilised its forces in self-defence, captured the guns that defended the town-hall and after a bloody struggle, during which it invaded the aristocratic quarter, took over the government of the city. It celebrated its victory by a triumphal procession and hoisted its ensign, the red flag, on the steeple of St Michael's church. Condé from the North instructed his lieutenants to give it their support and for a year, from the end of June 1652 to July 1653, its 'Chamber' was the ruler of Bordeaux. Since it won the municipal elections in July, it had the right to behave as the legitimate government of the city. It had to repress the conspiracies of the royalists, but it allowed most of its leading opponents to leave the town unmolested. None of them was executed.

In the North things were going ill for the Fronde. Early in July Turenne inflicted a severe defeat on Condé at the Porte Saint-Antoine in the outskirts of Paris. After this disaster, though his party made a desperate effort to rally its adherents, it soon became clear that the Parisians had reached the limit of their endurance. Mazarin, from his banishment, still directed the policy of the Queen-mother. He saw his opportunity and persuaded her to publish on 26 August, 1652, in the name of the boy king, a generous offer of amnesty to all who would lay down their arms. Condé in his pride rejected it, for he maintained (what was true) that the Italian Cardinal was still in control behind the scenes and predicted (what came to pass) that he would soon be back in office. By October the Queen and the King were able to return to Paris, where in February 1653 Mazarin, too wise to think of vengeance, rejoined them, avowedly the ruler of France. Condé had to retreat to Lorraine.

In Bordeaux the *Parlement* was, of course, for accepting the amnesty, but the *Ormée*, still bent on achieving a democratic republic, would not hear of surrender. In September it erected four gallows round the town-hall as a threat to all who dared to talk of peace. Meanwhile, the territory which Bordeaux and its army controlled was growing painfully less. But from the Commonwealth it received a first instalment of aid. It was allowed to import cannon-fodder from Ireland; for Limerick had fallen and its defenders, the legendary 'wild geese', might sell their lives abroad for what they would fetch. Some 1,500 of them arrived in the Gironde during 1652 and were set to garrison the strategically important little town of Lormont. As one of Condé's agents in London reckoned, they cost delivered f.o.b. only twelve *livres* (a trifle above 38s.) per man. More were available. If the Bordelais would send two ships laden with claret to the Thames, their cargoes would pay for yet another thousand Irishmen whom they might bring back on the return voyage.[11] This was an earnest of better things to come. According to the news that reached Bordeaux from London, the Parliament was eager to take that rebel city under its protection, whatever the cost might be. It was prepared to send 12,000 troops—meaning, one takes it, authentic Englishmen—packed aboard ships of war. But a treaty must first be concluded, for the English wanted a port to guarantee their expenses and serve as a base for their fleet.

Mazarin, who knew all that was going on, realised that for him and for France the fortunes of the day might turn on the disposition of the Huguenots of Guienne and Languedoc. If they took advantage of Sexby's mission to send out an urgent plea for succour, Cromwell might be moved to action. Accordingly, while the Fronde was still raging, he caused to be issued in the King's name on 21 May, 1652, a remarkable declaration addressed—to quote its cautious legal phraseology—to his subjects of *la religion prétendue réformée*. It confirmed their right, conferred by the Edict of Nantes, to the free and public exercise of the said religion in all the places specified therein, notwithstanding any judgments to the contrary, and desired that all who contravened the said edict should be punished as disturbers of the public peace.[12] The Huguenots were impressed by this assurance, so much so that the militia of their stronghold Montauban took the initiative in backing the King's forces against those of the Fronde. Mazarin rewarded the loyalty of this historic town by permitting it to rebuild the fortifications Richelieu had torn down.

While Mazarin reassured the Protestants, he mobilised all the forces of the Catholic church. All over the South the bishops fulminated against the Fronde. The Archbishop of Bordeaux, hitherto a moderate, took the extreme step of excommunicating all who rejected the amnesty. Richelieu had turned the monastic orders into the militia of the monarchy. Mazarin followed his example. A brilliant and romantic conspirator, who revelled in disguises and ciphers, Father Berthod, a Cordelier, had been the brain of every royalist conspiracy in Paris. At the close of the year he was sent to repeat his achievements in Bordeaux. There he failed, for all his plots were discovered and he exposed the faithful to the counter-measures of the *Ormée* and kept the city in a ferment of suspicion. The monastery in which he lodged was sacked and desecrated. From his intrigues the radical leader, de Villars, emerged with a tarnished record. Father Berthod escaped by disguising himself as one of the cavalry who were hunting him.

Life during the early months of 1653 was becoming difficult in Bordeaux. The country round about it was devastated and the trade of its port must have been interrupted. This would presumably lead to unemployment among its unskilled workers and the prices of food would be likely to rise. Its well-to-do citizens, both Protestants and Catholics, were now declaring openly for the King, while its gilded youth of both sexes took to wearing white ribbons and gathered in groups that called boldly for peace. Slowly but steadily, for all that Marsin could do in command of Condé's regulars and the volunteer trainbands of the *Ormée*, the King's forces were closing in on the city. The Spanish fleet had sailed back to its home port and the royal fleet under the Duke of Vendôme, a natural son of Henri IV, had entered the Gironde. Worst of all, Bordeaux was now exposed from the North-West, for Condé's chief ally, the Count du Daugnon, who controlled the Atlantic coast up to La Rochelle, had sold himself to Mazarin for 530,000 livres in cash, a dukedom and the baton of a Marshal of France.

During these anxious days of spring, the Bordelais realised that the only chance of survival for their republican experiment lay in the prompt appearance of an English fleet. Sexby saw his opportunity. He told the radicals that Condé's agents would never succeed in the negotiations which they were conducting in London, but that if the city of Bordeaux were to join them and call in the English the Commonwealth would send help enough to enable the province of Guienne to hold its own and win its freedom.[13] He and his colleague Arundel were negotiating not only with the Ormistes and the Huguenots, but also with the Prince de Conti and his sober, conservative adviser, Lenet. The upshot was that with Condé's approval the city decided in its own name and that of the princes to send three delegates to London with full powers to negotiate with the Commonwealth for aid in men, ships and money.

They were authorised to offer it a port on the shores of the Gironde which it might fortify; further, the Bordelais would support the English if they wished to acquire La Rochelle. The instructions foresaw the likelihood that the English would propose a new form of government for Bordeaux with guarantees for the freedom of the Protestants. In that case, the delegates were to reply that although the Huguenots were disaffected, they went in such fear of the King's government that they dared not associate themselves openly with this venture, but the moment they saw an English fleet and army in the Gironde they would join with all their might in the cry for freedom. These credentials were signed on 4 April, 1653 (N.S.), by the mayor of Bordeaux, the senior alderman (*jurat*) and eighteen citizens, and also by the Prince de Conti and Pierre Lenet, who described himself as the plenipotentiary of His Most Serene Highness the Prince of Condé. The princes were thinking only of tactics.

Sexby failed, it is clear, to get any countenance from the presbytery (*consistoire*) of the reformed church, but the *Ormée* backed him root and branch. It was ready to turn Guienne into a Leveller republic, and from this base it hoped to win, one day, the rest of France. The three delegates carried to London one of the most astonishing documents of that century. It is a declaration in which the two princes, Condé and Conti, the ministers, generals, magistrates, colonels, captains, officers and people of Bordeaux and the country round about it, 'declare jointly and severally in the presence of God that they will not lay down their arms . . . until they have achieved the true aim of a free people, a republic modelled on those which have come nearest to justice and good government'. After this solemn preamble, there follows, under the title of *L'Accord du Peuple*, a sketch of this ideal republic. It is a literal translation, into clumsy Anglo-Saxon French (with a few omissions), of the final version of the Agreement of the People, which the Levellers published on May Day 1649.[14] With it went the draft of a *Manifesto*, couched in simple and popular language, which set forth the reasons for making a republican revolution on the English model.

The Agreement was not composed in the Tower by Lilburne and his fellow-prisoners with the needs of the people of Bordeaux in mind. It was distilled from experiences that only Englishmen lived through. Clause by clause it set down the conclusions which Englishmen reached by arguing from principles and traditions embedded in the history of our island. But in class structure and therefore in political constitution England and France differed so radically in the seventeenth century that no scheme of reform would fit them both. Parliament and *Parlement* had in common little more than the three syllables of their names. Sects there were none in France; a catholic religion faced a reformed religion in head-on collision. Juries, all-important to the Levellers, were unknown in France till 1791. And so one might go on. If Sexby and his French comrades really proposed to publish the Agreement as it stood, without preface or commentary, they were behaving with a surprising lack of intelligence.

Yet when this is said, the fact remains that the Ormistes were perfectly capable of grasping the main principles on which the Agreement rested. They shared the class outlook of the Levellers and faced the same class-enemies—the City plutocrats, the clergy and the lawyers. They, too, were battling for the sovereignty of the people and democratic representation, though as yet the issue was joined only on the municipal plane. The bloody century that lay behind them had taught them even more of the evils of intolerance than Englishmen had experienced, and within their organisation Catholics and Protestants had learned to work happily together. Cast in a Latin mould, their minds would accept without demur the idea of human rights—*les droits de l'homme*—inscribed in a written constitution and a code of law.

The *Manifesto* that accompanied *l'Accord du Peuple* reads like the work of a French Protestant draftsman, though Sexby may have sat at his elbow and suggested to him an idea and even a phrase here and there. The result is a puzzling amalgam of

Calvinistic theology and Puritan morals with the Leveller passion for humanity and equality.

It opens with a spirited introduction which justifies the right of rebellion against a tyrant who breaks the contract that bound him to govern for his people's good. Its pages echo the Huguenot classics, from Béza to the *Vindiciae contra tyrannos*, which steeled the consciences of the rebels who followed Henry of Navarre. It ends, logically enough, in a passage that Sexby may have dictated, for it recalls Rainsborough's speeches and his own share in the memorable debates at Putney.

No man, [so it runs] is born a slave . . . The peasant is as free as the prince, for he wore neither sabots on his feet nor a saddle on his back when he came into the world, nor does the King's son bear a crown on his head. We are all by birth equally free, and, because we are so, have the power to choose the government by which we will be governed, for no man can be bound save by his representatives or by his own consent.

The next step in the argument is a demonstration that Frenchmen are living under a tyranny as greedy as it is lawless. The specific grievances of the Fronde receive a perfunctory mention; 'our heroic princes' are imprisoned while foreigners are promoted to the highest offices. But the passionate outcry is reserved for the wrongs of the common man. To put it briefly: 'the commanders of the armies that live on our children's bread use their power only to build their fortunes on our ruin. We are taxed till no man knows what he may call his own and a mere nobody, if he wears a sword in his belt, can lock us in prison or take our lives. The poor are neglected, the peasants robbed of their all, and thousands are ready to perish of hunger. Churchmen grow rich on money destined for the poor, and because the mercenary favourites of the court are installed in the seats of justice, our goods and our liberties are at their mercy.'

What, then, is to be done when the rebellion has succeeded? The answers of the *Manifesto* set out in twenty-one articles are often vague, though their tendency is clear enough. On three subjects, however, the *Manifesto* speaks not only boldly but with precision—toleration, Puritan morality and the incidence of taxation.

The intention of the programme is to create a democratic state in which all are equal before the law. No laws shall be valid, save those passed by a parliament (*parlement*) or representative of the people. No attempt is made to define its composition or method of election. There is to be no more arbitary taxation. All public officials are to be elected annually. Peasants shall come into court on an equal footing with their lords, even if these are princes. Base tenures (*titres serviles*), the chief support of tyranny, must be abolished. This last item must have come from the programme of the *Ormée*, for it did not figure in the final version of the Agreement. Though it had to wait for fulfilment till 1789, the will to make an end of feudalism was already articulate in Bordeaux.

The outstanding demand in the *Manifesto*, spread over five of its twenty-one articles, is for religious toleration. What the Edict of Nantes secured was something different and something less. It brought civil war to an end and confirmed the Protestants in the enjoyment of their rights, but only in the places, some two hundred of them, which they happened to hold at the cease-fire. The formula in the Agreement, which the Bordelais took over *verbatim*, set forth the general principle that government must not interfere either by compulsion or restriction with the free exercise of religion. Furthermore, Protestants should be eligible for all public offices and employments and should be free to erect their buildings for public worship where they please. Those who seek to divide the brethren of the two religions should be punished. In the name of Christ the reconciler, let no more controversial sermons be preached by either side.

Two articles proclaim the Puritan belief that God in His wrath is scourging Frenchmen for the sins in which they abound—drunkenness, profanity and lechery. His face will not shine upon them until they adopt the laws in force in England for the suppression of these crimes. Magistrates must be required, moreover, to enforce the strict observance of the Lord's day.

These Calvinist clauses are not easy to interpret. They did

not stem, needless to say, from the Leveller outlook on life; Sexby never talked in this strain. Were they adopted in order to attract the hesitating Huguenots, who were as austere in their outlook as their English brethren? Or was their purpose to appeal to Cromwell and the Commonwealth? The average man in Bordeaux would relish the prospect of the Puritan Sabbath as little as the average Englishman enjoyed the experience.

Yet another of these sharply outlined clauses looks forward to the Revolution. Already the middle sort of people in Guienne, peasants as well as craftsmen, were crying out for a republic, because the monarchy exempted from taxation those best able to bear it—aristocrats, bureaucrats and churchmen. The *Manifesto* lays it down that henceforward every man, whatever his rank or condition, shall pay his due share of taxation in proportion to his means, unless he can prove that his property amounts to less than 100 livres (about £16).

Such was the document that Councillor Trancas and his two colleagues from Bordeaux carried with them in the hope of deserving the sympathy and enlisting the aid of the English Republic. They would arrive in London a few days before Cromwell swept the Rump of the Long Parliament away. The Lord General was busy with his *coup d'état* and it was never his way, save on the field of battle, to make up his mind in a hurry. June came before the three Commissioners could report their success. Cromwell, so ran their dispatch, was prepared to send substantial help in men and money and would formally undertake to drive the royal forces out of Guienne. But the offer of one of the ports on the shores of the estuary did not satisfy him; he wanted Bordeaux itself for England.[15]

This the *Ormée* was prepared to grant and so was Marsin at the head of the army, but before a reply could be sent to London, the King's forces, whose commanders knew what was going on, quickened the pace of the campaign; for they dared not risk the appearance, under the redoubtable Blake, of the English fleet in the Garonne. On 3 July, the Spanish garrison of Bourg, whose pay was in arrears, capitulated after a brief and feeble resistance, and on the 17th the Irish in Lormont followed their example. By land and sea Bordeaux was now surrounded. The politic Cardinal saw his chance and by the 24th his offers of a lenient settlement were accepted. The great got off scot free, from Condé's family and the aristocrats who formed his staff down to the professional soldiers who served him. The ancient privileges of the city were confirmed. Vengeance fell only on the middle sort of people and on very few of them. The red flag came down from St Michael's spire and on 3 August, 1653, the Dukes of Vendôme and Candale were cheered by rich and poor alike as they marched in at the head of the royal troops. Of the five citizens excepted from the amnesty, the three members of the diplomatic mission were safe in London and De Villars escaped in disguise among the Prince de Conti's servants. Duretête suffered alone, broken on the wheel under the elms. As for the adaptable Conti, he deserted his still-belligerent brother and married one of Mazarin's nieces.

Cromwell, after listening to Sexby's personal report, did not at once abandon the dream of acquiring Bordeaux. In the autumn of 1653 he was still angling for reliable information. Major Joachim Hane (or was the name really Hahn?), a German engineer in the Commonwealth's service, was sent to report on the fortifications of the ports on the western coast. His story of his many escapes from death and torture is a moving tale of courage and endurance. Jean Baptiste Stouppe, pastor of the Huguenot church in the Savoy whom Bishop Burnet describes as 'a man of intrigue but of no virtue', after visiting most of the Calvinist communities in the South of France, reported that they were at their ease and meant to keep the peace; as for Condé, they thought him 'a man who sought nothing but his own greatness, to which . . . he was ready to sacrifice all his friends and every cause that he espoused'. This verdict seems to have persuaded Cromwell to accept Mazarin's overtures for a treaty of friendship, which led in due course to the acquisition of Dunkirk.

So ended the only attempt that was made to export the English Revolution. Only at Bordeaux, thanks to the Levellers, did the middle sort of people realise their fraternity across the salt water and the cultural gap that divided them. It happened again after the lapse of four generations, when Citizen Paine of London and Philadelphia was welcomed to Paris as a member of the Convention. Till 1792 the red flag that Duretête hoisted on St Michael's belfry lay furled to await the fullness of time.

NOTES TO CHAPTER XXXV

1. The best account from the English side of Cromwell's dealings with France is in the introduction by Sir C. H. Firth to the *Journal of Joachim Hane*. See also Gardiner, *Commonwealth and Protectorate*, II, pp. 156-7. From the French side two authorities are indispensable: (1) A. Chéruel, *Histoire de France sous le Ministère de Mazarin*, 2 vols. (esp. I, pp. 56-64) is the more objective of the two. (2) V. Cousin, *Madame de Longueville pendant la Fronde* (esp. pp. 464-75) is the more detailed and the more readable. Neither Chéruel nor Cousin realised that *l'Accord du Peuple* was a translation of a Leveller document. For the social history of the period I used *A History of the French People* by Guy de la Batut and Georges Friedmann (English translation, 1923). Professor Camille Jullian in his *Histoire de Bordeaux* gives a clear account of *l'Ormée*. For the organization of the *compagnons* see *Le Compagnonnage* by Martin Saint-Léon (Paris, 1901) and the vivid description in *Le Compagnon du Tour de France* by Georges Sand. For help in preparing this chapter I am indebted to my friend M. Olivier Lutaud of the Sorbonne [who has also been kind enough to extend his assistance to the editor].

2. *Mercurius Pragmaticus* (26 December, 1648).

3. For the *Croquants* see Batut and Friedmann, *op. cit.*, pp. 66-8, 99.

4. Chéruel, *op. cit.*, I, p. 56.

5. Loret, *Muse Historique*, Vol. I, pp. 32-3 (6 August, 1650), pp. 248-50 (2 June, 1652).

6. *Historical MSS. Commission, Thirteenth Report*, Appendix, Part IV, pp. 387, 392.

7. *C.S.P. Domestic, 1654*, pp. 160-1.

8. Pierre-Louis Berthaud's chapter in *L'Histoire, la Vie, les Moeurs et la Curiosité*, ed. John Grand-Carteret (1928).

9. One authority describes Duretête as a typical artisan, while another believes that he practised as a solicitor.

10. This account of *l'Ormée* is based on Jullian, *op. cit.*, pp. 491-4.

11. Cousin, *op. cit.*, p. 280 n.

12. *Ibid.*, p. 288.

13. *Ibid.*, p. 465.

14. Neither of the two MS. copies of this document bears a date. One of them, found among Mazarin's papers, is endorsed in his handwriting: 'Déclaration pour ériger en république la ville de Bordeaux, envoyée par MM. de Bordeaux [en Angleterre].' M. Chéruel (*op. cit.*, p. 159) thought that it may have been drafted towards the end of 1651, i.e. soon after Sexby's arrival. But his arguments do not strike me as conclusive. The

document does not seem to have been published in Bordeaux. It would have been published, presumably, when the help from England arrived. Condé gave his approval, as his letters to Lenet show, with no serious intention of setting up a republic. In his calculations, the scheme would serve, however, to keep the radicals and the Protestants from accepting Mazarin's amnesty (Cousin, *op. cit.*, p. 282). [M. Lutaud suggests that, contrary to Brailsford's view, this translation of the Agreement of the People may be by a Frenchman. The translator seems not to understand what the English Council of State was. M. Lutaud adds the interesting point that Mirabeau was well acquainted with the Agreement of the People; but his knowledge of it appears to derive not from the *Ormée's* translation but from Catherine Macaulay's *History of England from the Accession of James I to the Elevation of the House of Hanover* (1763-81).—Ed.]

15. The only authority for this statement is the Abbé de Cosnac (Cousin, *op. cit.*, p. 359, who took it from the Abbé's *Mémoires*, I, p. 68). De Cosnac was the chaplain of the Prince de Conti and acted as his secretary and political adviser. He would know all that was going on. Both Chéruel and Cousin regard him as a reliable witness. The only reason for questioning his statement is that England was still occupied with the Dutch War, though the issue was no longer doubtful.

A NOTE ON BOOKS

[Brailsford left no bibliography, but his notes show how full and careful his reading had been. I give here references to a few books and articles which he does not mention, most of them published since his death.]

J. Frank, *The Levellers* (Harvard U.P., 1955) is a general study.

Ed. F. A. Bates, *Graves Memoirs of the Civil War* (1927) contains material relevant to Joyce's seizure of the King, and to the Agitators' initiative in this affair (see Chapter X).

H. G. Tibbutt's edition of 'The Tower of London Letter-Book of Sir Lewis Dyve, 1646-7', in *Publications of the Bedfordshire Historical Record Soc.,* XXXVIII (1958), contains information about the Levellers and Agitators between September and November 1647, derived from Lilburne.

J. D. Hughes, 'The Drainage Disputes in the Isle of Axholme', in *The Lincolnshire Historian* (Vol. II, No. 1, 1954) is relevant to Chapter XXXI, p. 610.

A. Cole, 'The Quakers and the English Revolution', in *Past and Present* (No. 10, 1956), deals with the Leveller inheritance of the Quakers, along lines similar to those of Brailsford's Chapter XXXII.

Additional information about Winstanley's career after the suppression of the Digger colony is to be found in Paul H. Hardacre's 'Gerrard Winstanley in 1650', in *Huntington Library Quarterly* (Vol. XXII, No. 4, 1959); a possible notice of his death is recorded by Richard T. Vann in *Friends Historical Soc. Journal* (Vol. XLIX, No. 1, 1959).

Brailsford would also have enjoyed an article by K. V. Thomas, 'Women and the Civil War sects', in *Past and Present* (No. 13, 1958). I should like to think he would have been interested in some of the essays in my *Puritanism and Revolution* (1958), especially 'The Norman Yoke'.

Of forthcoming books, Miss Pauline Greg's *Life of John Lilburne* and Professor C. M. Williams's *Life of Henry Marten* should be mentioned.

But most of all Brailsford would have been excited by the chapter on the Levellers in Professor C. B. Macpherson's forthcoming book, *Possessive Individualism*. This will necessitate substantial modifications in the views hitherto held (by Brailsford among others) on the nature of Leveller ideas of democracy, since Professor Macpherson shows that the Levellers never advocated manhood suffrage. Brailsford might here have found the key to the problem which he raised in Chapter XXI (pp. 448-50), why the Levellers were so slow to agitate for the abolition of copyhold, the obvious rallying cry for a mass movement in the rural England of the seventeenth century. Yu. M. Saprikin suggested, in 'Some Questions in the History of the English Bourgeois Revolution' (in Russian), in *Sredniye Veka*, No. IV, 1953, that in so far as the Levellers looked for backing in the countryside at all, it was among the yeomen and better-to-do husbandmen and craftsmen. Professor Macpherson's essay seems to lend support to this argument.—Ed.]

Index